Admiralty Record®

Volume 9

PUBLISHED ADMIRALTY OPINIONS OF
THE SUPREME COURT OF THE UNITED STATES AND
THE UNITED STATES COURTS OF APPEALS ISSUED DURING
THE CALENDAR YEAR

2021

Cite as: 9 Adm. R. _____

REPORTED BY KIRK N. AURANDT, ESQ.
MEMBER OF THE BAR IN LOUISIANA AND PENNSYLVANIA

ADMIRALTY RECORD PUBLISHING COMPANY, L.L.C.
MANDEVILLE, LOUISIANA, U.S.A.

ISSN 2334-5411
ISBN 978-1-7337790-6-7

Admiralty record: published admiralty opinions of the Supreme Court of the United States and the United States Courts of Appeals issued during the calendar year ... Mandeville, Louisiana, U.S.A.: Admiralty Record Publishing Company, LLC, 2014-

KF1104.A75
ISSN: 2334-5411

https://lccn.loc.gov/2014200303

PREFACE

Volume 9—the ninth annual edition of the Admiralty Record®—reports the published admiralty opinions of the Supreme Court of the United States and the United States Courts of Appeals that were issued during the calendar year 2021. The opinions reported are the original majority, concurring, and dissenting opinions of the Court, with only minor changes in formatting to better suit a dual-column presentation. The pagination found in the Court's original opinion is indicated by the number contained inside of black brackets, *see, e.g.*, **[—15—]**. The pagination found in the official Reporter is indicated by the number contained inside of black braces, *see, e.g.*, **{–15–}**. Also, where applicable, I have added parallel citations to opinions reported in this Volume and in prior Volumes of the Admiralty Record®.

The decision to select an opinion to appear in Volume 9 of the Admiralty Record® was made solely by me following an examination of those opinions that each of the above-named courts designated for publication in 2021. Every effort has been made to ensure inclusion of all 2021 federal appellate court admiralty opinions that were designated for publication; however, to the extent that a relevant admiralty opinion has been inadvertently overlooked or otherwise mistakenly omitted, the error is regretted and is solely my own. A few opinions from appeals in civil cases that technically may not have fallen under a federal district court's admiralty or maritime jurisdiction have been reported if they touched upon admiralty matters, or were otherwise deemed to be of potential interest to the admiralty practitioner. Additionally, several opinions from criminal cases involving maritime crimes and civil cases arising under the Federal Employers' Liability Act have been included.

To assist the reader in locating those opinions from 2021 involving subject matters of interest, I have prepared an Index to the opinions. I have also prepared Tables of Authority, which supply page references to the cases, statutes, and rules cited in each opinion. Prior to relying upon any of the opinions reported herein, the reader is reminded to verify the current status of any particular case as valid precedent by checking the case with a reliable citator.

Additional copies of the Admiralty Record® may be ordered at www.admiraltyrecord.com. I hope that the Admiralty Record® will continue to be a valuable and ready reference source for not only the admiralty practitioner, but for anyone who is interested in reading the published admiralty opinions of the federal appellate courts.

KIRK N. AURANDT, ESQ.

This page intentionally left blank

TABLE OF CONTENTS[1]

(CASES ARRANGED CHRONOLOGICALLY BY COURT)

PAGE

[1] In 2020, there were no published admiralty opinions from the Supreme Court of the United States and the United States Court of Appeals for the Tenth Circuit.

This page intentionally left blank

United States Court of Appeals for the First Circuit

United States Court of Appeals
for the First Circuit

No. 19-1503

QBE SEGUROS
vs.
MORALES-VÁZQUEZ

Appeal from the United States District Court for the District of Puerto Rico

Decided: January 19, 2021

Citation: 986 F.3d 1, 9 Adm. R. 2 (1st Cir. 2021).

Before **BARRON** and **SELYA,** Circuit Judges, and **KATZMANN,** Judge.*

* Of the United States Court of International Trade, sitting by designation.

[—2—] **{–2–}** **SELYA,** Circuit Judge:

This appeal involves a dispute between a boat owner (who purchased a policy of marine insurance without disclosing, among other things, a prior grounding) and his insurance company. Resolving the appeal requires us to revisit the doctrine of uberrimae fidei—an entrenched principle of maritime law that imposes a duty of utmost good faith on the parties to marine insurance contracts. Concluding, as we do, that the district court faithfully applied this doctrine, we affirm the entry of judgment in favor of the insurer.

I. BACKGROUND

We briefly rehearse the relevant facts and travel of the case. In 2011, defendant-appellant Carlos Morales-Vázquez (Morales) purchased an insurance policy for his forty-foot Riviera yacht (the Riviera Policy) from Optima Insurance Company, an entity later acquired by another insurance **{–3–}** company, plaintiff-appellee QBE Seguros (QBE). As part of his application for this insurance policy, Morales left blank the spaces provided for answers to questions asking him to describe his prior boating history and all accidents related to any vessel he had previously owned, controlled, and/or operated. Morales renewed this policy (with QBE) in both 2012 and 2013.

In March of 2014, Morales applied for a separate insurance policy for his forty-eight-foot Cavileer yacht (the Cavileer Policy). Section seven of the application required **[—3—]** Morales to disclose any accidents or losses sustained in connection with any vessel he had owned, controlled, and/or operated. This time, Morales indicated that he had been involved in an accident some eleven years earlier, explaining that the accident was a "propeller strike" and that "[p]ropellers were replaced [and] shaft and rudders rectified." But Morales did not see fit to mention that in January of 2010 he had grounded a forty-foot Riviera Offshore yacht in Fajardo, Puerto Rico.

The omission of the earlier grounding was not Morales's only oversight. Section six of the application for the Cavileer Policy required Morales to recount his boat-ownership and boat-operating history. When responding, Morales listed only two of the seven boats that he previously had owned and/or operated (a forty-foot Riviera Offshore yacht and a forty-foot Riviera Sport Fisherman). He omitted the remaining information called for by section six even though the application form plainly stated that "[i]f incorrect answers are provided (either by error, omission or neglect), I will be in breach of this warranty and the policy, if issued, will be void from inception."

Morales submitted the application for the Cavileer Policy to an insurance broker, who contacted an underwriter at QBE. The broker indicated that the putative insured wanted to obtain a quote the same day. Thirty-six minutes after receiving the application, the underwriter quoted a premium to the broker. **[—4—]** In pricing the quotation, the underwriter relied, among other things, on the information contained in the applications for both the Riviera Policy and the Cavileer Policy, as well as Morales's "more than 15 years" of nautical "owner experience." *QBE Seguros v. Morales-Vázquez*, No. 15-2091, 2018 WL 3763305, at *1-3 (D.P.R. Aug. 7, 2018). She later testified at trial that she had evaluated the paperwork thoroughly before authorizing the issuance of the policy. The net result of the dealings between the broker and the underwriter was that, as of March 7, 2014,

Morales's Cavileer yacht was insured by QBE for the ensuing year in the face amount of $550,000.

On October 24, 2014, the Cavileer yacht sustained appreciable damage from a fire. Morales reported the loss to QBE, and QBE retained an independent adjustor to work with its own employees toward resolving Morales's claim. Following a number of surveys, QBE made a settlement offer in December of 2014: it offered to pay Morales $63,774.10 in satisfaction of the loss. Morales rejected the offer.

Negotiations between the parties continued over the next few months, and Morales rejected several other settlement offers from QBE. The tectonic plates shifted, though, in May of 2015, when QBE became aware of Morales's 2010 grounding. QBE exercised its right to question Morales under oath, and Morales admitted that he had not disclosed the 2010 grounding—nor had he disclosed **[—5—]** (in his application for the Cavileer Policy) the existence of five vessels that he previously had owned and/or operated.

With Morales's admissions in hand, QBE repaired to the federal district court in mid-2015. Invoking the court's admiralty **{-4-}** jurisdiction, *see* 28 U.S.C. § 1333, QBE sought a declaratory judgment voiding the policy on the grounds that Morales had failed to honor his duty of utmost good faith (known as "uberrimae fidei" in maritime law) in acquiring the Cavileer Policy and, in the bargain, had breached the warranty of truthfulness contained in the Cavileer Policy. Morales answered QBE's complaint, denied that QBE was entitled to the relief that it sought, asserted affirmative defenses of waiver and estoppel, and counterclaimed for damages arising out of QBE's alleged bad faith. The parties consented to proceed before a magistrate judge, *see* 28 U.S.C. § 636(c); Fed. R. Civ. P. 73, and—following preliminary motion practice and extensive pretrial discovery—they cross-moved for full or partial summary judgment. The district court denied both motions, but noted the relevance of the doctrine of uberrimae fidei and QBE's corresponding right to void the Cavileer Policy if Morales had made a material omission or misrepresentation.

A six-day bench trial ensued. The district court reserved decision, entertained post-trial briefing, and decided the case in a thoughtful rescript. The court concluded that QBE was entitled to void the policy for two independently sufficient **[—6—]** reasons: Morales had breached not only the duty of uberrimae fidei but also the policy's warranty of truthfulness. *See QBE*, 2018 WL 3763305, at *16. In connection with the latter holding, the court rejected Morales's affirmative defenses. *See id.* at *12-14. This timely appeal followed.

II. ANALYSIS

In this venue, Morales propounds four arguments. First, he asks that we hold the doctrine of uberrimae fidei inapplicable because of recent legal developments in the United Kingdom. Second, he says that even if the doctrine applies generally, the district court made no finding that QBE actually relied on his omissions and, thus, erred in holding that he had breached the duty. Third, he argues that the district court erred in finding that he breached the warranty of truthfulness. And finally, he argues that his affirmative defenses trump any right that QBE may have had to void the Cavileer Policy. The first two arguments are obviously related, and we discuss them together. As matters turn out, the resolution of those arguments suffices to lay this appeal to rest.

Given the thrust of Morales's first argument, we think it useful to start by sketching the evolution of the doctrine of uberrimae fidei. The Latin phrase "uberrimae fidei" loosely translates as "utmost good faith." *See* Black's Law Dictionary (10th ed. 2014). As relevant here, the doctrine requires parties **[—7—]** to a marine insurance contract to disclose all known facts or circumstances material to an insurer's risk. *See Windsor Mount Joy Mut. Ins. Co. v. Giragosian*, 57 F.3d 50, 54-55 (1st Cir. 1995). Under the doctrine, an insurer may void a marine insurance policy if its insured fails to disclose "*all* circumstances known to [the insured] and unknown to the insurer" that materially impact the insurer's risk calculus. *Caitlin at Lloyd's v. San Juan Towing & Marine Servs., Inc.*, 778 F.3d 69, 83, 3 Adm. R. 24, 34 (1st Cir. 2015) (emphasis in original); *cf. Stipcich v. Metro. Life Ins. Co.*, 277 U.S. 311, 316 (1928) (holding to like effect with respect to certain contracts outside marine insurance context).

The origins of the doctrine can be traced back to eighteenth-century London, which was—and remains—a global insurance hub. In its nascent form, the doctrine applied to a myriad of insurance contracts across a wide swath of industries. As early as 1766, Lord Mansfield recognized that insurance contracts impose a heightened **{-5-}** duty of good faith to prevent a party from omitting or concealing facts that would induce the counterparty "into a bargain, from his ignorance." *Carter v. Boehm* (1766) 97 Eng. Rep. 1162, 1164 (K.B.). Such a requirement was rooted in practical wisdom, recognizing that an insurer often lacked the ability to verify the insured's representations before issuing a policy. *See* Thomas J. Schoenbaum, *Admiralty and Maritime Law* § 19:14, at 460 (6th ed. 2018). This practical wisdom still **[—8—]** rings true when applied to marine insurance—an industry in which, for example, a policy may have to be issued in London, on a time-sensitive basis, for a vessel berthed halfway across the globe.

American courts first recognized the doctrine of uberrimae fidei in connection with marine insurance contracts in the early nineteenth century. *See McLanahan v. Universal Ins. Co.*, 26 U.S. (1 Pet.) 170, 185 (1828). In 1882, the Supreme Court confirmed the strict disclosure requirements that the doctrine imposed on an insured. *See Sun Mut. Ins. Co. v. Ocean Ins. Co.*, 107 U.S. 485, 510-11 (1883).

For some time, American and English law concerning marine insurance continued to develop in parallel through a parade of judicial decisions. Parliament, however, codified the by-then-venerable doctrine of uberrimae fidei by including it in the Marine Insurance Act of 1906 (1906 MIA). *See* Marine Insurance Act 1906, 6 Edw. 7 c. 41, § 17 (U.K.). Congress, however, remained silent; and American courts continued to develop their own federal common law of admiralty and continued to interpret marine insurance policies as incorporating, by implication, the doctrine of uberrimae fidei. *See, e.g., San Juan Towing*, 778 F.3d at 82, 3 Adm. R. at 33; *N.Y. Marine & Gen. Ins. Co. v. Cont'l Cement Co.*, 761 F.3d 830, 839, 2 Adm. R. 468, 473 (8th Cir. 2014); *AGF Marine Aviation & Transp. v. Cassin*, 544 F.3d 255, 263 (3d Cir. 2008); *Certain Underwriters at Lloyd's, London v. Inlet Fisheries Inc.*, 518 F.3d 645, 650 (9th Cir. 2008); *HIH* **[—9—]** *Marine Servs., Inc. v. Fraser*, 211 F.3d 1359, 1362 (11th Cir. 2000); *Puritan Ins. Co. v. Eagle S.S. Co. S.A.*, 779 F.2d 866, 870 (2d Cir. 1985).[1]

Parliament lately adopted a number of insurance reforms. As relevant here, Parliament passed the Insurance Act of 2015, which (among other things) effectively amended the 1906 MIA to preclude an insurer from voiding a marine insurance policy by recourse to the doctrine of uberrimae fidei. *See* Insurance Act 2015, c.4, § 14 (U.K.) ("Any rule of law permitting a party to a contract of insurance to avoid the contract on the ground that the utmost good faith has not been observed by the other party is abolished."). Even so, Congress did not follow Parliament's lead.

This lack of congressional action is significant. As the federal common law of admiralty developed, the Supreme Court acknowledged that congressional silence left room for courts, **[—10—]** among others, to fill

[1] There appears to be only a single outlier. *See Albany Ins. Co. v. Anh Thi Kieu*, 927 F.2d 882, 889 (5th Cir. 1991). This decision not only flies in the teeth of case law from both the Supreme Court and the overwhelming majority of circuits but also has been much-criticized. *See, e.g., Inlet Fisheries*, 518 F.3d at 653 (questioning the "logic chain" of *Anh Thi Kieu*); Thomas J. Schoenbaum, *The Duty of Utmost Good Faith in Marine Insurance Law: A Comparative Analysis of American and English Law*, 29 J. Mar. L. & Com. 1, 11 (1998) (calling into question *Anh Thi Kieu* decision because "no rule of marine insurance is better established tha[n] the utmost good faith rule").

the vacuum.[2] *See* **{–6–}** *Wilburn Boat Co. v. Fireman's Fund Ins. Co.*, 348 U.S. 310, 321 (1955) ("We, like Congress, leave the regulation of marine insurance where it has been—with the States.").

Against this backdrop, Morales contends that Supreme Court precedent requires courts to harmonize American and United Kingdom maritime law and that, therefore, uberrimae fidei would have to be scuttled (even if it included a requirement to prove reliance) to match what Parliament wrought in the Insurance Act of 2015. This contention poses a question of law, which engenders de novo review. *See Giragosian*, 57 F.3d at 53.

Morales does not dispute that uberrimae fidei is firmly entrenched in the jurisprudence of this circuit. *See San Juan Towing*, 778 F.3d at 80–81, 3 Adm. R. at 32 (holding "without further equivocation that the doctrine of *uberrimae fidei* is an established rule of maritime law in this Circuit"). He nonetheless urges us to disregard our own precedent, insisting that a trio of Supreme Court cases compels us to do so. *See Calmar S.S. Corp. v. Scott*, 345 **[—11—]** U.S. 427, 442-443 (1953); *Standard Oil Co. of N.J. v. United States*, 340 U.S. 54, 59 (1950); *Queen Ins. Co. of Am. v. Globe and Rutgers Fire Ins. Co.*, 263 U.S. 487, 493 (1924). The rule that Morales draws from these cases is that, in admiralty, federal common law should be tailored (or re-tailored, if necessary) to mirror developments in English law. This is magical thinking: the cases upon which Morales relies cannot bear the weight that he loads upon them. We explain briefly.

To begin, the quoted statements that Morales excerpts from his coveted trio of Supreme Court cases are dictum. None of them are meant to establish a binding analytic framework. And when all is said and done, Morales identifies no case in which the Court based a holding on English law. To confirm these points, we examine the cases that Morales cites.

In *Queen Insurance*, the Court was tasked with deciding, for insurance purposes, whether the sinking of a commercial vessel traveling with a military convoy resulted from "marine risks" or "war risks." 263 U.S. at 490. To resolve this conundrum, the Court looked primarily to a Court of Claims opinion, *see Morgan v. United States*, 5 Ct. Cl. 182, 194 (1869), which itself drew on English insurance law principles, *see Queen Insurance*, 263 U.S. at 492-93. Although Justice Holmes noted that "special reasons [exist] for keeping in harmony with the marine insurance laws of **[—12—]** England," *id.* at 493, the Court's holding was in no way based on English law.

In *Calmar*, the dispute involved a privately insured ship which—as a result of the attack on Pearl Harbor—was diverted to Australia and detained there. *See* 345 U.S. at 428-29. While detained, the ship was damaged by enemy bombing. *See id.* at 430. The parties quarreled over whether the ship's insurance policy afforded coverage, and the lower court based its resolution of this controversy in part on a House of Lords decision. *See id.* at 442 (citing *Rickards v. Forrestal Land, Timber and Rys. Co.* (1942) A.C. 50). On review, the **{–7–}** Supreme Court cited an analogous English case as "persuasive authority," but made plain that it was "not required" to adopt that particular interpretation. *Id.* at 443.

The third case to which Morales adverts also involved war risk insurance. There, the insured alleged that certain House of Lords decisions, which detoured from the traditional proximate cause inquiry, dictated the outcome. *See Standard Oil Co. of N.J.*, 340 U.S. at 59, 60 n.12 (citing *Yorkshire Dale S.S. Co. v. Minister of War Transp.* (1942) A.C. 691; *Bd. of Trade v. Hain S.S. Co.* (1929) A.C. 534; *Attorney-General v. Adelaide S.S. Co.*

---

[2] This means, of course, that questions sometimes arise in maritime cases as to whether federal or state common law should apply. *See San Juan Towing*, 778 F.3d at 76-80, 3 Adm. R. at 28–32. Here, however, the parties present their uberrimae fidei arguments exclusively in terms of federal common law, and we therefore may accept the parties' plausible view that federal common law supplies the substantive rules of decision. *Cf. Borden v. Paul Revere Life Ins. Co.*, 935 F.2d 370, 375 (1st Cir. 1991) (holding that, in diversity jurisdiction, court may accept parties' plausible agreement as to which state's law applies).

(1923) A.C. 292). Although the Court acknowledged the general "desirability of uniformity" between American and English law in the interpretation of marine insurance policies, it cautioned that "this does not mean that American courts must follow House of **[—13—]** Lords' decisions automatically." *Id.* at 59. Practicing what it preached, the Court declined to follow the English precedents hawked by the insured. *Id.* at 61.

Standard Oil offers us two important takeaways. First, American courts are not bound by legal developments in the United Kingdom. And even though the *Standard Oil* Court was speaking of judicial decisions, we think it follows, a fortiori, that acts of Parliament are equally non-binding. Second, although harmony between American and English admiralty law is desirable, "our practice is no more than to accord respect to established doctrines of English maritime law." *Id.* at 59. The respect accorded by American courts to English maritime law stems from the wisdom of the particular doctrine, not from either the acceptance or the rejection of that doctrine by Parliament. It follows, we think, that federal courts tasked with hearing admiralty cases should take heed of developments in English law, but they are not obliged to change course merely because Parliament acts to alter a previously entrenched principle.

Let us be perfectly clear. We do not gainsay that federal common law is intended to be dynamic and to evolve over time. *See, e.g., Nw. Airlines, Inc. v. Transp. Workers Union of Am., AFL-CIO*, 451 U.S. 77, 95-96 (1981) (discussing federal courts' role in developing "flexible" common law of admiralty). But Congress has been conspicuously silent on issues of marine **[—14—]** insurance, *see Wilburn Boat Co.*, 348 U.S. at 321, and the fact that federal common law has the capacity to evolve does not mean that it is captive to the vagaries of Parliament (or any foreign legislature, for that matter).

At any rate, abandoning the doctrine of uberrimae fidei in marine insurance cases would have rebarbative consequences, both upending settled law and disrupting an industry that has long been premised on insureds telling the whole truth to insurers. Given this grim prospect, we decline Morales's invitation to remove the doctrine of uberrimae fidei from service and place it in mothballs.

There are, of course, sound reasons to retain the challenged doctrine. Although the availability of information has improved dramatically in recent times, a marine insurer and its insured do not have equal access to the information needed to make underwriting decisions and to set premiums. Long ago, Lord Mansfield famously wrote that "[i]nsurance is a contract upon speculation. The special facts, upon which the contingent chance is to be computed, lie most commonly in the knowledge of the insured only." *Carter* 97 Eng. Rep. at 1164. This remains true in the sphere of marine insurance. Thus, even **{–8–}** though uberrimae fidei has been scuttled in other areas of insurance law, *see San Juan Towing*, 778 F.3d at 75, 3 Adm. R. at 27, the peculiarities of marine insurance underscore the case for its continued desirability. **[—15—]**

This proposition hardly can be disputed. Marine insurance is often needed at a moment's notice, and insurers are frequently located far away from the vessel that they are asked to insure. *See id.* at 80, 3 Adm. R. at 32. The insurer's task is made more formidable because the calculation of marine insurance premiums must take into account not only the vessel's history and particularities but also the maritime experiences of the owner and/or operator. Time is frequently critical to the issuance of marine insurance policies, and this wide constellation of facts is difficult for an insurer to ascertain on short notice unless it has the full and frank cooperation of the insured. *See generally* Mitchell J. Popham & Chau Vo, *Misrepresentation and Concealment in Marine Insurance Contracts: An Analysis of Federal and State Law Within the Ninth Circuit*, 11 U.S.F. Mar. L.J. 99, 104 (1998).

So, too, the asymmetry in the availability of information argues convincingly for the idea that the doctrine of uberrimae fidei is necessary for the maintenance of an economically efficient marine insurance industry. Requiring an insurer to ascertain difficult-to-find information about a risk will impose substantial costs on the industry—costs that are likely to be passed along to policyholders in the form of higher premiums. Placing the burden of disclosure on the insured (the party who knows or can most easily obtain the necessary information) will reduce processing costs and will help to keep premiums low. As **[—16—]** one commentator aptly observed, uberrimae fidei is not "based on 'old fashioned' moral principles . . . [i]t is a rule designed to minimize costs to both insurers and assureds." Schoenbaum, *The Duty of Utmost Good Faith*, *supra* note 1, at 3. The doctrine, therefore, remains "grounded in *economic efficiency*." *Id.*

This case is a poster child for the continuing relevance of the doctrine. Morales admits that QBE's underwriter was "pressed for time because Morales needed the insurance for that same day." To accommodate Morales, QBE moved rapidly; it delivered the requested coverage to Morales just thirty-six minutes after his broker submitted his application. In other words, the stringent burden of disclosure allowed Morales to obtain marine insurance in a matter of minutes.

Even so, clear sailing is not yet in sight. Morales argues that, even if uberrimae fidei remains applicable to marine insurance in American jurisprudence, the district court misapplied the doctrine because it did not make any finding that QBE actually relied on the insured's incomplete accident history and other omissions. To the extent that this claim of error turns on a question of law, our review is de novo. *See Giragosian*, 57 F.3d at 53. To the extent that it implicates the district court's factfinding, our review is for clear error. *See id.*

Morales's argument posits that QBE must show that it actually relied on his omissions in issuing the Cavileer Policy. **[—17—]** This argument strikes a novel chord: we have never held that actual reliance is a necessary prerequisite for an insurer to void a marine insurance policy under the doctrine of uberrimae fidei. Rather, we have held that the materiality of a false statement or an omission, without more, provides a sufficient ground for voiding such a policy. *See, e.g., San Juan Towing*, 778 F.3d at 83, 3 Adm. R. at 34; *Com. Union Ins. Co. v. Pesante*, 459 F.3d 34, 37-38 (1st Cir. 2006); **{–9–}** *Grande v. St. Paul Fire & Marine Ins. Co.*, 436 F.3d 277, 282-83 (1st Cir. 2006); *Giragosian*, 57 F.3d at 54-55. Several other courts of appeals likewise have concluded that a showing that an omission or a representation relates to a material fact is alone sufficient to void a marine insurance policy. *See, e.g., Inlet Fisheries*, 518 F.3d at 655; *AGF Marine Aviation*, 544 F.3d at 262; *HIH Marine Servs.*, 211 F.3d at 1363. The commenters agree that, under federal common law, the majority rule does not require actual reliance in marine insurance cases. *See, e.g.*, Schoenbaum, *Admiralty and Maritime Law*, *supra*, at 480; W. Benjamin Woody, *Sinking Uberrimae Fidei: How the Eighth Circuit's Decision in* St. Paul Fire & Marine Insurance Co. v. Abhe & Svoboda, Inc., *Accidentally Sank the Doctrine Before the Insurance Act 2015 Could*, 40 Tul. Mar. L.J. 573, 584-85 (2016).

In an effort to blunt the force of these authorities, Morales claims that three circuits—the Eleventh, Second, and **[—18—]** Eighth—have required a showing of actual reliance. Morales's claim, though, overstates the matter.

Caselaw from the Eleventh Circuit contravenes Morales's claim. The case that he cites stands only for the unremarkable proposition that misrepresentation of a prior loss *known to both parties* "could not have led [the insurer] to rely on that statement" and, thus, could "in no way constitute a material misrepresentation in breach of *uberrimae fidei*." *I.T.N. Consolidators, Inc. v. N. Marine Unders. Ltd.*, 464 Fed. Appx. 788, 794 (11th Cir. 2012) (dictum). That case was decided on other grounds, *see id.* at 795, and the Eleventh Circuit elsewhere has stated unequivocally that a material misrepresentation, without more, is a sufficient basis for voiding a marine insurance policy under uberrimae fidei, *see HIH Marine Servs.*, 211 F.3d at 1363.

The Second Circuit is more of a mixed bag. In the case that Morales cites, the court merely assumed, without deciding, that actual reliance was necessary. *See Fireman's Fund Ins. Co. v. Great Am. Ins. Co.*, 822 F.3d 620, 638, 4 Adm. R. 70, 81 (2d Cir. 2016). But our independent research indicates that the Second Circuit may, indeed, require actual reliance when applying uberrimae fidei. *See Puritan*, 779 F.2d at 871.

The Eighth Circuit case that Morales cites is favorable authority for his position. *See St. Paul Fire & Marine Ins. Co. v. Abhe & Svoboda, Inc.*, 798 F.3d 715, 721, 3 Adm. R. 522, 525 (8th Cir. 2015). Even **[—19—]** so, that court recognized that its holding was contrary to the weight of authority. *See id.*, 3 Adm. R. at 525–26. And in all events, the opinion is suspect because the *Abhe* court looked to insurance law outside the marine insurance context, *see id.* at 720-21, 3 Adm. R. at 524–25, and failed to acknowledge in any way the special relationship between marine insurance and the doctrine of uberrimae fidei.

In the end, we are not persuaded by Morales's argument. For one thing, binding precedent does not support the inclusion of an actual reliance requirement within the doctrine of uberrimae fidei. The Supreme Court has used only a materiality test—without any mention of actual reliance—in describing the preconditions for the application of uberrimae fidei in marine insurance cases. *See Sun Mut. Ins. Co.*, 107 U.S. at 509-10. And in this circuit's jurisprudence, materiality alone has consistently been recognized as a sufficient predicate for finding that an insured breached his duty of uberrimae fidei. *See, e.g., San Juan Towing*, 778 F.3d at 83, 3 Adm. R. at 34.

For another thing, Morales does not argue in the alternative that we should impose an actual reliance requirement regardless of controlling precedent. He does no more than cite some out-of-circuit cases that follow the minority rule to support his **{-10-}** claim that our precedent also requires actual reliance. These references are insufficient to support departure from our existing precedent. We hold, therefore, that the majority rule continues **[—20—]** to abide in this circuit; that under the majority rule, a showing of actual reliance is not required; and that QBE had no need to show that it actually relied on Morales's omissions in order to prevail under the doctrine of uberrimae fidei.[3]

Morales makes yet another effort to bail the water out of his sinking ship. He submits that certain language in the Cavileer Policy modified the traditional duty of uberrimae fidei and incorporated actual reliance into the contract. Specifically, he points to two provisions:

- A clause appearing on the bottom of each page of the application, which states, "I also agree that if the policy is issued, it was issued by you based upon and in reliance of the truthfulness and completeness of the answers provided herein."
- A sentence in the "General Conditions and Warranties" section of the Cavileer Policy, which states, "This policy was issued based upon and in reliance of the representations made by you or your representative in the Application."

Contrary to Morales's importunings, this language does nothing to water down the duty of uberrimae fidei. These provisions appear **[—21—]** to be little more than boilerplate contract terms, and we agree with the district court that neither of them amounts to an unambiguous statement modifying the duty of utmost good faith inherent in marine insurance contracts. *See QBE*, 2018 WL 3763305, at *7. To cinch the matter, other language in the Cavileer Policy makes pellucid that the parties did not intend to diminish the duty of uberrimae fidei:

> If the named insured has, before or after a loss made a false statement or representation with respect to this insurance or has concealed or misrepresented any material fact or circumstance relating to this insurance, this policy shall be void and without

[3] We note QBE's insistence that actual reliance occurred here. Like the district court, we have no need to reach that factbound issue.

> effect. The false statement or representation or concealment need not be related to the damages or loss claimed in order to void the entire policy.

This language embodies the core of the uberrimae fidei doctrine: that omission or misrepresentation of a material fact is a sufficient ground, in and of itself, to allow an insurer to void a policy of marine insurance.

For the sake of completeness, we note that our analysis of the contractual language does not offer any reason to move away from the overarching doctrine of uberrimae fidei. Quite the contrary: the contractual language provides strong support for the conclusion that the doctrine of uberrimae fidei is alive and well in marine insurance policies. Although the disclosure requirements in the contract align with those imposed by the **[—22—]** doctrine of uberrimae fidei, contractual requirements may operate as affirmative defenses. For example, waiver and estoppel may be affirmative defenses to a claim that an insured has committed a breach of a policy warranty, *see, e.g.*, *In re Frescati Shipping Co.*, 718 F.3d 184, 214, 1 Adm. R. 80, 102 (3d Cir. 2013); *Suydam v. Reed Stenhouse of Wash., Inc.*, 820 F.2d 1506, 1510 (9th Cir. 1987), and Morales asserts them here. But he develops no argument on appeal that these defenses apply against the doctrine of uberrimae **{–11–}** fidei. *See HIH Marine Servs.*, 211 F.3d at 1362 n.2.

It is true, of course, that omitted facts must be material in order to provide an avenue for an insurer to void an insurance policy under the doctrine of uberrimae fidei. *See San Juan Towing*, 778 F.3d at 83, 3 Adm. R. at 34; *Giragosian*, 57 F.3d at 54-55. For such purposes, materiality depends upon an objective standard. *See San Juan Towing*, 778 F.3d at 82, 3 Adm. R. at 33; *see also* Schoenbaum, *Admiralty and Maritime Law*, *supra*, at 480. Materiality is to be gleaned by evaluating the likely impact of facts that may influence a prudent insurer when considering whether to issue a particular policy. *See Pesante*, 459 F.3d at 38.

Here, the district court found that the incomplete accident history (most notably, the earlier grounding) crossed the threshold for materiality. *See QBE*, 2018 WL 3763305, at *8-9. On appeal, Morales makes no developed argument to the contrary. Given this unchallenged finding of materiality, the district court had **[—23—]** an impeccable predicate for applying the doctrine of uberrimae fidei.

We need go no further. From what we already have said, it is evident that the court below carefully threaded its way through the doctrinal complexities of uberrimae fidei and supportably concluded that the doctrine entitled QBE to a declaration that the Cavileer Policy was void.[4]

III. CONCLUSION

The judgment of the district court is

Affirmed.

---

[4] Given our conclusion that the district court did not err in ruling that Morales breached the duty of uberrimae fidei, we have no occasion to reach the parties' arguments concerning breach of the warranty of truthfulness, waiver, and estoppel.

United States Court of Appeals
for the First Circuit

No. 15-2377

UNITED STATES
VS.
AYBAR-ULLOA

Appeal from the United States District Court for the District of Puerto Rico

Decided: January 25, 2021

Citation: 987 F.3d 1, 9 Adm. R. 10 (1st Cir. 2021) (en banc).

Before **HOWARD,** Chief Judge, and **LYNCH, THOMPSON, KAYATTA,** and **BARRON,** Circuit Judges.*

* Judge Torruella heard oral argument in this matter and participated in the semble, but he did not participate in the issuance of the opinion in this case.

[—3—] {-2-} KAYATTA, Circuit Judge:

United States law enforcement authorities apprehended Johvanny Aybar-Ulloa ("Aybar") on a stateless vessel in international waters carrying packages of cocaine in violation of the Maritime Drug Law Enforcement Act ("MDLEA"), 46 U.S.C. §§ 70501–70508. In appealing his subsequent conviction, Aybar makes a two-step argument. First, he contends that Congress's authority to criminalize and punish conduct on the high seas under Article I, Section 8, Clause 10 of the United States Constitution ("the Define and Punish Clause") must be cabined by the limitations of international law on a nation's power to criminally prosecute conduct on the high seas. Second, he argues that the United States exceeded those limitations of international law by prosecuting him in this case.

In a divided opinion, a panel of this court trained its attention exclusively on the second part of Aybar's argument. *See United States v. Aybar-Ulloa*, 913 F.3d 47, 53-56, 7 Adm. R. 58, 61–64 (1st Cir. 2019). Relying on prior circuit precedent, the panel majority rejected that necessary part of Aybar's argument for two reasons: First, we previously held in *United States v. Victoria*, 876 F.2d 1009 (1st Cir. 1989) (Breyer, J.), that international law does indeed "give[] the United States . . . authority to treat stateless vessels as if they were its own." *Id.* at 1010 (second alteration in original) (quoting *United States v. Smith*, 680 F.2d 255, 258 (1st Cir. 1982)). Second, our prior opinion in *United States v.* **[—4—]** *Cardales*, 168 F.3d 548 (1st Cir. 1999), included certain statements construing international law as allowing a nation to define trafficking in controlled substances aboard vessels as a threat sufficient **{-3-}** to justify an assertion of jurisdiction under the "protective principle." *Id.* at 553.

As both the panel majority and the panel dissent observed, our prior opinion in *Victoria* "did not fully spell out" its reasoning. *Aybar-Ulloa*, 913 F.3d at 54, 7 Adm. R. at 62; *see also id.* at 61, 7 Adm. R. at 69 (Torruella, J., dissenting in part). *Cardales*, in turn, can be read as applying only to the circumstance where a foreign flag nation consents to the application of United States law to persons found on that nation's flagged vessel. *Id.* at 55-56, 7 Adm. R. at 63–64 (citing *Cardales*, 168 F.3d at 552-53). And the question of the United States' jurisdiction over persons on vessels on the high seas recurs in this circuit. For those reasons, we granted Aybar's petition to rehear this appeal en banc.

Following that rehearing, we now affirm Aybar's conviction. In doing so, we find that his prosecution in the United States for drug trafficking on a stateless vessel stopped and boarded by the United States in waters subject to the rights of navigation on the high seas violates no recognized principle of international law. To the contrary, international law accepts the criminal prosecution by the United States of persons like Aybar, who was seized by the United States while trafficking cocaine on **[—5—]** a stateless vessel on the high seas, just as if they were trafficking on a United States-flagged ship. We therefore need not and do not reach the question of whether the application of MDLEA to Aybar would be constitutional were international law otherwise. We also need not and do not rely on the protective principle, leaving its potential application for another day. Finally, for the reasons agreed upon by the full panel, we vacate Aybar's sentence and remand for resentencing under the Sentencing Commission's clarified guidance reflected in Amendment 794. *See id.* at 56-57, 7 Adm. R. at 64–65.

I.

A.

As Aybar urges, we take the facts as "[p]er the affidavit [filed by the government] in support of the complaint." On August 9, 2013, the HMS Lancaster, a foreign warship, launched a helicopter while on patrol in the Central Caribbean. Operators aboard the helicopter spotted a thirty-foot go-fast vessel dead in the water at 15-03N, 067-01W, an area approximately 160 nautical miles south of Puerto Rico constituting international waters.[1] The **[—6—]** vessel bore no indicia of nationality and was carrying numerous packages in plain view.

A Law Enforcement Detachment Team of the United States Coast Guard was embarked on the HMS Lancaster at the time of the incident. Members of this team launched a small boat to conduct a right-of-visit approach. Coast Guard personnel identified defendant Aybar and two others aboard the go-fast vessel. Aybar and another member of the vessel claimed to be citizens of the Dominican Republic, while the master of the vessel claimed Venezuelan citizenship. In response to inquiry from the Coast Guard personnel, the master of the vessel made no claim of nationality for the vessel. The Coast Guard personnel suspected contraband. **{-4-}**

Concluding that the vessel was without nationality, the Coast Guard personnel then boarded and searched the vessel. Following the search, the Coast Guard proceeded to take all three men and the packages found on board back to the HMS Lancaster, where the packages' contents tested positive for cocaine. The three men were then transferred to a United States Coast Guard vessel and taken to Ponce, Puerto Rico, where they were held in custody. **[—7—]**

B.

Shortly thereafter, a federal grand jury issued an indictment against Aybar, charging him under MDLEA with conspiring to possess with intent to distribute cocaine on board a vessel subject to the jurisdiction of the United States, 46 U.S.C. § 70506(b) (count one), and aiding and abetting possession with intent to distribute cocaine on board a vessel subject to the jurisdiction of the United States, 46 U.S.C. §§ 70502(c)(1)(A), 70503(a)(1), 70504(b)(1), 70506(a), 18 U.S.C. § 2 (count two). The indictment also included an allegation of forfeiture, 46 U.S.C. § 70507.

MDLEA provides that "[w]hile on board a covered vessel, an individual may not knowingly or intentionally . . . manufacture or distribute, or possess with intent to manufacture or distribute, a controlled substance." 46 U.S.C. § 70503(a)(1). As relevant here, a "covered vessel" includes "a vessel subject to the jurisdiction of the United States," *id.* § 70503(e)(1), which is defined to include "a vessel without nationality," *id.* § 70502(c)(1)(A). "[A] vessel without nationality," in turn, includes "a vessel aboard which the master or individual in charge fails, on request of an officer of the United States authorized to enforce applicable provisions of United States law, to make a claim of nationality or registry for that vessel." 46 U.S.C. § 70502(d)(1)(B). **[—8—]**

Aybar moved to dismiss the indictment for lack of jurisdiction, arguing that Congress's power under Article I "[t]o define and punish Piracies and Felonies committed on the high Seas, and Offenses against the Law of Nations," U.S. Const. art. I, § 8, cl. 10, did not

[1] The coordinates provided by the government nonetheless appear to place the defendant's vessel within the Exclusive Economic Zone ("EEZ") of the United States. Because the right of freedom of navigation on the high seas applies in the EEZ, we proceed with reference to the rules of interdiction applicable on the high seas. United Nations Convention on the Law of the Sea ("UNCLOS") arts. 58(1-2), 87, Dec. 10, 1982, S. Treaty Doc. No. 103-39, 1833 U.N.T.S. 397; *see generally id.* pt. VII, § 1. We **[—6—]** do not address any potential limitations on freedom of navigation in the EEZ that may be imposed in this area. *See id.* art. 58(3).

reach his conduct. After the district court denied his motion, Aybar proceeded to plead guilty. Aybar's plea accepted the facts substantiating the charges against him under MDLEA. Those facts, in turn, make clear that the vessel on which he was found was "a vessel without nationality" as defined in section 70502(d)(1)(B) because, while on board the vessel, the master made no claim of nationality when requested to do so by a United States officer authorized to enforce the United States drug laws. Despite his guilty plea and concessions, Aybar adequately preserved his challenge to Congress's constitutional power to criminalize his conduct pursuant to its Article I powers. *See Class v. United States*, 138 S. Ct. 798, 804-05 (2018). On January 9, 2019, a divided panel rejected that challenge, affirming his conviction. For unrelated reasons, the panel also vacated the district court's sentence and remanded for further proceedings.

II.

Our analysis proceeds in five parts summarized as follows: First, the "go-fast" ship upon which Aybar travelled was rendered "stateless" when its master on board failed upon request **[—9—]** to make a valid claim of nationality for it, flouting, among other things, the important requirement of international law that every vessel on the high seas sail under the flag of a nation state. Second, as a stateless vessel, the ship was susceptible to the exercise of jurisdiction by any nation intercepting the vessel on the high seas, just as if the vessel were one of that nation's own. Third, the exercise of **{-5-}** jurisdiction over Aybar's ship just as if it were a United States vessel included jurisdiction over drug trafficking on the vessel just as if it were drug trafficking on a United States vessel, which is considered to be the territory of the United States. Fourth, the application of that territorial jurisdiction to prosecute Aybar in a United States court for illegally trafficking cocaine is compatible with, and welcomed by, any relevant specific rules and undertakings governing the assertion of domestic power on the high seas. Fifth, we offer several important caveats.

A.

Under international law governing the seas, every vessel must sail under the flag of one, and only one, state. United Nations Convention on the Law of the Sea ("UNCLOS") art. 92, Dec. 10, 1982, S. Treaty Doc. No. 103-39, 1833 U.N.T.S. 397.[2] In **[—10—]** turn, every state maintains an obligation to "fix the conditions for the grant of its nationality to ships, for the registration of ships in its territory, and for the right to fly its flag," *id.* art. 91(1), and to "issue to ships to which it has granted the right to fly its flag documents to that effect," *id.* art. 91(2). While the type of registration papers may differ from state to state depending on domestic laws, every state must keep a register of "the names of all private vessels sailing under its flag," and ensure "that every vessel may be identified from a distance." 1 L.F.L. Oppenheim, *International Law* §§ 290 (Jennings et al. eds., 9th ed. 2008). "Without a flag or papers, a vessel may also traditionally make an oral claim of nationality when a proper demand is made." *United States v. Matos-Luchi*, 627 F.3d 1, 5 (1st Cir. 2010).

This "flag-state" system—by which all vessels are required to fly the flag of a state, and states are in turn required to approve the conditions for granting rights to fly their flag—serves several purposes. First, by subjecting vessels to the exclusive jurisdiction of the flag state, the flag-state system guarantees freedom of navigation in international waters, as states generally may not interfere with the passage on the high **[—11—]** seas of ships lawfully flying the flag of another state. *See* Richard A. Barnes, "Flag States," in *The Oxford Handbook on the Law of the Sea* 313 (Rothwell et al. eds. 2015); *cf.* UNCLOS arts. 87, 90. Second, the flag-state system provides clear guidance as to which

[2] The United States has signed but not ratified UNCLOS. We nevertheless cite to it as evidence of the customs and usages of international law. *See The Paquete Habana*, 175 U.S. 677, 700 (1900); *cf. United States v. Alaska*, 503 U.S. 569, 588 n.10 (1992) **[—10—]** (noting that the United States has stated that the "baseline provisions [of UNCLOS] reflect customary international law" (citation omitted)).

state bears the primary obligation to regulate conduct occurring on vessels on the seas. *See* R.R. Churchill & A.V. Lowe, *The Law of the Sea* 205 (1988); *cf.* UNCLOS art. 94. Third, the flag-state system indicates which state may bear responsibility for the conduct of a ship on the seas. *See* Churchill & Lowe, *supra*, at 205. Thus, the flag-state system is "[o]ne of the most important means by which public order is maintained at sea." *Id.*

Aybar concedes that the ship upon which he was found plainly did not comply with this system. It flew no flag, its master claimed no nationality, and no other indicia of registration or nationality were present when authorized United States officials stopped and boarded the ship. Presumably for these reasons, Aybar does not dispute that his vessel may be treated as "stateless" under international law. *See, e.g.*, **{-6-}** *Matos-Luchi*, 627 F.3d at 6 (stating that a vessel "may be deemed 'stateless' . . . if it fails to display or carry insignia of nationality and seeks to avoid national identification"). **[—12—]**

B.

International law plainly provides that a nation's warship (or law enforcement ship) may stop and board a stateless vessel on the high seas. *See* UNCLOS art. 110(1)(d); Restatement (Third) of the Foreign Relations Law of the United States § 522(2)(b) (1987) [hereinafter "Restatement (Third)"] ("[A] warship or clearly-marked law enforcement ship of any state may board [a nongovernmental ship] . . . if there is reason to suspect that the ship . . . is without nationality . . . ."); *see also Brownlie's Principles of Public International Law* 285, 292 (Crawford ed., 9th ed. 2019) [hereinafter "*Brownlie's Principles*"]; Malcolm Shaw, *International Law* 457 (8th ed. 2017) ("A ship that is stateless, and does not fly a flag, may be boarded and seized on the high seas."); Myres S. McDougal & William T. Burke, *The Maintenance of Public Order at Sea and the Nationality of Ships*, 54 Am. J. Int'l L. 25, 76-77 (1960) ("So great a premium is placed upon the certain identification of vessels for purposes of maintaining minimal order upon the high seas . . . that extraordinary deprivational measures are permitted with respect to stateless ships."). In short, "[b]ecause stateless vessels do not fall within the veil of another sovereign's territorial protection," the vessel is afforded no right of free navigation. *United States v. Rendon*, 354 F.3d 1320, 1325 (11th Cir. 2003) (quoting *United States v. Caicedo*, 47 F.3d 370, 373 (9th Cir. **[—13—]** 1995)); *see also United States v. Rubies*, 612 F.2d 397, 402-03 (9th Cir. 1979) ("A foreign flag[ged] vessel is thereby protected by her country of registration. . . . An unregistered, or 'stateless,' vessel, however, does not have these rights or protections.").

To say that international law grants to any state the authority to interdict and exercise physical control over a stateless vessel is to say that international law renders stateless vessels "susceptible to the jurisdiction of any State," Barnes, *supra*, at 314, including the United States. *See Smith*, 680 F.2d at 258 (recognizing that "[i]nternational law . . . allows any state to extend its authority over a stateless ship") (citing *United Nations Convention on the High Seas*, 13 U.S.T. 2313, T.I.A.S. No. 5200 (1958)); *see also United States v. Juda*, 46 F.3d 961, 967 (9th Cir. 1995); *United States v. Martinez-Hidalgo*, 993 F.2d 1052, 1055 (3d Cir. 1993); *Victoria*, 876 F.2d at 1010 (recognizing that international law "gives the United States . . . authority to treat stateless vessels as if they were its own"); *United States v. Alvarez-Mena*, 765 F.2d 1259, 1265 (5th Cir. 1985) ("[I]nternational law does not preclude any nation from exercising jurisdiction over stateless vessels on the high seas."); *United States v. Pinto-Mejia*, 720 F.2d 248, 260-61 (2d Cir. 1983); *United States v. Marino-Garcia*, 679 F.2d 1373, 1383 (11th Cir. 1982) ("[I]nternational law permits any nation to subject stateless **[—14—]** vessels on the high seas to its jurisdiction."); *United States v. Howard-Arias*, 679 F.2d 363, 371 (4th Cir. 1982); Malcolm D. Evans, "The Law of the Sea," in *International Law* 651, 656-60 (Malcolm D. Evans ed., 3d ed. 2010) ("[I]f a ship is stateless, or flies more than one flag so that its true State of registry is not clear, then any state can exercise jurisdiction over it.") (cited with approval in Restatement (Fourth) of the Foreign Relations Law of the United States § 408 n.3 (2018) [hereinafter "Restatement (Fourth)"]). **{-7-}**

In sum, there is no doubt that the United States could exercise jurisdiction over the stateless vessel upon which Aybar was found.

C.

Offering no persuasive reason why the United States could not exercise jurisdiction over the stateless vessel upon which he was found, Aybar narrows his focus to his prosecution. While it may be clear that international law allows any state to exercise jurisdiction over a flagless vessel, even to the point of stopping, boarding and seizing it should they wish to do so, he asserts that the prosecution of those on board the vessel under the laws of the seizing country is a different matter altogether.

With respect to United States-flagged vessels, the law does not distinguish between jurisdiction over the vessel itself and jurisdiction over the people on the vessel and their conduct **[—15—]** on board. It is well settled that the United States has jurisdiction over conduct occurring on United States-flagged vessels because: (1) "[t]he deck of a private American vessel . . . is considered . . . constructively as territory of the United States," *Ross v. McIntyre*, 140 U.S. 453, 464 (1891); and (2) a state's jurisdiction over conduct on its territory is one of "the most commonly recognized bases of jurisdiction," Restatement (Fourth) § 407 cmt. c; *see also id.* § 408 cmt. a ("A state may exercise prescriptive jurisdiction with respect to persons, property, and conduct within its territory."); *Smith*, 680 F.2d at 257 (similar). *Cf.* Restatement (Third) § 502 cmt. d (explaining that a flag state has jurisdiction over "the conduct of a ship" as well as "any activity aboard the ship").

Two centuries of case law strongly suggest that the same territorial principles apply to conduct aboard a stateless vessel. Shortly after our nation's founding, the United States Supreme Court issued a series of opinions addressing the scope of the United States' jurisdiction over conduct committed on board non-United States vessels. The Court rejected the assertion of jurisdiction in domestic courts over murders committed by and against foreigners on foreign vessels. *See United States v. Furlong*, 18 U.S. (5 Wheat.) 184, 196–98 (1820); *see also United States v. Klintock*, 18 U.S. (5 Wheat.) 144, 151 (1820). Murders committed by and against foreigners on stateless vessels, though, **[—16—]** could be prosecuted in the United States. *See Klintock*, 18 U.S. at 151–52; *United States v. Holmes*, 18 U.S. (5 Wheat.) 412, 417– 18; *see also Furlong*, 18 U.S. at 194–95 (stating that murder is "equally punishable" in the courts of the United States when committed on an American ship or on a stateless pirate ship, as opposed to on a foreign ship, which presented "a question of more difficulty").

While those cases dealt with vessels that were deemed stateless because of piratical conduct, the Court did not hold that piracy was the only means by which a vessel could be deemed stateless so as to justify United States prosecutorial jurisdiction. On that point, *Holmes* conveyed the opposite, signaling that conduct of persons on board a stateless vessel could be prosecuted whether the vessel was piratical or not:

> The said Circuit Court had jurisdiction of the offen[s]e charged in the indictment, if the vessel, on board of which it was committed, had, at the time of the commission thereof, no real national character but was possessed and held by pirates, or by persons not lawfully sailing under the flag, or entitled to the **{-8-}** protection of any government whatsoever.

18 U.S. at 419.

These founding-era cases also did not hold that a foreign national may be prosecuted in the United States for his conduct on the high seas only if he personally renounces his nationality by engaging in piracy. True, the Court certainly approved the **[—17—]** prosecution of "those who acknowledge the authority of no State." *Klintock*, 18 U.S. at 152. But the Court also repeatedly emphasized the statelessness of the ship, rather than the nationality of the persons on board, in upholding the United States' exercise of jurisdiction over those persons. For example, in *Klintock*, the Court held that "persons on board of a vessel not at the time belonging to the subjects of any foreign power, but in possession of a crew acting in defiance of all law, and acknowledging obedience to no government whatever, . . . are proper objects for the penal code of all nations." *Id.* To the extent that there is any ambiguity as to whether the phrase "acknowledging obedience to no government whatever" was intended to modify the "persons" or the "vessel" at issue, the Court clarified in *Holmes* that the status of the vessel was determinative:

> In Klintock's case, it was laid down, that to exclude the jurisdiction of the Courts of the United States, in cases of murder or robbery committed on the high seas, the vessel in which the offender is, or to which he belongs, must be, at the time, . . . the property of a subject of a foreign State, and . . . subject, at that time, to [its] control. But if the offen[s]e be committed in a vessel, not at the time belonging to subjects of a foreign State, but in possession of persons acknowledging obedience to no government or flag, and acting in defiance of all law, it is [punishable in the courts of the United States]. It follows, therefore, that murder or robbery committed on the high seas, may be an offen[s]e cognizable by the Courts of the United States, although it was committed on board of a vessel not belonging to citizens of the United States, [] **[—18—]** if she had no national character, but was possessed and held by pirates, or persons not lawfully sailing under the flag of any foreign nation.

18 U.S. at 416–17. Because the Court in *Holmes* held that the existence of jurisdiction depended on whether or not the vessel at issue was under the control of a foreign nation, "it made no difference, as to the point of jurisdiction, whether the [offenders] were citizens of the United States" or citizens of foreign nations. *Id.* at 419–20. As we have described, this approach comports with the overall system of flag-state jurisdiction. *See Furlong*, 18 U.S. at 198 (explaining that the distinction between foreign vessels and stateless vessels serves to avoid "offensive interference with the governments of other nations").

Our concurring colleague well develops the case for treating *Holmes* as binding authority dictating our holding in this case. This is certainly a defensible view. If murder, a crime over which there is no universal jurisdiction, can be prosecuted by the United States when committed by a foreigner upon a foreigner on a vessel that has no national character, why can the United States not also prosecute drug trafficking committed by a foreigner on such a vessel? Nevertheless, the sometimes challenging syntax in *Holmes*, *Furlong*, and *Klintock*, plus the possibility that international law itself now differs materially from international **[—19—]** law as understood 200 years ago, counsel against resting our conclusion solely on those cases if we do not need to do so. And we do not.

No other circuit has held that conduct aboard a stateless vessel seized by the United States on the high seas may not be **{–9–}** prosecuted as conduct committed on United States territory.[3] *See United States v. Moreno-Morillo*, 334 F.3d 819, 828 (9th Cir. 2003) (noting that "a showing of statelessness effectively moots the nexus requirement because those aboard stateless vessels effectively have waived their right to object to the exercise of jurisdiction over them by United States courts"); *see also Marino-Garcia*, 679 F.2d at 1383 (concluding that stateless status "makes the vessel subject to action by all nations proscribing certain activities aboard stateless vessels and subjects those on board to prosecution for violating th[ose] proscriptions"); *Juda*, 46 F.3d at 967 (recognizing no distinction between the right to seize stateless vessels and the right to

[3] Because we sustain MDLEA as applied to Aybar, we need not decide whether and to what effect MDLEA should be construed as reaching even more broadly.

prosecute persons on board them); *Alvarez-Mena*, 765 F.2d at 1266-67 (same).

While there is no unanimity among scholars on this point, *see* Douglas Guilfoyle, "The High Seas," in *The Oxford Handbook on the Law of the Sea* 218 (Rothwell et al. eds. 2015), the **[—20—]** longstanding unanimity among United States courts is especially significant, as "the state practice of the United States contributes to the development of customary international law when followed out of a sense of international legal right or obligation." Restatement (Fourth) § 402 cmt. b; *see also id.* n.2.

Treating conduct on stateless vessels in this manner furthers a basic aim of international law to achieve order on the high seas by disincentivizing the use of stateless vessels. *Marino-Garcia*, 679 F.2d at 1382-83. This approach also yields significant practical benefits, such as reducing complications when, for example, officials of the seizing nation are needed as witnesses in a subsequent prosecution of offenses committed on the vessel. Moreover, those who set out in stateless vessels cannot be said to possess the same reasonable expectation of sanctuary from foreign jurisdiction under international law as those on a flagged vessel would. *See Caicedo*, 47 F.3d at 372 (distinguishing properly flagged vessels, which have a "legitimate expectation" of being subject only to the laws of the flag state, from stateless vessels, which "subject themselves to the jurisdiction of all nations" such that a state's exercise of jurisdiction over them cannot, categorically, be said to be "arbitrary or fundamentally unfair"); *see also Moreno-Morillo*, 334 F.3d at 828; *Marino-Garcia*, 679 F.2d at 1382 (describing stateless vessels as "international pariahs" having "no internationally recognized right to navigate **[—21—]** freely on the high seas" and finding no categorical limits to the exercise of jurisdiction over stateless vessels under international law). Simply put, if a person intent on drug trafficking on the high seas wants to be prosecuted in his own country should he be caught, he should sail under that country's flag.

D.

Aybar contends that, notwithstanding the foregoing, his prosecution was prohibited by other, more specific rules and undertakings governing jurisdiction and the high seas. As we will explain, we find that the relevant and more specific rules and undertakings are entirely consistent with our conclusion that Aybar was properly subject to prosecution in the United States for his conduct on board the stateless vessel.

1.

Aybar first points to the 1988 United Nations Convention Against Illicit Traffic **{-10-}** in Narcotic Drugs and Psychotropic Substances ("UN Drug Trafficking Convention"), U.N.T.S. 27627 (1988), which was adopted to give effect to UNCLOS's call on states to "cooperate in the suppression of illicit traffic in narcotic drugs" on the high seas, UNCLOS art. 108. Specifically, he points out that the UN Drug Trafficking Convention does not explicitly address the possibility of states exercising jurisdiction over persons found engaging in drug trafficking on stateless vessels on **[—22—]** the high seas. *See* UN Drug Trafficking Convention art. 17. But it does not rule out such prosecutions either. To the contrary, at least one United Nations body has suggested that states may exercise jurisdiction under the convention over persons found engaging in illegal activities on stateless vessels, in combination with domestic sources of authority. *See* Commission on Crime Prevention and Criminal Justice, Outcome of the Expert Group Meeting on Transnational Organized Crime at Sea, held in Vienna, Austria, on 5-6 April 2016, U.N. Doc. E/CN.15/2016/CRP.3, ¶ 18 (May 19, 2016) (recognizing debate over enforcement activity against perpetrators found on stateless vessels but observing that "if a State is party to the [UN Drug Trafficking Convention], it should exercise jurisdiction over vessels without nationality").

To implement the UN Drug Trafficking Convention, several European states adopted the 1995 Council of Europe Convention on Illicit Traffic by Sea. That convention provides further support for the proposition that international law welcomes prosecutions by the seizing nation of those found engaged in drug trafficking on stateless vessels: It not only allows but *requires* parties to prosecute persons found trafficking drugs on stateless vessels. *See* Agreement on Illicit Traffic by Sea, Implementing Article 17 of the United Nations Convention Against Illicit Traffic in Narcotic Drugs and Psychotropic Substances art. 3, C.E.T.S. 156 (1995) (mandating that "each Party shall take such measures as may **[—23—]** be necessary to establish its jurisdiction over the relevant offen[s]es committed on board a vessel which is without nationality, or which is assimilated to a vessel without nationality under international law").[4]

Several other international law instruments similarly leave open the possibility of states taking law enforcement action against persons found on stateless vessels. Such instruments typically use language indicating that states may take action "in accordance with relevant domestic and international law" after searching a stateless vessel on the high seas. *See Brownlie's Principles*, *supra*, at 291 (explaining that this language "perpetuates the ambiguity regarding the exercise of prescriptive jurisdiction and enforcement over stateless vessels"). For example, the 2000 Migrant Smuggling Protocol indicates with respect to vessels without nationality that "[i]f evidence confirming the suspicion [of smuggling] is found," the boarding State "shall take appropriate measures *in accordance with relevant domestic and international law*." *See* Protocol Against the Smuggling of Migrants by Land, Sea and Air, Supplementing the **[—24—]** United Nations Convention Against Transnational Organized Crime art. 8(7), U.N.T.S. 2241 (2000) (emphasis added).

Likewise, the United Nations Straddling Fish Stocks Agreement suggests that states may take enforcement action against stateless fishing vessels for illegal **{-11-}** fishing "in accordance with international law," but does not specify what such action might entail. *See* Agreement for the Implementation of the Provisions of the United Nations Convention on the Law of the Seas of 10 December 1982 Relating to the Conservation and Management of Straddling Stocks and Highly Migratory Fish Stocks art. 21(17), Conference on Straddling Fish Stocks and Highly Migratory Fish Stocks, 6th Sess., U.N. Doc. A/CONF.164/37 (Sept. 8, 1995); *see also* Douglas Guilfoyle, *Shipping Interdiction and the Law of the Sea* 108 (2009) (observing that this language "accommodat[es] divergent views as to prescriptive and enforcement jurisdiction over stateless vessels at general international law"). Moreover, various regional fisheries organizations have encouraged states to take legal action where evidence is found of illegal fishing on stateless vessels.[5] *See* Guilfoyle, *Shipping Interdiction and the* **[—25—]** *Law of the Sea*, *supra*, at 129 (explaining that the Northeast Atlantic Fisheries Commission Scheme "appears to directly encourage the adoption of national laws permitting extraterritorial enforcement action against stateless vessels," even if, like the UN Drug Trafficking Convention, it does not itself provide for such enforcement measures); Rosemary Rayfuse, *Non-Flag State*

[4] *See also* Agreement Concerning Co-Operation in Suppressing Illicit Maritime Air Trafficking in Narcotic Drugs and Psychotropic Substances in the Caribbean Area (not yet in force) (signed by the United States on April 10, 2003) (providing the same).

[5] *See, e.g.*, International Commission for the Conservation of Atlantic Tunas (ICCAT), Recommendations by ICCAT on Vessel Sightings, ¶ 3 (June 20, 2020) ("If the vessel is confirmed to be without nationality, a competent authority . . . is encouraged to inspect the vessel, consistent with international law and, if evidence so warrants, the Contracting Party is encouraged to take such action as may be appropriate, in accordance with international law."); Northeast Atlantic Fisheries Commission, Scheme of Control **[—25—]** and Enforcement, art. 38(2) (Feb. 7, 2020); *see also* Indian Ocean Tuna Commission, Resolution 16/05 on Vessels Without Nationality (Sept. 27, 2016); United Nations Food and Agriculture Organization, Implementation of the International Plan of Action to Prevent, Deter and Eliminate Illegal, Unreported, and Unregulated Fishing 14-15 (2002) ("Taking action against [stateless] vessels should be a high priority, because their very statelessness frustrates the primary means to control fishing activity on the high seas—through flag State jurisdiction.").

Enforcement in High Seas Fisheries 330-31 (2004).

Moreover, certain bilateral instruments to which the United States is a party explicitly leave open the possibility of states taking enforcement action against persons found on board stateless vessels where the evidence so warrants. *See, e.g.*, Agreement between the Government of the United States of America and the Government of the Dominican Republic Concerning Maritime Counter-Drug Operations, U.S.-Dom. Rep., Mar. 23, 1995, T.I.A.S. No. 12620 (providing that counter-drug operations pursuant to the agreement may be carried out against vessels "without nationality," but also noting under the protocol to the agreement that law enforcement personnel are to act in accordance with **[—26—]** international law when engaging in boardings and searches); Agreement between the United States of America and Cyprus Concerning Cooperation to Suppress the Proliferation of Weapons of Mass Destruction, Their Delivery Systems, and Related Materials by Sea, U.S.-Cyp., July 25, 2005, T.I.A.S. 06-112 (including stateless vessels among the vessels against which operations may be undertaken under the agreement); Agreement between the United States of America and Belize Concerning Cooperation to Suppress the Proliferation of Weapons of Mass Destruction, Their Delivery Systems, and Related Materials by Sea, U.S.-Blz., Oct. 29, 2005, T.I.A.S. 05-1019 (same); *see also United States v. Bravo*, 489 F.3d 1, 4 (1st Cir. 2007) (recounting that the claimed flag **{-12-}** state could not confirm registry of the vessel and authorized the United States to proceed with law enforcement action under "international law").

2.

Aybar insists that UNCLOS nevertheless prohibits his prosecution. He relies on Article 110, which provides a right to visit ships suspected of being without nationality and to search those ships if suspicion of statelessness remains after checking the ship's documents. *See also Aybar-Ulloa*, 913 F.3d at 62-63, 7 Adm. R. at 69–71 (Torruella, J., dissenting in part) (arguing that the unilateral extension of domestic jurisdiction over a stateless vessel on the high seas without a nexus violates UNCLOS). But in recognizing a right to visit certain ships, including a ship "without **[—27—]** nationality," Article 110 does not prohibit the prosecution of those on board. It simply remains silent as to whether and when the visiting nation may prosecute persons found on the ship.

Aybar argues that we should draw a negative inference from that silence because other articles of UNCLOS do contain express grants of authority to penalize persons found on certain vessels. For example, Article 105 authorizes the arrest and punishment of persons found on pirate ships. Similarly, Articles 99 and 109 expressly grant the power to penalize persons for engaging in slavery and unauthorized broadcasting, respectively. We reject the negative inference Aybar would have us draw for two reasons.

First, and most simply, there are obvious differences between the examples given and that of a stateless vessel, undercutting any negative inference that could be drawn from the presence of express grants in some articles but not others. For starters, a ship engaged in piracy may retain its nationality. UNCLOS art. 104. So there was a reason for Article 105 to expressly confirm that any state can exercise universal jurisdiction to seize and prosecute individuals on such a ship—otherwise, it might have been possible to argue that only the ship's flag state would be able to seize and prosecute those individuals. Under this reading, Article 105 grants no new authority. Similarly, because vessels that engage in unauthorized **[—28—]** broadcasting can retain their nationality, an exception was needed to overcome the presumption of exclusive flag-state jurisdiction where it was desirable for impacted states to have the possibility of arresting "person[s] or ship[s] engaged in" this activity. *See id.* art. 109(4) (providing that states receiving transmissions or suffering from interference may exercise their jurisdiction to prosecute unauthorized broadcasting). Further, because slave ships also generally retain their nationality, Article 99 had to expressly impinge on flag-state jurisdiction in order to declare that enslaved persons found on any ship are ipso facto free. Without these provisions—which codify limitations on the rights of flag states where their ships engage in conduct of severe concern to the international community—other states may have presumed that their hands were tied.

Not so in the case of the stateless vessel. The presumption of flag-state jurisdiction, which arguably made the express grants of authority in Articles 99, 105, and 109 necessary, simply does not apply where the vessel at issue is stateless. Rather, as we have explained, stateless vessels are treated as subject to the exercise of authority by any nation. Accordingly, the absence of an express grant of authority to seize and prosecute persons on board a stateless vessel in Article 110 does not, on its own, establish that Aybar's seizure and prosecution are prohibited by UNCLOS. **[—29—]**

Second, Aybar's argument cannot be squared with the approach taken in the **{-13-}** international instruments and undertakings we have described. If a categorical rule against the extension of domestic jurisdiction over stateless vessels could be found in UNCLOS Article 110, it is unlikely that subsequent instruments mentioning stateless vessels could avoid it or that their drafters would have been unaware of it. Instead, it appears that in the decades since UNCLOS was concluded, the relevant international organizations and actors have resolved to leave the issue to the judgment of states. *See* Guilfoyle, "The High Seas," *supra*, at 218 (explaining that "[t]reaty law is silent" on the extension of national jurisdiction over stateless vessels without a nexus and "sometimes deliberately ambiguous" such that existing treaty language "covers divergent national (and academic) interpretations").

Our reading of international law does not render the United States an outlier. Other nations have also adopted laws and regulations permitting exercises of domestic jurisdiction over stateless vessels and persons found on board them. *See* United Nations Food and Agriculture Organization, Implementation of the International Plan of Action to Prevent, Deter and Eliminate Illegal, Unreported, and Unregulated Fishing 15 (2002) (discussing laws adopted by Canada and Norway to extend jurisdiction over stateless vessels); *see also Fisheries Jurisdiction Case (Spain v.* **[—30—]** *Canada)*, Jurisdiction, Judgment, 1998 I.C.J. Rep. 432, ¶¶ 19, 61 64, 75 (Dec. 4) (describing Canada's seizure of a vessel under its Coastal Fisheries Protection Act, adopted to cover high seas areas governed by the Northwest Atlantic Fisheries Organization, and the subsequent arrest and prosecution of its master for illegal fishing under that law, as well as Spain's response that such law enforcement actions were permissible only if the vessel were stateless); *Molvan v. Attorney-General for Palestine*, A.C. 351 (1948); Guilfoyle, "The High Seas," *supra*, at 218 (noting that the United States and United Kingdom have historically taken the view that no nexus is required to extend national jurisdiction over a stateless vessel).[6] That there is not even more evidence of similar state practices engenders no surprise, given the practical difficulties of seizing ships on the high seas. "[W]hile international law may allow states to arrest stateless vessels, states may not yet have appropriated that right unto themselves." Rayfuse, *supra*, at 330 (explaining that the absence of a widespread practice of arresting and prosecuting stateless fishing vessels may "reflect[] . . . the reality that few states have the physical capability to arrest these vessels on the high seas" and that **[—31—]** "states may lack a basis in their domestic legal framework permitting their authorities to take such action").

E.

We add, finally, several caveats.

---

[6] See generally Coastal Fisheries Protection Act (R.S.C., 1985, c. c-33) § 5.5 (Canada); Marine Resources Act no. 37 (6 June 2008) (Norway), available at https://www.fiskeridir.no/English/Fisheries/Regulations/The-marine-resources-act; Policing and Crime Act 2017, c.3 § 84(1)(b) (United Kingdom), available at https://www.legislation.gov.uk/ukpga/2017/3/section/84.

First, our holding makes no attempt to assert universal jurisdiction over drug trafficking offenses. The holding does not apply at all to the large majority of vessels sailing on the high seas. Rather, it applies only to vessels flouting order and custom on the high seas by eschewing the responsibilities and protections of the flag-state system.

Second, we do not suggest that international law does not apply to the seizure of the vessel or that persons on board such **{–14–}** vessels fall outside of the protection of international law. *See* Rayfuse, *supra*, at 57 (explaining that "a ship without nationality[] is not necessarily a ship without law[,] . . . [b]ut it is a ship without protection" (quoting D.P. O'Connell, 2 *The International Law of the Sea* 755 (1984))). Fundamental principles of customary international human rights law, and requirements of due process under United States law, may well still apply in circumstances not present in this appeal. *See Brownlie's Principles*, *supra*, at 285 (noting that stateless ships "are not outside the law altogether," as "their occupants are protected by elementary considerations of humanity"); Maarten Den Heijer, *Europe and Extra-territorial Asylum* 238 (2012) (recognizing that **[—32—]** the "taking of coercive measures" against stateless vessels "is likely to come within the ambit of human rights law"); *see also United States v. Ballestas*, 795 F.3d 138, 148, 3 Adm. R. 698, 703–04 (D.C. Cir. 2015); *United States v. Yousef*, 327 F.3d 56, 111-12 (2d Cir. 2003) (citing *United States v. Davis*, 905 F.2d 245, 248-49 (9th Cir. 1990)); *Cardales*, 168 F.3d at 553.

While the fundamental "arbitrariness or unfairness" of a prosecution may depend in some part on notions of "fair warning" under either domestic or international law, *see United States v. Van Der End*, 943 F.3d 98, 106, 7 Adm. R. 123, 127 (2d Cir. 2019), such "fair warning" has certainly been given in the case of drug trafficking. Although not a crime that gives rise to universal jurisdiction, *see* Restatement (Fourth) § 413 n.1 (explaining that "universal jurisdiction is limited to the most serious offenses about which a consensus has arisen for the existence of universal jurisdiction"); *United States v. Cardales-Luna*, 632 F.3d 731, 740-41 (Torruella, J., dissenting), drug trafficking has long been regarded as a serious crime by nearly all nations. *See* United Nations Treaty Depositary, Status of the United Nations Convention against Illicit Traffic in Narcotics (accessed August 9, 2020) (indicating that 191 states are party to the UN Drug Trafficking Convention); *see also* 46 U.S.C. § 70501(1) (recognizing that "trafficking in controlled substances aboard vessels is a serious international problem" that "is universally condemned"). **[—33—]**

Third, we opt not to decide one way or the other whether the United States may prosecute a foreign citizen engaged in drug trafficking on a stateless vessel where the United States never boarded and seized the vessel. Nor do we reach the question of whether the MDLEA by its own terms reaches such a situation. In this case the law has been applied to a person apprehended on board the stateless vessel when stopped and boarded by United States Coast Guard officers. Although the government seeks a broader ruling in its supplemental briefing, it does not abandon its argument that "MDLEA was not unconstitutional as applied to this case because Aybar's stateless vessel was intercepted on the high seas" by the United States. And resolving this "as applied" argument is all that is necessary to dispose of this appeal.

Finally, nothing in our reasoning forecloses a successful claim of diplomatic protection by a foreign state, should a foreign state make such a petition on behalf of its national. *See* Barnes, *supra*, at 315; Churchill & Lowe, *supra*, at 172. What we hold, instead, is that international law does not generally prohibit the United States from prosecuting drug traffickers found on a stateless vessel stopped and boarded by the United States on the high seas as if they had been found on a United States vessel subject to the territorial jurisdiction of the United States. Therefore, even if Congress's power under the **[—34—]** Define and Punish Clause is cabined by international **{–15–}** law, Aybar's prosecution under MDLEA would not exceed any such limitation.

III.

That leaves only Aybar's challenge to his sentence. For the reasons stated in the panel opinion, we vacate and remand for resentencing under the Sentencing Commission's clarified guidance, as reflected in Amendment 794. *See Aybar-Ulloa*, 913 F.3d at 56–57, 7 Adm. R. at 64–65 (citing *United States v. Sarmiento-Palacios*, 885 F. 3d 1, 6, 6 Adm. R. 8, 10–11 (1st Cir. 2018)).

IV.

For the foregoing reasons, we ***affirm*** the defendant's conviction, ***vacate*** the defendant's sentence, and ***remand*** for resentencing.

- Concurring Opinion Follows –

(Reporter's Note: Concurring Opinion follows on p. 22).

[—35—] {-15-} **BARRON**, Circuit Judge, concurring in the judgment:

Johvanny Aybar-Ulloa ("Aybar") contends that Article I, Section 8, Clause 10 of the United States Constitution, which authorizes Congress to "define and punish . . . Felonies committed on the high Seas," provides the sole constitutional source of power for the Maritime Drug Law Enforcement Act ("MDLEA"), 46 U.S.C. §§ 70501-70508. He further argues that there is an implicit limit on this power, rooted in the law of nations, and that this limit restricts Congress's authority to rely on this Clause to extend our country's domestic criminal laws to foreign nationals who violate them while they are outside the territorial jurisdiction of the United States. He therefore contends that his conviction under the MDLEA is unconstitutional, because he is a foreign national who is alleged to have engaged in drug trafficking while in international waters and on a vessel that is not registered to the United States.

In pressing this contention, Aybar asserts that his prosecution for violating the MDLEA cannot be deemed to accord with international law on the ground that the offense for which he was convicted is a crime against all nations. He emphasizes that this is so because international law does not recognize drug trafficking as a universal jurisdiction offense. He further asserts that there is no basis under international law for **[—36—]** permitting the United States to criminalize the conduct for which he was convicted based on an assertion of what is known as protective jurisdiction. This is so, he contends, because there was no nexus between his drug trafficking and the United States, as the vessel that he was on left from one foreign country and was headed to another. *See United States v. Robinson*, 843 F.2d 1, 3- 4 (1st Cir. 1988) (Breyer, J.) (noting "forceful argument" against application of protective principle to encompass drug trafficking on the high seas).

There is a fair amount of support for the contention that Article I's Define and Punish Clause is impliedly limited by the law of nations in ways that constrain Congress's authority to rely on that Clause to subject foreign nationals to our criminal laws for conduct that they engage on while they are on *foreign* vessels—even when those vessels are on the high seas. *See United States v. Furlong*, 18 U.S. (5 Wheat.) 184, 197-98 (1820) ("Congress . . . ha[s] no right to interfere" with other nations by "punishing [murders by foreign nationals] when committed within the [foreign] jurisdiction, or, (what is the same thing,) in the vessel of another nation."); *see also* Congressman John Marshall, Speech to the House of Representatives (Mar. 7, 1800), *in 10 Annals of Cong.* 607 (1800) (hereinafter "Speech of John Marshall") (arguing that the Define and Punish Clause cannot authorize federal "jurisdiction over offences, committed on {-16-} board a foreign ship **[—37—]** against a foreign nation" on the high seas); Justice James Wilson, Charge to the Grand Jury of the Circuit Court for the District of Virginia (May 23, 1791), *reprinted in 2 The Documentary History of the Supreme Court of the United States*, 1789-1800, at 179 (Maeva Marcus ed., 1988) (suggesting that "no state or states can; by treaties or municipal laws, alter or abrogate the law of nations" to the extent of reaching the crime of murder by a foreigner aboard a foreign flag ship).[7] But, without disputing that point, and without relying on either a claim that the crime involved here qualifies as a universal jurisdiction offense or that the MDLEA is the product of our nation's valid assertion of its protective jurisdiction, the majority nevertheless rejects Aybar's constitutional challenge.

The majority does so because, it rightly points out, although Aybar was on the high seas while he was in possession of the cocaine that led to his MDLEA charges, he was not at

[7] In fact, the United States itself early on took the position before the Supreme Court that the Define and Punish Clause was subject to this limitation, even though it takes the opposite view here. *See United States v. Palmer*, 16 U.S. (3 Wheat.) 610, 620 (1818) (argument of Mr. Blake on behalf of the United States) ("A felony, which is made a piracy by municipal statutes, and was not such by the law of nations, cannot be tried by the courts of the United States, if committed by a foreigner on board a foreign vessel, on the high seas; because the jurisdiction of the United States, beyond their own territorial limits, only extends to the punishment of crimes which are piracy by the law of nations.").

that time on a foreign vessel. Instead, he was on a stateless one that our **[—38—]** national authorities had interdicted in accord with international law. Thus, in the majority's view, Aybar was within the territorial jurisdiction of the United States when he violated the MDLEA no less than if he had been on a ship flying our nation's flag. *See* Slip Op. 4-5, 10-14. For that reason, the majority concludes, the premise on which Aybar's constitutional challenge rests—that he violated the MDLEA while he was *outside* the territorial jurisdiction of the United States—is mistaken. *See id.* at 33-34.

I do not disagree with the majority that Aybar's constitutional challenge must be rejected. I write separately, however, because I reach that conclusion through a different, albeit somewhat related, line of reasoning.

I.

The majority observes that, under the law of nations, a foreign national on a U.S.-flagged vessel is within the territorial jurisdiction of the United States even when that vessel is in international waters. *Id.* at 4-5, 14-15. The majority also notes that, under the law of nations, a country's war or clearly marked law enforcement ship may board and search a vessel in international waters when there is adequate reason to suspect that the vessel is stateless. *Id.* at 12-13; *see, e.g.*, Restatement (Third) of the Foreign Relations Law of the United States § 522(2)(b) & n.7 (1987) (hereinafter "Restatement (Third)") ("[A] warship or clearly- **[—39—]** marked law enforcement ship of any state may board . . . a ship . . . if there is reason to suspect that the ship . . . is without nationality"; "[a] stateless vessel is not entitled to . . . protection . . . against boarding and search."); *Brownlie's Principles of Public International Law* 285, 292 (James Crawford ed., 9th ed. 2019) (hereinafter "*Brownlie's Principles*") (noting statelessness as a "circumstance[] in which a warship may exercise the right of visit on the high seas"); Malcolm N. Shaw, *International Law* 457 (8th ed. 2017) ("A **{-17-}** ship that is stateless, and does not fly a flag, may be boarded and seized on the high seas.").

But, although the Third and Fourth Restatement of the Foreign Relations Law of the United States clearly establish the soundness of these twin propositions, *see* Restatement (Third) §§ 501 cmt. c, 502(2) & cmt. d, 522(2)(b) & n.7; Restatement (Fourth) of the Foreign Relations Law of the United States § 408 cmt. b & n.3 (2018), I do not read them to go further and establish that the prevailing view of the law of nations is that the interdicting country acquires the same territorial jurisdiction over the vessel's occupants as it acquires over the vessel itself. In fact, as the majority recognizes, Slip Op. 19, experts in international law have long noted the disagreement that exists over that very view, even in the case in which the interdicting country's officials have boarded the vessel. *See Brownlie's* **[—40—]** Principles at 292 (noting "two schools of practice" on the question of exercising jurisdiction over stateless vessels, one of which is the U.S. practice that also permits criminal prosecution of those aboard and the other which requires "some further jurisdictional nexus," and explaining that the latter "position [is] more consistent with existing treaty practice"); Douglas Guilfoyle, "The High Seas," *in The Oxford Handbook of the Law of the Sea* 216, 218 (Donald R. Rothwell et al. eds. 2015) ("[S]cholarly views vary" on "[t]he consequences of statelessness," and there are equally "divergent national . . . interpretations."); Douglas Guilfoyle, *Shipping Interdiction and the Law of the Sea* 17-18 (2009) (similar). Nor have these commentators suggested that, insofar as there is a prevailing view in this debate, it is one that is at odds with the understanding that Aybar asks us to conclude that international law embraces. *See* R.R. Churchill & A.V. Lowe, *The Law of the Sea* 214 (3d ed. 1999) ("[I]t has been held . . . that [stateless] *ships* enjoy the protection of no State," but the "better view appears to be that there is [still] a need for some [additional] jurisdictional nexus in order that a State may extend its laws to *those on board* a stateless ship and enforce the laws against them." (emphases added)); Richard Barnes, "The International Law of the Sea and Migration Control," *in Extraterritorial Immigration Control: Legal Challenges* 130-33 (B. Ryan and V. Mitsilegas eds., 2010) (noting that "US jurisprudence" **[—41—]** notwithstanding, "it is not at all clear that attempts to circumvent the requirement for a jurisdictional nexus . . . would be consistent with the law of the sea"; "the fact that right of visit and matters of enforcement are treated separately in the [United Nations Convention on the Law of the Sea] suggests that a positive right of visit does not imply wider enforcement powers").

Thus, insofar as the majority's understanding of the scope of territorial jurisdiction over Aybar under the law of nations is tied to the fact that the stateless vessel that he was on had been seized and boarded by the United States' authorities in the course of their attempt to determine the nation (if any) to which the vessel belonged, *see* Slip Op. 19 n.3, 33, I cannot find any clear support for that understanding in either the pertinent Restatements or the relevant learned commentary. I should add that I also am not aware of any precedent from U.S. courts that would provide such support.

There is precedent from our country's courts that stakes out a more expansive view of territorial jurisdiction under the law of nations than Aybar would have us countenance. But, that precedent, as I read it, does not tie that more expansive view to a showing that the officials from the nation that is claiming territorial jurisdiction **{–18–}** over the foreign national on a stateless vessel in international waters had seized and boarded the vessel in question pursuant to their recognized right under international **[—42—]** law to determine its status. Rather, that precedent appears to hold that foreign nationals on stateless vessels in international waters are subject to domestic prosecution by the United States for their conduct on board them pursuant to an assertion of the United States' territorial jurisdiction simply because there is support for all nations exercising such jurisdiction over vessels that are both stateless and in such waters. *See, e.g., United States v. Rendon*, 354 F.3d 1320, 1325 (11th Cir. 2003) ("Because stateless vessels do not fall within the veil of another sovereign's territorial protection, all nations can treat them as their own territory and subject them to their laws." (quoting *United States v. Caicedo*, 47 F.3d 370, 373 (9th Cir. 1995))); *Caicedo*, 47 F.3d at 373 ("Such vessels are 'international pariahs' . . . [and] subject themselves to the jurisdiction of all nations '*solely* as a consequence of the vessel's status as stateless.'" (quoting *United States v. Marino-Garcia*, 679 F.2d 1373, 1382-83 (11th Cir. 1982))); *United States v. Victoria*, 876 F.2d 1009, 1010 (1st Cir. 1989) (Breyer, J.) ("[A]s United States courts have interpreted international law, that law gives the 'United States authority to treat stateless vessels as if they were its own.'" (alteration omitted) (quoting *United States v. Smith*, 680 F.2d 255, 258 (1st Cir. 1982))); *United States v. Pinto-Meija*, 720 F.2d 248, 260-61 (2d Cir. 1983) ("[S]tateless vessels **[—43—]** on the high seas are, by virtue of their statelessness, subject to the jurisdiction of the United States.").

For these reasons, I see no clear support in either case law or commentary for the comparatively modest proposition that persons on stateless vessels that a foreign country's officials have seized and boarded pursuant to their recognized right to visit it are subject to that country's territorial jurisdiction under international law. Instead, I find no judicial precedent supporting that particular proposition, and much debate within the relevant commentary about its soundness.

There is another reason that prevents me from signing on to the majority's analysis. This reason has to do with the fact that I understand the MDLEA to have been premised on a broader theory of territorial jurisdiction under the law of nations than the majority is willing to embrace. That broader theory makes neither the physical presence of our authorities on a stateless vessel in the high seas or those authorities' interaction with that vessel of any legal significance in determining whether the occupants on that vessel come within our country's territorial jurisdiction. Instead, that broader theory makes the fact that the occupants are on a vessel that is both stateless and in international waters in and of itself the reason that their conduct while on board may be said to occur within the territorial jurisdiction of the United States. The notion that this more

[—44—] expansive theory of territorial jurisdiction under international law grounds the MDLEA finds support in the text of the statute itself. The MDLEA expressly criminalizes drug trafficking on any "vessel subject to the jurisdiction of the United States," 46 U.S.C. § 70503(e)(1), and then proceeds to define such vessels expansively to "include[]" not just those whose crews fail to make a claim that they belong to another nation "on request of an officer of the United States," *id.* § 70502(d)(1)(B) (deeming such vessels to be "without nationality," i.e., stateless), but also those vessels aboard which the crew's "claim of registry . . . is denied" or is "not affirmatively and unequivocally" affirmed "by the nation whose registry is claimed," without reference to a request being made by a {-19-} United States officer at all, *id.* § 70502(d)(1)(A), (C) (same). In these respects, the MDLEA notably fails to make the fact that U.S. authorities either have boarded the vessel or even interacted with the vessel's crew at the time of the commission of the offense a precondition for the vessel being subject to the jurisdiction of the United States. As a result, the MDLEA, by its terms, appears to make the bare fact that a foreign national engages in drug trafficking while on a stateless vessel in international waters a trigger for subjecting the foreign national to the reach of our domestic criminal laws.

To be sure, Aybar does not dispute on appeal that his vessel was in fact boarded by the U.S. authorities who interdicted [—45—] it. But, it is not evident to me that the jurisdictional basis for his MDLEA conviction was premised on any such finding, as it is not evident to me that any legal significance was attributed to that fact in convicting him of violating the MDLEA.[8]

For that reason, it is not surprising to me that the government describes the question concerning the scope of [—46—] territorial jurisdiction that Aybar's constitutional challenge to his MDLEA conviction implicates in terms that render both the physical presence of our authorities on his vessel and their interaction with it legally irrelevant. In fact, it would be surprising to me if the government were to embrace the view that, to ensure that the MDLEA would be enforced against a foreign national consonant with the law of nations, our law enforcement authorities must board the defendant's vessel (or even make contact with it) while he is both on it and in possession of the drugs. Such a view would appear to require the conclusion that our government could avoid flouting the law of nations in enforcing the MDLEA only by accepting that a foreign national on a stateless vessel on the high seas could protect himself from the statute's reach merely by dumping contraband from his vessel (stateless

[8] Aybar's indictment charging him with drug trafficking under the MDLEA mentioned only that he did so "on board a vessel subject to the jurisdiction of the United States; that is, a vessel without nationality," without noting the physical presence of U.S. officials on board the vessel at the time of the offense (or even any U.S. "interaction" with the vessel or the crew), and he did not admit to the vessel having been boarded in pleading guilty to the offense charged in the indictment, as he was not asked to do so, given that none of the elements of the offense made the fact of the boarding of legal relevance to his commission of it. The government's submissions to the District Court concerning whether Aybar was on board a vessel subject to U.S. jurisdiction, moreover, did not purport to make the finding that he was dependent on the fact of the vessel having been boarded by such officials. Finally, the District Court rejected Aybar's constitutional challenge on the ground that the United States had territorial jurisdiction over him while he possessed the cocaine at issue without purporting to premise that conclusion on the fact that U.S. officials had actually boarded his vessel. Thus, I am dubious that a conclusion that his conviction may be affirmed against this international-law-based constitutional challenge to Congress's Article I power is sustainable on the basis of the vessel having been boarded rather than on the more expansive theory that made his presence on a stateless vessel in international waters itself dispositive of whether he was subject to our nation's jurisdiction. *Cf. United States v. Lopez*, 514 U.S. 549, 559 (1995) (holding that the Gun- Free School Zones Act "exceeds the authority of Congress to 'regulate Commerce'" as it "neither regulates a commercial activity nor" "contains [a] jurisdictional element which would *ensure*, through case-by-case inquiry, that the firearm possession in question affects interstate commerce" (emphasis added) (quoting U.S. Const. Art. I § 8 cl. 3)); Richard H. Fallon, Jr., *As-Applied and Facial Challenges and Third-Party Standing*, 113 Harv. L. Rev. 1321, 1332-34 (2000).

though it is conceded to be) as soon as a ship carrying our country's law enforcement personnel is in view. **{-20-}** Yet, in fact, the government has enforced the MDLEA even when the defendant had finished possessing the drugs at issue before U.S. authorities had made any contact with the stateless vessel on which the offense had occurred. *See, e.g.*, *Rendon*, 354 F.3d at 1322–23; *Caicedo*, 47 F.3d at 371.

Of course, the fact that the government makes this broader assertion of territorial jurisdiction in asking us to reject Aybar's constitutional challenge does not mean that the **[—47—]** government's view of the scope of the United States' territorial jurisdiction under international law is correct. The Restatements and commentary described above provide no clear support for the notion that, under the law of nations, all countries are entitled to assert territorial jurisdiction over any foreign national in international waters who is on board a vessel that is stateless simply because that vessel is in those waters and does not belong to any nation. In fact, as I have explained, those materials do not even provide clear support for the relatively narrower but still broad proposition that a nation that exercises its right to visit a vessel in international waters that it suspects is stateless automatically acquires the right to assert domestic criminal jurisdiction over that vessel's foreign-national occupants.

I have noted above that a number of United States Circuit Courts have endorsed the view that, under the law of nations, a person's presence on a stateless vessel in international waters is in itself enough to make that person subject to a foreign nation's domestic criminal laws for the conduct in which he engages while on board—if, that is, the nation chooses to apply those laws to him. *See, e.g.*, *Rendon*, 354 F.3d at 1325; *Caicedo*, 47 F.3d at 372; *Pinto-Mejia*, 720 F.2d at 260-61. Thus, it is true that these courts have signed on to the government's expansive view of territorial jurisdiction under the law of nations. **[—48—]**

But, in doing so, these courts have supported that view merely by citing to other circuit-level precedents, *see, e.g.*, *Rendon*, 354 F.3d at 1325; *Caicedo*, 47 F.3d at 372; *Victoria*, 876 F.2d at 1010-11, or by treating international law authorities that clearly establish that a nation has territorial jurisdiction over a vessel in international waters that is stateless as if such authorities also establish that a nation has territorial jurisdiction over the foreign nationals who are on such a vessel, *see Pinto-Mejia*, 720 F.2d at 260-61; *Marino-Garcia*, 679 F.2d at 1382-83; *Smith*, 680 F.2d at 258. For that reason, I do not see how these precedents help to demonstrate that the law of nations is what the government says it is.

II.

The lack of clear authority for either the government's (or the majority's more modest but still broad) view of territorial jurisdiction under the law of nations does not necessarily compel us to hold that the United States lacks the constitutional authority to extend the MDLEA to Aybar's conduct. Even if we were to assume that the law of nations places limits on Congress's power under the Define and Punish Clause to subject foreign nationals on foreign vessels in international waters to our domestic criminal laws, and even if we were to assume that the United States may not assert protective jurisdiction over drug trafficking merely because it occurs on stateless vessels in international waters, **[—49—]** *see Robinson*, 843 F.2d at 3-4, it still may be that we are in no position to conclude that the application of the MDLEA to Aybar's conduct in this case would violate international law—and thus in no position to conclude that such application would transgress Article I. **{-21-}**

A rule of international law that would insulate foreign nationals on stateless vessels on the high seas from domestic criminal jurisdiction would raise practical difficulties for law enforcement authorities—and not only for those from our country. *See* Slip Op. 20-21. In light of those difficulties and the degree of legal uncertainty that exists in this realm, it may be that it would be proper for us to defer to our political branches' judgment as to what the law of nations permits here.[9] *Cf. United States v.* **[—50—]** *Smith,* 18 U.S. (5 Wheat.) 153, 159 (1820) (explaining that "there is a peculiar fitness in giving the power to define as well as to punish; and there is not the slightest reason to doubt that this consideration had very great weight in producing the phraseology in question"); *id.* at 169-72 (Livingston, J., dissenting) ("The special power here given to define . . ., can be attributed to no other cause, than to the uncertainty . . . in the law of nations, and which it must have been the intention of the framers of the constitution to remove, by conferring on the national legislature the power which has been mentioned.").

It may also be that, as the majority suggests, *see* Slip Op. 19-21, there is a "general usage and practice of nations," *Smith,* 18 U.S. (5 Wheat.) at 160-61, that supports the United States' position. Other nations do not appear to have affirmatively resisted our country's assertion of this expansive view of territorial jurisdiction, and we are dealing with the peculiar context of the high seas. Perhaps, then, it would be prudent to reject Aybar's constitutional challenge to his **[—51—]** conviction for this additional reason, notwithstanding that the evidence before us of this practice consists chiefly of what other nations have not done in response to what ours has. *See* Andrew W. Anderson, *Jurisdiction over Stateless Vessels on the High Seas: An Appraisal under Domestic and International Law,* 13 J. Mar. L. & Com. 323, 331-32 (1982); Myres S. McDougal, *The Law of the High Seas in Time of Peace,* 26 Naval War C. Rev. 35, 36 (1973); Myres S. McDougal & William T. Burke, *The Public Order of the Oceans: A Contemporary International Law of the Sea* 1047 (1962).

But, I am wary of rejecting Aybar's constitutional challenge by relying on either **{-22-}** a principle of deference to the political branches that I am not sure obtains or a state practice that is based only on the limited evidence of it that we have here. Rather, I conclude that we—as a lower court—must reject it due to the guidance supplied by the more than two-century-old Supreme Court precedent to which the majority gives great weight but ultimately concludes fails to dictate how we must decide this case. *See* Slip Op. 15-19.

III.

That precedent, *United States v. Holmes,* 18 U.S. (5 Wheat.) 412 (1820), was among the cases that the Supreme Court decided just decades after the Constitution's ratification and that are sometimes referred to as the "piracy cases," G. Edward White, *The Marshall Court and International Law: The Piracy Cases,* **[—52—]** 83 Am. J. Int'l L. 727 (1989). The cases in this line of authority dealt with the United States' power to prosecute defendants of a range of citizenships and

---

[9] Much like Congress in the MDLEA, the Executive Branch has before taken the position that our laws may punish drug trafficking by foreign nationals aboard stateless vessels in the high seas consistently with international law. *See, e.g., Stopping "Mother Ships" -- A Loophole in Drug Enforcement: Hearing on S. 3437 Before the Subcomm. to Investigate Juvenile Delinquency of the H. Comm. on the Judiciary,* 95th Cong. 28 (1978) (statement of Morris Busby, Acting Deputy Assistant Secretary, Dep't of St. Off. of Oceans Aff.) (explaining in supporting a precursor bill to the MDLEA that "making it a crime to possess drugs on the high seas with an intent to distribute, whether or not the intent was to distribute the[] drugs in the United States" "where you have a ship without any nationality on the high seas" "would comport with international law"); *Coast Guard Drug Law Enforcement: Hearing on H.R. 2538 Before the Subcomm. on Coast Guard and Navigation of the H. Comm. on Merchant Marine and Fisheries,* 96th Cong. 55 (1979) (statement of Morris Busby, Director, Dep't of St. Off. of Ocean Aff.) (elaborating that international law did, in his Department's view, create "an exception which allows us to board a vessel on the high seas which is without nationality," and further **[—50—]** "recommend[ing] . . . that [the United States] make it a [prosecutable] violation for [drug trafficking] to occur on board a vessel which is stateless"; "[w]hile ordinarily the United States does not favor a unilateral extension of jurisdiction . . . over the activities of non-U.S. citizens on board stateless vessels without proof of some connection to the United States, the serious nature of [the drug trafficking] problem, and the fact that persons on board these stateless vessels [generally] are engaged in narcotics trafficking aimed at the United States, warrant an extension in this particular case.").

circumstances who shared the attribute of having been indicted in our country pursuant to our criminal justice system for murder, robbery, or other wrongdoing on the high seas. *See Holmes*, 18 U.S. (5 Wheat.) 412; *Furlong*, 18 U.S. (5 Wheat.) 184; *Smith*, 18 U.S. (5 Wheat.) 153; *United States v. Klintock*, 18 U.S. (5 Wheat.) 144 (1820); *United States v. Palmer*, 16 U.S. (3 Wheat.) 610 (1818).

These cases were decided amidst the then-swirling debate over whether the law of nations permitted the United States to assert domestic criminal jurisdiction over foreign nationals who committed crimes while on the high seas. *Compare United States v. Robins*, 27 F. Cas. 825, 832 (D.S.C. 1799) ("There is no doubt that the circuit courts of the United States have a concurrent jurisdiction" that allows the U.S. government to prosecute the offense of murder aboard a British ship on the high seas, "and this arises under the general law of nations."), *with* Speech of John Marshall at 598-99 ("It is not true that all nations have jurisdiction over all offenses committed at sea. . . . [T]he jurisdiction of th[is] nation cannot extend to a murder committed by a British sailor, on board a British frigate navigating the high seas under a commission from his Britannic majesty. . . . It follows that no such common jurisdiction exists."). And *Holmes* **[—53—]** itself implicated that debate, as it concerned a challenge to the legal basis for a U.S. criminal prosecution of three defendants—two foreigners and one U.S. citizen—who had been indicted for knifing and throwing overboard an individual while they were on a vessel on the high seas that did not belong to the United States. *See Holmes*, 18 U.S. (5 Wheat.) at 412-13; *see also The Trial of William Holmes, Thomas Warrington, and Edward Rosewain on an Indictment for Murder on the High Seas Before the Circuit Court of the United States* 5 (Boston, Joseph C. Spear 1820) (hereinafter "The *Holmes* Trial").

Specifically, *Holmes* posed the following question: when, if ever, is "murder" by a foreign national "committed on the high seas, . . . an offence cognizable by the Courts of the United States"? *Holmes*, 18 U.S. (5 Wheat.) at 417. The Supreme Court answered as follows.

The Court first observed that, if the murder "be committed on board of a foreign vessel by a citizen of the United States, or on board of a vessel of the United States by a foreigner, the offender is to be considered . . . *as belonging to the nation under whose flag he sails*." *Id.* at 417 (emphasis added). But, the Court then continued, there would be jurisdiction in our nation's courts over such a prosecution "if [the vessel] had no national character, but was possessed and held by pirates, *or* **{-23-}** *persons not lawfully sailing under the flag of any foreign* **[—54—]** *nations*." *Id.* (emphasis added). And, the Court reiterated this same understanding in the certificate,[10] explaining: "the said Circuit Court had jurisdiction of the offence charged in the indictment [i.e., murder], if the vessel, on board of which it was committed, had, at the time of the commission thereof, no real national character but was possessed and held by pirates, *or by persons not lawfully sailing under the flag*, or entitled to the protection of any government whatsoever." *Id.* at 419 (emphasis added).

Holmes appears to state, then, that a foreign national is subject to the domestic criminal jurisdiction of the United States if he commits a felony while on a vessel on the high seas that is "*not lawfully sailing under the flag of any foreign nation*." *Id.* at 417 (emphasis added). For this reason, *Holmes* appears to sink Aybar's constitutional challenge—by rejecting the view that a stateless vessel in international waters is a foreign vessel, and by supporting the view that international law does not bar a nation from extending its domestic criminal laws to persons who are engaged in felonious conduct on board vessels **[—55—]** lacking any national character while those vessels are in international waters.[11]

[10] The "Certificate" "blend[ed] the views of all the justices together on the broadest common position." Alfred P. Rubin, *The Law of Piracy* 141 (1988).

[11] It is worth noting that the *Holmes* defendants were apprehended only after they eventually sailed their ship into a harbor in Scituate, Massachusetts; there is no indication that U.S. officials were aboard or interacted with the vessel at the time of the murder. *See* The *Holmes* Trial at 6.

Recognizing the potential threat that *Holmes* presents, Aybar seeks to keep his challenge afloat in the following way. He argues that *Holmes* is best read to address only the extent of Congress's power to regulate the conduct of "piracy committed either by a citizen or a foreigner . . . based on the universal jurisdiction of piracy." Accordingly, he contends, *Holmes* supplies no support for concluding that the law of nations permitted his prosecution under the MDLEA, given that "drug trafficking is not understood to be a universal jurisdiction offense."

The problem for Aybar is that the predicate offense in the foreign nationals' indictment in *Holmes* was "murder." 18 U.S. (5 Wheat.) at 413. That is significant because it was well understood at the time that general piracy was "rob[bery] . . . on the high seas" and that this single category of piracy offense was, under the law of nations, "punishable by all"—but "[n]o particular nation can increase or diminish the list of offences thus punishable." Speech of John Marshall at 600; *see also Smith,* **[—56—]** 18 U.S. (5 Wheat.) at 162 ("[T]he offence [of general piracy] is supposed to depend, not upon the particular provisions of any municipal code, but upon the law of nations, both for its definition and punishment."). Thus, because the charged offense at issue in *Holmes* was murder on the high seas rather than robbery on the high seas, there is little basis for concluding that the Court understood the foreign national defendants there to have been charged with general piracy—and thus with a universal jurisdiction offense—rather than with merely a domestic felony.

That the statute of conviction in *Holmes* provided that "if any person . . . shall commit, upon the high seas, . . . murder . . . every such offender *shall be deemed, taken, and adjudged to be, a pirate and felon,* and being thereof convicted, shall suffer death," Act of April 30th, 1790, for the Punishment of Certain Crimes Against the **{-24-}** United States, ch. 9 § 8, 1 Stat. 113 (emphasis added), does not suggest otherwise. It was understood at the time that "[a] statute may make *any* offence piracy, *committed within the jurisdiction of the nation passing the statute,* and such offence will be punishable by that nation"—but, unless the statutory offense was general piracy, "[t]he jurisdiction of the nation is [here] confined to its territory and to its own subjects." Speech of John Marshall at 600, 602 (emphases added); *see also id.* at 600-01 (rejecting the notion that all "piracies at common law" are "punishable by every nation," **[—57—]** and explaining that a statute might punish murder or other crimes as piracy, but such a "municipal regulation could not be considered as proving that those offences were . . . piracy by the law of nations"); Eugene Kontorovich, *The "Define and Punish" Clause and the Limits of Universal Jurisdiction,* 103 Nw. U. L. Rev. 149, 167 (2009) (explaining the then-familiar understanding that general piracy and municipal piracy were not equivalent).

Nor is there anything in *Holmes* that indicates that the Court understood the offense of murder that was at issue—denominated though it was in the underlying federal criminal statute as a species of piracy—to constitute "general" rather than "municipal" piracy. In fact, during the sentencing proceedings in *Holmes,* Justice Story, who not only participated in the case at the Supreme Court but also, while riding circuit, below in the First Circuit, referenced the defendants' mutiny aboard the vessel in question—noting that the knifing had been part of a plan to seize control of the ship—and informed the offenders that their conduct could have been indicted as a form of general piracy. *See* The *Holmes* Trial at 16-17. But, Justice Story made clear, the offense of murder on the high seas, for which the defendants had been indicted, was not itself such an offense. Indeed, he contrasted that offense with robbery on the high seas, which he concluded the defendants could have been indicted for in consequence of their "piratical usurpation and seizure of the **[—58—]** vessel," and which would have "left [them] only the character of general pirates and enemies of the human race, who had thrown off allegiance to all nations, and were justly amenable for [their] crime to the tribunal of all." The *Holmes* Trial at 16-17; *see also Report on the Trial of Samuel Tulley and John Dalton, on an Indictment for Piracy and*

Murder, Committed January 21st, 1812, Before the Circuit Court of the United States 30-31, 33 (Boston, J. Belcher 1812) (reporting a decision by Judge Davis, in which Justice Story concurred, which noted that "[t]he description of the offense [of piracy] in the first part of the 8th Section of [the Act of 1790] is analogous to the common law description" of piracy, as distinct from "piracy by the law of nations").

I do recognize that *Holmes* refers at one point to the vessel that the defendants were on as being "piratical." 18 U.S. (5 Wheat.) at 417. But, this reference also does not help Aybar in his attempt to show that *Holmes* fails to undermine the basis for his constitutional challenge to his conviction.

In describing the vessel from which the defendants committed the charged offense as "piratical," *Holmes* was not purporting to describe the nature of the defendants' charged offense as one that constituted general piracy. As we have seen, it was understood by those involved—Justice Story among them—that the offense did not qualify as such. *Holmes* was simply explaining why the vessel that the defendants had been on in the **[—59—]** high seas was fairly deemed to have no national character, or, otherwise put, to be stateless as opposed to foreign, such that the United States could subject those aboard to our **{-25-}** laws. For, a description of the evidence presented during the proceedings below reveals that the vessel on which the defendants had been when committing the murder on the high seas had earlier been unlawfully captured in those waters by pirate ships, at least if one followed the Court in disbelieving testimony that the seizing ships "were publicly fitted out at Buenos Ayres" and intended to "molest[] none but Spanish vessels." The *Holmes* Trial at 5, 7-8, 12; *see* Eugene Kontorovich, *Beyond the Article I Horizon: Congress's Enumerated Powers and Universal Jurisdiction over Drug Crimes*, 93 Minn. L. Rev. 1191, 1228 (2009) (arguing that the vessel in *Holmes* was "stateless by virtue of 'turning pirate'"); *see also Talbot v. Jansen*, 3 U.S. (3 Dall.) 133, 159 (1795) (opinion of Iredell, J.) ("[If] upon the enquiry it shall appear, that the vessel pretending to be a lawful privateer, is really not such, but uses a colourable commission for the purposes of plunder, she is to be considered by the law of nations . . . in the same light as having no commission at all."); The *Holmes* Trial at 10-11 ("If a murder be committed on board of a ship having no national character, as on board of ships owned and possessed by pirates, it is within the statute, if the ship be on the high seas when the crime is perpetrated. . . . *Palmer*'s case goes only to exclude the operation of the statute, **[—60—]** in cases where other nations have an exclusive jurisdiction."); *cf. Palmer*, 16 U.S. (3 Wheat.) at 632-33 ("The[r]e are offences against [a] nation *under whose flag the vessel sails*, and within whose particular jurisdiction all on board the vessel are. Every nation provides for such offences the punishment its own policy may dictate; and no general words of a statute ought to be construed to embrace them when committed by foreigners against a foreign government." (emphasis added)).[12]

Moreover, Aybar, who has waived any challenge to whether his vessel was actually stateless, makes no argument to us that the statelessness of a vessel in international

[12] *See* Letter from John Quincy Adams, U.S. Sec'y of State, to Francisco Dionisio Vives, Ambassador of Spain to the U.S. (May 3, 1820), *reprinted in* 5 Wheat. App. 154 (1820) (explaining that "[i]n the existing unfortunate civil war between Spain and the South American Provinces, the United States have constantly avowed, and faithfully maintained, an impartial neutrality," although the United States would—and did—prosecute "individuals guilty of piracy" that "*illegally* captured" "Spanish property" (emphasis added)); The *Holmes* Trial at 11 (reporting Justice Story's charge to the jury that "[i]f at the time when the crime was committed, . . . this vessel was under the exclusive jurisdiction of the Government of Buenos Ayres, then the statute does not reach the case [of murder aboard a foreign-flagged ship], and the Prisoners ought to be acquitted. And this depends on the fact, whether the capture was made by the privateers, under any authority derived from the Government of Buenos Ayres as a belligerent and independent nation . . . [and] sailed rightfully under its flag . . . [as this would mean] the capture was rightful, and the captured vessel immediately after the capture, may be justly deemed to have been exclusively under the jurisdiction of the Government of Buenos Ayres.").

waters permits the foreign national aboard it to be subjected to our domestic criminal **[—61—]** laws consistent with the law of nations only if the vessel is stateless by virtue of it having engaged in conduct that qualifies as general piracy. Aybar instead argues to us only that there is an important distinction to be drawn under the law of nations between offenses that are of universal jurisdiction and offenses that are not, and that the offense for which he was charged—drug trafficking—is of the latter kind.

Thus, the fact that *Holmes* deemed the foreign nationals who were the defendants in that case to be on a vessel lacking national character because it was piratical **{-26-}** lends little aid to Aybar's cause. The offense that was at issue in *Holmes* was a mere domestic felony, just like his, and it occurred on a vessel that was stateless, just like his.[13] **[—62—]**

Aybar also makes no argument to us that even if *Holmes* did take an expansive view of the United States' authority to assert domestic criminal jurisdiction over foreign nationals engaged in felonious conduct on a stateless vessel on the high seas, intervening developments in international law preclude us from construing Article I's Define and Punish Clause to permit Congress to rely on that power to enact this criminal statute on the understanding of the law of nations that *Holmes* embraced. His **[—63—]** only contention regarding *Holmes* is that it did not embrace that understanding of the law of nations even then.

IV.

For these reasons, I am convinced that *Holmes* requires that we conclude that the Define and Punish Clause is best understood not to contain an implicit limit that would prevent the United States from prosecuting foreign nationals for their felonious conduct on stateless vessels in international waters. The founding generation was attentive to the strictures of the law of nations. See David M. Golove & Daniel J. Hulsebosch, *The Law of Nations and the Constitution: An Early Modern Perspective*, 106 Geo. L. J. 1593, 1595-96 (2018) (describing "the prominent place of the law of nations in the constitutional reform project that culminated in the Philadelphia Convention"). And so, as between the uncertain or even skeptical views of more

---

[13] Interestingly, in his charge to the jury, Justice Story explained that the defendants could even be prosecuted if they had committed the murder while aboard *no* ship:

> The statute refers as to locality to "the high seas" only, and it would be far too narrow a construction, to limit its operation to crimes committed on board of ships or vessels. Murder may be committed on the high seas when neither the murderer, or the murdered is on board of any ship or vessel. A man may in the sea murder another who is in the sea swimming, or on a plank or raft; and it is obvious, that when the death is by drowning, the murder is committed literally on the high seas, wherever the murderer may at the time be. . . . *We see no reason in a case of this sort, where the murder is committed actually in the sea, why the case which is within the literal terms of the statute, should not be held within its purview, whether the murder were committed by* **[—62—]** *a citizen on a citizen, or by a foreigner on a citizen, or by a foreigner on a foreigner.* Such a case is not within the reason of Palmer's case. Every nation has concurrent jurisdiction with every other nation on the high seas; and when a crime is committed on the high seas, not on board of any ship or vessel, it is not exclusively within the jurisdiction of any nation; and every nation may, if it choose, punish such crime without doing any wrong to either nation.

The *Holmes* Trial at 10 (emphasis added). In *Holmes* itself, moreover, the Supreme Court agreed that

> it makes no difference whether the offence was committed on board of a vessel, or in the sea, as by throwing the deceased overboard and drowning him, or by shooting him when in the sea, though he was not thrown overboard. The words of the above act of Congress are general, and speak of certain offences committed upon the high seas, without reference to any vessel whatsoever on which they should be committed; and *no reason is perceived why a more restricted meaning should be given to the expressions of the law, than they literally import.*

18 U.S. (5 Wheat.) at 418 (emphasis added).

contemporary commentators on the law of nations and the seemingly unqualified statements of the Supreme Court in *Holmes*, I am persuaded that the latter must control our judgment as a lower court in this case—at least given that state practice is not clearly contrary to what the political branches of our country assert it to be. *See* **{-27-}** *United Nurses & Allied Prof'ls v. Nat'l Labor Rels. Bd.*, 975 F.3d 34, 40 (1st Cir. 2020) ("We are bound by the Supreme Court's 'considered dicta.'" (quoting *McCoy v. Mass. Inst. of Tech.*, 950 F.2d 13, 19 (1st Cir. 1991))). **[—64—]**

Accordingly, I would affirm Aybar's conviction against his constitutional challenge to Congress's exercise of its Article I power on the basis of *Holmes*, while leaving all other questions—including whether and when MDLEA prosecutions comport with the Fifth Amendment's Due Process Clause—for a case in which they are properly raised. I do note, though, that while I reach the same destination as the majority, the route that I take to get there may bear on the proper answer to at least one question that the case before us does not require us to resolve.

I do not dispute the majority's observation that "fair warning has certainly been given" that drug trafficking is commonly outlawed. Slip Op. 32. But, there is potentially a separate notice question concerning whether "fair warning" exists as to *where* that commonly outlawed offense may be prosecuted. *Cf. Int'l Shoe v. Washington*, 326 U.S. 310, 316 (1945) ("[D]ue process requires . . . that, in order to subject a defendant to a judgment *in personam*, if he be not present within the territory of the forum, he have certain minimum contacts with it . . . .").

It is not clear to me that our own Supreme Court's precedent (let alone precedents from lower U.S. courts such as ours) as to the scope of valid congressional power over misconduct by foreign nationals on stateless vessels on the high seas could supply fair warning on the "where" question to a foreign national. At least, I am not sure that it could do so if other authoritative **[—65—]** sources for determining the content of the law of nations—ones not generated solely by a single country's legal system—do not themselves provide fair warning that all nations possess territorial jurisdiction over the conduct of foreign nationals on board stateless vessels in international waters and thereby makes them potentially subject to prosecution in any nation under its domestic criminal laws.

Aybar, however, does not pursue a due process challenge to his conviction. I thus see no need to decide here whether the law of nations, uncertain though it appears to me to be in that respect, is nonetheless clear enough to provide a person who ventures into international waters in a stateless vessel the constitutionally requisite degree of warning of the risk of being prosecuted in a foreign forum for drug trafficking while on board that vessel. Nor do I see any reason to decide in this case whether *Holmes* itself requires us to conclude that, despite what more modern commentary suggests, the law of nations is clear enough on that score to mitigate any notice concerns that might be of a constitutional magnitude.

United States Court of Appeals
for the First Circuit

No. 19-1152

UNITED STATES
vs.
CASTILLO-VAZQUEZ

Appeal from the United States District Court for the District of Puerto Rico

Decided: April 16, 2021

Citation: 995 F.3d 14, 9 Adm. R. 33 (1st Cir. 2021).

Before **LYNCH**, **THOMPSON**, and **KAYATTA**, Circuit Judges.

[—2—] {-16-} **LYNCH**, Circuit Judge:

Juan Carlos Castillo-Vazquez was caught 39 nautical miles south of Puerto Rico smuggling 900 kilograms of cocaine into the United States on a 30-foot vessel. The district court sentenced him to 135 months' imprisonment. Castillo appeals his sentence on the grounds that the district court erred in refusing to grant a two-level reduction to his offense level based on his allegedly minor role in the offense or a departure based on Castillo's family ties and responsibilities. We affirm.

I.

On March 1, 2018, a Caribbean Air Marine Branch Maritime Patrol Aircraft observed a thirty-foot vessel loaded with packages travelling at high speed south of Ponce, Puerto Rico. The U.S. Coast Guard intercepted the vessel, seized thirty packages of cocaine weighing approximately 900 kilograms, and arrested the three men on the vessel. Castillo was one of these crew members.

On March 7, 2018, Castillo was charged with conspiracy to possess with intent to distribute five kilograms or more of cocaine on board a vessel subject to the jurisdiction of the United States in violation of 46 U.S.C. §§ 70502, 70503, and 70506, aiding and abetting in the possession with intent to distribute five kilograms or more of cocaine in violation of 46 U.S.C. §§ 70502, 70503, and 70506, and conspiracy to possess with intent to distribute for the purpose of unlawfully importing more than five **[—3—]** kilograms of cocaine into the United States in violation of 21 U.S.C. §§ 959, 960, and 963. Castillo pled guilty on all charges.

The Probation office filed an initial Presentence Report ("PSR") which calculated Castillo's advisory guidelines range to be 168 to 210 months' imprisonment and did not identify any grounds for a departure. The PSR was amended after Castillo participated in a safety-valve debriefing, which earned him a two-level reduction resulting in a guidelines range of 135 to 168 months. *See* 18 U.S.C. § 3553(f).

On January 14, 2019, Castillo filed a sentencing memorandum requesting that the court impose the statutory mandatory minimum sentence of 120 months' imprisonment and arguing that Castillo should receive a two-level reduction under USSG § 3B1.2(b) for his minor role in the offense and a downward departure from the guidelines range in light of his familial ties and responsibilities under USSG § 5H1.6. The government did not file a sentencing memorandum.

At the sentencing hearing on January 24, 2019, Castillo presented the arguments in his sentencing memorandum and the **{-17-}** government advocated for a middle-of-the-guidelines sentence of 150 months' imprisonment. The district court then confirmed that it had read Castillo's sentencing memorandum and explained its calculation of the guidelines sentencing range. It sentenced **[—4—]** Castillo to 135 months' imprisonment—the bottom of the guidelines range—on each count, to be served concurrently, and five years of supervised release. It stated that "a sentence at the lower end of the guideline range reflects the seriousness of the offense, promotes respect for the law, protects the public from further crimes by Mr. Castillo, and addresses the issues of deterrence and punishment."

After the sentence was announced, Castillo requested that the district court explain why it did not grant a reduction under USSG § 3B1.2(b) for Castillo's minor role in the offense or a departure under USSG § 5H1.6 based on Castillo's family ties and responsibilities. As to Castillo's role in the offense, the district court explained that under the First Circuit decision in *United States v. Arias-Mercedes*, 901 F.3d 1 (1st Cir. 2018), "a minor role shall not apply in cases such as this" and that there was "no way" that Castillo did not know "that there were 900 kilos of cocaine on the vessel." As to Castillo's family ties and responsibilities, the court stated that it "considered that and didn't think it was sufficient for a reduction." Castillo objected to these findings and timely appealed.

II.

Castillo argues again on appeal that the district court procedurally erred by failing to apply an adjustment for his role **[—5—]** in the offense and a departure based on his family ties and responsibilities.[1]

We review claims of sentencing error for abuse of discretion. *Arias-Mercedes*, 901 F.3d at 5. Within that standard, we review findings of fact for clear error, the interpretation and application of the sentencing guidelines de novo, and judgment calls for abuse of discretion. *United States v. Reyes-Torres*, 979 F.3d 1, 7 (1st Cir. 2020).

A. *The Minor Role Adjustment*

USSG § 3B1.2(b) authorizes a two-level reduction in a defendant's offense level if he was a "minor participant in any criminal activity" for which he is being sentenced. A defendant must show that he is "substantially less culpable than the average participant in the criminal activity." *Id.* § 3B1.2, cmt. n.3(A). "Role-in-offense determinations are notoriously fact-specific" and "absent a mistake of law, battles over a defendant's status . . . will almost always be won or lost in the district court." *Arias-Mercedes,* 901 F.3d at 5 (citations and internal quotation marks omitted). **[—6—]**

Castillo argues that the district court committed procedural error both by denying the minor role adjustment and by failing to explain "in a satisfactory manner . . . why it declined to grant the [] adjustment." These arguments fail.

As to Castillo's first argument, the district court did not err in denying Castillo a minor role adjustment. Here Castillo was one of a three-member crew on a small vessel and the amount of drugs was large. As explained in *Arias-Mercedes*, "[w]hen a person undertakes to provide material assistance in transporting a large **{–18–}** quantity of drugs as a member of a tiny crew in a hazardous voyage at sea, it ordinarily will not be clear error for the sentencing court to refuse him a mitigating role adjustment." 901 F.3d at 8. *Arias-Mercedes* also forecloses Castillo's argument that the district court should have considered Castillo's role in the larger drug conspiracy rather than his role in transporting this particular batch of drugs, and the argument that Castillo was entitled to a minor role adjustment simply because he was not the captain of the vessel. *See id.* at 6.

We also reject Castillo's argument that the district court's explanation was insufficient. There is no requirement that the district court must list expressly the factors enumerated in Application Note 3(C) when it denies a defendant a minor role reduction. *See United States v. Mendoza-Maisonet*, 962 F.3d 1, 24-25 (1st Cir. 2020). The district court's comparison to *Arias-* **[—7—]** *Mercedes* and the statements that Castillo must have been aware of the quantity of cocaine on board were sufficient to "allow for meaningful appellate review" of the denial of the downward adjustment. *Gall v. United States*, 552 U.S. 38, 50 (2007).

---

[1] Castillo also summarily states that these denials constituted substantive error. He has waived this argument by failing to adequately address the issue. *United States v. Zannino*, 895 F.2d 1, 17 (1st Cir. 1990) ("[I]ssues adverted to in a perfunctory manner, unaccompanied by some effort at developed argumentation, are deemed waived.").

B. *The Family Ties and Circumstances Departure*

Castillo next argues that the district court erred in refusing to grant a departure under USSG § 5H1.6 based on his "family ties and responsibilities." "As a general rule, a sentencing court's discretionary refusal to depart is unreviewable." *United States v. Sanchez,* 354 F.3d 70, 76 (1st Cir. 2004). Where, as here, the district court "knew he had the power to depart but deliberately chose not to do so," "we are foreclosed from second-guessing the court's discretionary decision not to depart from the [guidelines range]." *United States v. Teeter,* 257 F.3d 14, 30 (1st Cir. 2001); *see also United States v. Louis,* 300 F.3d 78, 81 (1st Cir. 2002) ("[A] district court's decision rejecting a downward departure is largely unreviewable."). Castillo is not entitled to relief on this ground.

III.

Affirmed.

United States Court of Appeals
for the First Circuit

No. 19-1112

AFUNDAY CHARTERS, INC.
vs.
ABC INS. CO.

Appeal from the United States District Court for the District of Puerto Rico

Decided: May 13, 2021

Citation: 997 F.3d 390, 9 Adm. R. 36 (1st Cir. 2021).

Before KAYATTA, LIPEZ, and BARRON, Circuit Judges.

[—4—] **{–390–}** KAYATTA, Circuit Judge: **{–391–}**

This admiralty proceeding arises out of the grounding and constructive total loss of a brand-new seventy-four-foot yacht. Afunday Charters, Inc., had purchased the yacht from its builder, Spencer Yachts, Inc. Those on board the yacht at the time of the grounding included Sean Alonzo—who was hired by Afunday's owner, Anthony Norman Sabga—and Joseph Daniel Spencer—an employee of Spencer Yachts. Afunday sued Spencer and Spencer Yachts, alleging that Spencer negligently ran the yacht aground and that Spencer and Spencer Yachts were jointly and severally liable for the yacht's loss. Spencer and Spencer Yachts each denied responsibility, raised an affirmative defense of negligence by Afunday's agents Sabga and Alonzo, and filed a third-party complaint against Sabga and Alonzo. This appeal arises out of the subsequent dismissal of the third-party complaints pursuant to Fed. R. Civ. P. 12(b)(6). *Afunday Charters, Inc. v. Spencer Yachts, Inc.*, Civil No. 16-3141 (GAG), 2018 WL 10878066 (D.P.R. Dec. 18, 2018). We have jurisdiction over this interlocutory appeal under 28 U.S.C. § 1292(a)(3). And our standard of review is de novo. For the following reasons, we affirm.

I.

As in a normal civil action, a defendant in an admiralty proceeding can file a third-party complaint contending that, if the defendant is liable to the plaintiff, a third party is in turn **[—5—]** liable to the defendant. *Compare* Fed. R. Civ. P. 14(a)(1) ("A defending party may, as third-party plaintiff, serve a summons and complaint on a nonparty who is or may be liable to it for all or part of the claim against it."), *with* Fed. R. Civ. P. 14(c)(1) (permitting an admiralty defendant to "bring in a third-party defendant who may be wholly or partly liable . . . to the third-party plaintiff"). An admiralty defendant may also file a different type of third-party complaint, alleging that the third party is directly liable "to the [original] plaintiff" for the damages claimed. Fed. R. Civ. P. 14(c)(1). This distinct feature of Rule 14(c) promotes efficient apportionment of liability in admiralty suits. *See generally* 6 Arthur R. Miller, Mary Kay Kane & A. Benjamin Spencer, *Federal Practice & Procedure (Wright & Miller)* § 1465 (3d ed. 2020). Here, Spencer and Spencer Yachts sought to include both types of third-party claims in their respective third-party complaints.

Sabga and Alonzo moved to dismiss the third-party complaints pursuant to Rule 12(b)(6), arguing that, as a matter of law, Spencer and Spencer Yachts could never have any recovery or benefit from the complaints. This was so, they contended, because if Sabga or Alonzo were responsible for the loss, that responsibility would reduce commensurately any liability of Spencer or Spencer Yachts to Afunday. Spencer and Spencer Yachts opposed the motions, arguing that Sabga and Alonzo's negligence **[—6—]** would not necessarily be attributable **{–392–}** to Afunday, a distinct legal entity. In reply, Afunday, Sabga, and Alonzo all conceded without reservation or right of rescission that any comparative fault on the part of Sabga or Alonzo would be attributed to Afunday and thus reduce to the extent of that fault any liability of Spencer or Spencer Yachts. Sabga and Alonzo argued that this concession supported dismissal because it made the third-party complaints duplicative of Spencer's and Spencer Yachts's affirmative defenses of negligence.

Some courts applying Rule 14(a) in non-admiralty proceedings have accepted this precise reasoning. *See, e.g., Gabriel Cap., LP v. Natwest Fin., Inc.*, 137 F. Supp. 2d 251, 266 (S.D.N.Y. 2000) (dismissing third-party claim for contribution "against a plaintiff's agent where that claim [was] identical to defendant's affirmative defense"); *cf. Loreley Fin. (Jersey) No. 3 Ltd. v. Wells Fargo Sec., LLC*, No. 12-cv-3723 (RJS), 2017 WL 985875, at *3 (S.D.N.Y. Mar. 10, 2017) (noting that this doctrine does not apply when "the third-party defendant acts outside of the scope of its agency"). Rule 14(a) provides a textual toehold for such a practical approach. It allows a defendant in the original action to bring a third-party complaint only against one "who is or may be liable to [the defendant] for all or part of the claim against [the defendant]." Fed. R. Civ. P. 14(a)(1). Where a third party's comparative negligence is properly attributed to the **[—7—]** original plaintiff, a Rule 14(a) complaint against the third party would do no work because the defendant in the original action will not be liable for the negligence attributed to the original plaintiff. So if an original plaintiff's concession means that a third party can never be liable to a defendant in the original action for any part of a claim against that defendant, then one can see how text might welcome practicality in such a case.

Here, though, we have third-party complaints under Rule 14(c) as well. The fact that there can never be any liability of Sabga and Alonzo to Spencer or Spencer Yachts does not by itself preclude the filing of Rule 14(c) complaints against Sabga and Alonzo, as long as Sabga and Alonzo may be directly liable to the original plaintiff, Afunday. Spencer and Spencer Yachts confusingly label the counts of their third-party complaints as claims for indemnification or contribution, but both complaints invoke Rule 14(c) and seek the entry of judgment in Afunday's favor against Sabga and Alonzo. *See* Fed. R. Civ. P. 14(c)(2) ("The third-party plaintiff may demand judgment in the plaintiff's favor against the third-party defendant.").

It is not clear that Spencer or Spencer Yachts have plausibly pleaded that Sabga and Alonzo are directly liable to Afunday. *Cf. Royal Ins. Co. of Am. v. Sw. Marine*, 194 F.3d 1009, 1018 (9th Cir. 1999) (holding that third-party complaints satisfied Rule 14(c) by referring to the rule and explaining how **[—8—]** and why third-party defendants were liable to the original plaintiff). The facts alleged do not suggest that Sabga and Alonzo acted as individuals rather than as Afunday's agents. And Spencer and Spencer Yachts have not contended that, as agents, Sabga and Alonzo would be liable to Afunday. But the district court does not appear to have relied on this arguable deficiency. And Spencer and Spencer Yachts also appeal the denial of leave to amend their third-party complaints to make pellucid the basis for claiming that Sabga and Alonzo acted independently, on Sabga's behalf. So we put to one side the issue of whether the third-party complaints' factual allegations are sufficient to state a Rule 14(c) claim.

We instead train our attention on whether the district court properly relied on **{–393–}** Afunday's concession accepting responsibility for any fault of Sabga or Alonzo as a basis to dismiss the Rule 14(c) complaints seeking to assert that the third-party defendants are directly liable to the original plaintiff. In the district court's view, the third-party complaints did not plausibly allege that Sabga and Alonzo "were acting in their own self-interest," and the court did not discern a difference between either holding them liable as individuals based on the third-party complaint or reducing Afunday's recovery in proportion to their comparative fault based on an affirmative defense. Put another way, the district court concluded that dismissal was warranted **[—9—]** because neither Spencer nor Spencer Yachts would incur any meaningful benefit from impleading Sabga and Alonzo.

Rule 14(c) itself contains no requirement that the pleading pose a potential benefit. On the other hand, Rule 16 bears on this matter. It grants the district court discretion to "take appropriate action" to "facilitat[e] . . . the just, speedy, and inexpensive disposition of the action." Fed. R. Civ. P. 16(c)(2)(P). It also allows a district court, when appropriate, to set a separate trial for the adjudication of a third-party claim, Fed. R. Civ. P. 16(c)(2)(M), and to otherwise "simplify[] the issues," Fed.

R. Civ. P. 16(c)(2)(A). Here, for example, the court could have simply reserved adjudication of the third-party complaints until after the respective faults of all parties were adjudicated in resolving Afunday's claim. At that point, at least as these parties describe the dispute, there would be nothing left to decide.

We therefore see no practical difference between delaying the adjudication of the third-party complaints and dismissing them. In either event, Spencer and Spencer Yachts would end up in exactly the same place because they are guaranteed that any negligence by Sabga and Alonzo would reduce a damage award against Spencer or Spencer Yachts. Far from creating a risk of duplicative proceedings, this method of apportioning comparative **[—10—]** fault obviates the need for follow-on litigation seeking contribution from Sabga and Alonzo.

If the third-party plaintiffs had shown that dismissal of their pleadings would harm them, we would likely reverse. When we explored the possibility of prejudice by asking for supplemental filings addressing possible prejudice to Spencer or Spencer Yachts, the Spencer parties pointed to an unsupported assertion that Sabga's personal insurance would be triggered only by a direct claim against him. This response hardly answered the question. Regardless of whether the policy covers the incident, neither Spencer nor Spencer Yachts will incur any liability or share of liability for fault attributed to Sabga for actions that Afunday concedes Sabga performed as its agent.

At oral argument, counsel for the Spencer parties suggested that the policy, once triggered, would pay for Spencer's legal defense. But if that is really the reason for objecting to the district court's ruling, one would have expected that reason to have been trotted out front and center in the district court, and certainly in the Spencer parties' various briefs on appeal. Forfeited arguments in civil cases fare poorly. *See Teamsters Union, Loc. No. 59 v. Superline Transp. Co.*, 953 F.2d 17, 21 (1st Cir. 1992). And arguments withheld from the briefs on appeal fare even worse. *See Piazza v. Aponte Roque*, 909 F.2d 35, 37 (1st Cir. 1990) ("Except in extraordinary circumstances . . . , a court of **[—11—]** appeals will not consider an issue raised for the first time at oral argument."). Noting that even now the Spencer parties do not explain how the policy works in the asserted manner, we see no extraordinary circumstances that **{-394-}** would justify our consideration of this argument forfeited in the district court and waived on appeal.

Spencer and Spencer Yachts have also suggested in their supplemental filing and at oral argument that discovery against Sabga might be easier if Sabga and Alonzo are parties to the action rather than witnesses. But we understand that Sabga and Alonzo—represented by Afunday's counsel to be Afunday's agents—will not attempt to gain any advantage not available to a party. And if that turns out to be wrong, or if there should develop any presently unforeseeable prejudice to Spencer or Spencer Yachts due to the lack of a third-party complaint, the district court on remand can always revisit the pleadings to the extent necessary. Fed. R. Civ. P. 15(a)(2) (allowing amendment "when justice so requires").

II.

For the foregoing reasons, we *affirm* the judgment of the district court. Each party shall bear its own costs.

– Dissenting Opinion Follows –

(Reporter's Note: Dissenting Opinion follows on p. 39).

[—12—] {-394-} **BARRON**, Circuit Judge, dissenting:

I read the District Court to have ruled that the claims for contribution that the third-party plaintiffs—Joseph Daniel Spencer and Spencer Yachts, Inc. ("Spencer")[1]—brought pursuant to Federal Rule of Civil Procedure 14 against Sean Alonzo and Anthony Norman Sabga fail plausibly to allege that either man was not acting merely as an agent of Afunday Charters, Inc., ("Afunday") at the relevant times, at least given the stipulation by Afunday, Alonzo, and Sabga that the two men *were* acting as Afunday's agents. I further read the District Court to have concluded that, in consequence of that pleading deficiency, these contribution claims under Rule 14(a) may not go forward because they are necessarily redundant of Spencer's own affirmative defense of comparative negligence that it asserts in response to the claims that Afunday has brought against Spencer.

But, while Spencer's complaint is hardly as fulsome as one might hope, it states that Sabga was acting "in his capacity as the chief executive officer or president of Afunday Charters, Inc., *or alternatively*, in his capacity as the sole shareholder of Afunday Charters, Inc.," (emphasis added), and that Sabga hired Alonzo. Under the notice pleading standard, *see* Fed. R. Civ. P. [—13—] 8(a), I cannot see why more was required for Spencer plausibly to allege that neither Alonzo nor Sabga was acting merely as an agent of Afunday during the period that mattered. Accordingly, as Spencer's comparative negligence defense is premised on the two men having acted as Afunday's agents, I conclude that the District Court has failed to offer an adequate rationale for dismissing Spencer's Rule 14(a) claims for contribution against Alonzo and Sabga insofar as they allege that the two men were acting for themselves and not for Afunday.

There remains to address the District Court's dismissal of Spencer's Rule 14(c) claims regarding Alonzo and Sabga. These claims are not for contribution. They allege instead that the two men are directly liable to Afunday. Here, too, I read the District Court to have dismissed the claims based on the understanding that they could not go forward because they plausibly plead only that Alonzo and Sabga were acting as Afunday's agents at the times that mattered and thus necessarily rise and fall with the comparative negligence defense {-395-} that Spencer asserts against the claims that Afunday brings. But, as I have explained, Spencer's complaint does not allege that the two men were acting only as Afunday's agents. It alternatively pleads that they were acting for themselves. Accordingly, I cannot see how the District Court's dismissal of these Rule 14(c) claims can be upheld either. [—14—]

Moreover, I read Spencer's briefing to us to argue that, even insofar as the Rule 14(c) claims characterize Alonzo and Sabga as Afunday's agents, they may go forward, notwithstanding the nature of the comparative negligence defense that Spencer asserts against the claims that Afunday brings as a plaintiff in its own right. And, I read the District Court to have dismissed this variant of Spencer's Rule 14(c) claims based solely on the finding of redundancy that it made as to the Rule 14 claims generally—and thus without accounting for this type of claim being one for direct liability under Rule 14(c) rather than contribution under Rule 14(a). I thus would require the District Court to address this variant of Spencer's Rule 14(c) claims on remand as well.

I do recognize that if we were to vacate the order dismissing Spencer's Rule 14 claims, as I conclude that we must, then the District Court on remand might well choose to proceed just as the majority concludes that it is entitled to under Federal Rule of Civil Procedure 16. But, even if the District Court chose to follow that course, Spencer then could challenge that exercise of discretion on appeal by advancing contentions like those that it has made to us about the advantages that keeping the Rule 14 claims in the case would have in

[1] As no party asserts there is any legally meaningful distinction between Spencer and Spencer Yachts with respect to the issues before us on appeal, I refer to both third-party plaintiffs collectively.

terms of discovery and enforcement of insurance policy terms. And, were Spencer to do so, we then would have the benefit of something that we now lack—an assessment of those contentions by the adjudicator most conversant **[—15—]** with the ins and outs of the case. Thus, slow as the usual process of adjudication may be, I would not short-circuit it by effectively affirming a ruling that has not yet been made.

For these reasons, I respectfully dissent.

United States Court of Appeals for the First Circuit

No. 18-2247

UNITED STATES vs. STEWART-CARRASQUILLO

Appeal from the United States District Court for the District of Puerto Rico

Decided: May 17, 2021

Citation: 997 F.3d 408, 9 Adm. R. 41 (1st Cir. 2021).

Before **BARRON** and **SELYA**, Circuit Judges, and **KATZMANN**, Judge.*

* Of the United States Court of International Trade, sitting by designation.

[—3—] {-413-} **KATZMANN**, Judge:

As police intercepted them racing shortly after dawn toward the coast of Ceiba, Puerto Rico, defendants James Stewart-Carrasquillo ("Stewart") and Harold Esquilin-Montañez ("Esquilin") were caught dumping bales of contraband off the side of a turbocharged "fishing" boat loaded, on deck and in plain view, with more than $12 million worth of cocaine (at street value) packed in twenty-five bales with a total weight of more than 1,200 pounds. Not crediting their defense at trial that they were innocent bystanders on a fishing trip where traps were laid into the waters for later retrieval of lobsters, a jury convicted both defendants of various narcotics offenses. They now appeal, claiming that the evidence was insufficient to support the **{-414-}** guilty verdicts, that the district court abused its discretion by excluding their homemade video "reenactment," and that prosecutorial misconduct during closing argument warrants reversal. We affirm.

I. *BACKGROUND*

A. *Facts*

"Since one of the claims addressed in this opinion is a challenge to the sufficiency of the evidence, we recount the facts in the light most favorable to the verdict," *United States v. Paz-Alvarez*, 799 F.3d 12, 18, 3 Adm. R. 61, 61 (1st Cir. 2015), deferring some details to our analysis of the issues raised on appeal.

In the very early morning of December 10, 2016, while on **[—4—]** a routine patrol off the island's eastern coast, three maritime agents from Puerto Rico's *Fuerzas Unidas de Rápida Acción* (FURA)[1]—Sergeant Magaly Diaz-Perez ("Diaz"), Agent Adalberto Del Valle-Jesus ("Del Valle"), and Agent Luis Feliciano—picked up from the FURA boat's radar an object "moving along a rocky area . . . towards the east of the island of Puerto Rico." In Agent Del Valle's experience, this was not "an area where boats typically travel through" because of the "rough" conditions and "the risk that it entails"; in fact, "the yawls that [he had] . . . seen [in that area] have basically been all engaged in drug trafficking." Describing his experience with drug-smuggling into Puerto Rico, he recounted that a boat bringing in drugs from the Caribbean meets in the waters with another boat for the transfer of the drugs to that vessel, which then returns to the Puerto Rican coast. Cocaine is packaged in kilos, wrapped, soaked in oil, and shaped into bales. According to Agent Del Valle, the boat-to-boat, drug-at-sea transfer of a multi-gram shipment typically requires three or four persons to move the drugs from one boat to another because a typical bale "containing 20 to 25 bricks of cocaine" would weigh in the "range of 50 to 55 pounds," and must be "move[d] . . . quickly" to avoid **[—5—]** detection.

As the FURA agents neared what appeared to be a blue and white fishing boat, Agent Del Valle "notice[d] that the manner in which the water [was] being displaced . . . was not normal," and "[t]he manner in which [the boat] was behaving was not the normal manner in which a fishing vessel conducts itself." He recalled that the boat "was going fast," and "displacing a large amount of water," indicating that it was "carrying a large

[1] "FURA is the Spanish acronym for a division of the Puerto Rico Police Department, the name of which can be translated as 'Forces United for Rapid Action.'" *Diaz-Roman v. Denis*, No. CIV. 08-1420 (GAG), 2010 WL 3069442, at *3 n.2 (D.P.R. Aug. 2, 2010).

amount of weight." This small "fishing" boat was equipped with "two 175-horsepower engines," which, Agent Del Valle testified, were necessary "to master the amount of weight that they ha[d] on the boat." In his view, "a lower horsepower engine, say 50 or 75 horsepower, would [not] be able to carry such a large amount of drugs."

When they were about forty yards from the boat, Agent Del Valle could make out "three individuals aboard." He "proceed[ed] to carry out . . . an approach to the stern," at which point he saw "two individuals on the left-hand side of the vessel throwing packages into the water." Sergeant Diaz also saw black packages being thrown overboard and identified defendants as the "individuals . . . throwing bales overboard." The agents gave "verbal orders to desist from this action" but were ignored. Agent Del Valle suspected that "they were in all likelihood throwing drugs into the water," and he "readied [his] crew . . . to interdict and intercept the vessel." **[—6—]** **{-415-}**

The two individuals "continue[d] to throw packages into the water" until the FURA boat was "literally by their side," at which point the fishing boat's "captain swerve[d] the wheel to ram" the agents' boat. The FURA boat instead successfully "rammed their vessel," which finally "stopped the action of throwing packages into the water." The agents then boarded the boat and arrested its captain—Carrasquillo[2]—and the other two persons aboard, whom the agents had seen jettisoning the bales—defendants. Agent Del Valle observed additional bales on an open area in front of the steering wheel.

With the suspects arrested, the agents attempted to recover the evidence strewn about in the water. Sergeant Diaz first tried to retrieve the four bales that defendants had thrown overboard, but she was unable to handle the weight. Agent Del Valle lifted them one-by-one and injured his leg while doing so. The agents eventually succeeded in bringing the four bales back on board.

Undertaking a search of the seized vessel, the agents found three fishing poles on the boat. There was no indication that the "poles had actually been used to conduct any fishing activities that day," nor was there any "bait for fishing," **[—7—]** "fishing boxes," "lobster boxes," "ice," "food," or "cell phones" on board.

As for contraband, in addition to the four bales the agents had recovered from the water, the agents found another twenty-one bales—identical to the other four, except that these were dry—on the boat floor. "[T]ied to the last bale of cocaine" was a "set of weights" weighing between 50 and 70 pounds, which, Agent Del Valle later testified, are "known . . . in the underworld as *potala*" and "are directly tied to the drug in case [traffickers] need to get rid of it, have it drop down directly to the deep, to the bottom." Agent Del Valle observed that the bales resembled "the traditional manner in which [traffickers] transport . . . drugs over to Puerto Rico" and agreed that, "in [his] 14 years as a FURA boat captain," he had never "seen or intercepted a boat carrying bales like that, that do not contain cocaine, or drugs."

A Homeland Security Investigations ("HSI") Special Agent "opened up" one of the bales "to reveal its content": "bricks neatly packed together, wrapped in a clear plastic wrapping," one of which "was opened up and . . . tested positive to characteristics of narcotics, of cocaine." "[W]hen it was finally counted," the seized cocaine totaled "499 bricks, with a total weight of 577.6 kilograms."

In its chemical analysis of the contraband, U.S. Customs **[—8—]** and Border Protection ("CBP") determined "an average purity rate of 78 percent" and a total drug content of "502,582 grams or the equivalent of 502 kilograms." Because "one kilogram or brick of cocaine traveling into Puerto Rico is worth approximately [$20,000] to $25,000" on the street, the seized shipment was "worth approximately $10 million to [$12.5] million."

[2] Juan Carrasquillo-Soto ("Carrasquillo") is Stewart's uncle. Defendants both worked for Carrasquillo in the construction business. He is not a party to these appeals.

B. *Proceedings*

A federal grand jury in the District of Puerto Rico returned a three-count indictment charging Stewart, Esquilin, and Carrasquillo with aiding and abetting the possession with intent to distribute a controlled substance onboard a vessel subject to the jurisdiction of the United States, in violation of 46 U.S.C. § 70503(a)(1) and 18 U.S.C. § 2 (Count 1); conspiracy to possess with intent to distribute a controlled substance onboard a vessel subject to the **{-416-}** jurisdiction of the United States, in violation of 46 U.S.C. § 7053(a)(1) and 46 U.S.C. § 70506(b) (Count 2); and aiding and abetting the possession with intent to distribute five kilograms or more of cocaine, in violation of 21 U.S.C. § 841(a)(1) and 18 U.S.C. § 2 (Count 3). Carrasquillo pleaded guilty to Count 3 of the indictment and did not proceed to trial. Defendants jointly filed a Motion to Dismiss the Indictment for loss or destruction of exculpatory evidence by the government, namely a "Fish Finder GPS Hummingbird 698." The district court denied the **[—9—]** motion.[3]

Defendants proceeded to a joint trial. At trial, the government presented four witnesses—FURA agents Del Valle and Diaz, HSI agent Ramos, and CBP specialist Figueroa—and adduced two stipulations as to the cocaine's purity and weight, as well as to its street value in Puerto Rico. At the close of the government's case-in-chief, both defendants moved for judgments of acquittal under Federal Rule of Criminal Procedure 29, which the district court denied.

Following the Rule 29 ruling, defendants put on evidence **[—10—]** in support of their defense that they were not willing participants in a drug trafficking venture but were invitees on a fishing trip who were merely present on a boat when it came upon packages of cocaine in the water. The thrust of their testimony was that Carrasquillo had captained the boat, that the trip began as an uneventful fishing trip where they unloaded lobster traps in the water, that subsequently the boat came upon the packages in the water, namely bales of cocaine packaged in black plastic floating in the water, and that Carrasquillo loaded those packages on to the boat himself because defendants refused to assist.

Stewart testified that around 4 AM on December 10, 2016, he, Esquilin, and Carrasquillo rode to the docks in Carrasquillo's pickup truck with lobster traps, that they then navigated for about one hour off the coast of Puerto Rico, and then laid approximately twenty lobster traps at sea. In support of his claim that the trip was a fishing trip, Stewart testified that as the lobster traps were laid, Carrasquillo would place in a device, a fish finder with a GPS, information about the coordinates, so that he could know where to locate them and the lobsters. After spending about thirty-five minutes laying the traps, Carrasquillo spotted some items floating in the water **{-417-}** and alerted defendants. Despite Carrasquillo's incessant

---

[3] As explained by the district court, Esquilin and Stewart sought a maritime expert to inspect a "Fish Finder" device that they claimed was used on the asserted December 10, 2016, fishing trip to place and locate lobster traps. According to the defendants, the fish finder's built-in GPS technology stored the coordinates where lobster traps were placed, and would corroborate the defendants' version of events. Property receipts indicated that the fish finder "was itemized (or accounted for) on the days of, and following the defendants' arrest." The record was not clear "on whether the law enforcement agents involved in the inspection and handling of the property ever removed the Fish Finder from the center console of the vessel." In any event, it was missing. The district court determined that the fish finder evidence "could hardly prove their unwilling or unknowing involvement in the salvage and transportation of $10 million worth of floating cocaine." "At best, that evidence, would provide a tangential portent of corroboration to the defendants' accounts . . . [and] lacks any apparently exculpatory value." Moreover, the district court determined that the defendants had not demonstrated bad faith by the government in the handling of the evidence. Accordingly, it denied the motion to dismiss the indictment. That ruling is not before us. At trial, as noted below, the defendants offered testimony about the fish finder and discussed it during closing arguments, telling the jury that due to "carelessness" and "sloppy and irresponsible" conduct, this "important piece of evidence" was lost and not available to the defense.

and profane directives that defendants aid him in loading the floating items (later identified as bales of cocaine) onto the vessel, they both refused to do so. According **[—11—]** to Stewart, over a span of about forty-five minutes to an hour, the twenty-five packages, some fifty pounds each, were pulled by rope with ease onto the boat solely by Carrasquillo, a fifty-nine year old man who was about "five-eight, five-nine" and "160 to 170 pounds." Stewart explained that he did not touch any of the packages that Carrasquillo loaded onto the vessel because he "presumed that it could be either drugs or money" and his "fear was that somebody would come there and kill us if he saw us taking something that was theirs." About an hour after Carrasquillo had loaded all the packages, he started shouting, "like, crazy, [t]hrow the packages to the water; throw the packages to the water." Stewart testified that Esquilin, who he thought was "scared," reacted and pushed one of the packages to the water, and "some two or three" then fell into the water. In sum, Stewart told the jury that he did not accompany Carrasquillo for the purpose of retrieving drugs, that he had no knowledge that drugs would be found that day, and that he never touched any of the packages that Carrasquillo loaded onto the vessel.

In his defense case, and in support of his contention that the trip was supposed to be a fishing expedition, and that he was a last-minute recruit to the trip, Stewart called Javier Hernandez-Peña ("Hernandez"), a construction worker who had worked for Carrasquillo. He testified that he had planned to go on the fishing trip of December 10, 2016, on Carrasquillo's boat and had **[—12—]** helped him load lobster traps on to the boat the day before, despite having twisted one of his ankles. He testified that he could not join the trip because of the twisted ankle. Stewart's wife, Nancylin Fernandez-Colon, also testified that Carrasquillo came to speak with his nephew for about two minutes on December 9. Finally, Stewart called his pastor as a character witness.

Esquilin did not himself testify, but presented two witnesses in his defense. His wife Nancy Claudio testified that her husband "likes to go fishing." Manuel Valentin-Laureano testified that he was a former FURA maritime officer and that in assisting the defense he had inspected the vessel and sought to obtain the fish finder which had been identified on the Inventory that had been compiled by the government, and which he testified would have been important in establishing that the trip was indeed a fishing trip as Esquilin contended.

At the conclusion of the defense case, defendants again moved for judgment of acquittal pursuant to Federal Rule of Criminal Procedure 29. The district court reserved decision on the renewed motions. After the jury returned guilty verdicts on all counts, the court denied the defendants' motions for judgment of acquittal. The defendants filed written post-verdict Rule 29 motions, which the court denied in a written opinion. The district court sentenced each defendant to 121 months of imprisonment, to be followed by five years of supervised release. They now appeal. **[—13—]**

II. *DISCUSSION*

A. *Sufficiency of the Evidence*

"We review de novo the district court's denial of a motion under Rule 29 for judgment of acquittal." *United States v. Santos-Soto*, 799 F.3d 49, 56 (1st Cir. 2015). We review the denial of such challenge to the sufficiency of the evidence in the light most favorable to the verdict, "giving 'equal weight to direct and circumstantial evidence.'" **{-418-}** *Paz-Alvarez*, 799 F.3d at 25, 3 Adm. R. at 67 (quoting *United States v. Appolon*, 715 F.3d 362, 367 (1st Cir. 2013)). We do not judge credibility; that is the province of the jury. *United States v. Downs-Moses*, 329 F.3d 253, 261 (1st Cir. 2003). "The verdict must stand unless the evidence is so scant that a rational factfinder could not conclude that the government proved all the essential elements of the charged crime beyond a reasonable doubt." *United States v. Rodríguez-Vélez*, 597 F.3d 32, 39 (1st Cir. 2010) (emphasis omitted). The "relevant inquiry is not whether a reasonable jury could have acquitted the defendant, but rather whether a reasonable jury 'could have found that the government proved each element of the crime beyond a reasonable doubt.'" *Paz-Alvarez*, 799 F.3d at 25, 3 Adm. R. at 67 (quoting *Appolon*, 715 F.3d at 367). The government need not succeed in "eliminating every possible theory consistent with the defendant's innocence." *United States v. Trinidad-Acosta*, 773 F.3d 298, 311 (1st Cir. 2014) (quoting *United States v. Troy*, 583 F.3d 20, 24 (1st Cir. 2009)), **[—14—]** *superseded on other grounds by* U.S. Sent'g Guidelines Manual §3B1.2 n.3(a). Thus, "[d]efendants challenging convictions for insufficiency of evidence face an uphill battle on appeal." *United States v. Lipscomb*, 539 F.3d 32, 40 (1st Cir. 2008) (alteration in original) (quoting *United States v. Hernández*, 218 F.3d 58, 64 (1st Cir. 2000)). That said, "we must 'reject those evidentiary interpretations and illations that are unreasonable, insupportable, or overly speculative.'" *United States v. Rodríguez-Martinez*, 778 F.3d 367, 371 (1st Cir. 2015) (quoting *United States v. Spinney*, 65 F.3d 231, 234 (1st Cir. 1995)).

At the outset, we review the defendants' claim of insufficiency of evidence to convict under Count 1, charging the defendants with aiding and abetting each other in violation of 46 U.S.C. § 70503(a)(1) and 18 U.S.C. § 2(a). To convict, the government needed to prove, beyond a reasonable doubt, that the vessel was subject to the jurisdiction of the United States; the material found on the vessel was a controlled substance; and the defendants knowingly or intentionally possessed the controlled substance with intent to distribute it. The first two elements are not disputed; what is disputed is the third element. In a case alleging "the defendants' knowing participation in the transportation of a controlled substance . . . the evidence is sufficient to convict if it adequately supports 'the requisite "two-step inference"': (1) that the vessel was engaged in obviously **[—15—]** illegal activity and (2) that each defendant was ready to assist in the criminal enterprise." *United States v. Guerrero*, 114 F.3d 332, 342 (1st Cir. 1997) (quoting *United States v. Jimenez-Perez*, 869 F.2d 9, 11 (1st Cir. 1989)).

With respect to the first prong of the two-step inference, abundant precedent yields guidance "when a jury may reasonably infer that a crewman or passenger on a boat had knowledge that the boat also carried drugs," *United States v. Carrasco*, 540 F.3d 43, 50 (1st Cir. 2008), focusing on facts such as the quantity of drugs aboard, the size and condition of the vessel, the closeness of the crew's relationship, and the absence of a legitimate purpose for the voyage. *Guerrero*, 114 F.3d at 342. Here, the jury heard evidence that crewmembers defendants were close associates of boat captain Carrasquillo -- as noted, Stewart was Carrasquillo's nephew, and defendants had both worked for Carrasquillo in the construction business. There was evidence of a massive quantity of drugs loaded on to the boat. Indeed, the defendants stipulated that the twenty-five bales on the small, turbocharged vessel were determined to contain 502 kilograms of cocaine, with a street value of $10 to $12.5 million. **{–419–}** Such a "quantity of drugs . . . was consistent with an intent to distribute" rather than with "possess[ion] . . . for personal use." *United States v. Henry*, 848 F.3d 1, 14 (1st Cir. 2017); *see United States v. Piedrahita-Santiago*, 931 F.2d 127, 131 (1st Cir. 1991) **[—16—]** ("[A] relatively small vessel carrying a large quantity of drugs is indicative of knowledge and involvement on the part of the crew."). Further support for a conclusion that the vessel was involved in illegal activity was supplied by Stewart himself, who, regarding the loaded bales, testified that he "presumed that it could be either drugs or money." The conclusion that the vessel was on an illicit endeavor and not on a legitimate fishing trip was supported by Agent Del Valle's testimony that there was no indication that the three fishing poles found on the boat had been used in fishing activities. Moreover, as noted, the police recovered no bait for fishing, fishing boxes, lobster boxes, ice or food when the boat was seized. While the defendants contend that they dropped lobster traps and were unable to prove that because of the loss of their fish-finder GPS, defense witness Hernandez testified that Carrasquillo's boat was not equipped with a wincher, an engine device used to pull up lobster traps. In sum, a rational juror could conclude that the vessel was engaged in illegal activity.

As to the second prong—that each defendant was ready to assist in the criminal enterprise—the evidence supports such a conclusion by the jury. A rational juror could infer that defendants were informed of Carrasquillo's plan and that they were not innocent bystanders, as they contend. "The quantity of drugs seized itself suggests strongly that each of the crew members knew **[—17—]** about the boat's drug smuggling purpose because 'drug traffickers would not entrust a multi-million-dollar shipment to anyone in whom they did not have confidence.'" *United States v. Angulo-Hernández*, 565 F.3d 2, 8 (1st Cir. 2009) (quoting *United States v. Rodríguez-Durán*, 507 F.3d 749, 760 (1st Cir. 2007)). "[U]nwitting bystanders would not have been hired to participate in the [boat's] obvious illegal transport of millions of dollars' worth of contraband." *Guerrero*, 114 F.3d at 344; *see also United States v. Cuevas-Esquivel*, 905 F.2d 510, 515 (1st Cir. 1990) ("It is entirely reasonable for the jury to conclude that conspirators, engaged in conduct which by its nature is kept secret from outsiders, would not allow the presence of innocent bystanders."). As noted, both defendants were associates of Carrasquillo, and moreover, Carrasquillo had spoken with Stewart about the voyage outside the presence of Stewart's family the day before the trip. While the defendants claim that the 59-year-old Carrasquillo alone lifted and loaded the twenty-five bales of cocaine weighing 975 kilograms (or more than 1,200 pounds) into the boat, the jury could have reasonably concluded that given the weight of the contraband and the rocky, treacherous, and shark-infested waters, both defendants must have assisted Carrasquillo in that task. *See Downs-Moses*, 329 F.3d at 261-62 ("[A] reasonable jury could have found that all twenty-eight bales of cocaine, elaborately and similarly packaged, . . . (weighing 975 kilograms, or more than **[—18—]** 2100 pounds) necessitated that a number of individuals participate in its transport . . . ."). The defendants' frantic efforts to unload the cocaine as the FURA police approached, as testified to by two FURA agents, also supports a conclusion that they were willing participants in the conspiracy. While they dispute the agents' testimony identifying them as dumping the cocaine, it is undisputed that there were only three people aboard, with one of them captaining the boat at the time of the interdiction. As defendants acknowledge **{-420-}** that the captain was Carrasquillo, a rational juror could have concluded that the two sighted dumpers were the defendants. Even "ancillary . . . services" performed "to advance the conspiracy's objective of avoiding police detection" are sufficient "for a reasonable jury to find that [the defendant] in fact intended to join the conspiracy and advance its goals." *Paz-Alvarez*, 799 F.3d at 25-26, 3 Adm. R. at 67–68.

In sum, on appeal, as they did in front of the jury, defendants advance their own interpretation for being on board a vessel loaded with more than $12 million worth of cocaine. The jury rejected that explanation. "On appeal, we cannot re-weigh the evidence or second-guess the jury's credibility determinations." *Santos-Soto*, 799 F.3d at 61. "[I]f the evidence can be construed in various reasonable alternatives, the jury is entitled to freely choose from among them." *United States v. Smith*, 680 F.2d 255, 259 (1st Cir. 1982). We conclude that the **[—19—]** defendants have not overcome the "daunting hurdles" of a sufficiency challenge. *United States v. Hatch*, 434 F.3d 1, 4 (1st Cir. 2006). We uphold the convictions under Count 1 for aiding and abetting the possession with intent to distribute a controlled substance onboard a vessel subject to the jurisdiction of the United States.

We also conclude, as did the district court in its thorough and persuasive Opinion and Order denying the defendants' motions for judgment of acquittal, that the evidence is sufficient to sustain the defendants' convictions under Count 2 (conspiracy to possess with intent to distribute a controlled substance on board a vessel subject to the jurisdiction of the United States) and Count 3 (aiding and abetting the possession with intent to distribute five kilograms or more of cocaine). Although the three offenses of conviction are comprised of distinct elements, the same evidence that permitted the jury to infer that Stewart, Esquilin, and Carrasquillo were working together to bring the cocaine back to shore for distribution supports the jury's verdict as to each. *See Carrasco*, 540 F.3d at 51 ("Because the jury could have inferred that both men knew of the drugs, it could also have inferred that appellants had agreed to transport them to Puerto Rico for the purpose of distributing them, which is the essence of the conspiracy charge."); *United States v. Page*, 521 F.3d 101, 109 (1st Cir. 2008) ("Since [the defendant] subsequently helped to **[—20—]** load these bags into the . . . vehicle for transport, the jury reasonably could infer both that [the defendant] had formed the requisite intent to possess that cocaine . . . and further that [the defendant] had implicitly joined in and aided the . . . conspiracy."); *United States v. May*, 343 F.3d 1, 6 (1st Cir. 2003) ("[B]y having an amount of the drug in his own possession however briefly, [defendant] was 'directly involved' with the drug, which suffices to hold him accountable for the contraband.") (citation omitted); *United States v. Romero*, 32 F.3d 641, 645 (1st Cir. 1994) (Finding that "[t]he government's evidence of possession was ample" for purposes of determining sufficient evidence existed to support defendants' convictions for possessing, while aboard a vessel subject to jurisdiction of the United States, cocaine intended for distribution, where law enforcement testified they saw people aboard defendants' vessel throwing bales overboard).

B. *Demonstrative Evidence*

Defendants contend that the district court committed reversible error by excluding a demonstrative aid in the form of a videotaped "reenactment" that they claim directly contradicted the government's case and established Carrasquillo's **{-421-}** ability to load twenty-five bales of cocaine onto his boat without their assistance. We are not persuaded.

During both the fourth and fifth day of trial, defendants offered as evidence a homemade video depicting a reenactment of **[—21—]** twenty-five bales being brought on board a vessel by "a normal housewife," a woman of similar age to Carrasquillo. Defense counsel explained that "because the Government has questioned the ability of Juan Carrasquillo to bring those bales on board . . . instead of doing the reenactment with a man, we decided to use conditions that were more onerous, and did the reenactment with a woman of similar age, who was able to load the 25 bales." Defense counsel urged that the video had "[Federal Rule of Evidence] 101 value" and it would be probative in that would help "the jury understand the testimony."

The government opposed admission of the video, stating that the defendants had not "show[n] a similarity of conditions and circumstances" between the original loading of the cocaine and the purported reenactment. The government objected that there was "no indication as to how the bales that were seen floating were actually constructed or packaged"; there was "dissimilarity in terms of the sea conditions"; the boat appeared to be "just slightly off a pier instead of in the middle of the ocean"; "in the video, you can see someone actually captaining the vessel or near the steering console" (in contrast to Stewart's testimony that Carrasquillo, in the middle of the ocean, had left the steering wheel for "40, 45 minutes" in order to "load all of the packages on board," during which time the boat just floated and "was being guided by the currents"); and the reenactment was done **[—22—]** "in the daylight hours."

The district court observed that "the boat [in the video] is not the same" one used by Carrasquillo and the defendants, that the reenactment video "could be confusing to the jury how actually the bales were put on," and that it was of minimal probative value since it was "in the record already" through the "testimony of Mr. Hernandez and Mr. Stewart to the effect that they have seen Mr. Carrasquillo for many years, and they see no weaknesses." After hearing the arguments from counsel, the district court denied admission of the video "reenactment" pursuant to Federal Rule of Evidence 403.

Under Rule 403, a district court may exclude evidence when its probative value is substantially outweighed by the danger of unfair prejudice. *United States v. Leoner-Aguirre*, 939 F.3d 310, 321 (1st Cir. 2019). "We give great deference to a district judge's balancing of probative value versus unfair prejudice," *United States v. Breton*, 740 F.3d 1, 14 (1st Cir. 2014), and review that determination for abuse of discretion, *Leoner-Aguirre*, 939 F.3d at 321. Although we have not had occasion to discuss the exclusion of demonstrative reenactment evidence in a criminal case, we have done so in a civil context. *See Fusco v. Gen. Motors Corp.*, 11 F.3d 259, 264 (1st Cir. 1993) (upholding the district court's exclusion of a video that General Motors had produced and offered as replication of an automobile accident on a test track). **[—23—]** We see no reason not to be guided by the analysis therein.

We observed in *Fusco* that with demonstrative recreation evidence, "courts have feared that the jurors may be misled because they do not fully appreciate how variations in the surrounding conditions, as between the original occurrence and the staged event, can alter the outcome." *Id.* Setting forth a "substantial similarity" test, we noted that "[i]n such cases the solution of many courts, including this one, has been to call for substantial similarity in conditions, or to stress the great **{-422-}** discretion of the trial judge to exclude the evidence where similarity is not shown, or both." *Id.* (first citing *Swajian v. Gen. Motors*, 916 F.2d 31 (1st Cir. 1990); and then citing 1 J. Strong, McCormick on Evidence § 202 (1992)). We further explained:

> [T]he concept of substantial similarity is a flexible one, and ought to be, for the benefits of the demonstration and the dangers of misleading the jury will vary greatly depending upon the facts. We think that the trial judge enjoys great discretion in this area. But here the circumstances were not similar: as in *Swajian*, the test occurred in controlled conditions, on a test track with a driver expecting the occurrence, and with a doctored piece of equipment rather than one the actually broke.

Id. Applying the teaching of *Fusco* to the demonstrative video enactment before us, we conclude that the district court did not abuse its discretion in finding that the defendants' proffer failed the "substantial similarity" test. The reenactment occurred "in controlled conditions," off a dock rather than in rocky, open **[—24—]** waters, on a different "piece of equipment" than Carrasquillo's boat, with the boat being captained during the loading rather than left adrift for forty or forty-five minutes. For these reasons, the district court did not abuse its broad discretion in excluding the evidence under Rule 403.

Finally, we note that in holding that the "substantial similarity" test also applies to recreations in the criminal context, we join other circuits. *See United States v. Jackson*, 479 F.3d 485, 489 (7th Cir. 2007); *United States v. Baldwin*, 418 F.3d 575, 580 (6th Cir. 2005); *United States v. Birch*, 39 F.3d 1089, 1092–93 (10th Cir. 1994); *United States v. Russell*, 971 F.2d 1098, 1106 (4th Cir. 1992). We reiterate that "substantially similar" is a flexible concept; it is not synonymous with "identical." When a demonstration is admitted, any dissimilarity is fair game for cross-examination. The application of the substantial similarity test is informed by the purpose for which the purported recreation is offered. However the proponent characterizes the reason for the introduction of the demonstrative aid, if that demonstration does not permit a fair comparison with the event at issue because it is "insufficiently comparable to the circumstances [of] the case," *Swajian*, 916 F.3d at 36, then the district court is well within its wide berth as gatekeeper of the evidence in excluding it. **[—25—]**

C. *Closing Argument*

Defendants contend that the prosecutor's misstatement in closing argument that defense witness Hernandez suffered from a "broken ankle" rather than a "twisted ankle" constituted reversible error. We disagree.

In support of the defendants' contention that they thought that the fishing trip captained by Carrasquillo was a legitimate lobster trip and that they did not understand it to be a drug trafficking venture, Hernandez testified that several days before December 10, 2016, Carrasquillo asked him to accompany him to lay lobster traps at sea. He testified that he planned to make the trip, but on December 9, he told Carrasquillo that he had twisted his ankle and would not be able to join him. Nonetheless, he loaded lobster cages onto the boat. The defense stated to the jury in closing argument that Hernandez was "the person that was supposed to go fishing with Juan Carrasquillo on December the 10th, and it was not until the afternoon before that he told Juan Carrasquillo that he twisted his ankle and couldn't go." The defendants argued that Carrasquillo's testimony supported their claim that they had been recruited at the last minute in light of **{-423-}** Hernandez's inability to make the trip in what they understood to be a legitimate lobster expedition: they were not willing participants in a structured and planned drug trafficking venture but were innocent bystanders. **[—26—]**

In his closing, referencing Hernandez's testimony, the prosecutor told the jury to "ask [them]selves" if it is "really possible for this individual [Hernandez] to be loading lobster cages with a broken ankle. . . . That's his story. His story is he loaded 20 lobster cages with a broken ankle, he baited them, and then he decided not to go on this fishing trip. What does that tell you?"

When the prosecutor concluded his summation, Stewart's counsel objected that "the testimony was not that Javier Hernandez had a broken ankle. He clearly said he had a twisted ankle, and there is a huge difference between that." Denying the objection, the district court stated that it did not think "it makes a difference" as to whether Hernandez had a broken ankle or a twisted ankle, and also noted that it had "already explained to the jury that it is their recollection that prevails in this case" and not statements made by counsel. In its instructions to the jury following the closing arguments, the court reiterated:

> The argument and the statements by the lawyers are not evidence. The lawyers are not witnesses. Whatever they may have said in their opening statements and in their closing arguments and at other times is intended to help you interpret the evidence, but it is not evidence. If the facts as you remember them differ from the way the lawyers have stated them, your memory of them is the one that controls.

Where a timely objection is lodged to a statement made by the government in closing argument, "[w]e review *de novo* whether **[—27—]** the challenged portion of the government's closing argument was improper and, if so, whether it was harmful." *United States v. González-Pérez*, 778 F.3d 3, 19 (1st Cir. 2015) (alteration in original) (quoting *Appolon*, 695 F.3d at 66). That is to say, "we may reverse [the] convictions on the basis of the prosecutor's remarks only if they were 'both inappropriate and prejudicial.'" *United States v. Amaro-Santiago*, 824 F.3d 154, 158 (1st Cir. 2016) (quoting *United States v. Matías*, 707 F.3d 1, 5 (1st Cir. 2013)). We have "fashioned a three prong test for examining whether the [remarks] 'so poisoned the well' that the trial's outcome was likely affected, thus warranting a new trial." *United States v. Joyner*, 191 F.3d 47, 54 (1st Cir. 1999) (quoting *United States v. Capone*, 683 F.2d 582, 586-87 (1st Cir. 1982)). "We examine: (1) whether the prosecutor's conduct was isolated and/or deliberate; (2) whether the trial court gave a strong and explicit cautionary instruction; and (3) whether it is likely that any prejudice surviving the judge's instruction could have affected the outcome of the case." *Id.* We thus review the challenged remarks under the three-pronged test.

First, the prosecutor's mischaracterization of Hernandez's twisted ankle as a "broken ankle" was isolated, occurring only twice and fleetingly.

Second, as noted, soon after the closing arguments were finished, the district court gave a cautionary instruction to the **[—28—]** jury that the "argument and the statements by the lawyers are not evidence" and instructed that "[i]f the facts as you remember them differ from the way the lawyers have stated them, your memory of them is the one that controls." As we have often observed, "juries are presumed to follow such instructions." *Amaro-Santiago*, 824 F.3d at 160 (quoting *United States v. Rodriguez*, 675 F.3d 48, 63 (1st Cir. 2012)). **{-424-}**

Third, even if any confusion about the extent of Hernandez's injury and his consequent ability to assist in loading lobster traps survived the district court's curative instruction, it is highly unlikely that any hypothetical misapprehension by a juror would have had any bearing on the outcome of the case. The prosecution did not discount the possibility that at some point lobster traps may have been present on the boat, and in fact during closing argument reminded the jury "the defense witness [Valentin] himself came up here and told you that lobster traps can be used to disguise drug trafficking." Whether or not Hernandez would have been able to lift the lobster traps was a tangential matter and not one that would have affected the outcome of the case.

In sum, the fleeting misstatement does not warrant a new trial.

CONCLUSION

For the reasons stated above, the judgments of conviction are **affirmed**.

United States Court of Appeals
for the First Circuit

No. 18-1710

UNITED STATES
vs.
DE LA CRUZ

Appeal from the United States District Court for the District of Puerto Rico

Decided: May 26, 2021

Citation: 998 F.3d 508, 9 Adm. R. 51 (1st Cir. 2021).

Before **LYNCH, SELYA,** and **KAYATTA,** Circuit Judges.

[—2—] {–508–} **LYNCH,** Circuit Judge: **{–509–}**

Ángel De la Cruz and two others were intercepted by the U.S. Coast Guard while smuggling drugs on a small ship in the waters north of Puerto Rico. The Coast Guard seized a large amount of cocaine from the ship and arrested De la Cruz and the other two crewmembers. They were brought to Puerto Rico and charged by indictment with several drug-related offenses, including violations of the Maritime Drug Law Enforcement Act ("MDLEA"), 46 U.S.C. §§ 70503 and 70506. The MDLEA offenses carried a mandatory minimum sentence of ten years' imprisonment. *See id.* § 70506(a)-(b); 21 U.S.C. § 960(b)(1)(B) (2018).

De la Cruz pleaded guilty to all counts. As to sentencing, he argued that he qualified for "safety valve" relief, which authorizes a district court to impose a sentence below the statutorily prescribed mandatory minimum sentence for certain enumerated offenses if the court makes several specific factual findings at sentencing. *See* 18 U.S.C. § 3553(f) (2018). The district court held that De la Cruz was ineligible for safety valve relief for his MDLEA offenses because they were not among those offenses specifically enumerated in the safety valve statute, and it sentenced him to the mandatory minimum sentence of ten years' imprisonment under the MDLEA. We now join the majority of circuits in holding that MDLEA offenses were not safety-valve eligible under the then-applicable safety valve provision and so affirm. **[—3—]**

I.

Because De la Cruz pleaded guilty, "we draw the facts from the plea colloquy, the unchallenged portions of the presentence investigation report, and the transcript of the sentencing hearing." *United States v. Padilla-Colón*, 578 F.3d 23, 25 (1st Cir. 2009).

On December 10, 2017, the U.S. Coast Guard detected a suspicious vessel traveling at a high rate of speed north of Fajardo, Puerto Rico. A Coast Guard team intercepted and boarded the ship and found three Dominican nationals on board, including De la Cruz, as well as fifty-three bales of suspected narcotics. The government of the Dominican Republic did not claim nationality over the ship. De la Cruz does not question that both he and the ship were subject to U.S. jurisdiction.

The Coast Guard team conducted field tests of the bales of suspected narcotics and they tested positive for cocaine. All three crewmembers were arrested and brought to Puerto Rico. About 1,325 kilograms of cocaine were seized from the ship.

De la Cruz was indicted on one count of conspiracy to possess with intent to distribute five kilograms or more of a controlled substance on board a vessel subject to the jurisdiction of the United States in violation of the MDLEA, 46 U.S.C. §§ 70503 and 70506; one count of aiding or abetting the MDLEA offense in violation **{–510–}** of §§ 70503 and 70506 and 18 U.S.C. § 2; and one count **[—4—]** of conspiracy to import into the United States five kilograms or more of a controlled substance in violation of 21 U.S.C. §§ 952, 960, and 963.

In March 2018, De la Cruz entered a straight plea of guilty to all three counts. He argued for a safety valve reduction, and the government opposed and argued that he was ineligible for safety valve relief as a matter of law because the applicable safety valve provision did not apply to MDLEA offenses. The government argued that Congress had deliberately chosen in the text of the safety valve statute to exclude MDLEA offenses from those eligible for safety valve relief by explicitly including other offenses in the safety valve statute, but not MDLEA offenses.

The district court agreed with the government and ruled that De la Cruz was ineligible for safety valve relief in a written memorandum and order in June 2018. The district court relied on a previous decision it had written in which it had held that the plain language of the safety valve statute did not apply to offenses under the MDLEA and that the history of the MDLEA and safety valve statute and case law from other circuits further confirmed that conclusion. *See United States v. Espinal-Mieses*, 313 F. Supp. 3d 376, 381-85 (D.P.R. 2018). The court went on to conclude that even though De la Cruz had also been convicted of non-MDLEA offenses, his sentence could not fall below the mandatory minimum of ten years' imprisonment for the MDLEA offenses. De la **[—5—]** Cruz filed a motion for reconsideration, which the district court denied.

At the sentencing hearing in July 2018, the district court denied De la Cruz's request for a minor role reduction.[1] Nonetheless, it varied downward and imposed the mandatory minimum sentence of ten years' imprisonment as to each count to be served concurrently.

De la Cruz timely appealed his sentence.

II.

De la Cruz makes two primary arguments: (1) that the district court erroneously determined that the 18 U.S.C. § 3553(f) safety valve provision did not apply to MDLEA offenses such that it could not sentence him below the ten-year mandatory minimum; and (2) that the court erred in denying the minor role reduction.[2] **[—6—]** The parties agree that, because the district court imposed the minimum statutory sentence required under the MDLEA, De la Cruz's challenge to the denial of the minor role reduction is moot if this Court rejects his safety valve argument.[3] **{-511-}**

The government does not challenge De la Cruz's assertion that, if eligible, he would meet the five fact-based criteria for safety valve relief. We review de novo the issue of whether the safety valve applied to MDLEA offenses because it is a purely legal issue of statutory interpretation. *See Padilla-Colón*, 578 F.3d at 29.

Three of our sister circuits have already decided this precise issue and held that the safety valve provision did not apply to offenses under the MDLEA under the plain language of the statute. *See United States v. Anchundia-Espinoza*, 897 F.3d 629, 633-34, 6 Adm. R. 233, 235–36 (5th Cir. 2018); *United States v. Pertuz-Pertuz*, 679 F.3d 1327, 1328-29 (11th Cir. 2012); *United States v. Gamboa-Cardenas*, 508 F.3d 491, 496-502 (9th Cir. 2007). Only one circuit has held that the safety valve provision did apply to such offenses, **[—7—]** reasoning that it did so based on the interaction between the MDLEA and the penalty provision of 21 U.S.C. § 960. *See United States v. Mosquera-Murillo*, 902 F.3d 285, 292-96, 6 Adm. R. 505, 509–13 (D.C. Cir.

[1] The court did apply a two-level reduction to De la Cruz's offense level under United States Sentencing Guidelines Manual § 2D1.1(b)(17), to which both the defendant and the government agreed. Under the then-applicable 2016 Guidelines, § 2D1.1(b)(17) provided for a two-level reduction if the defendant met the five fact-based criteria under 18 U.S.C. § 3553(f), even if the defendant did not qualify for the safety valve relief authorizing a sentence below the applicable statutory minimum. *See* U.S. Sent'g Guidelines Manual § 2D1.1(b)(17) (U.S. Sent'g Comm'n 2016); *id.* § 5C1.2(a)(1)-(5); *see also United States v. Warnick*, 287 F.3d 299, 303-04 (4th Cir. 2002) (applying a previous version of the two-level reduction).

[2] All references to § 3553(f) and the safety valve provision are to the previous version in effect at the time of the defendant's sentencing, unless otherwise stated.

[3] De la Cruz concedes on appeal that the safety valve issue that he raises is an open question in this circuit. Nonetheless, he cites *United States v. Rodríguez-Durán*, 507 F.3d 749, 772 (1st Cir. 2007), and *United States v. Bravo*, 489 F.3d 1, 11-12 (1st Cir. 2007), and argues that "the Court has previously assumed without deciding that the safety valve may apply to defendants convicted of violating the MDLEA." Neither of those cases states such an assumption and the Court did not consider the issue. *See Rodríguez-Durán*, 507 F.3d at 772-74; *Bravo*, 489 F.3d at 11-12.

2018). We agree with the majority view and hold that the applicable safety valve provision did not apply to offenses under the MDLEA based on the plain language of the statute as well as the history and structure of that statute and others.[4]

A. *The Relevant Statutes*

Because the language of the MDLEA, 21 U.S.C. § 960, and the safety valve provision is essential to both parties' arguments, we first discuss the language of those statutes and provide a brief history of each.

Congress enacted the MDLEA in 1980 "to facilitate increased enforcement by the Coast Guard of laws relating to the importation of controlled substances, and for other purposes." Pub. L. No. 96-350, 94 Stat. 1159, 1159 (1980) (codified as amended at 46 U.S.C. §§ 70501-70507).[5] The MDLEA provides that "[w]hile **[—8—]** on board a covered vessel, an individual may not," among other things, "knowingly or intentionally . . . manufacture or distribute, or possess with intent to manufacture or distribute, a controlled substance." 46 U.S.C. § 70503(a). A separate penalty section of the MDLEA, in turn, provides that an offense or a conspiracy or attempt to commit an offense under § 70503(a)(1) "shall be punished as provided in [21 U.S.C. § 960]" if it is the person's first felony drug offense. 46 U.S.C. § 70506(a)-(b); *see also* 21 U.S.C. § 962(b).

Congress enacted 21 U.S.C. § 960 in 1970 as part of the Controlled Substances Import and Export Act. Pub. L. No. 91-513, § 1010, 84 Stat. 1236, 1290 (1970) (codified as amended at 21 U.S.C. § 960 (2018)). Section 960 has several subsections. Section 960(a) provides the "[u]nlawful acts" which are punishable under the statute and specifically lists six other statutes **{–512–}** which constitute those unlawful acts under § 960. 21 U.S.C. § 960(a) (2018) (listing 21 U.S.C. §§ 825, 952, 953, 955, 957, and 959 as unlawful conduct for purposes of § 960). MDLEA offenses are not among those listed as "[u]nlawful acts" under § 960(a). Although the MDLEA did not exist at the time § 960 was first enacted, § 960 was later amended a number of times after the MDLEA was enacted, **[—9—]** including in the Maritime Drug Law Enforcement Prosecution Improvements Act of 1986. *See* Pub. L. No. 99-570, §§ 1005, 1302, 100 Stat. 3207, 3207-6, 3207-15 to -18 (1986). None of those later amendments to § 960 added the MDLEA to the list of offenses which constituted "[u]nlawful acts" under § 960(a).

Section 960(a) provides that the enumerated unlawful acts "shall be punished as provided in subsection (b)." It is pursuant to § 960(b) that MDLEA offenses under § 70503(a)(1) are punished. *See* 46 U.S.C. § 70506(a)-(b).

Section 960(b), titled "[p]enalties," describes how the drug-related offenses to which it applies should be punished based on the drug type and amount involved. It provides that when the violation involves "5 kilograms or more of a mixture or substance containing a detectable amount of [cocaine] . . . the person committing such violation shall be sentenced to a term of imprisonment of not less than 10 years" if there was no death or serious bodily injury resulting from the use of the controlled substance and the person has no prior conviction for a felony drug offense. 21 U.S.C. § 960(b)(1) (2018).

In 1994, Congress enacted the Violent Crime Control and Law Enforcement Act which, among other things, created the safety valve provision at issue. Pub. L. No. 103-322, § 80001(a), 108 Stat. 1796, 1985-86 (1994)

---

[4] The defendant has not argued on appeal that interpreting the safety valve provision not to apply to MDLEA offenses would somehow contravene the purpose of the safety valve statute, the MDLEA, or any other statute. Rather, he focuses his arguments on the language of the safety valve provision, the MDLEA, and 21 U.S.C. § 960, as interpreted in *Mosquera-Murillo*. The government responds with arguments based on the language of the statute, as well as its history and structure in the context of other statutes.

[5] The MDLEA, which was originally codified at 46 U.S.C. §§ 1901 to 1904, was amended several times between 1980 and when the safety valve provision was enacted in 1994, with the most **[—8—]** substantial amendment occurring in 1986. *See* Maritime Drug Law Enforcement Prosecution Improvements Act of 1986, Pub. L. No. 99- 570, §§ 3201-3202, 100 Stat. 3207, 3207-95 to -97.

(codified as amended at 18 U.S.C. **[—10—]** § 3553(f) (2018)). The version of the safety valve provision that applies to De la Cruz[6] provided that

> [n]otwithstanding any other provision of law, in the case of an offense under [21 U.S.C. §§ 841, 844, or 846] or [21 U.S.C. §§ 960 or 963], the court shall impose a sentence pursuant to guidelines promulgated by the United States Sentencing Commission . . . without regard to any statutory minimum sentence, if the court finds at sentencing, after the Government has been afforded the opportunity to make a recommendation, that [the defendant satisfies five criteria].[7] **[—11—] {-513-}**

18 U.S.C. § 3553(f) (2018). MDLEA offenses under §§ 70503 and 70506 were not among the five specifically enumerated offenses in § 3553(f).

B. *The Safety Valve Provision Did Not Apply to MDLEA Offenses Under the Plain Language of the Statute*

We begin with the safety valve statute's language in interpreting its meaning. *United States v. Vidal-Reyes*, 562 F.3d 43, 50 (1st Cir. 2009). "In so doing, we accord the statutory text 'its ordinary meaning by reference to the specific context in which that language is used, and the broader context of the statute as a whole.'" *Recovery Grp., Inc. v. Comm'r*, 652 F.3d 122, 125 (1st Cir. 2011) (quoting *Mullane v. Chambers*, 333 F.3d 322, 330 (1st Cir. 2003) (internal quotation marks omitted)). "When exhausting those [textual and structural] clues enables us to resolve the interpretive question put to us, our 'sole function' is to apply the law as we find it, not defer to some conflicting reading . . . ." *Niz-Chavez v. Garland*, 141 S. Ct. 1474, 1480 **[—12—]** (2021) (citation omitted) (quoting *Lamie v. U.S. Tr.*, 540 U.S. 526, 534 (2004)); *see also Recovery Grp.*, 652 F.3d at 125 ("If the statutory language is plain and unambiguous, we 'must apply the statute according to its terms,' except in unusual cases where, for example, doing so would bring about absurd results." (citation omitted) (quoting *Carcieri v. Salazar*, 555 U.S. 379, 387 (2009))).

The language of the safety valve provision plainly and unambiguously did not apply to offenses under the MDLEA. Section 3553(f) provided that the safety valve could apply to "an offense under" one of the five enumerated statutes listed in that provision. 18 U.S.C. § 3553(f) (2018). The MDLEA was not one of

---

[6] In December 2018, Congress enacted the First Step Act which, among other things, amended the § 3553(f) safety valve provision to explicitly include MDLEA offenses under §§ 70503 and 70506 as offenses eligible for relief from statutory minimums. Pub. L. No. 115-391, § 402(a)(1)(A)(ii), 132 Stat. 5194, 5221 (2018). The title of that section of the First Step Act is "Broadening of Existing Safety Valve." *Id.* § 402. Congress chose not to make the amendment to the safety valve provision apply retroactively. *Id.* § 402(b). Because De la Cruz was sentenced before the First Step Act was enacted, the previous version of the safety valve provision applies to him.

[7] Those five criteria are that:

> (1) the defendant does not have more than 1 criminal history point, as determined under the sentencing guidelines; (2) the defendant did not use violence or credible threats of violence or possess a firearm or other dangerous weapon (or induce another participant to do so) in connection with the offense; (3) the offense did not result in death or serious bodily injury to any person; (4) the defendant was not an organizer, leader, manager, or supervisor of others in the offense, as determined under the sentencing guidelines and was not engaged in a continuing criminal enterprise, as defined in section 408 of the Controlled Substances Act; and (5) not later than the time of the sentencing hearing, the defendant has **[—11—]** truthfully provided to the Government all information and evidence the defendant has concerning the offense or offenses that were part of the same course of conduct or of a common scheme or plan, but the fact that the defendant has no relevant or useful other information to provide or that the Government is already aware of the information shall not preclude a determination by the court that the defendant has complied with this requirement.

18 U.S.C. § 3553(f)(1)-(5) (2018).

those enumerated statutes. By explicitly listing certain statutes and excluding others, Congress clearly intended for the safety valve provision to apply only to offenses under the specific statutes listed and not to offenses under the MDLEA. *Anchundia-Espinoza*, 897 F.3d at 633, 6 Adm. R. at 235; *Pertuz-Pertuz*, 679 F.3d at 1328; *Gamboa-Cardenas*, 508 F.3d at 497-98; *see also United States v. Hernández-Ferrer*, 599 F.3d 63, 67-68 (1st Cir. 2010) (applying the "expressio unius est exclusio alterius" canon of statutory construction, "which translates roughly as 'the expression of one thing is the exclusion of other things'" (emphasis omitted)).[8] Congress had a **[—13—]** good reason for not including MDLEA offenses among those eligible for safety valve relief: at that time, Congress was especially concerned about drug trafficking over the seas and found that it was "a serious international problem and [was] universally condemned" and "present[ed] a specific threat to the security and societal well-being of the United States." Maritime Drug Law Enforcement Prosecution Improvements **{-514-}** Act of 1986, Pub. L. No. 99-570, § 3202, 100 Stat. 3207, 3207-95.

Nor are MDLEA offenses "offense[s] under" § 960, which was one of the statutes expressly included in the safety valve provision. *See* 18 U.S.C. § 3553(f) (2018). Section 960(a) lists six statutes the violation of any one of which constitutes the "[u]nlawful acts" under § 960. 21 U.S.C. § 960(a) (2018). Violations of one of those other listed statutes would be eligible for safety valve relief because they are offenses under § 960. *Anchundia-Espinoza*, 897 F.3d at 634, 6 Adm. R. at 236; *Pertuz-Pertuz*, 679 F.3d at 1329; *Gamboa-Cardenas*, 508 F.3d at 497. The MDLEA is not one of the statutes expressly listed under § 960(a), and so an MDLEA offense is not an offense under § 960 for purposes of safety valve relief. *Anchundia-Espinoza*, 897 F.3d at 634, 6 Adm. R. at 236; *Pertuz-Pertuz*, 679 **[—14—]** F.3d at 1329; *Gamboa-Cardenas*, 508 F.3d at 497-99; *see also Hernández-Ferrer*, 599 F.3d at 67-68.

The fact that MDLEA offenses are punished pursuant to § 960(b) does not change that conclusion. As our sister circuits have noted, the safety valve provision applies to "offense[s] under" one of the listed statutes, not to "offenses punishable under," "offenses penalized under," or "sentences under" one of those listed statutes. *See Anchundia-Espinoza*, 897 F.3d at 634, 6 Adm. R. at 236; *Pertuz-Pertuz*, 679 F.3d at 1329; *Gamboa-Cardenas*, 508 F.3d at 498-99; *see also* 18 U.S.C. § 3553(f) (2018). Section 960 provides its own offense conduct, by incorporation of other statutes, and the MDLEA provides its own offense conduct which is not incorporated into § 960. *See* 46 U.S.C. § 70506(a)-(b); 21 U.S.C. § 960(a) (2018). That § 70506 incorporates the penalty provision of § 960 does not change the fact that those separate statutes each defines and criminalizes different conduct which constitutes the offenses under those two statutes.

De la Cruz relies on the D.C. Circuit's decision in *Mosquera-Murillo* to support his § 960 argument. *Mosquera-Murillo*, in turn, states that it was relying on the Supreme Court's decisions in *Patterson v. New York*, 432 U.S. 197, 210 (1977), *Apprendi v. New Jersey*, 530 U.S. 466, 490 (2000), and *Alleyne v. United States*, 570 U.S. 99, 105-06 (2013) (plurality), in holding that MDLEA offenses are offenses under § 960 because the penalty **[—15—]** provision in § 960(b) provides elements of those offenses.[9] *See* 902 F.3d at 293, 6 Adm. R. at 510 (stating that "[o]ffenses are defined by the provisions that supply their elements" (citing *Patterson*, 432 U.S. at 210)).

[8] Other circuits have also strictly construed the § 3553(f) safety valve provision not to apply to offenses under other statutes which were not expressly included in the safety valve provision. *See, e.g., United States v. Koons*, 300 F.3d 985, [—13—] 993 (8th Cir. 2002) (holding that the safety valve provision did not apply to offenses under 21 U.S.C. § 860 because it was not one of the statutes specifically listed in the safety valve); *United States v. McQuilkin*, 78 F.3d 105, 108 (3d Cir. 1996) (same).

[9] The D.C. Circuit in *Mosquera-Murillo* also relied on the fact that the government had charged the defendants with violations of both the MDLEA and § 960 in the same count of the indictment as further support for the § 960 argument. *See* 902 F.3d at 293-94, 6 Adm. R. at 510–12. The indictment here charged violations of the MDLEA and § 960 in separate counts.

In our view, *Patterson*, *Apprendi*, and *Alleyne* are inapposite because none addresses the statutory interpretation issue here.[10] **[—16—] {-515-}**

Even if drug type and drug amount are elements of an MDLEA offense for purposes of punishment, as provided by § 960(b), and so those facts must be proven to a jury beyond a reasonable doubt as a matter of constitutional due process under *Patterson*, *Apprendi*, and *Alleyne*, those cases do not say anything about what "offense under" means for purposes of safety valve relief as a matter of statutory interpretation. That is a separate question about what Congress intended when it enacted the safety valve statute in 1994, and the plain and unambiguous language of 18 U.S.C. § 3553(f) simply did not apply to offenses under the MDLEA.

[10] *Patterson* addressed the issue of whether placing the burden of proving an affirmative defense at a murder trial on the defendant violates the Due Process Clause of the Fourteenth Amendment. 432 U.S. at 198. *Patterson* held that "the Due Process Clause requires the prosecution to prove beyond a reasonable doubt all of the elements included in the definition of the offense of which the defendant is charged" but does not require the prosecution to prove the nonexistence of an affirmative defense where the affirmative defense does not require the defendant to disprove an element of the charged offense. *Id.* at 210; *see also id.* at 206-07.

Apprendi addressed the issue of "whether the Due Process Clause of the Fourteenth Amendment requires that a factual determination authorizing an increase in the maximum prison sentence for an offense from 10 to 20 years be made by a jury on the basis of proof beyond a reasonable doubt." 530 U.S. at 469. The Supreme Court held that, as a matter of constitutional due process, "any fact (other than prior conviction) that increases the maximum penalty for a crime must be charged in an indictment, submitted to a jury, and proven beyond a reasonable doubt." *Id.* at 476 (quoting *Jones v. United States*, 526 U.S. 227, 243 n.6 (1999)); *see also id.* at 490. The Supreme Court in *Alleyne* concluded the same with respect to any fact that increases a mandatory minimum, holding that "[a]ny fact that, by law, increases the penalty for a crime is an 'element' that must be submitted to the jury and found beyond a reasonable doubt." 570 U.S. at 103 (citing *Apprendi*, 530 U.S. at 483 n.10, 490).

We cannot conclude that the technical definition of what an "offense" might mean under *Apprendi* and *Alleyne*, which postdate the enactment of the safety valve provision, was the definition that Congress intended in 1994. *See Niz-Chavez*, 141 S. Ct. at 1480 ("When called on to resolve a dispute over a statute's meaning, this Court normally seeks to afford the law's terms their ordinary meaning at the time Congress adopted them."); *Ngiraingas v. Sanchez*, 495 U.S. 182, 187 (1990). At that time, Black's Law Dictionary defined "offense" as "[a] felony or misdemeanor; a breach of the criminal laws; violation of law for which penalty is prescribed." *Offense*, Black's Law Dictionary (6th ed. 1990); *see also Taniguchi v. Kan Pac. Saipan, Ltd.*, 566 U.S. 560, 566-69 (2012) (using dictionary definitions to interpret a term in a statute). A "breach" or "violation" of the law connotes the **[—17—]** actions or conduct by the perpetrator which warrants the penalty prescribed by the law, but neither definition refers to the conduct that bears only on the degree of that penalty.

To the contrary, our understanding of "offense" comes from the Supreme Court's opinion in *McMillan v. Pennsylvania*, 477 U.S. 79 (1986). In *McMillan*, the Supreme Court held that sentencing factors which come into play only after the defendant has been found guilty beyond a reasonable doubt will not be considered elements of the substantive offense except under limited circumstances not involved here. *See id.* at 84-91 (relying on *Patterson*). At the time the safety valve provision was enacted, the Circuit Courts of Appeals applied the *McMillan* rule in holding that drug amount for purposes of sentencing was not an element of the substantive offense. *See, e.g., United States v. Lowden*, 955 F.2d 128, 129-30 (1st Cir. 1992); *United States v. Lam Kwong-Wah*, 966 F.2d 682, 685-88 (D.C. Cir. 1992); *United States v. Royal*, 972 F.2d 643, 649-50, 649 n.10 (5th Cir. 1992); *United States v. Harrison-Philpot*, 978 F.2d 1520, 1523-24 (9th Cir. 1992); *United States v. Perez*, 960 F.2d 1569, 1574-75 (11th Cir. 1992); *United States v. Madkour*, 930 F.2d 234, 237-38 (2d Cir. 1991); *United States v. Moreno*, 899 F.2d 465, 472-74 (6th Cir. 1990); **{-516-}** *United States v. Reynolds*, 900 F.2d

1000, 1002-04 (7th Cir. 1990); *United States v. Powell*, 886 F.2d 81, 84-85 (4th Cir. 1989); *United States v. Jenkins*, 866 F.2d 331, 333-34 (10th Cir. 1989); *United States* **[—18—]** *v. Woods*, 834 F.2d 1382, 1389-90 (8th Cir. 1987). It was not until years after the safety valve provision was enacted that *McMillan*'s definition of what constituted an "offense" and "offense elements" was overruled. *See United States v. Haymond*, 139 S. Ct. 2369, 2378 (2019) (stating that *Alleyne* expressly overruled *McMillan* and extended *Apprendi*).

C. *The History and Structure of the MDLEA, Safety Valve Provision, and Other Statutes Confirm That the Safety Valve Provision Did Not Apply to MDLEA Offenses*

The plain text resolves the statutory interpretation question. And in any event, our interpretation is further confirmed by other indicia. For confirmation, we look to the legislative history of the safety valve and other statutes. *See, e.g., Niz-Chavez*, 141 S. Ct. at 1484; *Telecomms. Regul. Bd. of P.R. v. CTIA-The Wireless Ass'n*, 752 F.3d 60, 66 (1st Cir. 2014). We also look to the structure of the safety valve provision in the context of the act which enacted it and in the context of other statutes. *See, e.g., Niz-Chavez*, 141 S. Ct. at 1482-84; *City of Providence v. Barr*, 954 F.3d 23, 31-44 (1st Cir. 2020); *Carnero v. Bos. Sci. Corp.*, 433 F.3d 1, 7-11 (1st Cir. 2006).

The MDLEA was enacted about fourteen years before—and subject to significant amendment eight years before—the safety valve provision was enacted. Congress was clearly aware of the MDLEA at the time it created the safety valve and could easily have included it among the safety valve's enumerated offenses if **[—19—]** it had so wanted. *See Anchundia-Espinoza*, 897 F.3d at 634, 6 Adm. R. at 236; *Gamboa-Cardenas*, 508 F.3d at 497-98. Moreover, § 960 was amended several times after the MDLEA was enacted, including as part of the act which amended the MDLEA in 1986 and the act which enacted the safety valve provision in 1994. None of those amendments added the MDLEA to the list of statutes that constituted the unlawful conduct under § 960. It would have been far easier for Congress simply to include MDLEA offenses under either § 3553(f) or § 960(a) if it intended for the safety valve to apply to such offenses, rather than rely on a complex analysis by which a court must infer safety valve relief through the MDLEA's incorporation of a penalty provision that does not itself discuss the safety valve. We cannot conclude that Congress intended to do indirectly what it could have done directly but did not. *See Anchundia-Espinoza*, 897 F.3d at 633-34, 6 Adm. R. at 235–36; *Pertuz-Pertuz*, 679 F.3d at 1328-29; *Gamboa-Cardenas*, 508 F.3d at 497-98; *see also Franklin Cal. Tax-Free Tr. v. Puerto Rico*, 805 F.3d 322, 338 (1st Cir. 2015).

That Congress eventually did amend the § 3553(f) safety valve provision in 2018 to explicitly include offenses under the MDLEA—eleven years after the first appellate opinion holding that the safety valve did not apply to such offenses, *see Gamboa-Cardenas*, 508 F.3d at 491—and chose not to apply that amendment retroactively is further evidence that the safety valve did not **[—20—]** previously apply to offenses under the MDLEA.[11] *See* **{-517-}** *Heckler v. Turner*, 470 U.S. 184, 209-11 (1985) (referring to later enacted legislation in interpreting an earlier statute and stating that "it carries . . . considerable retrospective weight" (collecting cases)); *Seatrain Shipbuilding Corp. v. Shell Oil Co.*, 444 U.S. 572, 595-96 (1980) (stating that "while the views of subsequent Congresses cannot override the unmistakable intent of the enacting one, such views are entitled to significant weight" (citation omitted)).

This later enactment in 2018 is entitled to weight, and it reinforces our conclusions based on the language of the statute. The fact that the title of the operative section of the First

[11] In his brief, De la Cruz refers to the "undue sentencing disparity" for defendants like De la Cruz who were sentenced shortly before the enactment of the First Step Act. But any disparity is the result of Congress's own choice to make the First Step Act's amendment to the safety valve provision not retroactive. And because all MDLEA defendants sentenced after December 2018 are now eligible for safety valve relief, only a small group of defendants is likely to be affected by this decision.

Step Act is called "Broadening of Existing Safety Valve," Pub. L. No. 115-391, § 402, 132 Stat. 5194, 5221 (2018), is further evidence that Congress understood the older version of the statute to have a narrower scope, *see Fla. Dep't of Revenue v. Piccadilly Cafeterias, Inc.*, 554 U.S. 33, 47 (2008) (stating that "statutory titles and section headings 'are tools available for the resolution of a doubt about the meaning of a statute'" (quoting *Porter v.* **[—21—]** *Nussle*, 534 U.S. 516, 528 (2002) (internal quotation marks omitted))). Indeed, it would have been unnecessary for Congress to "broaden" the existing safety valve to encompass MDLEA offenses if those offenses were already within its scope. The use of the term "broaden" in adding MDLEA offenses, rather than "confirm" or "clarify," also reinforces that even post-*Apprendi*, Congress did not have in mind *Mosquera-Murillo*'s technical, case law-based view of the word "offense" for purposes of the safety valve.

Furthermore, the structure of the act which enacted the safety valve provision, as well as the language used in surrounding statutes, confirm that the safety valve provision did not apply to offenses under the MDLEA. Congress enacted the safety valve provision in the Violent Crime Control and Law Enforcement Act of 1994. Pub. L. No. 103-322, § 80001(a), 108 Stat. 1796, 1985-86. In that same act, Congress added a subsection to 18 U.S.C. § 924 which made it unlawful to "smuggle[] or knowingly bring[] into the United States a firearm" "with intent to engage in or to promote conduct that . . . is punishable under the Controlled Substances Act (21 U.S.C. [§§] 801 et seq.), the Controlled Substances Import and Export Act (21 U.S.C. [§§] 951 et seq.), *or the Maritime Drug Law Enforcement Act* [(46 U.S.C. §§ 70501 et seq.)]." Pub. L. No. 103-322, § 110503, 108 Stat. 1796, 2016 (codified as amended at 18 U.S.C. § 924(k)) (emphasis added). That Congress explicitly referred to the MDLEA in another section of the same act which **[—22—]** created the safety valve provision to define another offense shows that Congress intended to exclude MDLEA offenses from the scope of the safety valve provision. *See Russello v. United States*, 464 U.S. 16, 23 (1983) ("[W]here Congress includes particular language in one section of a statute but omits it in another section of the same Act, it is generally presumed that Congress acts intentionally and purposely in the disparate inclusion or exclusion." (alteration in original) (quoting *United States v. Wong Kim Bo*, 472 F.2d 720, 722 (5th Cir. 1972))).

Congress also used the phrase "punishable under" in enacting the new subsection of 18 U.S.C. § 924 in the Violent Crime Control and Law Enforcement Act of 1994 to define the unlawful conduct covered by that subsection. **{-518-}** Pub. L. No. 103-322, § 110503, 108 Stat. 1796, 2016. If Congress had intended the safety valve provision to apply to offenses "punishable under" one of the statutes enumerated in that provision, Congress could have used that same language. That it instead chose to use different language in different parts of the same act which created the safety valve provision is important. *See Russello*, 464 U.S. at 23. And in the new subsection of 18 U.S.C. § 924 enacted in the Violent Crime Control and Law Enforcement Act of 1994, Congress listed the Controlled Substances Import and Export Act (which includes 21 U.S.C. § 960) and the MDLEA separately using the disjunctive "or." Referring to those statutes in that way is **[—23—]** further evidence that Congress did not intend for MDLEA offenses to be subsumed under § 960 through the MDLEA's incorporation of the penalty provision in § 960(b).

At the time Congress enacted the safety valve provision, there were numerous other statutes where Congress had specifically referred to the MDLEA when describing drug-related offenses, which is further evidence that Congress knew how to include MDLEA offenses when it so intended. *See, e.g.*, 18 U.S.C. § 924(c)(2) (1994) (defining "drug trafficking crime" as "any felony punishable under the Controlled Substances Act (21 U.S.C. [§§] 801 et seq.), the Controlled Substances Import and Export Act (21 U.S.C. [§§] 951 et seq.), *or the Maritime Drug Law Enforcement Act* [(46 U.S.C. §§ 70501 et seq.)] (emphasis added)); *id.* § 924(e)(2)(A)(i) (1994) (defining a "serious drug offense" using similar language); *id.* § 924(g)(2) (1994) (using similar language in making it unlawful to travel interstate with a firearm); *id.*

§ 929(a)(2) (1994) (using the same definition of "drug trafficking crime" as § 924(c)(2)); *id.* § 3142(e) (1994) (prescribing a rebuttable presumption of pretrial detention for defendants where "there is probable cause to believe that the person committed an offense for which a maximum term of imprisonment of ten years or more is prescribed in the Controlled Substances Act (21 U.S.C. [§§] 801 et seq.), the Controlled Substances Import and Export Act (21 U.S.C. [§§] 951 et seq.), *the Maritime Drug Law Enforcement* **[—24—]** *Act* [(46 U.S.C. §§ 70501 et seq.)], or an offense under section [18 U.S.C. §] 924(c)" (emphasis added)); 28 U.S.C. § 994(h) (1994) (providing that the Sentencing Commission's guidelines must specify a prison sentence "at or near the maximum term authorized for categories of defendants" who are at least eighteen years old and have been convicted of multiple felonies that each are "a crime of violence . . . or . . . an offense described in section 401 of the Controlled Substances Act (21 U.S.C. [§] 841), sections 1002(a), 1005, and 1009 of the Controlled Substances Import and Export Act (21 U.S.C. [§§] 952(a), 955, and 959), *and the Maritime Drug Law Enforcement Act* [(46 U.S.C. §§ 70501 et seq.)]" (emphasis added)).

And in several of these statutes which existed at the time Congress enacted the safety valve provision, Congress used the term "punishable under" when referring to § 960 which further demonstrates it distinguished between "offenses under" and "offenses punishable under." *See, e.g.*, 18 U.S.C. § 924(c)(2) (1994); *id.* § 924(g)(2) (1994); *id.* § 929(a)(2) (1994). Several of these statutes also listed both MDLEA offenses and § 960 offenses separately and in the disjunctive. *See, e.g.*, 18 U.S.C. § 924(c)(2) (1994); *id.* § 924(e)(2)(A)(i) (1994); *id.* § 924(g)(2) (1994); *id.* § 929(a)(2) (1994). These are further indicia that Congress did not intend for MDLEA offenses to fall under § 960. **[—25—]**

Finally, the plain language reading of the safety valve provision is supported by the possible effect the defendant's contrary **{-519-}** reading would have on the availability of safety valve relief. If we were to accept De la Cruz's argument and the position of the D.C. Circuit in *Mosquera-Murillo* that MDLEA offenses were eligible for safety valve relief because § 960 provides some of the elements for those offenses, that likely would have consequences as to other separate offenses also not explicitly listed. The government argues that offenses under both 21 U.S.C. §§ 859 and 860 would likely also be eligible for safety valve relief, even though neither was listed in 18 U.S.C. § 3553(f). After all, §§ 859 and 860 both refer to and incorporate a violation of 21 U.S.C. § 841(a)(1) (which is one of the statutes listed in the safety valve provision) as an element of the offense; add an additional element of distributing a controlled substance to someone under twenty-one years old, *see id.* § 859, or "distributing, possessing with intent to distribute, or manufacturing a controlled substance in or on, or within" certain protected areas, such as schools or public housing facilities, *id.* § 860(a)-(b), or hiring someone under eighteen years old to do so or to assist in doing so, *id.* § 860(c); and then set enhanced penalties which are calculated by reference to the penalties provided in § 841 that are based on drug type and drug amount, *see id.* §§ 841(b), 859, 860. **[—26—]**

Yet every circuit to have directly decided the issue has held that offenses under § 860 are not eligible for § 3553(f) safety valve relief. *See United States v. Phillips*, 382 F.3d 489, 499-500 (5th Cir. 2004); *Koons*, 300 F.3d at 993; *United States v. Kakatin*, 214 F.3d 1049, 1051-52 (9th Cir. 2000); *United States v. Anderson*, 200 F.3d 1344, 1346-48 (11th Cir. 2000); *McQuilkin*, 78 F.3d at 107-09; *see also United States v. Warnick*, 287 F.3d 299, 303-04 (4th Cir. 2002). *But see Mosquera-Murillo*, 902 F.3d at 296, 6 Adm. R. at 513 (discussing but not deciding the issue). That De la Cruz's and *Mosquera-Murillo*'s reasoning would indirectly expand the § 3553(f) safety valve to even more statutes which are not explicitly included in that safety valve provision is evidence that Congress did not intend this reading.[12]

---

[12] In his brief, De la Cruz argues that the "unfairness [of his sentence] is compounded by the government's documented practice of extending safety-valve relief to some MDLEA defendants while denying it to others." But De la Cruz does not develop that argument and so it is waived. *See*

III.

De la Cruz's sentence and the judgment of the district court are *affirmed*.

Henderson v. Mass. Bay Transp. Auth., 977 F.3d 20, 33 (1st Cir. 2020).

He also raised the rule of lenity for the first time at oral argument. Any argument based on the rule of lenity is also waived because it was not made in his opening brief. *See Bernardo ex rel. M & K Eng'g, Inc. v. Johnson*, 814 F.3d 481, 492 n.17 (1st Cir. 2016). Even bypassing that waiver issue, the rule of lenity does not apply here because the safety valve provision is not ambiguous. *See United States v. Pinkham*, 896 F.3d 133, 138 (1st Cir. 2018).

United States Court of Appeals
for the First Circuit

No. 19-2046

UNITED STATES
VS.
DE LEON-DE LA ROSA

Appeal from the United States District Court for the District of Puerto Rico

Decided: November 2, 2021

Citation: 17 F.4th 175, 9 Adm. R. 61 (1st Cir. 2021).

Before **KAYATTA** and **BARRON**, Circuit Judges, and **O'TOOLE,*** District Judge.

* Of the District of Massachusetts, sitting by designation.

[—3—] {-179-} BARRON, Circuit Judge:

Noel de Leon-De la Rosa ("De Leon") and Juan Batista Johnson-Debel ("Johnson") challenge their respective federal convictions in the District of Puerto Rico, as well as the resulting sentences. Those convictions are for destruction of a controlled substance while on a vessel, and conspiracy to destroy a controlled substance while on a vessel. Their prosecutions followed their indictment for these offenses -- as well as for others for which they also were convicted but that are not at issue here -- after U.S. Customs and Border Patrol ("CBP") agents in April 2017 interdicted off the coast of Puerto Rico the small boat that De Leon and Johnson were on at the time. We vacate the convictions that Johnson and De Leon each challenge, though we vacate Johnson's for different reasons than those that lead us to vacate De Leon's. **{-180-}**

I.

A.

The following facts are not in dispute. On the night of April 20, 2017, De Leon and Johnson were on a small boat about thirty miles off the northern coast of Puerto Rico, traveling southeast. The boat had no running lights.

At around 9:00 p.m., a CBP agent patrolling those waters by airplane detected the boat on the plane's forward-looking infrared camera. Suspecting drug smuggling, the agent called the **[—4—]** Coast Guard and the CPB's marine interdiction unit was dispatched to the boat's location.

The unit interdicted the boat just before midnight. After boarding the vessel, members of the unit determined that there was no contraband on board. CBP agents from the unit then detained Johnson and De Leon and brought the two of them—along with the boat—to the CBP facility in San Juan, Puerto Rico.

Once onshore at the CBP facility, at around 2:00 a.m., Johnson was interviewed by Francisco Calderón, an agent with U.S. Homeland Security Investigations. Calderón read Johnson the warnings required under *Miranda v. Arizona*, 384 U.S. 436 (1966),[1] and Johnson then answered questions that Calderón put to him about what had transpired aboard the boat. Johnson had also been interviewed immediately after the interdiction by Agent Miguel Borges.

The following morning, CBP Canine Enforcement Officer Adriel Castillo brought Honzo, a drug-detection dog, to inspect the boat. As Castillo walked the dog around the boat, Honzo "alerted" to the "[p]ossible contamination of narcotics."

That same day, Maritime Law Enforcement Specialist Matthew Tommie from the U.S. Coast Guard used a machine called an **[—5—]** Ionscan 400B to test swabs taken from the vessel. The scan revealed no trace residue of narcotics.

B.

Johnson and De Leon were indicted in the District of Puerto Rico on May 18, 2017, in an eight-count indictment. The indictment set forth the following charges against each defendant:

---

[1] Johnson filed a motion to suppress his statements below but has not renewed any *Miranda* claims on appeal.

Count One[:] Possession with the intent to distribute a controlled substance on board a vessel subject to the jurisdiction of the United States, aiding and abetting . . . in violation of [46 U.S.C. § 70503(a)(1) and 18 U.S.C. § 2].

Count Two[:] Conspiracy to possess with the intent to distribute a controlled substance on board a vessel subject to the jurisdiction of the United States . . . in violation of [46 U.S.C. §§ 70503(a)(1), 70506(b)].

Count Three[:] Possession with the intent to distribute a controlled substance . . . in violation of [21 U.S.C. § 841 and 18 U.S.C. § 2].

Count Four[:] Conspiracy to possess with the intent to distribute a controlled substance . . . in violation of [21 U.S.C. §§ 841, 846].

Count Five[:] Conspiracy to destroy property subject to forfeiture under [s]ection 511(a) of the Comprehensive Drug Abuse Prevention Act of 1970 . . . that is [a] . . . controlled substance [while on a vessel]. . . in violation of [21 U.S.C. § 881(a) and 46 U.S.C. §§ 70503(a)(2), 70504(b)(1), 70506(d)]. **{-181-}**

Count Six[:] Destruction of property subject to forfeiture under [s]ection 511(a) of the Comprehensive Drug Abuse Prevention Act of 1970 . . . that is . . . [a] controlled substance [while on a vessel] . . . in violation of [21 U.S.C. § 881(a), 46 U.S.C. §§ 70503(a)(2), 70504(b)(1), 70506(d), and 18 U.S.C. § 2]. **[—6—]**

The indictment also set forth two other counts. Count Seven charged Johnson alone with improper entry by a noncitizen in violation of 8 U.S.C. § 1325(a)(1). Count Eight charged De Leon alone with illegal reentry of a removed noncitizen in violation of 8 U.S.C. § 1326(a) and (b)(1).

Before trial, De Leon moved for severance. He did so on the ground that Johnson's statements to Calderón and Borges following the interdiction, if admitted in a joint trial with him, would violate De Leon's rights under the Confrontation Clause of the Sixth Amendment of the U.S. Constitution as interpreted in *Bruton v. United States*, 391 U.S. 123 (1968). The District Court denied the motion. De Leon moved for reconsideration, which the District Court denied.

De Leon then renewed his request at trial to exclude Johnson's statements to Agent Calderón based on *Bruton*. The District Court once again denied the request, explaining that "so long as [the confession] is sanitized then it's admissible." In charging the jury, the District Court instructed that the "statements . . . made by . . . Johnson [to Calderón]. . . can only be considered as evidence against [Johnson]" and "cannot be considered as evidence against [De Leon]."

At both the conclusion of the government's case and the close of evidence, the defendants argued that judgments of acquittal should be entered as to Counts One through Six for each **[—7—]** defendant because the government had failed to prove its case beyond a reasonable doubt. The District Court denied the motions.

The jury convicted Johnson and De Leon separately on Counts Seven and Eight, which set forth their respective immigration charges, and Counts Five and Six, which set forth their respective charges for destruction of property subject to forfeiture while aboard a vessel and conspiracy to commit the same offense. The jury acquitted both defendants of Counts One through Four, which set forth charges against each of them relating to possession with the intent to distribute a controlled substance. The jury verdicts entered on June 24, 2019.

Johnson and De Leon filed written motions for judgments of acquittal under Rule 29 of the Federal Rules of Criminal Procedure as to Counts Five and Six. The motions were denied.

The case proceeded to sentencing. Johnson was sentenced to fifty-seven months of imprisonment on his convictions for Counts Five and Six and three months' for his conviction on Count Seven, to be served consecutively for a total sentence of sixty months'. De Leon was sentenced to seventy-two months of imprisonment on his convictions on Counts Five and Six and twelve months' for his conviction on Count Eight, to be served concurrently.

Judgment entered against each defendant on September 25, 2019, and each filed a timely notice of appeal. *See* Fed. R. App. P. 4(b)(1)(A)(I). We have jurisdiction over their appeals of their **[—8—]** convictions under 28 U.S.C. § 1291 and over their appeals of their sentences under 18 U.S.C. § 3742(a).

II.

We begin with the defendants' challenges to the District Court's denial of their motions for judgments of acquittal as to their convictions on Counts Five and **{-182-}** Six. As we have explained, the latter count was for destruction of property subject to forfeiture while on a vessel, and the former count was for conspiracy to commit the same. *See United States v. Godin*, 534 F.3d 51, 61 (1st Cir. 2008). De Leon and Johnson each contends that the District Court erred because the evidence in the record does not suffice to support a finding of guilt beyond a reasonable doubt as to either offense.

Our review of the defendants' sufficiency-of-the-evidence challenges is de novo. *See United States v. Burgos-Montes*, 786 F.3d 92, 112 (1st Cir. 2015). In undertaking this review, we must consider the evidence "in the light most favorable to the verdict," *United States v. Stewart-Carrasquillo*, 997 F.3d 408, 417, 9 Adm. R. 41, 44 (1st Cir. 2021), mindful that "both direct and circumstantial evidence, whether alone or in concert, can sustain a conviction," *United States v. Clough*, 978 F.3d 810, 816 (1st Cir. 2020).

We have cautioned that in reviewing a sufficiency challenge we may not "stack inference upon inference in order to **[—9—]** uphold the jury's verdict." *United States v. Guzman-Ortiz*, 975 F.3d 43, 55 (1st Cir. 2020) (quoting *United States v. Valerio*, 48 F.3d 58, 64 (1st Cir. 1995). At the same time, we also have explained that we "may not pursue a divide and conquer strategy," *id.* (internal quotation marks omitted), that would isolate each piece of evidence without giving due weight to the picture that it helps to create when the evidence is considered as a whole. Instead, we must consider the evidence "in its totality," *id.* at 54, as the ultimate question that we must answer "is not whether a reasonable jury could have acquitted the defendant, but rather whether a reasonable jury 'could have found that the government proved each element of the crime beyond a reasonable doubt.'" *Stewart-Carrasquillo*, 997 F.3d at 418, 9 Adm. R. 44–45 (quoting *United States v. Paz-Alvarez*, 799 F.3d 12, 25, 3 Adm. R. 61, 67 (1st Cir. 2015)).

We agree with the government that, under the standards just described, there is no merit to the sufficiency challenges before us. To see why, it first helps to provide some more background about the government's case and the nature of the issues that are in dispute in relation to the defendants' sufficiency challenges. We then will turn to the specific arguments that each defendant makes about why the evidence is too thin, starting with Johnson's. **[—10—]**

A.

The indictment charged De Leon and Johnson each with violating 46 U.S.C. § 70503(a)(2) and 18 U.S.C. § 2 by destroying property subject to forfeiture as defined by 21 U.S.C. § 881(a), as well as conspiring to do the same. Section 881(a), in turn, provides that certain categories of property are subject to forfeiture, including "[a]ll controlled substances which have been manufactured, distributed, dispensed, or acquired in violation of [the Act]", *id.* § 881(a)(1), and "[a]ll raw materials, products, and equipment of any kind which are used, or intended for use, in manufacturing, compounding, processing, delivering, importing, or exporting any controlled substance," *id.* § 881(a)(2).

The indictment specified the property subject to forfeiture for each defendant as "a manufactured, distributed, dispensed, acquired, or possessed controlled substance." *Id.* § 881(a)(1). The indictment did not identify "equipment of any kind which are used, or intended for use, in manufacturing, compounding, processing, delivering, importing, or exporting any controlled substance" as constituting the predicate property subject to forfeiture for any of the charges against either De Leon or Johnson. *Id.* § 881(a)(2). **{-183-}**

Notwithstanding these features of the indictment, the District Court instructed the jury as follows as to what it would need to find to return a verdict of guilty for the charges **[—11—]** underlying the convictions at issue here. With respect to the charge for the underlying substantive offense, the District Court instructed, the jury would have to find beyond a reasonable doubt that: (1) "[O]n the date charged, [the] defendants were on board the vessel in this case and, at the time, destroyed property that was on board the vessel;" (2) "the property was a controlled substance *or equipment used for delivering controlled substances*" (emphasis added); and (3) "they did so knowingly and intentionally." With respect to the charge for the underlying conspiracy offense, the District Court instructed, the jury would have to find the same with the one difference being that the jury would have to find beyond a reasonable doubt that the defendant "conspired to destroy property [subject to forfeiture] that was on board the vessel" rather than that the defendant had in fact destroyed it.

The government does not dispute, however, the defendants' contention that, despite the instructions, the forfeitable property that serves as the predicate for the underlying convictions is a "controlled substance" and not "equipment used for delivering controlled substances." The government thus does not contend that the defendants' convictions may be upheld if the evidence suffices to show beyond a reasonable doubt that each destroyed—and conspired to destroy—such equipment rather than a controlled substance. In this respect, **[—12—]** the government does not dispute the defendants' contention that the evidence must suffice to show beyond a reasonable doubt that the forfeitable property that each defendant destroyed—and conspired to destroy—was a controlled substance.

Nonetheless, the government contends that the defendants are wrong to assert—insofar as they do—that their acquittals of the counts that charge each of them with the cocaine possession offenses in and of themselves require us to sustain their sufficiency challenges to the convictions for the distinct offenses that they challenge here. We agree. A conviction on one count may be upheld against a sufficiency challenge, even though it is seemingly inconsistent with that jury's verdict of acquittal on another count. *See Dunn v. United States*, 284 U.S. 390, 393 (1932) ("Consistency in the verdict is not necessary. Each count in an indictment is regarded as if it was a separate indictment."); *see also United States v. Powell*, 469 U.S. 57, 64-65 (1984) (confirming that *Dunn*'s rule remains good law).

The critical question for us, then, is whether, for each defendant, the evidence suffices to show beyond a reasonable doubt that each of them agreed to jettison cocaine from the boat and that each of them did so. For, if the evidence so suffices, then the defendants' challenges to the District Court's denial of their motions for acquittal necessarily fail. **[—13—]**

B.

Johnson contends that the evidence does not suffice to support his conviction for either the substantive or the conspiracy variant of the offense because "the only evidence showing destruction of cocaine was [his out-of-court confession]," and there was too little independent proof that tends to establish that the crimes to which he admitted in that confession occurred. He relies for this proposition on our decision in *United States v. Tanco-Baez*, 942 F.3d 7 (1st Cir. 2019). **{-184-}**

In *Tanco-Baez*, we explained why a defendant's out-of-court confession alone, due to a specific concern about its reliability, cannot be the sole basis to support a conviction. That concern arises when there is no substantial independent evidence in the record that the crime that the confession encompasses in fact occurred. Thus, we explained in *Tanco-Baez*, such a confession must be supported by "substantial" independent evidence that "tends to establish" that the crime admitted in the confession in fact occurred in order for that confession to be given weight in assessing whether the evidence as a whole suffices to support the conviction beyond a reasonable doubt. *Id.* at 20 (quoting *Opper v. United States*, 348 U.S. 84, 93 (1954)).

We emphasized in *Tanco-Baez*, however, that the kind of evidence that could serve this corroborating function need not be strong enough in its own right to support the conviction. *Id.* **[—14—]** Rather, such evidence need be strong enough only to provide the kind of support for the confession's reliability that, despite the out-of-court circumstances in which it is claimed to have been made, would permit it to be deemed reliable when considered along with the evidence in the record as a whole. *Id.* Thus, in the event such corroborating evidence is present, the confession may be relied upon to support the conviction against the sufficiency challenge. *Id.*

Against this legal backdrop, we begin our analysis by considering the evidence of what Johnson concedes constitutes the out-of-court confession by him to the crimes for which he was convicted. That confession was introduced at trial through the testimony of the law enforcement agents to whom Johnson spoke soon after the interdiction of the boat.

First, Agent Calderón testified, in response to questions from the prosecutor, about the statements that Johnson made to him. Specifically, he testified as follows in that regard:

> Q: And what, if anything, did [Johnson] say about the contents of the boat[] he left on?
> A: He stated that once he was in the boat, *eso*, referring to drugs[,] were in the boat.
> Q: And he used that word specifically, *eso*?
> A: *Eso*, correct.
> Q: And when have you heard that in your career?
> A: In previous drug trafficking investigations where they will refer to drugs as *eso*.
> Q: Does *eso* refer to a particular type of drug or just drugs in general?
> A: Mostly cocaine as that was smuggled over in this . . . area of responsibility. **[—15—]**
> Q: And what, if anything, did Defendant Johnson say about what happened when law enforcement approached the vessel on which he was?
> A: He stated that when he saw that he was going to be interdicted by the marine officers . . . he grabbed the small engine [to] which the bales were tied up, the *doce piezas* [was] the term that he used, called pieces, within two bales. Each one has six pieces, they were tied up to a rope to the small engine and he jettisoned [it] overboard, he threw them overboard into the water, so it would s[ink] and it [would]n't be recovered by law enforcement.
> Q: I want to unwrap that statement just a little bit. You stated that he said that there was a small outboard engine onboard?
> A: Correct.
> Q: Did he provide any details about that small outboard engine? **{–185–}**
> A: I believe -- if I recall correctly it was a 30 horsepower.
> Q: A 30 horsepower engine?
> A: Correct.
> Q: You said something about two sacks or bales.
> A: Correct. He stated that there were two small sacks or bales and each one contained six pieces, referring to bricks of cocaine, for a total of 12 pieces, that were tied up to a rope to the engine, and he lifted it and threw them overboard.

Second, Agent Borges testified about what Johnson said to him. In doing so, he recounted that he "specifically talked to Johnson. And during those preboarding questions [Johnson] said . . . that they threw overboard a small spare engine."

Johnson does not dispute that, from the testimony of these two agents about the statements that he made to them, a reasonable juror could find that he admitted that he was aboard **[—16—]** the boat with another person (De Leon), that the boat was transporting cocaine, that he tied the cocaine to a spare engine, and that "they" intentionally threw the engine overboard (thereby destroying the cocaine) upon learning that the boat had been detected by law enforcement.[2] In other words, he does not dispute that the statements—together—constitute a confession to the crimes at issue here. Johnson nevertheless contends that this out-of-court confession cannot suffice to support either of his convictions at issue because there was an absence of "substantial" independent evidence that "tends to establish" that the crimes that he admitted committing in his out-of-court confession occurred. *See Tanco-Baez*, 942 F.3d at 20 (quoting *Opper*, 348 U.S. at 93). We do not agree.

For starters, substantial independent evidence was introduced at trial that "tends to establish" that the boat on which Johnson was traveling did have a controlled substance—cocaine—aboard it just prior to its interdiction. Francisco González, the CBP agent patrolling the ocean by plane the night of **[—17—]** the interdiction, testified that he spotted the boat on which Johnson was found in the waters prior to its interdiction. He further testified that the images that he reviewed on the infrared camera on his plane—which were also introduced into evidence and that he testified were taken prior to the boat's interdiction—showed "bales or packages" that were "in the middle" of the boat and thus in a location on the vessel that would have made it possible for those on board to "get rid of" the "bales or packages" easily if the boat were intercepted.

González also testified that the boat that the defendants were on was traveling near "Highway 19," which he described as a common drug smuggling route off the coast of Puerto Rico, when it was interdicted and that he had participated in a number of operations in which large quantities of cocaine had been seized from vessels traveling close to Highway 19. He further testified that the boat had no navigational lights running when it was spotted, and that it was the most "common type" of vessel to be carrying controlled substances **{-186-}** because larger boats were typically used to smuggle migrants.

In addition, Calderón, who had questioned Johnson following the boat's interdiction, testified in his own right about the general practices of the drug trafficking operations that he had investigated during his time patrolling the waters around Puerto Rico. That testimony accorded with González's about how **[—18—]** such operations are usually conducted. It accorded as well with the description that Calderón had provided about what González had observed with respect to the boat on which Johnson was found.

This testimony—and the evidence from the infrared camera—was not the only evidence that the government introduced that bears on whether there was substantial independent evidence that "tends to establish" that cocaine was on board the boat. The government also introduced testimony from the handler of a drug canine, who testified that when the dog conducted a canine sniff of the boat, it alerted to "[p]ossible contamination of narcotics." The government also introduced testimony from an intelligence research analyst about the contents of a cell phone retrieved from the

---

[2] We note, in this regard, that in the testimony reciting Johnson's statements, the agents did not at any point assert that Johnson himself stated that the material he tied to the engine was "cocaine," as he instead referred to what was tied to the engine only as "*eso*" and "*doce piezas*." But, the agents testified that "*eso*" and "*doce piezas*" are common slang terms that drug smugglers use to refer to cocaine. Johnson does not contend that his statements—because they refer to "*eso*" and "*doce piezas*" and not "cocaine"—do not constitute a confession to the crimes charged.

defendants' boat, as well as a report that contained a translation of those messages. That evidence, together, showed that the phone's owner had some kind of transaction planned.

All of this evidence is independent of Johnson's out-of-court confession, and, at least when considered as a whole, it constitutes substantial evidence that "tends to establish" that cocaine was on board the boat prior to its interdiction. It thus serves the necessary corroborative function with respect to that aspect of Johnson's out-of-court statements to Calderón about his criminal conduct.

The government introduced similarly substantial evidence independent of Johnson's out-of-court confession that "tends to **[—19—]** establish" another critical aspect of it—namely, that there was a spare engine aboard to which Johnson had tied at least some of the cocaine that was aboard the boat. That evidence includes the evidence already described that indicates that the boat was involved in smuggling drugs—specifically cocaine. It also includes testimony from Agents Calderón and González that cocaine smugglers often travel with a spare engine on board their boat for the purpose of ensuring that they have a ready means of disposing of the cocaine while they are on the open waters.

Agent Calderón testified in that connection that typically "bale[s]" containing cocaine are "tied" to a "smaller engine" by drug smugglers so that any cocaine tossed overboard "will sink and it will not be recovered as evidence by law enforcement." González, the CBP officer, also testified that drug smugglers package cocaine in "bales" and then they "attach each . . . bale[] to another [bale] with a line,. . . and at the end of the line they put some weight"—often in the form of a "spare engine[]"—so that if "any law enforcement vessel detect[s] them, they're able to throw it [into] the water and s[i]nk it [in] no time." Thus, there is substantial independent evidence in the record that "tends to establish" the aspect of Johnson's confession in which he admitted that such an engine was on the boat and that cocaine was tied to it. **[—20—]**

Finally, the government provided independent evidence that "tends to establish" Johnson's admission that he intentionally jettisoned the engine after realizing that the boat had been detected by law enforcement. For example, González testified that, after the defendants appeared to hear the plane and the approaching interdicting vessel, and while he was moving the plane in for a closer look, he could no longer see **{–187–}** on the infrared camera the bales or packages that he had originally spotted in the middle of the boat. Moreover, when the boat was interdicted, no bales or packages were found on board or in the water.

Viewed as a whole, then, the record contains "substantial" evidence that "tends to establish" each of the key components of the statements attributed to Johnson that he does not dispute, in pressing his argument under *Tanco-Baez,* combined to constitute a confession to his destruction of cocaine on board a boat. Accordingly, Johnson's *Tanco-Baez*-based challenge fails as to his conviction for the destruction of a controlled substance offense.

We emphasize that *Tanco-Baez* reversed a conviction for possession of a firearm by an unlawful user of a controlled substance under 18 U.S.C. § 922(g)(3) only after finding that the government did not sufficiently corroborate "each essential fact that [was] admitted"—in that case, the defendant's statement to **[—21—]** law enforcement that he was a long-term marijuana user. 942 F.3d at 14-15, 25. And, *Tanco-Baez* did so only after determining that the government was unable to provide *any* independent evidence that corroborated the admission of habitual drug use. *Id.* at 24-25.

The government in this case, by contrast, provided substantial independent evidence that "tends to establish" *all* the relevant aspects of Johnson's admissions concerning the destruction of forfeitable property offense—his statements that "*eso*" or cocaine was on the boat and tied to an engine, and his confession that "they" intentionally threw the engine overboard. We do not mean to suggest in emphasizing this distinction that independent evidence of this comprehensive kind is needed to satisfy the requirements described in *Tanco-Baez* for permitting an out-of-court confession to be given weight. But, at least in the face of such comprehensively bolstering evidence, we must reject Johnson's contention that the evidence was not sufficient to support his convictions for the charged crime, given his conceded confession to it.

There does remain Johnson's challenge under *Tanco-Baez* to his conviction for conspiracy to destroy forfeitable property on a vessel. But, to the extent that more is needed under *Tanco-Baez* to corroborate the aspects of the confession that bear directly on whether he committed the conspiracy offense—namely, **[—22—]** his statement that "*they*" threw the engine overboard with twelve "*piezas*" tied to it—more was provided.

Calderón testified that the thirty-horsepower engine Johnson professed to have thrown overboard through his statements to law enforcement would have "weigh[ed] approximately 50 [or] 60 pounds." Calderón further testified that, based on his experience investigating drug trafficking, each "*pieza*" of cocaine typically would weigh 2.4 pounds. Thus, that testimony supplies independent evidence that "tends to establish" that Johnson, after setting out on a multi-day trip on a small boat carrying controlled substances with De Leon, did not act alone in lifting more than sixty pounds in the dark of night but instead was assisted by his boatmate. So, here, as well, Johnson's *Tanco-Baez*-based challenges come up short.

C.

We turn now to De Leon's sufficiency challenges to his convictions, which also are for destruction of property subject to forfeiture while aboard a boat and conspiracy to commit that offense. He challenges both convictions on the ground that the evidence of these charges was "circumstantial" and "improper[ly]" required the **{-188-}** "jury [to] mount[] inference over inference."

We first consider whether the evidence suffices to permit a reasonable juror to find beyond a reasonable doubt that cocaine was on the boat and that De Leon assisted Johnson in **[—23—]** destroying it. Because we conclude that it does, we conclude that De Leon's conviction for the destruction of forfeitable property as defined by § 881(a)(1) on a vessel is supported by sufficient evidence.

De Leon is right that we may not consider the statements that Johnson made to Calderón in which Johnson purportedly admitted either that "*eso*" or that a spare engine that had something tied to it was aboard the boat. The jury was instructed not to consider those statements for purposes of assessing whether there was evidence sufficient to find De Leon guilty of the charges that he faced, and so we set them aside for present purposes.

There is no bar, however, to our considering the inculpatory statements by Johnson that Agent Borges testified Johnson made to him. There was no similar prohibitory instruction by the District Court to the jury regarding those statements; they were admitted into evidence against De Leon. Nor does De Leon argue otherwise. Accordingly, we must take account of Johnson's statements that "they" threw the "engine" overboard, as he made that statement to Borges, in assessing whether the quantum of evidence in the record suffices to support De Leon's convictions.

With those preliminaries out of the way, the central question is whether Johnson's statement to Agent Borges that "they threw overboard a small spare engine" is sufficient to support De Leon's conviction for the destruction-of-forfeitable-property- **[—24—]** while-on-a-vessel offense when that statement is considered along with all the other evidence—other than, that is, Johnson's statements to Agent Calderón. We conclude that it is.

At trial, the government presented circumstantial evidence, previously described, that "tends to establish" that cocaine was on the boat on which De Leon was found. This evidence includes the infrared images suggesting that the boat the defendants were on carried cargo or "bales" of some kind; the evidence of the text messages from the phone found on the boat that suggested that the sender had a transaction of some kind planned; the testimony from Agent González stating that the boat was traveling without navigational lights, on a route infamous for drug smuggling, and was the type of vessel commonly used for drug smuggling; and the testimony by the canine handler that after the boat was interdicted, a canine sniff of the boat revealed "[p]ossible contamination of narcotics."

Moreover, Agents Calderón and González provided testimony that in their experience drug smugglers often have spare engines aboard their boats to weigh down the cocaine in the event that they need to jettison the drugs to avoid their detection by law enforcement. And—crucially—Agent Borges testified that Johnson told him that "they threw overboard a small spare engine" prior to the boat being interdicted. **[—25—]**

Thus, a rational juror could have concluded beyond a reasonable doubt that—in light of the circumstantial evidence that the boat contained cocaine, the testimony that drug smugglers use spare engines to quickly dispose of cocaine in the event of an interdiction, and Johnson's statement that "they threw overboard a small spare engine"—De Leon intentionally jettisoned cocaine from the vessel. The result is that we must reject De Leon's sufficiency challenge **{-189-}** to his conviction for the destruction-of-forfeitable-property offense.

There remains De Leon's challenge to the sufficiency of the evidence supporting his conviction of conspiring to destroy forfeitable property. It, too, falls short.

Most problematic for De Leon is Borges's testimony that Johnson told Borges that "*they* threw overboard a small spare engine" (emphasis added)—implying that Johnson worked with another person—when he jettisoned the engine. As De Leon was the only other person on the boat, it is no leap to conclude that he was that other person.

Problematic as well for De Leon is Calderón's testimony that the likely weight of the engine Johnson described was "approximately 50 [or] 60 pounds." That testimony when combined with the other testimony in the record that drug smugglers typically tie cocaine to the engine—which would add further weight to the already heavy engine—would allow a reasonable **[—26—]** juror to conclude that De Leon and Johnson had to have worked together to have been physically able to move the engine and throw it overboard in the few minutes between when they heard the plane and when the boat was pictured as no longer containing bales. The record thus contains sufficient evidence for a rational juror to find beyond a reasonable doubt that De Leon conspired to destroy cocaine on a boat. The District Court therefore did not err in denying De Leon's motion for judgment of acquittal as to Counts Five or Six.

III.

We next consider the defendants' arguments for vacating their convictions due to various alleged errors at trial. We begin with the arguments for vacating them that De Leon advances. We then consider Johnson's.

A.

De Leon contends, among other things, his rights under the Confrontation Clause of the U.S. Constitution as recognized in *Bruton* were violated by the use of Johnson's statements to Agents Calderón and Borges at his joint trial with Johnson, notwithstanding the District Court's instruction to the jury that it could not consider Johnson's statements to Calderón in De Leon's case. We described these statements in detail above in analyzing Johnson's sufficiency challenges. For present purposes, we emphasize only that, to Agent Calderón, Johnson reportedly said **[—27—]** that "*eso*" was on the boat in the amount of "*doce piezas*" and that it was tied to a spare engine, which "he" threw overboard, and that, to Agent Borges, Johnson reportedly said that "*they* threw overboard a small spare engine." (emphasis added).

De Leon argues that the "statements" attributed to Johnson by Calderón and Borges "are incriminating on their face, and did not become incriminating by [his] testimony or by the introduction of any other evidence." Put otherwise, he contends, under *Bruton*, these statements, together, rendered the admission of Johnson's confession impermissible "regardless of what the [District] Court instructed the jury to do with it."

The government does not dispute that De Leon's *Bruton* challenge is preserved.[3] We thus proceed on that understanding, which means that our review is de novo. *See United States v. Vega Molina*, 407 F.3d 511, 520 (1st Cir. 2005). Because we **{-190-}** find merit to De Leon's *Bruton* challenge, we must vacate his convictions on that ground alone. *Id.* at 522, 535. We thus do not address the various separate challenges that he makes to his sentence.

1.

The Confrontation Clause provides that "[i]n all criminal prosecutions, the accused shall enjoy the right . . . to **[—28—]** be confronted with the witnesses against him." U.S. Const. amend. VI. The Supreme Court of the United States held in *Bruton* that a defendant is deprived of that right "where the powerfully incriminating extrajudicial statements of a codefendant, who stands accused side-by-side with the defendant, are deliberately spread before the jury in a joint trial" and the "alleged accomplice . . . does not testify and cannot be tested by cross-examination." 391 U.S. at 135-36 (1968).

Notably, the Court set aside the defendant's conviction in *Bruton* despite "concededly clear instructions to the jury to disregard" the confession as to him. *Id.* at 137. The Court explained that it could not "accept limiting instructions as an adequate substitute for [Bruton's] constitutional right of cross-examination," *id.* at 137, given the "powerfully incriminating" nature of the confession as to the defendant himself, *id.* at 135.

In light of *Bruton*, the fact that there was a limiting instruction here—with respect to Johnson's statements to Calderón—is no bar to De Leon's challenge to the use of those statements. Insofar as the use of the statements is impermissible under *Bruton*, the instruction cannot cure it. We turn, then, to the question whether the use of the statements—along with those that Johnson made to Borges—is barred by *Bruton*. But, the answer to that question does not depend merely on what the Court said in *Bruton* itself. **[—29—]**

In *Richardson v. Marsh*, the Court held that *Bruton* does not apply where "the codefendant's confession is redacted to omit any reference to the defendant, but the defendant is nonetheless linked to the confession by evidence properly admitted against him at trial." 481 U.S. 200, 202, 211 (1987). The Court explained that the codefendant's confession in *Bruton* "'expressly implicat[ed]' the defendant as his accomplice" and "at the time that confession was introduced there was not the slightest doubt that it would prove 'powerfully incriminating.'" *Id.* at 208 (quoting *Bruton*, 391 U.S. at 124 n.1, 135). By contrast, the Court further explained, the confession at issue in *Richardson* "was not incriminating on its face, and became so only when linked with evidence introduced later at trial," namely, "the defendant's own testimony." *Id.* It then held that "[w]here the necessity of such linkage is involved," "the Confrontation Clause is not violated by the admission of [the] . . . confession" so long as there is "a proper limiting instruction." *Id.* at 208, 211; *see also Vega Molina*, 407 F.3d at 520 ("Statements that are incriminating only when linked to other evidence in the case do not trigger application of *Bruton*'s preclusionary rule.").

Richardson, however, does not itself mark the end of the story when it comes to *Bruton*. Thereafter, the Court weighed in on *Bruton*'s scope yet again in *Gray v. Maryland*, 523 U.S. 185 **[—30—]** (1998), and, it did so in a way

[3] In addition to conceding that de novo review applies, the government has not contended in its briefs or at oral argument that De Leon has waived any particular argument in support of his *Bruton* claim.

that is of direct relevance here, given the nature of the *Bruton* challenge that De Leon presses.

Gray recounted that "*Richardson* placed outside the scope of *Bruton*'s rule those statements that incriminate inferentially." **{-191-}** *Id.* at 195. But, *Gray* explained, "inference pure and simple cannot make the critical difference." *Id.* Instead, *Gray* held, the applicability of *Richardson* "depend[s] in significant part upon the *kind* of, not the simple *fact* of, inference." *Id.* at 196.

At issue in *Gray* was a codefendant's statement that included a response to the question, "Who was in the group that beat Stacey?" The answer had been redacted to read: "Me, deleted, deleted, and a few other guys." *Id.* at 196. The Court acknowledged "that the jury [was required to] use inference to connect . . . [such a] redacted confession with the defendant." *Id.* at 195. The Court nonetheless held that the redacted confession was facially incriminatory, *id.* at 197, notwithstanding the fact that statement did not expressly name Gray and even though it would be impossible to infer from the text of the codefendant's statement alone to whom "deleted" referred, *see id.* at 196.

Gray reasoned that a juror who put together the pieces of the evidence and the prosecutor's argument would naturally infer that the deleted reference in the confession must have been a reference to the defendant. *Id.* at 193; *see also id.* at 195 (noting that the "Court has assumed . . . that . . . specific **[—31—]** descriptions," such as "where confessions describe [a] codefendant as the 'white guy' and give[] a description of his age, height, weight, and hair color," "fall inside . . . *Bruton*'s protection" (quoting *Harrington v. California*, 395 U.S. 250, 253 (1969))); *Vega Molina*, 407 F.3d at 520 (comparing the efficacy of redaction in a case involving "numerous events and actors, such that no direct inference plausibly can be made that a neutral phrase like 'another person' refers to a specific codefendant" with its utility in a case "involv[ing] so few defendants that the statement leaves little doubt in the listener's mind about the identity of 'another person'"). The Court pointed out that a juror need not be well-versed in the law to make that inference with ease. Indeed, the Court explained, if the "blank" referred to someone else, a juror "might . . . wonder how . . . the prosecutor could argue the confession is reliable, for the prosecutor, after all, has been arguing that [the defendant], not someone else" committed the crime described in the confession. *Gray*, 523 U.S. at 193. Thus, *Gray* makes clear that, even when the jury must engage in some inferential reasoning in order to conclude that a codefendant's statement is incriminating, the statement still may fall within the scope of *Bruton*. For the statement to do so, though, the inference that is necessary to make it incriminating must be one "that a jury ordinarily could make immediately, even were the confession the very first item introduced at trial," such that the **[—32—]** statement "obviously" and "directly" implicates the defendant in the crime. *Id.* at 196.

2.

The government contends that, notwithstanding *Gray*, there is no *Bruton* problem here in part because the statements attributed to Johnson were made to different agents who each independently testified about what Johnson had said to each of them. In particular, the government asserts that when viewed separately, the two statements are not facially incriminating as to De Leon. Johnson's alleged statement to Agent Borges—that "they" threw the engine overboard—is not incriminating on its own, according to the government, as the government agrees that De Leon was not charged with jettisoning equipment used in connection with the transportation **{-192-}** of a controlled substance but rather just destruction of a controlled substance while on a vessel. According to the government, Johnson's purported statements to Agent Calderón also did not facially incriminate De Leon, because Calderón testified that Johnson only described what he himself had done without mentioning De Leon. In other words, the government's argument appears to be that the work that the jury would have to do to combine the statements would require too much inferential **[—33—]** reasoning to permit them to be deemed facially incriminating.[4] We do not agree.

Whether a statement by a non-testifying codefendant is "facially incriminatory" of the defendant himself turns on how readily a juror might make the inferences required for the statement to be incriminating. The government develops no argument—beyond a conclusory one—for determining that merely because the statements attributed to Johnson were introduced by the testimony of two different government witnesses it would take more than an immediately obvious inference for a juror to put them together. It is thus reasonable to conclude here that the jury immediately, and without having to resort to other evidence, would have discerned the significance of the collective import of these statements, whatever it may have been, despite the fact that they were delivered separately, in just the manner contemplated in *Gray*.[5] We therefore reject the notion that the government can **[—34—]** avoid creating a *Bruton* problem by simply splitting up a defendant's confession and having multiple government witnesses testify to pieces of it.

True, as we explain later, a juror would have been free to believe the testimony recounting some of Johnson's statements but not others precisely because different agents recounted hearing them in distinct circumstances. But, the fact that some portions of testimony about a codefendant's confession might be given more weight than others by a juror is not a reason to conclude that the confession itself, if believed, is not facially incriminating under *Bruton*. Even when a codefendant's confession is admitted by testimony given by a single witness a jury might find some portions of that witness's recounting of it more credible than others. That there is a possibility that a jury may not actually find evidence of a codefendant's confession persuasive or even credible is of no moment under *Bruton*, which requires that we assume that a confession will be given maximum weight by a jury. *See Bruton*, 391 U.S. at 135-36. Consequently, we consider Johnson's statements together.

3.

Considering Johnson's separate statements as one, then, we must decide whether they, together, constitute a facially **[—35—]** incriminating confession within the meaning of *Bruton*. Notably, we are not dealing here with a case that is just like **{-193-}** *Richardson* and *Gray*, as each of those cases arose in the redaction context. Notably, too, we are not dealing here with statements that require any inference—as the statements in *Richardson* and *Gray* did—as to whether the allegedly incriminating statements of the codefendant implicate the defendant in the conduct described. Johnson's statements, given *Gray*, obviously referred to De Leon as a participant in the conduct by admitting that "they" acted together. Nor does the government contend otherwise.

Thus, the *Bruton* challenge that De Leon raises turns on a question distinct from the one that arose in the Supreme Court's *Bruton* trilogy that we have detailed above. The question here concerns whether the codefendant's statement is a confession to any criminal conduct at all, even as to himself.

The issue arises in this way here because the statements by Johnson that are at issue do not refer expressly to "cocaine" or "controlled substances" at any point. They instead refer only to "*eso*" and "*doce piezas*."

This feature of the statements, however, does not necessarily preclude us from finding

---

[4] In his arguments to us, De Leon contends that Johnson's statements are testimonial such that the Confrontation Clause applies. The government does not contest this point, and thus we find the government to have waived any contention that the statements were not testimonial in nature.

[5] We note that our conclusion that the government cannot split a defendant's confession into pieces to evade a *Bruton* problem does not implicate the administrability concerns that informed the Court's holding in *Richardson*. The government had the entirety of Johnson's statement available to it at the outset of trial, and we are not concerned under such circumstances that it would have been "[im]possible [for the government] to predict the admissibility of **[—34—]** [that] confession in advance of trial." *Richardson*, 481 U.S. at 209.

a *Bruton* violation here. We have applied the *Bruton* framework in cases in which the question was not whether the anonymization was adequate but whether the admitted-to conduct was sufficiently inculpatory. *See, e.g.*, **[—36—]** *United States v. Lopez-Lopez*, 282 F.3d 1, 11-13 (1st Cir. 2002) (considering whether *Bruton* applied to a codefendant's statement that could be read as referring to the defendant but was questionably inculpatory); *United States v. Limberopoulos*, 26 F.3d 245, 253 (1st Cir. 1994) (rejecting a *Bruton* claim as to statements that did "not implicate" the defendant); *cf. Brown v. Maloney*, 267 F.3d 36, 42 (1st Cir. 2001) (concluding a state-court decision was not contrary to clearly established Supreme Court precedent where it found no *Bruton* issue because the codefendants' statements were only "somewhat incriminating" because they only had the effect of placing the defendant "close to the crime location"). And, although, for record-based reasons, we did not find a *Bruton* violation in any of those cases, *see, e.g., Lopez-Lopez*, 282 F.3d at 11-13 (rejecting the defendant's *Bruton* claim as to a codefendant's statement directing the defendant "don't answer" in response to a question by law enforcement because the "statement [was] not sufficiently close to a confession" to be "powerfully incriminating" as it "did not even mention any person or any crime or any criminal responsibility"); *Limberopoulos*, 26 F.3d at 253 (concluding that *Bruton* did not apply to statements made by a codefendant when he surrendered a license because the inference "that the [statement] was an obvious attempt at deceit and coverup" was not obvious or immediate but rather "require[d] a considerable chain of subsidiary inferences"), the government does not argue **[—37—]** that, because we are not dealing with a redaction or a question as to whether the defendant is implicated in the statements by the codefendant confessing to criminal conduct, *Bruton* is inapplicable here.

The government's sole contention as to why there is no *Bruton* violation—insofar as the statements at issue must be considered together—hinges on the fact that Johnson did not at any point in his statements expressly assert that he had tied a controlled substance to the engine that was jettisoned. Rather, the government stresses, Johnson referred in those statements only to "*eso*."

According to the government, that feature of Johnson's statements in and of itself ensures that there is no problem here under *Bruton*, because it ensures that those statements are not themselves "facially incriminating" of De Leon. According **{–194–}** to the government, the statements became so only when linked to the other testimony at trial that explained that "*eso*" and "*piezas*" are common slang terms for cocaine. We thus next take up that argument, which, as we will explain, fails to align with the logic set forth in *Gray*.

4.

The Court made clear in *Gray* that the bare text of the codefendant's confession in isolation does not control the *Bruton* inquiry. Instead, *Gray* instructs that where the record makes it **[—38—]** "obvious[]" that a statement that might be somewhat ambiguous taken alone is in fact facially incriminating, the inference required of the jury to find the statement incriminating is not "the kind of . . . inference" that would take the admission outside *Bruton*'s ambit. *Gray*, 523 U.S. at 196 (emphasis omitted).

As the Court explained, "confessions that use shortened first names, nicknames, descriptions as unique as the 'red-haired, bearded, one-eyed man-with-a-limp,' and perhaps even full names of defendants who are always known by a nickname" are all examples of statements which the Court "has assumed . . . [are] not outside . . . *Bruton*'s protection." *Gray*, 523 U.S. at 195 (quoting *United States v. Grinnell Corp.*, 384 U.S. 563, 591 (1966) (Fortas, J., dissenting)). Our decision in *Vega Molina* is to the same effect. It explains that the inquiry under *Bruton*, *Richardson*, and *Gray* "requires careful attention" not only "to the text of the statement itself" but also "to the context in which it is proffered," all with the aim of assessing whether a "direct inference [from the statement] plausibly can be made." 407 F.3d at 520.

Applying this guidance, we have no doubt that if Johnson referred to cocaine in a language other than Spanish or English, the statement containing that reference would not be insulated from *Bruton*'s reach just because the reference had to be translated to a different language to be understood by the jury. The same is **[—39—]** true, we think, if Johnson had used an obvious slang name for cocaine without using that word itself—notwithstanding that the slang name could, in theory and stripped of context, have a different meaning, as might be true of the word "crack." There, too, we would still deem the statement to be facially incriminating, just as a nickname may be.

The only question here, then, is whether Johnson's references to "*eso*" and "*piezas*" in answering questions put to him during a criminal investigation triggered by suspicions of drug smuggling about what he had tied to the engine when he jettisoned it are similarly facially incriminating. We conclude that they are.

We may assume that the government is right that the words "*eso*" and "*piezas*" themselves do not in the abstract necessarily carry as an ordinary meaning "cocaine." But, language is always used in context, as *Gray* instructs us to remember in assessing whether a *Bruton* violation occurred. *See Gray*, 523 U.S. at 195-96; *see also Vega Molina*, 407 F.3d at 520-21. Taking that instruction seriously, we note that the government has not argued that there is anything in the record from which the jury could have concluded that "*eso*" and "*piezas*," as used in the context in which the witnesses described Johnson as having used them (namely, answering questions during an interrogation regarding his suspected drug smuggling), referred to anything but cocaine. Thus, **[—40—]** while neither word inherently carries that meaning, any more than a nickname or a description of a red-headed, bearded man with a limp inherently refers to a defendant who happens to have that alias or **{-195-}** those characteristics, Johnson's statements were "facially incriminat[ing]" as to De Leon and fall within the ambit of *Bruton*. *Gray*, 523 U.S. at 196 (emphasis omitted) (quoting *Richardson*, 481 U.S. at 209)).

In accord with that conclusion, we are confident that "[a] juror who does not know the law," to use the Court's terminology from *Gray*, 523 U.S. at 193, would easily intuit that had the meaning of "*eso*" been ambiguous, Agent Calderón would have asked Johnson a follow up question—namely, "What is *eso*?" Given that Calderón did not acknowledge asking such a question, a juror would immediately infer here that the meaning of "*eso*" was unambiguous to Johnson's interlocutor. And, in coming to that conclusion, a juror would also immediately infer that "*eso*" must obviously mean cocaine—for if it did not mean as much, then Calderón would have continued to question Johnson about what was on the boat to determine if he would admit to possessing, destroying, and conspiring to destroy forfeitable property.

Because we determine that Johnson's purported statements to Agents Calderón and Borges were, when viewed together, facially incriminating, we find that the admission of those statements against Johnson in his joint trial with De Leon violated De Leon's **[—41—]** Sixth Amendment rights under *Bruton*. As such, the limiting instruction the District Court gave as to Johnson's statements to Calderón were insufficiently curative.[6] We consequently must vacate De Leon's convictions for Counts Five and Six.

IV.

We now turn to the challenges that Johnson brings in which he contends that, due to trial errors, his convictions must be vacated. He presents three such challenges: first, that one of the empaneled jurors was not impartial; second, that the District Court improperly allowed lay witnesses to testify to

[6] The government has developed no argument as to why, insofar as there is a *Bruton* violation, such a violation would constitute harmless error as to one or more of the counts of conviction that De Leon challenges. *See United States v. Wright*, 937 F.3d 8, 30 (1st Cir. 2019) (explaining that "we may deem any harmless error argument not briefed by the government as waived").

technical, specialized subjects; and third, that the jury instructions constructively amended the indictment.

"A constructive amendment occurs when the charging terms of the indictment are altered, either literally or in effect, by [the] prosecution or court after the grand jury has last passed upon them." *United States v. DeCicco*, 439 F.3d 36, 43 (1st Cir. 2006) (quoting *United States v. Fisher*, 3 F.3d 456, 462 (1st Cir. 1993)). An amendment can be "brought about by a literal alteration of the words in the indictment," by "a jury instruction which modifies the offense charged," or by "the admission of evidence of **[—42—]** an offense not charged by the grand jury." *United States v. Dunn*, 758 F.2d 30, 35 (1st Cir. 1985). Because we conclude that Johnson's assertion that his indictment was constructively amended and that he was prejudiced thereby has merit, we begin and end our analysis there.[7] **{-196-}**

We first address Johnson's constructive-amendment argument as it pertains to the substantive offense for which he was convicted. We then address that argument as it pertains to his conviction for conspiring to commit that same offense.[8] **[—43—]**

A.

Johnson acknowledges that the indictment "limited" his charged conduct, with respect to the substantive offense, to "the destruction of 'controlled substances.'" But, he points out that the jury instructions allowed the jury to find him guilty of that offense on grounds not included in the indictment. He contends in this regard that, under those instructions, the jury was told that it could find him guilty of the substantive offense even if it found that he had not destroyed controlled substances but instead had destroyed only "equipment . . . used . . . [in] . . . delivering . . . any controlled substance." (alteration in original).

Johnson does not dispute that he failed to raise this challenge below. Accordingly, Johnson must survive plain-error review to obtain relief on this ground. *See United States v. Brandao*, 539 F.3d 44, 47 (1st Cir. 2008). He thus must establish not only that there was an error, but "that it is 'clear or obvious,' that his substantial rights were prejudiced thereby, and that the 'fairness, integrity, or public reputation of judicial **[—44—]** proceedings' [was] 'seriously impaired,'" *United States v. Gaccione*, 977 F.3d 75, 81 (1st Cir. 2020) (quoting *United States v. Rodríguez-Milián*, 820 F.3d 26, 32-33 (1st Cir. 2016)). We conclude that he has made that showing.

---

[7] Johnson's challenge to the admission of the testimony of various law enforcement agents on the ground that they were not qualified as experts but provided expert testimony anyway does concern an issue that could be implicated in any re-trial that may ensue. Nonetheless, it is not clear how the government will present that case if it chooses to bring one. We do note that we have emphasized in the past that "the line between expert testimony under Rule 702 [of the Federal Rules of Evidence] and lay opinion testimony under Rule 701 is, in practice, 'not [an] easy [one] to draw.'" *United States v. Valdivia*, 680 F.3d 33, 50 (1st Cir. 2012) (second and third alterations in original) (quoting *United States v. Cólon Osorio*, 360 F.3d 48, 52-53 (1st Cir. 2004)). Generally, "testimony based on the . . . expertise a witness personally acquires through experience, often on the job," is lay testimony. *United States v. George*, 761 F.3d 42, 59 (1st Cir. 2014) (citation omitted). But, testimony that requires a witness to go beyond "simple logic and pattern recognition" and to rely instead on a "technical understanding of the government's . . . tools and . . . capabilities"—even if that technical understanding is developed on the job—is typically considered expert testimony under our precedent, requiring the witness to be qualified as such. *United States v. Montijo-Maysonet*, 974 F.3d 34, 48-49 (1st Cir. 2020) (internal quotation marks and citations omitted).

[8] We note that even if De Leon could have raised the same arguments that Johnson now advances in support of his assertion that the indictment was constructively amended, he did not do so. **[—43—]** As a result, we do not decide whether we would have vacated De Leon's convictions on the same constructive amendment grounds on which we vacate Johnson's convictions. *See United States v. Kilmartin*, 944 F.3d 315, 326 (1st Cir. 2019), *cert. denied*, 140 S. Ct. 2658 (2020) (noting that the court "ha[d] no duty" to consider a constructive amendment argument the defendant did not make on appeal).

1.

With respect to the first two prongs of plain-error review, Johnson contends that the District Court erred by "impermissibly add[ing] possible bases for conviction beyond that specified in the indictment" and that this error was clear or obvious. We agree.

In *Stirone v. United States*, 361 U.S. 212 (1960), the Supreme Court established that a constructive amendment occurs when jury instructions "broaden[] the possible bases for conviction from that which appeared in the indictment." *United States v. Miller*, 471 U.S. 130, 138 (1985) (emphasis omitted) (discussing **{-197-}** *Stirone*, 361 U.S. at 213). There, the district court submitted to the jury two different theories under which the defendant could be found guilty of violating the Hobbs Act, either of which could have independently supported a conviction under the Act. *Stirone*, 361 U.S. at 213-14. But, the government had specified only one of those theories in the indictment, *id.* at 213, and the Court concluded that the instructions thus constructively amended the indictment, *id.* **[—45—]**

The indictment in this case charged Johnson with "knowingly and intentionally destroy[ing] property subject to forfeiture"—specifying that the "subject property" was a "controlled substance." The indictment thus limited the theories under which a jury could convict Johnson of the crimes. By instructing the jury that it could find Johnson guilty if it found beyond a reasonable doubt that "the property was a controlled substance *or* equipment used for delivering controlled substances" (emphasis added), the District Court instructed the jury about a crime that was not contained in the indictment—and committed a "clear" and "obvious" error in doing so.

The government suggests that it was not an error to instruct the jury on both possible bases for conviction because 21 U.S.C. § 881(a), which lists the types of property subject to forfeiture, includes both "controlled substances" as well as "equipment of any kind . . . used [for] . . . delivering . . . controlled substances." 21 U.S.C. § 881(a). But, the fact that the government *could* have indicted Johnson for destroying "equipment used for delivering controlled substances" does not change the fact that the government did not.

The indictment limited the charges against Johnson to the one set forth in § 881(a)(1): destruction of a "manufactured, distributed, dispensed, acquired, or possessed controlled substance." We have previously found that when an indictment **[—46—]** quotes directly from a section of a statute, it can be understood to be referencing that specific section. *See, e.g., United States v. Kilmartin*, 944 F.3d 315, 326 (1st Cir. 2019). That is what we understand the indictment did here—the indictment quoted from § 881(a)(1), thereby limiting the charge to that provision.

Moreover, the jury instructions then broadened the charge offense to encompass the one set forth in § 881(a)(2). The written instructions stated that the jury could find each defendant guilty of "intentionally destroying property that is subject to forfeiture under section 511(a) of the Comprehensive Drug Abuse Prevention and Control Act of 1970. (Title 21, United States Code, *Section 881(a)(1))*"—defining the charged offense as the destruction of a controlled substance—if the jury found, among other facts, that "the property [destroyed] was a controlled substance *or* equipment used for delivering controlled substances" (emphasis added). The oral instructions were substantially similar.

In other words, the jury instructions—instructions that the government itself proposed—recognized that the indictment was limited to the offense of destruction of property defined by § 881(a)(1) but then instructed the jury that it could find Johnson guilty of that offense if it found that Johnson had destroyed property defined by § 881(a)(1) or § 881(a)(2). *See also Mathis v. United States*, 136 S. Ct. 2243, 2257 (2016) ("[A]n **[—47—]** indictment and jury instructions could indicate, by referencing one alternative term to the exclusion of all others, that the statute contains a list of elements, each one of which goes toward a separate crime."). By broadening the grounds on which a jury could convict **{–198–}** Johnson of destruction of forfeitable property, the District Court constructively amended the indictment and committed a clear and obvious error.[9]

2.

We turn, then, to whether Johnson has met his burden to show that his "substantial rights were prejudiced" by the clear or obvious error. *Gaccione*, 977 F.3d at 81. The prejudice requirement of plain-error review is not satisfied in this context when, "given the evidence at trial, the jury could not have found [the defendant] guilty of . . . the amended charge[] if it had not also found he had [committed the indicted charge]." *Brandao*, 539 F.3d at 63. In that situation, "[any] error" could not have affected whether the defendant had been convicted of the charged offense rather than the uncharged one set forth in the jury instructions. *Id.*

The government contends that is the situation here. It does not dispute that the jury may have, due to the instruction, **[—48—]** determined that Johnson was guilty of destroying equipment, which § 881(a)(2) concerns. It simply contends that he was not prejudiced thereby, because any finding of guilt on that basis necessarily depended on the jury also finding him guilty of destroying cocaine, which § 881(a)(1) concerns. In other words, the government contends, Johnson's convictions necessarily encompassed all the charged conduct, even accepting that the only charged conduct deemed the predicate forfeitable property to be a controlled substance. It thus follows, the government contends, that Johnson cannot make the prejudice showing that he must.

To assess that contention, we must determine whether it is reasonably probable that a jury instructed as this one was would have determined, in finding Johnson guilty, that he destroyed equipment associated with a controlled substance without also finding that he destroyed a controlled substance. If that outcome is reasonably probable, then Johnson would have met his burden as to prejudice on plain error review. *See id.*; *see also United States v. Takesian*, 945 F.3d 553, 566 (1st Cir. 2019).

Johnson contends that, on this record, the "instruction guided the jury to convict by . . . finding that Johnson jettisoned a spare engine, . . . and not necessarily . . . the destruction of drugs." (emphasis omitted). He asserts that due to the "contradict[ing]" nature of the evidence at trial that cocaine was on the boat and the "undisputed and admitted" nature of Johnson's **[—49—]** statement that he threw the engine overboard, "the jury might have convicted based on something different than the destruction of cocaine." (emphasis omitted).

The government responds that Johnson fails to account for the requirement that the jury find that the "equipment" jettisoned was "used for delivering controlled substances." It argues that the only way a rational juror could have found the required connection to drugs is if "the jury . . . [found] that drugs were on the [boat]." We are not persuaded.

One reason for our reluctance to accept the government's argument about prejudice is that this jury *acquitted* Johnson of the cocaine possession and conspiracy to possess cocaine charges that he faced. It is true that a jury's acquittal of a defendant of an offense that is seemingly inconsistent with the jury's verdict of guilt as to that same defendant as to another offense has **{–199–}** no bearing on whether the evidence is sufficient to support the finding of guilt as to that other offense. *See Powell*, 469 U.S. at 65. But, we are hesitant to accept the notion that such an acquittal adds nothing to a defendant's contention that it is reasonably probable that a plainly erroneous jury instruction of the sort at issue here caused prejudice because a jury found that defendant guilty of the uncharged offense without also finding him guilty of the charged one. **[—50—]**

[9] The government does not dispute the necessary premise of Johnson's challenge—that § 881(a)(1) and § 881(a)(2) set forth two distinct offenses rather than two means of committing the same offense.

Moreover, here, the jury learned of the statements in which Johnson admitted that he had thrown overboard a spare engine upon being espied by law enforcement from two different agents—only one of whom recounted that Johnson had said anything that indicated that cocaine had been tied to it. Indeed, the other agent, Agent Borges, who testified that Johnson had made the statement that the engine had been so jettisoned, did not indicate that Johnson made any reference to cocaine. Yet, that agent was the one who testified that Johnson had provided those answers in response to a standardized set of questions that were asked of all those aboard interdicted vessels before law enforcement boards them. By contrast, the agent who testified that Johnson had not only stated that he had thrown the engine overbroad but also had tied cocaine to it beforehand, Agent Calderón, reported that Johnson had so stated in an interrogation of him that occurred ashore several hours after the boat had been interdicted. No notes or transcript of that interrogation were introduced at trial. We thus conclude that, on this record, there is a reasonable probability that a juror would have weighed the testimony of the two agents differently and surmised, accordingly, that the spare engine had been jettisoned without also concluding that cocaine was tied to it.

That conclusion is reinforced by the fact that there was evidence in the record to indicate that the boat had been involved **[—51—]** in drug smuggling apart from the evidence that could support a finding that cocaine had been on the boat and jettisoned upon the boat's interdiction. That evidence included the alert from the drug canine indicating the possible presence of drug residue, the boat's location on a route infamous for drug smuggling, testimony that the boat was the type typically used for drug smuggling, and the text messages suggesting that a transaction of some sort was planned. It also included the testimony from Agents González and Calderón about the use that cocaine smugglers have for spare engines—to destroy evidence of cocaine in the event of detection by law enforcement.

Thus, there was evidence that the spare engine was forfeitable property in its own right, regardless of whether these defendants used the engine to destroy cocaine during the journey that led to their interdiction. *See, e.g., United States v. Latorre-Cacho*, 874 F.3d 299, 310-11 (1st Cir. 2017) (finding error in the jury instructions to be prejudicial on plain error review when there was not insubstantial evidence presented to the jury that would have allowed it to reach a verdict based on the erroneous instruction). As such, it would not have been unreasonable for a juror to conclude that Johnson jettisoned the spare engine to conceal it from law enforcement simply because of its character as "equipment," forfeitable under § 881(a)(2) due to its connection to drug smuggling. **[—52—]**

Accordingly, we conclude that, on this record, Johnson has met his burden to show that it is reasonably probable that a juror would have found that "the property [jettisoned] was . . . equipment used for delivering controlled substances" without also finding that controlled substances **{–200–}** were jettisoned from the boat during this specific voyage. *See Takesian*, 945 F.3d at 566 ("'A reasonable probability' . . . is more than a mere possibility, but less than a preponderance of the evidence." (quoting *United States v. Domínguez Benítez*, 542 U.S. 74, 83 n.9 (2004))). As a result, we hold that "the record could [have] 'rationally le[d] to a contrary finding" and the prejudice prong of plain error is satisfied. *Brandao*, 539 F.3d at 63 (quoting *Neder v. United States*, 527 U.S. 1, 19 (1999)).

3.

That brings us to the fourth and final prong of plain error, which requires that we consider whether the error "seriously impaired" the "fairness, integrity, or public reputation of judicial proceedings." *Gaccione*, 977 F.3d at 81 (citation omitted). The purpose of the prohibition on constructive amendments is "to preserve the defendant's Fifth Amendment right to indictment by grand jury, to prevent re-prosecution for the same offense in violation of the Sixth Amendment, and to protect the defendant's Sixth Amendment right to be informed of the charges against him." *Brandao*, 539 F.3d at 57. **[—53—]**

These rights are at the very core of our criminal justice system. Undermining these principles by allowing a constructive amendment would thus seriously impair the fairness and integrity of the judicial proceeding.

We therefore conclude that it was plain error for the District Court to constructively amend through its jury instructions the indicted offense of destruction of a controlled substance on a vessel. We consequently vacate Johnson's conviction of Count 6.

B.

We now consider Johnson's constructive amendment argument as it pertains to his conspiracy conviction. Here, too, our review is for plain error. *See Brandao*, 539 F.3d at 60. We again find the standard satisfied.

1.

By quoting directly from § 881(a)(1), the indictment specified that the object of the charged conspiracy was the destruction, while on a vessel, of forfeitable property as defined by § 881(a)(1)—"that is . . . a manufactured, distributed, dispensed, acquired, or possessed controlled substance." The District Court instructed the jury, however, that it could find the defendant guilty if it found that Johnson conspired to destroy, while on a vessel, "a controlled substance *or* equipment used for delivering controlled substances." (emphasis added). **[—54—]**

Thus, for the reasons explained above, when the indictment was limited to charging Johnson with conspiracy to destroy forfeitable property in the form of a controlled substance, the District Court could not then instruct the jury that it could find Johnson guilty if it found that he conspired to destroy "a controlled substance *or* equipment used for delivering controlled substances." (emphasis added).

To be sure, we have allowed for some variation between the means alleged in an indictment for a conspiracy offense and what is presented to the jury at trial. But, here, the government does not dispute the premise of Johnson's challenge—that the indictment alleged a conspiracy to commit one crime while the instructions permitted the jury to render a guilty verdict upon finding that the defendant conspired to commit a different crime because the forefeitable property was an element of the crime rather than a means of committing it. *See, e.g., United States v. Mueffelman*, 470 F.3d 33, 38 (1st Cir. 2006) (explaining **{-201-}** that the conspiracy offense was not constructively amended because "the titular crime was not altered"). Thus, we conclude that the District Court committed clear or obvious error in its jury instructions with respect to the conspiracy offense.

2.

There remain the questions of whether Johnson has met his burden to show that this error "prejudiced" his "substantial **[—55—]** rights" and it would "seriously impair[]" the "fairness, integrity, or public reputation of judicial proceedings." *Gaccione*, 977 F.3d at 81 (quoting *Rodríguez-Milián*, 820 F.3d at 32-33). We conclude that he has.

With respect to prejudice, we again rely on the test articulated in *Brandao* and consider whether, "given the evidence at trial, the jury could not have found [the defendant] guilty of . . . the amended charge[] if it had not also found he had [committed the indicted charge]." *Brandao*, 539 F.3d at 63. We find that test satisfied.

The government's case against Johnson at trial as to the conspiracy charge overlapped considerably with its case as to the substantive offense of destruction of a controlled substance while on a vessel. A juror could have credited Agent Borges's testimony that Johnson purportedly told him that "they threw overboard a small spare engine," found compelling the testimony that drug smugglers typically have spare engines on their boats that they use to weigh down any jettisoned cocaine, and believed that the vessel in this case was likely used to transport cocaine at some point but did not have cocaine on board on this trip given that no cocaine was found. In addition, as to the element of agreement, that same juror, having already credited Borges's testimony that Johnsons said that "*they* threw overboard a small spare engine," (emphasis added), could have also relied on Agent **[—56—]** González's testimony that the engine of the type Borges's testimony referred to would weigh fifty or sixty pounds, such that throwing the engine overboard would be a two-man job. Thus, we conclude that there was a reasonable probability that a juror could have convicted Johnson of conspiring to jettison equipment used to transport cocaine rather than of conspiring to jettison cocaine. *See Takesian*, 945 F.3d at 566 (explaining that "'[a] reasonable probability' . . . is more than a mere possibility, but less than a preponderance of the evidence" (quoting *Domínguez Benítez*, 542 U.S. at 83 n.9)).

With respect to the fourth prong of plain error review, we must determine whether the clear or obvious error "seriously impaired" the "fairness, integrity, or public reputation of judicial proceedings." *Gaccione*, 977 F.3d at 81. We conclude that it did, for reasons similar to those that we set forth above in finding this same prong satisfied in the context of the substantive destruction-of-forfeitable-property offense. We therefore conclude that it was plain error for the District Court to constructively amend the indictment as to the conspiracy-to-destroy-forfeitable-property offense.

V.

For the aforementioned reasons, we decline to reverse either Johnson's or De Leon's convictions on sufficiency-of-the-evidence grounds. We ***vacate*** De Leon's convictions of Counts 5 and **[—57—]** 6 and the associated sentence because the admission of Johnson's statements in their joint trial violated De Leon's rights under the Confrontation Clause to the Federal Constitution. As to Johnson, we ***vacate*** his convictions of Counts 5 and 6 and the associated sentences because the District Court constructively **{–202–}** amended the indictment through its instructions to the jury.

United States Court of Appeals
for the First Circuit

No. 20-1073

UNITED STATES
vs.
GARRAWAY

Appeal from the United States District Court for the District of Puerto Rico

Decided: November 15, 2021

Citation: 18 F.4th 33, 9 Adm. R. 81 (1st Cir. 2021).

Before **LYNCH**, **LIIPEZ**, and **BARRON**, Circuit Judges.

[—3—] **{–34–}** **LYNCH**, Circuit Judge:

Raymond Alexander Garraway and Cordwell Nathaniel Bennett, convicted at trial for possession with intent to distribute marijuana, successfully moved for a mistrial on the basis of improper arguments made by the prosecution at closing. The government now seeks to retry them, and Garraway and Bennett moved to dismiss, arguing that retrial would violate the Double Jeopardy Clause. The district court denied the motion to dismiss. *United States v. Trapp*, No. 16-159, 2019 WL 6974767, at *1 (D.P.R. Dec. 18, 2019). Because the district court did not abuse its discretion in finding that the prosecution did not intentionally provoke a mistrial, we affirm.

I.

On March 1, 2016, a U.S. Coast Guard law enforcement detachment aboard a Dutch naval ship came across an eighty-foot fishing vessel while on routine patrol in the Caribbean. The Coast Guard team captured video of the crew of the fishing vessel jettisoning objects overboard.

The Coast Guard deployed two rigid-hulled inflatable boats, one to intercept the fishing vessel and one towards the debris. **{–35–}** The boat dispatched in the direction of the jettisoned debris recovered nineteen bales of suspected narcotics. Samples from the bales were tested and found to be marijuana. In total, the marijuana bales weighed 399.4 kilograms. **[—4—]**

The second team questioned the individuals aboard the fishing vessel. The Coast Guard team took samples from the fishing vessel which were tested using an Ion Scan 400B device, which detects the presence of narcotics. No narcotics were detected. The Coast Guard team found no contraband aboard the fishing vessel. Two of the bales that had been recovered preliminarily tested positive for marijuana, and the Coast Guard took the crew into custody. On March 16, 2016, Garraway and Bennett, along with the third man aboard the fishing vessel, Michael Anthony Trapp, were indicted on two counts of possession with intent to distribute 100 kilograms or more of marijuana.

Their jury trial began on September 4, 2018. The prosecution introduced into evidence the video taken by the Coast Guard of objects being thrown out of the fishing vessel, testimony of a Coast Guard officer that the marijuana bales were recovered near the fishing vessel and that there were no other vessels in the area, and testimony that rope was found on the fishing vessel which appeared identical to the rope used to bind the bales of marijuana. The defense theory was that the bales of marijuana recovered by the Coast Guard had never been aboard their fishing vessel. The defendants pointed to the Ion Scan results which showed that marijuana was not detected aboard the fishing vessel, as well as the fact that the bales of marijuana were found between five and seven nautical miles from the fishing vessel. They also **[—5—]** introduced testimony that the seas had been rough, and that they were throwing garbage and debris, not bales of marijuana, off the fishing vessel because it endangered them to have loose debris rolling around the deck.

The prosecution and defense entered into several factual stipulations concerning the chain of custody of the bales of marijuana and the details of the Ion Scan testing and results. The defense relied on these stipulations to establish the negative Ion Scan results and where the bales of marijuana were found. The stipulations contained no information about whether or how wrapping the drugs would affect the accuracy of the Ion Scan results, and no evidence to that effect was presented. During the closing argument rebuttal, the prosecution argued to the jury that the wrappings on the bales of marijuana prevented the Ion Scan from detecting its presence on the fishing vessel. The jury convicted.

The defendants moved for an acquittal and for a mistrial. The district court denied the motion for acquittal. However, it granted the motion for mistrial on the basis of the prosecution's statements about the Ion Scan results being affected by the wrapping on the marijuana. The district court found the statements were not a permissible inference to argue from the evidence introduced at trial. It found that the prosecution made the statement deliberately, though not in bad faith, and that the court **[—6—]** could not be confident, given the totality of the circumstances, that the prosecution's argument did not affect the jury's decision to convict. The court did note in a footnote that there was no double jeopardy bar to retrial, finding that "there is no indication that in making the statement in question, the prosecutor had the intent to goad defendants into moving for a mistrial or to harass them out of fear of acquittal due to insufficient evidence in order to marshal a more favorable opportunity to **{-36-}** convict the defendants in a subsequent trial."

Nevertheless, when the prosecution began to retry the defendants, the defendants filed a joint motion to dismiss for violation of the Double Jeopardy Clause. They argued that the prosecution deliberately made the improper statement at closing in order to goad the defendants into moving for a mistrial, so that the prosecution would have a better chance at convicting in a subsequent trial.

The district court denied the motion, finding that the prosecution did not intend to provoke a mistrial. In making its decision, the district court also concluded that "this is not a case where the evidence led a reasonable person to conclude that acquittal was likely at the time of the objected comment, and that misconduct had to be engaged in to prevent it." **[—7—]**

II.

The standard of review applicable to a motion to dismiss on double jeopardy grounds following a mistrial is abuse of discretion. *United States v. Toribio-Lugo*, 376 F.3d 33, 38 (1st Cir. 2004). The district court's findings of fact are reviewed for clear error, while conclusions of law are reviewed de novo.[1] *Id.*

The Double Jeopardy Clause, U.S. Const. amend. V, cl. 2, "protects not only against double punishment but also against being 'twice put to trial for the same offense.'" *United States v. Suazo*, 14 F.4th 70, 74 (1st Cir. 2021) (quoting *Abney v. United States*, 431 U.S. 651, 661 (1977)). Not all reprosecution is barred, and mistrials are a common exception. *See Toribio-Lugo*, 376 F.3d at 38. Retrial is, however, barred after a mistrial where "the conduct giving rise to the successful motion for a mistrial was intended to provoke the defendant into moving for a mistrial." *Oregon v. Kennedy*, 456 U.S. 667, 679 (1982); *see also United States v. Gary*, 74 F.3d 304, 315 (1st Cir. 1996), *abrogated on other grounds by Johnson v. United States*, 576 U.S. 591 (2015).

Garraway and Bennett argue that the district court erred in finding that the prosecution did not intend to provoke them to **[—8—]** move for a mistrial by making improper arguments at closing. They contend that this intent can be inferred from what they characterize as a pattern of overreaching with respect to the stipulations by the government and a weak response to the defendants' motion for mistrial, the timing of the improper statement at a point when the defendants could no longer rebut it, and what they consider the overall weakness of the government's case. They also point out that the government now seeks to introduce new

[1] Because the defendants were tried together, raise the same issues, and make the same arguments in their briefs, we address their arguments together. The third co-defendant, Michael Anthony Trapp, is not involved in this appeal.

expert testimony while also compelling the defendants to enter into the same stipulations as in the first trial, which they argue is evidence that the prosecution intentionally threw the first case in order to make a stronger case on retrial.

The defendants do not challenge the legal standard the district court used to decide their motion; rather, they challenge only the district court's finding that the prosecution did not intend to provoke a mistrial. This finding is not clearly erroneous.

The district court determined that, at the time of closing argument, an acquittal was not likely. Though defendants characterize **{-37-}** the prosecution's case as "weak," the trial court's determination is supported by the record. The prosecution introduced video of the defendants throwing debris out of the fishing vessel. The prosecution showed that the Coast Guard had **[—9—]** recovered nineteen bales of marijuana from the water, and that there were no other vessels in the vicinity. Perhaps most damning, the prosecution introduced testimony that the rope used to bind the bales was the same as rope found on the fishing vessel. The defendants introduced evidence to try to neutralize the prosecution's case, including offering an alternative explanation for why the crew was jettisoning debris from the fishing vessel and emphasizing the Ion Scan's negative findings. However, given the substantial case mounted by the prosecution, the record supports the district court's assessment of the likelihood of acquittal.

In light of the district court's supportable finding that acquittal was not likely, the defendants' arguments about the timing of the statement also fail. Nothing about the timing of the improper argument suggests that the district court's finding was clearly erroneous and nothing in *Kennedy* supports a rule that improper arguments made late in the trial are necessarily intended to provoke a mistrial. *See United States v. Jozwiak*, 954 F.2d 458, 460 (7th Cir. 1992) ("Only a prosecutor who thinks the trial going sour—or who seeks to get just far enough into the trial to preview the defense—would want to precipitate a mistrial.").

The defendants' argument that the government has benefitted from previewing their arguments at trial and strengthening its own case on retrial ignores that the defendants **[—10—]** benefit similarly from the declaration of a mistrial. *See United States v. Garske*, 939 F.3d 321, 335 (1st Cir. 2019) (noting that "the purported advantage works both ways . . . . [as] the defendants have previewed the government's case and are now better positioned to defend against it"). The government, which bears the burden of proof, faces the risk at retrial that witnesses' memories may dull or witnesses may become unavailable, in addition to the need to expend limited resources to retry an entire case. *See United States v. Lun*, 944 F.2d 642, 646 (9th Cir. 1991) ("'If the defendant consents to a mistrial, the prosecutor must go to the time, trouble, and expense of starting all over with the criminal prosecution.' Witnesses may disappear or forget their testimony after the long delay." (citation omitted) (quoting *Kennedy*, 456 U.S. at 686 (Stevens, J., concurring))); *see also Jozwiak*, 954 F.2d at 460 ("Trying one defendant twice means, for a prosecutor with limited resources, letting some other defendant go.").

The defendants also argue the prosecution "barely objected" to their motion for a mistrial. Again, this is not so. The trial court found that the government had made a "comprehensive response." This too is supported by our review of the government's response to the defendants' motion for mistrial and is not clearly erroneous. Though the district court ultimately disagreed, the government defended its statements at closing as reasonable **[—11—]** inferences from the evidence it presented at trial and did not make merely a pro forma response to the defendants' motion. After overseeing the entire trial and considering the defendants' motion for a mistrial and the prosecution's opposition, the district court specifically found that the prosecutor believed he was arguing a permissible inference from the evidence.

In all, the record supports the government's contention, and the district court's finding, that the government did not intentionally provoke a mistrial. The government **{–38–}** presented a strong case at trial. At the point before the prosecution made its closing rebuttal argument, an acquittal was not likely. The prosecution vigorously opposed the defendants' motion for a mistrial. Any opportunity the prosecution will have to adjust its case in response to what occurred at the first trial will also be afforded to the defendants.

As the district court pointed out in denying the defendants' double jeopardy motion, it "presided over the trial," affording it a better vantage point than ours to assess the intent of the prosecution. Absent clear evidence from the record that the district court's finding as to the intent to provoke a mistrial is unsupported, we will not supplant its judgment with our own. No such evidence exists here; rather, the record amply supports the district court's decision. **[—12—]**

III.

The order of the district court is *affirmed.*

United States Court of Appeals
for the First Circuit

No. 20-1846

CURTIS
vs.
GALAKATOS

Appeal from the United States District Court for the District of Massachusetts

Decided: November 29, 2021

Citation: 19 F.4th 41, 9 Adm. R. 85 (1st Cir. 2021).

Before **THOMPSON** and **LIPEZ,** Circuit Judges, and **TORRESEN,*** District Judge.

* Of the District of Maine, sitting by designation.

[—2—] {–45–} THOMPSON, Circuit Judge:

On vacation in Greece, two U.S. citizens, Cindy Curtis and Demetre Cambouris, were ferrying along on a small boat, the M/V Marina. That is until another boat, the M/V Galani, smacked into the Marina and sunk it in the Paros-Antiparos Strait. On top of the marine wreckage, the crash also left Curtis with serious personal injuries. So she and her husband sued the U.S.-citizen owner of the Galani, Nicholas Galakatos, in federal court in Massachusetts seeking damages. Galakatos, though, told the district court that this was a suit meant for Greece—not the United States—and moved to dismiss on the ground of *forum non conveniens*. The district court agreed and sent the parties packing for a Greek court. Ever mindful of our deferential standard of review in this context, we nonetheless reverse.

THE FACTS

Curtis and Cambouris, spouses, hail from New York. In the summer of 2018, they crossed the pond to spend time in Greece, specifically in the area of the Paros-Antiparos Strait. While there, they (along with one other passenger) took a ride aboard Cambouris's boat, the M/V Marina, in the Strait.

That same day, Galakatos's M/V Galani, piloted by Greek citizen Dimitrios Faroupos, was also traveling the Strait. Faroupos (who we now know is the gardener at Galakatos's summer residence in Greece) was carrying six others on board the Galani **[—3—]** at the time. When the collision occurred, Galakatos was back home in Massachusetts.

With Faroupos at the helm, the Galani plowed into the stern (*i.e.*, the back) of the Marina, traversing its way over the passenger area before plunging back into the **{–46–}** water on the other side. In the process, the Galani's hull and propellers struck Curtis. Nearby vessels rescued all three passengers. The Marina, though, sunk, its wreckage ultimately towed out of the Strait.

After being pulled from the water, Curtis was brought to the local medical center and shortly thereafter transferred to a hospital in Athens. Physicians there diagnosed a host of serious injuries, including: ten broken ribs, eight of which were fractured front and back; fractures of her shoulder blade, collarbone, sternum, and lower arm; multiple fractures in her leg; and massive wounds on her thigh from the propeller blades. Various surgical procedures kept her in the Intensive Care Unit for about a month. After being hospitalized a bit longer in Athens, she made her way home to the United States, where she was admitted to New York Presbyterian Hospital in New York City. There, she underwent even more surgical procedures. Curtis has since gone through months of physical therapy. And more than a year after the shipwreck, Curtis still required a walker to balance.

Following the crash, the Paros Port Authority investigated. In that investigation, sworn depositions or **[—4—]** declarations have been provided in Greek by thirteen individuals. The case was then assigned to the Public Prosecutor by the First Instance Court of Syros to decide whether to prosecute anyone in the matter. At some point after the crash, Faroupos was arrested for provocation of a shipwreck and causing serious personal injury. He was later released. The criminal case is still ongoing.

About six months after the crash, Curtis and Cambouris filed suit against Galakatos in the United States. Rather than sue back in their Empire State, Curtis and Cambouris shipped up to Boston and filed suit in the federal court of Galakatos's hometown. They brought claims for maritime negligence, loss of consortium, and property damage.

Galakatos moved to dismiss the complaint for *forum non conveniens*, arguing that Greece, not Massachusetts, is the "most appropriate venue" for this case. In support of the motion, Galakatos submitted his own affidavit. In it, he declared that he was not in Greece at the time of the accident and felt it was important to proceed in Greece because "nearly all of the identifiable witnesses to this incident other than the Plaintiffs reside in Greece." Thus, he reasoned, trying this case in Massachusetts "would be damaging and prejudicial to [his] ability to defend the action." He also submitted an affidavit of a Greek attorney, who gave his opinion on a smattering of Greek-law issues. Importantly, the attorney also provided a list of names of the **[—5—]** thirteen individuals who gave depositions or declarations to the Port Authority, which he obtained from Faroupos's attorney. Given these facts, Galakatos agreed to submit to the jurisdiction of an appropriate Greek court and to waive any statute-of-limitations defense.

Persuaded, the district court dismissed the case, and Curtis and Cambouris now appeal. But before we dig into the issue raised here, we first get our bearings with the multifaceted law of *forum non conveniens*.

THE LAW TO APPLY

Forum non conveniens gives courts the discretion "to dismiss a case because the chosen forum (despite the presence of jurisdiction and venue) is so inconvenient that it would be unfair to conduct the litigation in that place." *Nandjou v. Marriott Int'l, Inc.*, 985 F.3d 135, 140 (1st Cir. 2021) (quoting **{-47-}** *Howe v. Goldcorp Invs., Ltd.*, 946 F.2d 944, 947 (1st Cir. 1991)).[1] Dismissal on that doctrinal basis "reflects a court's assessment of a 'range of considerations, most notably the convenience to the parties and the practical difficulties that can attend the adjudication of a dispute in a certain locality.'" *Sinochem Int'l Co. v. Malay. Int'l Shipping Corp.*, 549 U.S. 422, 429 (2007) **[—6—]** (quoting *Quackenbush v. Allstate Ins. Co.*, 517 U.S. 706, 723 (1996)). When a district court makes a *forum non conveniens* dismissal, the "practical effect" is that the plaintiffs have to re-file in a more convenient court, *Nandjou*, 985 F.3d at 140, perhaps a foreign one, *see Sinochem Int'l*, 549 U.S. at 430 (noting that common-law *forum non conveniens* applies when the alternative forum is abroad).[2]

Forum non conveniens is a balancing act. On the one hand, a plaintiff ordinarily holds a "heavy presumption weigh[ing] in favor of [her] initial forum choice." *Adelson v. Hananel*, 510 F.3d 43, 53 (1st Cir. 2007). Her forum choice "will be disturbed only rarely." *Nowak v. Tak How Invs.*, 94 F.3d 708, 719 (1st Cir. 1996). Still, it is not as though the plaintiff's choice of forum is "given dispositive weight" such that "dismissal [is] automatically barred when a plaintiff has filed suit in [her] home forum." *Interface Partners Int'l, Ltd. v. Hananel*, 575 F.3d 97, 102 (1st Cir. 2009) (quoting *Piper Aircraft Co. v. Reyno*, 454 U.S. 235, 254 n.23 (1981)); *see also Nandjou*, 985 F.3d at 142 (noting that a U.S. forum is a "home forum" even when the plaintiff is from another state where the alternative is a non-U.S. court). It just means that there's a "heavy burden" on a defendant to show **[—7—]** why the balance favors vetoing the plaintiff's forum choice. *Nandjou*, 985 F.3d at 141 (quoting *Adelson*, 510 F.3d at 52).

To meet that heavy burden, a defendant must show, on the other side of the scale, that

---

[1] For those who aren't fluent in Latin, *forum non conveniens* translates to "an unsuitable court." *Forum Non Conveniens*, *Black's Law Dictionary* (11th ed. 2019).

[2] If the more convenient forum is another U.S. federal court, we'd be looking not to common-law *forum non conveniens*, but the statutorily codified version of the doctrine. *See* 28 U.S.C. § 1404(a); *Sinochem Int'l*, 549 U.S. at 430.

the plaintiff's chosen forum is "so inconvenient that transfer is needed to avoid *serious unfairness*." *See id.* (emphasis in original) (quoting *Adelson*, 510 F.3d at 52). Indeed, we recognize that a plaintiff's forum choice may "'vex, harass, or oppress the defendant by inflicting upon [her] expense' or unnecessary trouble." *Id.* (quoting *Gulf Oil Corp. v. Gilbert*, 330 U.S. 501, 508 (1947)). Yet "a real showing of convenience by a plaintiff who has sued in his home forum will normally outweigh the inconvenience the defendant may have shown." *Id.* (quoting *Koster v. (Am.) Lumbermens Mut. Cas. Co.*, 330 U.S. 518, 524 (1947)). To overcome that presumption, the oppressiveness and vexation must be "out of all proportion to plaintiff's convenience," or the administrative and legal problems too much for the court to bear. *Am. Dredging Co. v. Miller*, 510 U.S. 443, 447–48 (1994) (quoting *Piper*, 454 U.S. at 241).

Meeting that heavy burden involves two steps. First, the defendant has a burden to show that an "adequate alternative forum exists." *Shinya Imamura v. Gen. Elec. Co.*, 957 F.3d 98, 106 (1st Cir. 2020). "[A]n adequate alternative forum exists when '(1) all parties can come within that forum's jurisdiction, and (2) the parties **{-48-}** will not be deprived of all remedies or treated **[—8—]** unfairly, even though they may not enjoy the same benefits as they might receive in an American court.'" *Id.* (quoting *Mercier v. Sheraton Int'l, Inc.* (*Mercier I*), 935 F.2d 419, 424 (1st Cir. 1991)). If the defendant fails to show there's another suitable court to hear the plaintiff's case, that's the end of the line for her *forum non conveniens* motion. *See Nandjou*, 985 F.3d at 141.

Second, if there's an adequate alternative forum, the defendant must *also* show that a balance of public and private interest factors "*strongly favor* litigating the claim in the second forum." *Nandjou*, 985 F.3d at 142 (citation omitted) (emphasis in original). If, on balance, the interest factors are about equal, that's not enough to surmount the defendant's heavy burden. *See id.* at 141.

As for the public interest factors that get thrown onto the scale, the Supreme Court has taught us this: we are to consider

> the administrative difficulties flowing from court congestion; the "local interest in having localized controversies decided at home"; the interest in having the trial of a diversity case in a forum that is at home with the law that must govern the action; the avoidance of unnecessary problems in conflict of laws, or in the application of foreign law; and the unfairness of burdening citizens in an unrelated forum with jury duty.

Piper, 454 U.S. at 241 n.6 (quoting *Gulf Oil,* 330 U.S. at 509).

The private interest factors require consideration of the practicalities of litigating a case in a particular forum that **[—9—]** may make it easy and inexpensive, or cumbersome and extra costly. *See Iragorri v. Int'l Elevator, Inc.*, 203 F.3d 8, 12 (1st Cir. 2000). These factors include "the relative ease of access to sources of proof; availability of compulsory process for attendance of unwilling, and the cost of obtaining attendance of willing, witnesses; [and the] possibility of view of premises, if view would be appropriate to the action." *Id.* (alteration in original) (quoting *Gulf Oil*, 330 U.S. at 508). As particularly relevant here, courts must consider "the nature of the plaintiff's claims and the evidence that would be relied upon to adjudicate them." *Nandjou*, 985 F.3d at 142. In doing so, courts ought to give "particular attention to where the witnesses that the parties would rely upon are located" and "how burdensome it would be for them to appear in either the home or the foreign forum." *Id.* Additionally, courts must give "due consideration . . . to how many . . . witnesses are third parties to the litigation and whether, despite their third-party status, they would be subject to compulsory process in either the home or the foreign forum." *Id.*

This list of public and private interest factors, though, isn't exhaustive. They're merely a "helpful starting point." *Imamura*, 957 F.3d at 107 (quoting *Iragorri*, 203 F.3d at

12); *see, e.g., Nandjou*, 989 F.3d at 146 (considering the physical and emotional toll to witnesses on returning to a location where **[—10—]** they experienced a traumatic experience); *Nowak*, 94 F.3d at 719 (considering as a private interest factor the ability of a plaintiff to use a contingent-fee arrangement). Indeed, "flexibility is the watchword" with *forum non conveniens* cases, *Iragorri*, 203 F.3d at 12, as the inquiry ultimately turns on the unique facts of each case, *Piper*, 454 U.S. at 249. The "ultimate inquiry" remains, all in all, "where trial will best serve the convenience of the parties and the ends of justice." **{-49-}** *Imamura*, 957 F.3d at 107 (quoting *Koster*, 330 U.S. at 527).

Given this multifaceted and fact-laden inquiry, our review of a district court's *forum non conveniens* conclusion is (as the Supreme Court has put it) only for a "clear abuse of discretion," *Piper*, 454 U.S. at 257, which we've since interpreted to be the same test as abuse-of-discretion review, *see, e.g., Imamura*, 957 F.3d at 106 (calling it "abuse of discretion" and citing *Piper*); *Mercier I*, 935 F.2d at 423 (same). As we've said in other contexts, though, the abuse-of-discretion standard isn't a rubber stamp. *Colón-Cabrera v. Esso Std. Oil Co. P.R.*, 723 F.3d 82, 88 (1st Cir. 2013); *accord Simon v. Republic of Hungary*, 911 F.3d 1172, 1190 (D.C. Cir. 2018) ("While we accord respectful deference to district courts' *forum non conveniens* determinations, we do not rubber stamp them."). An abuse of discretion in deciding a *forum non conveniens* motion occurs when a district court has "(1) failed to consider a material factor; (2) substantially relied **[—11—]** on an improper factor; or (3) assessed the proper factors, but clearly erred in weighing them." *Nandjou*, 985 F.3d at 142 (quoting *Interface Partners*, 575 F.3d at 101).

OUR TAKE

With that framework in mind, we dive into our analysis. Curtis and Cambouris say the district court abused its discretion in concluding "the overall balance" "strongly favors Greece as the more convenient and efficient forum." Although they now concede Greece is an adequate alternative forum, they stress that the district court erred in determining that the public and private interest factors strongly favor litigating in Greece. As we'll explain in some detail, we agree that the district court erred in considering the private interest factors and clearly erred in striking the overall balance, thus abusing its discretion.

A. The Public Interest Factors

We begin, though, with the public interest factors, as to which we find no error in the district court's determination that they weighed in favor of litigating in Greece. The court recognized the United States' interest in adjudicating the controversy between three U.S. citizens but determined that interest was outweighed by the fact that, in totality, the United States' connection to the events, even if Galakatos resides in **[—12—]** Massachusetts, was "attenuated."[3] The court emphasized that the collision occurred in Greece and presumably "much of the relevant evidence is located there." "Provided adequate recognition is accorded 'the substantial public interest in providing a convenient United States forum for an action in which all parties are United States citizens and residents,' the trial court may weigh, as a subsidiary consideration, any attenuated connection between the particular United States forum and the matter in litigation." *Mercier v. Sheraton Int'l, Inc. (Mercier II)*, 981 F.2d 1345, 1355 (1st Cir. 1992) (quoting *Mercier I*, 935 F.2d at 430). It was not error to find that the particular contacts with Massachusetts were limited and to balance that consideration against the United States' general interest in deciding disputes between its citizens. *See id.*[4] **{-50-}**

---

[3] We note that Curtis and Cambouris filed suit in Massachusetts, Galakatos's home state, rather than their home state of New York. But since the alternative forum was a non-U.S. court, Massachusetts still counted as the plaintiffs' "home forum"—even though they are New York residents. *See Nandjou*, 985 F.3d at 142.

[4] Our recent decision in *Nandjou* is not to the contrary. There, we affirmed that the district court didn't err in concluding that Massachusetts's interest in the dispute was a "neutral" factor where a Massachusetts citizen sued not only a U.S.-citizen defendant, but also a *Canadian*-citizen defendant,

Nor did the court err when in its analysis it placed weight towards dismissal on its unfamiliarity with Greek law. *See* **[—13—]** *Mercier I*, 981 F.2d at 1357 (noting courts may ascribe some weight to the unfamiliarity with foreign law, but cautioning that they not give it "undue importance" since "the task of deciding foreign law is a chore courts must often perform" (cleaned up) (quoting *Manu Int'l, S.A. v. Avon Prods., Inc.*, 641 F.2d 62, 68 (2d Cir. 1981))).[5] Though we note that, in the grand scheme of things, the court said this factor weighed only "somewhat" toward dismissal.

B. The Private Interest Factors

When it came to the private interest factors, the court thought those weighed in favor of sending this case to Greece. The court emphasized that the accident occurring in Greece weighed heavily in favor of Greece, and that the Greek authorities had investigated—examining physical evidence and taking sworn testimony from witnesses. The court concluded that "the vast majority of key fact witnesses, including eyewitnesses to the collision, Ms. Curtis'[s] Greek treating physicians, and the pilot of the Galani, all reside in Greece." And, because "only a Greek court has the power to compel the testimony of Greek witnesses," **[—14—]** the court thought this weighed toward litigating in Greece.[6] But according to Curtis and Cambouris, Galakatos, contrary to what the district court found, failed to meet his burden of showing that the witnesses were both unavailable to testify in the United States and relevant to this case. In consequence, they say, by failing to hold Galakatos to his burden, the district court committed legal error.

Galakatos, for his part, says that he has no burden to provide detailed information on the identity of witnesses or their relevance to the case. Regardless, he presses there is evidence that there were statements from twelve non-U.S. citizens given to the Greek Port Authority in the initial investigation and that fact suffices.[7] Thus, whatever may be his burden has been met.

In our view, the problem with Galakatos's argument is that the district court had insufficient evidence to support the purported residency of these twelve individuals as we'll discuss in more detail momentarily.[8] As for Galakatos's claim that **{-51-}** he has **[—15—]** no obligation to produce any detailed evidence regarding witnesses, we think Galakatos may be oversimplifying our case law.

True, we've said before, "there is no 'blanket rule' that a defendant affirmatively demonstrate, by affidavit, the unavailability of a foreign witness and the significance of the witness's testimony." *Interface Partners*, 575 F.3d at 104 (quoting *Mercier II*, 981 F.2d at 1356). Indeed, the Supreme Court has specifically rejected the contention that defendants seeking *forum non conveniens* dismissal must submit detailed "affidavits identifying the witnesses they would call and the testimony these witnesses would provide if

---

for an accident that occurred in Canada. *See* 985 F.3d at 143. But it is not error for the district court here to come out the other way.

[5] We also note that we reject Galakatos's argument that the court, under the public interest factors, should consider the "burden of requiring a Massachusetts jury to interpret and analyze issues of Greek law." Courts—not finders of fact—interpret and analyze issues of law. *See* Fed. R. Civ. P. 44.1 (noting the court's determination of foreign law is treated as a question of law); *Animal Sci. Prods. v. Hebei Welcome Pharm. Co.*, 138 S. Ct. 1865, 1873 (2018). Juries determine the facts and apply them to the law the court provides.

[6] This is so because parties lack the "authority to subpoena a foreign national located in a foreign country." *United States v. Aboshady*, 951 F.3d 1, 11 (1st Cir. 2020) (citing Fed. R. Crim. P. 17(e)(2)); *see* Fed. R. Civ. P. 45(b)(3) (providing, just as Fed. R. Crim. P. 17(e)(2), that 28 U.S.C. § 1783 governs service of subpoenas in a foreign country); *see also* 28 U.S.C. § 1783(a) (providing for service in a foreign country only if the witness is a U.S. national or resident).

[7] One of the thirteen statements was from Galakatos, and we know he's a U.S. citizen.

[8] Galakatos claims that the plaintiffs didn't raise any issue with the sufficiency of the evidence on the witnesses' nationality **[—15—]** below, and thus waived it. But the record makes plain that Curtis and Cambouris did object to Galakatos's lack of evidence on the unavailability of witnesses—just apparently not with as much specificity as Galakatos desires.

the trial were held in the alternative forum." *Piper*, 454 U.S. at 258. "Such detail," the Court said, "is not necessary." *Id.*

On the other hand, though, the *Piper* Court made clear that "[o]f course, defendants must provide *enough* information to enable the District Court to balance the parties' interests." *Id.* (emphasis added). Yet the Court didn't provide much guidance on what constitutes "enough"—although it found the defendants did present "enough" in *Piper. Id.*; *see Otto Candies, LLC v. Citigroup, Inc.*, 963 F.3d 1331, 1347, 8 Adm. R. 445, 455 (11th Cir. 2020) (noting the lack of clear guidance from *Piper* on what is "enough"). **[—16—]**

So, delving into what the *Piper* Court deemed sufficient will be instructive in gleaning a benchmark for what meets the defendant's evidentiary burden. But before we take a look at the evidence the *Piper* defendants offered, some context of the case will prove helpful.

Piper involved a dispute over a tragic airplane crash. The airplane, manufactured by U.S.-based Piper Aircraft Co., was on a flight from Blackpool, England to Perth, Scotland when it crashed in the Scottish Highlands after a potential failure with the propeller, manufactured by U.S.-based Hartzell Propeller, Inc. *Piper*, 454 U.S. at 238-39. All five passengers—who were all residents of Scotland—died in the crash. *Id.* The plane at the time was owned, maintained, and operated by United Kingdom-based entities. *Id.* A U.S. resident, Gaynell Reyno, brought suit in a U.S. court as the court-appointed administratrix of the estates of the five Scottish passengers (whom she wasn't in any way related to). *Id.* Asserting wrongful-death and strict-liability claims against the two U.S.-based manufacturers, Reyno admitted that she filed suit in the U.S. because the applicable laws and available relief were much more favorable than those in Scotland. *Id.* at 239–40.

The U.S.-based defendants moved to dismiss for *forum non conveniens*. *Id.* at 240-41. They argued, as relevant to us, that key witnesses on liability and damages—specifically those who **[—17—]** could testify about the aircraft's maintenance since manufacture, the training of the pilot, and the investigation of the accident—were based in the U.K. *Id.* at 242. The district court agreed, but the Third Circuit reversed. *Id.* at 243-44. The Third Circuit concluded that the defendants hadn't met their burden on witness inconvenience because they did not specify the witnesses they would call and the testimony the witnesses would provide. *Id.* at 244.

The Supreme Court, as we've already hinted, disagreed. Rejecting the Third Circuit's witness-convenience conclusion, the **{–52–}** Court indicated that "[s]uch detail is not necessary." *Id.* at 258. Still, as we've noted, the Court made clear that defendants "[o]f course . . . must provide enough information to enable the District Court to balance the parties' interests," which the defendants did there. *Id.*

In finding that the defendants submitted "enough," the high Court referred to the affidavits submitted by the defendants, particularly the one submitted by Piper Aircraft Co. *See id.* at 258–59 & n.27. In it, Piper Aircraft identified, with some detail, the individuals it would call as witnesses in a trial. *See* Aff. of Charles J. McKelvey, Pet. for Writ of Cert. of Piper Aircraft Co. at 1f–3f, *Piper*, 454 U.S. 235 (1981) (No. 80-848). Although it did not identify individuals by name, Piper Aircraft identified general groups of people (*e.g.*, individuals from the Scottish company that owned and operated the aircraft, and individuals from **[—18—]** the aircraft maintenance company) and the general topic of their testimony. And it submitted that all of these individuals were residents of Scotland—a fact that the plaintiff never disputed. *See Reyno v. Piper Aircraft Co.*, 479 F. Supp. 727, 732 (M.D. Pa. 1979) (noting that "[e]ven Plaintiff admits that all witnesses to damages reside in Scotland" and rejecting her argument "that the evidence going to legitimately raised defenses is irrelevant"). Rather, because she brought a claim only for strict liability, the plaintiff in *Piper* thought the only relevant witnesses were the U.S.-based manufacturer's employees. *See* Opp'ns to Pets. for Writs of Cert., *Piper*, 454 U.S. 236 (1981) (No. 80-848), 1980 U.S. S. Ct. Briefs LEXIS 1793, at *9–10. But the manufacturer pressed as a defense that events in Scotland in the seven years since the aircraft's assembly could have affected the manufacturer's liability. *See* Tr. Oral Arg. at 18–19, *Piper*, 454 U.S. 236 (1981) (No. 80-848). And, in furtherance of its request to move the venue, the manufacturer expressly agreed to bear the burden of transporting those U.S.-based witnesses to Scotland. *See id.* at 18.

The evidentiary support Galakatos offered up here is a far cry from that in *Piper*. First, it was undisputed in *Piper* that all the witnesses the defendant sought to call—save those U.S.-based-employee witnesses who would travel to Scotland at the defendant's expense—were located in Scotland. The *Piper* Court **[—19—]** thus could make the reasonable assumption that a Scottish court could compel those witnesses to testify. Here, Curtis and Cambouris have made no similar concession as to the residency of the witnesses Galakatos has identified. And, though we've scoured the record, we've found but one piece of evidence from Galakatos on this subject: Galakatos's statement that "nearly all of the identifiable witnesses to this incident other than the Plaintiffs reside in Greece." Further, all we have to explain that allegation is his counsel's "understanding" (again without any factual basis) that the eleven individuals with seemingly Greek surnames are citizens of Greece and not, as Cambouris was, merely vacationers.[9] *See Duha v. Agrium, Inc.*, 448 F.3d 867, 879 (6th Cir. 2006) (holding the district court abused its discretion in giving undue weight to information about witnesses "asserted **{-53-}** in [the defendant's] brief but not by affidavit or in any other record evidence"). Without such evidence identifying the witnesses' residency,[10] the district court did not have a sufficient basis to **[—20—]** conclude that a Greek court could compel testimony from these eleven individuals.[11] *See, e.g., SAS Inst., Inc. v. World Programming Ltd.*, 468 F. App'x 264, 266-67 (4th Cir. 2012) (per curiam) (finding abuse of discretion because the district court failed to hold the defendant to its burden by relying on a barebones affidavit stating that witnesses were in the U.K.). Its finding to the contrary was clear error, and its resulting emphasis on this factor was erroneous.

Further, putting aside the residency of the witnesses, the district court again erred when it placed undue weight on a Greek court's ability, if any, to compel witness testimony. As the Supreme Court has instructed, courts consider the "availability of compulsory process for attendance of *unwilling* **[—21—]** . . . witnesses." *Gulf Oil*, 330 U.S. at 508 (emphasis added).[12] Yet Galakatos made no

---

[9] Galakatos argues we can infer these individuals are Greek residents because the Port Authority report specifies that Curtis is of "USA Nationality," but doesn't say the same for others. It's not clear how the Port Authority decided to mark (or not mark) various nationalities in the report. However, as Curtis and Cambouris point out, the lack of similar notations of nationality for other individuals appears to be based off assumptions about last names. Cambouris (a U.S. citizen and resident of New York) doesn't have a "USA Nationality" notation after his name.

[10] Of course, it could be necessary to know not just the witnesses' *residency* but also their citizenship, as the district court could (so long as other requirements are met) have the **[—20—]** authority to compel the testimony of a U.S. citizen residing abroad. *See* 28 U.S.C. § 1783 (providing for service of a subpoena on a U.S. citizen on international soil if certain findings are made by the district court); *see also* Fed. R. Civ. P. 45(b)(3). Though residency of a non-U.S. citizen, too, would be relevant to the question of whether witnesses' testimony could be compelled, since a district court could have the authority to compel the testimony of a Greek citizen residing in the United States. See Fed. R. Civ. P. 45(b)(2); *Probulk Carriers Ltd. v. Marvel Int'l Mgmt. & Transp.*, 180 F. Supp. 3d 290, 292 (S.D.N.Y. 2016) (concluding subpoena on foreign national temporarily in the United States enforceable and noting that Fed. R. Civ. P. 45(b)(2) "does not distinguish between witnesses who are citizens or residents of the United States and witnesses who are not").

[11] Galakatos has provided no legal authority suggesting that a Greek court could compel the testimony of non-resident Greek citizens.

[12] Galakatos did not argue that the "cost of obtaining attendance of *willing*[] witnesses," *see Gulf Oil*, 330 U.S. at 508 (emphasis added), weighed in favor of litigating in Greece.

allegations that any of the witnesses would be unwilling to testify in the United States absent compulsory process—only (on appeal, without record support) that the witnesses are "*unlikely* to travel to Massachusetts to testify."[13] *See Mercier I*, 935 F.3d at 428 (noting the defendant "failed to establish that these witnesses would be unwilling to come to the United States"). Unlikely and unwilling do not equate, and the district court placed undue weight on the availability of compulsory process. *See, e.g., Hefferan v. Ethicon Endo-Surgery Inc.*, 828 F.3d 488, 499 (6th Cir. 2016) (the availability of compulsory process, though a consideration, "receives less weight 'when it has not been alleged or shown that any witness would be unwilling to testify'" (quoting *Duha*, 448 F.3d at 877)); *DiFederico v. Marriott Int'l, Inc.*, 714 F.3d 796, 807 (4th Cir. 2013) (noting a defendant "must do more than simply point to categories of witnesses who are outside the court's control" and that "a generalized assertion that the court cannot compel Pakistani witnesses to give testimony" doesn't establish unwillingness); *cf.* **[—22—]** *also Iragorri*, 203 F.3d at 17 (noting that a "mere suggestion of greater financial strain is meaningless unless and until the plaintiff demonstrates the nature and extent **{–54–}** of the supposed limitations").[14]

Moreover, even assuming the witnesses were outside the reach of necessary Massachusetts compulsory process, Galakatos also failed to demonstrate why the proposed witnesses had any relevance to his case. Looking back to *Piper*'s baseline standard, we see that the *Piper* defendant submitted "enough" when it listed different categories of witnesses and, equally important, the subjects upon which they were proposed to testify. Further to explaining what's "enough," we have also recently clarified that a defendant's long list of potential witnesses, without more, is not always "enough" to meet its burden on the witnesses factor. *See Nandjou*, 985 F.3d at 147. In *Nandjou*, we faced another tragic case where a father and son drowned in a hotel pool in Montréal. *Id.* at 138. The defendants, as part of their *forum non conveniens* **[—23—]** motion, contended there were twenty-five witnesses in Canada (including civilian first responders, police officers, paramedics, medical personnel, and the coroner) that could not be compelled to testify in a Massachusetts court. *Id.* at 144-45. The plaintiffs countered by identifying three U.S.-based third-party liability witnesses, multiple U.S.-based third-party damages witnesses, and two U.S.-based party witnesses—who also happened to be the only individuals who actually witnessed the drowning at issue. *Id.* at 145-46. On that record, we said the district court placed undue weight on the defendants' numeric list because the defendants "[did] not explain[] why live testimony from all of those witnesses [was] critical." *Id.* at 147. Indeed, we said so even where the defendants offered as evidence reports from many of their list of twenty-five witnesses, including six of the civilian first responders, six police officers, and the coroner. Defs.' Renewed Mot. to Dismiss, Ex. B, at 6-16, 34-44, *Nandjou v. Marriott Int'l, Inc.*, No. 18-CV-12230-ADB, 2019 WL 5551438 (D. Mass. Oct. 28, 2019), ECF No. 39; *id.*, Ex. C, at 1-9.

Here, though, Galakatos submitted a list of names omitting any even generalized detail on their role in the underlying incident (whether eyewitness to the crash, first responder, or participant in the investigation).[15] Yet he

---

[13] Indeed, he did not even make any allegation that Faroupos (the pilot of the Galani and gardener at his vacation home) would be unwilling—even though the Greek attorney submitting an affidavit on Galakatos's behalf was in contact with Faroupos's attorney.

[14] Our circuit's case law hasn't always been crystal clear on this requirement. After noting in *Mercier I* that the defendant didn't establish any witness's unwillingness to come to the United States, we said subsequently in *Mercier II* that a defendant need not, in every case, establish with record evidence that unwillingness. *See* 981 F.3d at 1356; *see also Interface Partners*, 575 F.3d at 104-05 (quoting *Mercier II* for this proposition). But, as we'll soon note, the necessary information to surmount a defendant's burden will vary from case to case. And, as we'll also soon explain, the concerns driving *Mercier II*'s observation aren't present here.

[15] The record contains a translated copy of the Port Authority's report on the incident, which happens to identify the **[—24—]** role that some of these potential witnesses played on the day of the

bore the **[—24—]** burden of giving the district court "enough" to evaluate the relative burdens related to the convenience of witnesses. *See Van Cauwenberghe v. Biard*, 486 U.S. 517, 528 (1988) (noting that to evaluate the access-to-evidence factor, the court must "evaluate what proof is required, and determine whether the pieces of evidence cited by the parties are critical, or even relevant, to the plaintiff's cause of action and to any potential defenses to the action"). The district court erred in failing **{-55-}** to require some showing from Galakatos as to how the witnesses were relevant. *See, e.g., Nandjou*, 985 F.3d at 147; *Bos. Telecomms. Grp., Inc. v. Wood*, 588 F.3d 1201, 1210 (9th Cir. 2009) (finding abuse of discretion in weighing witnesses factor where the defendant "provided very little information that would have enabled the district court to understand why various witnesses were material to his defense"); *cf. Iragorri*, 203 F.3d at 17 (emphasizing that "live testimony of key witnesses" can be essential if the defendant shows how those witnesses are critical (cleaned up) (quoting *Howe*, 946 F.2d at 952)). **[—25—]**

Contrary to Galakatos's suggestion, our requirement for more information (about residency, unwillingness, or relevance) would not, on the facts of this case, "defeat the purpose of the[] motion" by requiring "extensive investigation." *Piper*, 454 U.S. at 258. The *Piper* Court was obviously concerned with forcing defendants to bear an impossible burden by identifying the names and testimony of witnesses in a jurisdiction in which they have no power to compel information. *See id.* (noting that defendants "have moved for dismissal precisely because many crucial witnesses are located beyond the reach of compulsory process, and thus are difficult to identify or interview"); *see also Mercier II*, 981 F.2d at 1356 (noting that a "blanket rule 'would tend to inflict an impossible burden'" because defendants "cannot compel evidence, including the evidence necessary to argue for dismissal" (citation omitted)). But here, Galakatos had easy access to—at the very least—the location of at least six of the eleven individuals identified on the list. As the Port Authority's investigation report makes clear, five of those individuals were aboard the Galani with Faroupos (the sixth) when the accident occurred. And although Galakatos stresses in his appellate papers that he is "not in regular communication with the eyewitnesses," it is clear Galakatos has at least some access to Faroupos: the Greek attorney hired by Galakatos's counsel obtained the list of witnesses directly from Faroupos's attorney in the criminal investigation. **[—26—]** Content to rest on what he believed the bare minimum, Galakatos apparently made no attempt to utilize the information he *could* access to try to shoulder his heavy burden.

Thus, although we today reaffirm that there is no "blanket rule" that a defendant identify the substance of a proposed witness's testimony, *see Interface Partners*, 575 F.3d at 104, we echo, too, the Supreme Court admonition that a defendant must give the district court enough information to analyze whether the defendant has shouldered her heavy burden, *see Piper*, 454 U.S. at 258; *see also Iragorri*, 203 F.3d at 17 (making clear that a "mere suggestion" of burden without evidentiary support showing the "nature and extent of the supposed limitations" may be insufficient). Again, "flexibility is the watchword," *Iragorri*, 203 F.3d at 12, and a defendant may, in some cases, need to show why the inability to compel certain non-U.S.-based witnesses strongly outweighs the plaintiff's desire to try her case in her home forum of choosing, *see Lacey v. Cessna Aircraft Co.*, 862 F.2d 38, 44 (3d Cir. 1988) ("[T]here is no hard and fast rule, and . . . the amount of information that a defendant must provide depends upon the facts of the particular case."); *In re Air Crash Disaster near New Orleans*, 821 F.2d 1147, 1165 n.28 (5th Cir. 1987) (en banc) (noting the detail required will vary depending on the issues that are contested), *vacated and remanded on other grounds sub. nom. Pan Am. World Airways,*

---

crash. (Though we note as an aside that, further to Galakatos's apparent strategy of providing little-to-no information, it wasn't Galakatos that provided this document—it was Curtis and Cambouris.) But Galakatos still did not give the district court enough information to determine that any of the witnesses actually had relevant testimony to offer.

Inc. v. Lopez, 490 U.S. 1032, 1033 **[—27—]** (1989), *op. reinstated in relevant part*, 883 F.2d 17, 17 (5th Cir. 1989). But a mere reliance upon **{–56–}** assumptions—Galakatos assumes those deposed by Greek officials are in Greece and that all of them have something relevant to offer—will not do. *See Adelson*, 510 F.3d at 53; *Mercier I*, 935 F.2d at 426 ("the district court mistakenly relieved the moving defendant of its burden" in "assuming"). All that said, defendants who choose to try to meet their heavy burden with the bare minimum of what's "enough" do so at their own peril.

We also believe the district court gave inadequate consideration to the convenience of the plaintiffs' witnesses, in particular, the plaintiff herself.[16] The district court failed to take heed of the physical and emotional burden on Curtis in returning to Greece, as the plaintiffs requested it do. *See Nandjou*, 985 F.3d at 146 (noting the district court should have considered the burden on the plaintiffs who, "if forced to testify **[—28—]** in Montreal, would be required to return to the country of their loved ones' deaths" (citing *Guidi v. Inter-Cont'l Hotels Corp.*, 224 F.3d 142, 145 (2d Cir. 2000))); *see also Guidi*, 224 F.3d at 145 (reversing a *forum non conveniens* dismissal in part because the district court failed to consider the "emotional burden" it would impose on the plaintiffs to return to Egypt, where their loved ones were killed).

Galakatos claims any physical or emotional burden on Curtis (or her husband for that matter) doesn't need much consideration because, he claims, Greek courts "rel[y] heavily on written evidence and only rarely require[] live testimony, so the likelihood of Plaintiffs being required to travel back to Greece is very small." Yet the key words in there—even assuming their accuracy—are "rarely" and "very small" likelihood. Indeed, although Galakatos avers that "testimony by a litigant party is not permitted under Greek law," his Greek attorney's testimony on that point is inconsistent. Although the attorney states that "litigant parties are not entitled to swear affidavits or be examined as witnesses," he also states (emphases our own) that there could be the "*rare* event that the Court would ask the Plaintiffs . . . to appear before it in order to be examined," and that it would be "*very unlikely* for the Court to ask from any of the Plaintiffs to travel to Greece in order to be examined." The district court didn't make any legal conclusion on whether Curtis **[—29—]** could be called to testify in Greece and did not consider at all how this balanced against the location of the other witnesses. It should have considered the prejudice to Curtis of possibly—even if unlikely—having to return to Greece to prosecute her claims. *Cf., e.g., Mercier I*, 935 F.2d at 428 (no weight given to witnesses factor where the burdens between the two sides were "likely to be about equal").

Curtis and Cambouris do not dispute, though, that the district court correctly determined that some of the physical evidence being in Greece weighed in favor of litigating there. Still, we think that this factor alone cannot weigh "strongly" **{–57–}** in favor of a Greek forum. The district court did not explain why this factor *strongly* favored litigating in Greece given that the documents could be transmitted electronically. Nor are we convinced by Galakatos's repeated emphasis that the need to translate these documents counsels strongly toward a Greek court. The same need for translation exists if this case heads to Greece, as neither Curtis nor her U.S.-based physicians speak Greek.

[16] Curtis and Cambouris also argue that the district court erred when it concluded that Curtis's U.S.-based medical providers' unwillingness to travel to Greece did not weigh against dismissal. We spy no error, though, because the district court did *consider* this fact. It just didn't apply the weight Curtis and Cambouris would like. *Cf. Imamura*, 957 F.3d at 106 (reminding that we won't strike the balance of relevant factors anew). And, as the district court noted, not only could Curtis and Cambouris obtain testimony from one of the treating Greek physicians (one of whom is identified by name and hospital in the record), her U.S.-based physicians could also submit written testimony. True, U.S. courts prefer live testimony. *See Interface Partners*, 575 F.3d at 105. But Greek courts apparently generally rely on written testimony—a point Curtis doesn't dispute.

C. Putting It All Together

In review, the district court abused its discretion in failing to hold Galakatos to his burden of showing that the public and private interest factors displaced the "heavy presumption weigh[ing] in favor of [Curtis's] initial forum of choice," *Adelson*, 510 F.3d at 53, and that all in all, a trial in Greece **[—30—]** "will best serve the convenience of the parties and the ends of justice," *Imamura*, 957 F.3d at 107 (quoting *Koster*, 330 U.S. at 527). The district court clearly erred in striking the overall balance, and, in doing so, abused its discretion. *See Nandjou*, 985 F.3d at 147.

Before we close out, we have one more note. Below, Galakatos opposed Curtis and Cambouris's cross-motion for targeted discovery in support of their opposition to the *forum non conveniens* motion. Galakatos's position then was that he had given the district court enough information for it to rule in his favor.[17] However, we conclude he did not, and given that it was his heavy burden to show *forum non conveniens*, and given his decision below to advocate against the development of a stronger factual record, we will leave him to shoulder the burden of the inadequacy of his evidentiary offerings.[18] *See Iragorri*, 203 F.3d at 17 ("It is hornbook law that an appellate argument cannot survive the proponent's failure to supply a sufficient factual predicate for it."); *cf. Dow v. United Bhd. of Carpenters & Joiners*, 1 F.3d 56, 61 (1st Cir. 1993) (noting we are loath to "squander judicial **[—31—]** resources and give parties who . . . plunge headlong into the merits of a case without pausing to exhaust discovery options a second bite at the cherry"); *Bhatnagar v. Surrendra Overseas Ltd.*, 52 F.3d 1220, 1231 (3d Cir. 1995) (holding, without enacting a blanket rule disfavoring reconsideration of *forum non conveniens* motions with new evidence, that reconsideration on an expanded record should be "limited to exceptional circumstances").

SIGN OFF

Our voyage complete, we ***reverse*** the district court's judgment dismissing this case and ***remand*** to allow the case to proceed in the plaintiffs' chosen forum. Costs to appellants. Fed. R. App. P. 39(a)(3).

---

[17] Galakatos also says, on appeal, that Curtis and Cambouris didn't ask for discovery on the witnesses issue. But Curtis and Cambouris asked for discovery on the "issues raised in the *forum non conveniens* motion," which would include his and his counsel's statements that the witnesses are in Greece.

[18] Galakatos has not suggested on appeal that, if we found insufficient evidence, we should remand for further factfinding.

This page intentionally left blank

United States Court of Appeals for the Second Circuit

United States Court of Appeals
for the Second Circuit

No. 20-2268

BENSCH
VS.
ESTATE OF UMAR

Appeal from the United States District Court for the Western District of New York

Decided: June 23, 2021

Citation: 2 F.4th 70, 9 Adm. R. 98 (2d Cir. 2021).

Before **LIVINGSTON,** Chief Judge, **CABRANES** and **LYNCH,** Circuit Judges.

[—2—] {-72-} **LYNCH,** Circuit Judge:

This appeal requires us to decide whether maritime complaints seeking exoneration from or limitation of liability pursuant to the Limitation of Liability Act, **{-73-}** 46 U.S.C. § 30511 *et seq.*, must contain sufficient factual matter to satisfy the "plausibility" standard applicable to pleadings under Federal Rule of Civil **[—3—]** Procedure 8(a), as interpreted by the Supreme Court in *Bell Atlantic Corp. v. Twombly*, 550 U.S. 544 (2007), and *Ashcroft v. Iqbal*, 556 U.S. 662 (2009). We hold that such maritime complaints must satisfy the plausibility standard. We conclude, however, that the Petitioner's Second Proposed Amended Complaint met that standard, and that the district court exceeded its discretion in denying the motion for leave to amend.

BACKGROUND

The case arises from a tragic boating accident on the Niagara River in August 2018. Petitioner Christopher Bensch was piloting his boat, a 46-foot pleasure craft, in a marked channel on the river. The decedent, Ahmed Abdulla Umar, was operating a jet ski that he had rented from Waikiki Watercraft, LLC ("Waikiki"), with his young daughter as a passenger. Umar fell off the jet ski in front of Bensch's vessel, which struck and killed him. Umar's daughter fortunately survived. As described in more detail below, the parties dispute responsibility for the fatal collision in litigation in both state and federal courts.

I. Legal Background: Exoneration and Limitation of Liability

The Limitation of Liability Act, 46 U.S.C. § 30501 *et seq.*, limits the liability of a vessel owner to the value of the vessel (and any freight it is carrying, a factor **[—4—]** not relevant here) for any damage caused by a collision without the "privity or knowledge" of the owner. *Id.* § 30505(b). The animating premise of the statute is that the owner of a vessel is generally an absentee who entrusts the vessel to the command of a captain whom the owner has limited ability to supervise or control once the vessel is on the sea. Thus, in what we have described as an effort "to encourage the development of American merchant shipping," the Act loosens the normal rules of *respondeat superior* in admiralty cases by allowing shipowners to insulate their personal assets (beyond the value of the ship) in cases where any negligence is committed without the owner's privity or knowledge. *Complaint of Dammers & Vanderheide & Scheepvaart Maats Christina B.V.*, 836 F.2d 750, 754 (2d Cir. 1988), quoting *Lake Tankers Corp. v. Henn*, 354 U.S. 147, 150 (1957). This policy, and the literal language of the statute, might suggest that it applies only where the owner lacked knowledge of the accident itself, which occurred out of his sight. But it has long been held that "[p]rivity and knowledge is a term of art meaning complicity in the fault that caused the accident." *Blackler v. F. Jacobus Transp. Co.*, 243 F.2d 733, 735 (2d Cir. 1957) (internal quotation marks omitted). Thus, the fact that here the owner himself was operating the vessel at the time of the injury does not defeat the limitation of liability action. *See id.* In effect, the **[—5—]** statute creates a federal admiralty forum in which the owner may seek limitation of liability by establishing that he was not at fault with respect to the collision.[1] **{-74-}**

[1] It is unnecessary for purposes of this case to trace the complex interaction of federal and state jurisdiction arising from what the Supreme Court has called the "tension" between the Limitation of Liability Act and the Savings to Suitors clause in

Bensch seeks to avail himself of the benefits of that remedy by filing a complaint asserting that he was not at fault in connection with the death of Umar.

II. Procedural History

On October 30, 2018, Umar's widow, Ameera Umar, brought a wrongful death action on behalf of herself and Umar's estate (together, the "Claimants") in the Supreme Court of New York for Erie County against Bensch and Waikiki, alleging that Bensch operated his boat negligently and that Waikiki failed to provide adequate instruction regarding the proper operation of the jet ski.[2] On January 4, 2019, Bensch brought this limitation action against the Claimants in the United States District Court for the Western District of New York, invoking **[—6—]** its admiralty jurisdiction and seeking exoneration from or limitation of liability pursuant to the Limitation of Liability Act, 46 U.S.C. 30501 *et seq.*, and Rule F of the Supplemental Rules for Admiralty or Maritime Claims and Asset Forfeiture Actions (the "Supplemental Rules").[3]

Bensch did not include much detail about the accident in his initial complaint. Besides identifying the action as one for exoneration from or limitation of liability, describing the vessel and its value, and indicating that he had been sued by Claimants for negligence and that the claims asserted would exceed the value of his interest in the vessel, Bensch's initial complaint included only two paragraphs concerning the accident itself. The first addressed Umar's conduct, alleging that Umar "was recklessly operating a personal watercraft ('Jet Ski') at a high rate of speed across the channel without regards [*sic*] to navigation rules, wakes, water conditions, and marine traffic[,] . . . struck the wake of another vessel, and fell off of the Jet Ski directly ahead of Petitioner's Vessel." App'x at 8. As to his own conduct, Bensch alleged only that any damages **[—7—]** resulting from the accident "were not due to any fault, neglect, or want of care of Petitioner and occurred without Petitioner's privity or knowledge." *Id.* On September 26, 2019, Claimants moved to dismiss the complaint for failure to state a claim upon which relief can be granted. On November 8, 2019, Bensch opposed the motion to dismiss and also moved for leave to amend the complaint, attaching a slightly amended version of his complaint (the "First Proposed Amended Complaint"). The only material change from the initial complaint was to add a single sentence stating that "[t]he voyage was a recreational excursion to and from a dock located at 7619 Buffalo Ave, Niagara Falls, N.Y." App'x at 73.[4]

On January 9, 2020, United States Magistrate Judge Jeremiah J. McCarthy recommended that the motion to dismiss be granted and the motion for leave to amend be denied on grounds of futility. The magistrate judge concluded that while the allegations in the initial complaint adequately pled that Umar was negligent, "the Complaint contains no factual allegations showing **{-75-}** that Bensch was not also negligent." App'x at 82. Citing principally cases arising under Rule **[—8—]** 8(a) outside the admiralty context, including *Ashcroft v. Iqbal*, the magistrate judge (whose views on this point were in due course adopted by the district court) ruled that because a court is not bound to accept as true a legal conclusion couched as a factual allegation, Bensch's disavowal of any negligence on his own part was a mere legal conclusion that "fails to plausibly allege a basis for limiting his liability." App'x at 83. The magistrate judge, in short, applied the

28 U.S.C. § 1333(1), which preserves to admiralty plaintiffs all remedies, including trial by jury, to which they are otherwise entitled. *See Lewis v. Lewis & Clark Marine, Inc.*, 531 U.S. 438, 448 (2001).

[2] Waikiki is not involved in this appeal.

[3] On December 5, 2018, Bensch also removed the wrongful death action from state court to the United States District Court for the Western District of New York. In a ruling not challenged on this appeal, the district court remanded the wrongful death action to state court, where it remains pending.

[4] As noted below, this sentence was apparently intended to address the specific requirement of Supplemental Rule F(2) that a complaint for exoneration from or limitation of liability include certain details about the voyage, if any, on which the vessel was engaged at the time of the accident. *See infra* note 6.

same pleading standard to Bensch's complaint in this maritime claim for exoneration or limitation that would apply to a complaint in any other civil action under the governing pleading standard announced in *Twombly* and *Iqbal*. The magistrate judge further recommended denial on grounds of futility of the motion for leave to amend because the change in the First Proposed Amended Complaint did nothing to address the shortcomings of the initial complaint. *See Est. of Umar v. Bensch*, No. 18-CV-1414, 2020 WL 3491633, at *4 (W.D.N.Y. Jan. 9, 2020), *report and recommendation adopted*, No. 18-CV-1414, 2020 WL 3489674 (W.D.N.Y. June 26, 2020).

Bensch responded to the magistrate judge's Report and Recommendation by filing yet another motion for leave to amend the complaint and attaching a second amended complaint (the "Second Proposed Amended Complaint"). The **[—9—]** Second Proposed Amended Complaint added a number of additional allegations about Bensch, his boat, and his behavior on the day of the accident, including that Bensch was an "experienced operator," who was "familiar with boating on the Niagara River;" that his boat "was properly outfitted and equipped;" that at the time of the accident Bensch was "keeping a lookout ahead and to each side" and his "visibility was not impaired;" that he observed Umar, who was operating the jet ski "not on any particular course," "suddenly turn[ ] directly in front of [Bensch's] [v]essel's path;" and that he (unsuccessfully) "took appropriate action to avoid collision." App'x at 98.

Nevertheless, the magistrate judge recommended that Bensch's second motion for leave to amend be denied on grounds of bad faith. Because Bensch did not "suggest that [he was] unaware of the pleading requirements of Supplemental Rule F(2) and *Iqbal* and offer[ed] no excuse for [his] failure to satisfy those requirements," the magistrate judge concluded failing to meet those requirements until the second motion for leave to amend must have been deliberate and in bad faith. App'x at 104-05.

The district court (John L. Sinatra, Jr., *J.*) adopted, with some modifications, the substance of the magistrate judge's reports and recommendations discussed **[—10—]** above, dismissing Bensch's complaint and denying the motions to amend. The principal modification relevant to this appeal is that the district court denied the second motion for leave to amend for futility as well as on the basis of bad faith as the magistrate judge had recommended. *Est. of Umar v. Bensch*, No. 18-CV-1414, 2020 WL 3489674, at *1 (W.D.N.Y. June 26, 2020).[5] This appeal followed.

DISCUSSION

Bensch argues that the plausibility standard for assessing the sufficiency of a complaint **{-76-}** that applies in civil litigation under Federal Rule of Civil Procedure 8(a), as announced by the Supreme Court in *Twombly* and *Iqbal*, is inapplicable to maritime complaints for exoneration from or limitation of liability, which are also governed by the Supplemental Rules. We write principally to address that argument, which raises a question of first impression in this Court, and is of general importance to the admiralty bar and the district courts. We also address Bensch's specific argument as to whether he should have been permitted to file his Second Proposed Amended Complaint. **[—11—]**

I. The Proper Pleading Standard under Rule F(2)

To analyze the pleading standard applicable in this case, it is necessary to review the evolution and history of pleading under the Federal Rules of Civil Procedure, and of the relationship of those rules to claims under maritime law, particularly claims for exoneration from or limitation of liability.

The original text of the Federal Rules of Civil Procedure, adopted in 1937, provided that "[t]hese rules govern the procedure in the district courts of the United States of all suits of a civil nature whether cognizable as cases

[5] The district court also rejected the magistrate judge's recommendation that attorney's fees should be awarded to Claimants. That determination has not been appealed and therefore is not before us.

at law or in equity." Fed. R. Civ. P. 1 (1937). The rules thus unified the formerly distinct procedural regimes for cases in equity, which had been governed by the Federal Equity Rules and cases at law, which had been governed by the procedures applicable in the courts of the states where each federal court sat. *See* Order of the Supreme Court of the United States (June 3, 1935), *reprinted in* Advisory Committee on Civil Rules, Report of the Advisory Committee on Rules for Civil Procedure iii (1937). Maritime claims, however, continued to be governed by a separate set of admiralty rules.

That changed in 1966, when the admiralty rules were largely abolished, and the final phrase of Rule 1 as quoted above was amended to read "whether **[—12—]** cognizable as cases at law or in equity *or in admiralty*." Fed. R. Civ. P. 1 (1966) (emphasis added). That entire phrase was deleted as unnecessary in 2007, because, as the Advisory Committee noted, "[t]he merger of law, equity and admiralty practice is complete[, and t]here is no need to carry forward the phrases that initially accomplished the merger." Fed. R. Civ. P. 1 (advisory committee's note to 2007 amendment).

Even after the merger, however, the Advisory Committee recognized the need to preserve "[c]ertain distinctively maritime remedies," and, accordingly, to craft specific rules appropriate for cases invoking those remedies. Supplemental Rule A (advisory committee's note to 1966 adoption). Accordingly, the Federal Rules were supplemented with a specific set of Supplemental Rules applicable to a short list of specific types of maritime claims. *Id.*; *see also* Fed. R. Civ. P. 9(h). Among the particular remedies in admiralty actions subject to the Supplemental Rules are "actions for exoneration from or limitation of liability." Supplemental Rule A(1)(A)(iv). Supplemental Rule A(2) emphasizes, however, that even as to the listed categories of maritime claims, that "[t]he Federal Rules of Civil Procedure also apply to the foregoing proceedings except to the extent that they are inconsistent with these Supplemental Rules." **[—13—]**

The specific Supplemental Rule governing actions for limitation of liability is Rule F, which contains detailed provisions governing the contents of a complaint seeking that remedy. Under Rule F(2), as relevant here, a complaint "shall set forth the facts on the basis of which the right to limit **{-77-}** liability is asserted."[6]

On appeal, Bensch insists that even his initial complaint was sufficient to satisfy Supplemental Rule F, because it asserted, albeit in conclusory terms, that Umar's negligent operation of the jet ski "was the direct cause of the incident and that [Bensch] does not have knowledge or privity of that negligence." Appellant's Br. 10. Although this argument would appear contrary to the text of Rule F(2), which explicitly requires the complaint to "set forth the *facts*" on which the claim for liability is based (emphasis added), Bensch nevertheless maintains that the formulation in his complaint is "standard admiralty wording" and that "similarly worded complaints have withstood dismissal" in a number of district **[—14—]** courts in this Circuit. *Id.*[7] In effect, he argues that in maritime cases to which the Supplemental Rules apply, a distinctive customary admiralty standard of pleading governs, distinct from the Rule 8(a) standard as currently understood. As support for that contention, he relies on the venerable case of *Colonial Sand & Stone Co. v. Muscelli*, 151

---

[6] Supplemental Rule F(2) also requires certain specific factual allegations, most of which are not relevant to this case. One that is of some marginal relevance to this matter is the requirement that the complaint "shall state the voyage[,] if any, on which the demands sought to be limited arose, with the date and place of its termination." Supplemental Rule F(2). *See supra* note 4.

[7] As examples of such district court cases, Bensch cites *In re Franz*, 7 F. Supp. 3d 238, 243 (N.D.N.Y. 2014), *In re Yanicky*, No. 11-CV-6287, 2011 WL 5523600, at *2 (W.D.N.Y. 2011), and *Matter of Schnittger*, 431 F. Supp. 3d 109, 114 (E.D.N.Y. 2019). While some of the cited cases are arguably distinguishable, we need not quibble over the specifics of the particular cases, and readily acknowledge that some district courts seem to have upheld the sufficiency of complaints that say little or nothing more than Bensch alleged here.

F.2d 884 (2d Cir. 1945), authored by no less an authority than Judge Learned Hand.

Bensch accurately states the holding of *Colonial Sand.* At least as reflected in Judge Hand's opinion, the petition of the vessel owner in that case alleged no more, with respect to the owner's privity and knowledge concerning the causes of the claimant's injuries, than that those injuries "were suffered without the petitioner's knowledge, and were not caused by its fault or negligence, or that of any of its employees." *Id.* at 884. The claimant there, like the Claimants here, argued that this complaint was insufficient under then-governing Admiralty Rule 53, which, like the present Supplemental Rule F(2), required the petitioner in **[—15—]** an exoneration or limitation case to "state the facts and circumstances by reason of which exemption from liability is claimed." *Id.* at 885, quoting Admiralty Rule 53. The Court nevertheless held that the allegation in the petition was sufficient. *Id.*

Bensch, however, wrenches that holding from its historical context. Indeed, properly read in the context of the law of its time, *Colonial Sand* rejected the notion of a special admiralty pleading standard, and effectively assimilated the pleading standard under the admiralty rules to the general pleading standard of the Federal Rules of Civil Procedure, as that standard was understood at the time.

Notably, in *Colonial Sand,* it was the *claimant,* not the vessel owner, who argued against the applicability of the general pleading standard for civil cases under the Federal Rules to maritime complaints. Indeed, the claimant argued for a distinctive admiralty pleading standard, relying on the particular language of the old Admiralty Rules, and on what Judge Hand acknowledged was the "common custom in **{-78-}** the admiralty [bar] not to confine pleadings to the 'ultimate,' 'constitutive,' or 'operational,' facts on which the right or defense depends, as is **[—16—]** required in other branches of the law; but to set out a discursive narrative of the pleader's version of the events." *Id.*

But Judge Hand dismissed that custom and glided past the specific language of Admiralty Rule 53 to hold that there was no basis for applying a special pleading rule in limitation of liability cases and "every reason to sustain a pleading which is adequate under ordinary canons." *Id.* The general pleading rule in most admiralty cases, Judge Hand wrote, required only that the libel (the equivalent in traditional admiralty practice of a complaint) "shall 'allege in distinct articles the various allegations of fact upon which the libellant relies in support of his suit[.]'" *Id.*, quoting Admiralty Rule 22. And *that* standard, Judge Hand concluded, "is not different in substance from Rule 8(a) of the [Federal] Rules of Civil [Procedure.]" *Id.* All that was required to invoke the right to limit liability was that the owner had been sued for an injury that incurred without his "privity or knowledge," and, under the prevailing pleading rules in admiralty, as in civil cases, a general allegation of lack of negligence. *Id.*

Of course, when Judge Hand wrote, that was all that Federal Rule of Civil Procedure 8 required of civil complaints. The text of the rule, then as now, required only "a short and plain statement of the claim showing that the pleader **[—17—]** is entitled to relief." Fed. R. Civ. P. 8(a)(2). Crucially, however, the rule at that time was understood to institute a system of "notice pleading," under which a plaintiff was not required to plead extensive facts, but merely to identify the nature of the claim sufficiently to put the defendant on notice of the suit it needed to defend, with further factual development to be worked out through broad discovery and motion practice.[8]

That general philosophy of pleading was embodied in the Supreme Court's well-known decision in *Conley v. Gibson,* which sustained a complaint over the defendants' objection that it "failed to set forth specific facts to support its general allegations of discrimination," holding that the "notice pleading" regime enacted by the Federal Rules

[8] Judge Charles Clark, a member of the panel that decided *Colonial Sand,* was one of the principal drafters of the original Federal Rules adopted in 1937, and a vigorous proponent of the notice pleading system.

of Civil Procedure "do[es] not require a claimant to set out in detail the facts upon which he bases his claim," but rather required only "a short and plain statement of the claim that will give the defendant fair notice of what the plaintiff's claim is and the grounds upon which it rests." 355 U.S. 41, 47 (1957) (internal quotation marks and footnote omitted). Under *Conley*'s reading of Rule 8, for which the Court cited cases extending back to 1944, "a complaint **[—18—]** should not be dismissed for failure to state a claim unless it appears beyond doubt that the plaintiff can prove no set of facts in support of his claim which would entitle him to relief." *Id.* at 45-46.

Although Bensch continues to rely on the *Conley* formulation in support of his argument that even his initial complaint was sufficient, *see* Appellant's Br. 21, that philosophy of pleading was abandoned, and the *Conley* standard expressly disavowed, in *Twombly*, 550 U.S. at 560-63, in which the Supreme Court substituted a "plausibility" standard that requires civil complaints to plead not merely **{-79-}** legal conclusions but sufficient "factual content that allows the court to draw the reasonable inference" that the plaintiff is entitled to prevail on his claim. *Iqbal*, 556 U.S. at 678.

In *Colonial Sand*, Judge Hand ruled that there was no reason to read the language of what is now Supplemental Rule F(2) to adopt a different standard of pleading for maritime claims than the standard embodied in the Federal Rules of Civil Procedure for all civil complaints. 151 F.2d at 885. Accordingly, Judge Hand rejected the claimant's contention that the specific language of the Admiralty Rules, which required a description of the "facts and circumstances" warranting a finding that the petitioner lacked "privity and knowledge" of any negligence **[—19—]** resulting in the claimant's injuries, mandated that a maritime complaint contain *more* facts than what was required of a civil complaint under Federal Rule of Civil Procedure 8(a) as the courts then interpreted it. *Id.* Similarly, today we see no reason to interpret the language of Supplemental Rule F(2) to permit a complaint to proceed on *fewer* factual allegations than are required of a civil complaint under Rule 8(a) as the Supreme Court now reads it. To the contrary, the language of Rule F(2), which requires a recitation of "the facts on the basis of which the right to limit liability is asserted" is fully compatible with the emphasis on pleading concrete facts that was announced in *Twombly* and *Iqbal*.[9] Rule 8(a) of the Federal Rules of Civil Procedure, as interpreted in those cases, is fully consistent with the Supplemental Rules and thus applies in maritime cases under Supplemental Rule A(2). We therefore conclude that the district court was correct to hold that Supplemental Rule F(2) requires a vessel owner petitioning for exoneration from or limitation of liability to set forth sufficient facts to render his **[—20—]** claim of lack of "privity and knowledge" plausible as that phrase is defined in *Iqbal*.

IV. The Pleading Standard Applied

Applying the plausibility standard to the successive iterations of Bensch's complaint, we have little difficulty in affirming the district court's conclusion that his initial complaint and his First Proposed Amended Complaint were insufficient. As the magistrate judge stated in the first Report and Recommendation, while the factual allegations of the initial complaint "indicate that Umar was negligent, the Complaint contains no factual allegations showing that Bensch was not *also* negligent." App'x at 82. Although the conclusory disavowal of negligence in the initial complaint gives the Claimants notice of Bensch's assertion that he lacked "privity and knowledge" and therefore is entitled to exoneration from liability, App'x at 8 (¶ 6), the initial complaint contains no factual allegations that could render that assertion plausible. And the First Proposed

[9] *See* 5 Wright & Miller, Federal Practice and Procedure § 1227 (noting in general terms that while the pleading requirements of Rule 8 apply in admiralty and maritime claims, to the extent the Supplemental Rules apply in particular cases including claims for limitation of liability, "the effect of these provisions is to require a *higher* degree of specificity" than the standards applicable under the Civil Rules (emphasis added)).

Amended Complaint does nothing to address that problem: it adds a fact that plugs what is arguably a different hole in the initial complaint, *see supra* notes 4 and 6, but still pleads no facts that plausibly support Bensch's claim of lack of negligence. **[—21—]**

Bensch correctly points out that just as it is difficult to *prove* a negative, it is difficult to allege facts that would plausibly indicate a negative. But as the magistrate **{-80-}** judge observed, it is hardly impossible to imagine such facts:

> For example, an "important consideration in many collision cases is whether there was a failure to maintain safe speed and a proper lookout[."] 2 Schoenbaum, *Admiralty & Maritime Law* §14:3 (6th ed.). "The duty of the lookout is of the highest importance . . . . The rigor of the requirement rises according to the power and speed of the vessel in question." *The Ariadne*, 80 U.S. 475, 478-79 (1871). Bensch's Complaint contains no facts concerning the speed of his boat prior to the accident, or whether he observed Umar's reckless conduct in time to take evasive action.

App'x at 82-83. Allegations with respect to facts such as those specified by the magistrate judge may be sufficient to render a claim of lack of negligence plausible.

And indeed, Bensch then undertook, in his Second Proposed Amended Complaint, to allege such facts. As set forth above, Bensch proposed to add factual allegations that he was properly experienced in conditions on the waterway in question, that his vessel was properly maintained, that he kept a proper lookout, that he observed Umar on his jet ski, and that Umar's sudden **[—22—]** turn led him to take appropriate evasive action (although those efforts failed to avoid a collision).

It is true that those allegations could be more factually detailed. For example, as Claimants argue, the allegation that Bensch took "appropriate" evasive action is somewhat conclusory to the extent that it does not identify the particular actions that he took. Appellees Br. 11. Nor does Bensch specify the exact speed at which he was proceeding. But the plausibility standard does not require that a plaintiff plead every factual detail relevant to liability, or allege facts that, if proved to the factfinder's satisfaction, would rule out every possible defense to his claim. It is sufficient for the pleading to contain sufficient factual allegations to "nudge[ ] [the petitioner's] claims across the line from conceivable to plausible." *Twombly,* 550 U.S. at 570. We conclude that the Second Proposed Amended Complaint does just that.

V. The Second Motion to Amend

We review the denial of a motion for leave to amend for abuse of discretion. *Starr v. Sony BMG Music Ent.*, 592 F.3d 314, 321 (2d Cir. 2010). However, to the extent the denial of such a motion is based on futility, it rests on **[—23—]** a legal conclusion, which we review *de novo. Shimon v. Equifax Info. Servs. LLC*, 994 F.3d 88, 91 (2d Cir. 2021).

What we have already said is sufficient to overturn the district court's finding of futility as to Bensch's second motion for leave to amend and to file his Second Proposed Amended Complaint. The district court's holding in this regard is itself conclusory, offering no analysis of the additional allegations that Bensch proposed to include in his Second Proposed Amended Complaint and merely asserting that *both* proposed amended complaints "fail to set forth the substantive facts necessary to suggest absence of fault and make limitation of liability possible." App'x at 114. Nor did the magistrate judge, who recommended denial of Bensch's second motion for leave to amend on a different ground, find any fault with the legal sufficiency of the Second Proposed Amended Complaint. For the reasons set forth above, we conclude that Bensch's Second Proposed Amended Complaint was sufficient to plausibly state a claim upon which relief can be granted and that the district court exceeded its discretion in denying Bensch's second motion for leave to amend for futility. **{-81-}**

The magistrate judge's recommendation, adopted by the district court, that Bensch's second motion for leave to amend be denied on grounds of bad faith **[—24—]** presents a closer question. The magistrate judge was correct that Bensch did not suggest that he was unaware of the pleading requirements of Supplemental Rule F(2) and *Iqbal*. Moreover, the new facts alleged in the Second Proposed Amended Complaint were all within Bensch's personal knowledge when he initiated this action, and Bensch offered no excuse for his failure to include them in his initial complaint (or even in his First Proposed Amended Complaint), particularly after Claimants moved to dismiss on the grounds that the initial complaint failed to allege a factual basis for its assertion that Bensch had not been negligent. And as we have already ruled, the magistrate judge's determination that legal conclusions couched as factual allegations are not sufficient to plausibly state a claim upon which relief can be granted was indeed correct. We can sympathize, moreover, with the magistrate judge's frustration with Bensch's somewhat stiff-necked insistence on defending an outdated approach to pleading in the maritime context.

But we disagree with the magistrate judge's equation of Bensch's position on this point with "bad faith." Federal Rule of Civil Procedure 15(a) provides that courts should "freely give leave [to amend] when justice so requires." A district court may in its discretion deny leave to amend "for good reason, including **[—25—]** futility, bad faith, undue delay, or undue prejudice to the opposing party." *McCarthy v. Dun & Bradstreet Corp.*, 482 F.3d 184, 200 (2d Cir. 2007). Nothing in the record supports any implication that Bensch was either engaged in delay and imposing unnecessary additional litigation costs or inventing non-existent "facts" for which there was no good faith basis. *See, e.g., id.* at 201-02 (affirming district court's denial of leave to amend where "[p]laintiffs sought to amend their complaint after an inordinate delay" of "more than seven months" and where "discovery had closed, defendants had filed for summary judgment, and nearly two years had passed since the filing of the original complaint"). Rather than harboring some dilatory motive, it seems clear that Bensch was defending a legal proposition about the proper pleading standard in the maritime context that, while incorrect as we hold today, was believed in good faith by Bensch to be correct.

Nor can we dismiss Bensch's argument as to the proper pleading standard as frivolous. It was plausibly supported by decisions of several district courts, and by a reasonable if ahistorical reading of an opinion of this Court which, though old, has never been disavowed by subsequent binding authority. As explained above, we hold that Bensch misinterpreted that precedent. But the **[—26—]** analysis set forth in this Opinion was not articulated in the motion to dismiss and thus was not directly presented below. In a matter of some importance to the admiralty practice, we do not think counsel for Bensch acted in bad faith either in drafting the initial complaint, or in defending its sufficiency in response to Claimants' motion to dismiss.

Accordingly, we conclude that the district court exceeded its discretion in denying Bensch's second motion for leave to amend on the basis of bad faith.

CONCLUSION

For the reasons set forth above, we AFFIRM the judgment of the district court to the extent that it dismissed the initial complaint and denied Bensch's first motion for leave to amend, but we REVERSE the judgment to the extent it denied the second motion for leave to amend on grounds of futility and bad faith, **{-82-}** and REMAND the case for further proceedings consistent with this Opinion.

United States Court of Appeals
for the Second Circuit

No. 19-1076

CANGEMI
VS.
UNITED STATES

Appeal from the United States District Court for the Eastern District of New York

Decided: September 7, 2021

Citation: 13 F.4th 115, 9 Adm. R. 106 (2d Cir. 2021).

Before **RAGGI**, **SULLIVAN**, and **NARDINI**, Circuit Judges.

[—3—] **{-121-}** **SULLIVAN**, Circuit Judge:

Plaintiffs-Appellants, seaside property owners in the Town of East Hampton, New York ("Plaintiffs"), appeal from a final judgment of the district court in favor of Defendants-Appellees the United States and the Town of East Hampton (the "Town"). Plaintiffs challenge two decisions of the district court. In the first decision, the district court dismissed Plaintiffs' Federal Tort Claims Act **[—4—]** ("FTCA") claims against the United States for lack of subject matter jurisdiction on sovereign immunity grounds, citing the FTCA's discretionary function exception. *See Cangemi v. United States*, No. 12-cv-3989 (JS), 2017 WL 1274060, at *1 (E.D.N.Y. Mar. 31, 2017) ("*Cangemi III*"); Fed. R. Civ. P. 12(b)(1).[1] In the second, the district court **{-122-}** granted the Town's motion for judgment as a matter of law after trial on Plaintiffs' state-law private nuisance and trespass claims. *See Cangemi IV*, 374 F. Supp. 3d at 231, 239; Fed. R. Civ. P. 50(b). On appeal, Plaintiffs argue that (1) the FTCA's discretionary function exception does not apply to the federal government's management of the jetties abutting Lake Montauk Harbor; and (2) the Town was not entitled to judgment as a matter of law because, as the owner of the land underneath the jetties, it had a duty to mitigate erosion caused by those jetties. For the reasons set forth below, we reject these arguments and affirm the district court's judgment. **[—5—]**

I. BACKGROUND

A. Facts

1. The Jetties and Lake Montauk Harbor Federal Navigation Project

This case centers around two rock jetties standing at the mouth of Lake Montauk Harbor, which is located in the Town of East Hampton on the northern shore of the south fork of Long Island. The Lake Montauk Harbor jetties (the "Jetties") stabilize the inlet and provide access to the harbor, which houses a U.S. Coast Guard station and serves as the largest commercial fishing port in New York. The Jetties were first constructed in 1926 by a private development company managed by entrepreneur Carl Fisher, who owned much of the land surrounding Lake Montauk Harbor and used it primarily as a private yacht club.

Fisher's development company went into receivership during the Great Depression, so representatives from the Town of East Hampton urged the federal government to preserve access to the harbor. In response to these efforts, the U.S. Army Corps of Engineers ("USACE") surveyed the harbor and informed Congress that federal intervention to improve and maintain Lake Montauk Harbor was justified because it was the only harbor of refuge within fifty miles for large vessels navigating near the east end and South Fork of Long Island during rough weather, **[—6—]** and because the harbor benefitted the public by providing recreational and economic opportunities for the community. The USACE issued its recommendation to Congress in part because Fisher's development company had agreed to convey to the United States, free of charge, all

[1] Although Plaintiffs directly challenge only two of the district court's decisions, the district court issued four decisions involving the key issues on appeal: (1) *Cangemi v. United States*, 939 F. Supp. 2d 188 (E.D.N.Y. 2013) ("*Cangemi I*"); (2) *Cangemi v. United States*, No. 12-cv-3989 (JS), 2016 WL 915173 (E.D.N.Y. Mar. 7, 2016) ("*Cangemi II*"); (3) *Cangemi III*, 2017 WL 1274060; and (4) *Cangemi v. Town of East Hampton*, 374 F. Supp. 3d 227 (E.D.N.Y. 2019) ("*Cangemi IV*").

right of way to Lake Montauk Harbor, its bed, shores, and structures, and to dedicate them to permanent, public use as a navigable waterway.

To facilitate the federal government's involvement, in 1941, Fisher's development company transferred to the Town title to the Jetties and the land under Lake Montauk Harbor. In 1942, the Town then granted the federal government a permanent easement to use and develop the Jetties, the channel, and the waters of Lake Montauk Harbor as a Federal Navigation Project ("FNP"). The Town retained, and still retains, legal title to the Jetties and the land underneath Lake Montauk Harbor.

Congress formally approved the Lake Montauk Harbor FNP under the Rivers and Harbors Act of 1945. *See* Pub. L. No. 79-14, § 2, 59 Stat. 10, 13 (1945). As **{-123-}** an FNP, the Jetties, channel, and waters of Lake Montauk Harbor fell under the exclusive authority of the federal government. But in 1962, as a condition of continued federal involvement, the Town executed an "Assurance of Local **[—7—]** Cooperation" with the federal government, in which the Town reauthorized its 1942 easement and agreed to indemnify the federal government for "claims for damages that may occur from the construction and maintenance of the improvements" to Lake Montauk Harbor as part of the FNP. App'x at 4605.

Federal development of the harbor was completed in 1968, when the east and west Jetties were repaired and extended to their current lengths. Although the design of the Jetties has remained unchanged since 1968, the USACE repaired the eastern jetty in 1995 and performed periodic dredging of the Lake Montauk Harbor channel from 1966 to 2011. To this day, the USACE maintains the Jetties pursuant to the FNP; the Town does not control or manage them.

2. The 1991 Resolution and Reconnaissance Study

In 1991, the Senate Committee on Environmental and Public Works asked the USACE to "determin[e] if further improvements for navigation [were] advisable" in Lake Montauk Harbor. *Id.* at 385. As a general matter, when the USACE receives such congressional authority, it investigates possibilities for federal improvement and issues a "reconnaissance study," which is a preliminary **[—8—]** document stating whether federal interests exist in continuing to the next development phase—the issuance of a "feasibility study."[2]

In May 1995, the USACE completed the Lake Montauk Harbor Reconnaissance Study, which reported that navigation into Lake Montauk Harbor had become difficult due to deterioration of the east Jetty. The Reconnaissance Study recommended rehabilitating the Jetties, deepening the channel at the entrance to Lake Montauk Harbor, and using dredged and "bypassed" sand to replenish the shoreline to the west of the Jetties, which had experienced erosion.[3]

3. The Feasibility Cost Sharing Agreement

The USACE's 1995 Reconnaissance Study concluded that a feasibility study was needed to chart a course of action for rehabilitating Lake Montauk Harbor. In broad strokes, a feasibility study provides a detailed report of all engineering, design, and real estate activities required for a development project. *See* 33 U.S.C. § 2282(a)(2); *Army Corps of Engineers* at 11–12. Unlike a reconnaissance study, a **[—9—]** feasibility study is a complete decision document that presents a final recommendation to Congress. *Army Corps of Engineers* at 12. Congress may then accept or reject the USACE's recommendation, as only

---

[2] *See* Nicole T. Carter & Charles V. Stern, Cong. Rsch. Serv. R41243, *Army Corps of Engineers: Water Resource Authorizations, Appropriations, and Activities* 7–9 (2017) (hereinafter "*Army Corps of Engineers*").

[3] In this context, sand "dredging" referred to the removal of sand from the already-existing channel, while sand "bypassing" referred to the transportation of sand from the eastern shoreline to the western shoreline via truck, barge, or temporary hydraulic pipeline.

Congress has the final authority to approve and fund a project. *Id.*

The USACE cannot begin a feasibility study without a "feasibility cost sharing agreement" with a nonfederal sponsor that commits to sharing 50% of the cost of the study. *See* 33 U.S.C. § 2215(a)(1)(A). To **{-124-}** that end, in February 2002, the USACE entered into a feasibility cost sharing agreement (the "FCSA") with the New York State Department of Environmental Conservation. The FCSA provides, at Article II.A., that the USACE "shall expeditiously prosecute and complete the [Lake Montauk Harbor Feasibility] Study." App'x at 423. Further, Article X.A. of the FCSA states that either party may terminate the FCSA upon thirty days' written notice, and that upon such termination, "both parties shall conclude their activities relating to the [Feasibility] Study and proceed to a final accounting." *Id.* at 427. The preamble to the FCSA also specifies that nothing in the agreement "obligates either party to implement a project." *Id.* at 422. **[—10—]**

4. The Feasibility Scoping Meeting, 3x3x3 Paradigm, and DRAA

Progress on the Lake Montauk Harbor Feasibility Study ("LMH Study") slowed to a crawl in the years following the signing of the FCSA. Nevertheless, in September 2006, the USACE held a meeting for the LMH Study to explore different alternatives for the completed development project.

On February 8, 2012, Major General Michael J. Walsh, Deputy Commanding General for the USACE's Civil and Emergency Operations, issued a memorandum establishing the "3x3x3 Paradigm," which provided that certain USACE feasibility studies should be completed within three years, cost no more than three million dollars, and have three levels of review. Importantly, the 2012 memorandum made clear that the 3x3x3 Paradigm would apply only to feasibility studies that "ha[d] not reached a Feasibility Scoping Meeting (FSM) by 31 December 2011." *Id.* at 2053.

Anthony Ciorra, former Chief of the Civil Works Branch of the Programs and Project Management Division of the USACE New York District, testified that the September 2006 meeting for the LMH Study qualified as a "feasibility scoping meeting" within the meaning of the 3x3x3 Paradigm. *Id.* at 2046. Moreover, on April 3, 2014, the USACE updated its Lake Montauk Harbor Project Management **[—11—]** Plan to confirm that an "Alternatives" meeting – "another term used to refer to a feasibility scoping meeting" – had taken place in September 2006. *Id.* at 2047–48. Ciorra testified (and a strategy paper appended to the Project Management Plan confirmed) that, in light of the completion of this Feasibility Scoping Meeting prior to December 31, 2011, the LMH Study was "grandfathered" – *i.e.*, it was exempted from the requirements of the 3x3x3 Paradigm. *Id.* at 2046, 2048, 2061, 2094.

On January 29, 2013, Congress enacted the Disaster Relief Appropriations Act of 2013 ("DRAA"), which provided federal funding for various USACE feasibility studies, including the LMH Study, for projects that would help remediate damage caused by Superstorm Sandy. *See* Pub. L. No. 113-2, tit. II, 127 Stat. 4, 5 (2013). On April 13, 2015, Joseph Vietri, Chief of the Policy and Planning Division for the USACE North Atlantic Division, issued a memorandum setting "proposed . . . milestone" dates for feasibility studies "being conducted under the [DRAA]." App'x at 2101. Pursuant to this memorandum, the proposed completion date of the LMH Study was set for April 17, 2017. As of April 19, 2019 **[—12—]** —the date that Plaintiffs filed their Notice of Appeal—the final LMH Study Report had not yet been issued.[4] **{-125-}**

[4] According to the USACE's website, of which we may take judicial notice, *see 23-34 94th St. Grocery Corp. v. N.Y.C. Bd. of Health*, 685 F.3d 174, 183 n.7 (2d Cir. 2012), the USACE issued a draft feasibility report for public review in July 2019, and a final report was approved in February 2021. *See* USACE, *Fact Sheet – Lake Montauk Harbor Feasibility Study, NY*, USACE New York District Website (Apr. 9, 2021), https://www.nan.usace.army.mil/Media/Fact-Sheets/Fact-Sheet-Article-View/Article/487490/fact-sheet-lake-montauk-harbor-feasibility-study/.

5. The Lake Montauk Harbor Feasibility Study

During the course of its work on the LMH Study, the USACE considered twelve different options for improving the navigation into Lake Montauk Harbor and nine different options for reducing storm damage and shoreline erosion around Lake Montauk Harbor. The USACE rejected some of these alternatives for various reasons, including cost and efficacy. For instance, although the USACE appeared to recognize that the Jetties contributed to erosion on the western shoreline, it rejected a plan that would have addressed that erosion by modifying the Jetties. It explained that "[u]nless both Jetties are removed and [the] channel [is] closed, partial modification would not meet the purpose of restoring natural sediment transport . . . to prevent downdrift beach erosion." *Id.* at 482–83. The **[—13—]** USACE further noted that altering the Jetties would "contradict[] the navigation channel improvement purpose" of the plan. *Id.*

At a public meeting in March 2014, the USACE gave a presentation discussing three specific proposals for developing the Lake Montauk Harbor FNP. One option was to take no action. *Id.* at 509. "Alternative 1" was a "Navigation Only Plan," which involved deepening the channel, placing the dredged material on the western shoreline, and dredging on a five-year cycle, for a total cost of approximately $26 million. *Id.* at 510, 513. Another option, "Alternative 2," was a "Navigation and Coastal Storm Risk Management Plan," which involved all of the development under Alternative 1 but also included bypassing approximately 230,000 cubic yards of sand to address erosion on the western shoreline and continued sand bypassing on a regular basis. *Id.* at 511. Alternative 2 had an estimated cost of $41 million. *Id.* at 513.

6. The Town's Efforts to Mitigate Erosion

As discussed above, once the Town ceded control of the Jetties to the USACE, it no longer managed the Jetties themselves or the navigable waters of Lake Montauk Harbor. The Town did, however, recognize that the Jetties appeared to cause erosion to the shoreline to the west of the Jetties. As early as **[—14—]** 1994, Town representatives wrote to the USACE requesting the federal government's assistance in addressing "the severe downdrift scouring caused by the Federal jetties." *Id.* at 4617. And the Town undertook its own efforts to address erosion, including a Local Waterfront Revitalization Program ("LWRP"). The final LWRP report, approved by the New York Secretary of State in 2007, acknowledged that the Jetties caused "downdrift scouring" to the beaches along Soundview Drive to the west of the Jetties. *Id.* at 6062.

Consistent with the observations made in the LWRP report, the Town also proposed a sand bypass plan to address erosion to the west of the Jetties. Under that proposal, the Town would transport 5,000 to 10,000 cubic yards of surplus sand from the Town-owned portion of Gin Beach (east of the Jetties) to the eroded Soundview Drive shoreline to the west. This sand bypass plan progressed to the point that the Town Board approved resolutions to proceed with the project, and permits were obtained to perform the work. Town representatives **{-126-}** also attended meetings with state representatives regarding other sand bypass options that would not require federal involvement. Ultimately, however, the Town never commenced any of these sand bypass projects. **[—15—]**

B. Procedural History

1. State Court Action and *Cangemi I*

The parties' long-winding litigation began in January 2011, when Plaintiffs, a group of Montauk residents owning property west of the Jetties, sued the Town, Suffolk County, the State of New York, and several New York state officials in New York state court. The Plaintiffs asserted various state common-law claims, as well as state and federal constitutional claims, all premised on the erosion caused by the Jetties and the Town's and New York's failure to mitigate that erosion. On February 17, 2012, the New York Supreme Court dismissed Plaintiffs' state complaint on the ground that the United States was a necessary party because it was "the entity that performed the repairs and extensions of the [J]etties pursuant to the [FNP] and would be involved in mitigation measures." *Cangemi v. Town of East Hampton*, 2012 N.Y. Slip Op. 30538(U), at 4 (Sup. Ct. Feb. 17, 2012).

Plaintiffs then commenced this action in federal court against the Town and the United States on June 14, 2012.[5] In their operative Amended Complaint, filed **[—16—]** September 14, 2012, Plaintiffs asserted three claims relevant to this appeal. First, Plaintiffs alleged that both the Town and the United States were liable for private nuisance, under New York law, on the theory that the Jetties (owned by the Town and controlled by the federal government) interrupted "the natural east-to-west littoral movement of . . . sand," resulting in severe erosion to Plaintiffs' properties. App'x at 53. Second, Plaintiffs alleged that—for essentially the same reasons—"[t]he design, construction, maintenance[,] and continued presence of the Jetties constitute[d] . . . an absolute public nuisance." *Id.* at 59. Third, Plaintiffs alleged that the Town and the United States were liable for trespass, under New York law, on the theory that the Jetties caused the "unauthorized entry and acceleration of waters" onto Plaintiffs' property.[6] *Id.* at 64. **[—17—]**

On August 27, 2012, the Town moved to dismiss Plaintiffs' amended complaint.[7] As relevant to this appeal, the Town argued that Plaintiffs failed to plausibly allege **{–127–}** their private nuisance claim because they made no allegations that the Town had (1) acted intentionally to create erosion on Plaintiffs' properties or (2) acted negligently, since the Town had no duty to mitigate the effects of the Jetties that were operated entirely by the federal government. The Town also argued that Plaintiffs failed to properly plead their trespass claim because they failed to allege the requisite level of intent to give rise to a trespass.

In a March 29, 2013 memorandum and order, the district court denied the Town's motion to dismiss Plaintiffs' private nuisance, public nuisance, and trespass claims. *Cangemi I*, 939 F. Supp. 2d at 205–07. In pertinent part, the district court held that Plaintiffs plausibly alleged that the Town had engaged in intentional or negligent conduct with respect to the Jetties, such that the Town could be liable for nuisance and trespass. *Id.* at 198, 203–05. Moreover, the district court rejected the Town's argument that it did not have a duty to mitigate the **[—18—]** effects of the Jetties, reasoning that, as alleged in the amended complaint, the Town was more than "a mere instrumentality" of the federal government in managing the Jetties. *Id.* at 205 n.9 (internal quotation marks omitted).[8]

---

[5] Plaintiffs also named as defendants the State of New York, Suffolk County, several New York state officials, a Town official, the USACE, and a USACE official, but those additional defendants were subsequently dismissed from the case (either by stipulation or by order of the district court), and Plaintiffs do not challenge those dismissals on appeal. In addition, while Plaintiffs originally **[—16—]** filed their complaint in the Southern District of New York, the parties agreed to transfer the case to the Eastern District of New York in August 2012.

[6] Plaintiffs also alleged additional claims against the Town and the United States that are not directly at issue in this appeal, including: (1) New York common-law claims for (a) negligence, (b) unjust enrichment, and (c) appropriation of resources; (2) denial of due process under the U.S. Constitution; (3) denial of equal protection under the U.S. Constitution; (4) unlawful taking of property under the U.S. Constitution; (5) unlawful taking of property under the New York Constitution; and (6) as to the United States only, violation of the Administrative Procedure Act.

[7] More precisely, the Town moved to dismiss Plaintiffs' *original* complaint, but because Plaintiffs' amended complaint did not substantially alter the claims against the Town, the parties agreed—and the district court ordered—that the Town's motion to dismiss would be applied to the amended complaint.

[8] In that same decision, the district court dismissed several of Plaintiffs' other claims – including their federal takings, due process, and equal protection claims – on the ground that they were barred by the relevant statutes of limitations. *See id.* at 199–201.

2. *Cangemi II* and *III*

On March 6, 2015, the United States filed a motion to dismiss for lack of subject matter jurisdiction, asserting that Plaintiffs' claims against it were barred by the doctrine of sovereign immunity. Specifically, the United States argued that Plaintiffs' tort claims (including their private nuisance and trespass claims) fell within the FTCA's discretionary function exception, meaning that the United States had not waived its sovereign immunity as to such claims. The United States argued that the USACE was not subject to any mandatory directive prescribing a certain course of conduct with respect to the Jetties or the Lake Montauk Harbor FNP, and that the USACE's management of the Jetties was grounded in questions of public policy – the two elements necessary to satisfy the discretionary function exception. **[—19—]**

Initially, the district court denied the United States' motion to dismiss in a March 7, 2016 memorandum and order. *Cangemi II*, 2016 WL 915173, at *7. The court agreed with the United States that the USACE's management of the Jetties (including the LMH Study) was "either grounded in policy concerns or, at the very least, susceptible to policy analysis." *Id.* at *5 n.4. But the court concluded that the discretionary function exception did not apply because both the 3x3x3 Paradigm and the LMH Study FCSA "provide[d] a prescribed course of action"—specifically, that the USACE was required to complete the LMH Study within a certain timeframe so that the federal government could respond to the erosion caused by the Jetties. *Id.* at *6–7 (internal quotation marks and alterations omitted).

One year later, however, the district court reversed course. After the United States submitted a motion for reconsideration pointing to evidence in the record that the district court had overlooked, the court granted the United States' motion to dismiss for lack of subject matter jurisdiction. *Cangemi III*, 2017 WL 1274060, at *3–4. Although the court acknowledged that it had already concluded, in *Cangemi II*, that the USACE's actions were susceptible to a **{-128-}** policy analysis, it conceded that it had "overlooked the FCSA's termination provision" and other language in the FCSA showing that the FCSA did not impose a mandatory directive. *Id.* at *4. The **[—20—]** court also recognized that new materials submitted with the United States' motion (including an affidavit from Anthony Ciorra) made clear that the USACE *had* held a "Feasibility Scoping Meeting" before December 31, 2011, thereby exempting the LMH Study from the 3x3x3 Paradigm. *Id.* at *7. Accordingly, because *Cangemi II* had relied on the FCSA and the 3x3x3 Paradigm as the only sources of mandatory directives imposed on the USACE concerning the Jetties, the district court dismissed Plaintiffs' tort claims against the United States on sovereign immunity grounds. *Id.* at *4.

In the same decision, the district court nevertheless denied the Town's motion for summary judgment on Plaintiffs' private and public nuisance and trespass claims. *Id.* at *10–11. Relying extensively on the reasoning from *Cangemi I*, in which it had denied the Town's motion to dismiss, the court concluded that Plaintiffs' claims against the Town could not "be resolved as a matter of law at [that] stage." *Id.* at *11.

3. Trial and *Cangemi IV*

Plaintiffs' state-law private nuisance, public nuisance, and trespass claims against the Town proceeded to trial from June 4 to June 29, 2018. *Cangemi IV*, 374 F. Supp. 3d at 232. At the close of Plaintiffs' case and again at the close of the **[—21—]** Town's case, the Town moved for judgment as a matter of law pursuant to Federal Rule of Civil Procedure 50(a) on the grounds that (1) it had no duty to remediate the effects of the Jetties because it lacked control over the Jetties; and (2) it engaged in no intentional conduct that could give rise to liability for nuisance or trespass. *Id.* at 232, 235. The district court reserved decision on the motions and submitted the case to the jury. *Id.* at 232. The jury found for Plaintiffs on their claims for private nuisance and trespass, found for the Town on the public nuisance claim, and awarded Plaintiffs $355,961.27 in compensatory damages. *Id.*

After the verdict, the Town renewed its motion for judgment as a matter of law pursuant to Federal Rule of Civil Procedure 50(b) and, alternatively, moved for a new trial pursuant to Rule 59. *Id.*

In a March 15, 2019 memorandum and order, the district court granted the Town's renewed motion for judgment as a matter of law. *Id.* at 231, 238. Although "mindful" of its prior orders, in which it had stated "that Plaintiffs had 'at least plausibly suggested that [the Town] can maintain the Jetties without creating a nuisance or trespass by remedial actions,'" *id.* at 234 (quoting *Cangemi I*, 939 F. Supp. 2d at 198); *see also Cangemi III*, 2017 WL 1274060, at *8, the district court concluded that "the evidence at trial . . . convinced th[e] [c]ourt that the Town **[—22—]** simply could not and did not exercise control over the [J]etties sufficient to impose liability on it." *Cangemi IV*, 374 F. Supp. 3d at 234.

With respect to Plaintiffs' private nuisance claim, the district court held that, because the Town lacked control over the Jetties, Plaintiffs could not show the necessary intent or causation to prove an intentional private nuisance, since the Town was a "mere instrumentality" of the USACE and did not actually maintain the Jetties. *Id.* at 235 (internal quotation marks omitted). And although the court recognized that the *failure* to act can in some circumstances give rise to nuisance liability under New York law, such liability was inappropriate in this case because the Town was under no legal duty to act given its lack of **{-129-}** control over the Jetties. *Id.* at 236. The court similarly concluded that, because the Town had no duty to act, Plaintiffs could not show *negligent* private nuisance. *Id.* at 237.

With respect to Plaintiffs' trespass claim, the district court again focused on the Town's lack of intentional conduct concerning the Jetties, explaining that because "the Town did not act intentionally and willfully or negligently . . . , no **[—23—]** reasonable fact-finder could have found it liable for the intrusion of water upon Plaintiffs' property." *Id.* at 238.[9]

Following the district court's decision and entry of the final judgment, Plaintiffs filed a timely notice of appeal.

II. DISCUSSION

On appeal, Plaintiffs principally challenge two of the district court's decisions. First, they contend that the district court erred when it dismissed their tort claims against the United States on sovereign immunity grounds, arguing that those claims are not barred by the FTCA's discretionary function exception. Second, they argue that the district court improperly granted the Town's renewed motion for judgment as a matter of law because Plaintiffs' private nuisance and trespass claims were established at trial through evidence showing that the Town knew of harm caused by the Jetties but failed to remediate that harm, and through evidence showing that the Town authorized the building of the Jetties and derived a benefit from them. We address each of these challenges in turn. **[—24—]**

A. Plaintiffs' Claims Against the United States

On appeal from a dismissal pursuant to Rule 12(b)(1), including on sovereign immunity grounds, we review a district court's legal conclusions *de novo* and factual findings for clear error.[10] *See Makarova v. United*

---

[9] In the alternative, the district court granted the Town's motion for a new trial. *Id.* at 238. Essentially for the same reasons that it granted the Town's renewed motion for judgment as a matter of law, the court concluded that "the verdict was against the weight of the evidence" because "[t]he Town did not control the [J]etties, could not and did not engage in conduct, and lacked the requisite intent." *Id.*

[10] As a technical matter, Plaintiffs challenge the district court's grant of the United States' motion for reconsideration, a decision we have previously reviewed for abuse of discretion. *See Shrader v. CSX Transp., Inc.*, 70 F.3d 255, 257 (2d Cir. 1995). But because an error of law constitutes an abuse of discretion, *see RJE Corp. v. Northville Indus. Corp.*, 329 F.3d 310, 316 (2d Cir. 2003), and

States, 201 F.3d 110, 113 (2d Cir. 2000). "In resolving a motion to dismiss for lack of subject matter jurisdiction under Rule 12(b)(1), a district court . . . may refer to evidence outside the pleadings." *Id.*

"Absent an unequivocally expressed statutory waiver, the United States . . . [is] immune from suit based on the principle of sovereign immunity." *County of Suffolk v. Sebelius*, 605 F.3d 135, 140 (2d Cir. 2010) (internal quotation marks omitted). The FTCA provides for a limited waiver of sovereign immunity for "injury or loss of property . . . caused by the negligent or wrongful act or omission" **{-130-}** of a federal government employee "acting within the scope of his office or **[—25—]** employment." 28 U.S.C. § 1346(b)(1). But the FTCA is limited by a number of exceptions, including the so-called "discretionary function exception," which bars "[a]ny claim . . . based upon the exercise or performance or the failure to exercise or perform a discretionary function or duty on the part of a federal agency or an employee of the Government, whether or not the discretion involved be abused." 28 U.S.C. § 2680(a). Thus, for acts that fall under the discretionary function exception, the United States has not waived its sovereign immunity, and federal courts lack subject matter jurisdiction over claims premised on those acts. *See Fazi v. United States*, 935 F.2d 535, 537 (2d Cir. 1991).

The Supreme Court has developed a two-part framework, known as the "*Berkovitz/Gaubert*" test, for determining whether the discretionary function exception applies to a given claim. *See United States v. Gaubert*, 499 U.S. 315, 322–23 (1991); *Berkovitz v. United States*, 486 U.S. 531, 536–37 (1988). Under the *Berkovitz/Gaubert* test, the discretionary function exception bars a claim where "(1) the acts alleged to be negligent [or wrongful] . . . [are] discretionary, in that they involve an element of judgment or choice and are not compelled by statute or regulation and (2) the judgment or choice in question [is] . . . grounded in **[—26—]** considerations of public policy or susceptible to policy analysis." *Coulthurst v. United States*, 214 F.3d 106, 109 (2d Cir. 2000) (internal quotation marks omitted).

Because plaintiffs bear the initial burden of showing that their claims against the United States fall within the FTCA's limited waiver of sovereign immunity, plaintiffs also bear the initial burden of showing that their claims are not barred by the discretionary function exception. *See Molchatsky v. United States*, 713 F.3d 159, 162 (2d Cir. 2013) (citing *Gaubert*, 499 U.S. at 324–25). Plaintiffs can overcome a motion to dismiss premised on the discretionary function exception by showing that *either* (1) the United States' allegedly tortious act (or failure to act) was inconsistent with a "specific mandatory directive"—*i.e.*, a "federal statute, regulation, or policy [that] specifically prescribes a course of action for [the federal government] to follow," *Berkovitz*, 486 U.S. at 536, 544; *or* (2) the allegedly tortious "judgment or choice in question" is not "grounded in considerations of public policy or susceptible to policy analysis," *Coulthurst*, 214 F.3d at 109 (internal quotation marks omitted).

Here, Plaintiffs challenge the district court's dismissal of their claims against the United States on both grounds. First, Plaintiffs argue that the USACE was subject to and violated two sources of mandatory directives: (1) the FCSA and **[—27—]** (2) the 3x3x3 Paradigm. Plaintiffs contend that both of these directives required the USACE to conduct the LMH Study within a prescribed timeframe, and that the USACE failed to complete the LMH Study within that timeframe. Second, Plaintiffs argue that the extensive and unjustified delays associated with the LMH Study were not grounded in considerations of public policy. But as the district court correctly concluded, neither the

---

because Plaintiffs challenge the district court's dismissal under 12(b)(1), not its decision to reconsider its earlier order, we review the district court's dismissal *de novo*, *cf.*, *e.g.*, *Bayerische Landesbank v. Aladdin Cap. Mgmt. LLC*, 692 F.3d 42, 52 n.3 (2d Cir. 2012) (declining to review district court's order denying a motion for reconsideration for abuse of discretion because that decision was "essentially an affirmance" of the district court's prior ruling "on the merits" (internal quotation marks omitted)).

FCSA nor the 3x3x3 Paradigm actually imposed upon the USACE a mandatory timeline for completing the LMH Study. *See Cangemi III*, 2017 WL 1274060, at *4. And while Plaintiffs are correct that the LMH Study experienced significant (and largely unexplained) delays, the district court properly recognized that the USACE was afforded substantial discretion in undertaking that feasibility study and managing the FNP at **{-131-}** Lake Montauk Harbor—including the discretion *not* to take any action to mitigate the adverse effects of the Jetties. *See id.*; *Cangemi II*, 2016 WL 915173, at *5 n.4. Accordingly, the district court correctly found that both parts of the *Berkovitz/Gaubert* test were satisfied and properly dismissed Plaintiffs' FTCA claims against the United States.

1. Neither the FCSA nor the 3x3x3 Paradigm imposes a mandatory directive.

Though Plaintiffs look to the FCSA as the source of a mandatory directive, the very first section of that agreement makes clear that "entering into this **[—28—]** Agreement in no way obligates either" the State of New York or the federal government "to implement a project," and that "whether the [federal government] supports a project authorization and budgets it for implementation depends upon, among other things, the outcome of the [LMH] Study and whether the proposed solution is consistent with the . . . budget priorities of the Administration." App'x at 422. Article X.A. of the FCSA also provides that the federal government can terminate or suspend the agreement at any point prior to submitting the "feasibility report to the Office of Management and Budget" upon thirty days' written notice. *Id.* at 422, 427. Upon such termination, "both parties shall conclude their activities relating to the [LMH] Study and proceed to a final accounting . . . ." *Id.* at 427. These provisions in the FCSA reveal that the federal government was free to walk away from the LMH Study at any point.

Plaintiffs' sole argument for a mandatory directive in the FCSA comes from Article II.A., which provides that the federal government "shall expeditiously prosecute and complete the [LMH] Study." *Id.* at 423. The district court correctly rejected this argument for two key reasons. First, the term "expeditiously" is "undefined and does not constitute a fixed or readily ascertainable standard to prevent the government's conduct from falling into the discretionary function **[—29—]** exception." *Cangemi III*, 2017 WL 1274060, at *4 n.7 (internal quotation marks, alterations, and emphasis omitted). Indeed, Plaintiffs do not point to any specified time at which their claims premised on the FCSA accrued.

Second, Plaintiffs' reading of Article II.A. imposes an artificial obligation on the USACE to actually *complete* the LMH Study, which directly conflicts with the FCSA's preamble and Article X.A. Under Plaintiffs' theory, the USACE was under a mandatory duty to complete the LMH Study (in some "expeditious[]" yet undesignated timeframe), even though the USACE was explicitly under no obligation to complete any final project and could terminate the FCSA—automatically triggering the end of the LMH Study—upon thirty days' written notice. Plaintiffs' narrow reading of Article II.A. thus ignores the substantial discretion afforded to the USACE by the rest of the FCSA, and the district court properly held that the FCSA did not give rise to a mandatory directive.

Plaintiffs' arguments premised on the USACE's 3x3x3 Paradigm policy fare no better. The 3x3x3 Paradigm imposed a three-year timeline for the feasibility studies to which it applied, but the memorandum announcing the 3x3x3 Paradigm explicitly stated that this timeline applied only to "feasibility studies that have *not* reached a Feasibility Scoping Meeting . . . by 31 December 2011." App'x at 2053 **[—30—]** (emphasis added). As part of its motion to dismiss Plaintiffs' action for lack of subject matter jurisdiction, the United States submitted an undisputed declaration by Anthony Ciorra, an updated Lake Montauk Harbor Project Management Plan, and a **{-132-}** USACE strategy paper appended to that Plan, all making clear that the "Feasibility Scoping Meeting" for the LMH Study occurred in September 2006. *See id.* at

2046–48, 2061, 2084, 2094. The materials submitted with the United States' motion to dismiss thus reflect that the LMH Study did not violate the 3x3x3 Paradigm because it was "grandfathered" and therefore exempt. *Id.* at 2094.

Plaintiffs argue that the Ciorra declaration is "self-serving" and should not have been credited by the district court. But while the declaration was surely "self-serving" in the sense that it supported the United States' contention that the district court lacked subject matter jurisdiction, it was supported by references to the updated Lake Montauk Harbor Project Management Plan, the internal USACE strategy paper, and Ciorra's prior deposition testimony. After the United States presented this evidence supporting its motion to dismiss, it was *Plaintiffs'* burden to come forward with evidence supporting their assertion of jurisdiction. *See Carter v. HealthPort Techs., LLC*, 822 F.3d 47, 57 (2d Cir. 2016) (explaining that when plaintiffs oppose a motion to dismiss for lack of subject matter jurisdiction **[—31—]** supported by evidence outside the pleadings, they "need to come forward with evidence of their own to controvert that presented by the defendant if the affidavits submitted on a 12(b)(1) motion reveal the existence of factual problems in the assertion of jurisdiction" (internal quotation marks and alterations omitted)). Because they did not do so, the district court was entitled to rely on the Ciorra declaration, which conclusively establishes that the LMH Study was exempt from the strictures of the 3x3x3 Paradigm.[11]

2. The LMH Study is susceptible to policy analysis.

The district court also correctly held that the United States satisfied the second prong of the *Berkovitz/Gaubert* test because the LMH Study—along with the USACE's management of the FNP at Lake Montauk Harbor—is "susceptible to policy analysis." *Gaubert*, 499 U.S. at 325. Congress has enumerated a multitude of policy concerns that must be balanced in any USACE feasibility study, including **[—32—]** "the economic, environmental, and social benefits and detriments of the recommended plan and alternative plans considered by the Secretary and . . . the public acceptability, and the purposes, scope, and scale of the recommended plan." 33 U.S.C. § 2282(a)(2). Moreover, as the district court recognized, decisions regarding whether to ultimately approve and fund a given FNP are grounded in policy and thus are exclusively for Congress. *See Cangemi II*, 2016 WL 915173, at *3 ("[T]he decision to approve a USACE project is for Congress, not the judiciary." (citing *County of Vernon v. United States*, 933 F.2d 532, 535 (7th Cir. 1991)). Accordingly, the USACE's management of the **{-133-}** Lake Montauk Harbor FNP and the LMH Study are clearly susceptible to policy analysis.

Plaintiffs appear to argue that, even though these authorities granted the USACE broad discretion in conducting the LMH Study and operating the Lake Montauk Harbor FNP, the United States cannot satisfy the second prong of the *Berkovitz/Gaubert* test because the USACE *in this case* did not actually undertake a policy analysis in declining to abate the erosion caused by the Jetties in a timely manner. The record evidence undermines the assertion that the USACE failed to undertake a policy analysis in this case: the USACE weighed at least twelve different alternatives for improving navigation into Lake Montauk Harbor and **[—33—]** presented three of those in a public

[11] To the extent that Appellants argue that the LMH Study was subject to a mandatory deadline by virtue of the April 2015 USACE memorandum that set "start and end milestone dates" for the LMH Study pursuant to the DRAA, App'x at 2101–03, we also reject that memorandum as a source of a mandatory directive. Appellants appear to conflate the 3x3x3 Paradigm with the separate timeline established in the April 2015 memorandum. But putting that confusion aside, neither the DRAA nor the 2015 memorandum imposed a *mandatory* timeline for completion of the LMH Study. The 2015 memorandum merely established "proposed . . . milestone[s]" for completion. *Id.* at 2101. Accordingly, Appellants have not met their burden of showing that the deadlines imposed by this 2015 memorandum were mandatory rather than "involv[ing] an element of judgment or choice." *Coulthurst*, 214 F.3d at 109 (internal quotation marks omitted).

meeting in March 2014. *See* App'x at 478–83, 509. One of the three "Alternatives" presented at the meeting was to take no action to expand the FNP at Lake Montauk Harbor or to mitigate the effects of the erosion caused by the Jetties. *See id.* at 509. As noted above, the discretionary function exception applies not only where the federal government has *actually* undertaken a public policy analysis, but also where the decision at issue is merely "*susceptible* to policy analysis." *Gaubert*, 499 U.S. at 325 (emphasis added). Thus, even if the USACE had failed to engage in a policy analysis here, the broad discretion afforded to the USACE in undertaking the LMH, alone, is enough to satisfy the second prong of the *Berkovitz/Gaubert* test.

In sum, because neither the FCSA nor the 3x3x3 Paradigm prescribes a specific course of action abridging the USACE's broad discretion in carrying out the LMH Study, and because that study and the Lake Montauk Harbor FNP are clearly susceptible to policy analysis, Plaintiffs' FTCA claims against the United States were properly dismissed under the discretionary function exception.[12] **[—34—]**

B. Plaintiffs' Claims Against the Town

1. The district court had subject matter jurisdiction over Plaintiffs' state-law claims.

Before addressing the merits of the district court's decision to grant judgment as a matter of law to the Town on Plaintiffs' state-law claims, we must first determine whether the district court properly exercised jurisdiction over those claims after it dismissed the last of Plaintiffs' claims against the United States in 2017. Although neither Plaintiffs nor the Town challenges the district court's jurisdiction in this regard, "[e]very federal appellate court has a special obligation to satisfy itself not only of its own jurisdiction, but also that of the lower courts in a cause under review." *Cohen v. Postal Holdings, LLC*, 873 F.3d 394, 398 (2d Cir. 2017) (internal quotation marks omitted).

Here, Plaintiffs' assertion of subject matter jurisdiction over Plaintiffs' state-law claims against the Town appears to be premised on the existence of supplemental jurisdiction under **{-134-}** 28 U.S.C. § 1367(a).[13] Ordinarily, where a plaintiff **[—35—]** has asserted one or more federal claims pursuant to 28 U.S.C. § 1331, we review a district court's exercise of supplemental jurisdiction over additional state-law claims only for abuse of discretion. *See Lundy v. Cath. Health Sys. of Long Island Inc.*, 711 F.3d 106, 117–18 (2d Cir. 2013). This is true even where a district court exercises supplemental jurisdiction after dismissing all federal claims in a case on the merits. *See Kroshnyi v. U.S. Pack Courier Servs.*, 771 F.3d 93, 102 (2d Cir. 2014). Where a district court dismisses all federal claims under Rule 12(b)(1) of the Federal Rules of Civil Procedure, however, the district court is *precluded* from exercising supplemental jurisdiction over the remaining state-law claims. *See Cohen*, 873 F.3d at 399. This is

---

[12] Because we conclude that the district court properly dismissed Plaintiffs' claims against the United States under the discretionary function exception, we do not reach the United States' alternative argument that the district court also lacked subject matter jurisdiction over Plaintiffs' claims under the FTCA's "private analogue" requirement, 28 U.S.C. §§ 1346(b)(1), 2674, which bars claims "based on governmental action of the type that private persons could not engage in **[—34—]** and hence could not be liable for under local law." *Liranzo v. United States*, 690 F.3d 78, 86 (2d Cir. 2012) (internal quotation marks omitted).

[13] Neither Plaintiffs' amended complaint nor any of the district court's decisions cites to a specific statutory basis for subject matter jurisdiction over the Plaintiffs' state-law claims against the Town. While those claims could sound in diversity if Plaintiffs were all residents of states other than New York—after all, it is at least conceivable that the properties in question were all summer **[—35—]** homes and that none of the Plaintiffs were New York residents—Plaintiffs' amended complaint appears to foreclose such a scenario, as it states that Plaintiff Robin Racanelli "maintains a residence located in New York County, New York." App'x at 44. Because we conclude that the district court properly exercised supplemental jurisdiction over Plaintiffs' state-law claims against the Town, however, we need not determine whether the district court also could have exercised jurisdiction over those claims under 28 U.S.C. § 1332.

because, under the supplemental jurisdiction statute, "a district court cannot exercise supplemental jurisdiction unless there is first a proper basis for original federal jurisdiction." *Id.* (internal quotation marks omitted); *see also* 28 U.S.C. § 1367(a) (conferring supplemental jurisdiction "in any civil action of which the district courts have original jurisdiction"). **[—36—]**

Thus, while it ordinarily "makes little practical difference whether the district court labels its dismissal of an action as one for lack of subject matter jurisdiction under Rule 12(b)(1) or for failure to state a claim under 12(b)(6)," the distinction matters in cases like this one where a district court decides to retain jurisdiction over state-law claims after dismissing all federal claims. *Cohen*, 873 F.3d at 399 (internal quotation marks and alterations omitted). Because the district court dismissed Plaintiffs' tort claims against the United States in *Cangemi III* on sovereign immunity grounds, that was a jurisdictional dismissal under Rule 12(b)(1). *See Makarova*, 201 F.3d at 113. Were these claims the only ones purportedly giving rise to supplemental jurisdiction, the district court therefore would have been powerless to retain jurisdiction over Plaintiffs' remaining state-law claims against the Town. *See Cohen*, 873 F.3d at 399.

In an earlier decision, however, the district court dismissed several other federal claims raised by Plaintiffs (against both the Town and the United States) because they were barred by the statute of limitations applicable to 42 U.S.C. § 1983. *See Cangemi I*, 939 F. Supp. 2d at 199–201; *see also supra* note 8. Although the district court did not specify whether it was dismissing those claims under Rule 12(b)(1) or 12(b)(6), the law is clear that "[w]here the dates in a complaint **[—37—]** show that an action is barred by a statute of limitations," a motion to dismiss based on the statute of limitations is properly treated as one under Rule 12(b)(6) rather than Rule 12(b)(1). *Ghartey v. St. John's Queens Hosp.*, 869 F.2d 160, 162 (2d Cir. 1989); *see also Harris v. City of New York*, 186 F.3d 243, 247–51 (2d Cir. 1999) (examining motion to dismiss § 1983 claims on **{-135-}** statute-of-limitations grounds as one brought under Rule 12(b)(6)). Here, the district court dismissed Plaintiffs' § 1983 claims under the applicable statute of limitations by looking solely to the allegations appearing on the face of Plaintiffs' amended complaint, *see Cangemi I*, 939 F. Supp. 2d at 199–201, so the dismissal is properly treated as one under 12(b)(6). Accordingly, because there was no *jurisdictional* defect with those initial federal claims against the Town (as there was with Plaintiffs' tort claims against the United States that were barred by the discretionary function exception), the district court was not precluded from exercising supplemental jurisdiction over Plaintiffs' state-law claims against the Town. *See Cohen*, 873 F.3d at 400.

Of course, the fact that the district court was not *precluded* from exercising supplemental jurisdiction over Plaintiffs' state-law claims against the Town does not necessarily mean that it did not abuse its discretion in doing so. *See Cohen*, 873 F.3d at 404 (Calabresi, J., concurring) (explaining that, "after all federal claims have **[—38—]** been dismissed, the default rule is that federal courts should not decide related state-law claims unless there is good reason for doing so"). But we find no such abuse of discretion here because of the district court's long history with this case and familiarity with the issues by the time it dismissed Plaintiffs' claims against the United States in *Cangemi III*. *See Kroshnyi*, 771 F.3d at 102 (holding that the district court did not abuse its discretion in exercising supplemental jurisdiction, given "the advanced state of the litigation and the [district] [c]ourt's long familiarity with the issues in the case, combined with the likely hardship to both parties should plaintiff be forced to re-file in state court" (internal quotation marks omitted)).

We emphasize, however, that litigants should be diligent in establishing a firm basis for the district court's jurisdiction throughout *all* stages of a case, lest they risk needless and expensive litigation on the merits of an issue that no longer belongs in federal court (or never did in the first instance). "Federal courts are not courts of general jurisdiction," *Bender v. Williamsport Area Sch. Dist.*, 475 U.S. 534, 541 (1986), and district courts "lack the power to disregard such limits as have been imposed by the Constitution or Congress," *Durant, Nichols, Houston, Hodgson, & Cortese-Costa, P.C. v. Dupont*, 565 F.3d 56, 62 (2d Cir. 2009). Here, but for the **[—39—]** district court's earlier exercise of original jurisdiction over Plaintiffs' federal claims—which were eventually dismissed on statute-of-limitations grounds—the district court would have been powerless to retain jurisdiction over Plaintiffs' state-law claims against the Town following *Cangemi III*, and we would be similarly barred from considering the parties' arguments regarding the merits of those claims.

2. The district court properly granted the Town's renewed motion for judgment as a matter of law.

Having determined that the district court properly exercised supplemental jurisdiction over Plaintiffs' state-law claims against the Town, we now turn to the merits of Plaintiffs' challenge to the district court's order granting judgment to the Town as a matter of law on those claims. We review *de novo* a district court's resolution of a renewed motion for judgment as a matter of law under Federal Rule of Civil Procedure 50(b), considering the evidence in the light most favorable to the non-moving party and "giving that party the benefit of all reasonable inferences that the jury might have drawn in [that party's] favor from the evidence." **{-136-}** *Legg v. Ulster Cnty.*, 979 F.3d 101, 114 (2d Cir. 2020) (internal quotation marks omitted). A district court may grant such a motion against a party only when "the court finds that a reasonable jury would not have a legally sufficient evidentiary basis to find for the party." Fed. R. Civ. P. 50(a)(1). Plaintiffs argue **[—40—]** that the district court erred in granting the Town's renewed motion for judgment as a matter of law because the jury had a legally sufficient basis for finding the Town liable on Plaintiffs' private nuisance and trespass claims.

a. Private Nuisance

On appeal, Plaintiffs assert two principal theories for their private nuisance claims against the Town. First, they argue that the Town is liable for private nuisance because it knew that the Jetties (the nuisance) caused erosion on Plaintiffs' properties and it had the ability to mitigate that erosion (primarily through sand bypass projects) but failed to do so. Second, Plaintiffs argue that the Town consented to the creation of the Jetties and derived a benefit from those Jetties, which serves as an alternative basis for nuisance liability. Although the district court previously denied the Town's motion to dismiss and motion for summary judgment on similar grounds, it ultimately reached the correct conclusion when it rejected Plaintiffs' theories of nuisance liability and granted judgment as a matter of law in favor of the Town. The jury lacked a legally sufficient basis for finding in favor of Plaintiffs on their New York private nuisance claims because (1) the Town did not construct the Jetties and (2) the Town did not **[—41—]** and could not control the Jetties, which were the sole responsibility of the federal government.

Under New York law, a private nuisance claim may be brought under the theory that a defendant intentionally interfered with others' right to enjoy their land or that a defendant's negligence caused an interference with others' right to enjoy their land. *See Copart Indus. v. Consol. Edison Co.*, 41 N.Y.2d 564, 569 (1977) (citing Restatement (Second) of Torts § 822 (Am. L. Inst. 1975)). Where intentional nuisance is alleged, plaintiffs must prove five elements: "(1) an interference substantial in nature, (2) intentional in origin, [and] (3) unreasonable in character, (4) with a person's property right to use and enjoy land, (5) caused by another's conduct in acting or failing to act." *Id.* at 570. Where "a nuisance has its origin in negligence, negligence must be proven." *Id.* at 569 (internal quotation marks omitted).

Whether a nuisance action is premised on intentional conduct or negligence, "the duty to abate a private nuisance existing on real property arises from the power to possess the property and control the activities that occur on it." *Taggart v. Costabile*, 14 N.Y.S.3d 388, 392 (2d Dep't 2015). As such, a landowner that has relinquished control of its property "will not be liable for private nuisance that

[—42—] arises on the property if the landowner neither created the nuisance nor had notice of it at the time that possession of the property was transferred." *Id.*

The record reveals that the Jetties were first built by a private development company in 1926, and that the Town obtained a deed to the Jetties and the land underneath in 1941 to facilitate granting a permanent easement to the federal government to take control of the Jetties. At trial, Plaintiffs did not present any evidence suggesting that the Town constructed, repaired, or maintained the Jetties. Nor could they have, as federal law prohibits **{-137-}** the Town from interfering with the Jetties and the Federal Navigation Project at Lake Montauk Harbor. *See, e.g.*, 33 U.S.C. § 408. Moreover, at trial, a USACE representative testified that "maintenance responsibilities for the federal project [at Lake Montauk Harbor] are 100 percent federal," App'x at 3589, and several Town witnesses testified to the same. Indeed, Plaintiffs concede in their reply brief that "if the Town were to dismantle the [J]etties this would run afoul of the easement and of the [USACE's] navigational mandate." Pls.' Reply Br. at 7.

Despite acknowledging that the Town had no ability to control the Jetties, Plaintiffs contend that "[t]his case has never been about such an absurd postulation." *Id.* at 7–8. Rather, they argue that the Town should be held liable **[—43—]** for private nuisance because (1) it still owns the property on which the Jetties are located, (2) the Town was aware of the erosion occurring on Plaintiffs' properties, and (3) the Town could have taken remedial measures to address the erosion, such as undertaking a sand bypass project. But far from being "an absurd postulation," *id.* at 7–8, the Town's lack of control over the Jetties definitively resolves Plaintiffs' private nuisance claims.

As the Second Department has explained, "the duty to abate a private nuisance existing on real property arises from the power to possess the property and control the activities that occur on it." *Taggart*, 14 N.Y.S.3d at 392. This principle dates back almost a century to the decision of the New York Court of Appeals in *Wilks v. New York Telephone Co.*, 243 N.Y. 351 (1926), in which the court held that a landowner that did not originally construct the nuisance at issue (a faulty telephone wire) could not be held liable for private nuisance where the telephone wire was under the sole possession, control, and maintenance of the United States at the time of the accident. *Id.* at 356, 360–62. The key principle underlying *Wilks* and its progeny is that, where liability is premised on a failure to abate a nuisance, there must be a duty to act. *See* Restatement (Second) of Torts § 824 ("The conduct necessary to make the actor liable for . . . private nuisance may **[—44—]** consist of . . . a failure to act under circumstances in which the actor is under a duty to take positive action to . . . abate the . . . invasion of the private interest."). And where a landowner no longer controls the land at issue and did not create the nuisance in the first instance, there is no such duty.

Here, the Town simply had no ability to "possess the property" containing the alleged nuisance or "control the activities that occur on it." *Taggart*, 14 N.Y.S.3d at 392. Thus, it does not matter whether the Town may have been better positioned to undertake a sand bypass project than other entities; New York law is clear that it had no *obligation* to do so. The mere fact that the Town owned the property underneath the Jetties did not impose upon it a duty to take affirmative steps to remediate the downstream erosion the Jetties may have caused.[14] **[—45—]** **{-138-}**

[14] Plaintiffs also appear to argue that the Town's 1962 "Assurance of Local Cooperation" gave rise to a duty to mitigate the effects of the Jetties because the Town agreed to indemnify the federal government for "claims for damages that may occur from the construction and maintenance of the improvements" to Lake Montauk Harbor as part of the FNP. App'x at 4605. But even if this indemnification clause did reach Plaintiffs' private nuisance claims (an issue we do not decide), at most, this would simply require the Town to indemnify the *federal government* if it were found liable for private nuisance. *Cf. Raquet v. Braun*, 90 N.Y.2d 177, 183 (1997) (explaining the distinction between liability based on a duty running to the injured party and common-law indemnification, which involves "a separate duty owed [to] the

Plaintiffs alternatively argue that, even if the Town's mere ownership of the property under the Jetties did not give rise to a duty to mitigate their effects, the Town was still obligated to take action because it had knowledge of and thereby "consented" to the nuisance, and because the Town "continues to derive a benefit from the nuisance." Pls.' Br. at 43 (internal quotation marks omitted).[15] But a landowner's knowledge of or benefit from a nuisance does not give rise to nuisance liability under New York law unless the property owner was aware of or had reason to be aware of the nuisance *at the time it relinquished control of the property*. *See Taggart*, 14. N.Y.S.3d at 392 (granting defendant landowners' motion for summary judgment where the plaintiffs "did not allege that the defendants created the alleged nuisance, or that they knew or had reason to know that the **[—46—]** allegedly objectionable activities would take place at the time that the property was leased to the tenants"); *see also Wilks*, 243 N.Y. at 362; N.Y. Pattern Jury Instructions § 2:116 (Comm. on Pattern Jury Instructions 2019).

Here, Plaintiffs contend that the Town knew that the Jetties were causing erosion as early as 1994 and that the Town benefits from the Jetties because of the accumulation of sand on public beaches to the east of the Jetties and the municipal benefits generated by the harbor. But Plaintiffs presented no evidence at trial indicating that the Town knew or had any reason to believe that the Jetties would cause erosion to the private beaches to the west of the Jetties when the Town relinquished control of the Jetties in 1942. Thus, any awareness that the Town gained about the alleged nuisance *after* that transfer of title did not give rise to a duty to abate that nuisance, *see Taggart*, 14 N.Y.S.3d at 392; *Wilks*, 243 N.Y. at 362, and the district court properly granted judgment as a matter of law to the Town on Plaintiffs' private nuisance claims.[16] **[—47—] {-139-}**

b. Trespass

The district court also appropriately granted the Town's renewed motion for judgment as a matter of law on Plaintiffs' trespass claims. Under New York law, a trespass requires that a defendant "intend[] the act which produces the unlawful intrusion" onto another's property, "where the intrusion is an immediate or inevitable consequence of the act." *Volunteer Fire Ass'n of Tappan, Inc. v. County of Rockland*, 956 N.Y.S.2d 102, 105 (2d Dep't 2012). Here, as the district court recognized, "the only action the Town has taken" with respect to the Jetties "was to relinquish control over them." *Cangemi IV*, 374 F. Supp. 3d at 234. Thus, Plaintiffs' only plausible argument that the Town took *action* that caused waters to flow

---

indemnitee by the indemnitor"). It would not create a duty running from the Town to the Plaintiffs to mitigate all adverse effects of the Jetties.

[15] In passing, Plaintiffs argue that the Town "create[d] or participate[d] in the creation or maintenance of the nuisance," on the theory that the Town "function[ed] as the initiator of the [J]etty rehabilitation." Pls.' Br. at 36, 39. However, all of Plaintiffs' cases supporting this theory—most of which involve holding joint tortfeasors liable for *public* nuisance—pertain to defendants who directly participated in the creation of the nuisance, even if their relationship to the ultimate harm was relatively remote. *See, e.g., In re MTBE Prods. Liab. Litig.*, 725 F.3d 65, 121 (2d Cir. 2013) (rejecting the notion that Exxon was "too remote" from the contamination of a drinking well with MTBE because (1) "Exxon manufactured gasoline containing MTBE and supplied that gasoline to service stations in Queens" and (2) "Exxon knew station owners would store this gasoline in underground tanks that leaked"). By contrast, Plaintiffs point to no cases in which remote, indirect involvement of a defendant with no knowledge of the potential downstream consequences of its actions—such as the Town's advocacy for federal rehabilitation of the Jetties in the 1930s and 40s—qualifies as "creating" a nuisance under New York law.

[16] We also reject Plaintiffs' argument that the district court erred by deciding the issue of negligent nuisance, despite instructing the jury not to reach that issue if it found the Town liable for intentional private nuisance. With respect to negligent nuisance, the district court correctly concluded that the Town's lack of a legal duty to mitigate the effects of the Jetties precluded such a claim. *See Cangemi IV*, 374 F. Supp. 3d at 237. This was an issue of law that was proper for the district court to decide, and Plaintiffs point to no case law supporting their assertion that this decision somehow "usurped" the jury's function. Pls.' Br. at 52.

unnaturally onto their property is premised on (1) the Town's advocating for the Lake Montauk Harbor FNP in the 1930s and 40s and (2) the Town's grant of an easement to the federal government in 1942.

But, as already discussed, Plaintiffs presented no evidence at trial suggesting that the Town knew or had any reason to know in 1942 that the Jetty rehabilitation project (which would not be completed for another 26 years) would result in altering the flow of water in such a way as to cause erosion on properties subsequently acquired by Plaintiffs. *See Phillips v. Sun Oil Co.*, 307 N.Y. 328, 331 **[—48—]** (1954) (holding that a defendant is not liable in trespass for liquids intruding onto another's property "unless [the defendant] had good reason to know or expect that subterranean and other conditions were such that there would be passage from defendant's to plaintiff's land"). The disruption of the flow of water was therefore not "an immediate or inevitable consequence" of the Town's intentional conduct in passing control of the Jetties over to the federal government. *Volunteer Fire Ass'n of Tappan*, 956 N.Y.S.2d at 105.[17]

3. The law of the case doctrine did not compel denial of the Town's motion for judgment as a matter of law.

Finally, Plaintiffs contend that the district court erred by deviating from the "law of the case" when it reversed its prior rulings and granted the Town's Rule 50(b) motion. Plaintiffs argue that, because the district court denied the Town's motion to dismiss Plaintiffs' private nuisance and trespass claims in *Cangemi I* and denied the Town's motion for summary judgment on those claims in *Cangemi III*, it unduly prejudiced Plaintiffs by granting the Town's renewed motion for **[—49—]** judgment as a matter of law after trial in *Cangemi IV*. *See Colvin v. Keen*, 900 F.3d 63, 69 (2d Cir. 2018) (explaining that a district court abuses its discretion under the law of the case doctrine when it makes "a change of ruling" that "cause[s] prejudice to the appellant"). Plaintiffs' law of the case argument fails for two distinct reasons.

First, the district court's decision in *Cangemi IV* did not directly conflict with its previous decisions in *Cangemi I* and *Cangemi III*. Rather, as the district court explained in *Cangemi IV*, its apparent about-face on Plaintiffs' private nuisance **{-140-}** and trespass claims stemmed from the lack of any evidence presented at trial that the Town exercised control over (or even had the ability to exercise control over) the Jetties. *See Cangemi IV*, 374 F. Supp. 3d at 234. The law of the case doctrine cannot bar a district court from holding plaintiffs to their ever-increasing burden of proof over the course of a lawsuit. *See, e.g., Sagendorf-Teal v. County of Rensselaer*, 100 F.3d 270, 277 (2d Cir. 1996) (concluding that new evidence presented during trial justified the district court's reconsideration of a prior ruling); *McAnaney v. Astoria Fin. Corp.*, 665 F. Supp. 2d 132, 142 (E.D.N.Y. 2009) (explaining that the law of the case doctrine "is inapposite" to issues that have been developed through discovery **[—50—]** "because of the divergent standard of review applicable to motions to dismiss and motions for summary judgment").

Second, even if it could be said that the district court reconsidered its decisions in *Cangemi I* and *III* on purely legal grounds, the law of the case doctrine is "discretionary and does not limit a court's power to reconsider its own decision prior to final judgment." *Virgin Atl. Airways, Ltd. v. Nat'l Mediation Bd.*, 956 F.2d 1245, 1255 (2d Cir. 1992). While the district court perhaps could have addressed the legal arguments it considered in its 2019 decision at an earlier stage of the case, district courts are by no means obligated to deny a Rule 50 motion simply because earlier in the litigation they denied a motion to dismiss or a

[17] Because we affirm the district court's grant of the Town's renewed motion for judgment as a matter of law on these grounds, we need not consider the Town's alternative bases for affirming the district court's judgment—*i.e.*, that Plaintiffs' state-law claims are preempted by federal law and that any private nuisance or trespass caused by the Jetties was protected by a prescriptive easement. *See* Town's Br. at 54–59. We likewise need not reach the issue of whether the district court properly granted, in the alternative, the Town's motion for a new trial.

motion for summary judgment on the same issue. As we have recently explained, if the law of the case doctrine "were pushed so far as to call upon the reviewing court to vacate a changed, but correct, judgment, solely by reason of the change," the doctrine "would then mean that the initial incorrect ruling would bind not only the court that made it, but also the court of appellate review, whose function is to correct errors, rather than perpetuate them." *Colvin*, 900 F.3d at 72. Simply put, the district court eventually got it right with respect to Plaintiffs' private nuisance and **[—51—]** trespass claims, and it did not abuse its discretion in reconsidering its previous legal conclusions prior to a final judgment.

III. CONCLUSION

For the foregoing reasons, we **AFFIRM** the judgment of the district court.

United States Court of Appeals
for the Second Circuit

No. 19-4208

UNITED STATES
vs.
TORRES

Appeal from the United States District Court for the Southern District of New York

Decided: November 17, 2021

Citation: 18 F.4th 395, 9 Adm. R. 123 (2d Cir. 2021).

Before **CHIN** and **PARK,** Circuit Judges, and **BOLDEN,** District Judge.*

* Judge Victor A. Bolden, of the United States District Court for the District of Connecticut, sitting by designation.

[—3—] {-397-} CHIN, Circuit Judge: **{-398-}**

Defendants-appellants Ferney Salas Torres ("Torres") and Saul Calonjes Salas ("Salas") appeal from judgments entered December 10 and 12, 2019, respectively, following their guilty pleas, convicting them of conspiring to manufacture, distribute, or possess a controlled substance on a vessel in violation of 46 U.S.C. §§ 70504(b)(2) and 70506 and 21 U.S.C. § 960(b)(2)(B). The district court sentenced Torres principally to 240 months' imprisonment and Salas principally to 180 months' imprisonment. On appeal, Torres and Salas challenge their sentences on procedural grounds, arguing that the district court erred by denying minor-role reductions pursuant to U.S.S.G. §§ 3B1.2 and 2D1.1(a)(5)(iii) and applying two-level enhancements for their roles as pilot or navigator of a vessel carrying controlled substances pursuant to U.S.S.G. § 2D1.1(b)(3)(C). They **[—4—]** also contend that the district court did not give appropriate weight to the 18 U.S.C. § 3553(a) sentencing factors and therefore imposed substantively unreasonable sentences. For the reasons set forth below, the judgments of the district court are affirmed.

BACKGROUND

I. *The Facts*

The facts are drawn from the presentence reports (the "PSRs") to the extent the findings were adopted by the district court and from the evidence presented at a *Fatico* hearing held August 28, 2019. They may be summarized as follows:

A "go-fast boat" or "*panga*" is a thirty-to-fifty-foot fishing boat with a hidden compartment below deck used by drug-trafficking organizations ("DTOs") to transport narcotics. Investors in the Colombian drug trade hire DTOs to transport cocaine from Colombia to Central America and ultimately to the United States. DTO members communicate with the investors, coordinate logistics, track the cocaine's location by GPS, purchase gasoline, and serve as lookouts. The DTOs sometimes arrange for a go-fast boat to transport the cocaine from the Colombian coast through the Pacific Ocean to Central America. Typically, the go-fast boat will rendezvous with a second boat in the open ocean **[—5—]** fifty to one hundred miles, but as many as six hundred miles, off the coast, and the crews will move the cocaine to the second boat to continue the journey.

Three to four seasoned mariners typically make up the crew of a go-fast boat. The three main roles are captain, navigator, and mechanic, but all crewmembers "help each other out" by doing things like "driving the boat." The captain's responsibilities include driving the boat and communicating with the DTO via satellite phone. The mechanic maintains the engine. The navigator puts coordinates into a GPS and ensures the go-fast boat is going the right way by "steer[ing] the boat." Each mariner stands to earn between $40,000 and **{-399-}** $60,000 for about one week's work—seven to ten times what a Colombian police officer makes in a year— transporting a load of cocaine on a go-fast boat.

On March 17, 2018, the U.S. Coast Guard Cutter *Decisive* was patrolling eighty nautical miles southwest of Panama, an area known for narcotics trafficking, when it identified a vessel heading north at approximately thirty knots.[1] Thereafter the *Decisive* dispatched a small boat to investigate. The crew of the small boat discovered that the northbound vessel was a go-fast boat with three individuals aboard, approached within thirty yards with flashing **[—6—]** lights and sirens, and gave chase. Two of the individuals, Salas and Heyder Renteria Solis ("Solis"), jettisoned packages before they were stopped. The crew of the small boat determined that the third person, Torres, was the "pilot" of the go-fast boat.

The Coast Guard recovered thirty-four packages containing 945 kilograms of cocaine and 10 kilograms of amphetamine. On March 28, Coast Guard special agents transported Torres, Salas, and Solis to the United States, where they were arrested.

Torres and Salas are "typical mariners"; that is, they are fishermen having "low socioeconomic status" and "very little education" who live in Colombia. They were to be paid about $45,000 for the weeklong trip during which they were arrested. The go-fast boat had departed Buenaventura, Colombia, and the Coast Guard seized it "in the middle of the ocean"—eighty nautical miles offshore—just south of the border between Panama and Costa Rica.

Torres served as the captain of the go-fast boat, meaning that he was the primary "steerer" of the boat, most responsible, and most trusted by the DTO. **[—7—]** Salas also piloted the boat, served as navigator, and, as he concedes, "steered the boat." Salas App'x at 265; Salas Br. at 35.

Between 2004 and 2008, Torres participated in about ten narcotics-trafficking trips by crewing on boats transporting narcotics from Colombia to Central America. In 2008, he was arrested while serving as the captain of a go-fast boat transporting cocaine and was later convicted in the U.S. District Court for the Middle District of Florida of conspiracy to possess with intent to distribute cocaine while aboard a vessel. Torres was imprisoned until 2016 and then returned to Colombia.

Between 2005 and 2006, Salas participated in about six narcotics-trafficking trips. He was arrested in 2006 while crewing a go-fast boat transporting cocaine, was convicted of the same crime as Torres, and was imprisoned until 2011, also returning to Colombia thereafter.

In 2017, Torres and Salas began operating boats transporting narcotics again. They had completed three trips and, on the fourth, were apprehended by the Coast Guard.[2] **[—8—]**

II. *Proceedings Below*

In February 2019, Torres and Salas pleaded guilty to conspiracy to manufacture, distribute, or possess controlled substances on a vessel in violation of 46 U.S.C. §§ 70504(b)(2) and 70506 and 21 U.S.C. § 960(b)(2)(B). The PSRs indicated that **{-400-}** each was accountable for at least 450 kilograms of cocaine, which resulted in a base offense level of 38. The PSRs recommended a two-level mitigating-role reduction of the offense level because Torres and Salas were "minor participant[s] in the offense," U.S.S.G. § 3B1.2, as well as an additional four-level decrease for recipients of § 3B1.2 adjustments, § 2D1.1(a)(5).

After a three-level reduction for acceptance of responsibility, each defendant's total offense level was 29. Torres had a criminal history category of III, and the resulting Guidelines range was 108 to 135 months' imprisonment with a mandatory minimum of 60 months. Torres's PSR recommended a sentence of 84 months' imprisonment. Salas had a criminal history category of II, and the

[1] A nautical mile is 6076.115 feet, or 1.15 statute miles. *Nautical Mile, Merriam-Webster's Collegiate Dictionary* (11th ed. 2003).

[2] Torres and Salas contended below that they resumed drug trafficking to earn money to pay off extorters. Neither Torres nor Salas reported the extortion to Colombian authorities and the Government had minimal corroboration for the explanations. The **[—8—]** district court did not credit either defendant's extortion argument. Salas App'x at 321; Torres Dist. Ct. Dkt. No. 109 at 55-56.

resulting Guidelines range was 97 to 121 months' imprisonment with a mandatory minimum of 60 months. Salas's PSR recommended a sentence of 72 months' imprisonment. **[—9—]**

At Torres's initial sentencing hearing held May 17, 2019, the district court scheduled a *Fatico* hearing to determine whether Torres qualified for a minor-role reduction or a pilot enhancement under the Guidelines. Salas's initial sentencing hearing was adjourned for the same reason.

On August 28, 2019, the district court held the *Fatico* hearing. Special Agent Ronald Sandoval ("Sandoval") of the Drug Enforcement Agency testified for the government about the Colombian drug trade and his investigation into Torres and Salas. The district court did not rule on the issues at the conclusion of the hearing but set a schedule for posthearing submissions.

Torres's and Salas's sentencings were held on December 10 and 12, 2019, respectively. At Torres's sentencing the district court began with a base offense level of 38. The district court did not apply a minor-role two-level reduction, finding that Torres's compensation—$45,000 to $50,000—suggested the "importance" and "necessity" of his role on the boat. The district court applied a two-level pilot enhancement, finding that piloting a go-fast boat requires skill, an extended trip at sea, and a rendezvous in the open ocean, and concluding that Torres piloted the go-fast boat within the meaning of the enhancement. After applying a three-level reduction for acceptance of **[—10—]** responsibility, the district court concluded that the offense level was 37, the criminal history category was III, and the Guidelines range was 262 to 327 months.

During a discussion of the 18 U.S.C. § 3553(a) factors, Torres, through counsel, argued that he became reinvolved in drug trafficking to repay someone who paid a ransom for Torres's wife and daughter when they were kidnapped. The district court found this argument unpersuasive because it was not corroborated by letters from family members or by Special Agent Sandoval, and because Torres had a prior conviction for the same conduct. The district court also found Torres to be "unique" because he was previously convicted of the same crime, served a ten-year sentence, and reoffended within two years of his release. Thus, the district court concluded that Torres's sentence would not create an unwarranted disparity with other sentences because he was not situated similarly to other defendants. The district court sentenced Torres to 240 months' imprisonment, to be followed by five years of supervised release.

At Salas's sentencing on December 12, 2019, the district court began with a base offense level of 38. The district court found that Salas's role was "similar" to Torres's, and although Torres had "greater responsibility," defendants **[—11—]** were paid the same amount and both were "responsible at various times for directing and navigating the boat," which required "skill and experience." **{-401-}** Accordingly, the district court did not apply a minor-role two-level reduction. As to the pilot enhancement, the district court concluded that Salas played a "pilot or navigator" role on the boat based on inferences drawn from Special Agent Sandoval's testimony about the makeup of a typical crew and the evidence that Torres and Solis were the captain and mechanic, respectively. The district court added those two levels and subtracted three for acceptance of responsibility, leaving Salas with an offense level of 37, a criminal history category of II, and a Guidelines range of 235 to 293 months.

As to mitigating factors, the district court found that the extortion plot Salas described was "very implausible," did not "make a lot of sense," and ultimately did not mitigate Salas's wrongdoing. The district court sentenced Salas to 180 months' imprisonment, to be followed by five years of supervised release.

These appeals followed. **[—12—]**

DISCUSSION

Torres and Salas appeal the sentences on procedural grounds, arguing that the court erred in calculating the applicable ranges under the Guidelines by denying a reduction for minor role under U.S.S.G. § 3B1.2(b), which would have reduced the offense level by two levels and entitled defendants to an additional four-level decrease under U.S.S.G. §§ 2D1.1(a)(5),[3] and by wrongly applying a two-level increase for their roles as captain, pilot, or navigator of a vessel carrying narcotics under U.S.S.G. § 2D1.1(b)(3). They also appeal the sentences on substantive grounds.

In reviewing a sentence for substantive and procedural reasonableness, we apply a deferential abuse-of-discretion standard. *United States v. Thavaraja*, 740 F.3d 253, 258 (2d Cir. 2014). As to role adjustments, we review the district court's findings of fact as to the defendant's role for clear error, *United States v. Gomez*, 31 F.3d 28, 31 (2d Cir. 1994), and "reverse[] the district court's conclusion only for abuse of discretion," *United States v. Colon*, 220 F.3d 48, 51 (2d Cir. 2000) (citation omitted). Defendants must establish **[—13—]** entitlement to a minor-role reduction by a preponderance of the evidence. *United States v. Kerr*, 752 F.3d 206, 223 (2d Cir. 2014), *as amended* (June 18, 2014).

We review a district court's interpretation and application of the Guidelines *de novo, see United States v. Adler*, 52 F.3d 20, 21 (2d Cir. 1995) (per curiam), and its factual findings for clear error, *see United States v. Mulder*, 273 F.3d 91, 116 (2d Cir. 2001). "If we identify procedural error in a sentence, but the record indicates clearly that the district court would have imposed the same sentence in any event, the error may be deemed harmless, avoiding the need to vacate the sentence and to remand the case for resentencing." *United States v. Mandell*, 752 F.3d 544, 553 (2d Cir. 2014) (per curiam) (internal quotation marks omitted).

"Our review for substantive unreasonableness is particularly deferential." *Thavaraja*, 740 F.3d at 259 (internal quotation marks omitted). Because district courts are largely responsible for sentencing, our role is to "patrol the boundaries of reasonableness." *United States v. Cavera*, 550 F.3d 180, 191 (2d Cir. 2008). "We will identify as substantively unreasonable only those sentences that are so shockingly high, shockingly low, or otherwise unsupportable **{-402-}** as a matter of law that allowing them to stand would damage the **[—14—]** administration of justice." *Thavaraja*, 740 F.3d at 259 (internal quotation marks omitted).

We discuss the challenges in turn.

I. *Procedural Unreasonableness*

Torres and Salas argue that the district court committed procedural error when it denied them a reduction for minor role because they established by a preponderance of the evidence that they were minor participants in the offenses. Next, they argue that the district court erroneously applied the pilot enhancement because they did not possess the special skills or authority necessary to have the enhancement applied.

A. *Minor-Role Reduction*

Guideline § 3B1.2(b) allows for a two-level reduction in offense level when the defendant is a "minor participant," meaning that the defendant is "less culpable than most other participants in the criminal activity, but whose role could not be described as minimal." U.S.S.G. § 3B1.2(b) cmt. n.5. The minor participant determination is based on the "totality of circumstances," which may include the following:

> (i) the degree to which the defendant understood the scope and structure of the criminal activity; **[—15—]**
> (ii) the degree to which the defendant participated in planning or organizing the criminal activity;
> (iii) the degree to which the defendant exercised decision-making authority or influenced the exercise of decision-making authority;
> (iv) the nature and extent of the defendant's participation in the

[3] Torres and Salas both had a base offense level of 38. Hence, if they qualified for a mitigating role adjustment under § 3B1.2, the offense level would have been reduced by 4 levels. U.S.S.G. § 2D1.1(a)(5)(iii).

> commission of the criminal activity, including the acts the defendant performed and the responsibility and discretion the defendant had in performing those acts; [and]
> (v) the degree to which the defendant stood to benefit from the criminal activity.

Id. n.3.

We are not persuaded that the district court abused its discretion when it denied defendants minor-role reductions. Defendants contend that they had only limited knowledge of the criminal activity; no role in planning, organizing, or financing the activity; and no decision-making authority. Even assuming these facts to be true, however, the district court did not abuse its discretion when it gave these facts less weight than others because a reduction "will not be available simply because the defendant played a lesser role than his co-conspirators." *United States v. Carpenter*, 252 F.3d 230, 235 (2d Cir. 2001) (internal quotation marks omitted), *as amended* (July 19, 2001).

Indeed, the district court found that the minor-role reduction did not apply because Torres and Salas knew they were responsible for transporting nearly a ton of narcotics, employed skill in crewing the go-fast boat, were **[—16—]** recidivists, understood the scope of the conspiracy, and stood to earn about $45,000 each for their roles in the offense. As to Torres, the district court also found that he was in communication with other traffickers. The district court concluded that these facts underscored the "importance" and necessity" of Torres's role, Torres Dist. Ct. Dkt. No. 109 at 19, as well as the "skill" and "decision-making authority" employed by Salas, Salas App'x at 276-77. Even assuming defendants played a lesser role than others who planned, organized, and financed the narcotics activity, the district court did not abuse its discretion in concluding that defendants were not minor participants and declining to grant them the reduction. *See, e.g.,* **{-403-}** *United States v. Garcia*, 920 F.2d 153, 155 (2d Cir. 1990) (per curiam) (holding that although some narcotics "couriers" may receive a minor-role reduction "based upon their culpability in light of the specific facts," that conclusion "is by no means mandated").

B. ***Pilot Enhancement***

Pursuant to U.S.S.G. § 2D1.1(b)(3), a two-level enhancement is appropriate when "the defendant unlawfully imported or exported a controlled substance" and "acted as a pilot, copilot, captain, navigator, flight officer, or any other operation officer aboard any craft or vessel carrying a controlled **[—17—]** substance." When determining whether an enhancement is applicable, the district court uses the preponderance of the evidence standard. *United States v. Salazar*, 489 F.3d 555, 558 (2d Cir. 2007) (per curiam).

The Guidelines do not define the terms "pilot, copilot, captain, navigator, flight officer, or any other operation officer," nor has this Court defined these terms in the context of this enhancement. Defendants argue that the terms indicate possession of special skills or authority. Accordingly, they contend that the district court erred in applying the pilot enhancement because they merely "steered" the boat but did not have special skills or authority and, therefore, were not a pilot or navigator.

We are not persuaded. First, defendants' arguments fail as a matter of textual interpretation. Defendants' definitions are inconsistent with the plain meanings of "pilot" and "navigator." "Pilot" means "one employed to steer a ship." *Pilot, Merriam-Webster's Collegiate Dictionary* (11th ed. 2003). "Navigator" means "one [who] navigates or is qualified to navigate," and "navigate" means, among other things, "to steer or manage (a boat) in sailing." *Navigator, Navigate, Merriam-Webster's Collegiate Dictionary* (11th ed. 2003). Under these ordinary **[—18—]** dictionary definitions, "pilot" and "navigator" do not require possession of special skill, authority, or training.

Second, the circuits that have considered the meaning of "pilot" and "navigator" within § 2D1.1(b)(3)(C) have declined to interpret those terms to bear the more technical definitions advocated by defendants. *See United States v. Guerrero*, 114 F.3d 332, 346 (1st Cir. 1997) (affirming district court's finding that defendant "acted as a pilot" within the meaning of the pilot enhancement because defendant's conduct fell within "the common dictionary definition of 'pilot'": "a person hired to steer a vessel"); *United States v. Bautista-Montelongo*, 618 F.3d 464, 467 (5th Cir. 2010) (holding that no special skills are required; trial court properly applied pilot enhancement to person who "drove a boat containing contraband"); *United States v. Senn*, 129 F.3d 886, 896-97 (7th Cir. 1997) (holding that pilot enhancement does not require "proof of special skill"), *abrogated on other grounds by United States v. Vizcarra*, 668 F.3d 516 (7th Cir. 2012); *United States v. Cruz-Mendez*, 811 F.3d 1172, 1176, 4 Adm. R. 370, 372 (9th Cir. 2016) (applying a "common sense approach" rather than "rigid requirements of professionalism" to the "pilot/captain" enhancement and holding that district court properly applied enhancement to **[—19—]** person who "operated a boat . . . in open water" (internal quotation marks omitted)).[4]

Here, defendants' conduct is consistent with the ordinary meaning of "pilot" and "navigator," as they were both employed **{-404-}** to steer or navigate a boat. Each stood to earn $45,000 for operating the go-fast boat to transport a substantial load of narcotics. The Coast Guard observed Torres "piloting" the boat, and Torres identified himself as the captain to Special Agent Sandoval. Salas piloted and navigated the boat for at least part of the trip and, as he concedes, steered the boat. Additionally, go-fast boats are typically crewed by a captain, a mechanic, and a navigator, and Torres was the captain and Solis was the mechanic. The district court reasonably inferred that the third crewmember, Salas, must have filled the third role, navigator. *See United States v. Gaskin*, 364 F.3d 438, 464 (2d Cir. 2004) ("[A] sentencing court, like a jury, may base its factfinding on circumstantial evidence and on reasonable inferences drawn therefrom.").

Third, although the ordinary definitions of pilot and navigator do not require special skill, the district court found that defendants had special **[—20—]** skills. Piloting the boat required "real special skill" and "experience." Salas App'x at 265, 277. There was "more to it" than "putting [a destination] in your GPS to figure out how to get from here [to] Broadway." Torres Dist. Ct. Dkt. No. 109 at 20. The job required "a long time at sea" and traveling "hundreds of miles out into the open ocean." *Id.* As the district court observed, this was "no small feat" and was not something, for example, that the individuals in the courtroom other than defendants would have been able to do. Salas App'x at 264-65.

Defendants urge us to adopt the reasoning of a First Circuit dissent advocating the use of a nautical dictionary to define the term "navigate" as "'[t]o safely operate a vessel employing the elements of position, course and speed,'" which would require "extra abilities." *United States v. Trinidad*, 839 F.3d 112, 116, 119-20, 4 Adm. R. 25, 28, 31 (1st Cir. 2016) (Torruella, *J.*, dissenting) (quoting *Navigate*, Sea Talk Nautical Dictionary, http://www.seatalk.info/ (last visited Oct. 6, 2016)). But even if we were to employ a technical definition, we would not reach a different result because the district court properly found that defendants here had special skills.

Further, the *Trinidad* dissent provides no justification for employing a nautical dictionary rather than an ordinary one other than the avoidance of an **[—21—]** "unjust result." *Id.* at 119, 4 Adm. R. at 30. Nor does the Guideline itself warrant departure from ordinary meaning. Section 2D1.1(b)(3)(C) refers to crewmembers of boats and aircraft. The dissent's approach would require use of a nautical dictionary for some words and an aeronautical dictionary for others. The Guideline lacks technical references that could suggest that the drafters used "pilot" and "navigator" in a technical sense such as to warrant the use of a technical dictionary. *Cf. Taniguchi v. Kan Pac. Saipan, Ltd.*, 566 U.S. 560, 571 (2012) (considering technical definition where statute contained technical language). Finally, on this record, we are not

[4] *Guerrero*, *Bautista-Montelongo*, and *Senn* interpret U.S.S.G. § 2D1.1(b)(2), a previous version of § 2D1.1(b)(3)(C).

persuaded that the use of an ordinary dictionary would lead to an unjust result. Accordingly, we decline to employ a meaning other than ordinary meaning when interpreting the terms in U.S.S.G. § 2D1.1(b)(3)(C).

Defendants observe that the plea agreements and PSRs did not include the § 2D1.1(b)(3)(C) enhancement, but they do not argue that the district court committed procedural error by considering it *sua sponte*. In any event, the plea agreements explicitly provided that the district court was not bound by the agreements' Guidelines stipulations. **[—22—]**

Finally, even if the application of the enhancement were inappropriate, the district court made clear that it would have imposed the same sentences in any event. **{-405-}** First, the district court noted on the record at the sentencings that if the two-level pilot enhancement did not apply, a two-level enhancement for transporting methamphetamine would apply instead, as defendants were also transporting ten kilograms of methamphetamine. Torres Dist. Ct. Dkt. No. 109 at 21, 25; Salas App'x at 286. Second, when sentencing Torres, the district court found that "[a]nything less" than a twenty-year sentence "would not reflect [Torres's] culpability." Torres Dist. Ct. Dkt. No. 109 at 58. When sentencing Salas, the district court observed that a fifteen-year sentence was "appropriate" based on Salas's recidivism. Salas App'x at 322. Thus, any error would be harmless. *See Mandell*, 752 F.3d at 553 ("If we identify procedural error in a sentence, but the record indicates clearly that the district court would have imposed the same sentence in any event, the error may be deemed harmless, avoiding the need to vacate the sentence and to remand the case for resentencing." (internal quotation marks omitted)).

Accordingly, we hold that the sentencing court did not err in its findings or abuse its discretion in applying the pilot/navigator enhancement. **[—23—]**

III. *Substantive Unreasonableness*

Torres and Salas argue that the district imposed substantively unreasonable sentences because it failed to properly weigh the 18 U.S.C. § 3553(a)(2) factors, resulting in sentences "greater than necessary" to achieve sentencing goals.

District courts are to use the Guidelines as a "starting point" and then make an independent sentencing determination, taking into account the "nature and circumstances of the offense and the history and characteristics of the defendant" and all other statutory factors. 18 U.S.C. § 3553(a); *see Cavera*, 550 F.3d at 188-89. "The particular weight to be afforded aggravating and mitigating factors is a matter firmly committed to the discretion of the sentencing judge, with appellate courts seeking to ensure only that a factor can bear the weight assigned it under the totality of circumstances in the case." *United States v. Broxmeyer*, 699 F.3d 265, 289 (2d Cir. 2012) (internal quotation marks and citations omitted).

Torres's 240-month sentence and Salas's 180-month sentence were neither shockingly high nor unsupportable as a matter of law. Applying the particularly deferential standard for substantive reasonableness review, we **[—24—]** conclude that the district court's decision fell within the range of permissible decisions.

As to Torres, the district court considered the "incredibl[e] serious[ness]" and "impact" of the crime, his previous conviction for the same crime, and the need for deterrence. Torres Dist. Ct. Dkt. No. 109 at 54. The district court did not credit Torres's duress explanation, finding it to be unsubstantiated and inconsistent with testimony by Special Agent Sandoval. *Id.* at 55. After considering all the factors, the district court concluded that "[a]nything less" than a 240-month sentence would be "inappropriate" and "would not reflect [Torres's] culpability." *Id.* at 58.

Torres argues that the district court did not give "appropriate weight" to the duress he encountered, his educational and medical history, sentencing disparities, and other factors. But "[t]he particular weight to be afforded aggravating and mitigating factors is a matter firmly committed to the discretion of the sentencing judge," *Broxmeyer*, 699 F.3d at 289 (internal quotation marks and citations omitted), and the district court gave careful consideration to all of the relevant factors here. **[—25—] {-406-}**

As to Salas, the district court considered the "destructive harm" of the crime and "amount of drugs" involved, his previous conviction for the same crime, his duress argument, his personal history, sentencing disparities, his culpability vis-à-vis Torres, and the need for deterrence. The district court "balance[d]" and "weigh[ed]" those and other factors, and carefully considered them, noting on the record that the task was "very difficult" and that he had been "thinking about this case for quite some time" and "preparing for sentencing for many months." Salas App'x at 291. The district court concluded that a sentence of 180 months was "appropriate" while constituting a "significant," but not "deep," discount. *Id.* at 322-23.

Salas argues that the district court gave no weight to his life circumstances and other factors and did not give the appropriate weight to the need to avoid sentencing disparities. These arguments are belied by the record. The district court explicitly considered Salas's life circumstances, as well as other pertinent factors. The district court and counsel also discussed sentencing disparities and whether and how other defendants were similarly situated to Salas. Salas App'x at 305-06. **[—26—]**

Accordingly, Torres's and Salas's sentences are not substantively unreasonable, and the district court did not abuse its discretion in imposing them.

CONCLUSION

For the foregoing reasons, the judgments of the district court are AFFIRMED.

United States Court of Appeals for the Third Circuit

United States Court of Appeals
for the Third Circuit

No. 20-2269

NEDERLAND SHIPPING CORP.
VS.
UNITED STATES

Appeal from the United States District Court for the District of Delaware

Decided: November 16, 2021

Citation: 18 F.4th 115, 9 Adm. R. 132 (3d Cir. 2021).

Before **CHAGARES, JORDAN,** and **SCIRICA,** Circuit Judges.

[—2—] {-119-} JORDAN, Circuit Judge:

Delay is a serious problem in the transportation business, especially for shippers of perishable goods. So, when a ship called the M/V Nederland Reefer (the "Reefer" or the "Vessel"), carrying a cargo of fruit, arrived in the Port of **[—3—]** Wilmington, Delaware in February of 2019, its crew thought the layover would be brief. Things did not turn out that way. After a Coast Guard inspection of the ship revealed evidence of an illegal discharge of bilge water,[1] the Reefer was held in port pending an investigation. The Reefer's owner, Nederland Shipping Corporation ("Nederland"), wanted to get the ship back to sea as rapidly as possible and so entered into a contract with the United States government to allow for the release of the Reefer in exchange for, among other consideration, a surety bond to cover potential fines.

Although Nederland delivered the bond and met its other requirements under the contract, the Vessel was detained in Wilmington for at least two additional weeks. Nederland sued in the United States District Court for the District of Delaware, but the government moved to dismiss the suit, arguing among other things that the District Court lacked subject matter jurisdiction. **{-120-}** The District Court accepted that argument and dismissed the complaint, holding that Nederland's claims had to be brought in the United States Court of Federal Claims. More specifically, the District Court **[—4—]** held that the breach of contract claim did not invoke the Court's admiralty jurisdiction and that the statutory cause of action under the Act to Prevent Pollution from Ships (the "APPS") failed because the APPS did not waive the government's sovereign immunity. We disagree on both counts and will accordingly reverse and remand for further consideration.

I. BACKGROUND

The Reefer arrived at the Port of Wilmington, Delaware on February 20, 2019 for what Nederland expected to be a short stay. Upon shipboard inspection, however, the Coast Guard noticed evidence suggesting that the Vessel had violated the APPS.[2] Specifically, the Coast Guard suspected that the Vessel had discharged dirty bilge water directly overboard and misrepresented in its record book that the ship's oil water separator had been used to clean the bilge water prior to discharge. The Coast Guard accordingly detained the Reefer **[—5—]** by withholding a

[1] "Bilge," as a shorthand expression for bilge water, is sometimes used as a synonym for "nonsense," denoting disbelief and derision, *Bilge*, Cambridge Dictionary (2021), https://dictionary.cambridge.org/us/dictionary/english/bilge, but it has a literal maritime meaning too. Bilge water is the often noxious mixture of liquids that collects in the lowest compartment of a ship. *Bilge Water*, Cambridge Dictionary (2021), https://dictionary.cambridge.org/us/dictionary/english/bilge-water. Improperly disposing of it can lead to criminal liability, as further discussed herein.

[2] The Act to Prevent Pollution from Ships authorizes the Department of Homeland Security to enforce the 1973 International Convention for the Prevention of Pollution from Ships ("MARPOL") and to "prescribe any necessary or desired regulations to carry out" that treaty. 33 U.S.C. § 1903(c)(1); *see United States v. Abrogar*, 459 F.3d 430, 431-32 (3d Cir. 2006). It is a crime to "knowingly violate[ ]" those regulations or the APPS. 33 U.S.C. § 1908(a). "A ship operated in violation of" those laws "is liable in rem for any fine imposed[.]" *Id.* § 1908(d).

departure clearance, under 33 U.S.C. § 1908(e) of the APPS.[3]

The Coast Guard's Captain of the Port issued a letter to the Vessel's representative on February 22, 2019, explaining the Coast Guard's authority to withhold the departure clearance and that clearance could be granted if the Vessel entered into a surety agreement that included providing a financial bond. To negotiate that agreement, Nederland sought **[—6—]** out Commander Robert Pirone of the Coast Guard. On March 7, Commander Pirone repeated that departure clearance could be obtained upon the issuance of a bond as part of a security agreement. He also told Nederland that the alleged discharge of bilge water had been referred to the Department of Justice for criminal prosecution under the APPS.

Seeking to get the Reefer underway again, Nederland signed an "Agreement on Security" (the "Agreement") with the United States on March 8, 2019. Nederland agreed to post a surety bond of $1 million, which would act as security for any adjudicated fines or penalties for violations **{–121–}** of the APPS.[4] It also agreed to other provisions "[a]s consideration for surety satisfactory to the Secretary [of Homeland Security] for the release of the Vessel." (App. at 37.) Those provisions included consent to the jurisdiction of the United States over the criminal case and assurance that the thirteen crewmembers of the Reefer would remain in the United States to participate in the criminal trial, at the expense of Nederland. The Agreement also provided that "[a]ny dispute between the United States and Owner or Operator[, i.e., Nederland,] regarding payment under this paragraph shall be submitted to the United States District Court for the District of Delaware. ... [T]he party asserting that there has been a breach of the Agreement shall bear the burden of proof." (App. at 39.) In addition, the parties agreed that "the criminal and civil penalty claims of the United States against the Vessel in rem shall attach to the Vessel release's security as provided pursuant to the Federal Rules of Civil **[—7—]** Procedure, Admiralty, Maritime Claims, Supplemental Rule E(5)." (App. at 46.)

On that same day, March 8, Coast Guard agents served the Reefer's crewmembers with subpoenas to testify before a grand jury in April. Three days later, on March 11, Nederland's attorney informed Commander Pirone that all replacement crewmembers were on board the Reefer and had completed the handover from the thirteen crewmembers who were required to stay in Delaware. But the Vessel did not receive a departure clearance. After sending several emails asking for updates on the processing of paperwork for the detained crewmembers, Nederland's attorney told the government that the continuing delay of the Vessel had become unreasonable. He also highlighted Nederland's right to pursue damages under 33 U.S.C. § 1904(h).[5] In particular, he empha-

---

[3] The Coast Guard may "refuse or revoke" a vessel's departure clearance "if reasonable cause exists to believe" that the vessel may be subject to a fine under the APPS. 33 U.S.C. § 1908(e). The departure clearance may nonetheless be granted "upon the filing of a bond or other surety satisfactory to the Secretary" of Homeland Security. *Id.* Entitled "Ship clearance or permits; refusal or revocation; bond or other surety[,]" 33 U.S.C. § 1908(e) provides:

> If any ship subject to the MARPOL Protocol, Annex IV to the Antarctic Protocol, or this chapter, its owner, operator, or person in charge is liable for a fine or civil penalty under this section, or if reasonable cause exists to believe that the ship, its owner, operator, or person in charge may be subject to a fine or civil penalty under this section, the Secretary of the Treasury, upon the request of the Secretary [of Homeland Security], shall refuse or revoke the clearance required by section 60105 of Title 46 [to proceed from a port]. Clearance may be granted upon the filing of a bond or other surety satisfactory to the Secretary.

[4] Nederland ended up entering a guilty plea in the criminal case. It paid a $900,000 fine.

[5] Section 1904(h) provides: "Compensation for loss or damage [-] A ship unreasonably detained or delayed by the Secretary acting under the authority of this chapter is entitled to compensation for any loss or damage suffered thereby." 33 U.S.C. § 1904(h).

sized the economic losses that the Vessel would experience if the delay continued, including the costs associated with making alternative arrangements for its perishable cargoes and missing its next commercial commitment. Nederland continued to ask for updates from the government, with little to no response, until March 28, 2019, when the Vessel was finally permitted to leave port.

Approximately three months later, Nederland filed for declaratory relief in the District Court under 33 U.S.C. § 1904(h), seeking a declaratory judgment that the Agreement **[—8—]** was null and void *ab initio* and asking for damages for breach of contract and compensation for unreasonable delay in allowing the Vessel's departure. The government moved to dismiss for failure to state a claim and for lack of subject matter jurisdiction.

The District Court was persuaded by the government's attack on subject matter jurisdiction. As to Nederland's breach of contract claim, the Court held that it did not have jurisdiction in admiralty because the Agreement is not a maritime contract, as the "principal objective of the Agreement is to permit the ship's departure clearance while preserving the Government's ability to investigate." (App. at 9.) Without the waiver of sovereign immunity attendant to admiralty jurisdiction, the claim could not proceed, the Court said, because the Agreement itself did not amount to a waiver of that immunity. As to the APPS cause of action under **{-122-}** 33 U.S.C. § 1904(h), the Court held that § 1904(h) does not expressly waive sovereign immunity. According to the Court, the waiver of sovereign immunity found in the Tucker Act, 28 U.S.C. § 1491, could instead provide an avenue for relief for Nederland, but any such claim would have to be brought in the Court of Federal Claims.

Nederland now appeals.

II. DISCUSSION[6]

Nederland argues that the District Court erred in holding that it lacked subject matter jurisdiction in this case. **[—9—]** According to Nederland, the Agreement it entered with the government is maritime in nature and thus vested the Court with admiralty jurisdiction.[7] Nederland also contends that its statutory cause of action for monetary damages under 33 U.S.C. § 1904(h) provides subject matter jurisdiction because it is an independent cause of action that waives the government's sovereign immunity. The government counters that the Tucker Act waives sovereign immunity for non-tort monetary claims against the United States "founded ... upon ... any Act of Congress[,] ... or upon any express or implied contract with the United States," and also provides exclusive jurisdiction for such claims in the Court of Federal Claims, 28 U.S.C. § 1491(a)(1), so that Nederland's suit must instead be brought in that court.

To prevail in this jurisdictional dispute, Nederland must clear two hurdles: it has to demonstrate that Congress provided for subject matter jurisdiction in the district courts over the claims at issue and that Congress waived sovereign immunity. *See United States v. Bormes*, 568 U.S. 6, 9-10 (2012) (explaining plaintiffs may only sue the United States for **[—10—]** monetary damages where sovereign immunity has been waived and subject matter jurisdiction exists). The parties do not dispute that if there is admiralty jurisdiction in this case, both conditions are satisfied for the contract claim, since federal courts have power to hear "all

[6] We have appellate jurisdiction under 28 U.S.C. § 1291. Nederland asserted jurisdiction in the District Court **[—9—]** under 28 U.S.C. §§ 1331 and 2201. We address the District Court's jurisdiction herein. We exercise plenary review to determine whether the District Court enjoyed subject matter jurisdiction. *In re Allen*, 768 F.3d 274, 279 (3d Cir. 2014).

[7] Nederland also argues that the parties contracted for subject matter jurisdiction in the District Court. That argument plainly fails because parties cannot create subject matter jurisdiction. *See Samuel-Bassett v. KIA Motors Am., Inc.*, 357 F.3d 392, 396 (3d Cir. 2004) ("[P]arties may not confer subject matter jurisdiction by consent.").

Cases of admiralty and maritime Jurisdiction[,]" U.S. Const. art. III, § 2, cl. 1; 28 U.S.C. § 1333, and Congress has waived sovereign immunity for claims brought in admiralty, *Henderson v. United States*, 517 U.S. 654, 665 (1996); 46 U.S.C. § 30903. The fight over the contract claim is thus whether it is a maritime claim and so properly subject to admiralty jurisdiction. As to the APPS statutory claim, the fight is whether 33 U.S.C. § 1904(h) waives sovereign immunity.

A. The Agreement is a maritime contract.

Nederland argues that the Agreement is maritime in nature and thus invokes the District Court's admiralty jurisdiction. The government responds that the Agreement primarily sought to facilitate a criminal investigation pursuant to the APPS and so is not a maritime contract. Nederland has the better of the argument. **{-123-}**

The Supreme Court emphasized in *Norfolk Southern Railway Co. v. Kirby* that the primary interest of maritime jurisdiction is "the protection of maritime *commerce*." 543 U.S. 14, 25 (2004) (emphasis in original) (quoting *Exxon Corp. v. Cent. Gulf Lines, Inc.*, 500 U.S. 603, 608 (1991)). Consequently, we are looking to "the nature and character of the contract" at issue to determine whether it has "reference to maritime service or maritime transactions." *Id.* at 24 (quoting *N. Pac. S.S. Co. v. Hall Bros. Marine Ry. & Shipbuilding Co.*, 249 U.S. 119, 125 (1919)). A ship does not need to be directly **[—11—]** involved in the dispute for admiralty jurisdiction to attach, as "the admiralty and maritime jurisdiction ... extends to and includes cases of injury or damage ... caused by a vessel on navigable waters even though the injury or damage is done or consummated on land." *Id.* at 23-24 (quoting the Admiralty Jurisdiction Extension Act, 46 U.S.C. § 30101).

Following the two-step inquiry established more than a half-century ago in *Kossick v. United Fruit Co.*, 365 U.S. 731, 735 (1961), the *Kirby* Court asked first whether the contracts under review were maritime, and, second, whether they dealt with an inherently local dispute such that federal law should not control. *Kirby*, 543 U.S. at 22-23. It held that bills of lading for the transport of goods from Australia to Alabama were maritime contracts even though the final leg of the journey was via rail. *Id.* at 23-24. Because the bills of ladings' "primary objective" under the first step of *Kossick* was to "accomplish the transportation of goods by sea from Australia to the eastern coast of the United States[,]" the Court held that it was beside the point that part of the journey was by rail. *Id.* at 24. The Court also indicated, at the second step of *Kossick*, that no local interests had been suggested that would call federal jurisdiction into question. *Id.* at 27.

Following the same analytical path here, but in reverse order, we can quickly dispose of the "inherently local" issue. The dispute before us clearly implicates federal law—the APPS—and international concern with sea-going commerce and ocean pollution. It is thus obviously not inherently local. The issue, then, is the first question posed in *Kossick* and *Kirby*: what is the primary objective of the contract at issue. Not surprisingly, each party characterizes the Agreement's "primary objective" differently. *Id.* The government says the **[—12—]** primary objective of the Agreement was to allow "the criminal proceedings to continue to conclusion, including the payment of a potential criminal penalty." (Answering Br. at 23.) Nederland says instead that the primary objective of the Agreement was to provide sufficient security to obtain the Vessel's departure clearance so it could continue its trade. Both objectives are, it is true, contemplated in the Agreement, but the government's characterization ignores every interest but its own and, even at that, fails to acknowledge that the crime under investigation was itself particularly maritime in character. The government chooses to define its objective as simply pursuing a criminal prosecution, but that does not change the fact that the charge it was pursuing was a crime on the seas, outlawed by a maritime treaty. Nor does it change that both the Agreement (App. at 46) and the statute under which the government detained the vessel, 33 U.S.C. § 1908(d), speak in terms of liability in rem, which is language classically associated with admiralty jurisdiction. *See, e.g.*, **{-124-}** *Leon v. Galceran*, 78 U.S. 185, 190 (1870) ("[A] party may proceed *in rem* in the admiralty, and if he elects to pursue his remedy in that mode he cannot proceed in any other form, as the jurisdiction of the admiralty courts is exclusive in respect to that mode of proceeding[.]"). That is not determinative here, but it is telling.

What is determinative is that, contrary to the government's position, it did not need the Agreement to permit the criminal proceeding to continue to conclusion. The result of there having been no agreement and no surety bond would not have been the Reefer sailing away scot-free. It would have been the Coast Guard withholding the Vessel's departure clearance until the criminal proceedings ended. *Watervale Marine Co. v. U.S. Dep't of Homeland Sec.*, 807 F.3d 325, 330, 3 Adm. R. 707, 709–10 **[—13—]** (D.C. Cir. 2015) (Section 1908(e) "clearly provides authority in the Coast Guard to simply hold the ship in port until legal proceedings are completed."); *see also Angelex Ltd. v. United States* (*Angelex I*), 723 F.3d 500, 507, 1 Adm. R. 169, 173 (4th Cir. 2013) (Section 1908(e) "grants the Coast Guard broad discretion to deny bond altogether[.]"). So the essential character and purpose of the Agreement was not to secure the Vessel and crew in port; that was already done. The primary objective of the Agreement was rather to set the Reefer free to pursue maritime commerce.[8] **[—14—]**

The conclusion that the Agreement here has, as the saying goes, a "genuinely salty flavor," *Kirby*, 543 U.S. at 22 (citation omitted), is confirmed by other cases considering contracts that provide security in exchange for a vessel's freedom to continue on its journey. For example, in *Deval Denizcilik Ve Tigaret A.S. v. Agenzia Tripcovich S.R.L.*, the district court held that it had admiralty jurisdiction over a bank's guaranty to pay as a substitute for releasing cargo from arrest because it "ultimately hastened the delivery of the cargo by sea." 513 F. Supp. 2d 6, 9 (S.D.N.Y. 2007). Just as the ship's "cargo would not have been released had [the bank] not issued the guarantee[,]" Nederland's Vessel would not have been allowed to continue its maritime trade but for the Agreement. *Id.* Similarly, in *Great Eastern Shipping Co. v. Binani Cement Ltd.*, the district court held that a letter of indemnity promising to pay a bond to secure the release of a ship in exchange for the delivery of cargo was a maritime contract. 655 F. Supp. 2d 395, 399 (S.D.N.Y. 2009); *see also Compagnie Francaise De Navigation a Vapeur v. Bonnasse*, 19 F.2d 777, 778-79 (2d Cir. 1927) (holding admiralty jurisdiction existed over a contract to assume the performance of a bond "to release the res, or to prevent its arrest").

The government attempts to distinguish those cases by arguing that the security **{-125-}** agreements at issue in them were for inherently maritime obligations, while securing a potential criminal penalty is not a maritime obligation. In drawing that contrast, the government again views its Agreement with Nederland solely from its own perspective, not recognizing the obvious commercial benefit to Nederland of freeing the Reefer to go to sea. On top of that, the distinction the government draws is unfounded. The *Deval* court did not premise its decision on the underlying charter contract, but instead **[—15—]** emphasized

[8] The parties also discuss the purposes of the APPS and MARPOL, both pointing to various aims of the treaty and its enacting legislation to support their characterizations of their Agreement's primary objective. The government argues that the APPS was "passed to implement various environmental obligations that the United States assumed when it entered into" MARPOL. (Answering Br. at 16 (quoting *Watervale Marine Co. v. U.S. Dep't of Homeland Sec.*, 807 F.3d 325, 327, 3 Adm. R. 707, 707 (D.C. Cir. 2015)).) And Nederland contends that MARPOL not only sought to preserve the marine environment, but to balance those environmental concerns with "the desire not to impose laws which make shipping prohibitively expensive." (Reply Br. at 4-5 (quoting *United States v. Apex Oil Co. Inc.*, 132 F.3d 1287, 1291 (9th Cir. 1997)).) Such a concern was codified in § 1904(h), which provides a means by which ships unreasonably detained can seek compensation. 33 U.S.C. § 1904(h). Ultimately, however, "the nature and character of the contract" itself must guide our admiralty jurisdiction analysis—not a broader review of the treaty or the enabling legislation behind the particular contract. *Norfolk S. Ry. Co. v. Kirby*, 543 U.S. 14, 24 (2004) (citation omitted).

that the guaranty permitted maritime commerce to continue. 513 F. Supp. 2d at 9. That is a precise analog of deal in the Agreement here. So too in *Great Eastern Shipping*, the court stated that "Great Eastern's consideration was the prompt discharge of the cargo, a quintessentially maritime service, in forbearance of its right to demand the bills of lading on discharge, a quintessentially maritime right." 655 F. Supp. 2d at 399. It thus relied on its finding that the "overall purpose of the transaction ... was maritime" to conclude that the letter of indemnity was maritime in nature. *Id.* While the government rightly points out that both cases involved underlying commercial contracts, it was the discharge of the cargo to allow for uninterrupted maritime trade that rendered the contracts maritime in nature.

The government would prefer that we rely upon a case from the District of New Hampshire that was decided before *Kirby*. In *Chi Shun Hua Steel Co. v. Crest Tankers, Inc.*, the district court held that an agreement releasing the attachment of a vessel in exchange for posting security or bringing the vessel the following day to be reattached was a non-maritime contract. 708 F. Supp. 18, 22 (D.N.H. 1989). But, lacking the later guidance that the Supreme Court provided in the *Kirby* opinion, the *Crest Tankers* court determined whether the contract was maritime in nature by asking whether the contract "concerns transportation by sea, relates to navigation and concerns maritime employment." *Id.* Applying that outdated rule, the court held that the involvement of a ship did not bring the matter within its admiralty jurisdiction because "the settlement agreement itself was of a non-maritime nature." *Id.* Even if that reasoning were persuasive, it does not survive after *Kirby*. The *Kirby* Court specifically noted that "reference to maritime service or maritime transactions" can make a contract **[—16—]** maritime in nature. 543 U.S. at 24 (quoting *Hall Bros.*, 249 U.S. at 125). Reference to a vessel which has been detained, and which a surety agreement would free to continue its maritime trade, falls within the Supreme Court's definitional guidance.

For much the same reason, we are not persuaded by the cases that the District Court cited to support its jurisdictional conclusion. In saying it lacked jurisdiction, the Court first pointed to *Angelex I*, 723 F.3d at 509, 1 Adm. R. at 175, which is inapposite because, although it concerned the withholding of a departure clearance for a vessel accused of violating the APPS, there was no underlying contractual agreement in that dispute. There, the Fourth Circuit held that the withholding of a vessel's departure clearance for an indeterminate amount of time—where the vessel owner could not afford to post bond—was not "tantamount to an arrest of the ship" and thus did not invoke in rem admiralty jurisdiction. *Id.*, 1 Adm. R. at 175. Because in rem admiralty actions involve a vessel being "treated as the offender and made the defendant by name or description in order to enforce a lien[,]" and "discretionary action on the part of the Coast Guard under APPS" cannot be considered "an offense to the ship itself," the Fourth Circuit concluded that subject matter jurisdiction was lacking. *Id.* at 509-10, 1 Adm. R. at 176. That case would surely be on point and we **{-126-}** would have to address its analysis if Nederland and the government had failed to negotiate a security agreement. But the parties here *did* negotiate a contract, and our jurisdictional inquiry must focus on whether the Agreement they entered into, pursuant to § 1908(e), constitutes a maritime contract—a question not raised in *Angelex I*. **[—17—]**

The District Court also relied on *Retif Oil & Fuel, LLC v. Offshore Specialty Fabricators, LLC*, which held that a guaranty agreement to pay the debt owed on a contract for ship fuel and lube was a maritime contract. No. 17-7831, 2018 WL 4680125, at *5 (E.D. La. Sept. 28, 2018). The District Court in the instant case quoted *Retif Oil* for the proposition that "a 'surety agreement is held not to be an admiralty contract, since the obligation of the surety is only to pay damages in the event of liability on the underlying contract[.]'" (App. at 9 (quoting *Retif Oil*, 2018 WL 4680125, at *5).) The *Retif Oil* court concluded that the guaranty agreement before it, in contrast, was a promise to step into the shoes of the obligor and fully perform the underlying obligation by paying for the provisions if the other party did not. 2018 WL 4680125, at *6. So, the guaranty agreement at issue was more than a bare promise to pay damages and, thus, was a maritime contract. *Id.* But the hypothetical surety contract discussed in *Retif Oil* differs from the Agreement before us in a key aspect. Nederland did not merely promise to pay money in the event of liability; it promised to pay money and perform other undertakings in order to obtain a departure clearance so the Reefer could leave port and continue its maritime trade. In sum, both cases relied on by the District Court—*Angelex I* and *Retif Oil*—are distinguishable because they did not determine whether contracts providing security to allow a vessel to continue seagoing commerce are maritime in nature.

Finally, we note that the Agreement, which was drafted by the government, is premised on the explicit understanding that subject matter jurisdiction is proper in the District Court. For example, the Agreement provides that "the criminal and civil penalty claims of the United States against the Vessel in rem shall attach to the Vessel release's security as provided **[—18—]** pursuant to the Federal Rules of Civil Procedure, Admiralty, Maritime Claims, Supplemental Rule E(5)." (App. at 46.) We cannot conceive of a circumstance in which the government would contract to the applicability of Admiralty Supplemental Rule E(5) if it viewed potential breaches of the contract as not falling under admiralty jurisdiction.[9] In addition, the government agreed that "any" dispute "regarding payment under this paragraph shall be submitted to the United States District Court for the District of Delaware." (App. at 39.) At oral argument, counsel for the government said that this provision only refers to the United States' ability to sue Nederland for the payment of the bond. (See audio recording of oral argument held on April 14, 2021 at 30:00-31:57 (https://www2.ca3.uscourts.gov/oralargument/audio/20-2269_NederlandShippingv.USA.mp3).) But that assertion is belied by the very next sentence in the Agreement: "In any such dispute wherein one party claims a breach of the terms and **{–127–}** conditions herein, the party asserting that there has been a breach of the Agreement shall bear the burden of proof." (App. at 39.) The use of the generic term "party[,]" rather than specifying that only the United States may sue in the District Court, plainly means that either party could commence litigation in the District Court. While the parties to a contract cannot confer subject matter jurisdiction on federal courts, and while the government's past or present positions on jurisdiction do not determine our conclusion, it is nevertheless revealing that the government's pre-litigation view of the law, **[—19—]** as embodied in the form of contract it drafted, was that admiralty jurisdiction in a case like this existed in the District Court.

Given all of the foregoing, our view is that the District Court has admiralty jurisdiction over the breach of contract claim, as the primary objective of the Agreement was to secure the Vessel's departure clearance, so that it could continue its maritime trade.[10] **[—20—]**

---

[9] The Supplemental Admiralty and Maritime Claims Rule E contemplates jurisdiction over "actions in personam with process of maritime attachment and garnishment, *actions in rem*, and petitory, possessory, and partition actions[.]" Fed. R. Civ. P. Adm. Rule E(1) (emphasis added).

[10] Nederland fleetingly argues in the alternative that the contract is a "mixed" contract, meaning it contains both maritime and non-maritime elements. Mixed contracts do not fall within admiralty jurisdiction unless they are severable and may be separately adjudicated, *Berkshire Fashions, Inc. v. M.V. Hakusan II*, 954 F.2d 874, 880 (3d Cir. 1992), and Nederland suggests only in a conclusory manner that the Agreement is severable. Because the contract's primary objective is maritime in nature and thus falls within admiralty jurisdiction, we need not address that alternative argument.

We do, however, briefly note the government's subsidiary arguments. It says that the Agreement contains no maritime clauses or terms "that might require the district court to draw upon its maritime expertise[.]" (Answering Br. at 25.) It fails, however, to cite any precedent to support its suggestion that a contract can only be maritime in nature if it requires a court to analyze the meaning of a maritime term. Lastly, it relies on *Kirby* to contend that "the core purpose of admiralty jurisdiction, uniformity in the law," is best served if

B. The District Court erred in holding that it lacked subject matter jurisdiction over the APPS cause of action.

Nederland also contends that the District Court has federal question jurisdiction pursuant to 28 U.S.C. § 1331 over its statutory cause of action because Congress explicitly waived the government's sovereign immunity for damages claimed under the APPS in 33 U.S.C. § 1904(h).[11] The government argues that Nederland's § 1904(h) claim is not cognizable as an independent cause of action and thus must be transferred to the Court of Federal Claims under the waiver of sovereign immunity provided by the Tucker Act.[12] We agree with Nederland because the APPS explicitly waives the government's sovereign immunity, making the Tucker Act immaterial to this dispute.

The Tucker Act waives the government's sovereign immunity for non-tort monetary claims against the United States founded upon "any Act of Congress," the Constitution, **[—21—]** or contracts, but it vests jurisdiction only in the Court of **{-128-}** Federal Claims. 28 U.S.C. § 1491(a)(1).[13] With that waiver, the Tucker Act "supplied the missing ingredient for an action against the United States for the breach of monetary obligations not otherwise judicially enforceable." *Bormes*, 568 U.S. at 12. It does not provide a substantive right to damages but instead opens the door to government liability for claims falling under its purview. *Chabal v. Reagan*, 822 F.2d 349, 355 (3d Cir. 1987). For a claim to have the advantage granted by the Tucker Act, it need only "fairly be interpreted as mandating compensation by the Federal Government for the damage sustained." *United States v. White Mountain Apache Tribe*, 537 U.S. 465, 472 (2003) (citation omitted). That "'fair interpretation' rule demands a showing demonstrably lower than the standard for the initial waiver of sovereign immunity[,]" and thus "an explicit provision for money damages" is not necessary. *Id.* at 472, 477.

Not all claims against the government, however, are reliant on the Tucker Act. Claims premised upon statutes that provide for independent causes of action and that waive the **[—22—]** government's sovereign immunity need not be channeled through the Tucker Act. *See Bowen v. Massachusetts,* 487 U.S. 879, 910 n.48 (1988) ("Rather, [the Court of Federal Claims'] jurisdiction is 'exclusive' only to the extent that Congress has not granted any other court authority to hear the claims that may be decided by the Claims Court."); *Franklin-Mason v. Mabus*, 742 F.3d 1051, 1055 (D.C. Cir. 2014) ("If a separate waiver of sovereign immunity and grant of jurisdiction exist, district courts may hear cases over which, under the Tucker Act alone, the Court of Federal Claims would have exclusive jurisdiction." (citation omitted)); *Tritz v. U.S. Postal Serv.*, 721 F.3d 1133, 1137 (9th Cir. 2013) (While the Tucker Act "create[s] a presumption of exclusive jurisdiction in the Court of Federal Claims, ... that presumption can be overcome by an independent statutory grant of jurisdiction to another court."). Nederland argues that the APPS is one such statute, as it waives

---

APPS security agreements are always adjudicated in the Court of Federal Claims. (Answering Br. at 25-26.) But any uniformity concern cited by *Kirby* involved whether the contract at issue was inherently local or federal, not where in the federal system **[—20—]** the contract claim should be adjudicated. *Kirby*, 543 U.S. at 27-28.

[11] Nederland does not contend that the District Court enjoyed admiralty jurisdiction under 28 U.S.C. § 1333 over the statutory cause of action, and it is not necessary to consider that point.

[12] The government also says that Nederland forfeited its sovereign immunity waiver argument on appeal. Not so: Nederland argued that the APPS permits claims against the government through waiver of sovereign immunity.

[13] The Tucker Act provides:

> The United States Court of Federal Claims shall have jurisdiction to render judgment upon any claim against the United States founded either upon the Constitution, or any Act of Congress or any regulations of an executive department, or upon any express or implied contract with the United States, or for liquidated or unliquidated damages in cases not sounding in tort.

28 U.S.C. § 1491(a)(1).

sovereign immunity and provides jurisdiction in the district courts, so resort to the Tucker Act, and transfer to the Court of Federal Claims, is unnecessary. The government, on the other hand, contends that the APPS should be interpreted as providing a cause of action under the Tucker Act but not as an independent waiver of sovereign immunity.

The government does not dispute that if the APPS waives sovereign immunity, jurisdiction would be proper in the District Court.[14] The question before **{-129-}** us, then, is whether the **[—23—]** APPS indeed waives the government's sovereign immunity. The United States is immune from suit unless it expressly and unequivocally waives its immunity. *United States v. Mitchell*, 445 U.S. 535, 538 (1980). Statutory text purporting to waive governmental immunity is strictly construed "in favor of the sovereign." *United States v. Nordic Vill., Inc.*, 503 U.S. 30, 34 (1992) (internal quotation marks and citation omitted). Thus, "[a]ny ambiguities in the statutory language are to be construed in favor of immunity," and "[a]mbiguity exists if there is a plausible interpretation of the statute that would not authorize money damages against the [g]overnment." *F.A.A. v. Cooper*, 566 U.S. 284, 290-91 (2012). There is no particular set of words that must be invoked to waive sovereign immunity, but the waiver must be discernable and explicit through traditional tools of statutory interpretation. *Id.* at 291. Furthermore, "[a] statutory waiver of sovereign immunity ... defines the scope of a court's jurisdiction to entertain the suit." *Gentile v. Sec. & Exch. Comm'n*, 974 F.3d 311, 316 (3d Cir. 2020) (internal quotation marks and citations omitted). Consequently, "[t]o sustain a claim that the Government is liable for awards of monetary damages, the waiver of sovereign immunity must extend unambiguously to such monetary claims." *Lane v. Pena*, 518 U.S. 187, 192 (1996). **[—24—]**

With all of that in mind, we conclude that there is a waiver of sovereign immunity for monetary damages in the plain text of the APPS. Section 1904(h), under which Nederland brings its statutory cause of action, provides: "Compensation for loss or damage [-] A ship unreasonably detained or delayed by the Secretary acting under the authority of this chapter is entitled to compensation for any loss or damage suffered thereby." 33 U.S.C. § 1904(h). The Fourth Circuit has dubbed that provision an "after-the-fact damages remedy against the United States for unreasonable detention or delay." *Angelex I*, 723 F.3d at 509, 1 Adm. R. at 175.

By "entitl[ing] [a ship] to compensation for any loss or damage suffered" due to its detention or delay by the Secretary of Homeland Security, § 1904(h) clearly goes beyond providing a cause of action that is cognizable only under the Tucker Act. *Cf. White Mountain Apache Tribe*, 537 U.S. at 477 (comparing "the less demanding requirement" for finding a cause of action under the Tucker Act with the more demanding requirement for finding an independent waiver of sovereign immunity). We thus do not agree with the government that § 1904(h) provides a cause of action only in tandem with the Tucker Act's waiver of sovereign immunity. Rather, Congress provided "an explicit provision for money damages" by allowing for "compensation for any loss" caused by the Secretary's unreasonable detention of a ship. *Id.*; 33 U.S.C. § 1904(h). The provision need not explicitly state that "the United States" will pay compensation for any loss because, reading the provision in context as we must, *see King v. Burwell*, 576 U.S. 473, 486 (2015) ("Our duty ... is to construe statutes, not isolated provisions" (internal quotation marks and citation omitted)), no other actor could logically be held liable. The federal

---

[14] The government cites *Chabal v. Reagan*, where, in denying jurisdiction over a former U.S. Marshal's suit for reinstatement, back pay, and damages for an allegedly improper removal, we explained: "Jurisdiction over non-tort monetary claims against the United States is exclusively **[—23—]** defined by the Tucker Act, as codified at 28 U.S.C. §§ 1346, 1491, because it is only under the terms of the Tucker Act that the United States waives its sovereign immunity to non-tort claims seeking monetary relief." 822 F.2d 349, 353 (3d Cir. 1987). But, as later explained by the Supreme Court, that is merely an "assumption[,]" and Congress has the ability to waive sovereign immunity for other claims. *Bowen*, 487 U.S. at 910 n.48.

government causes the unreasonable **[—25—]** detention, and the federal government thus provides compensation for the resulting loss or damage. *Cf. Cooper*, 566 U.S. at 291 ("We have never required that Congress use magic words" to waive sovereign immunity.). Congress intended **{–130–}** to make the United States liable when a vessel is unreasonably detained by the Secretary of Homeland Security, and § 1904(h) is express and unequivocal in stating that waiver of sovereign immunity.[15] *Mitchell*, 445 U.S. at 538.

That conclusion comports with the opinion of the only other court of appeals to have considered a claim under § 1904(h). *See Angelex, Ltd. v. United States (Angelex II)*, 907 F.3d 612, 623, 6 Adm. R. 514, 521 (D.C. Cir. 2018) (affirming a grant of summary judgment for the government where a ship owner sought compensation under § 1904(h) for expenses after an allegedly unreasonable delay of its ship). In *Angelex II*, the D.C. Circuit **[—26—]** addressed a § 1904(h) claim on its merits without questioning or discussing subject matter jurisdiction. *Id.* at 618, 6 Adm. R. at 517. The district court in that case had noted at the motion to dismiss stage that the government did not contest jurisdiction. *Angelex, Ltd. v. United States*, 123 F. Supp. 3d 66, 74 n.4 (D.D.C. 2015). While the government is correct to point out that "drive-by jurisdictional ruling[s]" carry little precedential weight, *Del. Riverkeeper Network v. Sec'y Pa. Dep't of Env't Prot.*, 903 F.3d 65, 71 (3d Cir. 2018), it is notable that neither the district court nor the D.C. Circuit viewed subject matter jurisdiction over the § 1904(h) claim as worthy of discussion.

The government would have us reason that Congress may only displace the provisions of the Tucker Act through a statute with a "specific remedial scheme[,]" which the APPS does not have. (Answering Br. at 29 (quoting *Bormes*, 568 U.S. at 12).) Relying on *United States v. Bormes*, the government notes that the Supreme Court held a plaintiff could not avail himself of the Tucker Act's waiver of sovereign immunity because the Fair Credit Reporting Act contained its own self-executing remedial scheme, indicating that Congress intended to displace the Tucker Act. 568 U.S. at 10-11. When a litigant brings a claim under a statute with a self-executing remedial scheme that imposes monetary liability on the government, that law "supersedes the gap-filling role of the Tucker Act" because "precisely drawn, detailed statute[s] pre-empt[ ] more general remedies[.]" *Id.* at 12-13. So the government is quite right that *Bormes* described how "[t]he Tucker Act yields when the obligation-creating statute provides its own detailed remedies[.]" *Maine Cmty. Health Options v. United States*, 140 S. Ct. 1308, 1328 (2020) (citing *Bormes*, 568 U.S. at 13). But that case does not mandate deferral to the Tucker Act unless the other statute at issue has **[—27—]** a detailed remedial scheme. The issue is not the level of detail surrounding an alternative remedy; the issue is whether there is a clear waiver, and in the APPS there is.

Because there is no "plausible interpretation of the statute that would not authorize **{–131–}** money damages against the [g]overnment[,]" we conclude that § 1904(h) waives the federal government's sovereign immunity. *Cooper*, 566 U.S. 284 at 290-91. Thus, under 28 U.S.C. § 1331, the District Court enjoyed jurisdiction over the independent statutory cause of action provided in 33 U.S.C. § 1904(h).

---

[15] Nederland also argues that Congress waived sovereign immunity for claims brought under the APPS through § 1910. That provision, entitled "Legal Actions[,]" provides that "any person having an interest which is, or can be, adversely affected, may bring an action" upon certain stated grounds "in the United States district court for any judicial district wherein the ship or its owner or operator may be found." 33 U.S.C. § 1910(a), (c)(3). Because we read § 1904(h) to expressly waive sovereign immunity, we need not resort to other sections of the APPS to reach our conclusion.

As a reminder, the government does not dispute jurisdiction in the District Court if the APPS waives sovereign immunity. As contemplated by 33 U.S.C. § 1908(d), "[a] ship operated in violation of the MARPOL Protocol ... may be proceeded against in the United States district court of any district in which the ship may be found."

III. CONCLUSION

For the foregoing reasons, we will reverse the order of the District Court and remand for consideration of Nederland's claims.

United States Court of Appeals
for the Third Circuit

No. 20-2040

UNITED STATES
vs.
VASTARDIS

Appeal from the United States District Court for the District of Delaware

Decided: December 7, 2021

Citation: 19 F.4th 573, 9 Adm. R. 143 (3d Cir. 2021).

Before McKEE, RESTREPO, and FUENTES, Circuit Judges.

[—3—] {-576-} FUENTES, Circuit Judge:

This case requires us to determine whether the United States lacks prosecutorial authority over the presentation of falsified records to U.S. officials and other related deception that occurred while a defendant was docked in the Delaware Bay port because the crimes sought to be covered up were committed on the high seas. We hold that, although Vastardis cannot be convicted in a U.S. Court for crimes occurring in international waters, the convictions here were based on the presence of inaccurate records in U.S. waters. Accordingly, the District Court had subject matter jurisdiction even though the actual entries may have been made beyond the jurisdiction of the United States while on the high seas.

Nikolaos Vastardis, a citizen and resident of the Republic of Greece, appeals his conviction and sentence for crimes that allegedly took place while he was Chief Engineer onboard a Liberian-registered petroleum tanker named the *Evridiki*. Vastardis was convicted of four offenses related to maritime pollution: failing to maintain an accurate Oil Record Book from December 8, 2018 to March 11, 2019 in violation of 33 U.S.C. § 1908(a) (Count 1); falsifying high-seas Oil Record Book entries in violation of the Sarbanes-Oxley Act, 18 U.S.C. § 1519 (Count 2); obstructing justice in the Coast Guard's investigation of the *Evridiki* in violation of 18 U.S.C. § 1505 (Count 3); and making false statements in violation of 18 U.S.C. § 1001 (Count 4). The District Court imposed a **[—4—]** $7,500 fine, a $400 special assessment, and three years' probation. As a condition of probation, Vastardis was barred from entering the United States or applying for any visas to enter the United States. **{-577-}**

For the following reasons, we will affirm the convictions. However, we will vacate the portion of the District Court's sentence that precludes Vastardis from entering the United States while under court supervision.

I. INTERNATIONAL TREATIES ON MARITIME POLLUTION

The United States is a signatory to the 1973 International Convention for the Prevention of Pollution from Ships[1] and the Protocol of 1978 Relating to the International Convention for the Prevention of Pollution from Ships.[2] Both treaties relate to pollution on the high seas. Together, these treaties are referred to as "MARPOL" (short for "Maritime Pollution"), and their collective aim is to "achieve the complete elimination of international pollution of the marine environment by oil and other harmful substances."[3]

MARPOL is enforced by U.S. federal statute through the Act to Prevent Pollution from Ships ("Act to Prevent Pollution"), which criminalizes violations of MARPOL. The Act to Prevent Pollution designates the country in which a ship is registered as the "flag state," and the country receiving the **[—5—]** ship as the "port state."[4] Under MARPOL and the Act to Prevent Pollution, a ship's flag state may prosecute a violation "wherever the violation occurs."[5] By contrast, port states have jurisdiction over foreign ships only for conduct that occurs in their ports or waters and may only refer evidence of a foreign ship's high-

---

[1] Nov. 2, 1973, 1340 U.N.T.S. 184.

[2] Feb. 17, 1978, 1340 U.N.T.S. 61.

[3] 1340 U.N.T.S. at 128.

[4] *United States v. Abrogar*, 459 F.3d 430, 432 (3d Cir. 2006).

[5] MARPOL Art. 4(1)–(2), 1340 U.N.T.S. at 185.

seas misconduct to the flag state.[6] The Act to Prevent Pollution also authorizes the Coast Guard, an agency of the United States Department of Homeland Security, to "prescribe any necessary or desired regulations to carry out the provisions of . . . MARPOL."[7]

II. FACTUAL BACKGROUND

During ordinary operation, oceangoing petroleum tankers accumulate large volumes of oily wastewater in their bottoms ("bilges"), engine rooms, and mechanical spaces, which can potentially pollute the ocean. Regulations promulgated pursuant to the Act to Prevent Pollution accordingly prohibit tank vessels of 150 gross tons or more from discharging oily bilge water into the sea, unless (1) the discharge contains less than 15 parts per million ("ppm") of oil; and (2) the vessel has in operation certain pollution control equipment, including an Oily Water Separator that both filters waste and has an Oil Content Meter for monitoring waste levels in the discharge.[8] The Oil Content Meter is part of the Oily Water Separator and it monitors samples of wastewater about to be discharged. It is designed to sound an alarm and **[—6—]** automatically stop a discharge if the discharge contains more than 15 ppm of oil. Any bilge water that exceeds that pollution level must be retained by the vessel and taken to a "reception facility."[9] **{-578-}**

To track a ship's pollution, MARPOL and applicable regulations require tank vessels to "maintain an Oil Record Book."[10] The Oil Record Book is a running log that includes detailed entries for every onboard oil transfer operation. Regulations require the Oil Record Book to include entries for each tank-to-tank transfer of oil; each discharge of oily bilge water; each failure of oil filtering equipment; and any accidental or emergency discharge of oily waste exceeding the legal limit.[11] Regulations also require that individual line-by-line entries in the Oil Record Book be made without delay "on each occasion" that an oil operation occurs.[12] These entries must be signed by the person in charge of that operation, such as the supervising engineer, who is responsible for "maintenance" of the Oil Record Book.[13]

Nikolaos Vastardis was the Chief Engineer responsible for maintaining the Oil Record Book while onboard the *Evridiki*, a Liberian-registered 84,796-gross ton petroleum tanker. On March 11, 2019, the Coast Guard inspected the *Evridiki* after it entered the Delaware Bay port. They soon **[—7—]** became suspicious of the ship's Oil Content Meter.[14] After docking and inspecting the ship's international oil pollution prevention certificate, Coast Guard Officer Aaron Studie asked Vastardis to run the vessel's Oily Water Separator as he would at sea, to confirm its operability. The crew turned on the Oily Water Separator, and the Oil Content Meter displayed a reading of 0 ppm of oil. Vastardis

---

[6] *Id.* Art. 6(2), 1340 U.N.T.S. at 187; *Abrogar*, 459 F.3d at 432.

[7] 33 U.S.C. §§ 1903(c)(2), 1907.

[8] 33 C.F.R. § 151.10; MARPOL Annex I, Reg. 15.

[9] 33 C.F.R. § 151.10; MARPOL Annex I, Reg. 14.

[10] 33 C.F.R. § 151.25(a).

[11] 33 C.F.R. § 151.25; MARPOL Annex I, Reg. 17.

[12] 33 C.F.R. § 151.25(h).

[13] 33 C.F.R. § 151.25(j).

[14] Vastardis Br. at 7–10. Vastardis argues that the United States had no right to investigate the *Evridiki* because a valid international oil pollution prevention certificate was presented and no clear ground for further investigation was identified at the time of inspection, citing 33 U.S.C. § 1904(d) (investigation "*is limited to verifying whether or not a valid certificate is onboard, unless clear grounds exist*, which reasonably indicate that the condition of the ship or its equipment does not substantially agree with the particulars of the certificate."). However, in addition to its authority to confirm that a "valid [international oil pollution prevention] Certificate is on board," the Coast Guard also has the authority to confirm that the "condition of the ship and its equipment corresponds substantially with the particulars of the [international oil pollution prevention] Certificate" to determine whether the ship has discharged oil in violation of MARPOL, and to examine "the Oil Record Book, the oil content meter continuous records, and [conduct] a general examination of the ship." 33 C.F.R. § 151.23. Accordingly, federal statute authorized the Coast Guard's investigation.

responded by giving Studie "two thumbs up."[15] Studie was skeptical. He noticed that the valve supplying the discharge to the Oil Content Meter was closed, preventing the Oil Content Meter from testing the actual sample discharge. When that valve was opened, the **[—8—]** reading remained at 0 ppm. This surprised Studie because in his experience, a flat 0–2 ppm reading indicated that the Oil Content Meter was testing a sample of freshwater. If the Oil Content Meter were testing filtered oily bilge water, one would expect to see a fluctuating reading of 3–10 ppm. As Officer Studie tried to understand the anomaly, he physically traced the sample line until it reached behind the Oily Water Separator. There, he discovered a hidden valve that was also closed, blocking the Oily Water Separator sample from flowing through the Oil Content Meter. Once this valve was opened, the Oil Content Meter immediately jumped to a reading of 40 ppm or higher. This triggered an audible **{-579-}** alarm and caused the Oily Water Separator to go into recirculation mode.

After discovering the ship's hidden valve, Officer Studie reviewed the Oil Content Meter's memory chip to decipher the ship's past actions. He observed that the memory chip read a flat 0–2 ppm throughout the duration of all the recent discharges. Vastardis had recorded those discharges in the Oil Record Book as properly running through 15 ppm equipment. Officer Studie then realized that, given the configuration of the *Evridiki*'s Oily Water Separator, if the sample line were closed, the Oil Content Meter could be made to sample freshwater trapped in the device instead of the oily bilge water being discharged overboard. This explained why the Oil Content Meter displayed a reading of 0–2 ppm during the inspection, as well as the history recorded on the memory chip. Those recent discharges could not have been made through the 15 ppm Oil Content Meter equipment. Officer Studie suspected that during high seas operations, Vastardis "was keeping the valve closed and preventing the [Oily Water Separator's] oil content meter [from] getting an adequate **[—9—]** sample."[16] When the other Coast Guard officer conducting the inspection asked Vastardis what the position of the sample line valve was during normal operations, Vastardis repeatedly asserted that he always ran the Oily Water Separator with the valve in the "open" position.[17]

Between March 11–13, 2019, Coast Guard officers seized all of the ship's Oil Record Books for investigation. They duplicated all onboard computers and analyzed the Oil Content Meter's memory chip in greater depth. The analysis revealed that since 2018, the ship's Oily Water Separator operated 16 times, for a total of 55.5 hours, including on March 8, 2019, just three days before the inspection.[18] The Oil Record Book showed that Vastardis ran at least ten of those operations, discharging more than 62,000 gallons of oily bilge water into the ocean.[19] The Government claims that Vastardis falsified the ship's required Oil Record Book in order to indicate that the ship's oily waste discharges had been properly filtered and monitored through required pollution control equipment when the waste had actually bypassed the equipment on its way overboard.[20]

After the expanded inspection, the Coast Guard brought an *in rem* proceeding against the vessel under 33 U.S.C. § 1908(d) and (e). The Coast Guard sought criminal fines for **[—10—]** any violation of the Act to Prevent Pollution and claimed that the Government was entitled to a bond or other surety, including human surety, under § 1908(e).[21] The ship and her entire crew were detained while the Coast Guard negotiated an

15 Presentence Investigation Report ("PSR") ¶ 34.

16 Vastardis Br. at 11 (citing Motion Tr. at 42:23; omitted from App-II).

17 Supp. App'x. at 14-15.

18 PSR ¶ 38.

19 Gov't's Sent'g Memorandum and Opposition to Defendant's Motion for Variance, ECF 166 at 4; Supp. App. at 84.

20 Gov't Br. at 1.

21 33 U.S.C. § 1908 (d) and (e) provide criminal and civil penalties for certain persons who violate the MARPOL Protocol and allow the violating vessel to be seized and held "upon the filing of a bond or other surety satisfactory to the Secretary [of the Treasury]."

Agreement on Security, insisting that the crewmembers "remain within the jurisdiction of the U.S. District Court – District of Delaware," and attend "meetings with . . . [U.S.] law enforcement personnel" until a Government lawyer "advises that their presence is no longer necessary." **{-580-}** [22] After being held for the better part of a month without process, Vastardis and his thirty-two fellow foreign crewmembers petitioned for habeas relief in April 2019.[23] Ten days later, the Government filed a criminal complaint against Vastardis and secured *ex parte* material witness arrest warrants for the other ten crewmembers pledged as human surety.[24] Over the Government's objection, these witnesses were eventually allowed to give depositions and return to their homes overseas, subject to their agreement to return for trial unless at sea.

Vastardis was later charged in a four-count indictment with violations of the Act to Prevent Pollution and its regulations and for obstruction in connection with the Coast Guard inspection: (1) knowingly causing the failure to maintain an accurate Oil Record Book, aiding and abetting, in **[—11—]** violation of 33 U.S.C. § 1908(a), 33 C.F.R. § 151.25, and 18 U.S.C. § 2; (2) falsification of records, aiding and abetting, in violation of 18 U.S.C. §§ 1519 and 2; (3) obstruction of justice, in presenting false Oil Record Book entries and deceiving inspectors, aiding and abetting, in violation of 18 U.S.C. §§ 1505 and 2; and (4) false statements in connection with a federal investigation, aiding and abetting, in violation of 18 U.S.C. §§ 1001 and 2.

Vastardis moved to dismiss the indictment and to suppress evidence obtained during the inspection, but the District Court denied both motions. After a seven-day trial, a jury convicted him on all counts. Vastardis moved for judgment of acquittal based on sufficiency of the evidence, which the District Court denied. At sentencing, the District Court imposed a $7,500 fine, a $400 special assessment, and three years' probation, a condition of which was banishment from the United States and U.S. waters. This appeal followed.

III. JURISDICTION AND STANDARD OF REVIEW

The District Court had subject-matter jurisdiction over Vastardis's prosecution for federal crimes under 18 U.S.C. § 3231. We have appellate jurisdiction over the District Court's final judgment under 28 U.S.C. § 1291. We also have jurisdiction in sentencing appeals under 18 U.S.C. § 3742(a).

The parties raise several issues on appeal, each of which warrants a different level of review. We review the Government's various statutory and legal arguments on the application of the Act to Prevent Pollution *de novo*.[25] **[—12—]** Regarding the sufficiency of the evidence at trial, we afford "deference to a jury's findings" and draw "all reasonable inferences in favor of the jury verdict."[26] With regard to the confiscation of *Evridiki*'s Oil Record Book, we review the denial of Vastardis's motion to suppress for clear error as to the underlying factual findings and exercise plenary review over the District Court's application of the law to those facts.[27] Finally, we review Vastardis's challenge to the substantive reasonableness of his sentence under an abuse-of-discretion standard.[28] **{-581-}**

IV. MOTION TO SUPPRESS

As an initial matter, Vastardis argues that the District Court erred in denying his motion to suppress the Oil Record Book entries because they were unlawfully obtained by the U.S. Government.[29] In denying Vastardis's motion, the District Court concluded that "[b]inding Third Circuit precedent holds that

---

[22] App-II at 8–9.

[23] App-I at 8.

[24] *Id.* at 11.

[25] *United States v. Stock*, 728 F.3d 287, 291 (3d Cir. 2013).

[26] *United States v. Riley*, 621 F.3d 312, 329 (3d Cir. 2010) (internal citations omitted).

[27] *United States v. Burnett*, 773 F.3d 122, 130 (3d Cir. 2014).

[28] *See United States v. Richards*, 674 F.3d 215, 220 (3d Cir. 2012).

[29] Vastardis Br. at 51–53; *see also* Defs.' Joint Motion to Suppress, App-II at 112.

the Coast Guard can conduct a warrantless search of a vessel given reasonable suspicion of criminal activity."[30] We analyze Vastardis's argument in three steps: (1) "we ask whether a Fourth Amendment event, such as a search or seizure, has occurred"; (2) "we consider whether **[—13—]** that search or seizure was reasonable; and (3) if it was not, we then determine whether the circumstances warrant suppression of the evidence."[31] We conclude that, even assuming there was a seizure, it was reasonable. And even if unreasonable, the violation would not have warranted the suppression of the Oil Record Book entries.

Under 14 U.S.C. § 522(a), the Coast Guard has broad authority to inspect vessels and, in certain circumstances, to make searches and seizures, "upon the high seas and waters of which the United States has jurisdiction, for the prevention, detection, and suppression of violations of laws of the United States." As noted by the District Court, we have held that Section 522(a) authorizes "warrantless searches of vessels in U.S. territorial waters based solely upon a reasonable suspicion of criminal activity."[32] The Coast Guard also has specific authority to inspect vessels, including Oil Record Books, for compliance with MARPOL and the Act to Prevent Pollution, and it may expand such an inspection if "clear grounds exist which reasonably indicate that the condition of the ship or its equipment does not substantially agree with the particulars of" the ship's MARPOL certificate.[33] **[—14—]**

The Coast Guard's preliminary examination of the Oil Record Book and Oily Water Separator was within its inspection authority under the Act to Prevent Pollution. When the officers realized the Oily Water Separator was not filtering oil and observed prior Oil Content Meter readings showing 0–2 ppm, and when Vastardis appeared to conceal the fact that the Oily Water Separator was not operable, the officers had clear reason to suspect a criminal violation of the Act to Prevent Pollution. Given that reasonable suspicion, the warrantless seizure of the Oil Record Book was justified.

Vastardis argues that the Act to Prevent Pollution regulations provide that the United States, like all port states, is authorized only to *copy* foreign books—not to *seize* them. Annex I of MARPOL states:

> The competent authority of the Government of a Party to the present Convention may inspect the Oil Record Book Part I on board any ship to which this Annex applies while the ship is in its **{-582-}** port or offshore terminals and may make a copy of any entry in that book and may require the master of the ship to certify that the copy is a true copy of such entry. Any copy so made which has been certified by the master of the ship as a true copy of an entry in the ship's Oil Record Book Part I shall be made admissible in any judicial proceedings as evidence of the facts stated in the **[—15—]** entry. The inspection of an Oil Record Book Part I and the taking of a certified copy by the competent authority under this paragraph shall be performed as expeditiously as possible without causing the ship to be unduly delayed.[34]

The Government argues that while the MARPOL Annex authorizes certified copies, it does not *preclude* the Coast Guard's statutory authority to seize Oil Record Books.[35] Meanwhile, the Act to Prevent Pollution slightly modifies the language from the MARPOL Annex:

[30] App-I at 54 (citing *United States v. Varlack Ventures, Inc.*, 149 F.3d 212, 217 (3d Cir. 1998)).

[31] *United States v. Dupree*, 617 F.3d 724, 731 (3d Cir. 2010).

[32] *United States v. Varlack Ventures, Inc.*, 149 F.3d 212, 214 (3d Cir. 1998) (interpreting 14 U.S.C. § 89(a), now codified at 14 U.S.C. § 522(a)); *see also United States v. Benoit*, 730 F.3d 280, 284 (3d Cir. 2013) ("[A] reasonable suspicion requirement for searches and seizures on the high seas survives Fourth Amendment scrutiny." (citation and quotation marks omitted)).

[33] 33 U.S.C. § 1904(d); *see also id.* § 1907(c)(2)(A); 33 C.F.R. § 151.23(a)(1), (c); *Abrogar*, 459 F.3d at 432.

[34] MARPOL, Annex I, Reg. 17 ¶ 7.

[35] Gov't Br. at 45.

> An inspection under this section may include an examination of the Oil Record Book, the oil content meter continuous records, and a general examination of the ship. A copy of any entry in the Oil Record Book may be made and the Master of the ship may be required to certify that the copy is a true copy of such entry.[36]

Even if Vastardis were correct and only copying the Oil Record Book entries was permitted, that violation would not have required the suppression of the Oil Record Book. MARPOL allows a copy of the Oil Record Book to be made and a properly certified copy can surely be admitted as evidence in a judicial proceeding. Therefore, the Government's certified copy of the book would have put the same evidence in front of the jury.[37] Accordingly, the District **[—16—]** Court did not err in allowing the Oil Record Book entries into evidence, despite the records having been obtained, rather than copied, by the Government.

V. COUNT 1 – FAILURE TO MAINTAIN AN OIL RECORD BOOK

Count 1 of the indictment charged that "[o]n or about March 11, 2019, at the Big Stone Anchorage, Delaware Bay, Delaware," Vastardis "knowingly . . . cause[d] the failure to maintain an accurate Oil Record Book for the M/T EVRIDIKI," in violation of 33 C.F.R. § 151.25, 33 U.S.C. § 1908(a), and 18 U.S.C. § 2.[38] Sections 151.25 (d) and (j) of the Code of Federal Regulations require that: "[E]ntries shall be made in the Oil Record Book on each occasion . . . whenever any of [certain specified] machinery space operations take place . . . . The master . . . shall be responsible for the maintenance of [the Oil Record Book]." **[—17—]**

Section 1908(a) of the United States Code states:

> A person who knowingly violates the MARPOL Protocol, Annex IV to the **{-583-}** Antarctic Protocol, this chapter, or the regulations issued thereunder commits a class D felony. In the discretion of the Court, an amount equal to not more than ½ of such fine may be paid to the person giving information leading to conviction.

The Oil Record Book entries in question falsely documented bilge water discharges that occurred when the *Evridiki* was on the high seas. Vastardis argues that this divests the United States of the authority to enforce the penalties prescribed under MARPOL because the Act to Prevent Pollution is limited to conduct while in the navigable waters of the United States. We disagree. Instead, we—like some of our sister circuit courts— find that the arrival of the *Evridiki* in the Delaware Bay triggered the duty under Coast Guard regulations to "maintain an Oil Record Book" while in U.S. waters,[39] which brought Vastardis's conduct within U.S. jurisdiction under the Act to Prevent Pollution.

The word "maintain" in this context requires that the records be substantively accurate. Merriam-Webster's Dictionary defines "maintain" as, *inter alia*, "to keep in a state of repair, efficiency, or validity."[40] The recordkeeping **[—18—]** provision would make little sense if, as Vastardis proposes, it

---

36 33 C.F.R. § 151.23(c).

37 *See United States v. Wright*, 777 F.3d 635, 641 (3d Cir. 2015) (affirming the denial of a motion to suppress because the **[—16—]** Fourth Amendment violation "had no impact on the evidence that could be deployed against [the defendant] at trial" since "the agents would have collected precisely the same evidence, and [the defendant] would have been unable to stop them"); *United States v. Stabile*, 633 F.3d 219, 245 (3d Cir. 2011) (explaining that under the inevitable discovery doctrine, information that would have been discovered by lawful means should not be suppressed.).

38 App-I at 38–39. On each count, the Government charged Vastardis with aiding and abetting under 18 U.S.C. § 2.

39 33 C.F.R. § 151.25(a).

40 *Maintain*, Merriam-Webster's Unabridged Dictionary, https://www.merriamwebster.com/dictionary/maintain#:~:text=English%20Language%20Learners%20Definition%20of%20maintain%20%3A **[—18—]** %20to,etc.%20%3A%20to%20continue%20having%20or%20doing%20%28something%29.

required that ships only physically possess an Oil Record Book in any state of completeness or accuracy. Because an Oil Record Book must be accurately maintained under § 151.25, and because § 151.25 applies to foreign ships while they are in U.S. waters or in a U.S. port, the arrival in U.S. waters or a U.S. port of a ship with an inaccurate Oil Record Book constitutes a violation of that regulation. The Act to Prevent Pollution makes it a felony to violate that regulation knowingly.[41]

Two of our sister circuit courts—the Second and Fifth Circuits—have adopted this plain reading in holding that "the requirement that an oil record book be 'maintained' . . . impos[es] a duty upon a foreign-flagged vessel to ensure that its oil record book is accurate (or at least not knowingly inaccurate) upon entering the ports of navigable waters of the United States."[42] In both cases, the United States prosecuted the defendants under § 1908(a) for knowingly maintaining Oil Record Books in a U.S. port that falsely documented high-seas discharges in violation of § 151.25.[43] In reaching this **[—19—]** conclusion, the Second and Fifth Circuits rejected the argument that the obligation to "maintain" an Oil Record Book in U.S. waters imposes no substantive accuracy requirement.[44] In the recordkeeping context, "the duty to 'maintain' plainly means a duty to maintain a reasonably *complete* and *accurate* record," and "[n]o reasonable reader of [§ 151.25] could conclude, given the context, that the regulation merely imposes an **{-584-}** obligation to preserve the [Oil Record Book] in its existing state."[45]

One of our own cases similarly supports this plain reading.[46] In *United States v. Abrogar*, we articulated this offense as the "knowing failure to maintain an accurate oil record book within U.S. waters."[47] As here, the improper discharges occurred outside U.S. waters, and Abrogar falsely documented them while he was outside U.S. waters.[48] After a Coast Guard inspection uncovered the ship's conduct, Abrogar **[—20—]** pleaded guilty to failing to maintain an accurate Oil Record Book as required by § 151.25, in violation of § 1908(a).[49] Although we vacated the District Court's imposition of a six-level sentencing enhancement for an offense that "resulted in an ongoing, continuous, or repetitive discharge, release, or emission of a pollutant into the environment,"[50] this was because the high-seas discharges did not constitute "relevant conduct" for purposes of determining Abrogar's offense level under the U.S. Sentencing Guidelines.[51] The crime was, as here, the failure to maintain an accurate oil record book while in a U.S. port. Accordingly, Abrogar's offense did not "result[] in" any pollution, as required for the enhancement.[52]

Contrary to Vastardis's assertion, allowing the United States to prosecute this recordkeeping violation does not flout the division of authority set forth in MARPOL and the Act to Prevent Pollution. Rather, it adheres to that careful division and preserves the integrity of MARPOL. To be sure, Vastardis is correct that MARPOL vests

---

41 33 U.S.C. § 1908(a).

42 *United States v. Jho*, 534 F.3d 398, 403 (5th Cir. 2008); *see also United States v. Ionia Mgmt. S.A.*, 555 F.3d 303, 306 (2d Cir. 2009) (per curiam) ("[W]e join the Fifth Circuit in holding that [§ 151.25] imposes a duty on ships, upon entering the ports or navigable waters of the United States, to ensure that its [Oil Record Book] is accurate (or at least not knowingly inaccurate).").

43 *Ionia*, 555 F.3d at 305; *Jho*, 534 F.3d at 402–03.

44 *Ionia*, 555 F.3d at 307–09; *Jho*, 534 F.3d at 403.

45 *Ionia*, 555 F.3d at 309.

46 Because we find the text of the Act to Prevent Pollution and MARPOL to be unambiguous, Vastardis's reliance on the rule of lenity is unavailing. *See United States v. Kouevi*, 698 F.3d 126, 138 (3d Cir. 2012) ("The rule of lenity applies in those situations in which a reasonable doubt persists about a statute's intended scope even after resort to the language and structure, legislative history, and motivating policies of the statute.") (citation omitted).

47 459 F.3d at 435 (internal quotation marks omitted). We did not have occasion to squarely address the Government's jurisdiction to prosecute the offense, as Abrogar pleaded guilty.

48 *Id.* at 433, 436.

49 *Id.* at 433.

50 *Id.* (quoting U.S.S.G. § 2Q1.3(b)(1)(A)).

51 *Id.* at 437.

52 *Id.* at 436.

power in flag states to prosecute high-seas misconduct "wherever the violation occurs."[53] But MARPOL still vests concurrent jurisdiction to port states over conduct in their ports or waters.[54] Because the gravamen of Vastardis's crime occurred in the Delaware Bay port, it is appropriate for U.S. prosecution under MARPOL. Port states also play a key role in *detecting* (if not prosecuting) such **[—21—]** misconduct. Indeed, the ability of port states to refer violations to flag states hinges on the reliability of foreign ships' Oil Record Books, which port officers like the Coast Guard review in conducting inspections.[55] If foreign ships were free to maintain falsified Oil Record Books in U.S. ports, then "the Coast Guard's ability to conduct investigations **{-585-}** against foreign-flagged vessels would be severely hindered," allowing those vessels "to avoid detection."[56] Ships could carry two Oil Record Books: one accurate Oil Record Book for flag-state inspection, and one falsified Oil Record Book for port-state inspection. Under such a system, port states "would be severely hampered in their ability to report violations to the flag state for enforcement, and the international system of reporting and accountability under MARPOL would collapse."[57]

The jury convicted Vastardis on Count 1 after receiving an instruction that, to do so, it must find that the offense occurred "while the . . . *Evridiki* was in the navigable waters of, or at a port or terminal of the United States."[58] Because the Government was within its jurisdiction to prosecute the ship's failure to maintain an accurate Oil Record Book in a U.S. port, we will affirm that conviction. **[—22—]**

[53] MARPOL Art. 4(1)–(2), 1340 U.N.T.S. at 185.

[54] *Id.* Art. 6(2), 1340 U.N.T.S. at 187; *Abrogar*, 459 F.3d at 432.

[55] *See Abrogar*, 459 F.3d at 432 ("In conducting inspections, the Coast Guard typically relies on a ship's oil record book and statements of the crew."); *Jho*, 534 F.3d at 403 ("Accurate oil record books are necessary to carry out the goals of MARPOL and the [Act to Prevent Pollution].").

[56] *Jho*, 534 F.3d at 403.

[57] *Ionia*, 555 F.3d at 308.

[58] App-II at 318–19.

VI. COUNT 2 – FALSIFYING RECORDS, SARBANES-OXLEY

Count 2 of the indictment charged Vastardis with violating 18 U.S.C. § 1519 based on the falsified Oil Record Book. Section 1519 makes it a crime to knowingly "conceal[], cover[] up, or make[] a false entry in any record . . . with the intent to impede, obstruct, or influence the investigation or proper administration of any matter within the jurisdiction of any department or agency of the United States, . . . or in relation to or contemplation of any such matter or case."[59]

Vastardis argues that the Government failed to prove that he acted with the requisite specific intent of impeding a U.S. investigation because his falsification of the Oil Record Book would have been done with the intent to impede only a Liberian investigation, since only Liberia had jurisdiction to prosecute a recordkeeping offense. This argument fails.

The Coast Guard had statutory authority to conduct a compliance inspection and examine the ship's Oil Record Book while it was in the Delaware Bay. "While at a port or terminal under the jurisdiction of the United States, a ship is subject to inspection by the Coast Guard . . . [t]o determine whether a ship has been operating in accordance with and has not discharged any oil or oily mixtures in violation of the provisions of MARPOL."[60] Such an inspection "may include an examination of the Oil Record Book."[61] MARPOL itself **[—23—]** authorizes a port state to "inspect the Oil Record Book on board any ship . . . while the ship is in its port or offshore terminals."[62]

Under § 1519, "[i]t is sufficient that the 'matter' [under investigation] is within the jurisdiction of a federal agency as a factual

[59] 18 U.S.C. § 1519.

[60] 33 C.F.R. § 151.23(a); *see also* 33 U.S.C. § 1904(c)-(d); MARPOL Art 6(2), 1340 U.N.T.S. at 187.

[61] 33 C.F.R. § 151.23(c); *see also Abrogar*, 459 F.3d at 432.

[62] MARPOL Reg. 20(6), 1340 U.N.T.S. at 212.

matter."[63] The Government must prove only that "(1) [the defendant] intended to impede an investigation into 'any matter' and (2) the matter at issue **{-586-}** was ultimately proven to be within the federal government's jurisdiction."[64] The Government is "not required to prove that [the defendant] intended to obstruct or impede a specific federal investigation."[65] An Oil Record Book inspection by the Coast Guard is plainly a matter within its jurisdiction, and other circuit courts have affirmed § 1519 convictions for falsified Oil Record Books that were recorded on the high seas but presented to U.S. officials in port.[66] **[—24—]**

Viewing the record in the light most favorable to the Government, the evidence was sufficient to prove that Vastardis acted with the requisite intent to impede "any matter"—namely, an eventual inspection of the Oil Record Book. Vastardis was an experienced chief engineer responsible for signing Oil Record Book entries; he entered and signed the false Oil Record Book entries, he brought the Oil Record Book to the master for his signature before the ship's arrival in the Delaware Bay port, and the ship itself requested the Coast Guard inspection so that it could offload its cargo. Based on this evidence, a reasonable jury could conclude that Vastardis "knowingly falsified documents in 'contemplation of' an investigation of a 'matter,' which was proven to be within the jurisdiction of the federal government."[67] We therefore will affirm the conviction on Count 2. **[—25—]**

VII. COUNT 3 – IMPEDING A GOVERNMENT PROCEEDING

Count 3 charges Vastardis with obstructing justice under 18 U.S.C. § 1505. Section 1505 imposes criminal liability upon anyone who:

> corruptly . . . obstructs, or impedes or endeavors to influence, obstruct, or impede the due and proper administration of the law under which any pending proceeding is being had before any department or agency.

To convict under this section, the Government must establish: "(1) that there was an agency proceeding; (2) that the defendant was aware of that proceeding; and (3) that the defendant intentionally endeavored corruptly to influence, obstruct or impede the pending proceeding."[68] The term "proceeding" in the context **{-587-}** of § 1505 is construed broadly and encompasses agency investigative activities—including an agency's "search for the true facts."[69]

Count 3 charged that, during the Coast Guard's inspection of the ship's oil filtration

---

[63] *United States v. Moyer*, 674 F.3d 192, 210 (3d Cir. 2012) (alterations in original) (quoting *United States v. Yielding*, 657 F.3d 688, 714 (8th Cir. 2011)).

[64] *Id.*

[65] *Id.*

[66] *See, e.g., United States v. Oceanic Illsabe Ltd.*, 889 F.3d 178, 185–86, 6 Adm. R. 137, 139–41 (4th Cir. 2018); *Ionia*, 555 F.3d at 310; *see also United States v. Taohim*, 817 F.3d 1215, 1222 (11th Cir. 2013) (per curiam) (affirming § 1519 conviction in a similar context, rejecting the ship captain's argument that "he could not have intended to impede . . . the Coast Guard's investigation when he allegedly ordered the omission of [a] discharge from the garbage record book because at that time, the vessel was outside the territory of the United States," since § 1519 "does **[—24—]** not require that an investigation be pending or that the defendant be aware of one when he falsifies the record").

[67] *Moyer*, 674 F.3d at 211. Other courts of appeals have affirmed § 1519 convictions on similar records. *See, e.g., Taohim*, 817 F.3d at 1222 (explaining that a reasonable jury could credit testimony that the defendant was an experienced "old sea dog" and was "aware that the garbage record book would be reviewed during any Port State Control Inspection" as evidence that the book was "falsified 'in contemplation of' a future Port State Control Inspection"); *Oceanic Illsabe*, 889 F.3d at 190, 6 Adm. R. at 144 (citing evidence that the Oil Record Book "contained a plethora of inaccurate and false information, and . . . a vast amount of inculpatory information had not been properly recorded therein").

[68] *United States v. Smukler*, 991 F.3d 472, 483 n.7 (3d Cir. 2021) (quoting *United States v. Warshak*, 631 F.3d 266, 325 (6th Cir. 2010)).

[69] *See United States v. Leo*, 941 F.2d 181, 199 (3d Cir. 1991) (quoting *United States v. Browning, Inc.*, 572 F.2d 720, 724 (10th Cir. 1978)).

equipment, Vastardis "ran the Oil Content Meter with the sample line closed in order to trick the system into reporting an oil content of less than 15 **[—26—]** ppm" and, "when asked by [Coast Guard] inspectors to describe the position [of] the [Oil Content Meter] sample line valve during at-sea operations," he "falsely stated that the valve was 'open.'"[70] The Act to Prevent Pollution regulations authorize Coast Guard inspections not only "[t]o determine that a valid [international oil pollution prevention] Certificate is on board," but also "[t]o determine whether a ship has been operating in accordance with and has not discharged any oil or oily mixtures in violation of the provisions of MARPOL."[71] These regulations put ships on notice that inspections "may include an examination of the Oil Record Book, the oil content meter continuous records, and a general examination of the ship."[72] A Coast Guard inspection in a U.S. port is a "proceeding in the manner and form prescribed for conducting business before" that agency, and § 1505 reaches "all steps and stages in such an action from its inception to its conclusion."[73] Thus, contrary to Vastardis's argument, the Coast Guard's authorized investigation, even as an administrative inspection, is a "proceeding" within the meaning of § 1505.[74]

[70] App-I at 40–41 (under seal).

[71] 33 C.F.R. § 151.23(a)(1), (a)(3).

[72] *Id.* § 151.23(c).

[73] *Leo*, 941 F.2d at 199 (quoting *Rice v. United States*, 356 F.2d 709, 712 (8th Cir. 1966)).

[74] *See United States v. Technic Services, Inc.*, 314 F.3d 1031, 1044 (9th Cir. 2002) ("An administrative investigation is a 'proceeding' within the meaning of 18 U.S.C. § 1505." (citation and quotation marks omitted)), *overruled on other grounds by United States v. Contreras*, 593 F.3d 1135 (9th Cir. 2010) (en banc); *see also Taohim*, 817 F.3d at 1221 (affirming Section 1505 conviction where "the jury reasonably could have **[—27—]** inferred that [the ship's captain] knew that the garbage record book did not include the discharge of plastic into the sea and that he made that fraudulent book available to the Coast Guard with the intent to interfere with its investigation"); *Oceanic Illsabe*, 889 F.3d at 189 & n.18, 190 & n.19, 6 Adm. R. at 144 n. 18 & n. 19 (citing evidence that ship's crew lied to Coast Guard inspectors about the functioning of the ship's equipment as supporting § 1505 convictions).

We therefore will affirm Vastardis's conviction on Count 3. **[—27—]**

VIII. COUNT 4 – FALSIFYING A MATERIAL FACT

Count 4 charged Vastardis with making false statements in violation of 18 U.S.C. § 1001. Section 1001 imposes criminal liability upon anyone who:

> knowingly and willfully—falsifies, conceals, or covers up by any trick, scheme, or device a material fact; makes any materially false, fictitious, or fraudulent statement or representation; or makes or uses any false writing or document knowing the same to contain any materially false, fictitious, or fraudulent statement or entry.

Count 4 charged that, while at the Big Stone Anchorage in Delaware, Vastardis stated that when the ship's Oily Water Separator was run at sea during normal operations, the valve on the sample line to the Oil Content Meter was "open" when in **{-588-}** fact it was closed.[75] **[—28—]**

Here again, Vastardis argues that § 1001 does not apply because the matter being investigated was not within the jurisdiction of the Coast Guard, and that his conduct was only governed by Liberian law.[76] He is wrong. As the Government correctly notes, the actions relied upon for Count 4 were made during the inspection of the *Evridiki* while Vastardis was in the Delaware Bay port and thus were subject to the Coast Guard's jurisdiction. Moreover, the crew of the *Evridiki* requested the inspection in order to receive a certification necessary to operate in the United States. Accordingly, the Coast Guard's inspection, including its inquiries about the accuracy of the Oil Record Book entries and the related operability of the ship's equipment, fell well within the Coast Guard's jurisdiction.[77]

[75] App-I at 41–42.

[76] *See* Vastardis Br. at 2.

[77] *See United States v. Rodgers*, 466 U.S. 475, 481 (1984) (explaining that § 1001 reflects Congress's interest in protecting the integrity of

Although Vastardis insists that the valve was open, the Government introduced evidence that it was closed.[78] Vastardis's representation that the valve was open was clearly material to the Coast Guard's inquiry, and it was false. If the sample line had been even partially open—as Vastardis had told the inspectors—the Oil Content Meter would have detected oily wastewater. Yet the reading on the Oil Content Meter was instead 0–2 ppm. At trial, the Government proved that the Oil Content Meter had in fact been sampling trapped fresh water and that Vastardis had run the Oily Water Separator with the sample line closed. Given this evidence, which we view "in the light most favorable to the Government," we find **[—29—]** that Vastardis did violate 18 U.S.C. § 1001.[79] The District Court therefore did not err in denying Vastardis's motion for judgment of acquittal on Count 4.[80]

IX. BANISHMENT

Although we find no error among Vastardis's convictions, the District Court clearly abused its discretion in applying banishment as a condition of Vastardis's probation, when it stated that he may "not enter the United States, the waters of the United States, or apply for any [v]isas to enter the United States."[81] We have previously discussed the historical roots of banishment, summarizing it as a condition that "orders the probationer . . . to leave a broad geographic area."[82] We have also held that a "condition of probation may not circumvent another statutory scheme."[83] Through the Immigration and Nationality Act ("INA"), Congress outlined the sole and exclusive procedure through which foreigners may be deported from the United States.[84]

official inquiries, wherever there is a statutory basis for the inquiry).

[78] App-II at 251, 257–59.

[79] *United States v. Riley*, 621 F.3d 312, 329 (3d Cir. 2010) (internal quotation marks omitted).

[80] App-II at 182.

[81] App-II at 370.

[82] *United States v. Abushaar*, 761 F.2d 954, 960 (3d Cir. 1985).

[83] *Id.*

[84] *See id.* at 959.

While district courts generally have broad discretion to impose conditions of probation, such discretion must be viewed against the backdrop of the INA, **{-589-}** which provides the Attorney General with exclusive authority to admit, exclude, **[—30—]** and remove non-citizens.[85] A district court abuses its discretion, circumvents the authority of the Attorney General, and oversteps the bounds of the judiciary when it imposes banishment as a condition of probation.

Furthermore, the condition that Vastardis serve his probation outside the United States is unrelated to his rehabilitation or the protection of the public. This is another reason why a sentence that imposes banishment is an abuse of discretion.[86] Moreover, Vastardis is a seafarer whose career depends on travel in international waters, including U.S. waters. Because the condition of banishment impinges upon freedom of movement and has the potential to drastically interfere with the livelihood of a foreign national, it should be avoided. We will therefore vacate that condition of Vastardis's probation.

X. CONCLUSION

The United States had the authority to prosecute Vastardis. Vastardis aided the ship's presentation of a falsified Oil Record Book to U.S. officials and deceived them during an authorized inspection in an attempt to conceal the improper discharges. Such behavior forms the basis of federal recordkeeping and obstruction offenses because it harms the United States and goes to the heart of its ability to uncover **[—31—]** wrongdoing. Vastardis's light sentence—a $7,500 fine and three years' probation—reflects that his conviction reaches only his U.S.-based dishonesty and not his role in the ship's discharges of oily bilge water into the ocean while on the high seas.

[85] 8 U.S.C. § 1229a(a)(3) ("Unless otherwise specified in this chapter, a proceeding under this section shall be the sole and exclusive procedure for determining whether an alien may be admitted to the United States or, if the alien has been so admitted, removed from the United States.").

[86] *Abushaar*, 761 F.2d at 961.

With the exception of the condition of probation prohibiting Vastardis from entering the United States, we will affirm his conviction and sentence.

United States Court of Appeals for the Fourth Circuit

United States Court of Appeals
for the Fourth Circuit

No. 18-2438

ADDAX ENERGY SA
vs.
M/V YASA H. MULLA

Appeal from the United States District Court for the Eastern District of Virginia, at Norfolk

Decided: January 22, 2021

Citation: 987 F.3d 80, 9 Adm. R. 156 (4th Cir. 2021).

Before **MOTZ, AGEE,** and **KEENAN,** Circuit Judges.

[—2—] **{-82-}** **KEENAN,** Circuit Judge:

Addax Energy SA (Addax) filed this in rem action against M/V Yasa H. Mulla (the vessel), an ocean vessel, invoking the district court's admiralty jurisdiction under 28 U.S.C. § 1333. Addax had entered into a fuel supply agreement with the charterer of the vessel, a non-party to this action. When the charterer failed to pay the amount due, Addax filed the present in rem action against the vessel to enforce a maritime lien under the Commercial Instruments and Maritime Lien Act (the CIMLA), 46 U.S.C. § 31301 *et seq.*, and Supplemental Admiralty Rule C. In its defense, the vessel asserted that Addax's right to a maritime lien was extinguished when Addax settled its breach of contract claim with the charterer in a separate proceeding.

The district court granted summary judgment to Addax, concluding that the maritime lien arose by operation of law **{-83-}** and was unaffected by Addax's settlement agreement with the charterer. After a bench trial held to determine the amount of damages, the court entered judgment in favor of Addax.

Upon our review, we conclude that the settlement agreement did not extinguish Addax's right to a maritime lien, and that Addax was entitled to enforce that right in the district court. Additionally, we reject the vessel's arguments regarding the value of the lien, the expenses awarded to Addax, and the vessel's due process rights. We therefore affirm the district court's judgment. **[—3—]**

I.

Addax is based in Switzerland and supplies bunker fuel to ships and vessels. In February 2017, Addax entered into a fuel supply contract with non-party Windrose SPS Shipping & Trading (Windrose), the charterer of the vessel. The purchase price for the fuel was $320,997.77. Windrose failed to pay the amount due after receiving delivery of the fuel.

As a result of Windrose's default, Addax filed a claim against Windrose in a Swiss bankruptcy court. In those proceedings, Addax and Windrose entered into a settlement agreement in November 2017 (the settlement agreement). Under the settlement agreement, in exchange for Addax agreeing to suspend the Swiss proceedings, Windrose agreed to pay in installments a total of $344,481.81, including the invoiced amount plus interest and fees. As part of this total, the parties agreed that Windrose would assign to Addax Windrose's claim, worth at least $100,000, against third-party Cargill International (the Cargill claim). The vessel was not a party to the settlement agreement.

Since executing the settlement agreement, Windrose has paid Addax a total of $40,000 toward the debt.[1] In December 2017, Addax filed the present in rem action against the vessel in the Eastern District of Virginia. In its complaint, Addax sought to arrest the vessel to enforce its maritime lien pursuant to the CIMLA in order to recover the outstanding amount of the debt plus interest, fees, and expenses. **[—4—]**

On December 13, 2017, the district court issued an arrest warrant for the vessel, and a representative of the United States Marshals Service (Marshals Service) effectuated the arrest on December 27, 2017. The vessel was released on January 2, 2018 after its owner,

[1] Windrose paid Addax $20,000 immediately following execution of the settlement agreement. Windrose made a second $20,000 payment shortly after the complaint was filed in the present case.

Yasa Shipping, deposited cash security into the registry of the court. The parties proceeded to discovery and, in April 2018, the vessel filed a motion to vacate the arrest. In November 2018, the district court denied the vessel's motion to vacate, concluding that the settlement agreement did not extinguish Addax's right to a maritime lien. For the same reasons, the court also granted Addax's motion for summary judgment, holding that Addax was entitled to the requested lien.

The district court conducted a bench trial to determine the value of the maritime lien and the resulting damages to which Addax was entitled. The court deducted the $40,000 already paid by Windrose pursuant to the settlement agreement, and awarded Addax the balance due on the invoice, $280,997.77. The court also awarded Addax prejudgment interest and *custodia legis* expenses that Addax was required to pay to the Marshals Service and to the substitute custodian of the vessel **{-84-}** while the vessel was in custody. The vessel now appeals.

II.

The vessel primarily argues that the district court lacked admiralty jurisdiction, because the settlement agreement between Addax and Windrose, the charterer of the vessel, was a non-maritime contract that superseded the underlying fuel contract, thereby extinguishing Addax's maritime lien. The vessel also asserts that Addax lacks standing to **[—5—]** bring this in rem action, because Addax assigned its interest in the maritime lien to a third party. Additionally, the vessel contends that the district court (1) should have credited the value of the Cargill claim against the lien, (2) improperly awarded Addax *custodia legis* expenses, and (3) violated the vessel's due process rights by denying the vessel a prompt hearing under the admiralty rules. We will address each argument in turn.

A.

We first consider the vessel's contention that Addax lacks standing to assert its maritime claim, because Addax purportedly assigned its right to collect the receivables from the fuel invoice to a third-party financing company. According to the vessel, by assigning its contractual rights to a third party, Addax necessarily also assigned its right to enforce the lien in rem. The vessel thus contends that Addax has not satisfied its burden to establish it has suffered an injury in fact for purposes of Article III standing. We disagree with the vessel's analysis.

As an initial matter, we observe that the question whether Addax assigned its right to collect receivables to a third party does not implicate Addax's standing under Article III. The requirements of Article III standing ensure that a plaintiff has presented a live case or controversy over which the federal courts have jurisdiction. *See DaimlerChrysler Corp. v. Cuno*, 547 U.S. 332, 342 (2006). Addax plainly has satisfied the "irreducible constitutional minimum" of Article III standing, namely, that Addax was injured due to non-payment of the invoice it issued, and that this injury is traceable to the defendant vessel and is redressable by a favorable decision of the district court. *Spokeo, Inc. v. Robins*, 136 S. Ct. 1540, 1547 (2016) (citing *Lujan v. Defs. of Wildlife*, 504 U.S. 555, 560 (1992)). **[—6—]**

Rather than Article III standing, the true principle underlying the vessel's argument relates to whether Addax is the real party in interest under Federal Rule of Civil Procedure 17, which requires that "[a]n action [] be prosecuted in the name of the real party in interest." Fed. R. Civ. P. 17(a)(1). In making this determination, the question we must answer is whether Addax "was legally entitled to pursue" the maritime lien on its own behalf, or whether the claim belonged to a third-party assignee. *Martineau v. Wier*, 934 F.3d 385, 391 (4th Cir. 2019); *see also* 6A Charles Alan Wright, Arthur R. Miller & Mary Kay Kane, Federal Practice & Procedure § 1542 (3d ed. Supp. 2020) ("[I]f the [plaintiff] has assigned all interest in the claim before the action is instituted, the person no longer is the real party in interest."); *id.* § 1545 (discussing applicability of real party in interest rule to assignments).[2] {–85–}

A defendant may assert as an affirmative defense under Rule 17 that the plaintiff is not the real party in interest. *Cranpark, Inc. v. Rogers Grp., Inc.*, 821 F.3d 723, 730 (6th Cir. 2016). In such circumstances, when the plaintiff has moved for summary judgment, the defendant must show that there is a genuine dispute of material fact regarding whether the asserted claim belongs to the plaintiff or to a third party. *See* Fed. R. Civ. P. 56(a); *Celotex Corp. v. Catrett*, 477 U.S. 317, 323 (1986) ("The moving party is entitled to a judgment as a matter of law [when] the nonmoving party has failed to make a sufficient **[—7—]** showing on an essential element of her case with respect to which she has the burden of proof." (internal quotation marks omitted)).

In asserting that Addax assigned its right to the maritime lien, the vessel relies heavily on the June 2017 invoice that Addax submitted to Windrose seeking payment for the fuel delivery. The following language appeared at the bottom of the invoice:

> Please note that due to our financing structure, this invoice has been assigned in accordance with our legal and contractual obligations. The payment of this assigned invoice has to be made exclusively and irrevocably to our account as per following payment instructions.

The record before us lacks information about any such assignment, including the name of the assignee or the terms of any agreement reached. Indeed, other than the above language on the invoice, nothing in the record suggests that an assignment actually was made.

Addax's corporate designee testified at his deposition that the language at issue on the invoice was included as a matter of standard company practice, and that this language did not necessarily indicate that an assignment had been made. The corporate designee was unaware whether Addax had assigned its rights related to this particular invoice, and the vessel did not present other evidence that an assignment, in fact, had occurred.

Notably, the present record does not show that an assignee came forward to participate (1) in the Swiss bankruptcy proceedings, (2) in the settlement negotiations with Windrose, or (3) in the present in rem litigation. Thus, in effect, the vessel asked the district court to hold that an actual assignment had taken place although an unidentified assignee, who purportedly was owed several hundred thousand dollars, never materialized over the **[—8—]** course of these various proceedings. The district court properly declined to accept this speculative proposition.

Given the dearth of evidence in the record that Addax actually assigned its rights, we conclude that the vessel did not establish a genuine dispute of material fact that Addax was not the real party in interest to assert the maritime lien. Because summary judgment is intended to "isolate and dispose of factually unsupported … defenses," *Celotex*, 477 U.S. at 323-24, we conclude that the district court correctly rejected the vessel's affirmative defense that Addax was not the party legally entitled to bring this claim.

B.

We turn to consider the vessel's primary argument on appeal. Apart from its argument regarding standing, which we have rejected, the vessel concedes that Addax initially was entitled to a maritime lien under the CIMLA based on Addax's provision of fuel to the vessel. The vessel contends, **{–86–}** nevertheless, that the district court lacked admiralty jurisdiction over this in rem action because the settlement agreement, which is

---

[2] We respectfully disagree with the dissent's reliance on *In re Maco Homes, Inc.*, 180 F.3d 163 (4th Cir. 1999). There, we equated Article III standing with the real party in interest inquiry under Rule 17, without discussion. Although courts have at times collapsed the two issues, we explained in *Martineau* that the required inquiries are analytically distinct. *Martineau*, 934 F.3d at 391 & n.3.

not a maritime contract, superseded the underlying fuel supply contract. In the vessel's view, by failing to reserve expressly the right to a maritime lien in the settlement agreement, Addax settled both its in personam claim against Windrose and its in rem claim against the vessel. The vessel thus maintains that the settlement agreement precludes Addax from pursuing its in rem claim in this case. We disagree with the vessel's argument.

The CIMLA provides, in relevant part:

> [A] person providing necessaries to a vessel on the order of the owner or a person authorized by the owner— **[—9—]**
>
> (1) has a maritime lien on the vessel;
> (2) may bring a civil action in rem to enforce the lien; and
> (3) is not required to allege or prove in the action that credit was given to the vessel.

46 U.S.C. § 31342(a). A maritime lien "is a right in the vessel" that entitles a vessel's creditor to have the vessel sold in order to satisfy an outstanding debt. *Itel Containers Int'l Corp. v. Atlanttrafik Express Serv. Ltd.*, 982 F.2d 765, 768 (2d Cir. 1992) (citation omitted). When a creditor holds such a lien, "the vessel itself is viewed as the obligor, regardless of whether the vessel's owner is also obligated." *Triton Marine Fuels Ltd. v. M/V Pac. Chukotka*, 575 F.3d 409, 414 (4th Cir. 2009). The maritime lien is created by operation of law "from the moment the debt arises." *Itel Containers*, 982 F.2d at 768 (citation omitted); *see also Triton*, 575 F.3d at 416 ("[M]aritime liens are *stricti juris* and cannot be created by agreement between the parties; instead, they arise by operation of law." (citation omitted)).

The holder of a maritime lien generally may pursue an in rem action to enforce the lien against the vessel, as well as seek damages against the party responsible for breach of contract. *See Hawkspere Shipping Co. v. Intamex, S.A.*, 330 F.3d 225, 232-35, 240 (4th Cir. 2003); *Cal Dive Offshore Contractors, Inc. v. M/V Sampson*, 245 F. Supp. 3d 473, 478 (S.D.N.Y. 2017). Supplemental Admiralty Rule C expressly accounts for these parallel remedies. The Rule states that "[e]xcept as otherwise provided by law a party who may proceed in rem may also, or in the alternative, proceed in personam against any person who may be liable." Fed. R. Civ. P. Supp. R. C(1). Although a provider of necessaries may pursue both in personam and in rem remedies, the provider may not "double-recover" on **[—10—]** its debt. *See Hapag-Lloyd Aktiengesellschaft v. U.S. Oil Trading LLC*, 814 F.3d 146, 152 n.17, 4 Adm. R. 62, 66 n.17 (2d Cir. 2016). Thus, Addax was entitled to pursue both an in personam claim against Windrose and an in rem claim against the vessel to satisfy the maritime debt.

The vessel acknowledges this principle, but nonetheless contends that the settlement agreement, which failed to preserve expressly Addax's right to a maritime lien, precludes Addax from enforcing such a lien. This argument, however, misapprehends the nature of the claim that Addax advances here. Addax's complaint in this case does not arise under the settlement agreement, but instead asserts a single in rem claim under the CIMLA. Addax does not assert a claim for breach of the settlement agreement, nor does Addax name Windrose, the only other party to the settlement agreement, as a defendant. Addax similarly does not assert a breach of contract claim based on Windrose's failure to pay the amount owed under the original fuel supply contract. Thus, on the **{-87-}** face of the complaint, the terms of the settlement agreement do not affect Addax's in rem claim except insofar as Addax might be seeking a double recovery on the debt.

Moreover, the vessel, the only defendant in this case, was not a party to the settlement agreement between Addax and Windrose. The settlement agreement resolved only those claims between the signatories to that agreement involving Addax's in personam breach of contract claim against Windrose. Because the vessel was not a party to the settlement agreement, Addax was not required to expressly reserve in that agreement Addax's right to the maritime lien.

We will not assume that Addax intended to waive its in rem rights with respect to the vessel in a contract that the vessel had no role in negotiating and did not sign. And nothing in the language of the settlement agreement showed that **[—11—]** Addax intended to settle its maritime lien claim against the non-signatory vessel. To the contrary, the settlement agreement does not reference the maritime lien, and includes no language limiting the obligations of the vessel or Addax's ability to pursue an in rem action to satisfy the debt.[3]

Our conclusion is not altered by the vessel's contention that because Addax's maritime lien was "based on" the fuel supply contract, that lien later was extinguished by Addax's and Windrose's agreement to settle their dispute over the underlying fuel delivery. The right to a maritime lien was not a contractual benefit that Addax and Windrose could have negotiated in the fuel supply contract.[4] Maritime liens "cannot be created by agreement between the parties" but instead "arise by operation of law." *Triton*, 575 F.3d at 416 (citation omitted). Thus, the CIMLA created Addax's right to a maritime lien. Addax's and Windrose's later decision to renegotiate their obligations with respect to the fuel supply contract did not affect Addax's right to pursue its statutory in rem claim, except to preclude Addax from obtaining a double recovery on the debt. Accordingly, we conclude that the district court correctly held that Addax's settlement of its in personam **[—12—]** claim with Windrose did not extinguish Addax's right under the CIMLA to pursue a separate in rem claim against the vessel for the remaining amount due on the fuel contract.

C.

We next consider the vessel's assertion that the district court erred in declining to credit the value of the Cargill claim against the amount of the maritime lien, and that the court violated the vessel's due process rights by failing to hold a prompt hearing under Supplemental Admiralty Rule E(4)(f). We conclude that both these arguments lack merit.

i.

The vessel contends that the amount of Addax's lien must be reduced **{-88-}** by at least $100,000, the value of Windrose's claim against third-party Cargill International, which Windrose assigned to Addax as part of the settlement agreement. According to Addax, Windrose breached the settlement agreement by failing to cooperate with Addax's efforts to collect on the Cargill claim. The vessel, however, maintains that Addax reached this conclusion in bad faith, because Windrose complied with the requirements of the settlement agreement regarding the Cargill claim.

As discussed above, the terms of the settlement agreement are not at issue in this case. We therefore decline to opine on the question whether Windrose and Addax satisfied their obligations to each other under that agreement, to which the vessel was not a party. Relevant here, it is undisputed that Addax has not received any payment from Cargill International toward the underlying debt. We therefore conclude that the district court correctly declined to credit the value of the Cargill claim, which was a component part of the settlement agreement, toward the amount of the lien. **[—13—]**

---

[3] For these reasons, we find no merit in the vessel's reliance on Clause 13 of the settlement agreement, which provides that "[t]his agreement constitutes the entire Agreement between the Parties and supersedes and extinguishes all previous agreements, promises, assurances, warranties, representations and understandings between them, whether written or oral, relating to its subject matter." This clause plainly refers to the parties to the settlement and fuel supply contracts, namely, Addax and Windrose.

[4] The general terms and conditions governing the fuel supply contract included a choice of law provision, which provided that "the federal laws of the United States of America shall apply to the substantive issue of the existence and enforcement of a maritime lien." The fuel supply agreement otherwise was governed by English law.

ii.

The vessel also argues that its due process rights were violated when it did not receive a prompt hearing to challenge the arrest pursuant to Supplemental Admiralty Rule E(4)(f). That Rule, titled "Procedure for Release From Arrest or Attachment," provides in relevant part:

> Whenever property is arrested or attached, any person claiming an interest in it shall be entitled to a prompt hearing at which the plaintiff shall be required to show why the arrest or attachment should not be vacated or other relief granted consistent with these rules.

Fed. R. Civ. P. Supp. R. E(4)(f). As we have explained, "[a] shipowner challenging the validity of an arrest is constitutionally entitled to a prompt post-arrest hearing in which the plaintiff has the burden of showing probable cause for the arrest." *Amstar Corp. v. S/S Alexandros T.*, 664 F.2d 904, 912 (4th Cir. 1981).

Here, however, the district court did not violate the vessel's due process rights or improperly deprive the vessel of a hearing under Rule E(4)(f). The vessel was arrested on December 27, 2017, but did not file a motion to vacate the arrest until four months later, in the middle of the discovery proceedings.[5] Briefing on the motion to vacate was not completed until June, and the vessel did not timely request a hearing on the motion pursuant to the local rules of the Eastern District of Virginia. *See* E.D. Va. Local R. 7(E). **[—14—]**

The district court promptly issued rulings on the motion to vacate and the summary judgment motions following oral argument in November 2018. And, as the court observed, the vessel raised a due process argument for the first time at the damages trial, after the court had granted summary judgment to Addax. Also, the vessel did not include the issue in its proposed findings of fact and conclusions of law submitted to the district court. Under these circumstances, we cannot conclude that the district court erred in failing to hold an earlier hearing or that the court violated the vessel's due process rights.[6] **{-89-}**

III.

For these reasons, we affirm the district court's judgment.

AFFIRMED

(Reporter's Note: Dissenting Opinion follows on p. 162).

[5] Along with its answer to the complaint, on December 22, 2017, the vessel submitted a letter to the district court asking the court to hold a hearing and to vacate the arrest warrant pursuant to Rule E(4)(f). Because the vessel had not yet been arrested, this request for a hearing under Rule E(4)(f) was premature.

[6] We likewise reject the vessel's argument that the district court erred in awarding $14,197.51 in *custodia legis* expenses that Addax paid to the Marshals Service and the substitute custodian while the vessel was under arrest. The record before us lacks evidentiary support for this contention.

[—15—] {-89-} AGEE, Circuit Judge, dissenting:

While I generally concur with the Majority Opinion's analysis on the merits, I write separately regarding the threshold issue of jurisdiction. At this point, I am not satisfied that Addax Energy SA ("Addax") has standing to enforce a maritime lien against the M/V Yasa H. Mulla (IMO No. 9442512) (the "vessel"). Given the uncertainty surrounding whether Addax has assigned its rights to collect on the invoice at the heart of this dispute—as well as the dearth of record evidence concerning that point—I would remand the case to the district court for an evidentiary hearing to verify Article III standing for purposes of our jurisdiction.

The Majority Opinion suggests that any potential assignment, regardless of its scope, would have no impact on Addax's Article III standing. Rather, in their view, "the true principle underlying the vessel's argument relates to whether Addax is the real party in interest under Federal Rule of Civil Procedure 17." Maj. Op. 6. But our precedent suggests that standing may be implicated here. *See In re Maco Homes, Inc.*, 180 F.3d 163, 164, 166 (4th Cir. 1999) (holding that a party who had "previously assigned all of its rights, title, and interest in the disputed account . . . lack[ed] the requisite stake in the outcome" to confer Article III standing). To that end, until assured that Addax's assignment has not deprived it of standing—a question that could be easily answered through a limited remand—we should wade carefully.

At bottom, we are a Court of limited jurisdiction. Because the vessel has credibly called our jurisdiction into question—and Addax has done nothing to assuage any concern [—16—] surrounding it, despite bearing the burden to do so—I see no reason to gloss over this issue without the necessary record evidence informing our analysis.

I.

The Majority Opinion ably recounts the underlying facts, so I only emphasize the following points pertaining to Addax's potential assignment of its rights to collect on the invoice. As the Majority Opinion notes, Addax entered into a Supply Agreement with third-party charterer Windrose SPS Shipping & Trading ("Windrose") to deliver fuel bunkers to the vessel. After delivery, Addax issued Invoice No. 17345327 to Windrose in the amount of $320,997.77, which included a notation stating, "Please note that due to our financing structure, *this invoice has been assigned in accordance with our legal and contractual obligations*. The payment of this assigned invoice has to be made exclusively and irrevocably *to our account*." J.A. 110 (emphases added).[1] The invoice also provides instructions for how Windrose was to remit payment, which included submitting a telegraphic transfer in Addax's favor through JP Morgan Chase Bank New {-90-} York. There are no documents related to the underlying assignment in the record. Indeed, the foregoing reference on the invoice constitutes the sole direct evidence that such an assignment occurred. [—17—]

When asked about the invoice notation, Addax's Rule 30(b)(6) witness, Christophe Robert, testified that the banks that provide financing to Addax require this standard form wording to be printed on all of its invoices, regardless of whether those invoices are actually assigned. To that end, Robert acknowledged that when there is an assignment, "what happens is, once [Addax] sends the invoice, the right to collect receivables is typically transferred to the financing company." J.A. 332. That said, "based on [the] wording" in Addax's invoice to Windrose, Robert could not say "if there was a financing and if it was assigned or not." J.A. 332. Nevertheless, he conceded that "it [was] very possible . . . that Addax [did not] even have a right to collect on this invoice." J.A. 333.

[1] The General Terms and Conditions governing the Supply Agreement provide that Addax "shall be free to assign or transfer its *rights and obligations* under the [Supply] Agreement to any of its affiliated companies and/or third parties[.] [I]t is being understood that no prior written consent of [Windrose] shall be required." J.A. 105 (emphasis added).

Though the vessel included standing as an affirmative defense, it did not broach the issue before the district court until the pretrial conference.[2] The district court rejected the vessel's last-minute challenge, summarily concluding from the bench that it did not "believe that there[] [was] any merit to the claim that Addax, by assigning their recovery, [was] not the proper party plaintiff." J.A. 543. In the district court's opinion partially granting Addax's motion for summary judgment, it included a truncated analysis on this point:

> As a preliminary matter, *the record is not clear as to whether [Addax] assigned its rights* under the original fuel invoice to a financial institution. However, there was no evidence to support the proposition that any such assignment would have divested Addax of its right to pursue the instant claim. Furthermore, the evidence is uncontradicted that [Addax] did, in fact, pursue collection of the debt through settlement negotiations with Windrose as well as through the Swiss bankruptcy court and its *in rem* claim in this **[—18—]** Court, which resulted in the arrest of the Vessel. Accordingly, the Court **FINDS** that [Addax] has legal standing to maintain this claim under CIMLA.

J.A. 782 (italicized emphasis added and bolded emphasis in original). The vessel timely appealed and now contends that Addax lacks standing to enforce its maritime lien due to its purported assignment of its right to collect receivables from the Supply Agreement.

II.

"Every federal appellate court has a special obligation to satisfy itself not only of its own jurisdiction, but also that of the lower courts in a cause under review[.]" *Steel Co. v. Citizens for a Better Env't,* 523 U.S. 83, 95 (1998) (citation, alterations, and internal quotation marks omitted). And Addax, as the plaintiff here, bears the burden of establishing standing. *S. Walk at Broadlands Homeowner's Ass'n, Inc. v. OpenBand at Broadlands LLC,* 713 F.3d 175, 181 (4th Cir. 2013).

Before turning to the vessel's challenge, however, there are two threshold questions to address. First, are maritime liens assignable? Second, what effect, if any, would such an assignment have on the assignor's standing to bring suit to enforce that lien? **{-91-}**

A.

The Majority Opinion does not answer the first question. That said, there appears to be a wide consensus that suppliers like Addax can assign their rights to a maritime lien, thereby granting a third-party the ability to enforce it. *See, e.g., ING Bank N.V. v. M/V TEMARA, IMO No. 9333929,* 892 F.3d 511, 519–20, 6 Adm. R. 44, 48–49 (2d Cir. 2018) (holding that the assignee of receivables from a bunker transaction was entitled to assert a maritime lien **[—19—]** because the original supplier could have done so); *Barcliff, LLC v. M/V DEEP BLUE, IMO NO. 9215359,* 876 F.3d 1063, 1074, 5 Adm. R. 518, 526 (11th Cir. 2017) ("To begin with, we note that maritime liens are assignable."); *ING Bank N.V. v. M/V Temara,* 342 F. Supp. 3d 558, 561 (S.D.N.Y. 2018); Robert Force, Admiralty and Maritime Law, Fed. Judicial Ctr. 181 (Kris Markarian ed., 2d ed. 2013), https://www.fjc.gov/sites/default/files/2014/Admiralty2d.pdf ("Maritime liens are assignable; the assignee ordinarily assumes the rank of the assignor in determining lien priority."); 1 Thomas J. Schoenbaum, Admiralty and Maritime Law § 9:1 (6th ed. 2020) ("A maritime lien may be assigned, and one who advances money for the discharge of a lien occupies the position of an assignee."). I see no reason—and Addax offers none—to conclude otherwise.

B.

Having determined that maritime liens are assignable, the next consideration is whether an assignment could deprive the assignor of

[2] In doing so, the vessel argued Addax was not a "real party in interest" under Federal Rule of Civil Procedure 17. *See* J.A. 530–33. The vessel had listed this as a separate affirmative defense as well.

Article III standing to bring suit to enforce that lien. On this second threshold question, the Majority Opinion appears to conclude that an assignment can *never* have that effect, regardless of its scope. Rather, such an assignment would *only* implicate the assignor's status as a "real party in interest" under Federal Rule of Civil Procedure 17(a)(1).

To be sure, our precedent discussing the intersection between the standing and real-party-in-interest analyses in the context of assignments has not been a model of clarity. For example, in *Martineau v. Wier*, 934 F.3d 385 (4th Cir. 2019), we observed that our past decisions "have on occasion referred to th[e] real-party-in-interest question as one of 'standing,'" but noted that "in that context, the reference is not to Article III standing—the **[—20—]** basis for the district court's jurisdictional holding—but to prudential standing, reflecting courts' tendency to use the terms prudential standing and real party in interest interchangeably." *Id.* at 391 n.3 (citation omitted).

Yet, in *In re Maco*, decided twenty years before *Martineau*,[3] we expressly dismissed an appeal for lack of Article III standing because the assignor had transferred its rights to the disputed account. There, a real estate development corporation sued its lender for wrongful dishonor of its check and for wrongful setoff of funds in its money market deposit account. Before bringing suit, however, the corporation had "previously assigned all of its rights, title, and interest in the disputed account" to one of its subsidiaries. *In re Maco*, 180 F.3d at 164. Though we determined such an assignment meant the corporation was "not a real party in interest in this litigation" under Rule 17, *id.*, our ultimate holding was that it "lack[ed] the requisite stake in the outcome to participate in this appeal," *id.* at 166 (citing **{-92-}** *Friends of the Earth, Inc. v. Laidlaw Envtl. Servs. (TOC), Inc.*, 149 F.3d 303, 306 (4th Cir. 1998) (holding that federal jurisdiction requires a personal interest in the litigation that continues throughout all stages of review)). In other words, because the assignment was complete and by its terms "transferred away any right to assert a claim" to the disputed account, *id.*, the corporation "lack[ed] standing to challenge the ruling of the district court," *id.* at 164, thereby depriving us of "jurisdiction," *id.* at 166. **[—21—]**

And that holding is consistent with the generally accepted proposition that, depending on the state or country's law governing the assignment, "[a]n unequivocal and complete assignment extinguishes the assignor's rights against the obligor and leaves the assignor without standing to sue the obligor." *Aaron Ferer & Sons Ltd. v. Chase Manhattan Bank, N.A.*, 731 F.2d 112, 125 (2d Cir. 1984) (citation omitted); *accord Hacienda Records, L.P. v. Ramos*, 718 F. App'x 223, 227 (5th Cir. 2018) (per curiam) (observing that, under Texas law, "an assignor loses the ability to pursue an action after transferring the 'exclusive' right to do so"). In other words, an "[assignor's] assignment of its rights . . . deprive[s] it of any interest in [the] litigation." *Valdin Invs. Corp. v. Oxbridge Capital Mgmt.*, 651 F. App'x 5, 7 (2d Cir. 2016) (per curiam).

Of course, less than a total assignment may not deprive the assignor of standing:

> The distinction between a complete and a partial assignment also must be kept in mind. When all the rights to a claim have been assigned, courts generally have held the assignor no longer may sue. However, when there has been only a partial assignment the assignor and the assignee each retain an interest in the claim and are both real parties in interest.

6A Charles Alan Wright, Arthur R. Miller & Mary Kay Kane, Federal Practice & Procedure § 1545 (3d ed. Supp. 2020). But a partial assignment, depending on its degree and terms, may be sufficient to deprive the assignor of its status as a real party in

[3] "[W]e have made it clear that, as to conflicts between panel opinions, application of the basic rule that one panel cannot overrule another requires a panel to follow the earlier of the conflicting opinions." *McMellon v. United States*, 387 F.3d 329, 333 (4th Cir. 2004) (en banc).

interest to the case as well. *See, e.g.*, *Martineau*, 934 F.3d at 391–92 (conducting real-party-in-interest analysis in the context of a Chapter 7 debtor, who no longer maintains possession of the bankruptcy estate); *Wilson v. Dollar Gen. Corp.*, 717 F.3d 337, 342–44 (4th Cir. 2013) (same for Chapter 13 debtor, who retains possession of the bankruptcy estate). **[—22—]**

Thus, consistent with our precedent, I would look to the legal effect and scope of the assignment in question to determine whether it implicates our standing or real-party-in-interest analyses.

C.

For the foregoing reasons, in light of the present record, any analysis on the assignment at issue here would be murky, at best. Indeed, we do not know with certainty whether there was an assignment, much less its scope.[4] That said, in light of Addax's representations made in the invoice, its General Terms and Conditions, and through its Rule 30(b)(6) witness, there is a strong possibility that it has assigned its right to collect receivables from the Supply Agreement to a third party. Thus, at the very least, the vessel has presented a colorable claim that Addax may lack Article III standing to enforce the maritime lien, thereby depriving us of jurisdiction. **{-93-}**

Indeed, if there was an assignment which was unequivocal, complete, and transferred Addax's rights, title, and interest in their entirety, it likely lacks standing for the reasons noted above. If, however, the purported assignment effectuated anything less than a total transfer, then—and only then—would I apply the real-party-in-interest analysis. But I do not believe we are in a position to resolve this issue on the present record. **[—23—]**

And because it is Addax's burden to satisfy us that it has standing and it has pointed to no evidence contradicting the vessel's colorable claim that it may not, I am not satisfied at this time of our jurisdiction to hear this case.

III.

In light of the foregoing, I would remand the case to the district court to conduct the necessary factual inquiry in the first instance. As such, I respectfully dissent with regard to the standing issue.

---

[4] The Majority Opinion points to circumstantial evidence suggesting no assignment ever took place. I do not disagree with this assessment. Rather, because the question at issue concerns our jurisdiction, I would seek out and rely upon affirmative evidence to make such a determination, especially when that evidence is so easily obtainable.

United States Court of Appeals
for the Fourth Circuit

No. 20-2146

EAST COAST REPAIR & FABRICATION, LLC
vs.
UNITED STATES

Appeal from the United States District Court for the Eastern District of Virginia, at Norfolk

Decided: October 14, 2021

Citation: 16 F.4th 87, 9 Adm. R. 166 (4th Cir. 2021).

Before **MOTZ** and **AGEE**, Circuit Judges, and **KEENAN**, Senior Circuit Judge.

[—2—] {-88-} **MOTZ**, Circuit Judge:

This case arises from a dispute between East Coast Repair and the United States over contracts for the repair of three Navy ships. East Coast seeks to recover $473,600 that the Government withheld from payment under one of these contracts. Because the parties' settlement agreement precludes East Coast's claims, we affirm the judgment of the district court rejecting these claims.

I.

East Coast, a ship repair company, contracted with the U.S. Navy to repair three ships: the *USS Thunderbolt*, the *USS Tempest*, and the *USS Hurricane*. Though East Coast brought this suit under the *Hurricane* contract, the *Tempest* contract is central to it. In 2013, the Navy claimed it was entitled to $474,600 in liquidated damages under the *Tempest* contract because East Coast delivered the *Tempest* late. Because the Navy had already paid all but $1,000 for East Coast's work on the *Tempest*, it withheld a $473,600 setoff from **{-89-}** payment to East Coast under the *Hurricane* contract.

East Coast claimed the Navy caused the complained-of delay in delivery and sent a letter to the government contracting officer disputing the Navy's assessment of liquidated damages under the *Tempest* contract and requesting additional compensation for unanticipated work on the *Tempest*. In 2014, after the contracting officer denied that request, East Coast sued the United States under the *Tempest* contract in federal district court (the "*Tempest* suit"). In its complaint, East Coast referred specifically to the $473,600 setoff, stating that it "included those liquidated damages as part of its [request to **[—3—]** the government contracting officer] and as part of the calculation of the damages requested hereunder since they were assessed on the TEMPEST."

In 2014, while the litigation proceeded, East Coast submitted to the contracting officer a request for additional compensation under the *Hurricane* contract for its assertedly unexpected work on that ship. After six months without response, East Coast appealed to the Armed Services Board of Contract Appeals (the "Board") and ultimately moved for summary judgment before the Board seeking payment of the $473,600 "withheld from payments due under [the *Hurricane*] contract." For reasons unclear from the record, East Coast later withdrew the summary judgment motion.

East Coast and the Government settled the *Tempest* suit in 2017. In the settlement agreement, each party released the other from liability in broad, but not identical, terms. East Coast released the Government "from any and all actions, claims, . . . and liabilities of any type, whether known or unknown, suspected or unsuspected, foreseen or unforeseen, or open or hidden, which have existed, presently exist, or may exist in the future, arising out of or in any way relating to the [*Tempest*] Contract." The Government released East Coast from "any and all" claims "arising out of or in any way relating to the issues that were raised in the pleadings or could have been raised in the pleadings." Both releases contain an exception for retainage (a portion of the contract price the Government typically withholds from payment to ensure contractors complete their work). The district court dismissed the *Tempest* suit with prejudice.

In 2019, East Coast asserted a right to the same $473,600 in a third request to the government contracting officer. And in 2020, East Coast filed this action, claiming the [—4—] Government's refusal to pay the $473,600 breached the *Hurricane* contract. After the parties filed cross motions for summary judgment, the district court granted the Government's motion and denied East Coast's. The court held that (1) it lacked subject matter jurisdiction because East Coast made a binding choice to raise the setoff issue before the Board, and (2) the settlement agreement barred East Coast's claims. East Coast then filed this appeal.

II.

We first address the district court's jurisdictional holding. We review a court's dismissal for lack of subject matter jurisdiction de novo. *Ripley v. Foster Wheeler LLC*, 841 F.3d 207, 209 (4th Cir. 2016).

The district court based its conclusion that it lacked subject matter jurisdiction on Section 7104(b) of the Contract Disputes Act, 41 U.S.C. §§ 7101, *et seq.* That provision states that a contractor "may"—after first raising a claim with the designated "contracting officer"—bring the claim before a federal district court "in lieu of" appealing to the agency **{-90-}** board.[1] The Federal Circuit has interpreted Section 7104(b) to make binding a government contractor's choice to bring a claim before either the agency board or a federal district court. *See Nat'l Neighbors, Inc. v. United States*, 839 F.2d 1539, 1541–42 (Fed. Cir. 1988). Thus, once a contractor elects to bring its claim before one forum with jurisdiction, the other forum lacks subject matter jurisdiction over the same claim. *Bonneville Assocs. v.* **[—5—]** *United States*, 43 F.3d 649, 653 (Fed. Cir. 1994). The Federal Circuit commonly refers to this rule as the "Election Doctrine." *Id.* at 651. Relying on this doctrine, the district court concluded that East Coast made a binding choice of forum when it filed a motion for summary judgment raising the setoff issue before the Board in 2016. For this reason, the court held it lacked jurisdiction.

We have some question as to this holding. The district court did not consider the significance of the *Tempest* suit. The Government asserted before the district court that East Coast had earlier chosen federal district court as its preferred forum when it filed a complaint raising the setoff issue in the *Tempest* suit in 2014. If so, the filing of a summary judgment motion raising the same issue before the Board two years later would not constitute a binding election of forum. *Id.* at 653. Nor is it at all clear that the mere filing of a summary judgment motion constitutes a binding choice of forum under the governing statute, which states that a contractor may either "*appeal*[] the decision of a contracting officer . . . to an agency board" or "*bring an action directly*" in federal court. 41 U.S.C. § 7104(b) (emphasis added).

Rather than determine the answer to these difficult jurisdictional questions—questions that turn on principles never before applied in this Circuit—we take the "less burdensome course" and resolve this case on res judicata grounds. *See Sinochem Int'l Co. v. Malaysia Int'l Shipping Corp.*, 549 U.S. 422, 436 (2007). Where a court conclusively determines it lacks jurisdiction, it must dismiss the case on that basis. *Sinochem Int'l Co.*, 549 U.S. at 434. But a court may bypass a difficult jurisdictional question and "choose among threshold grounds for denying audience to a case on the merits . . . when **[—6—]** considerations of convenience, fairness, and judicial economy so warrant." *Id.* at 431–32; *Hicks v. Ferreyra*, 965 F.3d 302, 309 n.2 (4th Cir. 2020). Res judicata is one such threshold ground. *See Hoffman v. Nordic Naturals, Inc.*, 837 F.3d 272, 277 (3d Cir. 2016).

III.

Accordingly, we now turn to the district court's grant of summary judgment on the basis that res judicata bars East Coast's claims because East Coast released them in the 2017 settlement agreement. We review summary judgment decisions de novo. *Wilson*

[1] A contractor usually must choose between an agency board and the U.S. Court of Federal Claims. But in maritime cases like this one, a contractor may choose a federal district court. *See* 41 U.S.C. § 7102(d); Suits in Admiralty Act, 46 U.S.C. § 30901, *et seq.*

v. Prince George's Cnty., 893 F.3d 213, 218 (4th Cir. 2018). Summary judgment is appropriate if, construing all evidence in favor of the non-moving party, "there is no genuine dispute as to any material fact and the movant is entitled to judgment as a matter of law." Fed. R. Civ. P. 56(a).

Res judicata traditionally bars a party from asserting a claim in a later suit once a court has reached a final judgment on the merits of the same claim in an earlier suit. *Martin v. Am. Bancorp. Ret. Plan*, 407 F.3d 643, 650 (4th Cir. 2005). If a claim is resolved in a settlement agreement, **{-91-}** we look to the intent of the parties to determine whether the settlement agreement bars later claims. *Ohio Valley Envt'l Coal. v. Aracoma Coal Co.*, 556 F.3d 177, 211 (4th Cir. 2009) (citing 18A Charles Alan Wright, Arthur R. Miller, & Edward H. Cooper, *Federal Practice & Procedure* § 4443 (2d ed. 2002)). We use contract interpretation principles to discern the parties' intent. *Keith v. Aldridge*, 900 F.2d 736, 740–41 (4th Cir. 1990).

Here, East Coast released the Government from liability for "any and all" claims "arising out of or in any way relating to the [*Tempest*] Contract." The $473,600 setoff **[—7—]** clearly "relates" to the *Tempest* contract because the Navy withheld that amount as liquidated damages on the *Tempest* contract. We cannot read such a broad release to exclude a claim for a setoff taken as liquidated damages under the *Tempest* contract. *Cf. United States v. Gonzales*, 520 U.S. 1, 5 (1997) ("Read naturally, the word 'any' has an expansive meaning . . . ."); *Am. Recovery Corp. v. Comput. Thermal Imaging, Inc.*, 96 F.3d 88, 93 (4th Cir. 1996) (describing "arising out of or related to" formulation in an arbitration clause as "capable of an expansive reach"). And if we had any doubt as to whether East Coast believed the setoff relates "in any way" to the *Tempest* contract, we need only look to East Coast's complaint in the *Tempest* suit, which states that East Coast factored the $473,600 into its calculation of damages because the damages "were assessed on the TEMPEST."

East Coast insists, however, that we read its release to give meaning to the difference in wording between its release and the Government's. East Coast regards it as significant here that while it released any claims against the Government "arising out of or in any way relating to the [*Tempest*] Contract," the Government released any claims against East Coast "arising out of or in any way relating to issues that were raised in the pleadings or could have been raised in the pleadings" in the *Tempest* action. East Coast argues we must construe this difference to mean that "the parties intentionally omitted" a release of a claim for the setoff. Appellant's Br. at 25. But as it conceded at oral argument before us, East Coast offers no evidence of the parties' intent to do this in drafting the two releases. The difference in the language of the two releases alone does not require us to accept this "strained interpretation" of the text. *See Goodman v. Resolution Tr. Corp.*, 7 F.3d 1123, **[—8—]** 1126–27 (4th Cir. 1993). And when a settlement agreement's text is unambiguous, as it is here, we simply cannot rewrite its terms based on a party's protestation that it meant something other than what it said.

The absence of any reservation in the settlement agreement for the setoff further supports the conclusion that the settlement agreement bars East Coast's claims. *See Coakley & Williams Constr., Inc. v. Structural Concrete Equip.*, 973 F.2d 349, 353 (4th Cir. 1992) ("[B]ecause [a] release was very broadly phrased, it seems that if the parties intended to allow any future claims against each other, they would have done so specifically."). As the district court noted, the parties specifically included an exception in the settlement agreement for retainage and could have done the same for the setoff. Accordingly, we agree with the district court that the settlement agreement bars East Coast's claims.

IV.

For the foregoing reasons, the judgment of the district court is

AFFIRMED.

United States Court of Appeals for the Fifth Circuit

United States Court of Appeals
for the Fifth Circuit

No. 19-40718

GARCIA
VS.
UNITED STATES

Appeal from the United States District Court for the Southern District of Texas

Decided: January 19, 2021

Citation: 986 F.3d 513, 9 Adm. R. 170 (5th Cir. 2021).

Before **JOLLY, JONES,** and **WILLETT,** Circuit Judges.

[—1—] {-519-} WILLETT, Circuit Judge:

While patrolling the Brownsville Ship Channel around midnight, a United States Coast Guard vessel struck and killed Patricia Guadalupe Garcia Cervantes, a Mexican citizen who was attempting to enter the United States illegally by swimming across the Channel. Litigation ensued. Francisco Ortega Garcia, individually and on behalf of his and Cervantes' daughter, V.S.O.G., brought (1) negligence and wrongful death claims **[—2—]** against the United States and (2) products liability, gross negligence, and wrongful death claims against the manufacturers of the vessel and its engines, Safe Boats and Mercury Marine.

The district court dismissed everything. It dismissed the negligence claim against the United States, concluding that the United States owed no duty to Cervantes. It dismissed the products liability claims against Safe Boats and Mercury Marine, concluding that Cervantes, as a bystander, lacked standing to bring those claims. And, because it dismissed all the underlying tort claims, the district court dismissed the wrongful death claims. For the reasons below, we affirm the dismissal of all Garcia's claims against the United States, Safe Boats, and Mercury Marine.

I

A

The Brownsville Ship Channel (BSC) lies just three miles north of the mouth of the Rio Grande and connects the Port of Brownsville with the Gulf of Mexico.[1] The **{-520-}** BSC is a "high-traffic waterway, travelled day and night by various vessels from small fishing boats to large tankers."[2] In **[—3—]** general, "there is no posted speed limit" on the BSC,[3] and "[t]here are no lights along the [BSC], making it very dark at night."[4]

The United States Coast Guard maintains a station on South Padre Island, near the BSC. The station's "primary missions" include "search and rescue and maritime law enforcement." Coast Guard law enforcement patrols roughly 30 miles of the Texas coast and several nearby waterways, including the BSC. The purpose of the patrols is "to deter and interdict immigrants and narcotic smugglers, ensure safety and security of the maritime facilities within the Port of Brownsville, and to conduct commercial and recreational vessel boardings to enforce various safety and security laws and regulations."

The Coast Guard's patrol route follows a southwestern course, departing from the South Padre Island station, traveling along the BSC, passing the Shrimp Basin, and reaching the Port of Brownsville Turning

---

[1] *See United States v. Ruiz-Hernandez*, 890 F.3d 202, 206, 6 Adm. R. 199, 199 (5th Cir. 2018) (describing the BSC).

[2] *Id.*, 6 Adm. R. at 199.

[3] The one exception is the no-wake zone in the Shrimp Basin, a docking area on the BSC's north side where vessels must travel slowly. *Id.*, 6 Adm. R. at 199.

[4] *Id.*, 6 Adm. R. at 199. Although the Port of Brownsville commercial complex, located along the shores of the BSC between the Shrimp Basin and the Port of Brownsville Turning Basin, has "numerous commercial maritime facilities" that "have significant lighting that illuminates the general vicinity within the BSC," "[t]he remainder of the BSC, northeast from the Shrimp Basin"—where the incident occurred—"is mostly undeveloped with minimal shore side lighting."

Basin, at which point the patrol crew turns around and heads back to the station. Coast Guard crews conduct BSC patrols aboard a Special Purpose Craft-Law Enforcement (SPC-LE) vessel. The Coast Guard developed specifications for the SPC-LE, including that it be a "planing" vessel, a type of vessel in which the bow rises while it is accelerating, only to fall again when **[—4—]** it reaches "planing speed" of approximately 19.2 knots.[5] The Coast Guard awarded the SPC-LE manufacturing contract to Safe Boats. Safe Boats complied with the Coast Guard's "planing" vessel specifications when it supplied its SPC-LEs, and these vessels included engines with propeller drives manufactured by Mercury Marine.

* * *

At 9:53 p.m. on April 23, 2015, four United States Coast Guard members commenced a patrol of the BSC aboard an SPC-LE vessel.[6] At all relevant times, the vessel's navigation lights were on. Around 11:00 p.m., one of the crewmembers requested and received permission to accelerate the vessel to come up on plane. Two crewmembers assert that they looked forward before the vessel came up on plane and did not see anything in the water. In approximately 30 seconds, the vessel came up on plane. The vessel then transited for approximately 30 seconds at an average speed of 30.86 knots until the crew heard a "thud" or "thump" sound under the vessel's hull. The crew stopped the vessel, turned it around, and searched the area to identify the source of the sound. They spotted and recovered a pink plastic innertube. After this search, the crew continued **{–521–}** the patrol and returned to the Coast Guard station around 12:40 a.m.; they reported to Coast Guard officials and showed their superiors the recovered pink innertube.

Unbeknownst to the crew, Patricia Guadalupe Garcia Cervantes, a Mexican citizen, and Galdino Jose Ruiz-Hernandez, a human smuggler, had **[—5—]** been attempting to illegally enter the United States by swimming across the BSC.[7] Cervantes was using a pink innertube as a flotation device. Cervantes was struck by the Coast Guard crew's vessel approximately 30 seconds after the vessel had fully come up onto plane. An autopsy, conducted three days after this incident, revealed that the injuries on Cervantes' body were consistent with the shape of the vessel's propeller blades, and the coroner determined that Cervantes "died nearly instantly" after the collision "because of the initial blunt force trauma and blood loss." The Coast Guard conducted an investigation of the incident, which was summarized in a Major Incident Report, completed on July 14, 2015.

B

Francisco Ortega Garcia brought this suit in his individual capacity, as Cervantes' spouse and administrator of her estate, and on behalf of his and Cervantes' minor daughter, V.S.O.G. Garcia asserted several claims against three defendants: (1) negligence and wrongful death claims against the United States for the Coast Guard's operation of the vessel; (2) strict products liability, gross negligence, and wrongful death claims against Safe Boats regarding the vessel; and (3) strict products liability, gross negligence, and wrongful death claims against Mercury Marine regarding the vessel's engines.

The United States moved to dismiss parts of Garcia's negligence claim for lack of subject-matter jurisdiction.[8] Safe Boats moved for

---

[5] *See* Mark Corke, *Getting an Outboard Boat on Plane*, Boat U.S., https://www.boatus.com/magazine/2018/february/getting-on-plane.asp (describing how to get a boat "on plane").

[6] The four United States Coast Guard members will be referred to as the crew. The crew consisted of a certified coxswain, a break-in-coxswain, a boarding officer, and a crewmember.

[7] Ruiz-Hernandez was convicted of one count of conspiring to bring in, transport, and harbor an alien resulting in death and one count of transporting an alien within the United States for private financial gain and resulting in death. We upheld his conviction and sentence on appeal. *Ruiz-Hernandez*, 890 F.3d at 208, 213, 6 Adm. R. at 200–01, 204.

[8] The United States moved to dismiss the portions of Garcia's negligence claim alleging improper design of the vessel and lack of proper

partial **[—6—]** summary judgment on four different issues.[9] While all these motions were pending, the magistrate judge issued a Report and Recommendation (R&R), recommending that all of Garcia's claims be dismissed. Garcia timely filed objections to the R&R. The district court overruled Garcia's objections, adopted the magistrate judge's R&R in its entirety, and dismissed all of Garcia's claims with prejudice. Specifically, the district court determined that: (1) Garcia failed to identify what duty the United States owed to Cervantes; (2) he failed to show that Safe Boats and Mercury Marine had a duty to warn Cervantes; (3) he could not maintain the maritime products liability claims because Cervantes, as a "casual bystander," lacked standing to bring those claims; and (4) he could not maintain wrongful death claims because all the underlying tort claims were dismissed. Garcia appealed.

II

Before reaching the issues that Garcia raises on appeal, there are three threshold **{-522-}** matters: (1) whether the district court had subject-matter jurisdiction; (2) whether Garcia has standing to sue in his individual capacity; and (3) the proper standard of review. We address each in turn.

A

First, we address the parties' confusion about the basis for the district court's subject-matter jurisdiction.[10] Because Garcia brings claims against **[—7—]** the United States, our subject-matter jurisdiction analysis involves two inquiries: (1) Did the United States waive its sovereign immunity? And if so, (2) does diversity or admiralty subject-matter jurisdiction apply?

Turning to the first inquiry: To maintain a suit in district court against the United States, a plaintiff must bring claims under a statute in which Congress expressly waives the United States' sovereign immunity.[11] Garcia brings his claims under the Federal Tort Claims Act (FTCA)[12] or, in the alternative, the Suits in Admiralty Act (SIAA)[13] and the Public Vessels Act (PVA).[14] Determining which waiver statute applies matters because the FTCA excludes claims in admiralty, while the SIAA and PVA do not.[15] So, we must first decide whether Garcia's claims are admiralty claims.

A party seeking to invoke federal admiralty jurisdiction over a tort claim must demonstrate that the tortious activity (1) "occurred on navigable water" or that an "injury suffered on land was caused by a vessel on navigable water," and (2) bears a "connection with the maritime activity."[16] Garcia has done both. First, he alleges that Cervantes' death occurred on the BSC. **[—8—]** Second, he alleges that her death was caused by a Coast Guard vessel, which clearly bears a connection with maritime activity.[17]

---

training and supervision of Coast **[—6—]** Guard personnel, arguing those claims were barred by sovereign immunity and outside the discretionary function exception to the waiver of sovereign immunity.

[9] Safe Boats filed motions for partial summary judgment on the issues of (1) punitive damages, (2) Garcia's lack of standing, (3) proximate cause, and (4) the government contractor defense.

[10] The magistrate judge noted the "disagreement between the parties over the jurisdictional bases of [Garcia's] claims." "[S]ubject-matter jurisdiction is not waivable," **[—7—]** and we are "under a continuing duty to inquire into the basis of jurisdiction in the district court." *Warren v. United States*, 874 F.2d 280, 281–82 (5th Cir. 1989).

[11] *See Dunn-McCampbell Royalty Interest, Inc. v. National Park Service*, 112 F.3d 1283, 1287 (5th Cir. 1997) ("[T]he United States is immune from suit unless it consents, and the terms of its consent circumscribe our jurisdiction.").

[12] 28 U.S.C. § 1346(b)(1).

[13] 46 U.S.C. §§ 30901 *et seq.*

[14] 46 U.S.C. §§ 31101 *et seq.*

[15] 28 U.S.C. § 2680(d). *See also McCormick v. United States*, 680 F.2d 345, 348 (5th Cir. 1982); *Williams v. Central Gulf Lines*, 874 F.2d 1958, 1062 (5th Cir. 1989).

[16] *Jerome B. Grubart, Inc. v. Great Lakes Dredge & Dock Co.*, 513 U.S. 527, 534 (1995). See 28 U.S.C. § 1331.

[17] *See Yamaha Motor Corp., U.S.A. v. Calhoun*, 516 U.S. 199, 206 (1996) (citations omitted) (applying admiralty law in a case involving "a watercraft collision on navigable waters").

Federal Rule of Civil Procedure 9(h) specifies how a pleading may designate claims as admiralty claims.[18] A party need not make a specific reference to Rule 9(h) in his complaint, as long as the complaint contains "a simple statement asserting admiralty or maritime claims," which we have held sufficient to invoke a district court's admiralty jurisdiction.[19]

In his complaint, Garcia asserts that the district court has diversity subject-matter **{–523–}** jurisdiction under 28 U.S.C. § 1332. Although Garcia's complaint does not refer to Rule 9(h) or to the district court's admiralty subject-matter jurisdiction under 28 U.S.C. § 1333, Garcia's complaint does contain a simple statement asserting maritime claims, which is sufficient for admiralty jurisdiction purposes.[20] These are admiralty claims because they involve a vessel collision. Because Garcia's case is one in admiralty, the relevant sovereign immunity statutory waivers are the SIAA and PVA, not the FTCA. And these statutory waivers apply because this case—a collision between a Coast Guard vessel and an individual—falls within their statutory scope. Because the SIAA and PVA waive the United States' sovereign **[—9—]** immunity, the district court had subject-matter jurisdiction based in admiralty.

B

As a second threshold matter, we must address whether Garcia has standing to sue as Cervantes' surviving spouse.[21] To determine standing in maritime accident cases, we apply state wrongful death and survival statutes.[22] Texas law—the relevant state law here—provides that only the surviving spouse, children, and parents of a deceased individual may be the beneficiaries of wrongful death and survival suits.[23] Garcia admits that he and Cervantes were never formally married; he says that they had a common-law marriage. To prove a common-law marriage under Texas law, Garcia must provide evidence that that he and Cervantes (1) agreed to be married and after that agreement (2) lived together in Texas where (3) they represented to others that they were married.[24] Garcia and Cervantes never lived together in Texas, let alone represented to others in Texas that they were married. Because Garcia is unable to show that he is Cervantes' common-law spouse under Texas law, he does not qualify as Cervantes' surviving spouse and **[—10—]** therefore lacks standing in his individual capacity to bring wrongful death and survival claims.[25]

Notwithstanding his own lack of standing, Garcia may still maintain claims as next-of-friend for V.S.O.G., his child with Cervantes. Accordingly, we have jurisdiction to reach the merits of Garcia's claims.[26]

C

As a final preliminary matter, we must clarify the correct standard of **{–524–}** review. When the district court dismissed Garcia's claims, it had several motions before it, including the United States' motion to dismiss Garcia's negligence claim and Safe Boats' four motions for partial summary judgment. The

[18] FED. R. CIV. P. 9(h).

[19] *Teal v. Eagle Fleet, Inc.*, 933 F.2d 341, 345 (5th Cir. 1991).

[20] In addition, Garcia affirmatively stated that he did not object to the magistrate judge's R&R conclusion that Garcia had properly invoked admiralty jurisdiction as to all defendants, and the district court noted that Garcia elected to proceed under its admiralty jurisdiction.

[21] "The standing doctrine defines and limits the role of the judiciary and is a threshold inquiry to adjudication." *McClure v. Ashcroft*, 335 F.3d 404, 408 (5th Cir. 2003). Safe Boats raised the standing issue in its Motion for Partial Summary Judgment. Safe Boats and Mercury Marine again raise the standing issue in their brief. The United States does not raise this issue.

[22] *Yamaha*, 516 U.S. at 215–16.

[23] TEX. CIV. PRAC. & REM. CODE § 71.004(a) provides: "An action to recover damages . . . is for the exclusive benefit of the surviving spouse, children, and parents of the deceased." *See id.* § 71.004(b).

[24] TEX. FAM. CODE § 2.401(a)(2).

[25] Garcia relies on a Texas probate court's determination that he is an heir of Cervantes and designated as her spouse. But Texas family law, not the probate court's determination of marital status for purposes of inheritance law, determines standing for wrongful death and survival claims.

[26] We have jurisdiction under 28 U.S.C. § 1291.

district court did not explicitly state which motions it was addressing, and it did not state the standard(s) it was applying.[27]

The district court dismissed Garcia's negligence claim against the United States on the grounds that Garcia failed to establish that the United **[—11—]** States owed a duty to Cervantes and thus failed to allege a prima facie claim of negligence.[28] Determination of duty is a question of law that we review de novo.[29]

Turning to the remainder of Garcia's claims, the district court dismissed: (1) the failure-to-warn claims against Safe Boats and Mercury Marine because it found their duty to warn was owed to the United States, not to Cervantes; (2) the design defect claims against Safe Boats and Mercury Marine because Cervantes, as a "casual bystander," lacked standing to bring maritime products liability claims; and (3) the wrongful death claims against the United States, Safe Boats, and Mercury Marine because the underlying tort claims had been dismissed. In dismissing these claims, the district court relied on the R&R for the facts, which cited evidence outside the pleadings, so we treat the district court's order as a summary judgment ruling.

We review a district court's grant of summary judgment de novo, viewing all the facts and evidence in the light most favorable to the non- **[—12—]** movant.[30] Summary judgment is appropriate "if the movant shows that there is no genuine dispute **{–525–}** as to any material fact and the movant is entitled to judgment as a matter of law."[31] A genuine dispute of material fact exists when "the evidence is such that a reasonable jury could return a verdict for the nonmoving party."[32]

* * *

Summing up: We have subject-matter jurisdiction (because the United States waived its sovereign immunity under the SIAA and PVA) and the proper basis of subject-matter jurisdiction is in admiralty; Garcia does not have standing to sue in his individual capacity but may bring claims on behalf of V.S.O.G.; and we review the district court's grant of

---

[27] The magistrate judge's R&R also was unclear as to what motions it was addressing and what standard it was applying.

Although not raised as a stand alone issue, Garcia argues throughout his brief that the magistrate judge raised several of the reasons for dismissal *sua sponte*, including the magistrate judge's determination that Garcia failed to adequately identify the duty the Coast Guard owed Cervantes and that Cervantes was a "casual bystander" who lacked standing to bring products liability claims. Garcia argues this was improper because the United States had not filed a motion for summary judgment on his negligence claim, and Safe Boats and Mercury Marine had not moved for summary judgment on the "casual bystander" issue.

However, "district courts are widely acknowledged to possess the power to enter summary judgment *sua sponte*, so long as the losing party was on notice that she had to come **[—11—]** forward with all of her evidence." *Atkins v. Salazar*, 677 F.3d 667, 678 (5th Cir. 2011) (quoting *Celotex Corp. v. Catrett*, 477 U.S. 317, 326 (1986) (alteration omitted)). Applying a previous version of Federal Rule of Civil Procedure 56, we held that ten days' notice is sufficient to "grant summary judgment *sua sponte* on grounds not urged in a pending motion." *Lozano v. Ocwen Federal Bank, FSB*, 489 F.3d 636, 641 (5th Cir. 2007). Here, Garcia objected to the magistrate judge's R&R fourteen days after it was filed. The district court adopted the magistrate judge's R&R in its entirety almost three months after those objections were filed. Because Garcia had sufficient notice that the district court might grant summary judgment on grounds not raised by the defendants, Garcia's argument of insufficient notice—to the extent he makes this argument—fails.

[28] In a footnote, the district court tangentially addressed the United States' 12(b)(1) motion to dismiss based on the discretionary function exception. Because it dismissed the products liability claims based on Cervantes' lack of standing, the district court did not address the discretionary function exception to a waiver of sovereign immunity.

[29] *In re Great Lakes Dredge & Dock Co. LLC*, 624 F.3d 201, 211 (5th Cir. 2010) (quoting *In re Signal Int'l, LLC*, 579 F.3d 478, 490 (5th Cir. 2009)).

[30] *Juino v. Livingston Par. Fire Dist. No. 5*, 717 F.3d 431, 433 (5th Cir. 2013).

[31] Fed. R. Civ. P. 56(a).

[32] *Anderson v. Liberty Lobby, Inc.*, 477 U.S. 242, 248 (1986).

summary judgment and its duty determination de novo.

III

Garcia raises several issues on appeal.

- *Regarding his negligence claim against the United States,* Garcia argues that the district court erred in finding that the United States owed no duty to Cervantes based on the lack of foreseeability.

- *For his products liability claims against Safe Boats and Mercury Marine,* Garcia contends: (1) the district court erred in applying the Restatement (Second) of Torts, which forecloses Cervantes' standing to maintain the products liability claims; (2) the district court erred in construing his products liability claims as brought against the United **[—13—]** States, rather than Safe Boats and Mercury Marine; (3) the district court erred in dismissing the failure-to-warn claims and construing them as brought against the United States; and (4) the district court should have found that Safe Boats was not entitled to immunity as a government contractor.

- *Regarding the wrongful death claims against the United States, Safe Boats, and Mercury Marine,* Garcia argues that the district court erred in dismissing these claims by concluding that there were no underlying tort claims.

We address these arguments claim by claim.

A

We first address Garcia's negligence claim against the United States.

Garcia asserts in his complaint that the United States is vicariously liable for the Coast Guard crew's failures to operate the vessel at a safe speed and with sufficient lighting, to keep a proper lookout, and to render aid to Cervantes. He argues that the Coast Guard has "a duty . . . to not cause personal injury or death by their own wrongful or negligent acts or omissions" and "to not allow a situation to develop which would cause the death of another human being." The district court determined that the United States owed no duty to Cervantes—and was therefore not liable—because the Coast Guard crew did not have actual knowledge about the possibility of hitting Cervantes as she swam across the BSC. And, since it found that there was no duty, the district court dismissed Garcia's negligence claim for failure to make out his prima facie claim. On appeal, Garcia argues **[—14—]** that the district court erred because it failed to consider facts known to the Coast Guard that address the foreseeability of harm. **{-526-}**

We begin with the relevant law: "[N]egligence is an actionable wrong under general maritime law."[33] To maintain a negligence claim under admiralty law, the plaintiff must show "a duty owed by the defendant to the plaintiff, breach of that duty, injury sustained by [the] plaintiff, and a causal connection between the defendant's conduct and the plaintiff's injury."[34] We are concerned solely with the duty element.

Under general maritime law, "a tortfeasor is accountable only to those to whom a duty is owed."[35] More specifically, under the SIAA and PVA, the duty owed by the United States "is equal 'to that of a private person in like circumstances.'"[36] We must determine the

---

[33] *Withhart v. Otto Candies, L.L.C.*, 431 F.3d 840, 842 (5th Cir. 2005). *See also Norfolk Shipbuilding & Drydock Corp. v. Garris*, 532 U.S. 811, 820 (2001) ("The general maritime law has recognized the tort of negligence for more than a century . . . .").

[34] *In re Great Lakes*, 624 F.3d at 211 (quoting *Canal Barge Co. v. Torco Oil Co.*, 220 F.3d 370, 376 (5th Cir. 2020)). *See also Withhart*, 431 F.3d at 842 (providing that the elements of a negligence claim in maritime law are "essentially the same as land-based negligence under the common law").

[35] *Consol. Aluminum Corp. v. C.F. Bean Corp.*, 833 F.2d 65, 67 (5th Cir. 1987).

[36] *Southern Nat. Gas Co. v. Pontchartrain Materials, Inc.*, 711 F.2d 1251, 1254 (5th Cir. 1983)

existence and scope of that duty.[37] While our determination is guided by many factors, an especially important factor is "the foreseeability of the harm suffered by the complaining party."[38] And the foreseeability factor is the critical issue here: If the harm Cervantes suffered allegedly as a result of the Coast Guard crew's **[—15—]** negligence was not foreseeable, then the United States owed no duty to Cervantes and is not liable as a matter of law.

In the context of maritime torts,[39] we have deemed harm to be a foreseeable consequence of an act or omission "if harm of a general sort to persons of a general class might have been anticipated by a reasonably thoughtful person, as a probable result of the act or omission, considering the interplay of natural forces and likely human intervention."[40] This definition of foreseeability is in terms of *general* forms of harms and *general* classes of victims. So, our analysis focuses on the general risk of collision—not on the particular collision between the Coast Guard vessel and Cervantes—and on the general class of individuals—not on Cervantes.[41] And, when we consider the probability of harm, we do so "in terms of the 'natural and probable' risks that a reasonable person would likely take into account in guiding her practical conduct."[42]

Here, the general sort of harm—a collision between a vessel and an individual swimming across the BSC—was not foreseeable. The BSC is "a high-traffic waterway, travelled day and night by various vessels from small fishing boats to large **{-527-}** tankers."[43] Because the Coast Guard vessel's duty is equivalent to that of a private vessel in similar circumstances, Garcia must show that the private vessels that travel the BSC anticipated this general **[—16—]** kind of harm.[44] But Garcia provides no indication that any of these private vessels would reasonably anticipate a collision with a nighttime swimmer. Plus, "experience and common sense" weigh against the foreseeability of this general sort of harm.[45] The high-traffic nature of the BSC, compounded with its minimal lighting and absence of a speed limit, renders a nighttime crossing by a human not only dangerous, but also unforeseeable. Thus, a private vessel travelling at night in a high-traffic waterway would not reasonably anticipate encountering swimmers in the water. Accordingly, the presence of nighttime swimmers does not "guid[e] [the] practical conduct" of private vessels in the BSC.[46] Additionally, it bears emphasis that the harm involves individuals who are intentionally trying to avoid detection. Our caselaw on the foreseeability of harm in the maritime context has involved incidents between inanimate objects.[47] Of those cases, only *In re Signal* found that the harm was foreseeable, largely because the risk of danger was due to a discrete incident.[48] Here, because the harm involves individuals, rather than inanimate objects, it is far more difficult to foresee what an undocumented alien who is intentionally trying to avoid detection would do. For these reasons, the harm was not foreseeable.

Likewise, the general class of victims was not foreseeable. Here, the general class would be individuals swimming across the BSC. And, **[—17—]** importantly, this class of

(quoting *Canadian Pac. (Bermuda) Ltd. v. United States*, 534 F.2d 1165, 1168 (5th Cir. 1976)); *see* 46 U.S.C. §§ 30903(a), 31102(a)(1), 31103.

37 *See In re Great Lakes*, 624 F.3d at 211.

38 *Id.* (quoting *Consol. Aluminum Corp.*, 883 F.2d at 67).

39 *See id.*; *In re Signal*, 579 F.3d 478; *Consol. Aluminum Corp.*, 883 F.2d 65; *Southern Nat. Gas Co.*, 711 F.2d 1251.

40 *In re Great Lakes*, 624 F.3d at 211 (quoting *Consol. Aluminum Corp.*, 883 F.2d at 68).

41 *See In re Signal*, 579 F.3d at 492.

42 *Id.* at 491–92.

43 *Ruiz-Hernandez*, 890 F.3d at 206, 6 Adm. R. at 199.

44 *See Southern Nat. Gas Co.*, 711 F.2d at 1254 (quoting *Canadian Pac. (Bermuda) Ltd.*, 534 F.2d at 1168).

45 *Ashcroft v. Iqbal*, 556 U.S. 662, 679 (2009).

46 *In re Signal*, 579 F.3d at 492.

47 *In re Signal* involved a collision between two moored vessels and a bridge after Hurricane Katrina. *Consolidated Aluminum Corp.* involved the negligent rupturing of an oil pipeline. *Southern Natural Gas Co.* involved a dredging company's negligently striking of a pipeline. *In re Great Lakes* involved a private company's dredging activities.

48 *In re Signal*, 579 F.3d at 493.

victims includes individuals purposefully attempting to avoid detection.[49] Undocumented aliens' intention to evade detection mitigates the foreseeability of harm: If individuals are actively trying to avoid detection, then they do not wish to be foreseeable. Moreover, the relevant probability for duty is the natural and probable risks a reasonable person would likely take into account in guiding practical conduct, and Garcia provides no indication that private vessels in the BSC were in the practice of altering their conduct to accommodate the remote probability of encountering nighttime swimmers. Again, Garcia provides no indication that any of the private vessels that travel the BSC would reasonably anticipate causing harm to nighttime swimmers who were trying to avoid detection. Because the harm of a vessel–swimmer collision was not foreseeable, the United States owed no duty to Cervantes and is not liable for the asserted negligence of the Coast Guard crew. **{–528–}**

Garcia argues there were facts known to the Coast Guard that made the vessel–swimmer collision foreseeable. He offers as evidence testimony of several Coast Guard officials to show that the Coast Guard was aware—and had actual knowledge—that the entire BSC was used by undocumented aliens as a point of entry into the United States. However, as discussed below, the Coast Guard's awareness of undocumented alien crossings does not necessarily render the harm to Cervantes foreseeable.

First, Garcia cites the interview summary of Lieutenant Erica Kelly, relying on the statement that approximately two to four undocumented aliens **[—18—]** are apprehended by the Coast Guard each month in the BSC.[50] As an initial point, this evidence is inherently devoid of context since the interview summary lacks the questions to which Lieutenant Kelly was responding. Plus, while the interview summary may show that the Coast Guard knew that crossings occurred in the BSC, it also indicates that the Coast Guard did not have knowledge of how many crossings occur, where along the 17-mile-long BSC these crossings occur, with whom knowledge of these crossings was shared, and other important details that inform our foreseeability analysis.[51] And finally, Lieutenant Kelly's interview summary supports our holding that the Coast Guard does not owe a duty because Lieutenant Kelly indicated that private vessels in the BSC may not be aware of undocumented alien crossings:

> I'm not aware if there have been any Notices to Mariners saying this is a high traffic area for migrants. We provide some of that information to the facilities at working group meetings, but not for the shrimpers. I don't believe that anything has been given to the tug operators. We do not get much information, if any at all, from the commercial side on UDA activity.

The Coast Guard's knowledge cannot be attributed to private vessels. And, if private vessels do not possess knowledge of such crossings, it would not be foreseeable to these private vessels that undocumented aliens might swim across the BSC.

Garcia also cites the interview summary of Training Officer Portwood, who was told that the BSC's Shrimp Basin was a "point of entry" **[—19—]** into the United States and that "pretty much the entire BSC is known for crossings" to support his claim that the harm to Cervantes was foreseeable. And Garcia also relies on the interview summary of Lieutenant

[49] Garcia asserts that Cervantes was avoiding "nearby patrol boats," and the district court observed that she was "trying to cross undetected." The coxswain of the vessel on the night of the incident, Brandon Rae, also testified that undocumented aliens crossing the BSC "don't want to be seen."

[50] Lieutenant Kelly is the Chief of Intelligence at Sector Corpus Christi and collects and reports data on the BSC crossings.

[51] Garcia also relies on the interview summary's statement that the Coast Guard provided a weekly briefing about crossings. But the interview summary also indicates that "it is hard to determine who actually is listening to the brief."

Michael Bell, who said that he was briefed that undocumented aliens use trash bags, floats, and other flotation devices. Again, this evidence indicates that the Coast Guard had knowledge obtained through secondhand Coast Guard briefings and intelligence reports, but not necessarily firsthand experience of seeing undocumented aliens swimming across the BSC.[52]

Garcia fares no better in establishing that the crew on the night of the incident had firsthand experience of seeing such crossings. To show actual knowledge by the crew, Garcia must either provide evidence that the crew had firsthand experience of actually seeing an individual in the water or that the crew had previously encountered **{-529-}** someone swimming across the BSC at night. Garcia has not shown either. Instead, Garcia cites the testimony of the crew's coxswain, Brandon Rae, who agreed that there was an unspecified "probability" of nighttime swimmers in the BSC. Rae's testimony, when viewed in context, may demonstrate that he had knowledge of Coast Guard briefings and intelligence reports that crossings occurred along the entire 17-mile-long BSC. But Rae's testimony also confirms that he had no firsthand experience of seeing undocumented aliens swimming across the BSC. Garcia's argument that the crew had actual knowledge that would render harm to nighttime swimmers foreseeable therefore fails.[53] **[—20—]**

Garcia's cited evidence demonstrates that the Coast Guard was aware that undocumented alien crossings occurred along the BSC, but this knowledge was of a general nature. The Coast Guard did not know (1) the exact number of crossings, (2) the exact location of crossings, or (3) the exact timing of crossings, among other relevant details. These details are significant for our foreseeability analysis. The entire BSC is 17 miles long and approximately 500 feet wide; the Coast Guard patrols of the BSC cover a route of approximately 34.2 miles.[54] This is a very large area to cover, which affects our foreseeability analysis. Our decision in *Lloyd's Leasing Ltd. v. Conoco* is instructive. There, after a ship's tanks cracked, crude oil spilled into the waters of the Gulf of Mexico and washed ashore approximately 70 miles west of the site of the ship's grounding; the claimants were individuals who suffered damages from oil tracked onto their premises by tourists and beachgoers.[55] We held that the harm suffered by the plaintiffs was not foreseeable, emphasizing that the original oil spill occurred 70 miles away.[56] Because the oil spill had to wash ashore on a developed shore to create these damages of tracking oil, we noted that the amount of developed shoreline was a small percentage of the total coastline (60 miles out of 340 miles).[57] We ultimately held that, "[w]hile the appellee might reasonably anticipate that the oil would probably wash ashore somewhere, it had no reason to have anticipated that the oil would probably wash ashore in a heavily populated **[—21—]** area and then be tracked into businesses and homes."[58] Similarly, the cited evidence here may show that the Coast Guard might reasonably have anticipated encountering undocumented aliens somewhere in the BSC, but the Coast Guard did not have knowledge to anticipate where exactly in the BSC the undocumented aliens would be swimming.

Garcia also relies on our opinion in *United States v. Ruiz-Hernandez* to argue that the swimmer vessel collision was foreseeable. However, in *Ruiz-Hernandez*, we discussed foreseeability from the perspective of Ruiz-

[52] *See, e.g.*, *In re Great Lakes*, 624 F.3d at 210 (contrasting general and actual knowledge).

[53] Garcia also argues that the district court erred in citing our decision in *Republic of France v. United States*, 290 F.2d 395, 401 (5th Cir. 1961), which requires proof of actual knowledge. Garcia argues that *Republic of France* is "outdated and antiquated" and distinguishable from this case, but he overlooks that we have repeatedly reaffirmed *Republic* **[—20—]** *of France*'s actual knowledge requirement multiple times. *See, e.g.*, *In re Great Lakes*, 624 F.3d at 211–12; *Consol. Aluminum Corp.*, 833 F.2d at 68.

[54] *United States v. Ruiz-Hernandez*, 890 F.3d 202, 206, 6 Adm. R. 199, 199 (5th Cir. 2018).

[55] *Lloyd's Leasing Ltd. v. Conoco*, 868 F.2d 1447, 1449 (5th Cir. 1989).

[56] *Id.*

[57] *Id.*

[58] *Id.*

Hernandez: We held that it was foreseeable from a *swimmer's* perspective that vessels would be traveling through **{–530–}** the BSC.[59] But our holding there has little bearing on our duty analysis here because we must analyze foreseeability from the perspective of a *vessel* traveling through the BSC at night. Garcia also relies on *Ruiz-Hernandez* to argue that we should disregard the *manner* in which the harm occurred for purposes of determining foreseeability.[60] But the circumstances here—swimming at night in a high-traffic waterway that has minimal lighting and no speed limit—are relevant and bear upon the existence of an actionable duty.

Garcia also argues that the Coast Guard owes a special duty to undocumented aliens swimming across the BSC. He first argues there should be a duty because the purpose of BSC law-enforcement patrols is to search for, detect, and intercept undocumented aliens. But the specific functions that the Coast Guard performs has no bearing on the duty **[—22—]** determination because the duty owed, if any, is equal to that owed by private vessels, which do not perform such functions. Garcia also argues that the Coast Guard owes a duty to operate its vessels in a safe manner because its mission includes person-in-the-water recoveries. But the Coast Guard's safety responsibilities do not impose a special duty: Its duty is limited to ensuring the general safety of maritime facilities and commercial and recreational vessels in the BSC and in conducting search and rescue missions. And there is no evidence that the crew was undertaking a search and rescue as to Cervantes or otherwise providing rescue services in a manner that would impose a special duty.[61] In the absence of a special duty, the Coast Guard's duty is measured in accord with what all private vessels must do. Therefore, we hold that the Coast Guard did not owe a duty to Cervantes. Accordingly, the dismissal of Garcia's negligence claim against the United States for failure to state a prima facie case was proper.

B

Next, we address Garcia's products liability claims. Garcia brought defective design and failure-to-warn claims against Safe Boats and Mercury Marine under a theory of strict products liability.

Essentially, Garcia asserts two design defects: (1) the design of Safe Boats' vessel impaired the vessel-operator's forward visibility; and (2) the design of Mercury Marine's outboard engine lacked propeller guards. Garcia's failure-to-warn claims relate to these two asserted product defects. The district court dismissed the defective design claims against Safe Boats and Mercury Marine because, applying Restatement (Second) of Torts **[—23—]** § 402A, it found that Cervantes was neither a user nor a consumer and thus lacked standing to bring maritime products liability claims under the defective design theory. And the district court dismissed the failure-to-warn claims because any duty to warn would be owed to the United States, not Cervantes. **{–531–}**

Garcia raises several arguments regarding the dismissal of these claims. First, he argues that the district court incorrectly construed his products liability claims as brought against the United States. Next, he argues the district court erred in dismissing his products liability claims because it should have applied Restatement (Third) of Torts, not Restatement (Second) of Torts. Finally, Garcia argues that Safe Boats was not entitled to immunity based on the government contractor defense.

We address each argument in turn.

[59] 890 F.3d at 211, 6 Adm. R. at 203 (holding "it was reasonably foreseeable that a person swimming across a high-traffic ship channel in the dark of night would be struck by a passing ship").

[60] *Id.*, 6 Adm. R. at 203 (the "precise nature of the [resulting] injury and the manner of its infliction is immaterial . . . , so long as the injury is of a type that, in the circumstances, might reasonably have been expected to occur").

[61] *See Allen v. Walmart Stores, LLC*, 907 F.3d 170, 181 (5th Cir. 2018) (noting that Texas courts "have recognized that a duty to use reasonable care may arise when a person undertakes to provide services to another, either gratuitously or for compensation") (citation omitted).

1

Garcia first argues that the district court erred in adopting the magistrate's R&R in its entirety because it incorrectly construed the products liability claims as brought against the United States. Admittedly, the magistrate judge incorrectly characterized Garcia's products liability claims as claims brought against the United States, not Safe Boats and Mercury Marine. However, the district court did not do so: In its order, the district court correctly viewed the products liability claims as against Safe Boats and Mercury Marine. Plus, all parties agree that Garcia's products liability claims are against Safe Boats and Mercury Marine, not the United States. This argument thus fails.

2

We next address Garcia's argument that the district court erred in applying Restatement (Second) of Torts § 402A. Under § 402A, the **[—24—]** "ultimate user or consumer" who is harmed by an allegedly defective product may bring suit against the seller of that product.[62] But a casual bystander may not.[63] Garcia does not dispute that Cervantes was properly characterized as a casual bystander. Instead, he argues that, for maritime products liability claims, we should apply Restatement (Third) of Torts § 1, which more broadly exposes sellers to liability for harm to individuals and under which Cervantes might have standing to bring products liability claims.[64]

We and the Supreme Court apply the Second Restatement to maritime products liability cases.[65] Garcia claims that we already recognize that the Third Restatement supplies the applicable substantive law for maritime products liability law, but he bases this on our single decision in *Krummel v. Bombardier Corp.*[66] There, the user of a watercraft broke his leg after his foot became trapped in the watercraft; he sued the manufacturer on defective design and failure-to-warn claims under Restatement (Third) of Torts § 2(b) and Louisiana Products Liability Act (LPLA).[67] The district **[—25—]** court found the **{-532-}** manufacturer liable.[68] But we reversed because the district court based liability solely on the fact that an injury occurred and failed to perform the risk-utility analysis, as required by both the LPLA and the Third Restatement.[69] *Krummel* is distinguishable from this case: It involved claims by the product's user, not a casual bystander like Cervantes. So we had no reason in *Krummel* to discuss *who* may bring suits in maritime products liability cases under § 1—the provision Garcia claims should apply here. Instead, when we actually have confronted the issue of who has standing to bring maritime products liability claims, we have applied § 402A of the Second Restatement.[70] Thus, under our precedent, the Second Restatement, not the Third, supplies the substantive law for determining standing in maritime products liability claims. And, to the extent that Garcia argues we should adopt the Third Restatement, we may not: "Under our rule of orderliness, we may not overrule a prior panel decision absent an intervening change in the law, such as a statutory amendment or a decision from

[62] RESTATEMENT (SECOND) OF TORTS § 402A (AM. LAW INST. 1965).

[63] *See id.* § 402A cmt. o (Courts "have not gone beyond allowing recovery to users and consumers," and "[c]asual bystanders . . . have been denied recovery.").

[64] RESTATEMENT (THIRD) OF TORTS § 1 (AM. LAW INST. 1998).

[65] *See Saratoga Fishing Co. v. J.M. Martinac & Co.*, 520 U.S. 875, 979 (1997); *Vickers v. Chiles Drilling Co.*, 822 F.2d 535, 538 (5th Cir. 1987).

[66] 206 F.3d 548 (5th Cir. 2000). Garcia relies on other cases from our sister circuits, but those cases are distinguishable because they did not address § 1 of the Third Restatement. *See, e.g., Oswalt v. Resolute Indus., Inc.*, 642 F.3d 856, 860 n.2 (9th Cir. 2011) (discussing § 2 of the Third Restatement but declining to adopt the Third Restatement for all cases). Moreover, we are not bound by the decisions of our sister circuits. However, we are bound by the Supreme Court and our own caselaw, both of which apply § 402A of the Second Restatement.

[67] *Krummel*, 206 F.3d at 550–51.

[68] *Id.* at 551.

[69] *Id.* at 552.

[70] *See, e.g., Vickers*, 822 F.2d at 538.

either the Supreme Court or our en banc court."[71] The Restatement is neither.

Garcia also argues that we should apply Texas law, which permits bystanders to bring defective products liability claims.[72] But, in maritime cases, a federal court may only apply state law to "fill the gaps" of maritime **[—26—]** law.[73] Adopting Texas's broader standing for bystanders would be more than mere gap-filling: It would be a seismic shift in maritime law.[74]

Because § 402A of the Second Restatement supplies the substantive law in our circuit for maritime products liability claims, the district court correctly applied it to determine that Cervantes lacked standing to bring those claims. Therefore, the district court did not err in dismissing Garcia's defective design claims against Safe Boats and Mercury Marine.

3

Even assuming Garcia could bring these products liability claims, we have an additional reason to affirm the district court's dismissal: Garcia fails to show that the asserted defective products proximately caused Cervantes' death. Although the district court did not address proximate cause in its order, we may affirm the district court's dismissal on any ground supported by the record.[75] And the record amply supports a finding that Garcia failed to show that Safe Boats' and Mercury **{-533-}** Marine's asserted defective products were the proximate cause of Cervantes' fatality.

As the moving parties, Safe Boats and Mercury Marine have the burden of "identifying each claim or defense—or the part of each claim or defense—on which summary judgment is sought."[76] Since Garcia would ultimately bear the burden of proof on his products liability claims, Safe Boats **[—27—]** and Mercury Marine may satisfy their burden "by merely pointing out that the evidence in the record contains insufficient proof concerning an essential element of the nonmoving party's claim."[77] If they do so, the burden then shifts to Garcia to show that specific facts exist over which there is a genuine dispute.[78] But Garcia cannot rely on"[c]onclusory allegations, speculation, and unsubstantiated assertions" to make this showing.[79]

We begin with the relevant law: Maritime law incorporates products liability, including strict products liability.[80] And to prevail on his strict products liability claims, Garcia must show that (1) Safe Boats and Marine Mercury sold the products, (2) their products were unreasonably dangerous or defective when they left their control, (3) those defects caused Cervantes' injury, and (4) damages.[81]

We next turn to Safe Boats' and Mercury Marine's burden: They must demonstrate that the record is insufficient to establish causation for Garcia's products liability claims. Because Garcia asserts two design defects, we address

---

[71] *Thompson v. Dallas City Attorney's Office*, 913 F.3d 464, 467 (5th Cir. 2019).

[72] *See Darryl v. Ford Motor Co.*, 440 S.W.2d 630, 633 (Tex. 1969) (holding "recovery under the strict liability doctrine is not limited to users and consumers); *see also Hernandez v. Tokai Corp.*, 2 S.W.3d 251, 257 (Tex. 1999) (reaffirming the holding in *Darryl*).

[73] *Exxon Corp. v. Chick Kam Choo*, 817 F.2d 307, 316–17 (5th Cir. 1987).

[74] *See also Yamaha*, 516 U.S. at 210 ("[I]n several contexts, [the Supreme Court] ha[s] recognized that vindication of maritime policies demanded uniform adherence to a federal rule of decision, with no leeway for variation or supplementation by state law.").

[75] *Gilbert v. Donahue*, 751 F.3d 303, 311 (5th Cir. 2014) (stating that "we may 'affirm on any ground supported by the record'" even if "neither the appellant nor the district court addressed the ground, so long as the argument was raised below").

[76] FED. R. CIV. P. 56(a).

[77] *Norwegian Bulk Transp. A/S v. Int'l Marine Terminals P'ship*, 520 F.3d 409, 412 (5th Cir. 2008).

[78] *Anderson*, 477 U.S. at 250.

[79] *Ramsey v. Henderson*, 286 F.3d 264, 269 (5th Cir. 2002) (citation omitted).

[80] *East River S.S. Corp. v. Transamerica Delavel, Inc.*, 476 U.S. 858, 865 (1986). *See also Vickers*, 822 F.2d at 538.

[81] *Vickers*, 822 F.2d at 538–40; 1 THOMAS J. SCHOENBAUM, ADMIRALTY & MAR. LAW § 5.13 (6th ed. 2019) (citing RESTATEMENT (SECOND) OF TORTS § 402A).

the evidence for each. First, Garcia asserts that Safe Boats' vessel was defective because it had impaired forward visibility at the time of the incident. The uncontroverted evidence demonstrates that the vessel was **[—28—]** traveling more than 30 knots at the time of the impact.[82] And it is undisputed that, when the vessel travels at a speed greater than 30 knots, forward visibility is not reduced. So, whatever limitations may be present in the vessel's forward visibility at slower speeds, there is *no* impairment to the vessel's forward visibility when it is navigating in excess of 30 knots, as it was at the time of the incident. Because the vessel was travelling over 30 knots at the time of the incident, the asserted impaired visibility defect cannot be—and is not—the proximate cause of Cervantes' fatality. And Garcia fares no better with proving causation for the second asserted defect, the engines' lack of propeller guards. Based on the undisputed expert testimony, the force involved in the collision would have resulted in immediate death upon impact with **{-534-}** the vessel *even with* propeller guards. So the alleged failure to include propeller guards on the engines cannot be—and is not—the proximate cause of Cervantes' fatality.

Since Safe Boats and Mercury Marine meet their burden, the burden shifts to Garcia. Garcia must show that specific facts exist over which there is a genuine dispute about proximate cause. Garcia fails to do so. He provides no evidence that Safe Boats' and Mercury Marine's allegedly defective products proximately caused the incident. Instead, Garcia complains that the vessel was travelling too fast. But this concerns the operation of the vessel, not its design. Garcia's experts concede that the alleged limitation of the **[—29—]** vessel's forward visibility does not even come into play in this case.[83] Garcia's experts also concede that only if the vessel had been traveling at a slower speed at the time of impact would the propeller guards have eliminated Cervantes' injuries. Plus, the experts who evaluated the force involved in the collision testified that the force would have resulted in immediate death upon impact with the vessel, even with propeller guards.

Because Garcia fails to provide specific facts showing there is a genuine dispute about proximate causation, he fails to meet his burden on establishing proximate causation, so his products liability claims were properly dismissed by the district court.

4

Garcia also brought failure-to-warn claims against Safe Boats and Mercury Marine. The district court dismissed his failure-to-warn claims on the grounds that Safe Boats and Mercury Marine owed the duty to warn to the United States, not to Garcia; so, assuming there was a breach of that duty, only the United States could properly maintain negligent failure-to-warn claims against Safe Boats and Mercury Marine. Garcia does not contest that no duty to warn was owed to Cervantes—he even admits that Safe Boats' and Mercury Marine's duty was owed to the Coast Guard.

Garcia instead argues that the district court erred in treating his failure-to-warn claims as negligence, rather than strict liability, claims. In his second amended complaint, Garcia brings his failure-to-warn claim against **[—30—]** Safe Boats under a

---

[82] Safe Boats' expert, naval architect Robert Taylor, stated in his declaration and opined in his report that, at the time of the incident, the vessel was traveling at a speed of approximately 32–33 knots (36.8–38 mph). The Coast Guard's investigative report confirms this speed.

Importantly, for the 30 seconds before the impact, the vessel was fully on plane and the vessel's driver had an unobstructed view to the potential location of Cervantes. Only during the last 2.2 seconds before the impact—when Cervantes would have been too near the vessel to be visible—was the driver's forward visibility obstructed.

[83] Garcia's expert, Robert Swint, testified that the SPC-LE has "very good visibility up to about 10 [knots] and very good visibility at about 30 [knots]." He confirmed that an SPC-LE vessel would have *no* forward visibility issues at speeds above 30 knots. Similarly, CDI Engineering Solutions generated a report for the Coast Guard that concluded that, whatever limitations there may be on the vessel's forward visibility, they are *not* present when the vessel is traveling in excess of 30 knots.

strict liability theory. But Garcia also brought these claims under the alternative theory of negligence. Under the negligence theory, Garcia alleges Safe Boats and Mercury Marines were aware of the products' defects, had a duty to provide the Coast Guard with a post-sale warning and instructions, and breached that duty. The district court correctly applied the Second Restatement and found that any duty to warn was owed to the products' user (the United States), not to a bystander (Cervantes). "For the manufacturer of a product, the general duty of care includes a duty to warn when the manufacturer 'knows or has reason to know' that its product 'is or is likely to be dangerous for the use for which it is supplied' and the manufacturer 'has no reason to believe' that the product's users will realize that danger."[84] Because Safe Boats and Mercury **{–535–}** Marines owed no duty to Cervantes, the district court correctly dismissed Garcia's negligence failure-to-warn claims.

Assessing Garcia's failure-to-warn claims under the alternative strict liability theory, Garcia's claims still warrant dismissal because he does not establish causation. To maintain a failure-to-warn claim in strict liability, Garcia must present evidence that the absence of adequate warnings caused Cervantes' injuries. As with his design defect claims, Garcia does not show how the presence of warnings about the design of Safe Boats' vessel or Mercury Marine's engines would have prevented Cervantes' fatality.[85] In the absence of a showing that the inadequate instructions or warnings caused **[—31—]** Cervantes' fatality, Garcia's failure-to-warn claims were also properly dismissed.

5

Finally, Garcia argues that Safe Boats failed to bear its burden on the affirmative government contractor defense. But because we find that Safe Boats and Mercury Marine are not liable for either the design defect or the failure-to-warn claims, we need not address their government contractor defense.

C

Garcia also brought a gross negligence claim against Safe Boats and Mercury Marine, seeking exemplary damages. The district court did not explicitly address this gross negligence claim in its order, but it did dismiss all Garcia's "negligence-based claims." And because Garcia does not raise the gross negligence claim on appeal—and Mercury Marine and Safe Boats do not brief this claim—we do not address dismissal of this claim.

D

Finally, Garcia brought wrongful death claims against the United States, Safe Boats, and Mercury Marine, which the district court dismissed. Garcia argues that the district court erred in concluding there was no underlying tort to sustain his wrongful death claims.

Federal maritime law recognizes a wrongful death cause of action.[86] This extends to both negligence and strict products liability.[87] When a non-seafarer (someone other than a seaman or longshoreman) is killed within **[—32—]** state waters, the remedies applicable under the general maritime law may be supplemented by state law remedies, including state statutory wrongful death and survival remedies.[88] To recover these damages, a plaintiff must prove that the circumstances of the death meet the requirements of the relevant state law.

[84] *Air & Liquid Sys. Corp. v. DeVries*, 139 S. Ct. 986, 993, 7 Adm. R. 2, 4 (2019) (quoting RESTATEMENT (SECOND) OF TORTS § 388).

[85] Garcia points to Restatement (Third) of Torts § 2(c) and relies on our decision in *Krummel*. 206 F.3d 548 (5th Cir. 2000). As stated earlier, *Krummel* is distinguishable, and we apply the Second Restatement for cases in maritime law.

[86] *See Moragne v. State Marine Lines, Inc.*, 398 U.S. 375, 409 (1970).

[87] *See Norfolk*, 532 U.S. at 814; SCHOENBAUM, ADMIRALTY & MAR. LAW § 8:3.

[88] *See Yamaha*, 516 U.S. at 216 (holding that damages available for the jet ski death of an individual were governed by state law).

Here, Texas's Wrongful Death Act is the relevant law.[89] The Act "applies only if the **{–536–}** individual injured would have been entitled to bring an action for the injury if the individual had lived."[90] As discussed above, there are no claims that Cervantes would have been entitled to bring.

Garcia reiterates the arguments he makes for the other claims to assert that Cervantes would have been entitled to bring personal injury claims. His arguments fail because they are predicated on the assumption that the United States owed a duty to Cervantes and that Cervantes had standing to bring the products liability claims, both of which we rejected.

Accordingly, because Garcia has no sustainable claim against the United States, Safe Boats, and Mercury Marine, the district court did not err in dismissing his wrongful death claims.

IV

For these reasons, we AFFIRM the district court's dismissal of Garcia's claims against the United States, Safe Boats, and Mercury Marine.

---

[89] TEX. CIV. PRAC. & REM. § 71.002 *et seq.*

[90] *Id.* § 71.003(a).

United States Court of Appeals
for the Fifth Circuit

No. 19-30440

ALVARADO
vs.
BP EXPLORATION & PROD., INC.

Appeal from the United States District Court for the Eastern District of Louisiana

Decided: February 9, 2021

Citation: 988 F.3d 192, 9 Adm. R. 185 (5th Cir. 2021).

Before **HIGGINBOTHAM, ELROD,** and **HAYNES,** Circuit Judges.

[—3—] {-194-} PER CURIAM:

This case presents another in the line of cases related to the Deepwater Horizon **{-195-}** oil spill. Four appellants—Sandra Iames, Sheri Allen Dorgan, Brian Gortney, and Sergio Valdivieso—seek reversal of dismissals with prejudice for failure to comply with orders of the multidistrict litigation (MDL) judge to file particular information about their claims. Another appellant—Sergio Alvarado—seeks reversal of his dismissal with prejudice for failure to timely opt out of the settlement class. We affirm the district court's dismissals with prejudice of the claims of Iames and Alvarado and reverse and remand the dismissals of Dorgan, Gortney, and Valdivieso.

I.

A.

Thousands of claims arose out of the Deepwater Horizon oil spill—including the five at issue here. The MDL panel consolidated common claims before the district court, creating several "Pleading Bundles." The claims here were part of the B3 bundle claims for cleanup and personal injury. To facilitate the efficient resolution of claims, the district court in turn issued a series of pretrial orders (PTOs).

This appeal concerns PTO 66, issued on April 9, 2018, requiring remaining B3 plaintiffs to "provide more particularized information regarding their claims" to help "the Court and the parties to better understand the nature and scope of the injuries, damages, and causation alleged." It required remaining B3 plaintiffs to complete, sign, and serve on **[—4—]** counsel for BP and the Plaintiffs' Steering Committee a "Particularized Statement of Claim" (PSOC) form by July 9, 2018. The order warned that plaintiffs who failed to comply "may be required to show cause to this Court why his, her, or its claims should not be dismissed with prejudice."

PTO 66 further noted that some remaining B3 plaintiffs appeared to be members of the Medical Benefits Class Action Settlement Class (Medical Settlement Class), an earlier-approved settlement. Members of the Medical Settlement Class were given the opportunity to opt out of the settlement and pursue ordinary litigation by submitting a written request no later than November 1, 2012.[1] It further directed BP and the settlement's claims administrator to determine whether any remaining B3 plaintiffs were members of the Medical Settlement Class.

On September 20, 2018, the district court issued the PTO 66 Show Cause Order, identifying plaintiffs who either failed to respond to PTO 66 or whose response was materially deficient, including plaintiffs who still appeared to be members of the settlement class. The court ordered these plaintiffs to "show cause in writing on or before October 11, 2018 why this Court should not dismiss his/her/its B3 claim(s) with prejudice for failing to comply with the requirements of PTO 66."

On January 31, 2019, the district court issued the PTO 66 Compliance Order, dismissing with prejudice B3 claims that were deemed noncompliant with PTO 66, as well as those barred by settlement, including the claims of appellants here, and denied their motions for reconsideration. All five now seek reinstatement of their claims. **[—5—]**

[1] The original deadline to opt out was October 1, 2012, but it was later extended to November 1, 2012.

B.

In 2017, Iames, who cleaned beaches in Florida after the oil spill, filed her B3 complaint alleging personal injury. Although subject to PTO 66, she did not **{–196–}** respond to it, nor did she respond to the subsequent show cause order. Accordingly, the district court dismissed her claims with prejudice. Iames has offered no evidence that she ever came into compliance with PTO 66 by submitting a PSOC form.

C.

In 2017, Dorgan, claiming to have been exposed to oil and dispersants on the beach behind her house in Alabama, filed her B3 complaint alleging personal injury. Valdivieso, who cleaned waters in Louisiana after the oil spill, and Gortney, who lived near the oil spill's clean-up operations in Florida, filed their lawsuits in state court alleging personal injury. Both cases were removed and transferred to the MDL court and placed into the B3 bundle. All three plaintiffs—represented by the same counsel—failed to respond to PTO 66 but did respond to the district court's subsequent show cause order.

Gortney responded to the show cause order on October 11, 2018, with his PSOC form attached. Valdivieso also responded on October 11, 2018, but his response did not initially include his PSOC form. As his response explained, he had mailed his form to counsel, but it was delayed by Hurricane Florence. Valdivieso served a supplemental response eight days later with his PSOC form attached.[2] Dorgan also responded to the show cause order on October 11, 2018,[3] claiming that her PSOC form would be late because her **[—6—]** husband had a stroke on October 8, 2018.[4] She submitted her PSOC form on October 23, 2018.[5] All three concede that they mistakenly served their responses to the show cause order and their PSOC forms only on BP and failed to file them with the court.

BP filed various objections to the show cause responses, acknowledging that it received responses from Dorgan, Validivieso, and Gortney.[6] However, it argued that Dorgan and Gortney should be deemed noncompliant with PTO 66 for submitting their PSOC forms past deadline. It further argued that Valdivieso should be deemed noncompliant for failing to submit his form at all, but BP then discovered it did receive a form from him on October 19, 2018.

The district court dismissed Dorgan, Valdivieso, and Gortney's claims with prejudice, finding their PSOC forms were "significantly late or not submitted at all." The court further noted that these plaintiffs "appear[ed] to have served a show cause response on BP, but did not file a show cause response with the Court."

D.

In 2011, Alvarado, who worked as a deckhand on a vessel responding to the oil spill, filed a short-form joinder, a statement authorized by an earlier pretrial order that allowed plaintiffs to adopt an already-filed master complaint as their own. In 2013, Alvarado filed his individual B3 complaint alleging personal injury. **{–197–}**

The district court's show cause order identified him as a plaintiff in the Medical Settlement Class and required him to show cause why he should **[—7—]** not be dismissed with prejudice. In his response, Alvarado argued that he demonstrated his intention to opt out of the settlement class by filing his individual complaint. The district court rejected this argument and dismissed Alvarado's claims with prejudice, concluding

[2] The form was dated October 8, 2018.

[3] Although Dorgan's initial response to the show cause order was not a part of the record below, we grant her motion to take judicial notice of it, as BP concedes that it was served this response on October 11, 2018. *See* FED. R. EVID. 201(b).

[4] In briefing to this Court, Dorgan claims the stroke occurred on October 1, 2018.

[5] The form was dated October 7, 2018. When she submitted her PSOC form, Dorgan noted that her husband had died on October 16, 2018.

[6] It appears that BP was aware that these plaintiffs failed to file their responses with the district court.

he was a class member who had failed to opt out. He then sought reconsideration arguing that his claims should be allowed to proceed pursuant to Federal Rule of Civil Procedure 60(b) because his failure to opt out constituted excusable neglect. The court denied his motion.

II.

We first consider whether the district court erred in dismissing the claims of Iames, Dorgan, Gortney, and Valdivieso for their noncompliance with PTO 66 before turning to Alvarado's challenge to the district court's dismissal of his claims for failure to timely opt out of the Medical Settlement Class.

A.

We review a district court's dismissal for failure to comply with its orders mindful that the court has "broad discretion and inherent authority to manage its docket," including "the power to dismiss a case for a party's failure to obey the court's orders."[7] We review docket management for abuse of discretion, affording a district court "special deference . . . in the context of an MDL."[8]

At the same time, "because a dismissal with prejudice is an extreme sanction that deprives the litigant of the opportunity to pursue his claim, this court has limited the district court's discretion in dismissing cases with **[—8—]** prejudice."[9] Dismissals with prejudice for violations of docket management orders require "a clear record of delay or contumacious conduct by the plaintiff . . . where lesser sanctions would not serve the best interests of justice."[10] "[I]n most cases where this Court has affirmed dismissals with prejudice, we found at least one of three aggravating factors: (1) delay caused by the plaintiff himself and not his attorney; (2) actual prejudice to the defendant; or (3) delay caused by intentional conduct."[11]

1.

Iames makes several arguments contesting the dismissal of her case with prejudice. First, she argues that PTO 66 should be treated as a discovery order **{–198–}** rather than a docket management order. Second, she argues that the record does not show "delay or contumacious conduct" on her part, and, in any event, "lesser sanctions" would have served "the best interests of justice." Third, she argues that no aggravating factors in favor of dismissal are present. We address each argument in turn.

First, contrary to Iames's claim, we conclude that PTO 66 is a case-management order. PTO 66 was aimed at "streamlin[ing] the remaining B3 claims and facilitat[ing] the administration of this MDL." We have held that **[—9—]** similar pretrial orders, requiring sworn statements, are lawful exercises of the district court's docket management discretion.[12]

Second, the record shows a clear record of delay by Iames. While she eventually acknowledged PTO 66 through her motions for reconsideration, she never complied with the

---

[7] *In re Deepwater Horizon (Perez)*, 713 F.App'x 360, 362 (5th Cir. 2018) (unpublished) (per curiam).

[8] *In re Deepwater Horizon (Barrera)*, 907 F.3d 232, 234–35, 6 Adm. R. 270, 270–71 (5th Cir. 2018).

[9] *In re Deepwater Horizon (Graham)*, 922 F.3d 660, 666, 7 Adm. R. 251, 252 (5th Cir. 2019) (cleaned up). BP argues that the only orders properly before the Court as to Iames, Dorgan, Valdivieso, and Gortney are the district court's denials for reconsideration, since these plaintiffs first filed objections to their dismissal in the district court through their motions for reconsideration. BP cites no case law supporting this proposition, and even when plaintiffs in this litigation have not responded to a pretrial order and its subsequent show cause order, we have reviewed the underlying dismissal with prejudice. *See In re Deepwater Horizon (Park National)*, 805 F. App'x 262, 265 (5th Cir. 2020) (unpublished) (per curiam).

[10] *Barrera*, 907 F.3d at 235, 6 Adm. R. at 271 (internal quotation marks omitted) (quoting *Sealed Appellant v. Sealed Appellee*, 452 F.3d 415, 417 (5th Cir. 2006)).

[11] *Berry v. CIGNA/RSI-CIGNA*, 975 F.2d 1188, 1191 (5th Cir. 1992) (internal quotation marks and citation omitted).

[12] *See Park National*, 805 F. App'x at 264–65 (addressing PTO 65); *In re Deepwater Horizon (Cepeda)*, 765 F. App'x 980, 981 (5th Cir. 2019) (unpublished) (per curiam) (addressing PTO 64).

order by submitting her PSOC form. Under our precedent, Iames's repeated failure to comply with PTO 66 amounts to a clear record of delay.[13] In *Barrera*, another Deepwater Horizon case, we held that the record showed a clear record of delay when plaintiffs repeatedly failed to comply with a similar PTO—even when those plaintiffs, unlike Iames, responded to both the PTO and the show cause order in a timely fashion.[14]

And, it does not appear that lesser sanctions would have served the best interests of justice here. Lesser sanctions include "[a]ssessments of fines, costs, or damages against the plaintiff or his counsel, attorney disciplinary measures, conditional dismissal, dismissal without prejudice, and explicit warnings."[15] At the time of her dismissal, Iames had already been subject to explicit warnings: both PTO 66 and the subsequent show cause order specifically warned that noncompliance could lead to dismissal with prejudice. Given the district court's interest in streamlining the proceedings through PTO 66, additional lesser sanctions would only "further delay the district court's efforts to adjudicate the MDL expeditiously."[16] **[—10—]**

Third, while we agree with Iames that there are likely no aggravating factors present here, this alone does not warrant overturning a dismissal with prejudice.[17] Because the record shows a clear record of delay and lesser sanctions would not have served the best interests of justice, we conclude that the district court did not abuse its discretion in dismissing Iames's claims with prejudice.

2.

Unlike Iames, plaintiffs Dorgan, Valdivieso, and Gortney responded to the show cause order and submitted their PSOC forms. Because of their ultimate compliance with PTO 66, they argue that their claims were dismissed without a clear record of "delay or contumacious conduct." Moreover, they contend that no aggravating **{–199–}** factors counseling in favor of dismissal with prejudice are present. We agree.

In *Barrera* and *Graham*, we affirmed dismissals with prejudice after plaintiffs' total failure to comply with similar PTOs following "the district court's warnings and second chances."[18] But unlike those plaintiffs, after Dorgan, Valdivieso, and Gortney were alerted to their mistake by the district court's show cause order, they timely responded and came into compliance with PTO 66 by submitting their PSOC forms.[19] Admittedly, both Valdivieso **[—11—]** and Dorgan served BP with their PSOC forms over a week past the show cause order deadline, but ultimately, all three plaintiffs came into compliance with PTO 66 a little over three months after its

[13] *See Barrera*, 907. F.3d at 235–36, 6 Adm. R. at 271–72; *Park National*, 805 F. App'x at 265 (holding that failure to respond to both the order and the corresponding show cause order warranted dismissal with prejudice).

[14] *See Barrera*, 907. F.3d at 235–36, 6 Adm. R. at 271–72.

[15] *Rogers v. Kroger Co.*, 669 F.2d 317, 321 (5th Cir. 1982).

[16] *Barrera*, 907 F.3d at 236, 6 Adm. R. at 272.

[17] *See id.* at 235 n.1, 6 Adm. R. at 271 n.1 ("[A]ggravating factors are not required for a dismissal with prejudice.")

[18] *See Barrera*, 907 F.3d at 236, 6 Adm. R. at 272.

[19] *See id.*, 6 Adm. R. at 272 ("In fact, aside from a few untimely individuals, Plaintiffs *never* filed sworn declarations that complied with PTO 60."); *Graham*, 922 F.3d at 666, 7 Adm. R. at 253 ("[D]espite the extension, as in *Barrera*, the Lindsay Appellants failed to file anything by the new deadline."). On appeal, BP argues that Dorgan, Valdivieso, and Gortney further delayed proceedings by failing to initially file their show cause responses and PSOC forms with the court. Similarly, it argues that failure to file with the district court amounts to a violation of PTO 12, which explained the method for electronic service in this litigation. But BP did not raise these arguments blow, and thus, does not preserve them for appellate review. *See Celanese Corp. v. Martin K. Eby Const. Co.*, 620 F.3d 529, 531 (5th Cir. 2010) ("The general rule of this court is that arguments not raised before the district court are waived and will **[—11—]** not be considered on appeal."). Either way, it appears that the district court dismissed these plaintiffs only for belatedly complying with PTO 66, and it accepted compliance with PTO 66 on the date that plaintiffs served BP with their PSOC forms.

deadline and about a month after receiving a warning via the show cause order. This does not rise to the level of delay that justifies dismissal with prejudice.[20] Additionally, unlike the plaintiffs in *Barrera* and *Graham*, Dorgan, Valdivieso, and Gortney explained why they failed to timely comply with PTO 66 and included corroborating evidence.[21]

Further, the record in this case does not contain any of the three aggravating factors supporting dismissal with prejudice. Plaintiffs' attorney has repeatedly argued that failure to timely comply with PTO 66 was due to his fault alone. And BP has failed to show how it was prejudiced by plaintiffs' belated compliance with PTO 66. It only argues that allowing plaintiffs to return to the MDL would impede progression of the litigation and prejudice its interest in bringing the MDL to a close. However, BP offers no evidence **[—12—]** that plaintiffs' three-month delay actually prejudiced **{-200-}** its ability to defend the lawsuit.[22] Finally, the delay was caused by counsel's mistake, not plaintiffs' conduct; there is no evidence that the delay was intentional; it was not calculated to gain advantage and there is no suggestion that it impeded the proceedings or was contumacious.

B.

Alvarado challenges the district court's dismissal of his claims for failure to opt out of the Medical Settlement Class. Although Alvarado concedes that he is member of the settlement class and failed to opt out, he argues that his claims should be allowed to proceed because his failure to opt out constituted excusable neglect.[23]

In considering whether a party should be excused from an untimely filing, this Court applies the *Pioneer* factors.[24] We consider: (1) why the movant missed the deadline; (2) the length of the delay; (3) prejudice; and (4) evidence of good faith.[25]

As to why he missed the opt-out deadline, Alvarado contends that his wife mistakenly threw away the notices mailed to him. Alvarado admits that his wife received at least three notices of the settlement at their home. In addition to these mailed letters, notice of the settlement was broadly disseminated via "email, an extensive schedule of local newspaper, radio, television and Internet placement, well-read consumer magazines, a national daily business newspaper, highly-trafficked websites, and Sunday local **[—13—]** newspapers," plus the creation of a "neutral, informational notice website" that was "rendered in English, Spanish, and

---

[20] *See Millan v. USAA Gen. Indem. Co.*, 546 F.3d 321, 326–27 (5th Cir. 2008) ("[D]elay which warrants dismissal with prejudice must be longer than just a few months; instead, the delay must be characterized by significant periods of total inactivity." (internal quotation marks and citation omitted)); *Berry*, 975 F.2d at 1191 n.6 ("Generally, where a plaintiff has failed only to comply with a few court orders or rules, we have held that the district court abused its discretion in dismissing the suit with prejudice.").

[21] *See Barrera*, 907 F.3d at 235, 6 Adm. R. at 271 (concluding that plaintiffs' clear record of delay was evidenced by their failure to submit "any documentation or other evidence to the district court corroborating their explanation for the delay"); *Graham*, 922 F.3d at 666, 7 Adm. R. at 253 (determining that plaintiffs' record of contumacious conduct was evidenced by failure to submit any explanation for failure to timely comply with pretrial order). All three plaintiffs claimed that they failed to comply with PTO 66, because their counsel "did not see and was not aware of PTO 66." In their responses to the show cause order, all three plaintiffs attached sworn affidavits by counsel attesting that he did not become aware of PTO 66 until seeing the show cause order. When she submitted her PSOC form, Dorgan also attached evidence corroborating the timing of her husband's death.

[22] *Cf. Sealed Appellant*, 452 F.3d at 418 (explaining that failure to serve process within the statute of limitations may actually prejudice a defendant if it affects a defendant's preparations for suit).

[23] We review the district court's denial of Alvarado's Rule 60(b) motion for an abuse of discretion. *See Silvercreek Mgmt., Inc., v. Banc of Am. Sec., LLC*, 534 F.3d 469, 472 (5th Cir. 2008).

[24] *Id.*

[25] *Id.* (citing *Pioneer Inv. Servs. Co. v. Brunswick Assocs.*, 507 U.S. 380, 395 (1993)).

Vietnamese." Furthermore, it appears Alvarado was represented by counsel when he filed his short-form joinder in April 2011, and nothing in the record indicates that his counsel withdrew before the opt-out deadline. Alvarado does not address these additional notices or his counsel's role in his failure to opt out. And Alvarado's long length of delay weighs against him. Even if Alvarado's filing of an individual complaint in April 2013 counted as an implicit attempt to opt out—which we reject[26]—it came at least five months after the court-imposed deadline of November 1, 2012.[27] BP also offers the overarching contention that it would be prejudiced by a late opt out because the opt-out deadline was a negotiated term of the settlement. We agree that the interest in finality through settlement, while not determinative, also weighs against allowing Alvarado's late opt out.[28] **{-201-}**

In sum, we conclude that the district court did not abuse its discretion in finding that Alvarado's failure to opt out was inexcusable.

Finally, Alvarado urges that the district court violated due process by approving an opt-out deadline that preceded the running of the statute of limitations. This argument fares little better, as this Court has, in this MDL **[—14—]** litigation, approved settlement with an opt-out deadline set before the statute-of-limitations date.[29]

III.

For these reasons, we affirm the district court's judgment dismissing Iames and Alvarado's claims and reverse the dismissal of the claims of Dorgan, Gortney, and Valdivieso, remanding them for further proceedings consistent with this opinion.

(Reporter's Note: Opinion concurring in part, and dissenting in part follows on p. ***191****).*

---

[26] Alvarado argues that he implicitly opted out of the settlement class by filing his individual complaint. But we have previously rejected this argument, holding that "[g]iven the size and complexity of this MDL proceeding, the court and parties should not have to intuit an opt out from vague statements made in one of thousands of filings before the court." *See In re Deepwater Horizon (Mason)*, 819 F.3d 190, 197–98, 4 Adm. R. 248, 252 (5th Cir. 2016).

[27] *See Silvercreek*, 534 F.3d at 471–73 (concluding that the district court did not abuse its discretion in refusing to extend the opt-out date where the plaintiff waited a month after the deadline to file his opt-out request).

[28] *See In re Diet Drugs Prods. Liab. Litig.*, 92 F.App'x 890, 894-95 (3d Cir. 2004) (unpublished) (concluding that the "importance of accurately calculating initial opt-outs" weighs against a finding of excusable neglect).

[29] *See In re Deepwater Horizon (Deepwater Horizon II)*, 739 F.3d 790, 795, 2 Adm. R. 140, 140 (5th Cir. 2014). This settlement had the same opt-out date of November 1, 2012.

[—15—] {-201-} HAYNES, Circuit Judge, concurring in part, dissenting in part:

I concur in the judgment with respect to Iames and Alvarado. I respectfully dissent as to the other three. We review matters concerning docket management for abuse of discretion, affording a district court "special deference . . . in the context of an MDL." *In re Deepwater Horizon (Barrera)*, 907 F.3d 232, 234–35, 6 Adm. R. 270, 271 (5th Cir. 2018); *see also Coleman v. Sweetin*, 745 F.3d 756, 766 (5th Cir. 2014) (reviewing for abuse of discretion a district court's dismissal with prejudice for failure to comply with a court order). That "special deference" is important in these massive MDL cases: yes, of course, everyone is entitled to due process, whether in a single case or in an MDL. But "[t]he ability for 'judges to enforce orders pertaining to the progress of their cases' is most important in '[MDL] cases, where the very purpose of the centralization before the transferee judge is the efficient progress of the cases . . . .'" *Barrera*, 907 F.3d at 235, 6 Adm. R. at 271 (quoting *In re Asbestos Prod. Liab. Litig. (No. VI)*, 718 F.3d 236, 248 (3d Cir. 2013)). Accordingly, the need to ensure efficient and fair handling of massive litigation like this one warrants particular deference to the highly-involved district court's views on issues like the propriety of a delay—we should be hesitant to supplant our own views on whether that delay should be ignored.

Yet the majority opinion does just that, suggesting that Dorgan's, Valdivieso's, and Gortney's repeated failures to meet deadlines set by the district court can be overlooked because they "timely responded and came into compliance" after the show cause order. Unfortunately, that is not the case.

Dorgan admits in her brief that she did not respond to PTO 66 by the July 9, 2018 deadline, nor did she seek an extension. After being named in the show cause order, she sent a response to BP by the October 11, 2018 deadline—but she both failed to file that response with the court as required by PTO 12 and the show cause order *and* failed to include a particularized statement as required by PTO 66. On October 23, she then served a [—16—] "Supplemental Response to Court's Order to Show Cause Regarding PTO 66," this time including a particularized statement. In violation of PTO 12 and the show cause order, however, Dorgan did not file that response with the court. After her complaint was dismissed, she sought reconsideration acknowledging that her counsel "did not see and was not aware of PTO 66," "failed to {-202-} follow the requirements of PTO 66," and "erroneously thought" that various documents, like the response to the show cause order, had been filed when in fact they had not. The district court denied Dorgan's motion for reconsideration, explaining that her "attorneys' own fault" in complying with various orders did not warrant relief. Several motions later, she finally provided to the court her PTO 66 submission and response to the show cause order. The district court denied that motion and warned that monetary sanctions would be imposed if she filed another motion for reconsideration or similar request.

Similarly, Valdivieso and Gortney did not file their response to PTO 66 by the deadline. After being named in the show cause order, they did serve a response on BP by the October 11, 2018 deadline, but they did not file that document with the district court, a violation of both the show cause order and PTO 12. More importantly, the document they served on BP was deficient as to Valdivieso: although the unfiled response included a particularized statement for Gortney as required by PTO 66, it did not include one for Valdivieso. Hence, on October 19, 2018—more than a week after the show-cause deadline—Valdivieso and Gortney served a "supplemental" response, this time with the required particularized statement for Valdivieso. But they also failed to file this supplemental response with the district court, only including the document in a motion for reconsideration approximately four months later. Like Dorgan, Valdivieso and Gortney blamed their lawyers, a point the court found unavailing as their "attorneys' own fault" in failing to know about or comply with various orders did not justify relief. [—17—]

Notably, it was not until the court dismissed their cases that Valdivieso and

Gortney and, ultimately, Dorgan, filed their PTO 66 with the court. BP makes a good argument that our review on appeal is limited to the motions for reconsideration such that only Federal Rule of Civil Procedure 60 is at play here. Under Federal Rule of Civil Procedure 60(b)(1), the court may relieve a party from a final judgment for "mistake, inadvertence, surprise, or excusable neglect." However, the admitted attorney mistakes here—essentially, failures to meet clear filing deadlines—do not qualify. *See Pioneer Inv. Servs. Co. v. Brunswick Assocs. Ltd. P'ship*, 507 U.S. 380, 392 (1993) ("[I]nadvertence, ignorance of the rules, or mistakes construing the rules do not usually constitute 'excusable' neglect."); *Edward H. Bohlin Co. v. Banning Co.*, 6 F.3d 350, 356–57 (5th Cir. 1993) (concluding that denial of a Rule 60(b)(1) motion to set aside a dismissal "is not an abuse of discretion when the proffered justification for relief is the 'inadvertent mistake' of counsel"); *see also Rayford v. Karl Storz Endoscopy Am., Inc.*, 740 F. App'x 435, 436–37 (5th Cir. 2018) (noting that "[c]alendaring errors and mistakes about deadlines qualify as a careless mistake of counsel" and therefore do not entitle a movant to relief from judgment); *Brittingham v. Wells Fargo Bank, N.A.*, 543 F. App'x 372, 374 (5th Cir. 2013) (same). Indeed, because "[g]ross carelessness, ignorance of the rules, or ignorance of the law are insufficient bases for Rule 60(b)(1) relief," a district court "*would abuse its discretion* if it were to reopen a case under Rule 60(b)(1) when the reason asserted as justifying relief is one attributable solely to counsel's carelessness with or misapprehension of the law or the applicable rules of court." *Bohlin*, 6 F.3d at 356–57 (emphasis added).

Even if we ignore that the appeal concerns only the Rule 60 motions and we address the underlying dismissals themselves, I respectfully disagree with the majority opinion's analysis. The majority **{-203-}** opinion says that Dorgan's, Valdivieso's, and Gortney's conduct does not qualify as delay and does not contain the necessary aggravating factors. First of all, it is not necessary to show aggravating factors here, as the majority opinion **[—18—]** acknowledges with respect to Iames.[1] *Barrera*, 907 F.3d at 235 n.1, 6 Adm. R. at 271 n.1 ("[A]ggravating factors are not required for a dismissal with prejudice."). Second, there was more than enough delay for the district court to justifiably dismiss the complaints with prejudice. The original deadline which Dorgan, Valdivieso, and Gortney all failed to comply with was July 9, 2018. Dorgan did not actually submit her PTO 66 submission to the court until May 28, 2019. Valdivieso and Gortney did not submit a proper PTO 66 submission to the court until after the dismissal as part of their motion for reconsideration on February 8, 2019. Given the need to manage such a mammoth number of cases in this MDL, timeliness is important, and their failure to comply with deadlines constitutes the requisite delay. Thus, we should affirm in full. Because the majority opinion fails to do so, I respectfully dissent in part.

---

[1] Curiously, although the majority opinion (correctly) states that the lack of aggravating factors "does not warrant overturning" the dismissal of Iames's claims, it proceeds to treat the absence of aggravating factors as a primary reason for overturning the dismissal of Dorgan's, Valdivieso's, and Gortney's claims. Why it applies different analyses here is a mystery. The same rule applies to all four of these plaintiffs: the district court did not need to find aggravating factors to dismiss any of their claims. *See Barrera*, 907 F.3d at 235 n.1, 6 Adm. R. at 271 n.1.

United States Court of Appeals
for the Fifth Circuit

No. 20-20307

PLAYA VISTA CONROE
VS.
INSURANCE CO. OF THE WEST

Appeal from the United States District Court for the Southern District of Texas

Decided: March 5, 2021

Citation: 989 F.3d 411, 9 Adm. R. 193 (5th Cir. 2021).

Before **HIGGINBOTHAM, COSTA,** and **OLDHAM,** Circuit Judges.

[—1—] {–413–} OLDHAM, Circuit Judge:

A Texas condo association suffered property damage during Hurricane Harvey. It filed a property-damage claim against its insurer. The insurer refused to pay, so the condo association filed suit for breach of its insurance contracts. On cross-motions for summary judgment, the district court held the insurer liable. We affirm.

I.

Playa Vista Conroe is a condominium association located outside of Houston, Texas. Its property sits on the north shore of Lake Conroe, a **[—2—]** manmade lake on the San Jacinto River. Prior to Hurricane Harvey, that property included a dock with 22 boat slips. In May 2017, Playa Vista insured the dock and boat slips by purchasing insurance from Insurance Company of the West ("ICW"). Three policy documents are key to the parties' dispute:

- A "difference in conditions form": This document is 23 pages long and provides the framework for the parties' insurance agreement. We refer to the difference in conditions form as the "DICF."

- A "limited coverage—flood endorsement": This document is 1.5 pages long, and it replaces the background flood provisions in the DICF. We refer to the flood endorsement as the "FE."

- A "specified flood exclusion": This document is 0.5 pages long, and it adds an additional site-specific flood exclusion for "BOAT SLIPS/DOCKS." We refer to the boat slip exclusion as "BSE."

We refer to the DICF, FE, and BSE together as the "Policy."

In August 2017, Hurricane Harvey hit the State of Texas. The storm caused unprecedented rainfall and flooding. In order to prevent the Lake Conroe Dam from overflowing and failing, the San Jacinto River Authority released from the dam 79,141 cubic feet of water per second—nearly the flow rate of Niagara Falls. Playa Vista's boat slips were completely destroyed.

Those 22 destroyed boat slips are the only property at issue here. Playa Vista sought compensation for them based on **{–414–}** its Policy. It filed a notice of loss with ICW, describing the loss as "[d]estruction of various components of the condominium property from severe weather, including complete destruction of [the] boat dock, damage to condominium buildings, damage to garages, bulkhead damage, fencing damage, landscaping damage, pool damage, awning damage, and other miscellaneous damage." ICW initially **[—3—]** sent a reservation-of-rights letter. Then it denied coverage. ICW stated that the damage "appear[ed] to be the result of Hurricane/Tropical Storm Harvey," and that Playa Vista's "policy d[id] not cover flooding caused by a hurricane or tropical storm."

Playa Vista filed a notice and pre-litigation demand under Chapter 542A of the Texas Insurance Code. The notice claimed that Playa Vista "suffered immediate and severe damage to [its] commercial property as a result of an intense storm" and alleged ICW "improperly adjusted [Playa Vista's] claim so that [it] would not receive the coverage [it] had originally contracted to receive." Playa Vista attached a report estimating $208,117.44 in damages and listing "hurricane" as the type of loss. ICW responded by reiterating its denial of Playa Vista's claim.

Playa Vista filed suit in Texas state court. It raised several claims under state law, but only its breach-of-contract claim is relevant to this appeal. ICW removed the case to federal court. Then the parties cross-moved for summary judgment.

The district court denied ICW's motion and granted Playa Vista's motion. That order resolved Playa Vista's breach-of-contract claim, but it left damages and attorney's fees as issues for trial. Two weeks before the trial date, the parties submitted a joint agreed stipulation (the "Stipulation") in which they stipulated that Playa Vista incurred $190,827.50 in damages and $50,000.00 in attorney's fees. The district court approved and entered the Stipulation.

Playa Vista moved for entry of final judgment, *see* FED. R. CIV. P. 58(d), noting that "the only remaining issue . . . was the determination of the amount of damages which Playa Vista [wa]s entitled to under its breach of contract claim." The district court issued a final judgment awarding Playa Vista damages and attorney's fees pursuant to the Stipulation. The next day, **[—4—]** ICW filed a motion for leave to file a second motion for summary judgment. ICW claimed that by agreeing to the Stipulation, Playa Vista admitted that the loss fell within the Policy's exclusion for "[a]cts or decisions, including the failure to act or decide, of any person, organization or governmental body." Playa Vista did not respond. ICW then filed a motion to alter, amend, or reconsider the final judgment. Playa Vista objected, and the district court denied the motion. ICW appealed.

II.

We begin with the district court's summary-judgment order. "Where, as here, parties have filed cross-motions for summary judgment, each motion must be considered separately because each movant bears the burden of showing that no genuine issue of material fact exists and that it is entitled to a judgment as a matter of law." *Am. Int'l Specialty Lines Ins. Co. v. Rentech Steel, LLC*, 620 F.3d 558, 562 (5th Cir. 2010). Our review of the district court's application of this standard is *de novo*. *See id.* at 561–62.

Our review of the Policy language and the legal standards for insurance coverage also is *de novo*. *See Am. Nat'l Gen. Ins. Co. v. Ryan*, 274 F.3d 319, 323 (5th Cir. 2001). As to the Policy language, we use Texas's contract-interpretation **{–415–}** rules. *See ibid.* As to the legal standards for insurance coverage, Texas law provides:

> Initially, the insured has the burden of establishing coverage under the terms of the policy. If the insured proves coverage, then to avoid liability the insurer must prove the loss is within an exclusion. If the insurer proves that an exclusion applies, the burden shifts back to the insured to show that an exception to the exclusion brings the claim back within coverage.

Gilbert Tex. Constr., L.P. v. Underwriters at Lloyd's London, 327 S.W.3d 118, 124 (Tex. 2010) (citations omitted). We hold Playa Vista established coverage, and ICW failed to prove an exclusion applies. **[—5—]**

A.

We start with the coverage question. The DICF states that ICW "will pay for accidental direct physical loss or damage to Covered Property . . . caused by or resulting from a Covered Cause of Loss." It defines a "Covered Cause of Loss" as a "direct physical loss" that is not "excluded in Section[] C. . . . or [Section] D. . . . or excluded or limited in the Declarations or by endorsement." And Section C's "Property Excluded" provision states that ICW "will not pay for loss or damage to . . . docks" unless "a stated value is shown in Section E. . . . and/or a sub-limit of insurance is shown in Section A.1.a . . . in the Declarations or in an endorsement to this policy." Section A.1.a in the Declarations in turn includes a $220,000 "sublimit of insurance" for coverage of boat slips.

Therefore, Playa Vista met its burden to show that its boat slips are covered in the absence of an applicable exclusion.

B.

The burden thus shifts to ICW to prove that an exclusion applies. ICW points to three potential exclusions and insists that the language of the exclusions is sufficient standing alone to warrant judgment as a matter of law in its favor. That is wrong.

First, the DICF generally excludes losses arising from a "flood" and specifically excludes "damage resulting from waterborne material involved in the flood." But that same exclusion says: "if flood coverage is endorsed to and made part of this policy, we will way [sic] pay for loss subject to the limited coverage provided by that endorsement." Playa Vista did in fact purchase separate flood coverage—the FE—so the flood provisions in the DICF are irrelevant.

That is particularly true because the FE contains its own list of exclusions, several of which replicate the exclusions in the DICF. For example, the DICF excludes flood damage caused by "Underground waters **[—6—]** rising" and "Tsunami or tidal wave," and the FE likewise excludes flood damage caused by "Underground waters rising" and "Tsunami or tidal wave." This proves that ICW (as the drafter of the Policy documents) intended the coverage and exclusion provisions of the FE to replace those in the DICF. *See Progressive Cnty. Mut. Ins. Co. v. Sink*, 107 S.W.3d 547, 551 (Tex. 2003) (stating that "a court construing a contract must strive to give effect to the written expression of the parties' intent by reading all parts of a contract together" and an ambiguous insurance contract "will be interpreted in the manner that most favors coverage" (quotation omitted)); *CKB & Assocs., Inc. v. Moore McCormack Petroleum, Inc.*, 734 S.W.2d 653, 655 (Tex. 1987) (applying the *expressio unius* canon to the interpretation of a contract). The DICF flood exclusion therefore is irrelevant.

Second, the FE provides: "We will not pay for loss or damage caused by **{-416-}** 'flood', arising from . . . [a h]urricane or tropical storm." The FE further defines a "flood" as "a general and temporary condition of partial or complete inundation of 2 or more acres of normally dry land areas or of 2 or more distinct parcels of land (at least one of which is your property) with water." It is undisputed that the FE's definition of "flood" does not apply to Playa Vista's boat slips; they obviously existed on water, not two or more acres of normally dry land. Because the FE only applies to normally dry land, it too is irrelevant.[1] **[—7—]**

Third, the Policy also expressly excludes "flood" damage to boat slips and docks. This is the BSE. But the BSE suffers from the same problem as the second exclusion—it only applies to a "flood." It is unclear why ICW drafted its BSE to exclude "flood" damage to property that normally appears on water rather than dry land. But it was ICW's Policy to draft, so ICW must assume the perils of its chosen language. *See Ryan*, 274 F.3d at 323 ("Ambiguous insurance contracts will be interpreted against the insurer. The policy of strict construction against the insurer is especially strong when the court is dealing with exceptions and words of limitation." (quotations omitted)); *Goswick v. Emps.' Cas. Co.*, 440 S.W.2d 287, 289 (Tex. 1969) ("[W]e must presume that the objective of the insurance contract is to insure, and we should not construe the policy to defeat that objective unless the language requires it.").

But even if the FE or the BSE "flood" provisions could in theory apply, Playa Vista submitted competent summary-judgment evidence to show that its boat slips were not

[1] ICW's contrary argument is absurd. It argues that the FE *covers* "floods" only as "specifically defined" in the FE, Blue Br. 5—that is, "a general and temporary condition of partial or complete inundation of 2 or more acres of normally dry land areas or of 2 or more distinct parcels of land (at least one of which is your property) with water." But then it argues the FE *excludes* "floods" "as commonly understood (i.e. not defined), caused by [a h]urricane or tropical storm." Blue Br. 5–6 (quotation marks omitted). The FE says no such thing. It includes only one definition of "flood," and it applies equally to the FE's coverage provision and the FE's exclusion provision.

in fact destroyed by a "flood." In particular, Playa Vista's president Robert G. Copes testified by affidavit. *See* FED. R. CIV. P. 56(c)(1)(A) (listing affidavits as competent summary-judgment evidence). Copes testified that he personally observed the boat slips at 10:00 pm on the night before the San Jacinto River Authority "released the water from Lake Conroe Dam, and neither the dock nor any of the Boat Slips were damaged or destroyed at that time." When the River Authority released water from the dam, however, it:

> created a suction effect, like a sink drain that is unplugged, but on a much greater scale. Because of the rate at which water was being released, the water on the north side of [the] lake (where the Boat Slips are located) was below normal levels afterwards, despite the rainfall brought by Harvey. **[—8—]**

According to Copes, this super-powerful suction effect pulled debris from all over Lake Conroe, violently whipped it around the Lake, and destroyed Playa Vista's boat slips as the water drained southward out of the Lake. Thus, Copes testified, it was this "suction effect" and the *drop* of water levels—not an "inundation" or "flood" or *rise* of water levels—that destroyed Playa Vista's boat slips.

ICW chose not to dispute the Copes affidavit. Of course, Rule 56 did not obligate ICW to submit its own affidavit(s); it could simply "identify[] those portions of [the record] which it believes demonstrate **{–417–}** the absence of a genuine issue of material fact." *Celotex Corp. v. Catrett*, 477 U.S. 317, 323 (1986) (citing FED. R. CIV. P. 56). But in the face of an affidavit tending to establish that the boat slips were not destroyed by a "flood," ICW could not carry its legal burden to prove one of the "flood" exclusions by submitting nothing. That is particularly true where the Policy exclusions on their face do not apply to the loss of Playa Vista's boat slips. The district court did not err in granting summary judgment to Playa Vista.

III.

Finally, ICW makes two efforts to undo its litigation mistakes. Neither has merit.

ICW first argues that it creatively drafted its insurance contracts to avoid any burden to prove anything. As noted above, Texas law establishes a burden-shifting framework under which the insured must establish coverage, but then the *insurer* must prove an applicable exception. *See Gilbert*, 327 S.W.3d at 124. ICW says it anticipated this problem and drafted the DICF coverage provision to include an exclusionary clause—with the hope that its customers would get stuck with the burden of proving *both* coverage *and* the absence of an exclusion. We doubt that insurers can avoid Texas law so easily. It would be odd that insurers carry the burden to establish exclusions only **[—9—]** when the contract separates them from the coverage provisions and not when the coverage and exclusion provisions appear in the same contractual section. It would be particularly odd for that result to obtain when the insurer is the one who writes the contract. And it would be odder still for that result to obtain when ICW can point to no state-law authority for it.

But the issue is irrelevant here because ICW conceded in the district court that Playa Vista's boat slips are covered by the DICF coverage provision. ICW cannot take the opposite position now. *See Martinez v. Pompeo*, 977 F.3d 457, 460 (5th Cir. 2020) (per curiam).

Second, ICW says it snatched victory from the jaws of defeat by negotiating the Stipulation after losing at summary judgment. After the district court ruled in Playa Vista's favor at summary judgment, the only issue remaining for the district court was Playa Vista's request for damages and fees. The district court set those damages and fees for trial. But before trial, the parties submitted this Stipulation to obviate further proceedings:

> 1. The parties stipulate that [Playa Vista's] docks and boat slips were

> damaged from the San Jacinto River Authority's release of water from the Lake Conroe Dam at an unprecedented rate and volume, creating a suction effect that unmoored boats, causing these unmoored boats, fallen trees, and other debris to collide into the Plaintiff's docks and boat slips.
>
> 2. The parties stipulate [that Playa Vista's] property damaged as a result of the claim [is] valued at $190,827.50 and further stipulate that the recoverable attorney's fees are $50,000.00.

The district court approved the Stipulation and then issued a final judgment.

ICW says this Stipulation operates as a legal "gotcha," and that by agreeing to it, Playa Vista gave away its summary-judgment victory. After the district court entered final judgment, ICW argued that Playa Vista stipulated that its losses were caused by the decision of a governmental body—namely, **[—10—]** the San Jacinto River Authority—and hence triggered a theretofore unmentioned exclusion for "[a]cts or decisions, including the failure to act or decide, of any person, organization or governmental **{–418–}** body." That is far too little too late. If ICW wanted to rely on the governmental-body exclusion, it was obligated to raise it (at the latest) at summary judgment. *See, e.g.*, *Mid-Continent Cas. Co. v. Bay Rock Operating Co.*, 614 F.3d 105, 113 (5th Cir. 2010).

AFFIRMED.

United States Court of Appeals
for the Fifth Circuit

No. 19-20506

SANCHEZ
vs.
SMART FABRICATORS OF TEX., L.L.C.

Appeal from the United States District Court for the Southern District of Texas

Decided: May 11, 2021

Citation: 997 F.3d 564, 9 Adm. R. 198 (5th Cir. 2021) (en banc).

Before **OWEN**, Chief Judge, **DAVIS**, **JONES**, **SMITH**, **STEWART**, **DENNIS**, **ELROD**, **SOUTHWICK**, **HAYNES**, **GRAVES**, **HIGGINSON**, **COSTA**, **WILLETT**, **HO**, **DUNCAN**, **ENGELHARDT**, **OLDHAM**, and **WILSON**, Circuit Judges.

[—1—] {–566–} DAVIS, Circuit Judge:

We took this case en banc to attempt to define for this Circuit a more definitive test, consistent with Supreme Court caselaw, to distinguish seamen entitled to benefits under the Jones Act from other maritime workers generally covered under the Longshore and Harbor Worker's Compensation Act. **[—2—]**

We conclude that the plaintiff in this case, Gilbert Sanchez, a land-based welder directed by his employer to work on two discrete short-term transient repair jobs on two vessels, was not a seaman. Because Sanchez was not engaged in sea-based work that satisfied the requirement that he be substantially connected to a fleet of vessels in terms of the nature of his work, we AFFIRM the judgment of the district court.

I. FACTUAL BACKGROUND

The material facts in this case are not in dispute. The plaintiff, Gilbert Sanchez,[1] was employed as a land-based welder by Smart Fabricators of Texas, LLC ("SmartFab"), a contract welding firm engaged in steel fabrication, repairs to drilling equipment, and general contract welding work. SmartFab's work is performed to meet the demands of its customers on land and sometimes on jack-up drilling barges. The issues in this case revolve around Sanchez's work for SmartFab on two jack-up barges owned by SmartFab's customer, Enterprise Offshore Drilling LLC ("Enterprise").

Sanchez worked for SmartFab for a total of 67 days between August 2017 and August 2018. Six of those days were spent working on welding jobs either on land or vessels that are irrelevant to his status as a seaman because they were not owned or controlled by Enterprise. Sanchez spent the remaining 61 days—those pertinent to our inquiry—on two different jack-up drilling **{–567–}** rigs owned by Enterprise: the Enterprise WFD 350 and the Enterprise 263.

A. Enterprise WFD 350

Sanchez worked on the Enterprise jack-up barge WFD 350 for 48 days doing welding work on a discrete repair job. The entire time he worked on this vessel, it was jacked-up so that the deck of the barge was level with **[—3—]** Gabby's Dock in Sabine Pass, Texas, and separated from the dock by a gangplank. Sanchez could take two steps on the gangplank, and he was ashore. He commuted from his home to the vessel daily. His time on the WFD 350 comprised approximately 72 percent of his total work time with SmartFab.

B. Enterprise 263

Sanchez worked 13 days on one other Enterprise vessel, the Enterprise jack-up barge 263. His work on this vessel comprised approximately 19 percent of his time in SmartFab's employment. When Sanchez was dispatched to the Enterprise 263 in July 2018, it was located in West Cameron Block 38 on the Outer Continental Shelf ("OCS"). He was sent as part of a SmartFab crew that was contracted to perform repairs necessary to get the vessel in condition to satisfy requirements of the American Bureau of Shipping ("ABS"), the Bureau of Safety and Environmental Enforcement ("BSEE"), and the Coast Guard, so that the rig could begin drilling operations

[1] Payroll records indicate that Sanchez worked for SmartFab using the name Jorge Cruz.

at a new drilling site on the OCS. Sanchez was aboard the rig when it was moved by tugboats to the new drilling location, South Timbalier Block 125 on the OCS.

Sanchez performed welding and related work on the deck of the Enterprise 263. On August 8, 2018, he fell and sustained the injury that is the subject of this suit. Because Sanchez was sent ashore on August 9, 2018, following his injury, he was unable to complete his assignment and remain with the SmartFab crew until the repairs were completed on August 10, 2018. The rig began drilling on August 11, 2018.[2] Sanchez left the employ of **[—4—]** SmartFab after his injury and, as far as the record shows, did no more work on Enterprise vessels.

II. PROCEDURAL HISTORY

After his accident, Sanchez sued SmartFab in state court under the Jones Act. SmartFab promptly removed the case, but Sanchez moved to remand, arguing that the Jones Act precluded removal. The district court denied Sanchez's motion to remand and granted SmartFab's motion for summary judgment, both for the same reason: Sanchez did not qualify as a Jones Act seaman.[3]

A. District Court Rulings

The district court concluded that Sanchez failed to establish a substantial connection in terms of the nature of his work to the Enterprise fleet of jack-up barges he worked aboard.[4] The district court held that Sanchez spent more than 30 percent of his work time with SmartFab working on the Enterprise WFD 350 and 263, and that his repair work on those barges contributed **{–568–}** to the function of these vessels.[5] Because he contributed to the function of the vessels, he satisfied prong one of the seaman-status test.[6] The court also held that because Sanchez spent more than 30 percent of his work time with SmartFab working on those two barges, he met the substantial connection requirement as to duration.[7] However, the district court concluded that because less than 30 percent of his work on the two vessels **[—5—]** was performed away from the dock, he did not satisfy the nature element of the substantiality requirement and therefore Sanchez was not a seaman.[8] For this reason, the district court denied Sanchez's motion to remand the case to state court.[9] For the same reason, the district court granted SmartFab's motion for summary judgment.[10] Sanchez timely appealed both rulings.

B. Panel Opinion and En Banc Review

On appeal, the panel originally held that based upon binding Circuit precedent, Sanchez satisfied the requirements for seaman status. We based this on two of our earlier cases: *In re Endeavor Marine, Inc.*,[11] and *Naquin v. Elevating Boats, L.L.C.*[12] One

[2] Counsel for Sanchez confirmed during oral argument that the SmartFab work was completed on August 10 and drilling began on August 11, 2018 (Oral Argument Recording at 15:33-15:39), which is consistent with the affidavit of Glen Whitman, Rig Manager of the Enterprise 263.

[3] *See Sanchez v. Enter. Offshore Drilling LLC*, No. CV H-19-110, 2019 WL 2515307, at *4 (S.D. Tex. June 18, 2019); *Sanchez v. Enter. Offshore Drilling LLC*, 376 F. Supp. 3d 726, 733 (S.D. Tex. 2019).

[4] *Sanchez*, 376 F. Supp. 3d at 732.

[5] *Id.*

[6] *Id.*

[7] *Id.*

[8] *Id.*

[9] *Id.* at 733.

[10] *Sanchez*, 2019 WL 2515307, at *3–4.

[11] 234 F.3d 287 (5th Cir. 2000) (per curiam).

[12] 744 F.3d 927, 2 Adm. R. 200 (5th Cir. 2014). Most of the scholarship discussing our two earlier cases is critical of our holdings. *See* Kenneth G. Engerrand, *Escape from the Labyrinth: Call for the Admiralty Judges of the Supreme Court to Reconsider Seaman Status*, 40 HOUS. J. INT. L. 741, 763–74, 795 (2018); Timothy M. O'Hara, Comment, Naquin v. Elevating Boats, LLC: *The Fifth Circuit's Improper Expansion of Jones Act "Seaman Status" Qualification*, 36 PACE L. REV. 263, 286 (2015); Matthew H. Frederick, Note, *Adrift in the Harbor: Ambiguous- Amphibious Controversies and Seamen's Access to Workers' Compensation Benefits*, 81 TEX. L. REV. 1671, 1705 (2003); L. Taylor Coley, Note, *The "Perils of the Sea"- Man Status Question: The Fifth Circuit Falls Behind FELA's Advancements in Remedies in Favor of the Continued Confusion Surrounding the Seaman Definition*, 39 TUL. MAR. L. J. 371, 380–81 (2014).

member of the panel filed a concurring opinion, joined by the other members of the panel, questioning whether our precedent was in line with Supreme Court caselaw and proposing that we take the case **[—6—]** en banc to consider this question.[13] The case was voted en banc, and, for the reasons set forth below, the en banc court agrees that Supreme Court precedent requires us to affirm the judgment of the district court.

III. APPLICABLE LAW

We review both the denial of a motion to remand and the grant of summary judgment de novo.[14]

A. Jones Act and LHWCA

The Jones Act grants "a seaman" a cause of action against his employer in **{-569-}** negligence.[15] Only seamen may sue under the Jones Act and Jones Act claims are "not subject to removal to federal court."[16] Sanchez argues that because he was a seaman who brought his negligence action under the Jones Act in state court, the district court erred both in denying his motion to remand and in granting summary judgment for SmartFab. So, the only issue for us to decide to resolve this appeal is whether Sanchez is a seaman (or entitled to have a jury resolve the issue) entitled to the benefits of the Jones Act. **[—7—]**

In addition to the Jones Act, another important statute is relevant to our inquiry. Congress enacted the Longshore and Harbor Worker's Compensation Act (LHWCA) in 1927 to establish a federal compensation remedy for injuries to certain land-based workers occurring on navigable waters.[17] Generally, coverage under this compensation act excluded from its coverage "a master or member of a crew of any vessel."[18] The LHWCA, therefore, limits the definition of "seaman" in the Jones Act so as "to confine the benefits of the Jones Act to the members of the crew of a vessel plying in navigable waters and to substitute for the right of recovery . . . only such rights to compensation as are given by the LHWCA."[19] Thus, the seaman's remedy is limited to rights granted by the Jones Act, and rights granted to other maritime workers are provided exclusively by the LHWCA. The two remedies are mutually exclusive.[20]

Because Congress has not defined the term "seaman," the definition of and distinction between the two groups have been the subject of extensive litigation, and courts have struggled to establish workable tests to define the word "seaman." **[—8—]**

B. Supreme Court Trilogy

In the 1990s, the Supreme Court decided three cases that were enormously helpful in giving meaning to the term "seaman."

But see John R. Hillsman, *Still Lost in the Labyrinth: The Continuing Puzzle of Seaman Status*, 15 U.S.F. MAR. L. J. 49, 73–75 (2003). For a general discussion of these cases, see 1 Robert Force & Martin J. Norris, *The Law of Seamen* § 2:8 Westlaw (database updated Nov. 2020).

[13] *Sanchez v. Smart Fabricators of Texas, L.L.C.*, 970 F.3d 550, 555–56, 8 Adm. R. 222, 226–27 (5th Cir.), *reh'g en banc granted, opinion vacated*, 978 F.3d 976, 8 Adm. R. 235 (5th Cir. 2020).

[14] *Holmes v. Atl. Sounding Co.*, 437 F.3d 441, 445 (5th Cir. 2006), *abrogated on other grounds by Lozman v. City of Riviera Beach, Fla.*, 568 U.S. 115, 1 Adm. R. 2 (2013).

[15] "A seaman injured in the course of employment or, if the seaman dies from the injury, the personal representative of the seaman may elect to bring a civil action at law, with the right of trial by jury, against the employer. Laws of the United States regulating recovery for personal injury to, or death of, a railway employee apply to an action under this section." 46 U.S.C. § 30104.

[16] *Lewis v. Lewis & Clark Marine, Inc.*, 531 U.S. 438, 455 (2001) (noting that 28 U.S.C. § 1445(a), which bars removal of certain suits involving railroads, is incorporated into the Jones Act).

[17] 33 U.S.C. § 903(a).

[18] 33 U.S.C. § 902(3)(G).

[19] *McDermott Int'l, Inc. v. Wilander*, 498 U.S. 337, 347 (1991) (quoting *Swanson v. Mora Brothers, Inc.*, 328 U.S. 1, 7 (1946)).

[20] *See id.*

1. *Wilander*

First was *McDermott International, Inc. v. Wilander*.[21] The Court took this case primarily to resolve a split among the circuits on the question of whether a plaintiff, to establish seaman status, was required to show that he aided in the navigation of a vessel.[22] The Court rejected the circuit cases imposing this requirement and adopted the test set forth in Judge Wisdom's landmark decision in *Offshore Co. v. Robison*, requiring proof that the seaman "contributed to the function of the vessel or to the accomplishment of its mission" and have an employment-related connection **{-570-}** to a vessel.[23] The *Wilander* Court emphasized, "The key to seaman status is employment-related connection to a vessel in navigation."[24]

In order to give effect to the land-based/sea-based distinction, the Court "believe[d] the better rule is to define 'master or member of a crew' under the LHWCA, and therefore 'seaman' under the Jones Act, solely in terms of the employee's connection to a vessel in navigation."[25] The Court was persuaded that the connection requirement was consistent with "Congress' land-based/sea-based distinction," explaining: "All who work **[—9—]** at sea in the service of a ship face those particular perils to which the protection of maritime law, statutory as well as decisional, is directed."[26]

2. *Chandris*

The Supreme Court's next decision on seaman status came four years later in *Chandris, Inc. v. Latsis*.[27] In this case, the plaintiff, Latsis, was a supervising engineer who oversaw an engineering department for a fleet of six passenger cruise ships.[28] Latsis developed a detached retina while sailing on one of the vessels and sued because of an alleged delay by the employer in providing medical care.[29] Latsis's duties required him to divide his work between the office and aboard ship when he sometimes sailed for inspection and supervision of engineering work.[30] The Court was therefore asked to define the "relationship a worker must have to the vessel, regardless of the specific tasks the worker undertakes in order to obtain seaman status."[31] After discussing the judicial and legislative history of the passage of the LHWCA, the *Chandris* Court stated: "With the passage of the LHWCA, Congress established a clear distinction between land-based and sea-based maritime workers. The latter who owe their allegiance to a vessel and not solely to a land-based employer, are seamen."[32] The Court also pointed out that Congress, by enacting the LHWCA, had twice overturned the Supreme Court's extension of seamen's remedies to other maritime workers doing **[—10—]** seamen's work and incurring seamen's hazards.[33] Justice O'Connor summed up the effect of these two congressional acts: "Whether under the Jones Act or general maritime law, seamen do not include land-based workers."[34]

In explaining the importance of the requirement that a seaman have a substantial, enduring relationship to a vessel, the Court rejected a snapshot test for seaman status, denouncing a test that inspected "only the situation as it exists at the instance of injury" and noting that "a more enduring relationship is contemplated in the jurisprudence."[35] The Court emphasized that "a worker may not oscillate back and forth between Jones Act coverage and other remedies depending on the **{-571-}** activity in which the worker was engaged while injured."[36] The Court also recognized that "[s]eaman status is not co-extensive with seamen's risk."[37] "Some workers who

---

21 498 U.S. 337 (1991).
22 *Id.* at 340.
23 266 F.2d 769, 779 (5th Cir. 1959).
24 *Wilander*, 498 U.S. at 355.
25 *Id.* at 354.
26 *Id.*
27 515 U.S. 347 (1995).
28 *Id.* at 350.
29 *Id.* at 350–51.
30 *Id.* at 350.
31 *Id.*
32 *Id.* at 359.
33 *Id.*
34 *Id.* at 358.
35 *Id.* at 363.
36 *Id.*
37 *Id.* at 361.

unmistakably confront the perils of the sea, often in extreme form, are thereby left out of the seamen's protections."[38]

The Court then turned to apply these principles to the sufficiency of plaintiff's relationship to his employer's fleet of vessels to qualify for seaman status. It defined the substantial-connection test with two elements: "a seaman must have a connection to a vessel in navigation (or to an identifiable group of such vessels) that is substantial in terms of both its duration and its **[—11—]** nature."[39] In discussing the duration element, the Court stated that "the total circumstances of an individual's employment must be weighed."[40] The *Chandris* Court approved our rule of thumb as a guide to the degree of permanence required to satisfy the duration element. "A worker who spends less than about 30 percent of his time in the service of a vessel in navigation should not qualify as a seaman under the Jones Act."[41]

Because the record was unclear regarding how much of plaintiff's time was spent working on the employer's vessels as opposed to his land-based work, the Court remanded the case for application of the stated principles to the facts.[42]

3. *Papai*

The Supreme Court provided more guidance on the nature element of the substantiality requirement in *Harbor Tug and Barge Co. v. Papai*—the third case in this trilogy.[43] This case is closely analogous to the facts of the present case. In *Papai*, the shipowner, Harbor Tug, was one of several tugboat operators operating in San Francisco Bay that obtained workers through a union hiring hall.[44] Papai was engaged through the union hall to paint the housing of a Harbor Tug, the Pt. Barrow.[45] The entire time Papai worked on the Pt. Barrow, it was located dockside.[46] **[—12—]**

The Court stated that "[f]or the substantial connection requirement to serve its purpose, the inquiry into the nature of the employee's connection to the vessel must concentrate on whether the employee's duties take him to sea."[47] It further explained that "[t]his will give substance to the inquiry both as to duration and nature of the employee's connection to the vessel and be helpful in distinguishing land-based from sea-based employees."[48] The Court then considered Papai's actual duties and whether they satisfied the nature element. It determined, "[h]is actual duty on the Pt. **{–572–}** Barrow throughout the employment did not include any seagoing activity; he was hired for one day to paint the vessel at dockside and he was not going to sail with the vessel after he finished painting it."[49]

Papai contended that the entire group of vessels he worked on through the union hiring hall constituted an identifiable group of vessels and his connection to this "fleet" should be considered.[50] The Supreme Court rejected such a broad definition of "fleet." The Court stated: "In deciding whether there is an identifiable group of vessels of relevance for a Jones Act seaman-status determination, the question is whether the vessels are subject to common ownership or control."[51]

Papai then also argued that he qualified as a seaman if his jobs over the past two and a half months working on Harbor Tug's vessels were considered.[52] The Court answered, **[—13—]**

---

[38] *Id.* at 362. For example, Mississippi River pilots who do nothing but pilot ocean-going vessels through dangerous sections of the river are not seaman because the ships have no common ownership or control. *See Bach v. Trident S.S. Co., Inc.*, 947 F.3d 1290 (5th Cir. 1991).

[39] *Chandris*, 515 U.S. at 368.

[40] *Id.* at 370 (quoting *Wallace v. Oceaneering Int'l*, 727 F.2d 427, 432 (5th Cir. 1984)).

[41] *Id.* at 371.

[42] *Id.* at 374–75.

[43] 520 U.S. 548 (1997).

[44] *Id.* at 551.

[45] *Id.*

[46] *Id.* at 559.

[47] *Id.* at 555.

[48] *Id.*

[49] *Id.* at 559.

[50] *Id.* at 555.

[51] *Id.* at 557.

[52] *Id.* at 559.

Papai testified at his deposition that he worked aboard the Pt. Barrow on three or four occasions before the day he was injured, the most recent of which was more than a week earlier. Each of these engagements involved only maintenance work while the tug was docked. The nature of Papai's connection to the Pt. Barrow was no more substantial for seaman-status purposes by virtue of these engagements than the one during which he was injured . . . . In any event these discrete engagements were separate from the one in question, which was the sort of "transitory or sporadic" connection to a vessel or a group of vessels that, as we had explained in *Chandris*, does not qualify one for seaman status.[53] **[—14—] {-573-}**

C. Fifth Circuit Precedent

As stated above, the panel concluded that based on two of our cases, *Endeavor Marine* and *Naquin*, it was bound to hold that Sanchez was entitled to proceed with his Jones Act suit as a seaman.[54] The panel in a unanimous concurring opinion, however, concluded that those two cases were probably not consistent with the Supreme Court cases discussed above, namely *Wilander*, *Chandris* and *Papai*, and urged this Court to take the case en banc so that we could reconsider our circuit law on this question.[55]

In *Naquin*, the plaintiff, a vessel repair supervisor, was injured in a shipyard while working on a fleet of lift boats.[56] The lift boats he worked on were either moored, jacked-up, or docked in the shipyard canal.[57] We rejected the argument that this work did not expose the plaintiff to the perils of the sea and permitted him to pursue his suit under the Jones Act.[58] Because all of Naquin's work was performed on or near the dock, and we erred in analyzing *Naquin* based solely on the "perils of the sea" test, we must overrule it.

In *Endeavor Marine*, the plaintiff, a crane operator, was assigned to work aboard a derrick barge on the Mississippi River that

---

53 *Id.* at 559–60. The Second Circuit applied the previous Supreme Court cases to determine whether a maritime worker had a substantial connection in terms of duration and nature to satisfy the test for seaman's status in *Matter of Buchanan Marine, L.P.*, 874 F.3d 356, 5 Adm. R. 100 (2d Cir. 2017). In that case, the plaintiff, Volk, worked at a quarried rock processing facility on the Hudson River, inspecting and maintaining barges used to transport rock down the river. *Id.* at 360, 5 Adm. R. at 100. Volk was injured when he slipped from the narrow deck of one of the barges and sustained injuries. *Id.*, 5 Adm. R. at 100. The Second Circuit concluded that as a matter of law, Volk did not qualify as a seaman under the Jones Act. *Id.* at 368, 5 Adm. R. at 106. The court held that Volk "did not derive his livelihood from sea-based activities" and "Volk never operated a barge and only worked aboard the barges when they were secured to the dock." *Id.* at 366, 5 Adm. R. at 105 (internal quotation marks and citation omitted).

The Ninth Circuit applied the same Supreme Court cases in *Cabral v. Healy Tibbits Builders, Inc.*, 128 F.3d 1289 (9th Cir. 1997) to determine whether a barge-crane operator had a substantial connection in terms of duration and nature in order to be a seaman. The plaintiff crane operator was working in a quiet harbor with limited movement of the crane barge. *Id.* at 1293. Notably, the plaintiff was assigned to the barge for a specific project, and no evidence was presented that he would continue to work on the barge after the project was completed. *Id.* The Ninth Circuit concluded that the crane operator was not a seaman because he was "a land-based crane operator who happened to be assigned to a project which required him to work aboard [a crane barge]." *Id.*

In *Delange v. Dutra Const. Co., Inc.*, 183 F.3d 916, 920 (9th Cir. 1999), the Ninth Circuit concluded that a reasonable juror could find that the plaintiff carpenter was a seaman. Although the plaintiff's job as a carpenter was a land-based trade, the facts in the record **[—14—]** indicated that carpentry comprised only ten percent of the plaintiff's work. *Id.* The rest of the plaintiff's work "involved crewman and deckhand duties" where he was a lookout, cargo stower, line handler, and occasional pilot on a construction barge that moved to various construction sites. *Id.* Thus, facts clearly indicated that the plaintiff was a sea-based worker who did not have a "transitory or sporadic" connection to the vessel.

54 *Sanchez*, 970 F.3d at 555, 8 Adm. R. at 224–25.

55 *Id.* at 555–56, 8 Adm. R. at 226–27.

56 744 F.3d 927, 931, 2 Adm. R. 200, 200 (5th Cir. 2014).

57 *Id.* at 930, 2 Adm. R. at 200.

58 *Id.* at 935, 2 Adm. R. at 203–04.

was usually moored to the dock, where he loaded and unloaded cargo and helped to maintain the **[—15—]** crane.[59] Sometimes, the barge was moved from its base wharf to other wharfs for loading and unloading ships. On at least one occasion during the 18 months he worked on the barge, the plaintiff rode the barge from one location to another to operate and perform maintenance on the crane.[60] On other occasions, he drove his automobile to the new location where the barge was moved.[61] We reversed the district court and held that because the plaintiff was exposed to the perils of the sea, he was a seaman.[62]

Based on the fact that (1) plaintiff was permanently assigned to and worked on the same barge during his entire employment, (2) the barge was moved on occasion to different wharfs on the Mississippi River and the plaintiff moved to whatever new location the vessel was moved to, we cannot say the *Endeavor Marine* panel erred in holding the plaintiff was a seaman. However, as we explain below, we do not endorse the panel's rationale.

The panels in *Endeavor Marine* and *Naquin* asked whether those plaintiffs were subject to the "perils of the sea" as the primary test of their satisfaction of the nature element.[63] While this is one of the considerations in the calculus, it is not the sole or even the primary test. **[—16—] {-574-}**

D. Distilling the Principles from the Supreme Court Trilogy

In *Chandris*, the Court made clear that seamen and non-seamen maritime workers may face similar risks and perils, and that this is not an adequate test for distinguishing between the two.[64] We therefore conclude that the following additional inquiries should be made:

> (1) Does the worker owe his allegiance to the vessel, rather than simply to a shoreside employer?[65]
>
> (2) Is the work sea-based or involve seagoing activity?
>
> (3)(a) Is the worker's assignment to a vessel limited to performance of a discrete task after which the worker's connection to the vessel ends, or (b) Does the worker's assignment include sailing with the vessel from port to port or location to location?

Simply asking whether the worker was subject to the "perils of the sea" is not enough to resolve the nature element. Consider the captain and crew of a ferry boat or of an inland tug working in a calm river or bay, or the drilling crew on a drilling barge working in a quiet canal. No one would question whether those workers are seamen. Yet, their risk from the perils of the sea is minimal. Considering the more definitive inquiries set forth above by the Supreme Court, we now examine whether Sanchez was a seaman under the Jones Act during his employment with SmartFab. **[—17—]**

IV. DISCUSSION

As indicated above, Sanchez worked on two vessels during his 67 days of employment with SmartFab that are relevant to his seaman status. He worked aboard the Enterprise WFD 350 for 48 of his 67 days and 13 days aboard the Enterprise 263. His entire time aboard these two vessels was spent doing

---

59 234 F.3d 287, 289 (5th Cir. 2000).

60 *In re Complaint of Endeavor Marine, Inc.*, No. CIV.A. 98-0779, 1999 WL 76586, at *4 (E.D. La. Feb. 11, 1999).

61 *Id.* at *1.

62 *Endeavor Marine*, 234 F.3d at 292.

63 Much of the scholarship addressing seaman status emphasizes that "perils of the sea" alone is a problematic test for making the land-based and sea-based distinction. *See, e.g.*, Matthew H. Frederick, Note, *Adrift in the Harbor: Ambiguous-Amphibious Controversies and Seamen's Access to Workers' Compensation Benefits*, 81 TEX. L. REV. 1671, 1704 (2003).

64 *See Chandris v. Latsis*, 515 U.S. 347, 361–62 (1991).

65 *See id.* at 359 (citing *McDermott Int'l, Inc. v. Wilander*, 498 U.S. 337, 347 (1991)) ("Congress established a clear distinction between land-based and sea-based maritime workers. The latter, who owe their allegiance to a vessel and not solely to a land-based employer, are seamen.").

discrete welding jobs as part of repairs to the two vessels. This work certainly contributed to the function of these two vessels because that work was necessary to keep the vessels in condition to drill for oil and gas. Thus, Sanchez satisfied the first prong of the seaman-status test.[66]

Sanchez spent approximately 90 percent of his total employment time with SmartFab aboard the two Enterprise vessels. He therefore satisfied the duration prong of the substantiality test. As the Court stated in *Chandris*, generally if a worker spends at least 30 percent of his time aboard a vessel or a fleet of vessels, then he establishes the duration prong. **{–575–}** The question narrows to determine whether Sanchez spent at least 30 percent of his time aboard these two vessels doing work that satisfies the nature prong of that test.

As to the work Sanchez did aboard the WFD 350, the Supreme Court's decision in *Papai* makes it clear that this work was not "sea-based" and therefore did not satisfy the nature test. All of Sanchez's work on that **[—18—]** vessel was performed while it was jacked-up with the barge deck level with the dock and a gangplank away from shore. Just as Papai's actual duties on the Pt. Barrow moored at the dock did not include any "seagoing activity," neither did Sanchez's work on the WFD 350. The *Papai* Court explicitly stated that "maintenance work while the tug was docked" did not satisfy the nature test.[67] The Court also found significant the fact that there was no reason to assume that any particular percentage of Papai's work would be of a "seagoing nature" subjecting him to the "perils of the sea."[68] The *Papai* Court also found significant that Papai's "actual duty on the Pt. Barrow throughout the employment in question did not include any seagoing activity; he was hired for one day to paint the vessel at dockside, and he was not going to sail with the vessel after he finished painting it."[69]

It is clear from the above Supreme Court cases, that Sanchez, like Papai, who was working on a vessel at the dock, was not engaged in "seagoing activity." His duties on the WFD 350 did not "take him to sea;" his work on the docked vessel was not "of a seagoing nature;" and after he finished his **[—19—]** work at the dock, "he was not going to sail with the vessel" after he finished his work.

With respect to Sanchez's work on the Enterprise 263, the record reveals that he reported to that vessel located in the Gulf of

[66] While Sanchez was working aboard the Enterprise WFD 350 and Enterprise 263, both vessels were "in navigation" as that term has been defined by the Supreme Court. *See Chandris*, 515 U.S. at 374 (noting that a vessel is "in navigation" even though "moored to a dock, if it remains in readiness for another voyage" and recognizing general rule that "vessels undergoing repairs or spending relatively short period of time in drydock are still considered to be 'in navigation'") (internal quotation marks and citations omitted); *see also Stewart v. Dutra Const. Co.*, 543 U.S. 481, 495 (2005) (noting that "in navigation" requirement is "relevant to whether the craft is 'used, or capable of being used' for maritime transportation"); 1 Robert Force & Martin J. Norris, *The Law of Seamen* § 2:18 Westlaw (database updated Nov. 2020); 1B *Benedict on Admiralty* § 11b (2020).

[67] *Harbor Tug and Barge Co. v. Papai*, 520 U.S. 548, 559 (1997).

[68] *Id.* at 560.

[69] *Id.* at 559. Sanchez argued that *Southwest Marine, Inc. v. Gizoni*, 502 U.S. 81 (1991) supports his view that as a ship repairman, he should be considered a seaman. We disagree. The Court granted review in that case to consider whether a ship repairman is ineligible for seaman status because "ship repairmen" is one of the enumerated occupations under the term "employee" as defined in the LHWCA. The Court, without considering the merits of the plaintiff's claim to seaman status, stated: "While in some cases a ship repairman may lack the requisite connection to a vessel in navigation to qualify for seaman status, not all ship repairmen lack the requisite connection as a matter of law. This is so because '[i]t is not the employee's particular job that is determinative, but the employee's connection to a vessel." *Gizoni*, 502 U.S. at 492 (citations and footnote omitted). Therefore, Sanchez is clearly not barred from obtaining coverage under the Jones Act as a seaman simply because he was a ship repairer. If he could establish the requisite connection to the Enterprise fleet, he would be entitled to that protection. We hold he is not entitled to that protection because he failed to establish that required connection.

Mexico on the OCS in July 2018, as part of a SmartFab crew engaged to make discrete repairs on the vessel for a specific reason: to satisfy requirements of the ABS, BSEE, and Coast Guard, so that the rig could begin drilling at a new location on the OCS. It is undisputed that Sanchez worked for 13 days on the Enterprise 263 and that he was injured when he fell on the deck of the rig on August 8, 2018. After his injury, Sanchez was sent ashore for medical assistance.

The remainder of the SmartFab crew worked until August 10 or 11, 2018, when the repairs SmartFab agreed to perform were completed. The vessel began drilling on August 11, 2018, as planned at the new **{–576–}** location.[70] No evidence was presented that Sanchez planned to remain after the SmartFab crew completed their job, and there is no suggestion of any reason he would plan to do that.

Sanchez worked on the Enterprise 263 only 13 days, which would amount to less than 20 percent of his total time of his employment with SmartFab – well short of the 30 percent required for satisfaction of the duration prong of the substantiality test. Sanchez's work on the Enterprise 263, even though it was located on the OCS, was work performed on a discrete, individual job. When he and the SmartFab crew were finished, Sanchez would have no further connection to the vessel. **[—20—]**

Our case law reveals generally that two types of workers are found on drilling rigs. First, we have the drilling crew, who conduct the drilling operations (and workers who support that activity) and stay with the vessel when it moves from one drilling location to another.[71] These workers are the members of the crew of the vessel and are seamen. The second group are specialized transient workers, usually employed by contractors. These workers are engaged to do specific discrete short-term jobs.[72] Discrete transient jobs are like the work done by longshoremen when a vessel calls in port. As stated in *Papai*, these workers have only a "transitory or sporadic" connection to a vessel or group of vessels and do not qualify for seaman status.[73] Sanchez, as a transitory worker, falls into the second group, and thus does not satisfy the nature test. **[—21—]**

V. CONCLUSION

We conclude that Sanchez failed to create a genuine issue of material fact that he had a substantial connection to the Enterprise fleet of vessels as it related to the nature of his work. We therefore agree with the district court that Sanchez failed to meet the requirements for seaman status, and we AFFIRM the judgment of the district court.

---

[70] As previously noted, Counsel for Sanchez confirmed during oral argument that the SmartFab work was completed on August 10 and drilling began on August 11, 2018.

[71] *See Offshore Co. v. Robison*, 266 F.2d 769, 771–72 (5th Cir. 1959) (holding that an oilfield worker was a member of the crew that remained aboard the rig when it was moved to different well locations was a seaman); *Rogers v. Gracey-Hellums Corp.*, 331 F. Supp. 1287, 1288 (E.D. La. 1970), *aff'd*, 442 F.2d 1196 (finding that a roughneck permanently attached to a barge was a member of the crew); *Producers Drilling Co. v. Gray*, 361 F.2d 432, 436–37 (5th Cir. 1966) (finding that a roustabout who maintained a barge and its equipment as well as helped drill a well was a seaman).

[72] *See, e.g., Lirette v. N.L. Sperry Sun, Inc.*, 831 F.2d 554, 557 (5th Cir. 1987) (holding that a wireline worker was a "transitory maritime worker" and not a seaman). Lirette was a landbased wireline operator who performed "one specialized job for many different vessels." *Id.* We stated: "His duties closely resembled those of a transitory maritime worker. As we stated in *Barrett*, the distinction between seamen and transitory workers may not be blurred." *Id. See also Roberts v. Cardinal Serv., Inc.*, 266 F.3d 368, 378 (5th Cir. 2001) (discussing that a plugging and abandonment worker injured by a perforation gun attached to a wireline was not a seaman); *Ardleigh v. Schlumberger Ltd.*, 832 F.2d 933, 934 (5th Cir. 1987) ("[I]tinerant wireline workers are not Jones Act seamen."); *Wilcox v. Wild Well Control, Inc.*, 794 F.3d 531, 538–39, 3 Adm. R. 394, 397–98 (5th Cir. 2015) (holding that a welder was not a seaman because he was only assigned for one specific project which had a clear two month end date). *See also* 1B *Benedict on Admiralty* § 11e (2020) (collecting cases in Table 4).

[73] *Papai*, 520 U.S. at 559–60.

(Reporter's Note: Concurring Opinion follows on p. 208).

[—22—] {-576-} DENNIS, Circuit Judge, concurring: {-577-}

I concur in the majority opinion because it decides the present case consistently with the Supreme Court's decisions in *McDermott International, Inc. v. Wilander*, 498 U.S. 337 (1991), *Chandris, Inc. v. Latsis*, 515 U.S. 347 (1995), and *Harbor Tug and Barge Co. v. Papai*, 520 U.S. 548 (1997). I write to note that in future, perhaps more challenging, cases concerning contours of the Jones Act's coverage of maritime workers, I would look, in addition to the majority's authorities and reasoning, to the enduring writings of the late Professor David W. Robertson, a leading scholar and practitioner of maritime law.[1] As the majority endeavors to do here, in his article, *The Supreme Court's Approach to Determining Seaman Status: Discerning the Law Amid Loose Language and Catchphrases*, Prof. Robertson "provides a template for translating the U. S. Supreme Court's controlling seaman status cases" under the Jones Act. 34 J. MAR. L. & COM. 547, 548 (2003). This article remains, in my view, a pinnacle of scholarship synthesizing the Court's jurisprudence on the seaman status issue and serves as a useful guide for future cases.

---

[1] In addition to benefitting over the years from Prof. Robertson's outstanding body of scholarship on maritime and tort law, I also consider myself fortunate to have counted Prof. Robertson as a friend dating back to our service together on the LOUISIANA LAW REVIEW. I was indeed lucky to have David serve as my first student editor.

United States Court of Appeals
for the Fifth Circuit

No. 19-60610

OWENSBY & KRITIKOS, INC.
VS.
DIRECTOR, OFFICE OF WORKERS' COMPENSATION PROGRAMS

Petition for Review of an Order of the Benefits Review Board

Decided: May 14, 2021

Citation: 997 F.3d 587, 9 Adm. R. 209 (5th Cir. 2021).

Before **BARKSDALE, SOUTHWICK,** and **GRAVES,** Circuit Judges.

[—1—] {-589-} BARKSDALE, Circuit Judge: **{-590-}**

Primarily at issue, in the light of *Pacific Operators Offshore, LLP v. Valladolid*, 565 U.S. 207 (2012) (establishing substantial-nexus test), is **[—2—]** whether an onshore injury en route to a rig platform on the Outer Continental Shelf (OCS) is recoverable under the Longshore and Harbor Workers' Compensation Act (LHWCA), 33 U.S.C. § 901 *et seq.*, as extended by the Outer Continental Shelf Lands Act (OCSLA), 43 U.S.C. § 1331 *et seq.* When injured, James Boudreaux was employed by Owensby & Kritikos, Inc., as an equipment-testing technician on platforms located on the OCS. His injury resulted from an automobile accident on his way to his work for Owensby on the OCS. Boudreaux sought benefits under LHWCA, as extended by OCSLA; an administrative law judge (ALJ) ruled in his favor, and the Benefits Review Board (BRB) affirmed. Owensby's petition for review is DENIED; Boudreaux's cross-application is DISMISSED; and Boudreaux's request for attorney's fees is GRANTED.

I.

The facts are not in dispute. Boudreaux's work for Owensby as an Automated/Advanced Ultrasonic Testing (AUT) field supervisor required his operating a magnetic arm to scan storage tanks—primarily located on rig platforms on the OCS—in which extracted materials from drilling operations, including petrochemicals, were deposited. This work, both offshore and onshore, ensured continued, safe use of the tanks.

Boudreaux spent significant amounts of time offshore for the job—at one point he was on a rig for two-and-a-half months. During the year before the accident, Boudreaux worked 2,880 hours, 89% of which were offshore. While Boudreaux was onshore and proceeding to an OCS rig, Owensby paid him for mileage and driving time based upon the distance from Owensby's office in Broussard, Louisiana, to Boudreaux's pickup-point for offshore transportation. Owensby also paid for time Boudreaux spent on a helicopter or boat out to a platform. On the other hand, Boudreaux did not receive travel pay for a trip to his onshore office. **[—3—]**

On the day of the accident, Boudreaux left his home in Church Point, Louisiana, to drive to Freshwater City, Louisiana, for pickup for offshore transportation, stopping only for breakfast early that morning. As he normally did for travelling offshore, he had his inspection equipment in his vehicle. Near Freshwater City, another vehicle hit Boudreaux's, causing the accident. After the collision, an Owensby employee travelled to the accident site to retrieve Boudreaux's tank-testing equipment and transport it offshore.

Boudreaux sustained significant injury. His doctors, *inter alia*, prohibited his returning to offshore work. Owensby changed Boudreaux's job responsibilities **{-591-}** after he recovered; he now performs mostly office work and annually earns approximately $50,000 less than he did as an AUT.

Owensby paid Boudreaux various disability benefits from shortly after the accident until October 2016. Since then, it has paid him temporary total disability benefits and will do so until he reaches maximum medical improvement.

Because the parties could not resolve whether Boudreaux's claim for additional benefits falls under the jurisdiction of

LHWCA, as extended by OCSLA, or the Louisiana Workers' Compensation Act, the matter was referred to an ALJ. The ALJ determined: Boudreaux's injury occurred "in the course and scope" of his employment; and "the work he performed in testing the tanks . . . was directly related to outer continental shelf operations", based on the substantial-nexus test adopted by the Supreme Court in *Valladolid*.

Owensby appealed to the BRB, asserting: the ALJ improperly applied the *Valladolid* test because Boudreaux's injury was not *caused by* operations on the OCS; and, the ALJ applied a test rejected by the Court in *Valladolid*. The BRB rejected both assertions, concluding Boudreaux had satisfied **[—4—]** *Valladolid*'s substantial-nexus test, and his claim was covered by LHWCA, as extended by OCSLA.

After the BRB twice remanded to the ALJ to resolve lingering factual determinations, the ALJ determined Boudreaux was entitled to an award based on permanent total disability. Consequently, Owensby requested and received a summary affirmance from the BRB in order to petition our court for review.

II.

Owensby claims the BRB improperly applied the substantial-nexus test in holding Boudreaux's injury compensable under LHWCA, as extended by OCSLA. Boudreaux seeks, *inter alia*, attorney's fees under LHWCA, 33 U.S.C. § 928.

A.

When no factual dispute exists, as in this instance, coverage of an injury under LHWCA, as extended by OCSLA, is "a pure question of law" reviewed *de novo*. *Wood Grp. Prod. Servs. v. Dir., Off. of Workers' Comp. Programs*, 930 F.3d 733, 736–37, 7 Adm. R. 287, 288 (5th Cir. 2019) (citation omitted). In conducting our review, however, our court "afford[s] deference to interpretations of the LHWCA [as extended by OCSLA] by the Director of the Office of Workers' Compensation Programs". *Baker v. Dir., Off. of Workers' Comp. Programs*, 834 F.3d 542, 545, 4 Adm. R. 276, 277 (5th Cir. 2016) (first alteration in original) (quotation marks and citation omitted).

The two statutes under review—LHWCA and OCSLA—provide, in relevant part: "The term 'injury' means accidental injury or death arising out of and in the course of employment", 33 U.S.C. § 902(2) (LHWCA); and, "[w]ith respect to disability . . . of an employee resulting from any injury occurring as the result of operations conducted on the outer Continental **[—5—]** Shelf for the purpose of . . . removing . . . the natural resources . . . of the outer Continental Shelf, compensation shall be payable under . . . [LHWCA]". 43 U.S.C. § 1333(b) (OCSLA).

In determining whether an injury is covered under LHWCA, as extended by OCSLA, we apply the two-part test adopted in *Valladolid*. 565 U.S. at 222. As quoted above, OCSLA generally extends coverage under LHWCA to injuries occurring as the result of OCS operations. 43 U.S.C. § 1333(b); *see Valladolid*, 565 U.S. at 212 ("Section 1333(b) . . . makes LHWCA workers' **{-592-}** compensation benefits available for the 'disability or death of an employee resulting from any injury occurring as the result of operations conducted on the outer Continental Shelf' for the purpose of extracting its natural resources."). By extending LHWCA, any covered injury under OCSLA must first satisfy the limitations imposed by LHWCA.

This leaves us with two steps in our analysis to determine whether Boudreaux sustained a covered injury: first, did the injury arise out of, and occur within the scope of, his employment, under LHWCA's relevant provision, 33 U.S.C. § 902(2); and, second, was the injury sustained as the result of operations conducted on the OCS, under OCSLA's relevant provision, 43 U.S.C. § 1333(b)?

The ALJ's analysis followed this framework, primarily relying upon *Valladolid* and applying the substantial-nexus test to the facts at hand. The ALJ determined: Boudreaux's injury arose out of, and occurred in the course of, his employment by Owensby; and, Boudreaux's injury had a substantial nexus to extractive operations on the OCS. Along these lines, the BRB affirmed the ALJ's order because of "the broad discretion afforded . . . in applying the substantial nexus test" and the ALJ's fidelity in doing so. **[—6—]**

1.

As for the first part of the test, and as discussed *supra*, Boudreaux's job required him to spend most of his time offshore; at one point he was on a rig for two-and-a-half months straight, and he worked offshore 89 percent of the year prior to the accident. Additionally, and as also discussed *supra*, Boudreaux was compensated for his travel to and from the OCS—including the portion of his journey onshore—based on the distance from Owensby's office to Boudreaux's job site. The parties, including the Director, agree: Boudreaux was acting within the course and scope of his employment. *See* 33 U.S.C. § 902(2). (Employees travelling to-and-from work are generally not within the course and scope of their employment under LHWCA, *see Cardillo v. Liberty Mut. Ins. Co.*, 330 U.S. 469, 479 (1942), but the trip-payment exception recognizes employees *are* within the course and scope when their employer, *inter alia*, pays for the employee's transportation. *Id.* at 479–80 (discussing coming-and-going rule and exceptions under LHWCA as applied through the District of Columbia Workmen's Compensation Act); *see also Foster v. Massey*, 407 F.2d 343, 345–46 (D.C. Cir. 1968) (describing trip-payment exception).)

2.

Owensby's dispute is with application of the second part of the test. It urges rejecting the BRB's ruling because it claims the BRB applied a "but-for" test rejected by the Supreme Court. *See Valladolid*, 565 U.S. at 221 ("The . . . 'but-for' test . . . is also incompatible with § 1333(b)."). This rejected test was derived from a case with facts similar to those at hand. *See Curtis v. Schlumberger Offshore Serv. Inc.*, 849 F.2d 805, 806 (3rd Cir. 1988). In so doing, Owensby contends: the appropriate test instead requires claimant to "establish [a] substantial nexus . . . between the work performed by [his] employer on the OCS and the accident". **[—7—]**

The Director, however, urges our considering as instructive the ninth circuit's opinion in *Valladolid v. Pacific Operators Offshore, LLP*, 604 F.3d 1126 (9th Cir. 2010), *aff'd* 565 U.S. 207 (2012), which stated an "injury in a helicopter en route to the [OCS] likely would be" covered by LHWCA, as extended by OCSLA, *id.* at 1139. With the **{-593-}** benefit of both the Supreme Court and earlier-related ninth circuit *Valladolid* opinions, the Director contends *Curtis*' but-for test was rejected because it would bring accountants into the scope of LHWCA and OCSLA coverage, not because its facts are incongruous with a holding satisfying the substantial-nexus test. *See Valladolid*, 565 U.S. at 221 ("[T]he 'but for' test would extend workers' compensation coverage to all employees of a business engaged in the extraction of natural resources from the OCS, no matter where those employees work or what they are doing when they are injured.").

Although the Supreme Court's *Valladolid* opinion overruled *Curtis*' "but-for" test, it did not bar holding covered an injury resulting from an onshore accident while an employee was traveling onshore to go offshore. *See id.* (rejecting "but-for" test because the test's scope is over-inclusive, but making no mention of factual delineations). On the contrary, *Valladolid* rejects a factual-line-drawing approach and only decides the legal test to be applied by "ALJs and courts . . . to determine whether an injured employee has established a significant causal link between the injury he suffered and his employer's on-OCS extractive operations" based on "the individual circumstances of each case". *Id.* at 222.

Additionally, the Court rejected the situs-of-injury test, which undoubtedly utilized factual-line-drawing based on the exact location of the injury sustained to determine coverage, *vel non*. *Id.* at 222 (rejecting situs-of-injury test because it was unsupported by the text of § 1333(b)). Taken together, the Court avoided declaring which factual scenarios would be covered by the substantial-nexus test. **[—8—]**

Owensby's urging that our holding claimants are required to establish a substantial nexus between their employer's work performed on the OCS and the accident misreads the text of the two statutes by blurring the requirements of LHWCA's § 902(2) with those of OCSLA's § 1333(b). Owensby's interpretation reads § 902(2)'s course-and-scope requirement into the operating-on-the-OCS requirement of § 1333(b). Essentially, Owensby sees OCSLA as making compensable "any injury occurring as the result of, and in the course and scope of, operations conducted on the outer Continental Shelf". OCSLA does not include that limitation.

To show he sustained an injury "as the result of operations" on the OCS, claimant must establish a substantial nexus between the injury and extractive operations. 43 U.S.C. § 1333(b); *Valladolid*, 565 U.S. at 222. Section 1333(b) says nothing about the scope of the employee's job or his employer. *Valladolid* makes clear the only question § 1333(b) asks is whether the injury occurred as the result of OCS operations.

Our court last considered *Valladolid* in *Mays v. Chevron Pipe Line Co.*, 968 F.3d 442, 8 Adm. R. 213 (5th Cir. 2020). Pursuant to *Mays*, we look only to whether there is a "substantial nexus between the injury and extractive operations on the shelf" to determine whether an injury qualifies under OCSLA. *Id.* at 448, 8 Adm. R. at 216 (quoting *Valladolid*, 565 U.S. at 211). The substantial-nexus test "requires a link *only* between the employee's 'injury' and extractive 'operations conducted on the [OCS]'". *Id.* at 449, 8 Adm. R. at 217 (quoting 43 U.S.C. § 1333(b)) (emphasis added).

Mays' statutory analysis frequently emphasizes OCSLA's lack of limiting language. *E.g., id.* at 449, 8 Adm. R. at 217. Given the lack of limiting language, claims to narrow **{–594–}** the statute fail for lack of textual support. *Id.*, 8 Adm. R. at 217. Along those lines, and, as the Court in *Valladolid* implied, OCSLA does not preclude recovery for an injury suffered en route to the OCS. *See* 565 U.S. at 219–20 (declining **[—9—]** to preclude recovery under specific facts by rejecting situs-of-injury test). Again, answering whether an injury is covered "will depend on the individual circumstances of each case". *Id.* at 222.

Applying the two-part framework to the facts before us, we hold Boudreaux's injury is covered under OCSLA. Among the facts relevant to our inquiry, we find persuasive Boudreaux's: being compensated by Owensby for both time and onshore mileage while traveling to and from the OCS; being on-the-job when he was injured; necessarily traveling to an intermediary pickup location to be transported from onshore to the OCS; and transporting his testing equipment in his vehicle. *Cf. Baker*, 834 F.3d at 548–49, 4 Adm. R. at 280 (holding employee is not covered because, *inter alia*, his "particular job . . . did not require him to travel to the OCS *at all*") (emphasis in original). And, as noted, Owensby had another employee pick up Boudreaux's testing equipment to take it to the OCS after his accident. Each of these factors supports Boudreaux's injury occurring as the result of operations conducted on the OCS.

B.

Boudreaux seeks: enforcement of the BRB's order granting him relief; and attorney's fees. We first address enforcement, *vel non*.

1.

Prior to submitting his brief in our court, Boudreaux filed, pursuant to Federal Rule of Appellate Procedure 15(b)(1), a cross-application to enforce the BRB order granting him relief. In oral argument, however, Boudreaux's counsel advised this relief is unnecessary if Owensby's petition is denied and Boudreaux receives his awarded compensation.

In any event, we lack jurisdiction to consider the cross-application. *See* 33 U.S.C. § 921(d) (conferring jurisdiction to enforce a cross-application **[—10—]** on "the Federal district court"). Accordingly, the cross-application is dismissed.

2.

Boudreaux requests attorney's fees under 33 U.S.C. § 928 for defending against Owensby's petition. LHWCA provides attorney's fees under certain circumstances for each stage of the proceedings to a successful claimant in a litigated case. § 928; *see FMC Corp. v. Perez*, 128 F.3d 908, 909–10 (5th Cir. 1997) (holding attorney's fees allowable under § 928(b) when "the dispute has been the subject of an informal conference", the parties disagree as to the compensation due under LHWCA, the case is litigated, and the claimant wins).

Given our holding for Boudreaux, Owensby is ordered, pursuant to § 928(b), to pay Boudreaux's attorney's fees for defending against the petition at hand. Owensby does not contest such an award. Accordingly, Boudreaux shall submit his fee-request, Owensby its response, and Boudreaux his reply. We will then determine the fee award.

III.

For the foregoing reasons, Owensby's petition for review is DENIED; Boudreaux's cross-application is DISMISSED; and his request for reasonable attorney's fees incurred in defending against the petition **{-595-}** is GRANTED, pending our deciding the amount to be awarded.

United States Court of Appeals
for the Fifth Circuit

No. 20-30240

MILLER
VS.
RELIANCE STANDARD LIFE INS. CO.

Appeal from the United States District Court for the Eastern District of Louisiana

Decided: June 2, 2021

Citation: 999 F.3d 280, 9 Adm. R. 214 (5th Cir. 2021).

Before **HAYNES, DUNCAN,** and **ENGELHARDT,** Circuit Judges.

[—1—] {-281-} DUNCAN, Circuit Judge:

Michael Miller sued Reliance Standard Life Insurance Company for denying his long-term disability claim under a plan Reliance insures. The district court granted summary judgment to Reliance. It concluded that Miller's absence on medical leave at the time Reliance took over his group policy created a gap in Miller's coverage and rendered his complained-of disability an excluded preexisting condition. Because the district court misread the policy, we reverse and render judgment for Miller and remand for determining the amount of Miller's benefits. **[—2—]**

I.

Miller is a ship pilot who has worked since 1989 for Lake Charles Pilots, Inc. ("LCP"), navigating ships in the Calcasieu Ship Channel connecting the Port of Lake Charles, Louisiana, to the Gulf of Mexico. Reliance insures LCP's group disability plan. The parties do not dispute the facts underlying Miller's claim, only the plan's application to those facts.

Prior to the claim disputed here, Miller had an extensive history of health problems, injuries, medical procedures, and disability leave. Crucially, he was out on short-term disability leave—and had been for almost two months—on September 1, 2015, when Reliance took over LCP's insurance **{-282-}** plan from another insurer, Prudential. On October 23, Miller was cleared to return to work and was scheduled to work on November 4, but he suffered a fall that evening and reinjured himself. Reliance approved a claim for short-term disability benefits for this injury, which it now claims was a mistake.[1]

Miller briefly returned to work in July and August 2016 but stopped again on August 10 after nearly falling off a Jacob's ladder while boarding a ship. After that incident, believing that ailments in his wrist and knee would sideline him for some time, Miller applied to Reliance for short-term disability benefits. Reliance approved his claim, and when these benefits were exhausted, Miller, still unable to work, applied for long-term benefits.

Reliance denied this claim. It determined that Miller's coverage took effect only on the first of the month after he returned to active work: August 1, 2016. Because his date of reported disability was therefore within a year of the start of Miller's coverage, and because he had received medical treatment **[—3—]** for the same issues in the three months prior to the effective date, Reliance found the disability was an excluded preexisting condition.

Miller appealed Reliance's decision. He argued, *inter alia,* that Reliance was required to credit him, for purposes of the preexisting conditions limitation, for his time insured through LCP's plan by Prudential. Pointing to the Reliance policy's Transfer of Insurance Coverage Provision ("Transfer Provision"), he argued that he fulfilled all the policy's criteria for coverage from September 1, 2015, continuous with his coverage under the Prudential plan. That meant, Miller argued, that his many years on that plan should count toward satisfying the preexisting conditions limitation and, in his case, wipe it out entirely.

[1] Miller had filed claims for this injury with both Prudential and Reliance. Prudential denied his claim because it was distinct from the previous injuries he had suffered during the term of Prudential's coverage.

After Reliance failed to render a timely decision on his appeal, Miller sued in federal district court for benefits under the Employee Retirement Income Security Act ("ERISA"), 29 U.S.C. § 1132(a)(1)(B). The parties filed cross motions for summary judgment, and the district court ruled for Reliance. The court found that Miller's coverage with Reliance became effective only on August 1, 2016, when he returned to active work after Reliance's policy had taken effect. It then rejected Miller's argument that, because the policy's Transfer Provision credited him for his time insured through LCP's plan with Prudential, this would prevent the Reliance policy's preexisting condition limitation from barring his claim. The court did not apply the Transfer Provision to Miller because it found he could not fulfill two of its requirements: payment of premiums and being "Actively at Work" on the policy's original effective date (September 1, 2015). Having thus concluded that the policy's preexisting conditions limitation applied to Miller, the court found the limitation excluded his claimed disabilities, due to recent treatments he received for them. The district court therefore granted Reliance summary judgment. Miller appealed. **[—4—]**

II.

"Standard summary judgment rules control in ERISA cases." *Green v. Life Ins. Co. of N. Am.*, 754 F.3d 324, 329, 2 Adm. R. 245, 247 (5th Cir. 2014) (citation omitted). We review a summary judgment *de novo*. *In re La. Crawfish Producers*, 852 F.3d 456, 462, 5 Adm. R. 226, 228 (5th Cir. 2017). "The court shall grant **{-283-}** summary judgment if the movant shows that there is no genuine dispute as to any material fact and the movant is entitled to judgment as a matter of law." FED. R. CIV. P. 56(a). "When parties file cross-motions for summary judgment, we review each party's motion independently, viewing the evidence and inferences in the light most favorable to the nonmoving party." *Green*, 754 F.3d at 329, 2 Adm. R. at 247 (citation omitted).

We also review *de novo* a nondiscretionary denial of benefits challenged under ERISA, regardless of whether the denial is based on factual determinations or interpretation of the plan's language. *See generally Firestone Tire & Rubber Co. v. Bruch*, 489 U.S. 101, 115 (1989); *Ariana M. v. Humana Health Plan of Texas, Inc.*, 884 F.3d 246 (5th Cir. 2018) (en banc). In this case, Reliance's decision is subject to *de novo* review, as the district court determined.[2]

III.

Whether Miller was entitled to disability benefits depends on the meaning of the plan's Transfer Provision, which determines whether employees covered under the group's previous plan with Prudential remained continuously insured when Reliance's policy took effect. If this **[—5—]** provision applies to Miller, it makes his coverage effective on September 1 and exempts him from the policy's limitation on preexisting conditions, which Reliance invoked to deny his claim.

A.

"When construing ERISA plan provisions, courts are to give the language of an insurance contract its ordinary and generally accepted meaning if such a meaning exists." *Green*, 754 F.3d at 331, 2 Adm. R. at 248 (citation omitted). We apply the rule of *contra proferentem* to ambiguous terms—construing them strictly in favor of the insured—but "[o]nly if the plan terms remain ambiguous after applying ordinary principles of contract interpretation." *Ramirez v. United of Omaha Life Ins. Co.*, 872 F.3d 721, 725 (5th Cir. 2017); *see also Todd v. AIG Life Ins. Co.*, 47 F.3d 1448, 1451–52 (5th Cir. 1995).

The Transfer Provision reads in full, with the disputed sections emphasized:

[2] Although Reliance suggests an arbitrary-and-capricious standard may have been correct, *see Corry v. Liberty Life Assurance Co. of Boston*, 499 F.3d 389, 397 (5th Cir. 2007), it does not contest on appeal the district court's determination that *de novo* review applies. It also points to no language in the policy conferring discretion to award benefits.

TRANSFER OF INSURANCE COVERAGE

> If an employee was covered under any group long term disability insurance plan maintained by you prior to this Policy's Effective Date, that employee will be insured under this Policy, provided that he/she is Actively At Work and meets all of the requirements for being an Eligible Person under this Policy on its Effective Date.
>
> If an employee was covered under the prior group long term disability insurance plan maintained by you prior to this Policy's Effective Date, *but was not Actively at Work due to Injury or Sickness on the Effective Date of this Policy and would otherwise qualify as an Eligible Person,* coverage will be allowed under the following conditions:
>
> (1) The employee must have been insured with the prior carrier on the date of the transfer; and
>
> (2) *Premiums must be paid*; and **[—6—]**
>
> (3) Total Disability must begin on or after this Policy's Effective Date. **{-284-}**

The district court concluded the provision did not apply to Miller for two reasons. First, the court found Miller had not shown that his premium had been paid on the policy's effective date, as the Transfer Provision requires. Second, the court found Miller could not show he was an Eligible Person on the policy's effective date. On appeal, though, Reliance concedes the record shows that Miller's premiums were paid.[3] We therefore focus on whether the language of the Transfer Provision's second paragraph covers Miller. Concluding that it does, we resolve the appeal on that basis.

B.

The relevant Transfer Provision language allows coverage of an employee insured under the previous plan who was "not Actively at Work due to Injury or Sickness on the Effective Date of this Policy and would otherwise qualify as an Eligible Person." The parties agree that Miller was "not Actively at Work" when Reliance's policy took effect but dispute whether he "would otherwise qualify as an Eligible Person."

The term "Eligible Person" begins a string of cross-referenced definitions, provisions, and undefined terms within the policy. "Eligible Person" is defined as "a person who meets the Eligibility Requirements of this Policy." The policy defines its "Eligibility Requirements" as being "a member of an Eligible Class, as shown on the Schedule of Benefits page." **[—7—]** That page, in turn, lists only the following Eligible Class: "Each *active, Full-time Employee*, except any person employed on a temporary or seasonal basis" (emphasis added). That definition contains one more defined term: "Full-time" means "working . . . for a minimum of 30 hours during a person's regular work week." Notably, "active" is not a defined term. On the other hand, the policy does define "Actively at Work," as used in the Transfer Provision, to mean "actually performing on a Full-time basis the material duties pertaining to his/her job," with allowance for "approved time off such as vacation, jury duty and funeral leave, but . . . not . . . time off as a result of an Injury or Sickness."[4]

Stitching these provisions together, Miller must show that he was an "active" employee in every respect other than actually performing his duties as of the policy's

[3] Invoices in the supplemental administrative record show Miller on a list of employees and their premiums as of September 1, 2015, along with a record of payment for all premiums. Reliance argued to the district court, but no longer maintains on appeal, that this list is from October *2016*, not 2015. The discrepancy seems to be a matter of low-quality photocopies, but the invoices in the record appear on close inspection to be from September and October 2015, not 2016. Reliance's preliminary claim notes also indicate premiums were paid.

[4] "Injury" and "Sickness" both refer to conditions resulting in "Total Disability," *i.e.* a condition eligible for long-term disability benefits.

effective date. He must also show that he was a "Full-time" employee, working at least thirty hours during his "regular work week." The parties dispute exactly what this requires, especially with respect to the terms "active" and (to a lesser extent) "regular work week." In Miller's view, the policy only requires him to be a current employee of LCP, as opposed to retired, and full-time as opposed to a merely seasonal or part-time hire. Reliance, however, argues that to be an "active" employee, Miller would have to be actually working, and to be "full-time," he would have to have an actual "regular work week" around the transfer date. **{-285-}**

The Sixth Circuit recently interpreted this same language—also in a Reliance policy—in the insured's favor. *See Wallace v. Oakwood Healthcare, Inc.*, 954 F.3d 879 (6th Cir. 2020). Reading an identical Transfer Provision, the court held that "active," as used in the policy, was ambiguous. "'Active' **[—8—]** could mean that a party is able and available to work, but not present on that day. . . . 'Active' could also mean non-retired." *Id.* at 893–94. The court noted that "non-retired" was a plausible reading especially because plans under ERISA often cover a policyholder "both during the years of the employee's active service and in his or her retirement years." *Id.* at 894 (quoting *Boggs v. Boggs*, 520 U.S. 833, 839 (1997)). The court also found the definition of "Full-time" and its reference to a "regular work week" ambiguous: "This provision could be reasonably interpreted to mean that a person must currently work thirty hours a week, but it could also be reasonably interpreted to mean that a person's job description requires that person to work thirty hours a week." *Ibid.*[5] Faced with competing reasonable interpretations, the court therefore held that both terms must be interpreted in favor of the insured according to the rule of *contra proferentem. Ibid.* Noting the "nearly identical" facts in his case and *Wallace*, Miller urges the same result here.

We agree with the Sixth Circuit that, in the context of the Transfer Provision, the phrase "active, full-time" employees must be construed in the insured's favor to include those who, on the relevant date, are current employees even if not actually working. We also agree that the term "regular work week" must be construed to refer to an employee's job description, or to his typical workload when on duty. To hold otherwise, as Reliance urges, would render the second paragraph of the Transfer Provision virtually **[—9—]** redundant with the first. On Reliance's reading, the paragraph would cover employees who actually maintain a full-time work schedule at the time of transfer. But this is barely different, if at all, from the previous paragraph's provision for employees who at the time are "Actively at Work," defined to mean "*actually performing* on a Full-time basis the material duties pertaining to his/her job" (emphasis added). Effectively, Reliance's reading is that the second paragraph covers employees who are not "actually performing" work duties but are "otherwise" actually working. We reject this convoluted construction as the unambiguous meaning of the provision.

C.

Reliance unpersuasively tries to distinguish *Wallace*. Mainly it argues *Wallace* does not help Miller because there the court did not make a finding on eligibility but remanded for additional fact-finding. But the Sixth Circuit listed the six points on which further factfinding was needed in that case, *see* 954 F.3d at 898, and no similar fact issues are disputed here. In particular, the record is clear, and Reliance does not dispute, that Miller worked full-time for LCP when healthy and on the job. That the Sixth Circuit did not

[5] *See also Carlile v. Reliance Standard Life Ins. Co.*, 988 F.3d 1217, 1224 (10th Cir. 2021) ("We . . . reject Reliance's argument that the dictionary definition of 'active' unambiguously means 'actually working.'"). *Carlile* concerned the same language in a Reliance plan as here. *Id.* at 1222. Although it considered how long existing coverage continued in light of an employee's impending termination, *id.* at 1219–20, 1223, its reading of "active" is still instructive on the issue of when coverage becomes effective. *Carlile* also rejected the argument that the plan's definition of "Full-time" required an employee to be working an hourly minimum at a particular, relevant time. *Id.* at 1226–27 & nn. 7–8.

have {-286-} enough facts to make an eligibility determination does not distinguish the legal question in *Wallace* from the one in this case.

Reliance also attempts to rebut *Wallace* with other sister-circuit cases, all of which differ from this case in crucial respects. In one, the plan defined "active, full-time employee" more strictly, as one "actively at work an average of 40 or more hours per week." *See Fendler v. CNA Grp. Life Assurance Co.*, 247 F. App'x 754, 759 (6th Cir. 2007). In another, the policy provided that for employees not "actively at work" on the date coverage became effective, insurance "will become effective on the date the employee returns to active work." *Turner v. SafeCo Life Ins. Co.*, 17 F.3d 141, 143 (6th Cir. 1994). Another is a one-page summary calendar opinion which does not [—10—] divulge its reasoning at all. *See Lewis v. Life Ins. Co. of N. Am.*, 578 F. App'x 176, 177 (4th Cir. 2014). Finally, a Tenth Circuit case cited by Reliance suggested—but did not in fact decide—that an "active" requirement in a plan's effective-date provisions would have excluded an employee who went on medical leave, if such a requirement had applied. *Bartlett v. Martin Marietta Operations Support, Inc. Life Ins. Plan*, 38 F.3d 514, 517–18 (10th Cir. 1994). But the plan in that case had no such requirement at the relevant time, so the court held the plan covered an employee on leave without having to consider whether an "active" requirement would have commanded a different outcome. *Id.* at 519.[6] None of these cases undermines our conclusion about the policy language before us.[7]

Finally, Reliance argues the Transfer Provision's second paragraph is narrow by design: it is meant to protect employees who are "regularly working but are out of work on the transfer date," not employees who are on a lengthy disability leave. We disagree. The first paragraph of the provision already includes just such an allowance for regularly working employees, so [—11—] there is no reason to adopt Reliance's cramped reading of the second paragraph. The policy defines "Actively at Work"—the key operative term in the first paragraph—to include not only employees who are physically present on a particular day, but also all those who are "actually performing on a Full-time basis [at least thirty hours per week] the material duties pertaining to his/her job." This definition reasonably includes an employee who is on a full-time schedule at the relevant time, even if not physically present on a specific day. Furthermore, it makes allowance for any "approved time off such as vacation, jury duty and funeral leave." Thus, the {-287-} first paragraph already covers most situations in which an employee might be "regularly working" but "out of work on the transfer date" on some short but ill-timed absence. We see no reason to read the second paragraph, as Reliance urges, to make it largely duplicative of the first. At the very least, the Transfer Provision does not require such a construction, and we therefore construe it in favor of the insured.

IV.

In sum, we hold that the Transfer Provision applies to Miller. The plan therefore covered Miller when it took effect on September 1, 2015, during his leave, and so

[6] The case also appears to have used "active" and "actively at work" interchangeably, *see id.* at 517–18, a construction the Transfer Provision here forecloses.

[7] Reliance also cites decisions by two district courts in this circuit, neither of which supports its narrow construction of the term "active." The first considered a policy under which only "full-time active employees" were eligible, but the *pro se* plaintiff had been terminated *before* suffering his alleged disability and failed to offer any evidence of his eligibility. *Ferguson v. Dynamic Indus., Inc.*, No. 2:10-CV-316, 2011 WL 1113545, at *1 (W.D. La. Mar. 24, 2011). In the second, the court did suggest that the absence of the word "active" from the policy's definition of eligible employees prevented the insurer from excluding an employee on disability leave. That might seem to help Reliance here, but the district court went on to indicate that even a policy with the term "active" would have been ambiguous. *Patton v. Jacobs Eng'g Grp.*, No. 3:05-CV-1282, 2009 WL 89699, at *4–6 (M.D. La. Jan. 13, 2009); *see also Campbell v. Unum Life Ins. Co.*, No. 2:03-CV-1445, 2004 WL 1497712, at *14 (E.D. La. July 2, 2004) (holding "that the 'active employment' provision in [a contested] Policy is ambiguous as a matter of law").

Reliance wrongly denied his disability claim. The district court erred by concluding otherwise.[8] We therefore REVERSE the district court's summary judgment for Reliance; RENDER judgment for Miller; and REMAND the case to the district court to determine the amount of benefits to award to Miller, consistent with this opinion.

---

[8] Because reversal is warranted on this basis alone, we do not address the other issues the parties dispute, including other injuries Miller raises as disabling.

United States Court of Appeals
for the Fifth Circuit

No. 20-30552

TAYLOR ENERGY CO., L.L.C.
VS.
COUVILLION GROUP, L.L.C.

Appeal from the United States District Court for the Eastern District of Louisiana

Decided: June 30, 2021

Citation: 3 F.4th 172, 9 Adm. R. 220 (5th Cir. 2021).

Before **SMITH, STEWART,** and **HO,** Circuit Judges.

[—2—] {–173–} STEWART, Circuit Judge:

Taylor Energy Company, L.L.C. ("Taylor") seeks reversal of the summary judgment for Couvillion Group, L.L.C. ("Couvillion"). We AFFIRM.

I. Factual and Procedural History

Taylor leased and operated oil wells and production platforms including a platform in the Mississippi Canyon Block 20 Area. The area is located approximately ten miles offshore from the Louisiana coast at the mouth of the Mississippi River. Through 2008, Taylor leased and operated the MC20 Platform, wells, and associated facilities.

In September 2004, Hurricane Ivan hit the Gulf Coast and caused a massive seafloor collapse, toppling the MC20 platform and jacket. The collapse buried the MC20 wells, and oil leaked across the ocean floor and surface for more than sixteen years ("the MC20 Incident").

Taylor responded to the MC20 Incident and notified the Coast Guard of the platform's fall. The Coast Guard designated Taylor as the "Responsible Party" under the Oil Pollution Act of 1990. Taylor was also added to the Unified Command group, which was established to respond to the MC20 Incident and monitor the MC20 Site.

After an oil spill, the Clean Water Act ("CWA") requires a federal official to be designated the "On-Scene Coordinator." 33 U.S.C. § 1321(d)(2)(K). If a spill "poses or may present a substantial threat to public health or welfare of the United States," the On-Scene Coordinator "shall direct all federal, state, or private actions to remove the discharge, as appropriate." 40 C.F.R. § 300.322(b). Captain Kristi Luttrell of the Coast Guard served as the On-Scene Coordinator for the MC20 Response.

After consulting with multiple government authorities and the Coast Guard, Taylor successfully drilled nine intervention wells to seal and reduce **[—3—]** the oil leak. For over a decade, Taylor and the Coast Guard worked together to respond to the MC20 Incident and monitor the remaining **{–174–}** wells. Taylor spent more than $480 million to address the MC20 Incident.

In October 2018, the Washington Post published an article about the MC20 Incident that negatively described Taylor and its remediation efforts. On October 23, 2018, the Coast Guard rescinded its previous administrative order with Taylor after determining that some wells were actively discharging and that hundreds of barrels were discharged each day. The Coast Guard issued a new administrative order that required Taylor to instate a containment system to capture, contain, and remove oil from the erosional pit near the former Dome C location. The new order warned that a failure to comply could lead to the Government's full or partial assumption of the remediation efforts.

In November 2018, Taylor submitted proposals pitching itself as a potential contractor to install the containment system. Captain Luttrell also solicited proposals from other contactors, including Couvillion. Captain Luttrell selected Couvillion over Taylor, citing Taylor's previous failed efforts at containment. When selecting Couvillion, Luttrell issued a Notice of Federal Assumption, which meant that the Coast Guard would work directly with Couvillion to install the containment system and Taylor would be on the hook for the bill.

Couvillion entered into a Basic Ordering Agreement with the Coast Guard. The agreement requires Couvillion to provide "[l]abor, [e]quipment, and materials to contain, cleanup, and/or mitigate the harmful effects of oil spills and hazardous substance incidents." The Coast Guard also issued Authorization to Proceed Letters from November 2019 through April 2019 that authorized Couvillion to "proceed with work as ordered by the Federal On-Scene Coordinator . . . ." The Statement of Work provides goals and **[—4—]** tasks for Couvillion to propose and accomplish with the approval of the On-Scene Coordinator.

Captain Luttrell issued several memoranda that describe the Government's oversight of Couvillion's work. She described the meetings where various Government officials received progress reports on Couvillion's progress. In particular, she assigned several personnel to oversee different parts of the project, and Coast Guard teams were available to consult and provide their expertise. Her documents and memoranda indicate where she approved and monitored Couvillion's progress.

Despite the evidence of Captain Luttrell's and the Coast Guard's involvement with Couvillion, Taylor argues that the Government did not actually exercise control over the project. According to Taylor, Couvillion's contract with the Coast Guard lacks details and gives Couvillion leeway in deciding how to run the capture and cleanup operation. Taylor concludes that the "barebones contract" and lack of oversight by the Coast Guard allowed Couvillion to charge more than $40 million for its services (despite Couvillion's proposal estimate that the work would cost no more than $3 million). Taylor filed a notice to vacate the Coast Guard's Administrative Order and all actions taken under it, including the Notice of Assumption and the agreement with Couvillion.

At issue in this appeal is Taylor's Declaratory Judgment Action against Couvillion.[1] No contractual relationship exists between Taylor and Couvillion, but Taylor seeks tort damages and equitable relief for Couvillion's trespass and "unauthorized activities **{-175-}** at the MC20 Site." **[—5—]** Couvillion moved to dismiss on several grounds, including lack of subject-matter jurisdiction because it is a government contractor. The court denied Couvillion's Motion to Dismiss and ordered limited discovery on the jurisdictional issue. After discovery, Couvillion moved for summary judgment on two grounds: (1) because it was entitled to immunity under *Yearsley v. W.A. Ross Construction Company*, 309 U.S. 18 (1940), and (2) because Taylor's claims were preempted. The district court granted Couvillion's motion for summary judgment, concluding that Couvillion was immune under *Yearsley*. This appeal follows.

II. Standard of Review

"We review a district court's grant of summary judgment de novo, applying the same standard as the district court." *Fairmont Cash Mgmt. L.L.C. v. James*, 858 F.3d 356, 360 (5th Cir. 2017). Summary judgment is warranted where "the movant shows that there is no genuine dispute as to any material fact and the movant is entitled to judgment as a matter of law." *Id.* (quoting Fed. R. Civ. P. 56(a)).

Yearsley immunity is an affirmative defense, and Couvillion bore the burden of proof on the defense at trial. Accordingly, Couvillion must have demonstrated that there were no material factual disputes about whether the Coast Guard authorized and directed Couvillion's work. *See Rizzo v. Children's World Learning Ctrs.*, 84 F.3d 758, 762 (5th Cir. 1996).

III. Discussion

The district court determined that Couvillion was entitled to *Yearsley* immunity and granted Couvillion's motion for summary judgment. In *Yearsley*, a group of plaintiffs sued a contractor after the contractor

[1] Taylor filed a separate suit (now consolidated with this appeal) against Captain Luttrell and the Coast Guard, arguing that the Administrative Orders violated the Administrative Procedure Act and its right to due process.

extended a river dike near the plaintiffs' land and hastened the land's erosion. 309 U.S. at 19–20. The contractor defended itself on the grounds that its work was authorized and directed by the Government of the United States. *Id.* at 20. **[—6—]** The Court agreed and held that where "it is clear that [] authority to carry out [a] project was validly conferred, that is, if what was done was within the constitutional power of Congress, there is no liability on the part of the contractor for executing its will." *Id.* at 20–21.

Yearsley immunity is "derivative sovereign immunity." *Campbell-Ewald Co. v. Gomez*, 577 U.S. 153, 160 (2016). Such immunity shields contractors whose work was "authorized and directed by the Government of the United States" and "performed pursuant to [an] Act of Congress." *Id.* at 167 (quoting *Yearsley*, 309 U.S. at 20).

In Taylor's view, Couvillion is not entitled to *Yearsley* immunity for two reasons: (1) because Couvillion's actions were not authorized and directed by the Government, and (2) because Couvillion exceeded the bounds of the Coast Guard's authority under federal law. Neither argument prevails.

A. Authorized and Directed

Taylor argues that there were material factual disputes about whether the Government authorized and directed Couvillion's work. Taylor points to the documents memorializing Couvillion's agreement with the Government and Couvillion's representative's deposition testimony, contending that the evidence demonstrates the Government's lack of control over Couvillion.

For actions to be authorized and directed by the Government, the contractor's actions should comply with federal **{–176–}** directives. *See Campbell-Ewald Co.*, 577 U.S. at 167 n.7.

The Government's directives to Couvillion are contained in three sets of documents—the Basic Ordering Agreement, Authorizations to Proceed, and the Statement of Work. Taylor argues that the documents lack specificity **[—7—]** and thus indicate that the Government neither authorized nor directed Couvillion's actions.

The Statement of Work refutes Taylor's argument. The Statement of Work describes the MC20 Incident, the MC20 Site, and the conditions surrounding the site like water depth and currents, condition of the seafloor, and the location of the fallen jackets. The Statement of Work says "[t]he purpose of this effort is [to] eliminate the surface sheen at Mississippi Canyon Block 20 (MC20)."

The Statement of Work details the expectations of Couvillion and its subcontractors. It lists nine tasks and eleven deliverables (to be completed at various checkpoints during the life of the agreement). Tasks included, *inter alia*, mobilizing to create an MC20 Containment Project Management Plan, developing and implementing a Rapid Response Solution containment design, and working with the Source Control Support Coordinator and Branch Director to begin a review of relevant site data. The corresponding deliverables required Couvillion and the subcontractors to deliver the MC20 Containment Project Management Plan, to present the Rapid Response Solution containment design, and to complete an assessment report of possible sub-surface control response options. All deliverables were due within a set number of days from mobilization.

Given the specific expectations and due dates outlined in the Statement of Work, we agree with the district court's conclusion that there was no material factual dispute about the Government's authorization of and direction over Couvillion's work.

Taylor also argues that Couvillion's representative's deposition raised a genuine factual dispute. The representative testified that Couvillion (rather than the Coast Guard) designed various components of Couvillion's containment system. **[—8—]**

Taylor misunderstands the *Yearsley* analysis. *Yearsley* did not focus on whether the Government designed the river dikes that led to the plaintiffs' injuries, but whether the contractor's work was "done pursuant to a contract with the United States Government, and under the direction of the Secretary of War and the supervision of the Chief of Engineers of the United States . . . ." 309 U.S. at 19. The appropriate inquiry is whether Couvillion adhered to the Government's instructions as described in the contract documents. *See In re KBR, Inc., Burn Pit Litig.*, 744 F.3d 326, 345 (4th Cir. 2014) ("[T]he contractor must adhere to the government's instructions to enjoy derivative sovereign immunity; staying within the thematic umbrella of the work that the government authorized is not enough to render the contractor's activities the act[s] of the government." (internal quotation marks omitted)).

There are no genuine factual disputes about Couvillion's adherence to the Government's directives. The Government directed Couvillion to come up with an MC20 site assessment procedure for the Rapid Response Solution containment project. The Government authorized Couvillion's plan, the design of the response system, and the installation of the system.

The representative's testimony supports this conclusion as well. He further testified that as designs and components changed throughout the life of the project, a Coast **{–177–}** Guard officer and other Government officials (referred to as the "acceptance team") approved various components of Couvillion's design. The Coast Guard routinely met with Couvillion, and Couvillion went to the Coast Guard for approval before taking the next steps in the project.

To the extent that Taylor argues that the Government could not have authorized and directed Couvillion because Couvillion failed to fully remove the oil sheen, we also disagree. The Statement of Work says that the "purpose of this effort is [to] eliminate the surface sheen at Mississippi Canyon Block 20 (MC20)." Couvillion's actions eliminated at least some of **[—9—]** the sheen, and this evidence does not create a genuine fact dispute as to whether the Government authorized and directed Couvillion's work.

B. Validly Conferred Authority from Congress

The second prong of *Yearsley* immunity requires a contractor's authority to be validly conferred by Congress. *See Yearsley*, 309 U.S. at 20– 21. ("[A]uthority to carry out the project was validly conferred . . . if what was done was within the constitutional power of Congress."). Thus, we ask whether the On-Scene Coordinator's delegation of work to Couvillion was valid. If not, then Couvillion's actions are not immunized under *Yearsley*. *See Cunningham v. Gen. Dynamics Info. Tech., Inc.*, 888 F.3d 640, 648 (4th Cir. 2018) (explaining, in a suit against a contractor under the Telephone Consumer Protection Act, that "[t]he question is not whether informing applicants of their enrollment eligibility violated the [TCPA], but rather whether Congress had the authority to assign [the contractor] to complete that task.").

Taylor argues that the On-Scene Coordinator did not have authority to hire Couvillion. Relevant here, 33 U.S.C. § 1321(c)(1)(B) permits the President to

> (i) remove or arrange for the removal of a discharge, and mitigate or prevent a substantial threat of a discharge, at any time;
> (ii) direct or monitor all Federal, State, and private actions to remove a discharge; and
> (iii) remove and, if necessary, destroy a vessel discharging, or threatening to discharge, by whatever means are available.

Further, 40 C.F.R. § 300.322(b) gives the On-Scene Coordinator similar abilities. Taylor maintains that Couvillion and the Coast Guard **[—10—]** exceeded the limits of federal law by trespassing on the MC20 jacket since neither the jacket nor the other MC20 components are "vessels."[2]

---

[2] A vessel refers to "every description of watercraft or other artificial contrivance used, or capable of being used, as a means of transportation on water; and, as defined by section 311(a)(3) of the CWA, means every description of watercraft or other artificial contrivance used, or capable of being

We disagree with Taylor's analysis of the relevant statutes. Section 300.322(b)(1) and (2) empower the On-Scene Coordinator to remove discharges and mitigate substantial threats of discharge.[3] When the Government contracted with Couvillion and Couvillion placed its containment system at the MC20 site, the site was either actively discharging or threatening to discharge. Couvillion's actions on behalf of the Government fit within the language of the relevant federal statutes. Thus, Couvillion's authority to **{–178–}** carry out its actions was validly conferred by Congress.

IV. CONCLUSION

For the aforementioned reasons, we AFFIRM the summary judgment.

---

used, as a means of transportation on water other than a public vessel." 40 C.F.R. § 300.5.

[3] Section 1321(c)(1)(B)(i) similarly empowers the President to remove discharges and mitigate substantial threats of discharge.

United States Court of Appeals for the Fifth Circuit

No. 20-30693

WHEELER
vs.
NORFOLK S. RY. CO.

Appeal from the United States District Court for the Eastern District of Louisiana

Decided: July 29, 2021

Citation: 6 F.4th 626, 9 Adm. R. 225 (5th Cir. 2021).

Before **SMITH** and **HO,** Circuit Judges, and **BARKER,** District Judge.*

* U.S. District Judge for the Eastern District of Texas, sitting by designation.

[—1—] {–628–} BARKER, District Judge:

James Wheeler was employed by Hulcher Services, Inc. while working at a New Orleans railyard. After he lost several fingers in an accident at the railyard, he sued the railyard's owner, Norfolk Southern Railway Company, **[—2—]** under a federal law that allows suit by railroad employees injured on the job. *See* Federal Employers' Liability Act (FELA), 45 U.S.C. § 51 *et seq.* That claim presented the question whether Wheeler was an employee of Norfolk. On summary judgment, the district court held that he was not, so he could not recover under FELA. Wheeler now appeals. Because he does not show that Norfolk controlled the performance of his work or retained the right to do so, we affirm the district court's judgment.

I.

Norfolk asked Hulcher to clean up a derailment at Norfolk's New Orleans railyard, and Hulcher assigned Wheeler and other Hulcher employees to the project. At the time, Wheeler had worked for Hulcher for about three months, serving over a dozen Hulcher customers. He had never before worked at Norfolk's railyard.

The Hulcher crew serviced the derailment site and was packing up its heavy equipment when a novice Hulcher employee made a dangerous error. The employee failed to reverse a cable line that Wheeler was holding while rigging down a boom. The slack in the line evaporated in an instant, trapping Wheeler's right hand between a heavy steel cable and a load line. His middle, ring, and pinky fingers were severed.

Wheeler brought and settled a workers-compensation claim against Hulcher. He then brought this FELA suit, alleging that he was Norfolk's employee and was injured by its negligence. To show his employee **{–629–}** status, Wheeler relied on (1) the agreement between Hulcher and Norfolk and (2) the testimony of two Norfolk supervisors on duty during his accident. Those materials are described in further detail below.

1. Hulcher performed work for Norfolk under a Master Agreement for Derailment Cleanup and Repair Services. It provided for Hulcher **[—3—]** to work on derailments on an "as-needed, as-requested basis," with Norfolk not required to use Hulcher for any given derailment.

If requested to work on a derailment, Hulcher was required to provide trained personnel, equipment, and services to clean up the derailment site. Its work would include "(a) clearing, removing and/or rerailing locomotives, railcars and other rolling stock; (b) repair, reconstruction and replacement of damaged or destroyed trackage or track components . . . ; and (c) such other services as [Norfolk] may request to complete repair and cleanup of a derailment site." Norfolk determined the scope of those services and the equipment to be used on a case-by-case basis.

The agreement obligated Hulcher to "respond[] to derailments as promptly as possible . . . twenty-four (24) hours per day, seven (7) days per week." Regarding personnel, the agreement required Hulcher to follow federal law and mandated that Hulcher perform certain background checks on any employee assigned to the Norfolk railyard. The agreement provides that "[n]othing in this background investigation requirement [prevents Hulcher] from hiring any particular individual or requiring [Hulcher] to terminate such individual if already hired[.]" The agreement also imposes some of Norfolk's internal rules on Hulcher and its employees. For example, it requires Hulcher employees to comply with Norfolk's safety rules, attend job briefings conducted by Norfolk, stay up to date on environmental and hazardous-materials trainings, and wear safety gear at derailment sites.

The paragraph titled "Independent Contractor" states that Hulcher would "remain an original and independent party[.]" Hulcher's services were to be "its own separate business, under its management, supervision and direction." The agreement provides that Hulcher was to "employ, pay[,] . . . and discharge all persons engaged in the performance of" its services, and those persons were to "remain the sole employees of [Hulcher]." Nothing in **[—4—]** the agreement "is intended to create a joint venture or to constitute either party as agent . . . of the other."

The agreement gives Norfolk employees the right to inspect Hulcher's work and demand that Hulcher remedy any deficiencies. It also provides that Norfolk may assign its personnel to work alongside or in the vicinity of Hulcher employees, and it clarifies that the employees of each party "shall remain under the direction and control of [their] supervisors, there being no intention to render the employees of either as 'loaned' employees of the other[.]"

2. Wheeler submitted a declaration alleging that Norfolk employees "had the right to direct [his] work if they desired" and that, if they had directed him to do something, he "would have done it." He claims that he understood that he was supposed to follow Norfolk's safety rules, that he should stop if ordered to do so by a Norfolk employee, and that his failure to do either could lead to his removal from Norfolk's railyard. Wheeler supports his claims with the testimony of two Norfolk employees.

First, Wheeler relies on the testimony of Stacey Brown, Norfolk's Senior General Foreman at the railyard. Although Brown **{-630-}** was on duty the day that Wheeler was injured, Brown was unaware the accident had occurred. Brown was Norfolk's point person for Hulcher's services at the railyard. In the event of a derailment, Brown would call Hulcher and tell them the scope of the project and what equipment he believed was needed. Hulcher would then determine the number of its employees needed to clean up the site.

Brown stated that he did not make a habit of policing how Hulcher employees entered the yard, but he agreed that he had the authority to do so. He also agreed that he could order a Hulcher employee to stop working "for any reason." He represented that he did not have authority to order Hulcher employees to do something in a particular way, however, and that "I just tell **[—5—]** [the Hulcher employee] to stop, and then his supervisor would determine how they're going to do it." Brown knew that he could remove a contractor from the railyard, but he had never heard of someone's being removed in his 22 years at Norfolk.

Second, Wheeler relies on the testimony of Preston Hunter, the Norfolk yardmaster on duty during the accident. Hunter too was unaware of Wheeler's accident until this lawsuit was filed. As the yardmaster, Hunter controlled the railyard, but he never interacted with Hulcher or directly supervised its work or crews. He explained that, when a derailment occurs, Norfolk's mechanical department asks for permission to clear the affected tracks, after which the mechanical department contacts Hulcher. Hunter acknowledged that he could order the mechanical department to stop Hulcher from working in an emergency or if he saw something unsafe. But he stated, "that's just something I would never . . . do[,]" because from where Hunter was located in the tower, he "really wouldn't know what Hulcher is doing[.]"

II.

Employment by a railroad is required for a plaintiff to recover under FELA. 45 U.S.C. § 51. Whether an injured worker was acting as an employee of a railroad at the time of an injury is a question of fact. *Lindsey v. Louisville & Nashville R.R. Co.*, 775 F.2d 1322, 1324 (5th Cir. 1985). The district court entered summary judgment for Norfolk, holding that no genuine dispute of material fact existed on that point and that the record would not support a finding that Wheeler was Norfolk's employee at the time of his accident. On appeal, we review that summary judgment de novo.

In FELA, the words "employee" and "employed" are used in their natural sense, so principles of common law govern the issue of employment. *Kelley v. S. Pac. Co.*, 419 U.S. 318, 323 (1974). At common law, a person may **[—6—]** establish his employee status, despite his nominal classification as an independent contractor, under three recognized doctrines. As applied to a railroad, the person could (1) be the railroad's borrowed servant, (2) serve two employers simultaneously, or (3) be a subservant of a company that in turn serves the railroad. *Id.* at 324. Under each of those doctrines, a worker's employment status turns on "whether the railroad has control of the employee or the right to control the employee." *Lindsey*, 775 F.2d at 1324.

The railroad need not have full supervisory control, but its supervisory role must be significant. *Id.* The mere reservation of authority to ensure performance as contemplated by a contract is not sufficient control to turn a nominal contractor into an employee. *See* **{-631-}** *Sullivan v. Gen. Elec. Co.*, 226 F.2d 290, 291 (6th Cir. 1955). The control necessary to establish an employment relationship is also more than just the power of "mere suggestion as to details or the necessary cooperation, where the work furnished is part of a larger undertaking." *Kelley*, 419 U.S. at 329 (cleaned up). Likewise, "the passing of information and the accommodation . . . obviously required in a large and necessarily coordinated operation" do not prove sufficient supervisory control. *Id.* at 330 (citation omitted). Rather, to establish an employment relationship, the communications between the railroad and the contractor "must assume a supervisory character." *Id.*

Under those standards and on the summary-judgment record here, Wheeler's argument that he was Norfolk's employee fails as a matter of law. The undisputed evidence demonstrates that Norfolk did not control the manner and details of Wheeler's work, nor did it retain the right to do so. *See id.* at 325.

First, Norfolk personnel did not, in fact, supervise Wheeler's work. Wheeler identifies no instance in which a Norfolk employee instructed him to do something. The only Norfolk employees whom he identifies as being in **[—7—]** the railyard at the time of his accident—Brown and Hunter—were not even aware of the accident until this suit was filed. *Cf. Lindsey*, 775 F.2d at 1324 (upholding a finding of employee status based in part on testimony that workers "received specific orders and instructions from [railroad] employees").

Nor does Wheeler identify evidence that Norfolk personnel had the right of significant supervisory control over his work. Wheeler points to Hunter's general authority over the railyard and Brown's authority to tell anyone there to stop working. But those facts do not, alone or in conjunction with the other evidence, support a finding of significant supervisory control over Wheeler's rerailment work. This is not a case like *Baker v. Texas & Pacific Railway Co.*, 359 U.S. 227 (1959). There, the evidence sufficed to raise a question for the jury on employee status because a railroad supervisor "exercised directive control over the details of the job performed by the individual workmen, including the precise point where the mixture should be pumped, when they should move to the next point, and the consistency of the mixture." *Id.* at 228–29. Here, in contrast, the evidence could show only a retained authority by Brown and Hunter to order a Hulcher employee to stop working at the railyard—a far cry from the directive control described in *Baker*. It falls short of the affirmative control necessary to allow a finding of substantial supervisory power. It also stands in contrast with the directive control described in *Collins v. Union Pacific Railroad Co.*, 143 Cal. Rptr. 3d 849, 857–59 (Cal. Ct. App. 2012), on which Wheeler relies. There, the railroad employees would tell a worker "what [they] wanted done and *how to do it*." *Id.* at 859 (emphasis added). Here, the record lacks such evidence.

Second, no evidence shows that Wheeler's selection for Hulcher's work at the railyard was directed by Norfolk. Wheeler helped service over a dozen other Hulcher customers before starting the Norfolk project, and no evidence shows that anyone but Hulcher decided when and where Wheeler would be assigned. Hulcher retained complete authority over its employees' **[—8—]** schedules. The Norfolk–Hulcher agreement does not give Norfolk the power to hire employees for Hulcher or require any specific Hulcher employee to work at Norfolk's railyard. Hulcher was required to provide a sufficient workforce, not a specific workforce. And it is uncontroverted **{-632-}** that Hulcher paid Wheeler's wages.

Wheeler relies on the master agreement's requirements that Hulcher employees pass a background check, follow Norfolk safety rules, and attend job briefings and safety meetings. The Sixth Circuit addressed similar arguments in *Campbell v. BNSF Railway Co.*, 600 F.3d 667 (6th Cir. 2010), holding that such requirements are unsurprising in the context of an independent-contractor relationship: "[i]t was certainly reasonable for [the railroad] . . . to be concerned about workers performing potentially hazardous work on its land[,]" *id.* at 674. That reasoning applies with equal force here.

Third, the Norfolk–Hulcher agreement disclaims authority by either company to terminate or demand the termination of the other company's employees. Norfolk did not have authority to terminate Wheeler from Hulcher's employment. Wheeler argues that Norfolk had authority to ban him from the railyard, but he fails to explain why that is any different than the authority Norfolk could exercise against a trespasser, especially where Hulcher had numerous other customers. It does not support a finding of employment by Norfolk. *See Robertson v. Yazoo & Miss. Valley R.R. Co.,* 159 F.2d 31, 31 n.1, 35 (5th Cir. 1947) (acknowledging a railroad's power to remove a contractor's employees from its railyard but nonetheless holding that a worker failed to raise a fact issue as to his employment by the railroad).

Fourth, Hulcher was responsible for bringing the necessary equipment to the railyard. The agreement does give Norfolk authority to designate equipment for Hulcher to bring, but Wheeler fails to explain why that step goes beyond the cooperation "obviously required in a large and necessarily **[—9—]** coordinated operation." *See Kelley*, 419 U.S. at 330 (citation omitted). The ability to designate the equipment that Hulcher will bring allows Norfolk to anticipate the cost of each engagement with Hulcher. And the fact that Hulcher owned and provided its own specialized equipment for servicing derailments implies that Wheeler was an independent contractor, not Norfolk's employee, in performing that work. *Cf. Watts v. Mont. Rail Link, Inc.*, 975 P.2d 283, 292–93 (Mont. 1999) (concluding that a contractor's reliance on a railroad for "tools, equipment, and parts[,]" among other factors, established an employment relationship).

Fifth, although the work was performed at Norfolk's railyard, that seems almost unavoidable when an independent contractor's line of work is cleaning up derailments. As the district court recognized, the place of injury alone is insufficient to create an issue of fact as to a worker's employment by a railroad. *See Campbell*, 600 F.3d at 674, 676 (upholding summary judgment in favor of a railroad although a contractor was injured on railroad property).

Finally, Wheeler gains no ground in arguing that reliance on the Norfolk–Hulcher agreement is barred by § 55 of FELA. Section 55 reads in pertinent part: "Any contract, rule, regulation, or device whatsoever, the purpose or intent of which shall be to enable any common carrier to exempt itself from any liability created by this chapter, shall to that extent be void[.]" 45 U.S.C. § 55. Wheeler argues that § 55 prevents Norfolk from "escap[ing] FELA liability by contracting out its railroad activity to third parties[.]" But Wheeler failed to raise this argument in district court, so it is forfeited. *See Leverette v. Louisville Ladder Co.*, 183 F.3d 339, 342 (5th Cir. 1999). In any event, Wheeler cites no authority applying § 55 to bar a railroad's argument that a contract **{–633–}** for services shows that a worker of the service provider was not an employee of the railroad. The distinction between an employee and an independent contractor underlies and defines the scope of FELA liability; it is not an "exempt[ion]" from that liability under that Act. *See Robinson v.* **[—10—]** *Balt. & Ohio R.R. Co.*, 237 U.S. 84, 94 (1915) (remarking that Congress, aware "that there were . . . persons engaged in various services for other masters" on railroads, "did not use any appropriate expression . . . indicat[ing] a purpose to include such persons . . . under the act").

* * *

Summary judgment for Norfolk is proper because Wheeler cannot satisfy the railroad-employee element of his FELA claim. Accordingly, the judgment of the district court is affirmed.

United States Court of Appeals
for the Fifth Circuit

No. 20-30689

MOORE
VS.
BP EXPLORATION & PROD., INC.

Appeal from the United States District Court for the Eastern District of Louisiana

Decided: August 3, 2021

Citation: 17 F.4th 528, 9 Adm. R. 230 (5th Cir. 2021).

Before **CLEMENT, HAYNES,** and **WILSON,** Circuit Judges.

[—1—] {-529-} PER CURIAM: [—2—]

This case is another in the line of cases related to the *Deepwater Horizon* oil spill. **{-530-}** Eight individuals (collectively, "Plaintiffs") appeal the district court's order dismissing their claims with prejudice. We AFFIRM.

I. Background

To effectively resolve claims arising under MDL 2179—the multidistrict litigation handling all lawsuits against BP and other related defendants (collectively, "BP") stemming from the *Deepwater Horizon* oil spill—the district court established pleading bundles for different categories of cases. Plaintiffs are all part of the B3 pleading bundle, which includes personal-injury claims, and allege that they sustained medical conditions arising from exposure to the oil spill. As B3 plaintiffs, Plaintiffs were required to comply with several pretrial orders ("PTOs"). They complied with all PTOs up until PTO 68, which was issued on October 21, 2019. The question of compliance with that order prompted this appeal.

Of relevance, PTO 68 required Plaintiffs to provide past and present information about their medical conditions, which would be treated as interrogatory answers: the dates those conditions were diagnosed and first treated, names of their diagnosing healthcare providers, and whether treatment was currently being obtained. After requesting and receiving one extension, Plaintiffs responded to PTO 68 with conflicting information; they answered "N/A" or "Did not seek treatment" as to the past, but they then indicated they were still receiving treatment in the present. Plaintiffs revised their answers after conferring with BP, but the inconsistencies remained. Thus, BP noted Plaintiffs' noncompliance with PTO 68 in its status report to the district court.

The district court agreed that Plaintiffs' responses were noncompliant and issued a show cause order requiring Plaintiffs to explain by May 18, 2020 "why their claims should not be dismissed for failing to comply with PTO **[—3—]** 68." Plaintiffs conceded that their initial responses were internally inconsistent; but they argued that they could sufficiently cure those inconsistencies with another revision by saying they "d[id] not recall" as to the past. Plaintiffs accordingly filed another revision. In sum, Plaintiffs thrice attempted to comply with PTO 68, answering "N/A," "Did not seek treatment," or "does not recall" about the past but also answering that they were currently seeking treatment.[1]

Concluding that Plaintiffs' responses were "puzzling" and "hard to make sense of" at the show cause hearing, the district court held that Plaintiffs failed to comply with PTO 68 and dismissed their claims with prejudice. Plaintiffs timely appealed.

II. Standard of Review

We review docket-management matters for an abuse of discretion. *In re Deepwater Horizon* (*Barrera*), 907 F.3d 232, 234, 6 Adm. R. 270, 271 (5th Cir. 2018) (per curiam). A district court abuses its discretion when "its ruling is based on an erroneous view of the law or a clearly erroneous assessment of the

[1] Certain Plaintiffs answered that they did not recall the requested dates and diagnosing doctor in their initial response and/or their first revision. Despite the district court finding those answers noncompliant, those Plaintiffs did not revise their answers; instead, all other Plaintiffs followed suit, copying their "d[id] not recall" answers.

evidence." *Id.*, 6 Adm. R. at 271 (quotation omitted).

III. Discussion

Plaintiffs argue that the district court abused its discretion in dismissing their claims with prejudice. The parties agree that dismissal with prejudice is permissible here only when two conditions are satisfied: (1) there is "a clear record of **{-531-}** delay or contumacious conduct by the plaintiff" and (2) "lesser sanctions would not serve the best interests of justice." *Id.* at 235, 6 Adm. R. at 271 **[—4—]** (quotations omitted). Because our "independent review of the record confirms that both prongs are satisfied," we hold that the district court did not abuse its discretion. *See In re Taxotere (Docetaxel) Prods. Liab. Litig.*, 966 F.3d 351, 359 (5th Cir. 2020) (noting that district courts need not make "specific factual findings" on each prong to dismiss with prejudice).

A. Clear Record of Delay

There is a clear record of delay by Plaintiffs in complying with PTO 68. Plaintiffs had nearly seven months—from the date of PTO 68's issuance on October 21, 2019 to the date when Plaintiffs were required to respond to the show cause order on May 18, 2020—to obtain the necessary medical records and recall the required dates and diagnosing doctor to submit compliant responses. That time period included an extension and two additional opportunities to comply that Plaintiffs failed to take advantage of.

Although PTO 68 required Plaintiffs to provide information concerning their alleged claims of personal injuries that occurred about ten years ago, their inability to remember (or, at least, keep track of) such foundational information is suspect. They knew or should have known that they were going to pursue a claim against BP immediately upon the *Deepwater Horizon* oil spill. Consequently, Plaintiffs should have been keeping track of their claims. Thus, the information concerning when they first sought treatment for their alleged injuries and who their diagnosing doctor was should have been "reasonably available" to them. *Areizaga v. ADW Corp.*, 314 F.R.D. 428, 437 (N.D. Tex. 2016). At the very least, Plaintiffs should have been "diligent" and made a "good-faith" effort to obtain the necessary medical information in the nearly seven months the district court provided. They also should have explained, with a description of their efforts, why they could not obtain such records in the time provided. *McLeod, Alexander, Powel & Apffel, P.C. v. Quarles*, 894 F.2d 1482, 1485–86 (5th Cir. 1990). Therefore, **[—5—]** Plaintiffs' "N/A," "Did not seek treatment," and "does not recall" answers fail to meet PTO 68's directive that Plaintiffs provide responses equivalent to interrogatory answers. Further, the internal inconsistencies in Plaintiffs' answers and revisions yet again constitute part of the delay; Plaintiffs' briefing does not provide any cogent explanation.[2]

Accordingly, Plaintiffs' continuous and self-imposed failure to comply with PTO 68 amounts to clear delay. *See Barrera*, 907 F.3d at 234–37, 6 Adm. R. at 270–72 (affirming the district court's dismissal of the plaintiffs' claims with prejudice for failure to comply with PTO 60's deadline because the plaintiffs had been given one extension and a show cause order to come into compliance and failed to explain, with corroboration, why they could not comply within the given amount of time);[3]

---

[2] Plaintiffs state that in some cases, they provided "N/A" because the deadline was too short; per Plaintiffs, they "had not sought medical treatment until shortly before the issuance of PTO 68, which was recently enough that [their] counsel did not have time to obtain the medical records from the providers." Plaintiffs, however, did not provide this explanation to the district court, so it does not affect our analysis. *See Barrera*, 907 F.3d at 234, 6 Adm. R. at 271 (noting that an abuse of discretion requires a clearly erroneous assessment of the evidence before the district court). Even if we considered it, their argument continues to have inconsistencies.

[3] Although Plaintiffs met PTO 68's deadline—unlike the *Barrera* plaintiffs, who failed to submit any documentation by the deadline (or submitted it late)—that difference is not dispositive. Receiving noncompliant filings is in many ways just as bad as receiving no filings at all. *See Moore v. CITGO Refin. & Chems. Co., L.P.*, 735 F.3d 309, 314, 317 (5th Cir. 2013) (affirming a district court's dismissal with prejudice of plaintiffs' claims

cf. In re Deepwater Horizon (*Graham*), 922 F.3d 660, 667–68, 7 Adm. R. 251, 254 (5th Cir. 2019) (reversing the district court's **{-532-}** dismissal of certain plaintiffs' claims with prejudice for failure to comply with a PTO because the plaintiffs had followed erroneous advice from the Plaintiffs' Steering Committee). **[—6—]**

B. Lesser Sanctions

No lesser sanction than dismissal with prejudice would serve the interests of justice. Indeed, the district court already tried a lesser sanction—its show cause order. *See Rogers v. Kroger Co.*, 669 F.2d 317, 321 (5th Cir. 1982). Because that lesser sanction did not produce compliance, it is unclear what other lesser sanctions could have been appropriate, since "[a]ny sanction other than dismissal would not achieve the desired effect of [a] PTO[], and would further delay the district court's efforts to adjudicate the MDL expeditiously." *Barrera*, 907 F.3d at 236, 6 Adm. R. at 272.

IV. Conclusion

Plaintiffs' conduct satisfies both prongs for the standard for dismissing with prejudice. The district court did not abuse its discretion in dismissing Plaintiffs' claims with prejudice.[4] Accordingly, we AFFIRM.

---

because they responded, but failed to comply with, the district court's two discovery orders).

[4] In so holding, we reiterate that, in the MDL context, we do not require—and need not consider—any aggravating factor for a dismissal with prejudice. *See Barrera*, 907 F.3d at 235–37, 235 n.1, 6 Adm. R. at 271–72, 271 n.1 (noting that "aggravating factors are not required for a dismissal with prejudice" and affirming the district court's dismissal with prejudice for failure to comply with PTO 60 without addressing those factors); *In re Deepwater Horizon* (*Cepeda*), 765 F. App'x 980, 982–83 (5th Cir. 2019) (per curiam) (affirming the district court's dismissal with prejudice for failure to comply with a PTO without addressing the aggravating factors); *see generally In re Taxotere*, 966 F.3d at 358–59 (noting that, due to the complexity of managing an MDL, district courts require "greater flexibility to dismiss a plaintiff," and that the two-pronged test, sans aggravating factors, "helps animate the goals of strict enforcement and efficient management").

United States Court of Appeals for the Fifth Circuit

No. 20-20338

**PETROBAS AM., INC.
VS.
SAMSUNG HEAVY INDUS. CO.**

Appeal from the United States District Court for the Southern District of Texas

Decided: August 11, 2021

Citation: 9 F.4th 247, 9 Adm. R. 233 (5th Cir. 2021).

Before **ELROD, WILLETT,** and **ENGELHARDT,** Circuit Judges.

[—1—] {-251-} **PER CURIAM**:

Petrobras appeals the Rule 12(b)(6) dismissal of its fraud claims, arguing that Samsung did not establish that Petrobras's claims are barred by the applicable statute of limitations. Because the pleadings do not establish as a matter of law that Petrobras had actual or constructive notice of its injury before March 2015, dismissal at the pleading stage was improper. Therefore, we REVERSE and REMAND. **[—2—]**

I.

Petrobras America, Inc. is the American subsidiary of a Brazilian oil and gas producer. It alleges that Samsung Heavy Industries, a Korean shipbuilding company, secretly bribed Petrobras executives to finalize a drilling-services contract between Petrobras and Pride Global Limited—the lynchpin to Samsung's own construction contract with Pride.

In 2007, Samsung entered into a construction contract with Pride Global Limited.[1] The contract contained an option for Samsung to build a deep-sea drillship if Pride secured a drilling-services contract with another company. Hamylton Padilha Jr., an independent consultant retained by Pride, initiated negotiations between Pride and Petrobras to secure the drilling-services contract that would trigger the Samsung–Pride construction option. Nestor Cuñat Cerveró and Renato de Souza Duque, Petrobras executives, represented Petrobras in these negotiations.

Employees of the Petrobras International Division, headed by Cerveró, objected that there was no need for drilling services from another drillship. To overcome this hurdle, Padilha contacted a Samsung executive in Houston, Texas to arrange a bribe. Samsung arranged to pay $10 million to Cerveró and Duque and $10 million to Padilha as a commission. To fund the bribes, Samsung increased the labor and material costs charged to Pride for what later would become the "DS-5." Pride passed these costs to Petrobras by modifying its drilling-services contract proposal to reflect a $20 million cost increase.

Cerveró accepted this proposal on behalf of Petrobras. In December of 2007, the Samsung–Pride contract for the construction of the DS-5 was **[—3—]** signed. In January **{-252-}** 2008, the Petrobras–Pride drilling-services contract for the DS-5 was finalized.

After the construction of the DS-5 was complete in 2011, Petrobras had no work for the vessel. Petrobras therefore assigned the drilling-services contract to two other companies to mitigate losses. In 2015, Petrobras decided to put the DS-5 on permanent standby.

In March 2015, Petrobras began an internal audit to review the contracting procedures for the DS-5 and three other drillships.[2] The audit team discovered that a

[1] We construe all facts in the light most favorable to Petrobras, as we must at this stage. *Arnold v. Williams*, 979 F.3d 262, 265 n.1 (5th Cir. 2020).

[2] At the 12(b)(6) stage, the court may consider the complaint in its entirety, including "documents incorporated into the complaint by reference." *Funk v. Stryker Corp.*, 631 F.3d 777, 783 (5th Cir. 2011) (quoting *Tellabs, Inc. v. Makor Issues & Rts., Ltd.*, 551 U.S. 308, 322 (2007)); *accord Doe v. United States*, 853 F.3d 792, 800 (5th Cir. 2017). Petrobras referenced the audit report in its amended complaint, and the parties do not dispute that it is properly before the court on this motion to dismiss.

broker and Padilha visited with Cerveró during the DS-5 negotiations. The team concluded that the DS-5 contract's terms were unfavorable to Petrobras and based on inaccurate forecasts. Lastly, they recommended that Petrobras inform prosecutors of the audit's findings. The audit report was released May 18, 2015.

In October 2015, Brazilian prosecutors unsealed a plea agreement that Padilha had entered into in July 2015. In the plea agreement, Padilha revealed the details of the DS-5 bribery scheme. Three months later, Petrobras notified Pride that they were cancelling the DS-5 drilling-services contract as a product of fraud.

Meanwhile in 2014, news broke of "Operation Carwash,"[3] a widespread investigation into corruption throughout Brazil. Operation Carwash included a separate bribery scheme—which is not the subject of this **[—4—]** case—in which Samsung contracted directly with Petrobras to construct two other ships. According to a Reuters article, Samsung bribed Petrobras's Cerveró to finalize a contract between Petrobras and Samsung for the construction of the *Vitória 10,000* and the *Petrobras 10,000*. *See* Caroline Stauffer, *Another Former Petrobras Executive Charged in Brazil Scandal*, Reuters (Dec. 15, 2014). A Washington Post article reported that Petrobras's Duque was arrested in March 2014 for his actions in Operation Carwash. *See* Dom Phillips, *'Operation Carwash' in Brazil Causes Normally Staid Business Meeting to Go off Script*, Wash. Post (Nov. 17, 2014). Petrobras noted the *Vitória 10,000* and *Petrobras 10,000* bribery scheme, as well as related criminal charges against its executives Duque and Cerveró, in a May 2015 filing with the Securities and Exchange Commission. Neither the newspaper articles nor the SEC filing mentioned the DS-5.

On March 5, 2019, Petrobras filed a complaint in Texas state court against Samsung for its role in the bribery that led to the Petrobras–Pride contract for the DS-5's drilling services. The complaint alleged that Samsung engaged in both common-law fraud under Texas state law and racketeering under the Racketeer Influenced and Corrupt Organizations Act (RICO), 18 U.S.C. § 1962(c) and (d).

Samsung removed the case to federal court and moved to dismiss under Federal Rule of Civil Procedure 12(b)(6) on statute-of-limitations grounds. The district court took judicial notice of Petrobras's 2014 SEC filing and the two newspaper articles from the Washington Post and Reuters. Each of these documents detailed the bribery scheme underlying the Samsung–Petrobras **{–253–}** contract for the construction of the *Vitória 10,000* and *Petrobras 10,000*, but they did not mention the Petrobras–Pride contract for the DS-5's drilling services. From these, the district court inferred that Petrobras was on notice in 2014, at the latest, that the DS-5 contract was suspect. Holding that "the specific drillship in this case is not subject to its **[—5—]** own limitations clock," the district court granted Samsung's motion to dismiss. Petrobras timely appealed.

II.

We review orders on 12(b)(6) motions to dismiss for failure to state a claim *de novo*. *Life Partners Creditors' Tr. v. Cowley (In re Life Partners Holdings, Inc.)*, 926 F.3d 103, 116 (5th Cir. 2019). We accept all well-pleaded facts as true, viewing them in the light most favorable to the plaintiff. *Arnold v. Williams*, 979 F.3d 262, 265 n.1, 266 (5th Cir. 2020). We consider all "documents incorporated into the complaint by reference, and matters of which a court may take judicial notice." *Tellabs, Inc. v. Makor Issues & Rts., Ltd.*, 551 U.S. 308, 322 (2007). Rule 12(b)(6) dismissal under a statute of limitation is proper only when the complaint makes plain that the claim is time-barred and raises no basis for tolling. *Jones v. Alcoa, Inc.*, 339 F.3d 359, 366 (5th Cir. 2003).

III.

Petrobras argues that the district court erred in its determination that Petrobras was on notice in 2014 of the facts that gave rise to

---

[3] "Operação Lava Jato" in Portuguese.

its RICO claims. The statute of limitations is four years for both Texas fraud claims and civil RICO claims. Tex. Civ. Prac. & Rem. Code § 16.004(a)(4); 18 U.S.C. §§ 1962(c)–(d), 1964(c); *Agency Holding Corp. v. Malley-Duff & Assocs., Inc.*, 483 U.S. 143, 152 (1987). The statute of limitations for a RICO claim does not accrue until a plaintiff discovers, or through reasonably diligent investigation should discover, the injury.[4] *Rotella v. Wood*, 147 F.3d 438, 440 **[—6—]** (5th Cir. 1998), *aff'd*, 528 U.S. 549 (2000); *Jensen v. Snellings*, 841 F.2d 600, 607 (5th Cir. 1988) ("A plaintiff who has learned of facts which would cause a reasonable person to inquire further must proceed with a reasonable and diligent investigation, and is charged with the knowledge of all facts such an investigation would have disclosed."). The Texas discovery rule similarly requires the limitations period to "run from the date the plaintiff [(1)] discovers or should have discovered, in the exercise of reasonable care and diligence, the nature of the injury," or (2) "had knowledge of such facts as would cause a reasonably prudent person to make an inquiry that would lead to discovery of the cause of action." *Hoover v. Gregory*, 835 S.W.2d 668, 671 (Tex. App.—Dallas 1992, writ denied); *accord Exxon Corp. v. Emerald Oil & Gas Co.*, 348 S.W.3d 194, 209 (Tex. 2011) ("Knowledge of injury initiates the accrual of the cause **{-254-}** of action and triggers the putative claimant's duty to exercise reasonable diligence to investigate the problem, even if the claimant does not know the specific cause of the injury or the full extent of it.").

In Petrobras's view, it did not and could not have discovered its injury until May of 2015, when it completed an internal audit of the drilling services contract for DS-5. Samsung disagrees, arguing that Petrobras knew as far back as 2007, and certainly no later than 2014, that it had been injured. Because a "statute of limitations is an affirmative defense for which the [defendant] has the burden of proof," we will address Samsung's proposed dates of notice in turn. *Trinity Marine Prods., Inc. v. United States*, 812 F.3d 481, 486 (5th Cir. 2016); *accord* Fed. R. Civ. P. 8(c)(1). **[—7—]**

A.

In asserting that Petrobras had notice in 2007, Samsung argues that Cerveró's and Duque's knowledge of the bribes is imputed to Petrobras. According to Petrobras, only Cerveró and Duque knew about the DS-5 bribes; no other officials at Petrobras knew that Petrobras had been defrauded in the DS-5 contract. Samsung says this is enough because Petrobras is charged with the knowledge of its officers. *See Askanase v. Fatjo*, 130 F.3d 657, 666 (5th Cir. 1997).[5]

An officer's knowledge will not be imputed to his employer if he "was acting adversely to the [employer] and entirely for his own or another's purpose." *Id.* Taking the complaint's factual allegations as true, Cerveró and Duque acted in their own interests by accepting $10 million in bribes and in Samsung's interest "by causing Petrobras to hire a drillship it did not need." Thus, Cerveró and Duque are clearly adverse agents of Petrobras. Their knowledge cannot be imputed to Petrobras. *See id.*

On appeal, Samsung presents another basis for dismissal that the district court did not rely on in its order: Petrobras's injury lies in being stuck with the unfavorable terms of

---

[4] Knowledge of the wrongdoer is not required to start the clock on the statute of limitations; knowledge of the injury alone suffices for the claim to accrue. *See Love v. Nat'l Med. Enters.*, 230 F.3d 765, 773 (5th Cir. 2000) (citing *Rotella v. Wood*, 147 F.3d 438, 440 (5th Cir. 1998), *aff'd*, 528 U.S. 549 (2000)) ("[A] civil RICO claim accrues when the plaintiff discovers, or should have discovered, the injury."). However, the plaintiff may be **[—6—]** entitled to tolling by fraudulent concealment when: (1) the wrongdoer fraudulently conceals the "facts forming the basis for the claim," including the wrongdoer's own identity as the wrongdoer; and (2) the plaintiff cannot access these facts through reasonably diligent investigation. *Texas v. Allan Constr. Co.*, 851 F.2d 1526, 1533–34 (5th Cir. 1988).

[5] Samsung also points to a non-prosecution agreement Petrobras entered into in which it accepted responsibility for certain corruption schemes involving Cerveró and Duque. This agreement, however, did not address the DS-5 bribery scheme. The non-prosecution agreement is simply inapplicable to this case.

the DS-5 contract despite not having enough work for the vessel; Petrobras officials knew as early as 2007 that it might not need the DS-5; thus Petrobras knew about its injury as far back as 2007.

In its reply, Petrobras attacks this argument on two fronts. First, Petrobras contests the assertion that it knew from the start that there would **[—8—]** not be enough work for the DS-5. Second, Petrobras objects to Samsung's characterization of its injury as a lack of work for the DS-5.

On the first front, Petrobras contests the inferences drawn from Samsung's evidence. Samsung relies primarily on internal Petrobras e-mails from 2007,[6] in which the Petrobras International Division "discussed and agreed that there was no need for a third drillship." Petrobras, however, says that those e-mails and related documents also included projections and drilling plans that would support the need for the DS-5.

Regardless of whether Petrobras or Samsung is correct in its reading of these e-mails and documents, they do not conclusively **{-255-}** establish that the statute of limitations had run by March 5, 2019. Rather, they create a fact issue about Petrobras's knowledge. The 2007 e-mails and related documents are not a proper basis for 12(b)(6) dismissal. *Cf. Trinity Marine*, 812 F.3d at 490; *Sec. Indus. Ins. Co. v. United States*, 702 F.2d 1234, 1251 (5th Cir. 1983).

On the second front, Petrobras contends that Samsung mischaracterizes Petrobras's injury. In Samsung's view, Petrobras was injured by the "unfavorable terms" in the DS-5 contract, which it ultimately did not need. In its reply brief, Petrobras characterizes the injury as "a wholly unnecessary contract that was procured through Samsung's *fraud*."

Fraud is the key to Petrobras's injury. An unfavorable contract alone is not a legally cognizable injury. A contract procured through fraud is. *See Shandong Yinguang Chem. Indus. Joint Stock Co. v. Potter*, 607 F.3d 1029, 1032–33 (5th Cir. 2010) (citing *Ernst & Young, L.L.P. v. Pac. Mut. Life Ins. Co.*, 51 S.W.3d 573, 577 (Tex. 2001)); *Nat'l Enters., Inc. v. Mellon Fin. Servs. Corp. No. 7*, 847 F.2d 251, 254 (5th Cir. 1988) (determining that simple non- **[—9—]** payment under a contract, without more, does not amount to "a cognizable injury" under RICO). Petrobras's complaint clearly alleges an injury of fraud. We hold that Samsung "has not met its burden of conclusively establishing that" Petrobras knew or should have known about its injury as far back as 2007. *Trinity Marine*, 812 F.3d at 490.

B.

In support of its argument that Petrobras knew of its injury no later than 2014, Samsung presented to the district court two newspaper articles and Petrobras's 2014 Form 20-F Annual Report, filed in 2015 with the U.S. Securities and Exchange Commission. The district court took judicial notice of these documents. We review a district court's decision whether to take judicial notice for abuse of discretion. *See Taylor v. Charter Med. Corp.*, 162 F.3d 827, 829 (5th Cir. 1998).

Under Federal Rule of Evidence 201, a district court may take judicial notice of facts that are "(1) generally known within the trial court's territorial jurisdiction; or (2) can be accurately and readily determined from sources whose accuracy cannot reasonably be questioned." Fed. R. Evid. 201(b)(1)–(2). The newspaper articles in this case were not proper material for judicial notice. It was not established that the accuracy of the articles could not reasonably be questioned, nor that the facts were "generally known within the" district court's jurisdiction. *Id.*; *see also Eberhardt v. Merck & Co.*, 106 F. App'x 277, 279 (5th Cir. 2004).

The SEC filings, however, may be properly judicially noticed to the extent that they are "considered only for the purpose of determining what statements the documents contain, not to prove the truth of the documents' contents." *Lovelace v. Software*

[6] Petrobras referred to these e-mails in its amended complaint and attached them as exhibits 5, 7, 10, 13, and 14. Thus, they may be considered on 12(b)(6) review.

Spectrum Inc., 78 F.3d 1015, 1018 (5th Cir. 1996). Petrobras itself prepared the SEC filings, so they are relevant to Petrobras's knowledge of the statements in the documents. Assuming that **[—10—]** the district court considered the documents only as evidence of what Petrobras knew or should have known at the time, it did not abuse its discretion. *See id.*

Regardless of whether it was proper to consider these documents, they do not conclusively establish that the statute of limitations began running prior to March 5, 2015. The SEC filing and news articles do not mention Pride or DS-5 at all. Pride—not Samsung—entered into the DS-5 contract with Petrobras. Samsung's involvement was "camouflaged." The Samsung–Petrobras **{-256-}** contract involved the construction of the *Vitória 10,000* and *Petrobras 10,000*; the Petrobras–Pride contract involved the drilling services of the DS-5. The separate bribery schemes involved separate parties, separate contracts, and separate ships.

Because of the nature of the DS-5 bribery scheme, a reasonable person may not have thought to inquire into the Pride drilling-services contract after Cerveró was criminally charged in connection with the *Vitória 10,000* and *Petrobras 10,000* fraud. *See Jensen*, 841 F.2d at 607. Nor can it be said as a matter of law that a reasonably diligent investigation at the time, without the benefit of a full audit or the details of Padilha's plea agreement, would have uncovered the basis for Petrobras's fraud claim.

In short, Samsung's arguments at best raise fact questions not suitable for disposition under Rule 12(b)(6). *See Acad. of Allergy & Asthma in Primary Care v. Quest Diagnostics, Inc.*, 998 F.3d 190, 200 (5th Cir. 2021) (reversing 12(b)(6) dismissal on statute-of-limitations grounds because Defendants failed to conclusively establish that Plaintiffs should have discovered their injury through a diligent inquiry); *cf. Abdul-Alim Amin v. Universal Life Ins. Co. of Memphis*, 706 F.2d 638, 640 (5th Cir. 1983) ("While a statute-of-limitations defense may be raised in a motion to dismiss under Fed. R. Civ. P. 12(b)(6), such a motion should not be granted unless 'it appears beyond **[—11—]** doubt that the plaintiff can prove no set of facts in support of his claim which would entitle him to relief.'" (quoting *Mann v. Adams Realty Co.*, 556 F.2d 288, 293 (5th Cir. 1977))).

* * *

Samsung has not conclusively established at the 12(b)(6) stage that Petrobras's RICO and Texas fraud claims accrued before March 5, 2015. Accordingly, we REVERSE and REMAND for proceedings consistent with this opinion.

United States Court of Appeals
for the Fifth Circuit

No. 20-30765

POINCON
VS.
OFFSHORE MARINE CONTRACTORS, INC.

Appeal from the United States District Court for the Eastern District of Louisiana

Decided: August 13, 2021

Citation: 9 F.4th 289, 9 Adm. R. 238 (5th Cir. 2021).

Before **WIENER, ELROD,** and **HIGGINSON,** Circuit Judges.

[—1—] {-292-} ELROD, Circuit Judge:

Offshore Marine Contractors, Inc.'s employee Sonia Poincon injured her neck in a collision caused by an REC Marine Logistics, L.L.C. vessel in 2015. After Poincon injured her neck again by slipping and falling on an **[—2—]** Offshore Marine vessel in 2018, Offshore Marine sought contribution from REC for Poincon's maintenance and cure. The district court granted summary judgment to REC. Because under governing Fifth Circuit precedent Offshore Marine has brought forth genuine issues of material fact as to whether REC caused in part Poincon's need for maintenance and cure, we REVERSE and REMAND.

I.

In 2015, an REC vessel collided with an Offshore Marine liftboat. Sonia Poincon was working for Offshore Marine as a cook aboard the liftboat at the time. The collision threw her against a cabinet, injuring her head and neck.

She was taken to a doctor on shore and diagnosed the same day with a mild cervical strain and contusion. She did not seek further medical treatment after that out of fear of losing her job. She testified, however, that she continued to feel pain in her neck radiating down to her left hand in 2018. She worked through the pain and did not receive maintenance and cure for that accident. **{-293-}**

In 2018, Poincon was working aboard another Offshore Marine vessel when she slipped and fell while attempting to clear ice from the floor of the vessel's walk-in freezer. Immediately, pain shot up her neck and down her back. Poincon testified that this pain was the same type of pain that she had been experiencing since the 2015 REC collision, but now more intense: "When I fall, I felt like my whole spine shoot out of my head." At another point, though, Poincon declared that this new pain was "severe, constant and unique from any type of neck or back pain that I had experienced before the February 7, 2018 incident." She also said that she experienced "headaches unlike any headaches I had experienced before the February 7, 2018 incident." **[—3—]**

Poincon sought medical treatment for her fall. She related to her doctor the details of her 2015 injury and the subsequent ongoing symptoms. Her doctor observed that "[a]s a result of two separate work-related accidents on a ship, the patient sustained injuries primarily to the cervical paraspinal region on the left, causing cervicogenic headaches, pain in the cervical paraspinal area radiating down the left upper extremity." Based in part on the results of an MRI of Poincon's neck, the doctor concluded that the force from Poincon's 2018 fall "aggravated the cervical injuries from [her] previous [accident] with headaches again reported, severe neck pain, and pain down the left arm." As part of her ongoing treatment, Poincon underwent surgery on her neck in October 2018 and another surgery on her lower back in May 2019.

Poincon sued both Offshore Marine and REC. As a Jones Act seaman, Poincon asserted a Jones Act negligence claim, an unseaworthiness claim, and a claim for maintenance and cure against her employer Offshore Marine for her 2015 and 2018 injuries. Poincon asserted a single negligence claim against REC for her 2015 injuries.[1] Poincon's complaint stated that "[j]urisdiction

[1] REC has settled with Poincon on this claim.

of [the district court] is based on the Jones Act (46 U.S.C. § 30104, *et. seq.*), and under the general maritime law." It stated further that Poincon "desires and is entitled to a trial by jury on the issues sued upon herein."

The district court severed Poincon's claims related to the 2015 accident from her claims related to the 2018 accident because "there exist no common questions of fact concerning the ***liability*** of the distinct sets of defendants involved in the two incidents." (emphasis in original). This left **[—4—]** Offshore Marine as the sole defendant in the case concerning the 2018 accident.

Offshore Marine then filed a third-party complaint against REC seeking contribution to maintenance and cure paid for the 2018 injury. In response, REC moved for summary judgment on the third-party complaint. The district court granted summary judgment in favor of REC, concluding that the 2018 accident was not a foreseeable consequence of the 2015 collision and that the 2018 accident "was an intervening and superseding cause that cut off any liability REC may have had for maintenance and cure" related to the 2015 injury. The district court denied Offshore Marine's subsequent motion to reconsider. Offshore Marine timely appealed.

II.

Before proceeding to the merits, we must assure ourselves of appellate jurisdiction. Offshore Marine initially premised jurisdiction for this interlocutory appeal on 28 U.S.C. § 1292(a)(3), which authorizes appeals of interlocutory orders "determining **{-294-}** the rights and liabilities of the parties to admiralty cases." After initial briefing, we noticed a possible jurisdictional defect, so we asked the parties to submit supplemental briefs on whether § 1292(a)(3) applies to this case. They did so. After oral argument, Offshore Marine moved for the district court to certify its summary judgment order as final under Federal Rule of Civil Procedure 54(b), and the district court did so. We hold that this is a civil, rather than admiralty, case, and so our interlocutory appellate jurisdiction comes from the district court's Rule 54(b) certification, not § 1292(a)(3).

In her complaint, Poincon asserted a statutory claim under the Jones Act and maritime claims under the general maritime law. *See Powell v. Offshore Navigation, Inc.*, 644 F.2d 1063, 1068 (5th Cir. Unit A May 1981) ("A Jones Act claim is therefore a different cause of action altogether from **[—5—]** claims that can be brought in federal court under admiralty jurisdiction; the parameters of this cause of action are defined by the statute and not by the general maritime law."). Plaintiffs asserting maritime claims retain their right to pursue available civil remedies and invoke any applicable non-admiralty bases for federal jurisdiction. 28 U.S.C. § 1333 (conferring admiralty jurisdiction but "saving to suitors in all cases all other remedies to which they are otherwise entitled"). Poincon therefore had the option to file her complaint either on the "civil side" of the federal courts under federal question jurisdiction, *id.* § 1331, or on the "admiralty side" under federal admiralty jurisdiction, *id.* § 1333.[2] *See Bodden v. Osgood*, 879 F.2d 184, 186 (5th Cir. 1989); *Romero v. Int'l Terminal Operating Co.*, 358 U.S. 354, 380–81 (1959).

When a plaintiff asserts claims that can be brought under either the civil or admiralty jurisdiction of the federal courts, the plaintiff must elect admiralty jurisdiction under Federal Rule of Civil Procedure 9(h) to proceed in admiralty. *Bodden*, 879 F.2d at 186. The complaint does not have to explicitly cite to Rule 9(h), but it must at least include "a simple statement" invoking admiralty jurisdiction. *Id.* (quoting *T.N.T. Marine Serv.,*

[2] Traditionally, the term "admiralty" refers to the courts, jurisdiction, and procedure of maritime law, and "maritime" refers to the substantive law itself. David W. Robertson, Steven F. Friedell & Michael F. Sturley, *Admiralty and Maritime Law in the United States* 4 (3d ed. 2015). That distinction has faded over time, and "admiralty" and "maritime" are now used largely synonymously. *Id.* The distinction is helpful in this context, though, to conceptually separate the claims Poincon states (both maritime and statutory) from the jurisdiction she invokes (either admiralty or civil).

Inc. v. Weaver Shipyards & Dry Docks, Inc., 702 F.2d 585, 588 (5th Cir. 1983)).

Here, Poincon did not cite to Rule 9(h). We therefore look to the "totality of the circumstances" to determine if Poincon made the required "simple statement" to "properly invoke the district court's admiralty **[—6—]** jurisdiction." *Id.*; *accord T.N.T. Marine Serv.*, 702 F.2d at 587–88; *see also Apache Corp. v. Glob. Santa Fe Drilling Co.*, 435 F. App'x 322, 325 (5th Cir. 2011).

Poincon's original complaint included the following jurisdictional statement:

> Jurisdiction of this Honorable Court is based on the Jones Act (46 U.S.C. § 30104, *et. seq.*), and under the general maritime law for general maritime negligence and unseaworthiness and for maintenance and cure. Venue is proper in accordance with 28 U.S.C. § 1391(b)(1).

The complaint also requests a jury, which is not available in admiralty. **{-295-}** *Powell*, 644 F.2d at 1070 ("There is not the slightest indication of any intention, or of any professional or lay demands for a change in the time-sanctioned mode of trying suits in admiralty without a jury . . . ." (quoting *Romero*, 358 U.S. at 369)).

Poincon's citation to the Jones Act as a basis for jurisdiction signals a desire to rely on federal question jurisdiction under 28 U.S.C. § 1331. *See Romero*, 358 U.S. at 381. Her jury demand likewise signals a desire to proceed on the civil side of the district court.[3] *See Borne v. A & P Boat Rentals No. 4, Inc.*, 755 F.2d 1131, 1133 (5th Cir. 1985). The maritime claims Poincon asserts are all *in personam* claims rather than *in rem* claims, so none of her claims fall exclusively within admiralty. *See T.N.T. Marine Serv.*, 702 F.2d at 587–88 (noting that the plaintiff stated an *in rem* claim against the Tug *OCEAN WIND*, which "falls within the exclusive admiralty jurisdiction"); *see also* **[—7—]** *Luera v. M/V Alberta*, 635 F.3d 181, 190–91 (5th Cir. 2011) (permitting a plaintiff to proceed under the court's civil diversity jurisdiction for *in personam* maritime claims while proceeding in admiralty for *in rem* maritime claims). Nowhere in her complaint is there an indication that she wishes to proceed in admiralty. In light of the totality of the circumstances, it is clear that Poincon did not elect admiralty jurisdiction, and therefore this is a civil case. *See, e.g., Bodden*, 879 F.2d at 186; *Borne*, 755 F.2d at 1133; *see also Russell v. Jack Jackson, Inc.*, No. 02-31036, 2003 WL 21683485, at *2 (5th Cir. July 18, 2003); *Bayham v. Grosse Tete Well Serv., Inc.*, 510 F. App'x 329, 329–30 (5th Cir. 2013); *Lejano v. Soriamont S.S. Agencies, Inc.*, 33 F. App'x 704, at *3 (5th Cir. 2002).

The fact that Offshore Marine brought a maritime third-party claim against REC for contribution to Poincon's maintenance and cure does not change this result. Just like Poincon's maritime claims against Offshore Marine, Offshore Marine's contribution claim can be brought on the civil side of the federal courts based on the federal question jurisdiction conferred by Poincon's Jones Act claim. *See Romero*, 358 U.S. at 380–81; *Fitzgerald v. U.S. Lines Co.*, 374 U.S. 16, 20–21 (1963). Moreover, the decision whether to proceed in admiralty belongs to Poincon as the plaintiff. *Harrison v. Flota Mercante Grancolombiana, S.A.*, 577 F.2d 968, 987 (5th Cir. 1978). If we were to allow a defendant to re-designate a case as an admiralty case simply by seeking an interlocutory appeal under § 1292(a)(3), we would "emasculate the election given to the plaintiff by Rule 9(h)" and jeopardize the plaintiff's Seventh Amendment right to a jury trial. *Id.*; *see Bodden*, 879 F.2d at 186; *see also Fitzgerald*, 374 U.S. at 20–21. Simply put, Offshore Marine's appeal does not undermine Poincon's election.

"Since [Poincon]'s action does not come within the district court's admiralty

---

[3] Requesting a jury is not by itself dispositive. Had Poincon made a proper Rule 9(h) designation and proceeded in admiralty, the district could have simply denied Poincon's jury demand. *Bodden*, 879 F.2d at 186 ("Generally, merely requesting a jury trial does not change an admiralty claim, identified as such, to a non-admiralty claim. In such cases the district court should simply deny the request.").

jurisdiction and because the order from which appeal is taken does not dispose of all claims and parties, [Federal Rule of Civil Procedure] 54(b) **[—8—]** governs any appeal of the district court's decisions." *Bodden*, 879 F.2d at 186. Under Rule 54(b), district courts "may direct entry of a final judgment as to one or more, but fewer than all, claims or parties only if the court expressly **{-296-}** determines that there is no just reason for delay." Fed. R. Civ. P. 54(b); *accord Stewart v. Miss. Transp. Comm'n*, 586 F.3d 321, 327–28 (5th Cir. 2009).

Offshore Marine moved for the district court to expressly certify its summary judgment order in favor of REC as a final order under Rule 54(b). The district court did so, and we supplemented the record on appeal with that order. Accordingly, even though we do not have jurisdiction under § 1292(a)(3)'s special admiralty provision, we do have jurisdiction to proceed with this appeal based on the district court's Rule 54(b) certification. *Cf. Metallurgical Indus., Inc. v. Fourtek, Inc.*, 771 F.2d 915, 916 (5th Cir. 1985). Rule 54(b), rather than § 1292(a)(3), is the proper route to appellate jurisdiction over appeals of interlocutory decrees in civil cases presenting maritime claims.

III.

"We review a grant of summary judgment de novo, applying the same standard as the district court." *Combo Mar., Inc. v. U.S. United Bulk Terminal, LLC*, 615 F.3d 599, 604 (5th Cir. 2010) (quoting *QBE Ins. Corp. v. Brown & Mitchell, Inc.*, 591 F.3d 439, 442 (5th Cir. 2009)). Summary judgment is proper when "there is no genuine dispute as to any material fact and the movant is entitled to judgment as a matter of law." Fed. R. Civ. P. 56(a). "A genuine dispute of material fact exists 'if the evidence is such that a reasonable jury could return a verdict for the nonmoving party.'" *Brackeen v. Haaland*, 994 F.3d 249, 290 (5th Cir. 2021) (*en banc*) (quoting *Anderson v. Liberty Lobby, Inc.*, 477 U.S. 242, 248 (1986)). In reviewing the record, we **[—9—]** view "all the facts and evidence in the light most favorable to the non-movant." *Ortega Garcia v. United States*, 986 F.3d 513, 524, 9 Adm. R. 170, 174 (5th Cir. 2021).

IV.

The district court granted summary judgment to REC by relying on its own new rule for contribution claims involving multiple accidents: "a first accident's maintenance and cure obligation ends where a second accident's begins." This new statement of law foreclosed Offshore Marine's contribution claim against REC because the 2018 accident succeeded the 2015 accident caused by REC. The district court, however, erred by adopting a new rule of maritime law because our precedents, which analyze contribution claims under familiar tort principles of causation, ably address a sequence of accidents such as this. Under our governing precedent, Offshore Marine has established a genuine issue of a material fact, and therefore summary judgment is improper.

A.

On appeal, both parties agree that three cases—*Bertram*, *Adams*, and *Savoie*—developed the right of maritime employers to seek contribution to maintenance and cure in the Fifth Circuit and that those cases govern here. *Bertram v. Freeport McMoran, Inc.*, 35 F.3d 1008, 1013 (5th Cir. 1994); *Adams v. Texaco, Inc.*, 640 F.2d 618 (5th Cir. Unit A Mar. 1981); *Savoie v. Lafourche Boat Rentals, Inc.*, 627 F.2d 722 (5th Cir. Unit A 1980). In the view of Offshore Marine, the district court erred by creating a new rule of law unmoored from these governing cases. REC counters that the district court, despite its clear statements to the contrary, simply applied the *Bertram*, *Adams*, and *Savoie* rule to correctly render judgment in its favor.

The district court, however, approached this case as a novel set of facts requiring new law. It "searched in vain" for a perfectly factually analogous case in our caselaw **{-297-}** and, having come up empty, made its new rule: **[—10—]**

> The clearest way, then, to sort responsibility for an injured seaman's maintenance and cure as between a shipowner/employer and a third-party tortfeasor is on an accident-by-accident

basis, analyzing each accident—and the maintenance and cure incurred or paid for the same—as a discrete, distinct, and self-contained unit. In other words, a first accident's maintenance and cure obligation ends where a second accident's begins.

In crafting this new rule, the district court departed from the clear law governing contribution claims in this circuit: a third party is liable for an employer's expense of maintenance and cure to the extent that the third party's negligence "caused or contributed to the employee's injury" and need for maintenance and cure. *Savoie*, 627 F.2d at 724; *accord Bertram*, 35 F.3d at 1013; *Adams*, 640 F.2d at 620–21; *In re 4-K Marine, L.L.C.*, 914 F.3d 934, 938, 7 Adm. R. 192, 193 (5th Cir. 2019). Thus, to succeed on a claim for contribution, the maritime employer must show (i) negligence and (ii) causation. *Bertram*, 35 F.3d at 1013; *In re 4-K Marine*, 914 F.3d at 938, 7 Adm. R. at 193. The negligence element of a contribution claim is relatively straightforward, particularly in collision cases: did the third-party breach its duty of care? *See Combo Mar.*, 615 F.3d at 604–05 (relating the presumption that a drifting or moving vessel is at fault in an allision or in a collision with a stationary vessel). The causation element proves more difficult, particularly when there may be a superseding cause. *See id.* at 606.

Although a seaman's maintenance-and-cure claim against the seaman's maritime employer "is implied in the employment contract between" the two, a maritime employer's claim against a third party for contribution to the expenses of maintenance and cure arises from the principles of common law tort adopted by the general maritime law. *Bertram*, 35 F.3d at 1013 (quoting *Brister v. A.W.I., Inc.*, 946 F.2d 350, 360 (5th Cir. 1991)). In particular, the "common law negligence doctrines of proximate **[—11—]** causation and superseding cause apply" to maritime claims. *Stolt Achievement, Ltd. v. Dredge B.E. LINDHOLM*, 447 F.3d 360, 367 (5th Cir. 2006) (citing *Exxon Co., U.S.A. v. Sofec, Inc.*, 517 U.S. 830, 836–39 (1996)). Familiar tort principles thus govern causation in claims for contribution to maintenance and cure. "Questions of causation in admiralty are questions of fact," and they are best left to the factfinder—in this case, a jury—when there is a genuine dispute. *Stolt Achievement*, 447 F.3d at 367.

Instead of applying this law to the causation question in this case, the district court crafted its new rule that, as a matter of law, a second accident relieves a third party of liability for contribution to maintenance and cure. According to the district court, "[t]he difficulties posed by applying the *Adams/Savoie/Bertram* regime to the different factual circumstances presented by two separate accidents (including different parties, injuries, fault, causation, shares of fault, etc.) are intractable and could be insurmountable."

The district court's pragmatic concern is unfounded. Complicated questions of fact are routinely submitted to the factfinder. For example, in *Stolt Achievement*, an *in rem* action, the judge as factfinder ably parsed complicated fact disputes—such as the intensity of one ship's bow wave, the degree of the other ship's sheer, and the effect of both ships' speed and positioning—to apportion fault for a collision in the Houston Ship Channel. 447 F.3d at 362–63. Similarly, in *Davis v. Odeco, Inc.*, the plaintiff alleged that exposure to hydrocarbons **{–298–}** while aboard the defendant's vessels caused in part the plaintiff's Goodpasture's Syndrome. 18 F.3d 1237, 1239 (5th Cir. 1994). The jury, "entitled to infer causation from unexplained events," decided the complicated medical causation question in the plaintiff's favor and awarded damages under the Jones Act for negligence. *Id.* at 1242–43, 1247–48. **[—12—]**

There is no reason to doubt that a jury, guided by tort principles, can navigate even the choppiest causation question. The potential complexity of Offshore Marine's case for causation simply provides no basis for taking that fact question away from the jury. *Cf., e.g., United Gas Pub. Serv. Co. v. Texas*, 303 U.S. 123, 140 (1938) ("[W]e have never held that it is beyond the power of the state to provide for the trial by a jury of questions of fact because they are complicated. Cases at law triable by a jury in the federal courts often involve most difficult and complex questions . . . ."); *La. Generating, L.L.C. v. Ill. Union Ins. Co.*, 831 F.3d 618, 634 (5th Cir. 2016) ("We discern a genuine dispute of material fact in this complicated back-and-forth. Thus, summary judgment was improper . . . .").

The district court justified its new rule in part on the principle of "superseding cause," but this makes the district court's departure from precedent especially problematic because its rule effectively absolves REC of its burden of proving the superseding-cause affirmative defense at trial. *See, e.g., Michaels v. Avitech, Inc.*, 202 F.3d 746, 752 (5th Cir. 2000); *see also Stolt Achievement*, 447 F.3d at 367–68. Typically, the defendant has the initial burden of demonstrating that a superseding cause cuts off its liability for an injury. *Michaels*, 202 F.3d at 752. Under the district court's new rule, the plaintiff would have to preemptively establish that a subsequent accident, if any, is not a "second accident" within the contemplation of the district court's rule. Such burden shifting departs from the simple negligence-and-causation showing required by *Bertram*, *Adams*, and *Savoie*. *See Bertram*, 35 F.3d at 1012–13 (first citing *Savoie*, 627 F.2d at 723; and then citing *Adams*, 640 F.3d at 620).

In short, the district court erred by adopting its own new rule instead of analyzing REC's summary judgment motion according to governing Fifth Circuit precedent. When a third party injures a seaman in an initial accident and a subsequent accident then aggravates that injury, giving rise to the need **[—13—]** for maintenance and cure, the subsequent accident raises the fact-bound question of the extent to which the initial accident caused the need for maintenance and cure. Under longstanding Fifth Circuit precedent, familiar tort principles of causation—including the affirmative defense of superseding cause—govern the result.

B.

Offshore Marine has established a genuine dispute of material fact as to whether REC caused in part Poincon's need for maintenance and cure. *See* Fed. R. Civ. P. 56(a); *Savoie*, 627 F.2d at 723–24. In its motion for summary judgment, REC pointed to an absence of evidence of causation and also asserted a superseding-cause affirmative defense. Once REC pointed to an absence of evidence of causation, the burden shifted to Offshore Marine to offer some evidence that raises a genuine dispute. *In re La. Crawfish Producers*, 852 F.3d 456, 462, 5 Adm. R. 226, 228 (5th Cir. 2017) (citing *Lindsey v. Sears Roebuck & Co.*, 16 F.3d 616, 618 (5th Cir. 1994)). Since REC bears the burden of proving its affirmative defense at trial, *see Michaels*, 202 F.3d at 752, REC "bears the initial responsibility of demonstrating the absence of [a genuine **{-299-}** dispute] of material fact with respect to" superseding cause, *Lindsey*, 16 F.3d at 618. Offshore Marine has met its burden, but REC has not.

Offshore Marine points to three main pieces of evidence to support its contention that the 2018 slip and fall aggravated Poincon's 2015 injury. First, in her deposition Poincon testified that she experienced continuing neck pain from 2015 onward and that her 2018 fall intensified that same neck pain. Second, the physician who treated Poincon recorded in his notes that the 2018 fall "aggravated the cervical injuries" from the 2015 collision. Third, **[—14—]** Offshore Marine's proposed expert opined in his report that "the 2015 accident [was] the reason for her cervical issues."[4]

Offshore Marine's evidence, if credited, would allow a finder of fact to conclude that REC caused Poincon's neck injury in 2015 and that the injury was later aggravated in 2018. Aggravation of a prior injury can be the basis

[4] REC criticizes Offshore Marine's proposed expert testimony as incompetent summary judgment evidence because the report is unsworn. *Cf.* Fed. R. Civ. P. 56(c)(2) ("A party may object that the material cited to support or dispute a fact cannot be presented in a form that would be admissible in evidence."). Offshore Marine, however, did not need to produce an admissible form of the expert's testimony to overcome summary judgment. *Celotex Corp. v. Catrett*, 477 U.S. 317, 324 (1986). It is enough that the evidence can be made admissible for trial. *See id.* REC has not supported its flat assertion that it cannot be.

for a contribution claim. *See* 1B *Benedict on Admiralty* § 47 (2020) ("Where a seaman is injured aboard one vessel and subsequently the injury becomes aggravated or reactivates on another vessel or vessels, all vessels involved are liable for maintenance and cure equally. However, if the injury was caused by the negligence or unseaworthiness of the first vessel, the later vessels may be entitled to reimbursement from the first vessel for their maintenance and cure payments."); 1 Thomas J. Schoenbaum, *Admiralty and Maritime Law* § 6.35 (6th ed. 2018); *see also Gauthier v. Crosby Marine Serv., Inc.*, 499 F. Supp. 295, 297–98, 300 (E.D. La. 1980), *aff'd*, 752 F.2d 1085 (5th Cir. 1985); *Gooden v. Sinclair Refin. Co.*, 378 F.2d 576, 581 (3d Cir. 1967); *Gore v. Clearwater Shipping Corp.*, 378 F.2d 584, 586–87 (3d Cir. 1967). Offshore Marine has therefore demonstrated a genuine dispute as to a material fact.

REC, conversely, has not shown the absence of a genuine dispute as to its superseding-cause affirmative defense. "The superseding cause doctrine applies where the defendant's negligence in fact substantially contributed to the plaintiff's injury, but the injury was actually brought about **[—15—]** by a later cause of independent origin that was not foreseeable." *Stolt Achievement*, 447 F.3d at 367–68.

On appeal, REC argues that there is no evidence that Poincon would have required treatment for her 2015 neck injury without the subsequent 2018 injury. But that assertion slightly misstates the superseding-cause issue. Offshore Marine must show that REC in some part caused the need for maintenance and cure. *Bertram*, 35 F.3d at 1014 ("[A] party whose neglect has caused or contributed to the need for maintenance and cure payments should reimburse the cost of those payments." (quoting *Savoie*, 627 F.2d at 723)). It is plausible that if Poincon had not suffered her 2015 neck injury from the REC collision, her 2018 slip and fall would not have injured her neck to the point of needing maintenance and cure. In that sense, the 2015 collision would be a proximate cause of the need for maintenance and cure—*i.e.*, the 2015 collision caused the injury and the 2018 slip **{–300–}** and fall aggravated it. *Cf. Michaels*, 202 F.3d at 751 (determining that a genuine dispute of material fact existed as to whether a pilot's negligence was the sole proximate cause of a malfunctioning airplane's crash).

Poincon's deposition, her medical records, and Offshore Marine's proposed expert's report support the conclusion that Poincon had the same neck injury from the time of the 2015 injury onward, and that the 2018 slip and fall simply worsened it to the point of Poincon needing maintenance and cure. Because there is a genuine dispute here, REC has not shown that it is "entitled to judgment as a matter of law" on its superseding-cause affirmative defense. Fed. R. Civ. P. 56(a).

* * *

For the reasons set forth above, the judgment of the district court is REVERSED, and the case is REMANDED for further proceedings consistent with this opinion.

United States Court of Appeals for the Fifth Circuit

No. 19-30907

ADAMS
VS.
ALL COAST, L.L.C.

Appeal from the United States District Court for the Western District of Louisiana

Decided: September 30, 2021

Citation: 15 F.4th 365, 9 Adm. R. 245 (5th Cir. 2021).

ON PETITION FOR REHEARING EN BANC
(Opinion February 11, 2021, 988 F.3d 203)

[—1—] {-366-} PER CURIAM: {-367-}

The court, having been polled at the request of one of its members, and a majority of the judges who are in regular active service and not disqualified not having voted in favor (FED. R. APP. P. 35 and 5TH CIRC. R. 35), the petition for rehearing en banc is DENIED. **[—2—]**

In the en banc poll, two judges voted in favor of rehearing (Judges Jones and Elrod), and fifteen judges voted against rehearing (Chief Judge Owen, and Judges Smith, Stewart, Dennis, Southwick, Haynes, Graves, Higginson, Costa, Willett, Ho, Duncan, Engelhardt, Oldham, and Wilson).

It is ORDERED that our prior panel opinion, *Adams v. All Coast, L.L.C.*, 988 F.3d 203 (5th Cir. 2021), is WITHDRAWN and the following opinion is SUBSTITUTED therefor.

* * * * *

Before **SMITH, CLEMENT,** and **OLDHAM,** Circuit Judges.

[—2—] {-367-} CLEMENT, Circuit Judge:

William Adams filed this collective action on behalf of himself and others employed on All Coast's fleet of liftboats. Although All Coast hired Adams and the other plaintiffs to serve in various maritime jobs, the employees claim they spent most of their time doing something completely terrestrial: using cranes attached to the boats to move their customers' equipment on and off the boats, the docks, and the offshore oil rigs.

All Coast did not pay the plaintiffs overtime because it classified them as seamen, who are exempt from the overtime pay rules in the Fair Labor Standards Act ("FLSA"), 29 U.S.C. §§ 201 *et seq.* Persuaded by All Coast's reading of the FLSA, the district court entered summary judgment for All Coast because the employees' work served the liftboats' operation "as a means of transportation." 29 C.F.R. § 783.31. We disagree. Such a reading strays from the statutory and regulatory text and our jurisprudence. As we explain below, All Coast was not entitled to summary judgment. Accordingly, we reverse and remand.

I.

All Coast hired Adams as an able-bodied seaman to work on its fleet of liftboats that service offshore oil and gas platforms in the Gulf of Mexico.[1] **[—3—]** But despite his job title, Adams maintains that his main duty had nothing to do with maritime work. Instead, Adams spent much of his time operating a hydraulic crane to move personnel and equipment between the liftboat and the dock, offshore worksite platforms, and other vessels, as well as on the liftboat itself. Adams claims that because he was really a crane operator and not a seaman, All Coast owes him unpaid overtime wages under the FLSA. **{-368-}**

Adams filed a collective action on behalf of himself and other similarly-situated All Coast mates, deckhands, ordinary seamen, and able-bodied seamen, who all say their job titles

[1] "A lift-boat is a self-propelled, self-elevating, offshore supply vessel. Although it functions and navigates much like any other supply vessel, a typical lift-boat is equipped **[—3—]** with three column-like legs that can be quickly lowered to the seafloor to raise the vessel out of the water and stabilize it for marine operations." *Naquin v. Elevating Boats, L.L.C.*, 744 F.3d 927, 930 n.1, 2 Adm. R. 200, 200 n.1 (5th Cir. 2014); *see* 46 C.F.R. § 90.10–20 ("Liftboat means an offshore supply vessel with moveable legs capable of raising its hull above the surface of the sea.").

hide their true task: crane operator. Along with the crew members, liftboat cooks joined the class, alleging that they too are entitled to overtime pay since they spent their time cooking for third parties and these allegedly non-seamen crew members.

Adams and the other crew member plaintiffs say they spent no less than 80 percent of their time in the jacked-up, stationary position. Indeed, for some jobs or "hitches," the boats were jacked up 100 percent of the time. And regardless the duration of the hitch, they never used the cranes when the boats were underway. All told, the district court found that the plaintiffs "spent between 25% and 90% of their day operating the crane." The plaintiffs all ate, slept, and worked aboard a boat. And, when they weren't operating the cranes, they performed traditional maritime functions under the command of the boat's captain.

The plaintiffs claim their work servicing offshore oil and gas wells consisted of "the types of things that anyone engaged in oil and gas exploration does regardless of whether drilling onshore or offshore." All Coast job tickets list tasks like "Coil tubing ops," "Crane ops," "Working **[—4—]** with divers," and "Working with welders." Similarly, the plaintiffs' deposition testimony explains how they used the cranes to hold coil tubing units in place for their customers on oil rigs, and to lower divers into the water and retrieve equipment the divers placed into the crane basket. On the other hand, the record also makes plain that the crew never stepped foot on the oil platforms, nor did they directly drill for oil and gas.

All Coast did not pay the crew and cooks overtime because it classified them as exempt seamen under the FLSA. *See* 29 U.S.C. § 213(b)(6). All Coast first filed a motion to dismiss, which the district court converted to summary judgment and then denied as premature. But the district court later granted summary judgment for All Coast. The court found that the cooks were exempt seamen because All Coast crew members ate at every meal the cooks prepared. And although the crew spent as much as 90 percent of their time operating the cranes, they too were exempt seamen because the liftboat crane operation was a "service which is rendered primarily as an aid in the operation of such vessel as a means of transportation." 29 C.F.R. § 783.31. Plaintiffs timely appealed.

II.

We review a grant of summary judgment de novo, "applying the same legal standards as the district court." *Petro Harvester Operating Co., L.L.C. v. Keith*, 954 F.3d 686, 691 (5th Cir. 2020). "Summary judgment is appropriate when 'the movant shows that there is no genuine dispute as to any material fact and the movant is entitled to judgment as a matter of law.'" *United States v. Nature's Way Marine, L.L.C.*, 904 F.3d 416, 419, 6 Adm. R. 258, 259 (5th Cir. 2018) (quoting FED. R. CIV. P. 56(a)).

In a dispute about an FLSA exemption, the employer has the burden of establishing that the exemption applies by a preponderance of the evidence. *Faludi v. U.S. Shale Sols., L.L.C.*, 950 F.3d 269, 273 (5th Cir. 2020). The Supreme Court has "clarified that courts are to give FLSA exemptions 'a fair reading,' as opposed to the narrow interpretation **[—5—]** previously espoused by this and other circuits." *Carley v. Crest Pumping Techs., L.L.C.*, 890 F.3d 575, 579 (5th Cir. 2018) (quoting **{-369-}** *Encino Motorcars, L.L.C. v. Navarro*, 138 S. Ct. 1134, 1142 (2018)).

III.

The FLSA's baseline requirement is that any employee who works "longer than forty hours" in a workweek must be compensated "at a rate not less than one and one-half times the regular rate at which he is employed." 29 U.S.C. § 207(a)(1). "An employee is not protected by this broad prohibition, however, if he falls within an exemption." *Coffin v. Blessey Marine Servs., Inc.*, 771 F.3d 276, 279, 2 Adm. R. 367, 368 (5th Cir. 2014). Among them, "any employee employed as a seaman." 29 U.S.C. § 213(b)(6). Although the FLSA does not define "seaman," we determined shortly after the FLSA's enactment that the exemption applies only when an employee performs nautical *duties*:

> Since the Act does not define the word seaman, it must be taken in its ordinary meaning. . . . [T]he words of the exemption are: "Employees *employed as* seamen." The italicized words mean something; they are not mere tautology. They warn us to look to what the employees do, and not to rest on a mere matter of a name, or the place of their work. The entire Act is pervaded by the idea that what each employee actually does determines its application to him.

Walling v. W.D. Haden Co., 153 F.2d 196, 199 (5th Cir. 1946).

Even so, our later decisions have recognized that the statute has its limits. For that reason, we look "primarily" to the Department of Labor's regulations, "which we have held to be entitled to great weight." *Coffin*, 771 F.3d at 279, 2 Adm. R. at 369 (citing *Dole v. Petroleum Treaters, Inc.*, 876 F.2d 518, 521 (5th Cir. 1989)); *see Tony & Susan Alamo Found. v. Sec'y of Labor*, 471 U.S. 290, 297 (1985) (describing the regulation's definition of "business purpose" under the FLSA as "entitled to considerable weight in construing the Act"). According to those criteria, an employee is a seaman if: "(1) the employee is **[—6—]** subject to the authority, direction, and control of the master; and (2) the employee's service is primarily offered to aid the vessel as a means of transportation, provided that the employee does not perform a substantial amount of different work." *Coffin*, 771 F.3d at 281, 2 Adm. R. at 370 (citing 29 C.F.R. § 783.31).

The parties do not dispute the first part of the test. There is no doubt that the employees all ate, slept, and worked aboard the vessels and were subject to a captain's authority. The dispute revolves around the second prong, particularly whether using a crane aids in a liftboat's operation *as a means of transportation*. The district court concluded that it did: "The amount of time the plaintiffs spent operating the crane, whether 10% of their time or 100%[,] is irrelevant because crane operation is seaman's work that aids the vessel as a means of transportation." That conclusion runs contrary to the regulatory language and our decisions interpreting it.

A.

One salient example in the regulation says that "assisting in the loading or unloading of freight at the beginning or end of a voyage" is not "connected with operation of the vessel as a means of transportation." 29 C.F.R. § 783.32. Another explains that "employees on floating equipment who are engaged in . . . construction . . . and employees engaged in dredging operations or in the digging or processing of sand, gravel, or other materials are not employed as seamen within the meaning of the Act but are engaged in performing essentially industrial or excavation work." *Id.* § 783.34. By the regulation's plain language, when the crew assists with loading **{-370-}** or unloading, or with "essentially industrial" tasks, that portion of their time is not seaman's work.

The record shows that the plaintiffs spent a significant amount of time doing just that. Based on the plaintiffs' depositions, the district court found that they "spent between 25% and 90% of their day operating the crane" "to transport personnel, supplies, and equipment back and forth between the **[—7—]** liftboat and the dock, the liftboat and the worksite platform, the liftboat and other vessels, and within the liftboat itself." And other deposition testimony confirms that the crew members used the cranes only when the liftboats were stationary, never underway. In short, the plaintiffs performed "loading or unloading of freight at the beginning or end of a voyage." 29 C.F.R. § 783.32.

Nor does the regulation suggest anything unique about the plaintiffs' loading and unloading that would lead us to a different conclusion. The regulation recognizes that *all* vessels will have cargo on board during transport. Yet the work of handling that cargo does not qualify as seaman's work. The district court found that All Coast's customers chartered the liftboats "to transport people and equipment on the liftboat to a worksite offshore." Hardly a unique task for a seagoing vessel. But contrary to All Coast's argument, the regulation suggests there is nothing special about the nature of All Coast's charters that would pull crane operations into the vessel's ambit "as a means of transportation." 29 C.F.R § 783.31. Consider the alternative. If that were so then *all* loading and unloading would qualify as seaman's work. Yet the regulation says the opposite. If anything, the use of a hydraulic crane makes the work less like a typical seaman's, not more.

Recall too that All Coast's customers chartered the liftboats to support their industrial activity at offshore rigs. The plaintiffs used the cranes to support divers and hold coil tubing units in place. To be sure, the plaintiffs were not the divers or the welders. But they were akin to support crew that allowed the divers and welders to perform their industrial work. We would not say—indeed, we have not said, *see* section III.C, below—that these plaintiffs were engaged in seaman's work if they performed the same functions from the rigs themselves. Why should that conclusion change because they stayed on the liftboats? The inquiry is "the character of the work" the plaintiffs did, "not on what it is called or the place where it is performed." *Coffin*, 771 F.3d at 280, 2 Adm. R. at 370 (quoting 29 C.F.R. § 783.33); *see* 29 C.F.R. § 783.34. **[—8—]**

Regardless, All Coast argues that "crane operation was one of many fully integrated seaman's duties that aided in the safe operation of the vessel as a means of transportation of personnel and equipment." Instead of consulting the Department of Labor's guidance, which All Coast urges "does not have the force of law and is persuasive only," All Coast refers the court to dictionary definitions of "seaman" from the time of the FLSA's enactment.[2] **{-371-}**

This court often looks to dictionary definitions to determine the ordinary meaning of key statutory terms. Indeed, in *W.D. Haden*, we consulted the same Webster's definition that All Coast proffers here: "one whose occupation is to assist in the management of ships at sea; a mariner." *W.D. Haden*, 153 F.2d at 198 (quoting *Seaman*, Webster's New Int'l Dictionary (2d ed. 1934)). But, as we have said, this court has long looked to the Department of Labor's regulations too, precisely because the meaning of "seaman" is undefined in the statute. *Coffin*, 771 F.3d at 279, 2 Adm. R. at 368–69.

And the definitions that All Coast cites do not dissuade us from our normal interpretive methods. Black's Law Dictionary said that a seaman must "in some capacity assist in [a ship's] conduct, maintenance, or service." *Seamen*, Black's Law Dictionary (3d ed. 1933). Similarly, the **[—9—]** Oxford English Dictionary said that a seaman's "occupation or business is on the sea," but, "Also, with qualifying word: One skilled in navigation." *Seaman*, Oxford English Dictionary (1st ed. 1933). Of these, only the first, unqualified, Oxford definition might support All Coast's reading of the term "seaman," but only then because of its breadth. "That a definition is broad enough to encompass one sense of a word does not establish that the word is *ordinarily* understood in that sense." *Taniguchi v. Kan Pac. Saipan, Ltd.*, 566 U.S. 560, 568 (2012). Instead, the ordinary

---

[2] All Coast primarily takes aim at the Department of Labor's guidance that work other than seaman's work is substantial if it accounts for more than 20 percent of an employee's work hours. *See* 29 C.F.R. § 783.37; *see also Coffin*, 771 F.3d at 281, 2 Adm. R. at 370. We take up that argument in section III.D, below. However, we have also considered All Coast's criticism as targeting the portion of the regulation delineating seaman's work. All Coast relies on the Second Circuit's opinion in *Munoz-Gonzalez v. D.L.C. Limousine Service, Inc.*, 904 F.3d 208 (2d Cir. 2018). But *Munoz-Gonzalez* concerned the Department of Labor's Handbook, not its regulations. *See id.* at 216 ("[T]he Department of Labor's Handbook lacks the force of law, and 'is entitled to deference only to the extent that it has the 'power to persuade.'" (quoting *Chen v. Major League Baseball Props., Inc.*, 798 F.3d 72, 83 (2d Cir. 2015))). In contrast, of course, we have repeatedly emphasized that the Department's regulations are entitled to "great weight." *Coffin*, 771 F.3d at 279, 2 Adm. R. at 369 (citing *Dole*, 876 F.2d at 521). Finding no conflict here between the statute's plain meaning and the regulatory guidance, we will continue to give them that weight.

meaning from this survey of definitions reinforces the Department's regulations: a seaman's duty must serve the ship's operation *as a ship*.

When read in concert, the natural reading of those regulations is that these plaintiffs were engaged in seaman's work when they performed their nautical duties, but not when using the hydraulic cranes. During the periods when they were underway, the crew performed only the nautical duties listed in their job descriptions.[3] But when the liftboats were jacked up, the crew spent more time operating the cranes than performing their nautical tasks. Thus, the plain meaning of 29 C.F.R. § 783.31, and the illustrative examples in §§ 783.32 and 783.34, suggest the employees were not engaged in seamen's work when operating the cranes.

B.

1.

Our previous decisions only reinforce that conclusion. The district court primarily focused its analysis on two of our cases analyzing the seaman exemption for plaintiffs who performed loading and unloading duties. In *Owens v. SeaRiver Maritime,* this court held that a tankerman who primarily **[—10—]** loaded and unloaded petroleum products from a permanently moored barge was not a seaman. 272 F.3d 698, 704 (5th Cir. 2001). But then in *Coffin*, we distinguished *Owens* and held that vessel-based tankermen who loaded and unloaded liquids were exempt seamen. **{-372-}** 771 F.3d at 282–84, 2 Adm. R. at 370–73. The district court reasoned that this case is closer to *Coffin*.[4] We disagree.

The plaintiff in *Owens* was an experienced tankerman who had been reassigned from seagoing vessels to a stationary landing barge, which was an old oil barge that was removed from navigation and permanently moored. 272 F.3d at 700. The employees who worked on the landing barge loaded and unloaded the petroleum product like a towboat crew. But unlike a normal barge, the landing barges were never towed or attended by a boat crew. The court noted that the skills the tankerman used on the landing barge "were similar to those he used when he was a towboat crewman, although [he] attended the [landing] barges only for the purposes of loading and discharging the product." *Id.* The court held that the tankerman's loading and unloading duties did not "aid in the operation of [a] vessel as a means of transportation." *Id.* at 704 (quoting 29 C.F.R. § 783.31); *see also id.* ("Workers who are primarily concerned with loading and unloading cargo are not, generally speaking, seamen." (citing 29 C.F.R. § 783.36)).

The defendant company in *Owens* argued that the loading and unloading was seaman's work because "if a barge was loaded or unloaded improperly it could not be safely moved or towed, and could even break apart." *Id.* The court rejected that "extremely broad and unsupportable construction of 'aid in the operation' of a 'vessel as a means of transportation.'" *Id.*

> Of course, the unloading and loading would have to be done in a safe or proper way, but that only *prepares* the vessel for **[—11—]** navigation; it does not aid in its actual *operation* as a means of transportation. A rule that includes within the definition of "seaman's work" for FLSA purposes all work that prepares a vessel for navigation would include quite a few activities, most of which would not fit comfortably within a commonsense definition of "seaman's work." And, [this] broad definition of "seaman's work" neglects the primary purpose of

[3] Among those duties, the crew stood lookout, checked the engine room, attached lifting devices to cables, spliced rope, cleaned and painted, steered the boat, and performed other traditional maritime duties related to navigation and upkeep. In addition, one job description in the record notably lists the position as FLSA Non-Exempt. Neither party explains that contradiction, so we do not address it.

[4] The district court also considered *Johnson v. Canal Barge*, 181 F. Supp. 3d 413 (S.D. Tex. 2016). There, the district court followed *Coffin* in holding that a vessel-based tankerman was a seaman despite his loading and unloading duties. *Id.* at 418.

> the loading and unloading—to get cargo on or off the barge. Even though Owens's loading and unloading duties were technical, specialized, and had to be done properly in order to assure proper navigation of the barge, they were still primarily cargo loading and unloading duties.

Id.; *see also id.* at 704 n.6 (noting that under the defendant's definition, "a land-based worker who installs navigation equipment on vessels would be a seaman, as would a worker at a refueling dock—both tasks . . . aid in the operation of a vessel as a means of transportation to the same degree as loading or unloading cargo").

In contrast, we held that the vessel-based tankermen in *Coffin* were seamen. There, the company was also in the business of shipping liquid cargo on barges. *Coffin*, 771 F.3d at 278, 2 Adm. R. at 367. The crew—including the plaintiff tankermen—lived and worked on the towboat and answered to the captain. The tankermen were responsible for the duties of a deckhand plus the "complex" process of loading and unloading the liquid from the barges. *Id.*, 2 Adm. R. at 367. Those tankermen argued that their duties associated with loading and unloading were nonseaman work, "while acknowledging their many other duties" were those of a seaman. *Id.* at 279, 2 Adm. R. at 368.

After identifying the Department's criteria in 29 C.F.R. § 783.31, the court rejected **{-373-}** another proposed categorical rule. Just as the court had refused to adopt a "broad and unsupportable" construction of the regulation in *Owens*, 272 F.3d at 704, the court similarly declined the tankermen's argument that "loading and unloading a vessel is *always* nonseaman work," *Coffin*, 771 F.3d at 280, 2 Adm. R. at 369. Instead, the court emphasized that "we *always* **[—12—]** consider the factual context when deciding whether an employee is exempt." *Id.*, 2 Adm. R. at 370. The court then highlighted that this is a case-specific inquiry:

> While the DOL regulations suggest that in many cases loading and unloading duties are nonseaman work, we recognized [in *Owens*] that such a rule cannot be categorical in the light of the DOL's crucial qualification that the application of the seaman exemption "depends *upon the character of the work* [an employee] actually performs and not on what it is called or the place where it is performed."

Id. at 280–81, 2 Adm. R. at 370 (quoting 29 C.F.R. § 783.33) (emphasis and second bracket in *Coffin*).

Several critical factors distinguished the vessel-based tankermen in *Coffin* from the plaintiffs in *Owens*. They "ate, slept, lived, and worked aboard [the] towboats," and "worked at the direction of the captain." *Id.* at 282, 2 Adm. R. at 371. Additionally, "their loading and unloading duties were integrated with their many other duties." *Id.* at 283, 2 Adm. R. at 372. But most important of all, "safe loading and unloading contributed to the efficient movement of the barge." *Id.* at 282, 2 Adm. R. at 371. Indeed, we have since interpreted the distinction between *Owens* and *Coffin* as coming down to "whether the 'primary purpose' of the particular individual's work is safe navigation of the ship." *Halle v. Galliano Marine Serv., L.L.C.*, 855 F.3d 290, 294, 5 Adm. R. 239, 241 (5th Cir. 2017) (citing *Owens*, 272 F.3d at 703–04; *Coffin*, 771 F.3d at 283–84, 2 Adm. R. at 371–73).

To underscore that importance, *Coffin* referred to the standards of 29 C.F.R. § 783.36 as a rebuttable "presumption that loading and unloading duties are nonseaman work because those duties are usually performed by harbor-based personnel who have little to no role in the barge's navigational mission." *Coffin*, 771 F.3d at 282, 2 Adm. R. at 371 (citations omitted). That presumption was overcome by the undisputed evidence in *Coffin* that the "vessel-based tankermen performed their loading and unloading duties with an eye toward navigation *and* were required to perform such duties safely so that the vessel could safely operate on inland and oceanic waterways." *Id.* at 284, 2 Adm. R. at 372. **[—13—]**

2.

Here, the plaintiffs were not doing seamen's work when they were operating the cranes. Yes, they were "subject to the authority, direction, and control of the master" of the vessel. 29 C.F.R. § 783.31. Like the plaintiffs in *Coffin*, the employees here lived and worked on the liftboats and answered to the captain. But the parties do not dispute that part of the test.

The disputed question is whether their service operating the cranes was "offered to aid the vessel as a means of transportation." 29 C.F.R. § 783.31. It was not. To be sure, the plaintiffs performed many tasks that *do* satisfy that test. When the boats were underway, they acted as a normal nautical crew. And they remained responsible for their nautical tasks even when the boats were jacked up. They attended safety meetings, cleaned up the liftboats, and performed regular inspections. But unlike in *Coffin*, the plaintiffs' loading and unloading duties were not "integrated with their many other duties." *Coffin*, 771 F.3d at 283, 2 Adm. R. at 372. Instead, once they finished their duties as the boat's crew, the plaintiffs turned their attention exclusively to operating **{–374–}** the cranes. It was as though they were performing two discrete jobs: upkeep of the boat and operation of the crane.

The district court found that the "crane operations had implications for the seaworthiness and efficient movement of the vessel." That might be so, in the broadest sense; one false move of a hydraulic crane could certainly hazard the safety of the boat. Yet that invokes the same "broad and unsupportable construction" of the regulation that we rejected in *Owens*, 272 F.3d at 704. The fact that the liftboats moved under their own power does not change the nature of the crane operations, particularly because the plaintiffs operated them only while the boats were stationary. As we said in *Owens*, "unloading and loading . . . only prepares the vessel for navigation; it does not aid in its actual operation as a means of transportation." *Id.*

In any event, the record evidence suggests the real danger was to personnel, not the liftboats. The plaintiffs testified that it was critical to **[—14—]** operate the cranes safely, mostly to avoid striking any personnel with the crane basket. But this merely reinforces common sense. Unlike the tankerman in *Coffin* who "regularly walk[ed] his barge to make certain that the barge was level" for fear that it would "get stuck when traveling down a river or canal," *Coffin*, 771 F.3d at 283–84, 2 Adm. R. at 372, the liftboat crew's safety concerns had less to do with the impact on the liftboats as boats than with the dangers incidental to hydraulic cranes as cranes. In short, the use of the cranes was not in furtherance of the "safe navigation of the ship." *Halle*, 855 F.3d at 294, 5 Adm. R. at 241.

C.

Additionally, the loading and unloading duties do not address the plaintiffs' other compelling framing of the issue: that they also used the cranes to support their customers' industrial activities on the oil platforms. The plaintiffs point to *W.D. Haden*, a case involving dredge boat crew members. Like the crew here and in *Coffin*, the dredge boat crew were "in the general sense seamen." *W.D. Haden*, 153 F.2d at 199. They lived on their vessels, stood watch, and could "be called on for any service like the ordinary sailor." *Id.* Their nautical work involved "management of the dredge boat and barges as vessels," whereas their industrial work involved "the mining and handling of shells . . . carried on by means of a floating mining plant." *Id.* We held that they were not exempt seamen under the FLSA because their industrial work "clearly" dominated, while their nautical work was "incidental and occasional, taking but a small fraction of the work time." *Id.*; *see* 29 C.F.R. § 783.34 (citing *W.D. Haden*).

All Coast argues *W.D. Haden* is "easily distinguished" because the dredge boats had no motive power of their own and were used only to dredge for shells. *See id.* at 197–99. That argument belies the finding that the crew indeed performed a nautical function; it was just outweighed by their industrial duties. *Id.* at 199. Still, it is undisputed that the employees in this case did not directly drill for oil and gas. Nor does All Coast directly collect **[—15—]** its customers' spoils. Instead, the charters pay All Coast for the support it renders, whether their drills produce oil or not.

But purely industrial activity is not required. In *Dole v. Petroleum Treaters*, this court held that plaintiffs who serviced and maintained oil wells were not exempt seamen, even though they "clearly [performed] some seamen duties in that they [operated] their vessels . . . between oil wells." *Dole*, 876 F.2d at 521. The plaintiffs spent at least half their time maintaining the wells. That, we held, entitled them to FLSA overtime under *W.D. Haden*. *Id.* All **{-375-}** Coast is correct that the liftboat crews never left their boats or conducted maintenance on the oil platforms. But the liftboats spent even more time jacked up, adjacent to the oil platforms, than the *Dole* plaintiffs spent maintaining oil wells. *See id.* And there is no question that the liftboat crews used the cranes to support their customers' maintenance efforts. They delivered equipment to the platforms, held casings in place, placed divers in the water, and retrieved equipment that the divers placed in the crane baskets. Like the plaintiffs in *W.D. Haden* and *Dole*, these were industrial activities that had no bearing whatsoever on the liftboats' operation or navigation.

The Seventh Circuit's analysis in *Harkins v. Riverboat Services*, 385 F.3d 1099 (7th Cir. 2004), is also instructive. There, the plaintiffs were crewmembers of a gambling riverboat. "[T]hey were not waiters or croupiers, but instead were responsible for the operation of the ship." *Harkins*, 385 F.3d at 1100. But a curiosity of the ship's operation was that it spent "at least 90 percent of its time moored to a pier in East Chicago." *Id.* As a result, "their life differ[ed] only slightly from that of ordinary casino workers." *Id.*

The Seventh Circuit noted that the seaman exemption would not apply "in a case in which a person employed on a ship was engaged in activities that had no maritime tincture whatever." *Id.* at 1103; *see* 29 C.F.R. § 783.34 ("Concessionaires and their employees aboard a vessel" are generally not seamen.). But "none of the plaintiffs [was] a croupier, cashier, **[—16—]** bouncer, dealer, waiter, or entertainer; all [were] . . . members of the ship's operating crew." *Id.* So the court posed this critical question:

> We can ask the question this way: do the plaintiffs spend their time performing duties that are necessary to the operation of the *Showboat* because it is a ship or because it is a casino? A blackjack dealer does not become a seaman by virtue of leaving his job at Harrah's land-based casino and taking a job at Harrah's riverboat casino, but likewise a helmsman does not cease to be a seaman because he transfers to a casino boat that spends most of its time moored.

Id. at 1104 (citation omitted).[5]

When we pose the same question here, the answer becomes obvious. Surely the crew members were not performing duties that were necessary to the operation of the liftboats as boats, but merely as platforms for the hydraulic cranes. If the crew had *only* serviced the liftboats while they stood stationary next to the oil platforms, that would have been seamen's work without question. *See id.* at 1104. But their use of the cranes had nothing to do with the operation of the liftboats—other than the obvious fact that they had brought the cranes with them. There is no evidence in the record from which we could conclude that those activities aided the liftboats at all as a means of transportation. Those tasks do not even meet the failed standard that they "*prepare[d]* the vessel for navigation." *Owens*, 272 F.3d at 704.

Accordingly, we hold that the plaintiffs' crane operation was not seaman work for purposes of the FLSA exemption. Whether the plaintiffs qualify for the exemption otherwise will be decided on remand. The district court

[5] The plaintiffs' appeal in *Harkins* followed a jury's verdict in favor of the riverboat company, finding the plaintiffs were exempt seamen. 385 F.3d at 1101.

thus erred in granting summary judgment for All Coast. As the district court said, because of the substantial amount of time the plaintiffs spent operating the cranes, "if crane operation—in this context—is not seaman's **[—17—]** work[,] then **{-376-}** Plaintiffs . . . cannot qualify as seamen." It was not, and they cannot—not while they were operating the cranes. We remand to the district court for further proceedings consistent with our holding.

D.

It follows that All Coast was not entitled to summary judgment as to the cooks either. Like any other crew member, a cook is a seaman "if, as is the usual case, [his] service is" "rendered primarily as an aid in the operation of such vessel as a means of transportation, provided he performs no substantial amount of work of a different character." 29 C.F.R. §§ 783.31, 32. "A cook is *usually* a seaman because he usually cooks *for* seamen." *Martin v. Bedell,* 955 F.2d 1029, 1036 (5th Cir. 1992). But this is not the usual case for two reasons.

First, the district court must consider this question again in view of our holding that the liftboat crew members were not engaged in seamen's work when operating the hydraulic cranes. Our statement in *Martin* recognized a cook's service to the vessel as a means of transportation by way of the crew he feeds. *See id.* If that crew is not serving the vessel as a means of transportation, then neither is the cook. Just as there is a fact issue on remand about the amount of time the crew spent operating the cranes, there is a corollary question about the amount of time the cooks spent in service to the vessel as a means of transportation.

Second, the district court must also consider how much time the cooks spent preparing food for All Coast's chartered passengers. The district court concluded in its summary judgment opinion that the cooks were seamen because "for every meal [they] cooked, All Coast crew members ate." But even if the crew members were exempt seamen (which we have held they were not), that finding alone does not support summary judgment. The question is not so simple as whether All Coast crew members ate some of the food at each meal the cooks prepared. Instead, the question is whether the cooks rendered a service that was *"primarily* [an] aid in the operation of such **[—18—]** vessel as a means of transportation, provided [they] perform[ed] no *substantial* amount of work of a different character." 29 C.F.R. § 783.31 (emphasis added).

The regulations adopt a position that "such differing work is 'substantial' if it occupies more than 20 percent of the time worked by the employee during the workweek." *Id.* § 783.37. We have often recognized that 20 percent figure as a guide, even if we have not been quite so mathematically precise. In *Martin,* we adopted the 20 percent figure outright when we remanded to the district court to "determine if the cooks spent more than 20 percent of their time preparing food for non-crew members." *Martin*, 955 F.2d at 1036 (cleaned up). In *Owens*, we applied a more flexible approach that eschewed "apply[ing] the twenty percent rule in a strict, mechanical fashion." *Owens*, 272 F.3d at 702 n.5.[6] And in both *Coffin* and *Halle*, we **{-377-}** considered whether non-seaman's work made up more than "approximately" 20 percent of an employee's time. *See Halle*, 855 F.3d at 296, 5 Adm. R. at 242 (citing *Coffin*, 771 F.3d at 279–80, 2 Adm. R. at 369). With the regulatory cutoff as a guide, a cook who spends more than roughly 20 percent of his time cooking for non-crew members or, as

[6] Our concern in *Owens* may have been colored by a conflation of the FLSA's seaman exemption and seaman status under the Jones Act. As we have said, "the definition of 'seaman' in the Jones Act is not equivalent to that in the FLSA." *Halle*, 855 F.3d at 294, 5 Adm. R. at 240 (citing *Dole*, 876 F.2d at 520). Thus, we should not have been concerned in *Owens* that crew members who spent more than 20 percent of their time on differing work would "lose their seaman status for the few weeks a year their vessels were in port." *Owens*, 272 F.3d at 702 n.5. That concern betrayed a Jones Act inquiry irrelevant to the crew members' entitlement to overtime pay under the FLSA, a betrayal emphasized by our citation to *Chandris v. Latsis*, a Jones Act case. *See id.* (citing *Chandris v. Latsis*, 515 U.S. 347, 371–72 (1995)).

here, crew members who are non-exempt seamen, has spent a "substantial" amount of time on differing work. 29 C.F.R. § 783.31.

The district court's initial inquiry did not address that question. It was not enough to say that the liftboat crew members ate at each meal the cooks prepared, because that did not address the amount of time the cooks **[—19—]** devoted to the task. The liftboats were usually manned by a crew of four. It is unclear from the record how many passengers they typically chartered to the rigs. But suppose that there was an equal number of passengers and crew. Or, just as likely, suppose that the passengers outnumbered the crew. Perhaps a cook who must prepare food for the crew can double or triple his output without substantially increasing the cooking and prep time. Then again, perhaps not.

These fact questions preclude summary judgment for All Coast. On remand, the district court will need to determine how much time the cooks spent preparing food for the crew when they were not performing seamen's work, and how much time they spent preparing food for non-crew members. If that adds up to a "substantial" amount, then they, like the crane-operating crew members, were not doing seamen's work. *See* 29 C.F.R. § 783.31; *Martin*, 955 F.2d at 1036.

IV.

For the foregoing reasons, we REVERSE the district court's summary judgment and REMAND the case for further proceedings.

(Reporter's Note: Dissenting Opinion follows on p. 255).

[—20—] {-377-} **JONES,** Circuit Judge, joined by **ELROD,** Circuit Judge, dissenting:

For the second time in two months, this court flouts *Encino Motorcars, L.L.C. v. Navarro*, 138 S. Ct. 1134 (2018). There, rectifying decades of misreading, the Supreme Court held that the Fair Labor Standards Act exemptions call for a fair—not narrow—reading. *Id.* at 1142. Vague notions of the FLSA's remedial purpose, the Court noted, could not support the lower courts' atextual narrow-construction principle. *Id.* After all, FLSA exemptions serve no purpose when the courts' tendentious and incomplete readings of statutory and regulatory text encourage costly litigation and the threat of large damages the Act authorizes.

But this court has not figured that out. Recently, this court misinterpreted the executive, administrative, and professional exemption, 29 U.S.C. § 213(a)(1), and its accompanying regulations, 29 C.F.R. §§ 541.0-541.710, to award overtime to an offshore oil toolpusher who managed at least a dozen employees and earned over $200,000 annually. *Hewitt v. Helix Energy Sols. Grp.*, No. 19-20023, 2021 WL 4099598 (5th Cir. Sept. 9, 2021) (en banc). Today's victim is the "seaman" exemption, 29 U.S.C. § 213(b)(6), and its regulations, 29 C.F.R. §§ 783.0-783.51. At least the employer here has a chance to persuade a jury that its liftboat crewmembers are exempt seamen—but the panel's broad holding threatens uncertainty throughout the maritime industry.[1] **[—21—]** {-378-}

The plaintiffs are Coast Guard licensed mariners who served as mates, deckhands, ordinary seamen, and able-bodied seamen aboard All Coast's liftboats.[2] A liftboat is an "offshore supply vessel with moveable legs capable of raising its hull above the surface of the sea." 46 C.F.R. § 90.10-20. They are considered "vessels" in navigable water, even when in the jacked-up position. *Strong v. B.P. Expl. & Prod., Inc.*, 440 F.3d 665, 669 (5th Cir. 2006). A crew of about six navigates these large, special-purpose vessels far out into the Gulf of Mexico to deliver or retrieve supplies, workers, and machinery, just like any other commercial vessel. Voyages are typically 14-day hitches, during which the plaintiffs live, sleep, and work on board under direction of the vessel's captain. The liftboats' mission and navigation are coterminous with trips to and from port.

At their offshore destinations, liftboats use cranes to move cargo and personnel from the liftboats' deck to oil platforms. In addition, the cranes may assist in diving and other oil production operations. But even when the liftboat is jacked up, the crewmembers retain responsibility for standing look-out, checking the engine room, splicing rope, cleaning, and performing other quintessential seaman's work. Crewmembers, therefore, alternate in working the cranes and serving other vessel functions.

As is the case for all commercial vessels, a raft of Coast Guard regulations governs liftboats. *See* 46 C.F.R. §§ 134.100-134.180. With their legs **[—22—]** precariously planted hundreds of feet down on the soft seabed, the liftboats' stability is a matter of paramount importance to avoid capsizing[3] or experi-

---

[1] *See* Br. of Amici Curiae, Offshore Marine Serv. Ass'n and Nat'l Ocean Indus. Ass'n in Support of Applicant for Reh'g En Banc, *Adams v. All Coast, L.L.C.*, No. 19-30907, Doc. No. 515799315 (5th Cir. Mar. 29, 2021); Amicus Curiae Br. of the Am. Maritime Ass'n in Support of All Coast, L.L.C.'s Pet. For Reh'g En Banc, *Adams v. All Coast, L.L.C.*, No. 19-30907, Doc. No. 515799406 (5th Cir. Mar. 29, 2021).

[2] My critique applies equally to the plaintiffs that served as cooks. For them, the panel opinion looks to *Martin v. Bedell*, 955 F.2d 1029 (5th Cir. 1992). The court there held that a "cook is *usually* a seaman because he usually cooks *for* seamen," but recognized that may not always be the case. *Id.* at 1036 (emphasis in original). The panel directs the district court to consider whether the cooks spent a substantial amount of time serving non-seamen but gives little direction on what that means. *Ante*, at 17-19. Does it mean the employer must compare the servings of stew given to the crew qua seamen versus the crew qua non-seaman? Or whether all dine at the same table? Either way, the inquiry is unwieldy.

[3] *See Marine Accident Brief, Overturning of the Liftboat Kristin Faye*, Nat'l Transp. Safety Bd. (Nov. 4, 2020), https://www.ntsb.gov/investigations/AccidentReports/Rep orts/MAB2036.pdf (detailing how a liftboat

encing "uncontrolled descent" from the jacked-up position, 46 C.F.R. § 134.150, a hazard that can occur from mechanical failures or unbalanced loads on deck. Crew safety is also critical, as the loss or incapacitation of a single crewmember may render the vessel unable to move according to Coast Guard regulations.[4] 46 C.F.R. § 15.501.

The FLSA exempts from minimum wage requirements any person "employed as a seaman." 29 U.S.C. § 213(b)(6). A series of regulations, largely intact since the Act's early days, governs the exemption. **{-379-}** [5] 29 C.F.R.§§ 783.0-783.51. Courts look to the ordinary meaning of "employed as a seaman," which entails a functional analysis of an employee's work.[6] As a result, each case depends on its particular facts. *Coffin v. Blessey* **[—23—]** *Marine Servs., Inc.*, 771 F.3d 276, 280, 2 Adm. R. 367, 370 (5th Cir. 2014) (citation omitted). And the employer bears the burden of showing employees are exempt. *Faludi v. U.S. Shale Sols., L.L.C.*, 950 F.3d 269, 273 (5th Cir. 2020).

All Coast argued, and the district court agreed as a matter of law, that the plaintiffs are exempt as persons "employed as seamen," in the ordinary meaning of that phrase, because crane operation is integral to the mission, transportation function, and seaworthiness of the liftboats.[7] I agree. The regulations support All Coast's characterization of the plaintiffs as exempt seamen. The panel's errors lie in (a) artificially compartmentalizing the crew-members' tasks into those connected with sailing the vessels and operating the cranes and (b) analogizing liftboat crane operations to "industrial work" like dredging.

Start with the general definition: "an employee will ordinarily be regarded as 'employed as a seaman' if he performs, . . . subject to the authority, direction, and control of the master aboard a vessel, service which is rendered primarily as an aid in the operation of such vessel as a means of transportation, provided he performs no substantial amount of work of a different character." 29 C.F.R. § 783.31. More specifically, the "term 'seaman' includes members of the crew such as sailors, engineers, radio operators, firemen, pursers, surgeons, cooks, and stewards if, as is the usual case, their service is of the type described in § 783.31. . . . However, an employee employed as a seaman does not lose his status as such simply because, as an incident to such **[—24—]** employment, he performs some work not connected with operation of the vessel as a means of transportation, such as assisting in the loading or unloading of freight at the beginning or end of a voyage . . . ." 29 C.F.R. § 783.32. The regulations continue by stating

capsized as a result of the crew's failure to conduct adequate pre-load tests before engaging in crane operations).

[4] Other regulations govern the structural standards necessary to handle adverse conditions, 46 C.F.R. § 134.140, and the contents of a liftboat's operating manual, 46 C.F.R. § 134.170, which, among other things, must include "[d]esigned limits for each mode of operation" like wave height and period, wind, current, temperatures, and "[o]ther environmental factors."

[5] In 1961, among other changes, seamen on American vessels were brought within the Act's minimum wage coverage, but they remain outside the overtime provision. 29 C.F.R. § 783.28. Speculation is that the differing conditions of work "between maritime and landside labor" led to seamen's continued exemption from overtime. *Tate v. Showboat Marina Casino P'ship*, 431 F.3d 580, 584 (7th Cir. 2005) (Posner, J.).

[6] *See Gale v. Union Bag & Paper Corp.*, 116 F.2d 27, 27-28 (5th Cir. 1940) ("The word 'seaman' has a plain, ordinary meaning universally applied. Whether a person is a seaman depends upon the character of his duties. If they are maritime in character and rendered on a vessel in commerce, in navigable waters, he is a seaman.") (citing *Int'l Stevedoring Co. v. Haverty*, 272 U.S. 50, 47 S. Ct. 19 (1926)); *see also* 29 C.F.R. § 783.29(b) ("the exemption was intended to exempt employees employed as 'seamen' in the ordinary **[—23—]** meaning of that word"); *Coffin v. Blessey Marine Servs., Inc.*, 771 F.3d 276, 281, 2 Adm. R. 367, 370 (5th Cir. 2014) ("This reading is consistent with our own precedent in which we attempt to give the term seaman its ordinary meaning").

[7] Ordinary Seaman Migues testified, for instance, that in operating the crane, it is important to be mindful of environmental conditions like the weather and the sea. ROA.2382. Other crewmembers emphasized hazards to the cargo and to personnel on both the liftboat and the receiving platform or vessel. ROA.2408.

that "[m]erely because one works aboard a vessel . . . , or may be articled as a seaman . . . , or performs some maritime duties . . . , one is not employed as a seaman . . . unless one's services are rendered primarily as an aid in the operation of the vessel as a means of transportation." 29 C.F.R. § 783.33. Finally, the regulations specify that some employees aboard vessels are not "employed as seamen," for example, "[c]oncessionaires **{-380-}** and their employees" and those working on floating construction equipment or a dredge. 29 C.F.R. § 783.34.

Fairly read, the regulations show that these plaintiffs are employed as seamen. Sections 783.31 and 783.32 create a strong presumption that the plaintiffs are employed as seamen because liftboat employees are crewmembers of a vessel, subject to a captain's authority, travelling on 14-day voyages to transport goods, personnel, and equipment offshore as well as assist in oil and gas operations. The crane operations are a sine qua non of the liftboat's function as a means of transportation; without the cranes, the liftboat serves no transportive purpose. And even when the liftboat is jacked up, the crewmembers continue to have seaman responsibilities other than their crane work. The panel's piecemeal treatment of the plaintiffs' duties ignores the intimate connection between the crane work and the liftboats' purpose as a means of transportation. Moreover, § 783.32 deems as "seamen" those employees who bear conventional maritime titles and roles (i.e. common law seamen), like these plaintiffs. That provision emphasizes that incidental work like loading or unloading the vessel at the beginning or end of a voyage does not disqualify traditional crewmembers from the seaman exemption. Thus, even if the employees perform certain crane operations when the liftboat is preparing to leave port or after it arrives in port, the common law **[—25—]** seamen are still exempt seamen. *See, e.g., Coffin*, 771 F.3d at 282-84, 2 Adm. R. at 371–73 (holding that vessel-based tankermen were employed as seamen when their duties included loading and unloading the barges, a task integrally connected to the barge's seaworthiness). Finally, § 783.33 identifies three characteristics of seaman's work, none of which alone shows that a person is employed as a seaman, but the plaintiffs and their work involve all three characteristics—voyaging aboard the liftboats, being articled seamen, and performing maritime duties. In short, the plaintiffs fit squarely into the regulations' definition of "employed as a seaman."

The regulations also explain types of employees who are not "employed as seamen," and the plaintiffs are not those types. Persons not "employed as seamen," include employees "engaged in the construction of docks, levees, revetments, or other structures, and employees engaged in dredging operations or in the digging or processing of sand, gravel, or other materials." 29 C.F.R. § 783.34. The regulations also exclude employees engaged in stevedoring or longshoring activities, 29 C.F.R. §§ 783.33, 783.38, and "concessionaires and their employees," 29 C.F.R. § 783.34; employees aboard vessels who are primarily engaged in performing such work are not within the seaman exemption.[8] It is absurd to class the plaintiffs here with those types of employees given these plaintiffs' constant attention to the performance of the liftboats qua vessels.[9] Insofar as the plaintiffs here are **[—26—]** articled seamen, undertaking voyages at the captain's command, and responsible for the vessel, their duties manifestly include the vessel's safe operation **{-381-}** when discharging cargo or personnel, regardless whether the liftboat is positioned on the seabed or moored near the receiving platform.

---

[8] The panel seriously erred, in my view, by analogizing this case to *Owens v. SeaRiver Maritime, Inc.*, 272 F.3d 698 (5th Cir. 2001), in which the plaintiffs were land-based workers who principally removed petroleum products from moored barges, like stevedores. Operating cranes from a liftboat at sea is entirely different from sucking petroleum products out of docked barges.

[9] Another helpful juxtaposition, explained by a sister circuit, is between the waiters and blackjack dealers on a floating, but largely stationary, casino boat, who are not exempt seamen, and the vessel's "marine crew," who, as a jury found, are exempt seamen. *Harkins v. Riverboat Servs. Inc.*, 385 F.3d 1099, 1104 (7th Cir. 2004).

Read holistically, the regulations do not preclude considering plaintiffs' crane operation as part of their overall seaman's duties; factually, there is more than enough to consider those operations as integral to the liftboats' transportation function. After all, if the cargo cannot be delivered at sea, the liftboat has no role. As a result, the panel's focus on the plaintiffs' contention that they spent more than 20 percent (and allegedly up to 90 percent) of their workday aboard the liftboats operating the cranes is misplaced. And anyway, that contention arises from self-serving deposition testimony and is subject to further examination at trial.[10]

The panel's decision is novel. Research has not uncovered a single case in which a blue-water crewmember, like the articled-mariner plaintiffs here, was held not to be an exempt seaman. The regulations in fact presume that crewmembers are "ordinarily" exempt seamen and may perform incidental loading or unloading activities while maintaining that status. 29 C.F.R. §§ 783.31, 783.32. The panel's analysis thus stands in serious tension with a reasonable and holistic interpretation of FLSA regulations. Moreover, this decision has far-reaching consequences for the liftboat industry. The panel appears to allow workers to walk in and out of FLSA exempt status [—27—] and thereby necessitates detailed and, frankly, meaningless timekeeping ordeals aboard ship.[11]

One may reply to this dissent that the regulations are the regulations, and a "textual" approach is all that matters. But, of course, what text matters most is the question here. In dissenting, I rely on the fact-specific approach and careful delineation of exceptions to the seaman exemption that the regulations embody. Moreover, if the result of the panel's narrow "textual" reading of these regulations is to splice and dice the seaman exemption into portions of "seaman" and "non-seaman" work within the space of each voyage—then the exemption is practically worthless.

That this case will go to a jury for ultimate resolution of the exemption offers some comfort, perhaps, to All Coast, but to the maritime industry as a whole, legitimate and longstanding expectations as to the FLSA's seaman exemption have been upended. I respectfully dissent from the failure to rehear this case en banc.

---

[10] Moreover, the regulation from which the 20% guideline derives, 29 C.F.R. § 783.37, concerns the amount of work per week that may be deemed substantial "non-seaman's work" for the government's "enforcement purposes." *Id.* So, as the panel seems to agree, the 20 percent guideline is just that, a guideline. *Ante*, at 18.

[11] For instance, the regulations plainly state that loading or unloading can be incidental to bona fide exempt seaman status, 29 C.F.R. § 783.32, but where does the panel opinion leave an employer? Can loading or unloading be seaman work *unless* it is unloading material onto an offshore platform, at which point it becomes non-exempt "industrial" work? Or, though loading or unloading work at the platform can be seaman work, is using cranes to hold coil tubing units or lower divers into the water to retrieve equipment never seaman work? If the latter is the panel approach, would that not require a granular assessment of the relative percentages of "industrial" crane work versus "incidental" loading or unloading? From a larger perspective, must the crane work be accounted for daily, weekly, or on a voyage-by-voyage basis? And how, under any of these scenarios, will the employer reasonably be able to comply with the FLSA other than to ignore the seaman exemption?

United States Court of Appeals for the Fifth Circuit

No. 20-30776

NEPTUNE SHIPMANAGEMENT SERVS. PTE
VS.
DAHIYA

Appeal from the United States District Court for the Eastern District of Louisiana

Decided: October 1, 2021

Citation: 15 F.4th 630, 9 Adm. R. 259 (5th Cir. 2021).

Before **JONES, SOUTHWICK,** and **COSTA,** Circuit Judges.

[—1—] {-632-} **COSTA,** Circuit Judge:

Last year, we noted that arbitration does not always fulfill its goal of avoiding court and "increas[ing] the speed of dispute resolution." *OJSC Ukrnafta v. Carpatsky Petroleum Corp.*, 957 F.3d 487, 493 (5th Cir. 2020) (quoting *AT&T Mobility LLC v. Concepcion*, 563 U.S. 333, 345 (2011)). That international dispute was tied up in arbitration and courts for thirteen years. *Id.* **[—2—]**

This case involves even more protracted litigation arising out of an arbitration agreement. In a dispute dating back to the **{-633-}** last century, the parties have turned to Louisiana state court, federal court, civil court in India, and arbitration to resolve their dispute. Although Vinod Kumar Dahiya has secured an arbitral award for his maritime injuries, he continues to pursue litigation against the alleged wrongdoers—and he still disputes that there was an enforceable agreement to arbitrate at all.

The district court concluded that, after two decades, the dispute was finally at an end. It confirmed the Indian arbitration award and enjoined further litigation. We agree and affirm.

I.

In the fall of 1999, Dahiya, an Indian national, began working as an engine cadet for the Singapore-based ship crewing agency Neptune Shipmanagement Services. He was soon assigned to the *M/T Eagle Austin*, an oil tanker owned by Talmidge International, bareboat chartered[1] to American Eagle Tankers, insured by the Britannia Steam Ship Insurance Association, and crewed by Neptune (collectively known as "the Vessel Interests").

Dahiya's employment contract—which the parties refer to as "the Deed"—bound him to sail for Neptune, but it did not mention Talmidge, American Eagle, or Britannia. Only Dahiya signed it. The Deed contained a **[—3—]** clause stating that any dispute arising out of the agreement would be subject to arbitration in either Singapore or India and governed by Indian law.

Dahiya joined the *Eagle Austin* crew in Texas and sailed on the vessel as it travelled along the Gulf Coast, making stops in Beaumont, Lake Charles, and other oil ports. In late 1999, while in international waters en route to Louisiana, Dahiya was severely burned as he operated the vessel's trash incinerator. He was evacuated by helicopter to Baton Rouge and treated for second- and third-degree burns and an infection.

After recovering, Dahiya sued the Vessel Interests in Louisiana state court. The Vessel Interests sought to compel arbitration under the Deed. They removed the case to federal court, invoking jurisdiction under the removal provision relating to the Convention on the Recognition and Enforcement of Foreign Arbitral Awards (New York Convention). *See* 9 U.S.C. § 205. But the district court denied the motion to compel arbitration, holding that forum selection clauses in employment contracts "contravene strong Louisiana public policy." *Dahiya v. Talmidge Int'l, Ltd.*, 2002

[1] In a bareboat charter, "the vessel owner transfers full possession and control to the charterer, who in turn furnishes the crew and maintenance for the vessel (thus the term 'bareboat')." *Forrester v. Ocean Marine Indem. Co.*, 11 F.3d 1213, 1215 (5th Cir. 1993). The charterer therefore becomes responsible "for the negligence of the crew and the unseaworthiness of the vessel." *Id.*

WL 31962151, at *2 (E.D. La. Oct. 11, 2002). The court also determined that, because the forum selection clause was invalid, no basis for removal existed, so it remanded the case to state court. *Id.*

We dismissed the Vessel Interests' appeal of that order. *Dahiya v. Talmidge Int'l, Ltd.*, 371 F.3d 207, 208 (5th Cir. 2004). The statute governing removal procedure, we explained, bars appellate review of a remand order "no matter how erroneous."[2] *Id.* at 209 (quoting **{-634-}** *Arnold v. State Farm Fire & Cas. Co.*, 277 F.3d 772, 775 (5th Cir. 2001)); *see* 28 U.S.C. § 1447(d). **[—4—]**

Back in state court, the trial court also denied the Vessel Interests' motion to compel arbitration. At the end of the resulting trial, the court awarded Dahiya more than $579,000.

It was a short-lived victory. A Louisiana appellate court reversed the judgment on the ground that the Deed's arbitration clause was enforceable. *Dahiya v. Talmidge Int'l Ltd.*, 931 So. 2d 1163, 1171–73 (La. Ct. App. 2006). It thus remanded the case to the trial court with instructions to stay the lawsuit and compel arbitration in India. *Id.* at 1173.

On remand, Dahiya argued that the case should be stayed only against Neptune because the remaining Vessel Interests were not parties to the Deed containing the arbitration clause. But the trial court stayed the case "in its entirety pending arbitration," halting Dahiya's lawsuit against all the defendants.

The parties then shifted their focus to arbitration. After various delays and procedural blunders in India, Dahiya at last obtained an award in early 2020. The arbitrator awarded Dahiya 95 Lakh (about $130,000) against Neptune; Dahiya had not named the other Vessel Interests as respondents. Although the Vessel Interests offered to satisfy the award, Dahiya refused to accept payment, preferring instead to rekindle the state-court litigation.

Following the award, Dahiya returned to Louisiana court. With the stay now expired, he sought to reinstate the previously rendered $579,000 **[—5—]** judgment or obtain a new trial. The Vessel Interests again removed the lawsuit to federal court.

The Vessel Interests also filed a new federal lawsuit to confirm the Indian arbitration award under the New York Convention (this time invoking 9 U.S.C. § 207) and to enjoin Dahiya from pursuing any further litigation. Although both of these cases were pending before the same district court, the court declined to consolidate them.

Dahiya then moved to dismiss the new, award-confirmation suit brought by the Vessel Interests, arguing that the district court's remand in the original case prevented federal jurisdiction from ever again being exercised over the dispute. Undeterred, the Vessel Interests sought summary judgment confirming the award and reiterated their request for injunctive relief "to bring this interminable litigation to an end."

The district court granted summary judgment, terminating Dahiya's "increasingly quixotic bid to win greater damages in the United States." *Neptune Shipmanagement Servs. (PTE.), Ltd. v. Dahiya*, 2020 WL 6059647, at *1 (E.D. La. Oct. 14, 2020). The court thus enforced the Indian arbitration award and enjoined all pending and future

---

[2] The district court has since acknowledged that it made a mistake and should have enforced the arbitration clause. *Lejano v. Bandak*, 2004 U.S. Dist. LEXIS 27341, at *3 n.1 (E.D. La. May 27, 2004) (recognizing the error); *see Lim v. Offshore Specialty Fabricators, Inc.*, 404 F.3d 898, 906 (5th Cir. 2005) (holding that Louisiana law does not invalidate **[—4—]** arbitration clauses in employment contracts of foreign seamen). But even apart from whether the district court correctly ruled on the clause's enforceability, removal jurisdiction exists under 9 U.S.C. § 205 as long as "there is a conceivable connection to an arbitration agreement." *OJSC Ukrnafta*, 957 F.3d at 495. "Removal to federal court may thus be proper even when it turns out there is no arbitration agreement." *Id.* at 496. The district court improperly raised this "low bar" for removal by assessing the validity of the agreement in the course of determining its jurisdiction. *Id.* at 495.

legal actions arising from Dahiya's 1999 injuries.

Following its ruling, the district court entered final judgment confirming Dahiya's arbitral award in the amount of $300,580, a figure the parties proposed that includes accrued interest. Days later, **{-635-}** the Vessel Interests paid that amount in full.

These rulings came in the Vessel Interests' newly filed federal case seeking confirmation of the arbitration award. But as a result of the injunction it issued, the district court closed the original state-court case that the Vessel Interests had again removed to federal court. Dahiya appeals only **[—6—]** from the new federal case; he did not file a separate appeal of the removed action.

II.

Dahiya challenges the district court's subject matter jurisdiction to confirm the arbitral award, the enforceability of the arbitration clause itself, and the court's determination that the award prevents him from pursuing litigation even against the Vessel Interests that were not parties in the arbitration.

Our review begins with Dahiya's challenge to the district court's jurisdiction to confirm the award. Federal courts have the power to enforce awards subject to the New York Convention because these actions "arise under the laws and treaties of the United States." 9 U.S.C. § 203. Any party to an arbitration that falls under the Convention may apply to a federal court "for an order confirming the award as against any other party." *Id.* § 207. This case fits well within the heartland of that jurisdictional grant.[3]

Dahiya nonetheless argues that the district court lost its jurisdiction to enforce the award—or preside over any aspect of this dispute—in 2002, when it remanded the prearbitration suit to state court. He is mistaken. A **[—7—]** remand order issued nineteen years ago in a different lawsuit has no impact on the district court's ability to confirm the award.

To support his view that the 2002 remand binds this case, Dahiya emphasizes that "[a]n order remanding a case to the State court from which it was removed is not reviewable on appeal." 28 U.S.C. § 1447(d). True enough, and we followed that command when we dismissed the Vessel Interests' direct appeal from the 2002 remand order. *Dahiya*, 371 F.3d at 209. But the removal statutes also contemplate that a lawsuit not removable at its inception may later become removable. *See* 28 U.S.C. 1446(b)(3). Accordingly, we held that an earlier remand did not preclude a second removal based on diversity jurisdiction when a postremand deposition made clear the amount-in-controversy requirement was satisfied. *S.W.S. Erectors, Inc. v. Infax, Inc.*, 72 F.3d 489, 492 (5th Cir. 1996) ("The Fifth Circuit recognizes a defendant's right to seek subsequent removals after remand."). Thus, even in the same case, a defendant may seek removal more than once, so long as the request rests on different grounds, like new pleadings or ensuing events that reveal a basis for federal jurisdiction. *Id.* **{-636-}**

Surely, then, a federal court may hear a separate action premised on new factual developments that support federal jurisdiction. That describes this new case, as it seeks to confirm an arbitration award that did not exist back in 2002. This case was never pending in state court; it is a new action distinct from the litigation seeking to compel arbitration.

[3] As the district court held, Dahiya's award falls under the Convention's umbrella because it was issued in a signatory state (India), the parties seek enforcement in another signatory state (the United States), it arises from a commercial dispute, and it involves at least one non-U.S. citizen (Dahiya). *See Asignacion v. Rickmers Genoa Schiffahrtsgesellschaft mbH & Cie KG*, 783 F.3d 1010, 1015, 3 Adm. R. 304, 305–06 (5th Cir. 2015).

It may be that, as the only plaintiff to participate in the arbitration, Neptune alone has a claim to confirm the award. But that provides the jurisdictional hook for the suit. The claims of the other Vessel Interests seeking to enjoin Dahiya from engaging in further litigation would come into federal court through supplemental jurisdiction. *See* 28 U.S.C. §§ 1367(a), 1441(a).

Dahiya attempts to circumvent this problem by arguing that even a new suit can be an impermissible collateral attack on a remand order issued in an earlier one. *See New Orleans Pub. Serv., Inc. v. Majoue*, 802 F.2d 166, 167–68 (5th Cir. 1986) (holding that there was no federal jurisdiction over an action that was "nothing more than an artful, if not subtle, attempt to circumvent . . . § 1447(d)"). Such a collateral attack occurs when the same **[—8—]** arguments advanced in new litigation "were fully before the court on the petition for removal and subsequent petition for remand." *Id.* That is not what is happening here. The first lawsuit sought to compel arbitration before it had occurred. This one seeks to confirm an arbitration award that has now issued. This recent factual developmental—an award in an arbitration falling under the New York Convention—gives rise to federal jurisdiction. *See* 9 U.S.C. § 207.

Consider a suit alleging state-law unfair competition and trade secret claims. Absent diversity, such a case would not be removable. But if the plaintiff later obtains a patent on the technology at issue, she could then file an infringement suit in federal court. A remand in the first suit would not matter because the second one is based on an intervening event—the acquisition of a patent—that gives rise to federal jurisdiction.

As this hypothetical illustrates, a remand order in an earlier case is not controlling in a new case with a new basis for federal jurisdiction. Yet Dahiya still pushes back, arguing that we must ignore the arbitral award in determining jurisdiction because the remand order in the earlier case held that no enforceable arbitration agreement existed. That earlier ruling, Dahiya contends, gave rise to issue preclusion.

The issue preclusion argument also fails, however, because an unappealable ruling like a remand order is not entitled to preclusive effect. *Beiser v. Weyler*, 284 F.3d 665, 673 (5th Cir. 2002) (explaining that when "a litigant, as a matter of law, has no right to appellate review, then he has not had a full and fair opportunity to litigate and the issue is not precluded"); *see Winters v. Diamond Shamrock Chem. Co.*, 149 F.3d 387, 395 (5th Cir. 1998) (suggesting that "collateral estoppel may not be applied offensively to a jurisdictional decision—such as one granting a motion to remand—that is not capable of being subjected to appellate review"); 18A CHARLES ALAN **[—9—]** WRIGHT ET AL., FEDERAL PRACTICE AND PROCEDURE § 4433 n.39 (3d ed. 2021).[4]

The unappealability of remand orders is why, after a remand, a state court may revisit the federal court's jurisdictional reasoning. **{-637-}** *Kircher v. Putnam Funds Tr.*, 547 U.S. 633, 647 (2006); *Mo. Pac. Ry. Co. v. Fitzgerald*, 160 U.S. 556, 583 (1896). We recognized this principle in dismissing the appeal of the 2002 remand: "[T]he district court determined that the arbitration clause was invalid in the process of ascertaining whether it had subject matter jurisdiction," which meant the ruling "has no preclusive effect in state court." *Dahiya*, 371 F.3d at 211. The state court could freely reexamine the issue and "reach a different conclusion about [the] dispute's arbitrability." *Beiser*, 284 F.3d at 674.

The Louisiana Fourth Circuit Court of Appeal did just that, holding that federal law preempted the state statute prohibiting forum selection clauses and that the arbitration clause was enforceable. *Dahiya*, 931 So. 2d at 1172. The remand order lacked preclusive effect then as it does now. It determined the forum for the suit seeking to compel arbitration and nothing more. *See Kircher*, 547 U.S. at 647.

---

[4] There is another reason issue preclusion does not apply: this case and the earlier one do not involve an "identical issue." *See B&B Hardware, Inc. v. Hargis Indus. Inc.*, 575 U.S. 138, 153 (2015) (observing that issue preclusion applies only when "the issues in the two cases are indeed identical" (quoting 6 J. THOMAS MCCARTHY, TRADEMARKS AND UNFAIR COMPETITION § 32:99, at 32–244) (4th ed. 2014)). As we have explained, the issue in this case—whether a federal court has jurisdiction in a suit to confirm an arbitration award falling under the New York Convention—is not the same one decided in 2002 before Dahiya and Neptune arbitrated.

III.

Although a district court's remand order does not have preclusive effect, the judgment of a state appellate court surely may. That is the **[—10—]** problem with Dahiya's final two arguments: first, that the arbitration clause is invalid because Neptune never signed it, and second, that Dahiya was not required to arbitrate his claims against the remaining Vessel Interests.

A.

To begin, Dahiya contends that the district court erred in confirming the arbitral award against Neptune because Neptune did not sign the contract containing the arbitration clause. He cites Article II of the New York Convention, which defines arbitration agreements as "agreement[s] in writing," a term that "include[s] an arbitral clause in a contract or an arbitration agreement, signed by the parties or contained in an exchange of letters or telegrams." Convention on the Recognition and Enforcement of Foreign Arbitral Awards art. II, June 10, 1958, 21 U.S.T. 2517, 330 U.N.T.S. 3. Because Neptune never signed the Deed, and federal courts only have jurisdiction over awards "falling under the Convention," 9 U.S.C. § 207, Dahiya claims the district court had no authority to confirm the award.

But this case is not the first time Dahiya has raised an Article II issue with the Deed. Before the arbitration, he argued in front of the Louisiana appellate court that the agreement violated Article II because it was "signed only by him and not by Neptune." The state court did not buy the argument. It held that "Mr. Dahiya's arbitration clause easily meets all four requirements of the Convention," including Article II's agreement-in-writing provision. *Dahiya*, 931 So. 2d at 1172.

This ruling prevents us from revisiting whether the Deed contains an enforceable arbitration clause. Federal courts must "give preclusive effect to state-court judgments whenever the courts of the State from which the judgments emerged would do so." *Allen v. McCurry*, 449 U.S. 90, 96 (1980) (citing 28 U.S.C. § 1738). And under Louisiana law, "[a] judgment in favor of either the plaintiff or the defendant is conclusive, in any subsequent action **[—11—]** between them, with respect to any issue actually litigated and determined if its determination was essential to that judgment." *In re Keaty*, 397 F.3d 264, 270 (5th Cir. 2005) (quoting LA. STAT. ANN. § 13:4231(3)). It would be hard to find an issue more essential to a decision compelling arbitration than the court's determination that there is a binding arbitration agreement. **{-638-}**

Dahiya's argument that Neptune's signature was required would have fared no better in our court. Fifth Circuit caselaw holds that Article II does not require a signature when the arbitration clause is part of a broader contract. *Sphere Drake Ins. PLC v. Marine Towing, Inc.*, 16 F.3d 666, 669 (5th Cir. 1994). Our view may now be in the minority,[5] but even so, we did not compel arbitration here—the state court did. Preclusion principles prevent us from revisiting that ruling. And the reliance interests that preclusion law protects are especially strong here as the parties have spent years pursuing arbitration in India. *See Montana v. United States*, 440 U.S. 147, 153–54 (1979) (explaining that preclusion protects against "the expense and vexation attending

[5] Other circuits, led by the Second Circuit, have rejected *Sphere Drake*'s approach and held that Article II requires both stand-alone arbitration agreements and contracts containing an arbitration clause to be signed by the parties. *Kahn Lucas Lancaster, Inc. v. Lark Int'l Ltd.*, 186 F.3d 210, 218 (2d Cir. 1999), *abrogation on other grounds recognized by Marks on Behalf of SM v. Hochhauser*, 876 F.3d 416, 420 (2d Cir. 2017); *see also Yang v. Majestic Blue Fisheries, LLC*, 876 F.3d 996, 1001, 5 Adm. R. 437, 440 (9th Cir. 2017) (calling *Sphere Drake* an "outlier decision" and questioning whether our court would reach the same conclusion today), *abrogated on other grounds by GE Energy Power Conversion Fr. SAS, Corp. v. Outokumpu Stainless USA, LLC*, 140 S. Ct. 1637, 1642 (2020); *Czarina, LLC v. W.F. Poe Syndicate*, 358 F.3d 1286, 1290–91 (11th Cir. 2004) (following *Kahn Lucas* in holding that Article II requires a signed agreement); *Standard Bent Glass Corp. v. Glassrobots Oy*, 333 F.3d 440, 449 (3d Cir. 2003) (adopting *Kahn Lucas*).

multiple lawsuits, conserves judicial resources, and fosters reliance on judicial action by minimizing the possibility of inconsistent decisions"). **[—12—]**

B.

Finally, Dahiya argues that the district court erred in barring him from litigating against Talmidge, American Eagle, and Britannia because only Neptune was a party to the Deed. But the state court's ruling is preclusive on this question, too.[6]

Dahiya argued before the Louisiana appellate court that "[e]ven if Neptune were entitled to have its liability arbitrated, there is no basis for an arbitration defense for any of the other defendants." The court disagreed, ruling that "the *defendants'* Exceptions of No Right of Action, Improper Venue and Arbitration should have been sustained and the case stayed pending arbitration." *Dahiya*, 931 So. 2d at 1173 (emphasis added). Even more important than what the court said is what it did--reverse the verdict that had been entered against all the Vessel Interests. *Id.* The arbitration agreement was the only reason cited for undoing that verdict not just as to Neptune but for all the defendants. *See id.* Despite Dahiya's efforts, nothing in the state court's opinion segregated his claims against the different parties on the basis of only some being subject to arbitration.

After the Louisiana appellate court remanded the case for the trial court to issue a stay, Dahiya again argued that he should be allowed to litigate against the Vessel Interests other than Neptune. He maintained before the state trial court that the "defendants other than [Neptune were] not parties to the arbitration agreement, **{-639-}** and have no right to avoid suit in favor of an arbitration to which they will not be a party." The state trial court **[—13—]** nonetheless stayed the litigation "in its entirety." In doing so, the court rejected Dahiya's attempt to proceed to trial against some of the Vessel Interests while the arbitration was ongoing. *See M.J. Farms, Ltd. v. Exxon Mobil Corp.*, 998 So. 2d 16, 26 (La. 2008) ("Generally, when a trial court judgment is silent as to a claim or demand, it is presumed the relief sought was denied." (citations omitted)). We must respect the state court's judgment. *See* U.S. CONST. art. IV, § 1.

After the Louisiana courts halted the litigation, ordering Dahiya to arbitrate his claims, Dahiya had the opportunity to do just that. He could have named all the Vessel Interests as respondents in the arbitration. In fact, Dahiya's submissions to the arbitrator included allegations, such as unseaworthiness, most appropriately directed at the *Eagle Austin*'s owner (Talmidge) or charterer (American Eagle). *See Forrester v. Ocean Marine Indem. Co.*, 11 F.3d 1213, 1215 (5th Cir. 1993). Yet Dahiya named only Neptune as the respondent.

Dahiya's failure to include Talmidge, American Eagle, and Britannia in the arbitration constitutes a failure to prosecute his claims against those entities. *See Griggs v. S.G.E. Mgmt., L.L.C.*, 905 F.3d 835, 845 (5th Cir. 2018) (affirming dismissal for failure to prosecute after plaintiff refused to initiate arbitration as ordered by court). Having secured an arbitral award for his injuries, Dahiya cannot now double dip via litigation.

* * *

The judgment is AFFIRMED.

---

[6] The district court also held that Dahiya's claims against the Vessel Interests were intertwined, meaning that the entities excluded from the Deed could enforce its arbitration clause under the doctrine of equitable estoppel. *See Grigson v. Creative Artists Agency, L.L.C.*, 210 F.3d 524, 526–27 (5th Cir. 2000). We need not address this question as issue preclusion alone provides sufficient grounds to affirm the judgment.

United States Court of Appeals for the Fifth Circuit

No. 20-40811

COLEMAN vs. BP EXPLORATION & PROD., INC.

Appeal from the United States District Court for the Southern District of Texas

Decided: November 29, 2021

Citation: 19 F.4th 720, 9 Adm. R. 265 (5th Cir. 2021).

Before **HIGGINBOTHAM, WILLETT,** and **DUNCAN,** Circuit Judges.

[—1—] {–725–} WILLETT, Circuit Judge:

High ocean winds caused an oil-platform worker to injure his back while building scaffolding. He sued the companies managing both the day-to-day construction and the overall construction project. Neither company was his direct employer. Because a reasonable jury could not find either company liable for the worker's injury, we AFFIRM summary judgment for Defendants. **[—2—]**

I

Shell Pipeline Co. LP wanted to expand a fixed oil platform that it operated out on the Outer Continental Shelf ("OCS"), off Louisiana's coast. Not wanting to manage the expansion project itself, Shell engaged BP Exploration & Production. BP then delegated the project's day-to-day management to Grand Isle Shipping, LLC. From there, Grand Isle engaged Brand Energy Services to build some scaffolding on the platform. One of Brand's scaffold builders was Ledell Coleman, the plaintiff appellant.

Safety out on the platform was paramount. BP made everyone adopt and receive training on its safety rules; required Grand Isle to "take full responsibility for the . . . safety of all its operations and methods"; used onsite safety supervisors; and delegated to everyone authority to "stop work" if conditions were unsafe. Grand Isle did similarly. It required Brand to expressly warrant that its workers could perform the work "safely"; also used on-site safety supervisors; tightly controlled access to the tools that Brand used to build the scaffolding; and issued applicable safety equipment to Brand's employees. Brand, in turn, retained autonomy over when it would work. It completed a "Job Safety Environmental Assessment" before every shift and, as part of that assessment, considered "weather conditions" when deciding "the right time" to work.

The right time to work was not when Coleman first arrived at the platform. High winds kept Coleman on a housing vessel, located adjacent to the platform, for five days after he arrived. On the fifth day, though, BP told Brand that the wind had died down to "like, 22" knots. Brand decided **{–726–}** that "now [is] the right time to [do] the work." BP then began to transport Coleman and other Brand workers onto the platform.

Though the wind continued, Coleman arrived at the platform and began to build the scaffolding. To build the scaffolding, Coleman had to carry **[—3—]** heavy, eight-foot-long scaffolding boards. At some point while he was carrying a board, the wind gusted and "got up under it." Coleman tried to "snatch[] it to keep it from going overboard." Something in his back "popped" and his back began to hurt. Coleman informed his supervisor and returned to the housing vessel. He was evacuated the next day.

Coleman sued BP and Grand Isle in Texas state court for negligence.[1] Grand Isle removed the case to federal district court. Following discovery, each Defendant moved for summary judgment on Coleman's remaining claims. They argued that Louisiana's independent-contractor rule barred holding them liable for Brand's negligence. They further argued that no evidence supported that they committed independent negligent acts against Coleman. The district court agreed, granted both motions, and then entered a final judgment

[1] Coleman brought other claims as well, but he agreed to dismiss them prior to Defendants' motions for summary judgment.

dismissing Coleman's claims. Coleman appealed.

II

We review summary judgment de novo and apply the same standard as the district court.[2] We may affirm only if no genuine dispute of material fact exists and Defendants were entitled to judgment as a matter of law.[3] Defendants may satisfy their burden by demonstrating "a complete failure of proof" on an "essential element" of Coleman's case.[4] Still, we must view all evidence and draw all justifiable inferences in favor of Coleman, the **[—4—]** nonmovant.[5] A "genuine" fact dispute exists only if a reasonable jury could return a verdict for Coleman based on the evidence.[6] "Conclusional allegations and denials, speculation, improbable inferences, unsubstantiated assertions, and legalistic argumentation do not adequately substitute for specific facts showing a genuine issue for trial."[7]

The parties agree that we should look to Louisiana law in evaluating Coleman's claims against the summary-judgment standard. We agree with a caveat. The platform where Coleman was injured was located off Louisiana's coast and affixed to the OCS. *Federal* law exclusively governs out on the OCS.[8] Not the state of Louisiana's. But given the platform's location, we will *adopt* Louisiana law "as surrogate federal law" when it is "applicable **{-727-}** and not inconsistent with . . . other Federal laws."[9]

Louisiana vicarious-liability and negligence law is applicable and not inconsistent with other federal laws in this case. As the Supreme Court recently explained, we adopt state law "only where there is a gap in federal law's coverage."[10] If "a federal law addresses the issue at hand," then no gap exists.[11] The parties do not point us to any federal laws that address the merits **[—5—]** in this case. Therefore, we will adopt Louisiana law—as surrogate federal law—in deciding it.

III

Coleman contends that a genuine dispute of material fact exists on whether Defendants are vicariously liable for Brand's negligence. He bases his contention on three different theories: (A) that Brand was not an independent contractor with respect to Defendants; (B) even if Brand was an independent contractor, then Defendants exercised operational control over it; and (C) even if Brand was an independent contractor, then Defendants are vicariously liable for authorizing unsafe work practices. We are unpersuaded.

A

Coleman's first vicarious-liability theory is that Brand was not Defendants' independent contractor, but their employee. Adopting Louisiana law, "a principal is not liable for the negligent acts of an independent contractor acting pursuant to the contract."[12] The five "*Hickman*" factors govern deciding whether Brand qualified as an independent contractor.[13] On this evidence their balance weighs in Defendants' favor. **[—6—]**

---

2 *Hall CA-NV, L.L.C. v. Old Republic Nat'l Title Ins. Co.*, 990 F.3d 933, 936 (5th Cir. 2021) (citation omitted).

3 *Id.*

4 *Celotex Corp. v. Catrett*, 477 U.S. 317, 323 (1986).

5 *Old Republic*, 990 F.3d at 936 (citation omitted).

6 *TIG Ins. Co. v. Sedgwick James of Wash.*, 276 F.3d 754, 759 (5th Cir. 2002).

7 *Id.*

8 *Rodrigue v. Aetna Cas. & Sur. Co.*, 395 U.S. 352, 357 (1969) (holding that "federal law is 'exclusive' in its regulation" of "artificial islands and fixed structures erected" out on the OCS (quoting Outer Continental Shelf Lands Act, ch. 345, sec. 4, 67 Stat. 462, 462 (1953) (codified as amended 43 U.S.C. § 1333) [hereinafter OCSLA])).

9 *Id.* (quoting OCSLA section 4).

10 *Parker Drilling Mgmt. Svcs., Ltd. v. Newton*, 139 S. Ct. 1881, 1892, 7 Adm. R. 36, 41 (2019).

11 *Id.*, 7 Adm. R. at 41.

12 *E.g.*, *Graham v. Amoco Oil Co.*, 21 F.3d 643, 645 (5th Cir. 1994) (citation omitted).

13 *Hickman v. S. Pac. Transp. Co.*, 262 So. 2d 385, 390–91 (La. 1972); *see also Tower Credit, Inc. v. Carpenter*, 825 So. 2d 1125, 1129 (La. 2002) (summarizing the *Hickman* factors).

(1)

The first *Hickman* factor is whether "there is a valid contract between the parties."[14] The parties do not dispute the validity of the contracts in the record between Brand and Grand Isle, and between Grand Isle and BP. Therefore, the first *Hickman* factor weighs in Defendants' favor.

(2)

The second *Hickman* factor is whether "the work being done is of an independent nature such that the contractor may employ non-exclusive means in accomplishing it."[15] At least one Louisiana court has held that this factor weighs against independent-contractor status when a worker is required to use specific tools.[16]

The second factor applies differently to each Defendant. No evidence supports that BP interfered with the means that Brand chose for constructing the scaffolding. Not so for Grand Isle. Grand Isle admitted in **{-728-}** deposition that it "own[ed]" the tools that Brand "utiliz[ed]" to complete the scaffolding work: the "hammers," "wrenches," "safety harnesses," and "things like that." Grand Isle also stored these tools for Brand in "tool houses." On this evidence a reasonable jury could find that Grand Isle required Brand to use specific tools to complete the scaffolding work. Therefore, this factor weighs in BP's favor, but against Grand Isle's. **[—7—]**

(3)

The third *Hickman* factor is whether "the contract calls for specific piecework as a unit to be done according to the independent contractor's own methods, without being subject to the control and direction of the principal, except as to the result of the services to be rendered."[17] Still, principals may exercise control and direction over the end result of the work without creating an employer-employee relationship.[18] Further, Louisiana courts are reluctant to incentivize dangerous work practices by creating an employer-employee relationship based merely on workplace-safety standards.[19]

The third factor weighs in BP's favor. Coleman argues that BP's safety rules, on-the-platform supervision, and reporting requirements were so pervasive that BP effectively specified Grand Isle and Brand's work-performance standards. We disagree. No evidence supports that BP's general safety rules prescribed how Brand needed to build scaffolding.[20] **[—8—]** Further, BP was entitled to exercise direction and control over the end result of Brand's services through reporting requirements. Coleman also equates BP's control over transportation to and from the platform with specifying Brand's work hours. But the record reflects that BP did not make transportation decisions unilaterally.

---

[14] *Carpenter*, 825 So. 2d at 1129.

[15] *Id.*

[16] *See Kibodeaux v. Progressive Ins. Co.*, 4 So. 3d 222, 226 (La. Ct. App. 2009) (noting that an inspector "would most likely not have been allowed to substitute his own badge or his own inspection cards, in place of those provided").

[17] *Carpenter*, 825 So. 2d at 1129. Louisiana courts have found that certain facts make this factor weigh against finding an independent-contractor relationship—for example, unilaterally specifying work-performance standards, work hours, and work location, *Kibodeaux*, 4 So. 3d at 226; *Simon v. Farm Bureau Ins. Co.*, 297 So. 3d 147, 152 (La. Ct. App. 2020), or causing workers to fear termination for non-compliance with any of these, *Simon*, 297 So. 3d at 152–53.

[18] *Carpenter*, 825 So. 2d at 1129.

[19] *See Davenport v. Amax Nickel, Inc.*, 569 So. 2d 23, 28 (La. Ct. App. 1990) ("Imposing liability based on that theory could lead to the absurd result of encouraging owners to ignore and condone safety violations by independent contractors in order to avoid liability.").

[20] Even if they did, it would take an exceptional case before workplace-safety rules could cause the third *Hickman* factor to weigh against an independent-contractor relationship. The law encourages workplace safety out on the OCS. Not vice-versa. *Id.*; *see also LeJune v. Shell Oil Co.*, 950 F.2d 267, 270 (5th Cir. 1992) (commenting that, under Louisiana law, "[t]he fact that a principal takes an active interest in the safety of the employees of its independent contractor does not, in and of itself, constitute direct **[—8—]** operational control." (quoting *Duplantis v. Shell Offshore, Inc.*, 948 F.2d 187, 193 (5th Cir. 1991))).

Brand decided when to work, and BP decided when to transport. Without more, we can only speculate that BP actually specified Brand's work hours. Because speculation cannot support a genuine fact dispute, this argument fails to persuade as well.[21]

The third factor also weighs in Grand Isle's favor. Despite Coleman pointing to Grand Isle's routine supervision on the platform, no evidence supports that Grand Isle ever prescribed how Brand needed to build scaffolding. **{-729-}**

(4)

The fourth *Hickman* factor is whether "there is a specific price for the overall undertaking agreed upon."[22] The record and parties' arguments are unclear on how we should weigh this factor. We therefore hold that the fourth factor is neutral.

(5)

The fifth *Hickman* factor is whether "the duration of the work is for a specific time and not subject to termination or discontinuance at the will of either side without a corresponding liability for its breach[.]"[23] This factor **[—9—]** weighs in both Defendants' favor. No evidence supports and Coleman does not argue that BP could unilaterally terminate Brand. Coleman does argue, though, that Grand Isle could. He quotes the Grand Isle–Brand contract: "[Grand Isle] may terminate any particular work or service being performed under this contract at any time at its sole discretion." Coleman contends that this clause is an at-will-termination-without-liability provision. We disagree. We construe contracts by reading them as a whole.[24] The contract's preceding sentence expressly provides that "termination" would not relieve either party "of its respective obligations and liabilities arising from or incident to work performed or services rendered." Simply put, Grand Isle could terminate the contract at will, but Brand would still have a claim for breach. Therefore, this clause is no evidence that Grand Isle could terminate Brand at will without incurring liability for breach.

* * *

In sum, the *Hickman* factors weigh in favor of holding that Brand was Grand Isle and BP's independent contractor. For Grand Isle, the first, third, and fifth factors weigh in favor of an independent-contractor relationship. Only the second factor casts some doubt on that conclusion. But standing alone, that one factor in this case is not enough for a reasonable jury to return a verdict that Brand was Grand Isle's employee. The answer is even clearer for BP. No factor casts doubt on Brand's status as BP's independent contractor. Therefore, a reasonable jury could not return a verdict that Brand was BP's employee either. **[—10—]**

B

Coleman's second vicarious-liability theory is that even if Brand was an independent contractor, Defendants are still vicariously liable because they exercised operational control over Brand. Though the independent-contractor rule generally bars vicarious liability, some exceptions apply. One is the operational-control exception. As we have recognized before, when a principal either "retains"[25] or "exercises" operational control over the independent contractor's acts, then the principal remains vicariously liable.[26] Retention and actual exercise of control do not weigh equally. We clarified in **{-730-}** *Echeverry v. Jazz Casino Co.* that contractual

---

[21] *TIG*, 276 F.3d at 759.

[22] *Carpenter*, 825 So. 2d at 1129.

[23] *Id.* Here too, Louisiana courts have found that certain facts make this factor weigh against finding an independent-contractor relationship—for instance, if one party **[—9—]** may unilaterally terminate the contract without liability for breach. *Simon*, 297 So. 3d at 155–56.

[24] *Ogea v. Loffland Bros. Co.*, 622 F.2d 186, 189 (5th Cir. 1980) (declining to adopt a contractual interpretation that "would ignore the well-recognized principle under Louisiana law that [a] contract must be viewed as a whole" (citation omitted)).

[25] *Graham*, 21 F.3d at 645.

[26] *Bartholomew v. CNG Producing Co.*, 832 F.2d 326, 329 (5th Cir. 1987).

retention weighs heavier.[27] The district court found that the operational-control exception did not apply as to either BP or Grand Isle. Coleman disputes this on two fronts. He attacks both the standard that the district court used and its application. We agree with the district court.

(1)

Coleman argues that the district court applied too-narrow a standard in deciding operational control. Coleman argues that operational control exists anytime a principal does not give an independent contractor "complete" or "*absolute freedom* to perform work as [it] deem[s] fit."

Coleman's standard is much too broad. The district court faithfully applied the operational-control standard that we have articulated before: **[—11—]** Operational control requires evidence of "direct supervision" by the principal "over the step-by-step process of accomplishing the work."[28] That standard is not met merely because the principal contractually retained general rights—for example, the right to "order the work stopped or resumed," "inspect its progress," "receive reports,"[29] or demand that an independent contractor develop and implement safety procedures.[30] Neither is that standard met merely because a principal keeps a representative physically present at the jobsite to ensure compliance with the contract.[31]

Therefore, we disagree with Coleman's operational-control-exception formulation. The district court got the standard right.

(2)

Coleman further contends that he raised a fact dispute under the operational-control standard. Applying the above standard, we disagree. Coleman argues that Defendants exercised operational control by giving Brand work priorities. But setting general work priorities does not prescribe the step-by-step process for building scaffolding. Coleman argues that BP and Grand Isle established operational control by requiring compliance with BP safety rules. But safety rules generally do not establish operational control as a matter of public policy. Coleman argues Grand Isle established **[—12—]** operational control by having on-site supervisors that determined the equipment to be issued and used. Even accepting this as true, this actual exercise of control is less weighty than what the Grand Isle-Brand contract provided: that Grand Isle would leave to Brand "the methods and details of performance, Grand Isle being interested only in the **{–731–}** results obtained, and having no control over the manner and method of performance." Moreover, providing tools does not equate to giving step-by-step instructions on how to build scaffolding. Finally, Coleman argues that Defendants exercised operational control by directing or "influenc[ing]" Brand when to "begin its work." Even assuming they did, that falls squarely within a principal's general right to order the work stopped or resumed.

C

Coleman's third vicarious-liability theory is that even if Brand was an independent contractor, then there is still a fact dispute

---

[27] *See* 988 F.3d 221, 232 (5th Cir. 2021) ("The supervision and control that is actually exercised by the principal is less important than the right to control that is contractually reserved."); *see also Sandbom v. BASF Wyandotte, Corp.*, 674 So. 2d 349, 354 (La. Ct. App. 1996) ("The decisive element is whether the principal has retained the right of direct supervision of the step-by-step process of accomplishing the work.").

[28] *Fruge ex rel. Fruge v. Parker Drilling Co.*, 337 F.3d 558, 561 (5th Cir. 2003).

[29] *Renwick v. PNK Lake Charles, L.L.C.*, 901 F.3d 605, 613 (5th Cir. 2018) (quoting *LeJune*, 950 F.2d at 270).

[30] *Duplantis*, 948 F.2d at 193; *see also Davenport*, 569 So. 2d at 28 (declining to hold that imposing safety procedures can create vicarious liability through the operational-control exception because it would "encourag[e] owners to ignore and condone safety violations by independent contractors in order to avoid liability").

[31] *Davenport*, 569 So. at 28 ("The fact that [the principal's] personnel may have pointed out obvious violations of safety rules and may have sought to have them corrected does not make [the principal] liable for the consequences of such violations.").

over Defendants' vicarious liability under the unsafe-work-practices exception. When a principal "expressly or impliedly authorizes an unsafe practice," then the principal remains vicariously liable.[32] We agree with the district court: No genuine dispute of material fact exists on this issue. **[—13—]**

(1)

We recently explained in *Echeverry* that the unsafe-work-practices exception applies only when the principal "expressly or impliedly authorized the *particular manner*" which rendered the work unsafe.[33] Observing but failing to object to an unsafe work practice does not create a fact dispute.[34] And if the independent contractor "participated" in deciding to use the unsafe work practice, that also "weighs heavily against" finding a fact dispute.[35] Still, defining the unsafe work practice is no easy task. It first "requires determining at what level of generality to view the work practice."[36] That means "start[ing] with the underlying action" and then "add[ing] some specifics of the occasion."[37]

The parties disagree about what the unsafe work practice was. Coleman contends that it was "[p]erforming scaffolding work in inclement weather." The inclement weather being the "dangerous wind speeds" that day. Grand Isle appears to accept Coleman's framing, but BP does not. BP contends that the unsafe work practice was "using a scaffolding board on an offshore platform" and then "carrying [it] in gusting winds."

Our decision in *Echeverry* is instructive in deciding between the parties' competing definitions. In *Echeverry*, a casino hired a wildlife-removal company to remove birds from palm trees. The removal company injured a **[—14—]** pedestrian that was standing at a crosswalk by running her over with the manlift it was using for the work. The "flagman" had failed to alert her to its approach.[38] Under those facts, the underlying **{-732-}** action was "using a manlift."[39] After adding occasion specifics, the unsafe work practice became "moving a manlift against vehicular traffic at a busy intersection when there was substantial pedestrian traffic."[40]

Using *Echeverry* as our guide, we agree with BP's formulation. Specifically, the underlying action in *Echeverry* tracked the instrumentality that caused injury (the manlift) and not the work's overall purpose (bird removal). Here the work's purpose was to build scaffolding. But the instrumentality that caused Coleman's injury was the scaffolding board. As for the occasion specifics, in *Echeverry* we focused on what specifically made the underlying action unsafe: using a manlift "against vehicular traffic"; "at a busy intersection"; and while "there was substantial pedestrian traffic."[41] Here what specifically made using a scaffolding board unsafe was using it on an offshore platform while winds were gusting. Therefore, we agree with BP's unsafe-work-practices articulation: carrying scaffolding boards on an offshore platform in gusting winds.

(2)

No evidence supports that Defendants expressly or impliedly authorized Coleman to carry scaffolding boards on an offshore

---

32 *Bartholomew*, 832 F.2d at 329 (quoting *Ewell v. Petro Processors of La., Inc.*, 364 So. 2d 604, 606–07 (La. Ct. App. 1978)). Our cases have sometimes referred to the unsafe-work-practices exception collectively with the operational-control exception. *See, e.g., Voces v. Energy Res. Tech., G.O.M., L.L.C.*, 704 F. App'x 345, 349 (5th Cir. 2017) (per curiam) (labeling both "the operational control exception"). We note, however, that both are distinguishable exceptions to the independent-contractor rule under Louisiana law, complete with bespoke inquiries.

33 *Echeverry*, 988 F.3d at 233 (quoting *Davis v. Dynamic Offshore Res., L.L.C.*, 865 F.3d 235, 236 (5th Cir. 2017)).

34 *See id.* ("A company man's observing and failing to object to the independent contractor's unsafe work practices is insufficient evidence of authorization to defeat a motion for summary judgment.").

35 *Id.*

36 *Id.*

37 *Id.* at 234.

38 *Id.* at 227.

39 *Id.* at 234.

40 *Id.*

41 *See id.*

platform in gusting winds. Coleman points to how BP transferred him to the platform in an overloaded personnel basket in wind speeds exceeding BP's safety rules, **[—15—]** and that Defendants had a pecuniary motive to resume work after a multi-day work stoppage. However Coleman got to the platform and whatever Defendants' motives at the time, though, we have already discussed how Brand retained control over deciding when to work. And the record is clear: Brand chose to build scaffolding that day despite the wind speeds. Even if Defendants "influenced" that decision, Brand's participation in it weighs heavily against finding a genuine fact dispute. And once the work started, that BP and Grand Isle supervisors stood by and did nothing to stop Brand cannot create a fact dispute either.

IV

Coleman contends that even if the independent-contractor rule bars holding Defendants vicariously liable for his injuries, then each is still directly liable for its own negligence. Adopting Louisiana law, we have explained before that a principal owes "no duty" to its independent contractors "to provide a safe work place."[42] But the no-duty rule does not apply when the principal either affirmatively assumes that duty[43] or creates a workplace hazard.[44] Coleman contends that a fact dispute exists for both exceptions. The district court disagreed. We agree with the district court. **[—16—]**

A

For a principal to affirmatively assume a duty to provide its independent **{-733-}** contractors with a safe workplace, it must do more than merely observe unsafe work habits.[45] That *more* can be met, though, when the principal "voluntarily and affirmatively" goes beyond the contract to "reprimand[] the independent contractor for various safety violations."[46] The key, however, is that the injury must be caused by induced reliance on the principal's safety rules. Merely providing general safety rules is not enough.[47] Applying this standard, no evidence supports that either Defendant assumed a duty to keep Coleman safe.

(1)

Coleman contends that a genuine fact dispute exists over whether BP assumed a duty towards him. We disagree. Coleman argues that BP assumed a duty by enforcing safety rules on the platform. But no evidence supports that these safety rules governed carrying scaffolding boards in gusting winds. Coleman argues that BP assumed a duty by stationing safety supervisors on the platform. But merely observing an unsafe work practice is not enough to assume a duty. Coleman argues that BP's safety supervisors had the authority to and actually did determine the "applicable" safety equipment used on the platform. No evidence supports that contention. The deposition Coleman cites to in support is actually for a *Grand Isle* employee, not a BP employee. Further, the BP-Grand Isle contract expressly provided that **[—17—]** Grand Isle would "take full responsibility for the . . . safety of all its operations and methods necessary" to build the scaffolding.

(2)

Coleman also argues that Grand Isle assumed a duty towards him. We disagree with most of his arguments for many of the same reasons that we reject that BP assumed a duty. No evidence supports that Grand Isle enforced safety rules over carrying scaffolding boards in gusting winds. And Grand Isle did

---

42 *Graham*, 21 F.3d at 647.

43 *Cf. id.* (recognizing that a principal can "assume an ex-contract duty to provide a safe work place," but rejecting that the principal had in that case).

44 *Cf. Zephrin v. Conoco Oil Co., Inc.*, 884 F.2d 212, 213 (5th Cir. 1989) ("This court has consistently held . . . that a principal . . . who hires an independent contractor, over which it exercises no operational control, has no duty to remedy hazards created by its independent contractors." (citations omitted)).

45 *Graham*, 21 F.3d at 648.

46 *Id.*

47 *See LeJune*, 950 F.2d at 271 ("Nothing in the record before us, however, indicates that LeJeune was painting the rack on some kind of reliance induced by the Manual.").

not assume a duty merely based on what its safety supervisors observed.

Admittedly, though, Grand Isle's safety supervisors were more involved than BP's in one respect—issuing safety equipment. Coleman points to how Grand Isle's employee admitted at deposition that its safety supervisors determined "all applicable equipment" to be "used" by Brand on the platform. But that does not matter here. At most it supports a reasonable inference that Grand Isle undertook a duty to issue Coleman safety equipment applicable for building scaffolding. But it would be unreasonable for a jury to conclude from this evidence that Grand Isle undertook a broader duty to protect Coleman from *all* hazards on the platform. In fact, the record directly contradicts such a broad proposition. In its contract with Grand Isle, Brand expressly warranted that its workers could perform the work "safely." Moreover, nothing in the record supports that some unspecified piece of non-issued equipment would have or could have prevented Coleman's injury. Therefore, Grand Isle's admission does not change our analysis.[48] **[—18—] {-734-}**

B

Coleman finally argues that Defendants were independently negligent because they created the hazard that injured him. We disagree. As we have already noted, a principal is not liable for injuries sustained by its independent contractor when the independent contractor "created" the hazard.[49] A principal does not create the hazard when it does not "control the operation of the particular activity during which the plaintiff was allegedly injured."[50] Simply put, a reasonable jury could not conclude on this evidence that Defendants *controlled* the hazard that Coleman alleges injured him: the decision to start working in high winds. Coleman argues that Defendants controlled the decision to start work since BP controlled the decision over when to transport Brand employees to the platform. But deciding when to transport is not the same thing as deciding when to start building scaffolding. And on that front, the record not only reflects that Brand independently decided that "now [is] the right time to [do] the work," but also that everyone on the platform had the authority to stop working if conditions were unsafe. While Coleman contends he feared for his job if he exercised his stop-work authority, no evidence supports that Brand harbored similar fears if it did.

V

As to these Defendants, the district court got it right—a reasonable jury could not conclude on this record that either Defendant is vicariously or directly liable for Coleman's back injury. Therefore, we AFFIRM the district court.

48 *See Zervas v. Faulkner*, 861 F.2d 823, 836–37 (5th Cir. 1988) (equating an "overly attenuated chain of inferences" with "speculation and conjecture").

49 *E.g.*, *Zephrin*, 884 F.2d at 213.

50 *Id.*

United States Court of Appeals
for the Fifth Circuit

No. 20-30767

IN RE BONVILLIAN MARINE SERV., INC.

Appeal from the United States District Court for the Eastern District of Louisiana

Decided: December 2, 2021

Citation: 19 F.4th 787, 9 Adm. R. 273 (5th Cir. 2021).

Before **BARKSDALE, ENGELHARDT,** and **OLDHAM,** Circuit Judges.

[—1—] {-788-} **ENGELHARDT,** Circuit Judge: **{-789-}**

The Limitation of Liability Act of 1851 provides vessel owners like Appellant Bonvillian Marine Service a means of limiting their vessel's tort liability to the value of the vessel plus pending freight. *See* 46 U.S.C. **[—2—]** §§ 30501–30512. Section 30511(a) of the Act requires vessel owners to "bring a civil action in a district court of the United States for limitation of liability . . . within 6 months after a claimant gives the owner written notice of a claim."

After finding Bonvillian's action untimely under § 30511(a), the district court applied our precedent that "a challenge to the timeliness of a limitation action is a challenge to subject matter jurisdiction" and dismissed the action for lack of subject matter jurisdiction. *See In re Bonvillian Marine Serv., Inc.*, 502 F. Supp. 3d 1078, 1083–84, 1088 (E.D. La. 2020) (citing *In re Eckstein Marine Serv. L.L.C.*, 672 F.3d 310, 315–16 (5th Cir. 2012)).

The district court was not free to overturn the rule we announced in *Eckstein*. Because subsequent Supreme Court decisions have effected an intervening change in the law that warrants a change in course, we overturn the *Eckstein* rule today and REVERSE the district court's adept decision accordingly.

I.

On January 19, 2019, a vessel belonging to Bonvillian allided with the M/V MISS SADIE ELIZABETH, a crew boat docked on the Mississippi River near Port Sulphur, Louisiana. MISS SADIE ELIZABETH crew member and Appellee Junior Joseph Pellegrin, Jr., sustained a variety of personal injuries in the allision. On August 23, 2019, Pellegrin sued Bonvillian in Louisiana state court. On December 16, 2019, Bonvillian filed a verified limitation complaint in the Eastern District of Louisiana. Baywater Drilling, LLC, the owner of the MISS SADIE ELIZABETH and Pellegrin's co-Appellee, moved to dismiss Bonvillian's action for lack of subject matter jurisdiction.

Baywater's argument for Federal Rule of Civil Procedure 12(b)(1) dismissal was straightforward: because Bonvillian filed its limitation action **[—3—]** more than six months after receiving written notice of a claim with a reasonable probability of exceeding the value of its vessel,[1] its action was untimely under 46 U.S.C. § 30511(a) (requiring a limitation action to "be brought within 6 months after a claimant gives the [vessel] owner written notice of a claim"); and, because Bonvillian's action was untimely, the district court lacked subject matter jurisdiction under the Fifth Circuit rule announced in *In re Eckstein Marine Service L.L.C.*, in which a prior panel of this court observed that "[t]his circuit, like several other courts, has held that a party alleging a limitation petition was not timely filed challenges the district court's subject matter jurisdiction over that petition." 672 F.3d at 315 ("While many statutory filing deadlines are not jurisdictional, we have long recognized that some are. The Limitation Act's six-month filing requirement is one of these." (footnote omitted)).

[1] The factual grounds for Baywater's Rule 12(b)(1) motion are hotly contested by the parties, but because we remand on pure legal grounds, we refrain from discussing the parties' factual disputes over the agency of Bonvillian's claims adjuster and the likely value of the claims against Bonvillian.

The district court heard argument on Baywater's motion to dismiss and concluded: (1) that Bonvillian's action was indeed untimely under § 30511(a); (2) that the Fifth Circuit's *Eckstein* rule remained controlling (despite Bonvillian's contention that the Supreme Court implicitly overruled **{-790-}** *Eckstein* in the 2015 case of *United States v. Kwai Fun Wong*, 575 U.S. 402 (2015)); and (3) that, as a result, the court lacked subject matter jurisdiction.

The district court applied the *Eckstein* rule correctly in this regard, but as explained below, we now overturn that rule. **[—4—]**

II.

This case requires us to determine as a threshold matter whether to maintain and apply the rule this court announced in *Eckstein* (as the Appellees urge) or to adopt a rule that is better suited to the Supreme Court's intervening pronouncements in *Kwai Fun Wong* and related cases (as Bonvillian urges). Since the central issue is the interplay between *Eckstein* and *Kwai Fun Wong*, we begin with a brief introduction of those cases.

A.

In *Eckstein* in 2012, a panel of this court confronted a similar set of facts in reviewing a district court's Rule 12(b)(1) dismissal of a vessel owner's untimely limitation action. *See* 672 F.3d 310. In response to the appellant vessel owner's argument that timeliness under the Limitation Act "is not a jurisdictional issue," the *Eckstein* panel officially categorized "[t]he Limitation Act's six-month filing requirement" as a statutory filing deadline that *is* jurisdictional, as opposed to "many statutory filing deadlines [that] are not." *Id.* at 315 (citing *In re Tom-Mac, Inc.*, 76 F.3d 678, 682 (5th Cir. 1996) ("In their motion to dismiss, Claimants asserted that Tom-Mac's limitation of liability action was not timely filed, thus challenging the district court's jurisdiction to hear Tom-Mac's petition.")).

In the nine years since, *Eckstein* has been cited for this particular rule of law in just two Fifth Circuit cases. The lone published[2] decision citing *Eckstein* for the proposition that the Limitation Act's timeliness requirement is jurisdictional is *In re RLB Contracting, Inc.*, 773 F.3d 596, 601, 2 Adm. R. 378, 380 (5th Cir. 2014) (per curiam) ("A party who contends that a limitation action was not **[—5—]** timely filed challenges the district court's subject matter jurisdiction.").[3] The second and final Fifth Circuit case citing *Eckstein* for the rule at issue is our unpublished decision in *In re Marquette Transportation Co.*, 524 F. App'x 989, 991 (5th Cir. 2013) (per curiam) ("We review de novo the district court[']s ruling on a motion to dismiss for lack of subject matter jurisdiction under Fed. R. Civ. P. 12(b)(1), including the determination as to whether the limitation action was timely filed.").

The district court here correctly found itself bound by the rule we set forth in *Eckstein* and restated in *RLB Contracting*, but the Supreme Court's intervening decision in *Kwai Fun Wong*—which postdated both *Eckstein* and *RLB Contracting*—makes clear that our rule has fallen out of step with the Supreme Court's most recent jurisprudence on the jurisdictional import of statutory "procedural rules" like § 30511(a)'s time bar.

B.

In *United States v. Kwai Fun Wong*, the Supreme Court deemed time limitations in the Federal Tort Claims Act **{-791-}** (FTCA) *non*jurisdictional and reiterated a burgeoning "clear statement" rule for interpreting statutory procedural rules in general. As relevant here, the Court observed that given the "harsh consequences" of deeming such a rule jurisdictional, "procedural rules,

---

[2] 5TH CIRCUIT RULE 47.5 provides that unpublished opinions of this court are not precedent except under the limited—and in this scenario, inapplicable—circumstances set forth in 5TH CIRCUIT RULE 47.5.4.

[3] *RLB Contracting*, in turn, has been cited for the rule at issue just once—in the unpublished case of *In re Brown*, 766 F. App'x 30, 33 (5th Cir. 2019) ("We treat [§ 30511(a)'s] time limit as a jurisdictional requirement subject to our de novo review.").

including time bars, cabin a court's power only if Congress has 'clearly state[d]' as much." 575 U.S. at 409 (alteration in original) (quoting *Sebelius v. Auburn Reg'l Med. Ctr.*, 568 U.S. 145, 153 (2013)); *see also id.* at 409–10 ("Absent such a clear statement, courts should treat [a] restriction as nonjurisdictional. That does not mean Congress must incant magic words. **[—6—]** But traditional tools of statutory construction must plainly show that Congress imbued a procedural bar with jurisdictional consequences." (cleaned up)). Thus, the Court noted, "even when [a] time limit is important (most are) and even when it is framed in mandatory terms (again, most are)," it should—absent a clear statement by Congress—be deemed nonjurisdictional. *Id.* at 410. In keeping with this clear statement rule, "[t]ime and again" the Supreme Court has described filing deadlines like the one set forth in § 30511(a) as "'quintessential claim-processing rules,' which 'seek to promote the orderly progress of litigation,' but do not deprive a court of authority to hear a case." *Id.* (quoting *Henderson ex rel. Henderson v. Shinseki*, 562 U.S. 428, 435 (2011)).

Kwai Fun Wong was not the first case in which the Supreme Court applied a clear statement rule to distinguish jurisdictional procedural rules from nonjurisdictional ones, but Bonvillian contends that *Kwai Fun Wong* bears special importance here because our court's *Eckstein* panel drew significant support for its ruling from a Fifth Circuit case that *Kwai Fun Wong* directly abrogated—namely, *In re FEMA Trailer Formaldehyde Products Liability Litigation*, in which this court deemed the FTCA's similar filing deadline jurisdictional. *See* 646 F.3d 185, 189 (5th Cir. 2011), *abrogated by Kwai Fun Wong*, 575 U.S. 402.

Bonvillian is correct that *Kwai Fun Wong* is particularly salient here. As Bonvillian correctly observes, *FEMA Trailer* was indeed a logical linchpin of the *Eckstein* panel's decision to stick with "this Circuit's prior conclusion that the Limitation Act's six-month filing deadline is a jurisdictional requirement" in spite of the Supreme Court's "recent[] conclu[sion] that many filing deadlines are probably not jurisdictional." *See Eckstein*, 672 F.3d at 315 n.12. With greatest respect to the *Eckstein* panel, none of the four citations accompanying *FEMA Trailer* in *Eckstein*'s footnote 12—the footnote containing the *Eckstein* panel's citations and rationale for the rule in **[—7—]** question—are of comparable value in supporting the rule the *Eckstein* panel chose to reassert.[4] It is thus correct **{-792-}** to regard *FEMA Trailer* as a cornerstone of the *Eckstein* rule Bonvillian asks us to overturn in light of new legal developments.

Those legal developments leave our Circuit today in a quandary: the Supreme Court's 2015 decision in *Kwai Fun Wong* both (1) repeats a clear statement rule that our *Eckstein* panel did not apply in stating the rule at issue, and (2) abrogates the Fifth Circuit decision on which our *Eckstein* panel *did* principally rely in continuing to assume that the Limitation Act's six-month filing requirement is jurisdictional in nature. For these reasons, the *Eckstein* rule is ripe for revisitation—if the rule of orderliness allows it.

III.

"It is a well-settled Fifth Circuit rule of orderliness that one panel of our court may not overturn another panel's decision, absent an intervening change in the law, such as by a statutory amendment, or the Supreme Court, or our *en banc* court." *Jacobs v. Nat'l Drug Intel. Ctr.*, 548 F.3d 375, 378 (5th Cir. 2008).

---

[4] The three cases immediately following *FEMA Trailer* in *Eckstein* footnote 12—namely, this court's unpublished decisions in *Khan v. Gonzales*, 223 F. App'x 417 (5th Cir. 2007) (per curiam), and *Anderson v. Parsons State Hospital & Training Center*, 180 F. App'x 514 (5th Cir. 2006) (per curiam), and the Supreme Court's habeas corpus decision in *Bowles v. Russell*, 551 U.S. 205 (2007)—are decisions concerning statutory deadlines for *appeals* (which are *classically*, and unquestionably, jurisdictional in nature). A fourth and final citation—referencing the Supreme Court's statement in *Henderson ex rel. Henderson v. Shinseki*, 562 U.S. 428 (2011) that *Bowles* "did not hold categorically that every deadline for seeking judicial review in civil litigation is jurisdictional"—is a catch-all that merely confirms that the *Eckstein* rule has not been categorically ruled *out*.

This rule is strict and rigidly applied. Thus, "for a Supreme Court decision to change our Circuit's law, it 'must be more than merely illuminating with respect to the case before [the court]' and must 'unequivocally' overrule prior precedent." *Tech. Automation Servs. Corp. v.* **[—8—]** *Liberty Surplus Ins. Corp.*, 673 F.3d 399, 405 (5th Cir. 2012) (alteration in original) (quoting *Martin v. Medtronic, Inc.*, 254 F.3d 573, 577 (5th Cir. 2001)). Whether an intervening Supreme Court decision "merely illuminates" or "unequivocally overrules" is a judgment call—there is no hard-and-fast requirement, for instance, that a Supreme Court decision explicitly overrule the circuit precedent at issue, or specifically address the precise question of law at issue. Rather, a latter panel must simply determine that a former panel's decision has fallen unequivocally out of step with some intervening change in the law.[5] As we observed in a similar context,

> Whether a Supreme Court decision implicitly overrules a prior Fifth Circuit decision depends on context. That two decisions involve different statutes is not dispositive. Sometimes a Supreme Court decision involving one statute implicitly overrules our precedent involving another statute. Sometimes it does not. The overriding consideration is the similarity of the issues decided.

Gahagan v. U.S. Citizenship & Immigr. Servs., 911 F.3d 298, 302–03 (5th Cir. 2018) (footnote omitted) (citations omitted).

In basic terms, then, a "Fifth Circuit precedent is implicitly overruled if a subsequent Supreme Court opinion 'establishes a rule of law inconsistent with' that precedent." *Id.* at 302 (quoting *Gonzalez v. Thaler*, 623 F.3d 222, 226 (5th Cir. 2010)). One situation in which this may naturally occur is "where 'an intervening Supreme Court decision fundamentally change[s] the focus' of the relevant analysis." *Acosta v. Hensel Phelps Constr. Co.*, 909 **[—9—]** F.3d 723, 742 (5th Cir. 2018) (alteration in original) (quoting *Robinson v. J & K Admin. Mgmt. Servs., Inc.*, 817 F.3d 193, 197 (5th Cir. 2016)).

That, we hold, is the circumstance here. The Supreme Court's jurisprudence on the jurisdictional significance of statutory procedural rules "fundamentally changes" the analysis this court must perform in determining whether § 30511(a)'s six-month filing requirement imposes a jurisdictional **{–793–}** barrier to suit or a mere claim-processing rule. As such, whereas the *Eckstein* panel largely assumed—by citation to a prior panel's unsupported assumption in *Tom-Mac*,[6] and by analogy to this court's since-abrogated interpretation of the *FTCA*'s statute of limitations[7]—that a limitation action's untimeliness deprives a district court of jurisdiction, *this* panel has been instructed in *Kwai Fun Wong* and other intervening cases that the essential hallmark of a *jurisdictional* procedural rule is a clear congressional statement, which is nowhere to be found in the Limitation Act.

Put simply, it is doubtful that the *Eckstein* panel today would conclude that the Limitation Act's six-month filing requirement imposes a jurisdictional bar to suit. Indeed, as the Eleventh Circuit noted as the first court of appeals to interpret § 30511(a)'s time bar in the time since *Kwai Fun Wong*, there is "'no clear textual indication' that § 30511(a)'s six-month time bar 'was intended to limit courts' subject matter jurisdiction' . . . because, in short, [§ 30511(a)] does nothing 'special, beyond setting an exception-free deadline.'" *See Orion Marine Constr., Inc. v. Carroll*, 918 F.3d 1323, 1329, 7 Adm. R. 463, 367 **[—10—]** (11th Cir. 2019) (first quoting *Sec'y v. Preston*,

[5] When this occurs, the latter panel has both "the authority and *obligation* to declare and implement [the] change in the law" it perceives. *United States v. Tanksley*, 848 F.3d 347, 350 (5th Cir. 2017) (emphasis added).

[6] Because the 1996 *Tom-Mac* panel provided no citation for its statement that the claimants challenged the district court's *jurisdiction* by asserting that the vessel owner's limitation action was untimely, it is unclear where the panel drew that notion from (or its pedigree in this Circuit, to whatever extent that may be relevant). *See Tom-Mac*, 76 F.3d at 682.

[7] *See Eckstein*, 672 F.3d at 315 n.12 (citing *FEMA Trailer*, 646 F.3d at 189).

873 F.3d 877, 882 (11th Cir. 2017); then quoting *Kwai Fun Wong*, 575 U.S. at 410).

The Eleventh Circuit is correct. Section 30511(a) "speaks only to a claim's timeliness, not to a court's power."[8] *Cf. Kwai Fun Wong*, 575 U.S. at 410. Its mandatory phrasing makes no explicit reference to (much less any clear statement regarding) jurisdiction.[9] And its location within the United States Code—"among provisions that describe the standards and procedures that govern the cause of action . . . and (well) away from those that allocate jurisdiction," *Orion*, 918 F.3d at 1329, 7 Adm. R. at 466—further counsels against "imbu[ing]" its "procedural bar with jurisdictional consequences." *Cf. Kwai Fun Wong*, 575 U.S. at 410.

Consequently, the *Eckstein* rule clearly runs afoul of *Kwai Fun Wong* and its family of Supreme Court cases, and this panel is behooved to adjust our Circuit's stance accordingly. *See, e.g., Gahagan*, 911 F.3d at 302–03 (subsequent panel may depart from prior panel's decision where intervening Supreme Court pronouncement requires it to do so); *United States v. Tanksley*, 848 F.3d 347, 350 (5th Cir. 2017) (subsequent panel has *obligation* to declare and implement perceived change in law). **[—11—] {-794-}**

The appellees' counterarguments on this point are unavailing. In addition to arguments that clearly fail for reasons previously described, the appellees contend that this court *already* declined to overturn *Eckstein* and *RLB Contracting*[10] in *In re Brown*, 766 F. App'x 30 (5th Cir. 2019) (reciting the *Eckstein* rule without discussion). But the *Brown* panel made no mention of *Kwai Fun Wong* in its unpublished decision, which severely undermines the appellees' position, as "[a]n opinion restating a prior panel's ruling does not *sub silentio* hold that the prior ruling survived an uncited Supreme Court decision." *Gahagan*, 911 F.3d at 302. That's exactly what happened in *Brown*: the parties failed to mention *Kwai Fun Wong* in their briefs and instead took for granted this court's *Eckstein* rule, however shaky that rule's legal footing may have been at the time.

As a result, ours is the first Fifth Circuit panel to squarely address this question in light of *Kwai Fun Wong*, which both (1) places our Circuit's *Eckstein* rule in clear tension with binding Supreme Court precedent, and (2) directly abrogates another Fifth Circuit precedent (*FEMA Trailer*) which was a pillar at the core of the *Eckstein* rule. In short, then, *Kwai Fun Wong* indeed effects an intervening change in the law that warrants this panel's departure from the rule our court announced in *Eckstein*.

This panel is obliged to acknowledge the Supreme Court's implicit overruling of *Eckstein* and now holds that the time limitation set forth in 46 U.S.C. § 30511(a) is a mere claim-processing rule which has no bearing on a district court's subject matter jurisdiction. **[—12—]**

IV.

The district court held that "under current Fifth Circuit precedent, the Court lacks jurisdiction over this limitation action, and it must be dismissed." *Bonvillian*, 502 F. Supp. 3d at 1088. Our decision to overrule that precedent today renders the district court's able decision no longer valid.

The judgment of the district court is REVERSED, and the case is REMANDED for

[8] In full, § 30511(a) provides as follows: "The owner of a vessel may bring a civil action in a district court of the United States for limitation of liability under this chapter. The action must be brought within 6 months after a claimant gives the owner written notice of the claim."

[9] Several statutory rules featuring far more strenuous language than § 30511(a)'s relatively tepid time bar have been deemed nonjurisdictional by the Supreme Court. Indeed, under the strict test announced in *Kwai Fun Wong* and related cases, "Not even sweeping proscriptions like 'no action shall be brought' and 'shall be forever barred' [have been held to] do the trick." *Orion*, 918 F.3d at 1329, 7 Adm. R. at 466 (citations omitted) (first quoting *Jones v. Bock*, 549 U.S. 199, 220 (2007); then quoting *Kwai Fun Wong*, 575 U.S. at 416).

[10] Which, importantly, was decided before *Kwai Fun Wong*.

further proceedings consistent with this opinion.

United States Court of Appeals for the Fifth Circuit

No. 21-10068

TANGO MARINE S.A. vs. ELEPHANT GROUP LTD.***

Appeal from the United States District Court for the Northern District of Texas

Decided: December 3, 2021

*****Opinion withdrawn on rehearing on Mar. 11, 2022.**

Citation: 19 F.4th 808, 9 Adm. R. 279 (5th Cir. 2021).

Before **JONES, SOUTHWICK,** and **ENGELHARDT,** Circuit Judges.

[—1—] {-810-} SOUTHWICK, Circuit Judge:

A maritime case was filed in the Northern District of Texas against two Nigerian business entities. The district court vacated the initial default against the Nigerian entities, but subsequent procedural errors led to a second default judgment that the district court refused to vacate. We AFFIRM.

FACTUAL AND PROCEDURAL BACKGROUND

Tango Marine S.A., a Grecian corporation, filed suit in the Northern District of Texas against two Nigerian businesses, Elephant Group Limited **[—2—]** and Elephant Group, P.L.C. (collectively, "Elephant Group"). Tango alleges that the Elephant Group chartered one of its vessels to deliver cargo to Lagos, Nigeria in 2016. Upon arrival in Lagos, though, the Nigerian port authorities prevented the unloading of the cargo. Tango alleges that the vessel was detained for two and a half years due to the Elephant Group's failure to obtain proper permissions for the cargo, which caused damages for demurrage, supply, and maintenance charges. Tango also sought maritime attachment and garnishment pursuant to Federal Rule of Civil Procedure Supplemental Rule B.

Serving process on the Nigerian entities proved difficult. The district court granted Tango's request to serve the Elephant Group via email or mail. Approximately one month after this alternative service **{-811-}** occurred and no response arrived, Tango sought entry of default, which the clerk entered. When no motion for default judgment appeared before the court, the court ordered Tango to file its motion for default judgment or explain its failure. Only after Tango filed its motion for default judgment did the Elephant Group participate in the suit by filing a motion for extension of time to file an answer and a notice of appearance. It also sought to have the default set aside, claiming that it was entering a restricted appearance under Supplemental Rules for Admiralty or Maritime Claims Rule E(8). It stated it was appearing solely to contest the merits of the claim underlying the attachment. The court set aside the initial default but required the Elephant Group to pay Tango's attorneys' fees for their legal work up to that point.

With the initial default set aside, the Elephant Group filed a motion to dismiss under Federal Rule of Civil Procedure 12(b), arguing that (1) the court lacked jurisdiction (both personal and subject matter), (2) the complaint failed to comply with Rule 8(a)(2), and (3) Tango failed to join an indispensable party. **[—3—]**

In response, Tango filed two pleadings on the same day. First, it filed an amended complaint. It also filed a "response opposing [the] motion to dismiss," which argued the amended complaint cured the defects identified in the motion to dismiss. The Elephant Group responded only to this response to the motion to dismiss and never filed an answer to the amended complaint. Its reply to the motion to dismiss response referenced the amended complaint several times and specifically asked the district court to "dismiss, with prejudice, the Amended Complaint and the causes of action pled therein pursuant to" Rule 12(b). Importantly for later rulings by the district court, no answer to the amended complaint was filed.

Two days after the Elephant Group filed that reply to the response in opposition to the motion to dismiss, Tango asked the clerk for a second entry of default due to the Elephant Group's failure to answer the amended complaint. The Elephant Group filed an objection to this motion on the same day. Nevertheless, the clerk entered "default for want of answer or other defense."

The Elephant Group moved to have this second default set aside, which the district court denied. The district court determined that the Elephant Group's default was "willful" and that "willfulness of the default ends the inquiry." The district court also held that, even if the default were not willful, the Elephant Group failed to show that it had any meritorious defenses. It thus granted Tango's subsequent motion for default judgment and entered final judgment for $4,491,784.17, plus post-judgment interest, over the Elephant Group's objections. The Elephant Group appealed.

DISCUSSION

The Elephant Group makes two arguments on appeal. First, it maintains that the district court never acquired personal jurisdiction over it. Tango counters both that there is personal jurisdiction and that the Elephant **[—4—]** Group waived the personal-jurisdiction argument by not making such argument in its very first filing. Second, the Elephant Group argues that the district court abused its discretion in entering the default judgment. Tango asserts that default judgment was appropriate. We consider the Elephant Group's arguments that the district court lacked personal jurisdiction as part of our default judgment analysis, as the two issues require some common analysis. **{-812-}**

Under the federal rules, "a district court may set aside an entry of default or default judgment for 'good cause.'" *Lacy v. Sitel Corp.*, 227 F.3d 290, 291–92 (5th Cir. 2000). We review a refusal to set aside a default or default judgment for an abuse of discretion. *Wooten v. McDonald Transit Assocs., Inc.*, 788 F.3d 490, 495 (5th Cir. 2015). "Because of the seriousness of a default judgment, and although the standard of review is abuse of discretion, even a slight abuse of discretion may justify reversal." *Lacy*, 227 F.3d at 292 (quoting *CJC Holdings, Inc. v. Wright & Lato, Inc.*, 979 F.2d 60, 63 n.1 (5th Cir. 1992)).

We have identified three factors to determine whether good cause exists: (1) the willfulness of the default, (2) the prejudice to the opposing party if the default is set aside, and (3) the presence of any meritorious defenses for the defaulting party. *Id.* A district court may properly refuse to set aside a default judgment if the defendant "fails to present a meritorious defense sufficient to support a finding on the merits for the defaulting party." *Id.* at 293.

The default here was the failure to answer the amended complaint. The Elephant Group did reply to the response to the motion to dismiss that was filed simultaneously with the amended complaint, referred to the amended complaint in that reply, but clearly never filed an answer. The district court's entry of default was primarily based on its conclusion that the **[—5—]** Elephant Group acted "willfully"; it also commented that no meritorious defenses were presented. We doubt that "willful" is the right label for counsel's failure to file an answer. It did, after all, quickly make a filing referring to the new complaint. Inadvertence, clumsiness, or related labels come to mind. Whatever the inaction should be called, there was no filed answer. In the first order refusing to set aside the clerk's entry of default, the district court stated that the "willfulness of the default ends the inquiry," which is what our caselaw provides. *See id.* at 292. The district court nonetheless went on to conclude that no meritorious defenses existed either.

Relieving the Elephant Group of its default is not controlled by whether we disagree with the finding of willfulness. Even without willfulness or even prejudice to the other party, "a district court may have the discretion not to upset a default judgment if the defendant fails to present a meritorious defense sufficient to support a finding on the merits for the defaulting party." *Id.* at 293. That makes sense, as setting aside the default in the absence of a meritorious defense just postpones the inevitable. Thus, we examine the proposed defenses.

The Elephant Group first contends that the district court had no personal jurisdiction and the absence amounts to a meritorious defense. Components of that argument are that it was a group of Nigerian businesses with its principal place of business outside the United States. Further, it had no continuous and systematic contacts with the forum state, Texas, and did not even have any property there. Tango responds by saying the Elephant Group waived its arguments about a lack of personal jurisdiction by failing to present that argument in its first responsive pleading. Tango also argues that the Elephant Group did have minimum contacts in the forum state.

Some of the arguments raise issues of the existence of a distinction between general and special appearances in litigation. The Federal Rules of **[—6—]** Civil Procedure have abolished any distinction. The Civil Rules require only that a party raise **{–813–}** certain defenses by motion or in its first responsive pleading, including the lack of personal jurisdiction. *See* FED. R. CIV. P. 12(b)(2), 12(h). Those Rules, though, do not supplant the Supplemental Rules for Admiralty that are relied upon by Tango in this case. *E.g.*, *Sembawang Shipyard, Ltd. v. Charger, Inc.*, 955 F.2d 983, 989 (5th Cir. 1992). Those Supplemental Rules continue to recognize both a general and a more limited category of appearance:

> Restricted Appearance. An appearance to defend against an admiralty and maritime claim with respect to which there has issued process *in rem*, or *process of attachment and garnishment*, may be expressly restricted to the defense of such claim, and in that event is not an appearance for the purposes of any other claim with respect to which such process is not available or has not been served.

FED. R. CIV. P., SUPP. RULE E(8) (emphasis added). As we stated long after the distinction between special and general appearances was otherwise abolished, failure to appear specially to contest *in personam* jurisdiction can amount to waiver of that defense in maritime actions. *See Sembawang Shipyard*, 955 F.2d at 989.

Tango argues that the Elephant Group ignored the perils of admiralty appearances and entered an unrestricted general appearance. Our review of the record reveals that the Elephant Group attempted to restrict its appearance in its initial motion to set aside default. Prior to this motion, though, counsel for Elephant Group (1) filed an application for admission *pro hac vice*; (2) filed a motion for extension of time; and (3) entered a "Joint Notice of Appearance." Did any of these filings constitute a general appearance on behalf of Elephant Group? **[—7—]**

When determining whether a party has made a general appearance, we inquire whether the party has made "some presentation or submission to the court." *Cactus Pipe & Supply Co. v. M/V Montmartre*, 756 F.2d 1103, 1108 (5th Cir. 1985). This can arise from filing an answer without raising jurisdictional defects or impliedly "from a defendant's seeking, taking, or agreeing to some step or proceeding in the cause beneficial to himself or detrimental to plaintiff other than one contesting only the jurisdiction or by reason of some act or proceedings recognizing the case as in court." *Id.* (quotation marks and citation omitted).

None of the filings prior to the motion to set aside default were general appearances. None of these actions evince the "seeking, taking, or agreeing to some step or proceeding in the cause" required to constitute a general appearance. *Id.* Rather, they are best viewed as early maneuvering prior to any answer or motion; we agree with another circuit that they give "no hint that the answer will waive personal jurisdiction defects." *Benny v. Pipes*, 799 F.2d 489, 493 (9th Cir. 1986), *amended by* 807 F.2d 1514 (9th Cir. 1987).

We now examine the language of the Elephant Group's initial motion to set aside default to see if it was a restricted appearance. In the final few pages of the motion, the Elephant Group maintains that it is specially appearing "to defend against the claim underlying the attachment or arrest," and cites Supplemental Rule E(8) for this proposition. Though the Elephant Group does not drape its entire motion in the protection of a restricted appearance, we are satisfied that this invocation of Rule E(8) is sufficient to constitute a restricted appearance.

The Elephant Group's restricted appearance, though, does not mean that there was no *in personam* jurisdiction over the Elephant Group. In this case, Tango **{-814-}** specifically sought attachment and garnishment pursuant to Rule B of the Supplemental Rules of Civil Procedure because it believed **[—8—]** Elephant Group was not present in the district. Supplemental Rule B is "an adjunct to a claim *in personam*." *Sembawang Shipyard*, 955 F.2d at 987. Functionally, Rule B establishes a *quasi in rem* proceeding which "allows a district court to take jurisdiction over a defendant in an admiralty or maritime action by attaching property of the defendant." *Submersible Sys., Inc. v. Perforadora Cent., S.A. de C.V.*, 249 F.3d 413, 421 (5th Cir. 2001). One treatise labels Rule B attachment as a *quasi in rem* process for *in personam* maritime claims. 29 JAMES W. MOORE ET AL., MOORE'S FEDERAL PRACTICE § 705.04 (Matthew Bender 3d Ed. 2021). Importantly, it is the "good-faith allegation in the complaint that the *res* is present within the geographical jurisdiction of the court" — not the successful attachment of that *res* — that is "*the* jurisdictional fact which gives the court *in personam* jurisdiction over the defendant purported to own the *res*." *Great Prize, S.A. v. Mariner Shipping Party, Ltd.*, 967 F.2d 157, 159 (5th Cir. 1992). This is confirmed by the fact that the court maintains its jurisdiction even after a successful attachment has been vacated. *See J. Lauritzen A/S v. Dashwood Shipping, Ltd.*, 65 F.3d 139, 142 (9th Cir. 1995).

In this case, Tango alleged, and the district court approved, writs of attachment for various assets owned by the Elephant Group that Tango believed were present in the district. Tango's good faith allegations in its complaint were the "jurisdictional facts" that generated Rule B *in personam* jurisdiction over the Elephant Group. When the district court entered the second default, this jurisdiction existed. Thus, even assuming that a lack of personal jurisdiction amounts to a meritorious defense, here there was jurisdiction over the Elephant Group.

The Elephant Group claims it asserted two other meritorious defenses: pleading defects under Rule 8(a)(2) and failure to join an indispensable party. The Elephant Group simply cites Fifth Circuit precedents but does not analyze their application here. Recitations of law **[—9—]** without a "definite recitation of facts" supporting the applicability of that law to this case are insufficient to establish a meritorious defense. *Moldwood Corp. v. Stutts*, 410 F.2d 351, 352 (5th Cir. 1969).

Looking beyond that briefing defect, we see that Tango's first amended complaint set out extensive facts and included exhibits upon which its claims were based. No pleading defect appears there. Further, at no point did the Elephant Group identify the indispensable third party that needed to be joined, instead unhelpfully referring to it as "the charterer." The decision not to identify the allegedly indispensable party may have served some important purpose for the Elephant Group, but it failed to aid in the purpose of setting aside a default.

We agree with the district court that neither claimed defense suffices. The presentation of meritorious defenses requires "definite factual allegations, as opposed to mere legal conclusions." *Jenkens & Gilchrist v. Groia & Co.*, 542 F.3d 114, 122 (5th Cir. 2008). Legal conclusions were all that were presented.

AFFIRMED.***

******(Reporter's Note: On March 11, 2022, the U.S. Fifth Circuit withdrew this opinion on rehearing.)******

United States Court of Appeals for the Fifth Circuit

No. 21-30047

TERRAL RIVER SERV., INC.
VS.
SCF MARINE INC.

Appeal from the United States District Court for the Western District of Louisiana

Decided: December 15, 2021

Citation: 20 F.4th 1015, 9 Adm. R. 283 (5th Cir. 2021).

Before **HIGGINBOTHAM, STEWART,** and **WILSON,** Circuit Judges.

[—1—] {–1016–} **HIGGINBOTHAM,** Circuit Judge:

As provided in their contract, SCF Marine Inc. ("SCF") delivered its Barge SCF 14023 to a loading facility operated by Terral River Service, Inc. ("Terral"). The barge sank while secured at Terral's facility. Terral then sued SCF. The district court granted summary judgment to SCF on all of Terral's claims. Under our jurisdiction pursuant to 28 U.S.C. § 1292(a)(3), we affirm. **[—2—]**

I.

Prior to delivering the barge to Terral, SCF had the barge cleaned and inspected **{–1017–}** by C&M Marine, Inc on May 2, 2018. A C&M employee inspected the barge. He reported no leaks and only trace amounts of water within the void tanks, but not an amount warranting his concern.

Following the inspection, a towing company took the barge from the C&M facility up the Mississippi River to the Terral facility as part of a fleet of other barges. A Terral harbor boat there took custody of the barge, towing it into the Terral facility. Cory Pemberton, a Terral employee, inspected the barge and completed a Barge Inspection Report upon the barge's delivery on May 7, 2018. Pemberton reported that he inspected the barge's knuckles and void tanks but saw no water or sunlight in the void tanks, which would have indicated a fracture.

The Terral harbor boat crew then moored the barge at a dock for loading. Over the following two days, the barge was partially loaded with rice. On May 11, 2018, the Terral harbor boat crew checked the barge at 5:30 a.m. and saw no issues. When the harbor boat crew checked the barge again at 5:50 a.m., the barge had partially sunk.

Terral hired a salvor who raised the barge. Surveyors hired by Terral and SCF examined the barge and found a fracture measuring twelve inches long and three quarters of an inch wide on the port bow rake knuckle, an area of the hull covering a void tank. Green witness marks around the fracture were identified following the salvage.

Terral sued SCF for general maritime negligence, unseaworthiness, breach of contract, and indemnity. Underlying all of these claims is the allegation that "[t]he fracture preexisted delivery of the [b]arge to Terral and is estimated to have been two (2) to four (4) weeks old as of May 11, 2018." In its Second Amended Complaint Terral added contribution and salvage **[—3—]** claims. The contribution claim was based upon the same factual allegation as the four other claims presented in Terral's initial complaint. The salvage claim sought recovery as a salvor of SCF's barge. SCF counterclaimed against Terral for negligence and breach of duty and moved for summary judgment on Terral's claims.[1]

SCF also filed *Daubert* motions to exclude the testimony of two of Terral's expert witnesses, Frank Budwine and Bob Bartlett.[2] The district court granted SCF's motion to exclude Budwine's testimony regarding the age of the hull fracture and granted in part SCF's motion to exclude the testimony of Bob Bartlett. The district court excluded Bartlett's testimony that the fracture likely occurred before the barge was delivered, but allowed Bartlett to testify that the green witness marks indicated the fracture was likely

[1] SCF's counterclaim was not addressed by the district court in its order granting summary judgment and thus is not part of this appeal.

[2] *Daubert v. Merrell Dow Pharms., Inc.*, 509 U.S. 579 (1993).

caused by a collision between the gray barge and a green object. After ruling on the *Daubert* motions, the district court granted SCF's motion for summary judgment and dismissed all of Terral's claims with prejudice. Terral timely appealed.

II.

We review *de novo* a district court's grant of summary judgment.[3] Summary judgment is proper "if the movant shows that there is no genuine dispute as to any material fact and the movant is **{-1018-}** entitled to judgment as a matter of law."[4] However the movant "need not negate the elements of the **[—4—]** nonmovant's case."[5] "The moving party is entitled to a judgment as a matter of law because the nonmoving party has failed to make a sufficient showing on an essential element of her case with respect to which she has the burden of proof."[6] A summary judgment ruling "will be affirmed by this court when the nonmoving party fails to meet its burden to come forward with facts and law demonstrating a basis for recovery that would support a jury verdict,"[7] and we may affirm on any grounds supported by the record and presented to the district court.[8]

III.

Turning first to the burden of proof, Terral argues that SCF bears the burden of proving that the barge was seaworthy at the time of delivery, an allegation underlying all of Terral's non-salvage claims. SCF claims that Terral bears the burden of proving that it provided an unseaworthy vessel.

A vessel's owner is duty bound to furnish a vessel reasonably fit for its intended purpose.[9] "Ordinarily, when a charterer claims that a shipowner has breached the charter party by providing an unseaworthy vessel, the burden of proving such a breach rests upon the claimant."[10] Although it was **[—5—]** not a charterer, Terral is here the claimant and therefore bears the burden of proving that the barge was unseaworthy.

The parties do not dispute that the barge was the subject of a bailment with SCF as the bailor and Terral as the bailee. Terral urges that the bailment shifts the burden to SCF. Terral points to *Richmond Sand & Gravel Corp. v. Tidewater Const. Corp,*[11] but *Richmond* involved the paradigmatic situation in which a vessel's owner-bailor sued a defendant-bailee for the bailee's negligence that led to the vessel's capsizing.[12] Well enough, but under the paradigmatic example, SCF, as the bailor, would sue Terral, the bailee. Here, Terral is suing SCF.

The district court was correct that "[i]n the 'somewhat unusual situation' of a barge loader suing a barge owner for the sinking of the owner's barge, it is the plaintiff barge loader who bears the burden of proving that the barge was unseaworthy at the time the plaintiff barge loader took custody and control of the barge."[13] Terral bears the burden of proof for all its claims.

IV.

The district court granted summary judgment against Terral's five non-salvage **{-1019-}** claims: maritime negligence, unsea-

---

[3] *Martin Res. Mgmt. Corp. v. AXIS Ins. Co.*, 803 F.3d 766, 768 (5th Cir. 2015).

[4] FED. R. CIV. P. 56(a).

[5] *Little v. Liquid Air Corp.*, 37 F.3d 1069, 1075 (5th Cir. 1994).

[6] *Celotex Corp. v. Catrett*, 477 U.S. 317, 323 (1986) (internal quotations marks omitted).

[7] *Little*, 37 F.3d at 1071.

[8] *Hernandez v. Velasquez*, 522 F.3d 556, 560 (5th Cir. 2008).

[9] *Morales v. City of Galveston*, 370 U.S. 165, 169 (1962); *The Southwark*, 191 U.S. 1, 9 (1903).

[10] *Texaco, Inc. v. Universal Marine, Inc.*, 400 F. Supp. 311, 320 (E.D. La. 1975); *see also Cooper v. Pinedo*, 212 F.2d 137, 140–41 (5th Cir. 1954).

[11] 170 F.2d 392 (4th Cir. 1948).

[12] *Id.* at 393.

[13] *Terral River Serv., Inc. v. SCF Marine, Inc.*, 510 F. Supp. 3d 415, 419 (W.D. La. 2020) (*quoting Consolidation Coal Co. v. U.S. Steel Corp.*, 364 F. Supp. 1071, 1074 (W.D. Pa. 1973), *and citing Dunkard Mining Co. v. Mon River Towing*, No. 88-2181, 1989 WL 121053, at *3 (W.D. Pa., October 3, 1989)).

worthiness, indemnity, contribution, and breach of contract. Terral argues that summary judgment was improper as there were several issues of material fact remaining. But the "several" are a variation on a single theme—whether the barge's hull was **[—6—]** fractured prior to delivery. SCF presented evidence that the fracture was not present when SCF transferred the barge to Terral: the C&M inspection report and Terral's own inspection report did not note any fracture. The barge traveled hundreds of miles along the Mississippi River and then sat partially loaded for two days before sinking.

Terral continues to primarily rely on the assertions of Budwine and Bartlett, but their testimony was properly excluded under *Daubert* and Federal Rule of Evidence 702. Terral does present two arguments that do not rely on the excluded testimony. First, Terral argues that Pemberton's inspection from the deck of the barge would not place him at an angle to see a fracture in the hull. However, Terral's inspection procedures include looking for water and sunlight within the void tank—both indicators of a fracture—yet Pemberton did not detect either. Second, Terral argues that there was no green object at its facility that could have collided with the barge to explain how it received the witness marks. But neither of these arguments satisfies Terral's burden of proof to establish that the barge was already damaged when it was delivered. Without the excluded testimony, Terral lacked sufficient evidence to show that the hull was fractured prior to the barge's delivery.

With this weakness in its proof of an essential element of Terral's case for which it would bear the burden of proof at trial, the district court properly entered summary judgment as to Terral's maritime negligence, unseaworthiness, indemnity, and contribution claims. We affirm the district court's dismissal of these claims.

While the district court did not separately address it, the district court did not err in dismissing the breach of contract claim. Where a district court provides little or no reasoning as to its decision to grant summary judgment, we may still affirm the district court's decision on any basis presented to the **[—7—]** district court.[14] SCF argued that because Terral could not present evidence of the fracture existing prior to delivery, none of its claims could succeed. As the same lack of genuine issue of material fact that frustrated Terral's other non-salvage claims also underlies the breach of contract claim, we affirm the grant of summary judgment and its dismissal.

V.

As Terral's salvage claim does not depend on proof of when the fracture occurred, the district court's stated reasoning for granting summary judgment does not address the salvage claim. SCF argues either that Terral waived its salvage claim or that there is a sufficient alternative basis in the record to affirm the dismissal.

Generally, we will not consider arguments first raised on appeal.[15] To preserve an argument for appeal, a litigant must have presented the argument to such a degree that the district court had an opportunity to rule on it.[16] Terral presented **{–1020–}** its salvage claim in its Second Amended Complaint and SCF addressed and denied the salvage claim repeatedly below. Terral also raised its salvage claim in responding to SCF's motion for summary judgment. Terral sufficiently presented its salvage claim to the district court.

That said, Terral's preexisting duty of care as the barge's bailee here steps forward as an alternative basis for summary judgment and dismissal of the salvage claim, which has three elements: 1) marine peril, 2) service voluntarily rendered when not required by an existing duty or special contract, and 3) success in whole or in part, or that the service rendered **[—8—]** contributed to such

---

[14] *LeMaire v. La. Dep't of Transp. & Dev.*, 480 F.3d 383, 387 (5th Cir. 2007).

[15] *Est. of Duncan v. Comm'r*, 890 F.3d 192, 202 (5th Cir. 2018).

[16] *F.D.I.C. v. Mijalis*, 15 F.3d 1314, 1327 (5th Cir. 1994).

success.[17] Terral fails as to the second element because it had a preexisting duty as the barge's bailee, a duty of ordinary care owed to SCF,[18] that forecloses its salvage claim. We affirm the grant of summary judgment and the dismissal of the salvage claim.

VI.

As the non-movant at the summary judgment stage, Terral cannot show that there is a genuine issue of material fact over an essential element of each of its claims for which it bears the burden of proof. The district court properly granted summary judgment to SCF on Terral's five non-salvage claims and its salvage claim is foreclosed by its pre-existing duty as the barge's bailee. We AFFIRM the ruling of the district court.

---

[17] *The Sabine,* 101 U.S. 384, 384 (1879); *W. Coast Shipping Brokers Corp. v. Ferry "Chuchequero"*, 582 F.2d 959, 960 (5th Cir. 1978).

[18] *Stegemann v. Mia. Beach Boat Slips,* 213 F.2d 561, 564 (5th Cir. 1954).

United States Court of Appeals
for the Fifth Circuit

No. 20-60357

RIVERA
vs.
DIRECTOR, OFFICE OF WORKERS' COMPENSATION PROGRAMS

Petition for Review of the Decision and Order of the Benefits Review Board

Decided: December 21, 2021

Citation: 22 F.4th 460, 9 Adm. R. 287 (5th Cir. 2021).

Before **ELROD, WILLETT,** and **ENGELHARDT,** Circuit Judges.

[—1—] {-462-} **ELROD,** Circuit Judge:

Ramon Rivera was injured on the job while employed by Ameri-Force. He successfully obtained a workers' compensation award after filing a claim with the Office of Workers' Compensation Programs of the U.S. Department of Labor. The question before us is whether he is also entitled to attorney's fees under 33 U.S.C. § 928(b). Because Rivera is entitled to attorney's fees **[—2—]** under the plain text of that provision, we REVERSE the decision of the Benefits Review Board and REMAND for further proceedings.

I.

Rivera brought a hearing-loss claim with the Department of Labor against Ameri-Force and its insurer. In December of 2015, Ameri-Force responded by paying Rivera for two weeks of disability benefits based on an average weekly wage of $212.17. But Ameri-Force disputed that it was the "last responsible employer" and thus liable under the Longshore and Harbor Workers' Compensation Act, 33 U.S.C. §§ 901–950. On July 28 of the following year, the claims examiner assigned to the **{-463-}** dispute issued a memorandum noting that Rivera sought benefits based on 35.31% binaural hearing loss and an average weekly wage of $1,027.37. The claims examiner recommended that Rivera had made a *prima facie* case against Ameri-Force and that Ameri-Force is the last responsible maritime employer. The claims examiner asked the parties to consider that recommendation and reach an agreement on the disputed issues.

On August 5, 2016, Ameri-Force notified the claims examiner and Rivera by letter that it accepted its designation as the responsible employer. But Ameri-Force explained that negotiations concerning Rivera's average weekly wage were ongoing and that it would submit further documentation on that issue if the parties could not agree. It also explained that it organized an additional medical evaluation with Dr. Seidemann, a doctor of its choosing, to take place on August 23, 2016. Ameri-Force expressed that it "would appreciate the opportunity to present the doctor's findings before any final recommendations are made concerning the binaural hearing loss." Two weeks later, Ameri-Force sent another letter to the claims examiner arguing that Rivera's average weekly wage should not include his *per diem* payments and that the value should be $274.11. **[—3—]**

Shortly thereafter, on August 24, 2016, a newly assigned claims examiner issued a recommendation. The recommendation stated that Ameri-Force was Rivera's last responsible employer, Ameri-Force was responsible for costs associated with Rivera's 35.31% binaural hearing loss and his hearing aids, and that Rivera's average weekly wage should include *per diem* payments.

Immediately upon receiving the recommendation letter on August 29, 2016, Ameri-Force sent a letter to the new claims examiner asking him to "reconsider and withhold" the recommendation until Ameri-Force provided the findings from the second medical evaluation on Rivera's hearing loss and the claims examiner was able to review it. Three days later, Ameri-Force sent the claims examiner another letter. Enclosed were the results of Dr. Seidemann's evaluation, which concluded Rivera had suffered a 21% binaural hearing loss. The letter also stated:

> Based on our conversation, it is my understanding that[,] after considering the IME report from Dr. Seidemann and the wage information which we have provided, you will be issuing supplemental recommendations and that the parties will have 14 days from the issuance of these recommendations in which to advise whether they are accepted or rejected. If I am in error, please advise.

On September 7, the claims examiner indeed issued a "Supplemental Informal Conference Recommendation." The document purported to supplement both the July 28 and August 24 recommendations. In it, the claims examiner recommended that Rivera suffered a 28.16% hearing loss, a rate which represented the average of the competing rates proposed by the parties. The document also explained that under that rate, the average weekly wage would be $439.55 and the total benefits award due would be $24,755.46. Finally, it advised that any party who rejected the **[—4—]** recommendation should initiate the process for a formal hearing within 21 days. Neither party did so.

But on September 12 and 13, Ameri-Force offered to settle the dispute. It told Rivera that it agreed to pay $25,151.05 in disability indemnity benefits, use an average weekly wage of $659.33, and provide $5,000 in medical benefits if Rivera did not seek attorney's fees from Ameri-Force. If Rivera rejected the offer, Ameri-Force explained, it would pay benefits in accordance **{–464–}** with the September 7 recommendation. Rivera rejected the offer a couple days later, and on September 16 Ameri-Force paid $24,755.46, the amount set forth in the September 7 recommendation. Two weeks later, the claims examiner issued another supplemental recommendation concluding that Ameri-Force in fact owed $25,151.05, which was based on a 28.61% hearing loss, not a 28.16% hearing loss; Ameri-Force paid the difference shortly thereafter.

In November of 2016, Rivera filed a petition seeking an award of $8,153 in attorney's fees under 33 U.S.C. § 928 for the work performed on this matter. Ameri-Force objected. The district director concluded that Rivera was entitled to the fees under subsection (b) because Ameri-Force did not timely pay Rivera in accordance with the August 24 recommendation and Rivera ultimately obtained a greater award than Ameri-Force was initially willing to pay after that recommendation. Ameri-Force appealed to the BRB. On February 28, 2018, the BRB reversed, holding that the August 24 recommendation was rendered moot by the September 7 recommendation. In the BRB's view, because Ameri-Force timely paid Rivera in accordance with the September 7 recommendation, the criteria for attorney's fees under § 928(b) were not satisfied.

Rivera moved for reconsideration, and on October 24, 2018, the BRB granted the request only to remand for the district director to consider whether Rivera was entitled to fees under § 928(a). It rejected his request as **[—5—]** to its determination under § 928(b). Ameri-Force challenged the BRB's decision as to subsection (a), and on February 28, 2020 the BRB agreed and reversed the prior decision by *en banc* vote. But it granted a remand to the district director to consider the availability of attorney's fees under § 928(c). Rivera petitioned this court for review of the BRB's reversal of the district director's award of fees under § 928(b). So, the sole issue before us is whether that provision's criteria for attorney's fees are satisfied.

II.

As a preliminary matter, Ameri-Force asks us to dismiss as untimely Rivera's petition for review of the BRB's § 928(b) determination. We decline to do so.

Under 33 U.S.C. § 921(c), any petition for review of a final order of the BRB must be filed with the appropriate Court of Appeals within sixty days of the BRB's order. Rivera filed his petition on April 28, 2020. He claims that it was timely because it was filed within sixty days of the BRB's February 28, 2020 *en banc* order. Ameri-Force contends that the petition was untimely because it was not filed within sixty days of the BRB's October 24,

2018 order, which was when the BRB first made its determination regarding fees under § 928(b).

We consider the timeliness of the petition in relation to the February 28, 2020 *en banc* order, not the October 24, 2018 order. Rivera's initial request for a fee award sought fees and costs under both subsection (a) and (b) of § 928. In its October 24, 2018 order, the BRB remanded for the director to consider the availability of fees under subsection (a). But in doing so it remanded the *case*. Thus, although the BRB had already resolved the subsection (b) portion of the fee request in the October 24, 2018 order, it did not issue a final resolution of the fee request, which included the subsection (a) request, until February 28, 2020. The sixty-day timeline to file a petition under § 921(c) began then. *See Newpark Shipbuilding & Repair, Inc. v.* **[—6—]** *Roundtree*, 723 F.2d 399, 400–01 (5th Cir. 1984) (explaining that a "final" decision for purposes of § 921(c) is one that **{-465-}** "ends the litigation on the merits and leaves nothing for the court to do but execute the judgment" (quoting *Firestone Tire & Rubber Co. v. Risjord*, 449 U.S. 368, 373–74 (1981)). We therefore hold that Rivera's petition was timely filed.

III.

Turning to the substance of Rivera's claim, the only issue before us is whether Rivera is entitled to an award of attorney's fees under § 928(b). We hold that he is.

"This Court conducts a de novo review of the BRB's rulings of law, owing them no deference because the BRB is not a policymaking agency." *Carey v. Ormet Primary Aluminum Corp.*, 627 F.3d 979, 982 (5th Cir. 2010) (quoting *Pool Co. v. Cooper*, 274 F.3d 173, 177 (5th Cir. 2001)). As for fact issues, we "only determine whether evidence exists to support the [director's] findings." *Pool Co.*, 274 F.3d at 178. We therefore consider "whether the BRB properly concluded that the ALJ's factual findings were [or were not] supported by substantial evidence on the record as a whole." *James J. Flanagan Stevedores, Inc. v. Gallagher*, 219 F.3d 426, 429 (5th Cir. 2000).

An employee may collect attorney's fees under § 928(b) if: (1) an informal conference is held; (2) the BRB or a deputy commissioner issues a written recommendation; (3) the employer refuses to adopt the recommendation within fourteen days; and (4) the employee procures a lawyer's services to achieve an award greater than that which the employer was willing to pay after the written recommendation was issued. 33 U.S.C. § 928(b); *see also Carey*, 627 F.3d at 982. All those criteria were met here.

The claims examiner held an informal conference with Rivera and Ameri-Force on July 26, 2016. On August 24, 2016, the replacement claims **[—7—]** examiner issued a written recommendation declaring that Ameri-Force was responsible for the costs associated with Rivera's 35.31% hearing loss and Rivera's hearing aids, and that average weekly wage should include Rivera's *per diem* payments.[1] Ameri-Force did not accept that recommendation.[2] Instead, it asked the claims examiner to reconsider its recommendation, asserting that benefits should be calculated based on 21% hearing

[1] Ameri-Force received the recommendation on August 29, 2016.

[2] Ameri-Force argues that the § 928(b) fee-shifting provision is not triggered because it did not "reject" the August 24 recommendation. But, as this court has explained, § 928(b) "gives an employer an opportunity to avoid the payment of attorney's fees by either (1) accepting the Board's or Commissioner's recommendations or (2) refusing those recommendations but tendering a payment that is accepted by the claimant." *FMC Corp. v. Perez*, 128 F.3d 908, 910 (5th Cir. 1997). Ameri-Force did neither. It asserts that on September 12, 2016 it extended an offer to Rivera to pay $25,151.05 in disability and $5,000 in medical benefits if Rivera did not seek attorney's fees; and if Rivera chose to seek attorney's fees, Ameri-Force would pay $24,755.46 in disability and would authorize medical payments subject to audit. The first of these offers was not an acceptance of the August 24 recommendation because it was conditioned on Rivera not seeking attorney's fees. The second offer was, if anything, an acceptance of the September 7 recommendation, not the August 24 recommendation.

loss, not 35.31%. In the end, Ameri-Force paid benefits corresponding to a 28.61% hearing loss. Simply put, a conference was held, a recommendation was issued, Ameri-Force refused to adopt the recommendation, and, with counsel's assistance, Rivera ultimately obtained an award greater than that which Ameri-Force was initially willing to pay after the **{-466-}** recommendation. Under § 928(b), then, Rivera is entitled to attorney's fees.

The BRB erred when it concluded that the August 24, 2016 recommendation did not apply for the purposes of attorney's fees under § 928(b) because the claims examiner's September 7, 2016 recommendation rendered it moot. Ameri-Force asserts that requiring it to accept the August 24 recommendation after the September 7 recommendation supposedly rendered it moot would "lead to absurd consequences and glaringly unjust **[—8—]** results." It likens such a requirement to requiring a party to obey a moot *order*.

Ameri-Force provides no legal authority showing that a subsequent recommendation renders a prior one moot.[3] And the plain language of § 928(b) suggests no such thing. That provision merely states that after a recommendation is issued, the employer may open itself up to attorney's fees liability if it refuses to accept the recommendation within fourteen days. 33 U.S.C. § 928(b). The statute says nothing about the effect of follow-up recommendations, so such recommendations do not undo the direct consequences of the statute's plain terms.

Moreover, Ameri-Force's analogy to a moot order crumbles under the weight of examination. A party *must* follow a court order. If it does not, it may be held in contempt of court. *See Walling v. Crane*, 158 F.2d 80, 83 (5th Cir. 1946). So, if a later order contradicts an earlier one, a party can only follow one of them. In such circumstances, it makes sense only to require a party to follow the later order, so that the party has an open path to avoid contempt. But a recommendation by a claims examiner is different. Parties have no legal duty to follow such a recommendation. An employer *may* become liable for attorney's fees later *if* it refuses to follow the recommendation, *and* the employee then pays for an attorney's services, *and* the employee ultimately obtains an award greater than the employer's post-recommendation offer. 33 U.S.C. § 928(b); *Carey*, 627 F.3d at 982. So, whereas two conflicting orders cannot operate simultaneously without forcing a party into contempt, two active recommendations can overlap without creating a Catch-22. **[—9—]**

Nor may the August 24, 2016 recommendation be ignored on the ground that the recommendation was issued in a manner inconsistent with a party's expectations. If a claims examiner issues a recommendation, then a recommendation has been issued for the purposes of § 928(b). That does not change just because the parties may have expected otherwise. The regulations promulgated under the statute confirm this understanding. They provide that if parties do not agree with the claims examiner's post-conference recommendations, then further conferences can be scheduled. 20 C.F.R. § 702.316. But that provision cautions that if a party disagrees with a recommendation, the attorney's fees provision may apply. *Id.* ("If they disagree (*Caution: See § 702.134*), then the district director may schedule such further conference or conferences as, in his or her opinion, may bring about agreement . . . ." (emphasis added)). That fees provision, like § 928(b), explains that the employer owes attorney's fees if it refuses to accept the claims examiner's recommendation and the employee procures a lawyer's services to obtain a greater award than that which the employer initially was willing to pay. 20 C.F.R. § 702.134(b). **{-467-}**

It is true that the regulations do not specifically contemplate when a claims examiner issues a subsequent *recommendation* without a new conference. But the regulations make clear that if an employer wishes to seek reconsideration of an initial recommendation by way of a new conference, it may do so but may be liable for attorney's

[3] At oral argument, Ameri-Force's counsel admitted there was no legal authority one way or the other on the issue of whether a subsequent recommendation invalidates a prior recommendation.

fees depending on the result. All that to say, the regulations indicate that an employer must accept a recommendation within fourteen days *even if* the employer anticipates additional proceedings and determinations by the claims examiner.

Section 928(b) does identify an exception, but it does not apply here. Under that exception, attorney's fees are not due if: (1) the employer agrees to a medical examination by a physician employed or selected by the Secretary (an Independent Medical Examiner, or "IME"); and (2) the **[—10—]** employer agrees to pay compensation in accordance with the IME's findings. 33 U.S.C. § 928(b).

In this case, however, Ameri-Force asked for the claims examiner to reconsider the August 24 recommendation because of an anticipated report from a medical examiner *arranged by Ameri-Force*—not an IME.[4] The statute reasonably allows an extension of the fourteen-day period when an employer promises to abide by an independent examination. But a request to reconsider in light of an employer's own report is simply an objection to the recommendation. An employer certainly is entitled to submit its own evidence contradicting the employee's assertions regarding the severity of injury. But under the statute the employer cannot avoid attorney's fees liability by delaying the claims examiner's recommendation simply because the employer thinks the claims examiner got it wrong.

Ameri-Force also argues that the claims examiner's August 24, 2016 recommendation was not a "recommendation" at all for the purposes of § 928(b) because it did not include a specific dollar amount due for average weekly wage or total compensation. We disagree.

Section 928(b) provides that if a controversy develops over the compensation an employee is due, "the deputy commissioner or Board shall set the matter for an informal conference and following such conference the deputy commissioner or Board shall *recommend in writing a disposition of the controversy*." 33 U.S.C. § 928(b) (emphasis added). We hold that the recommended-disposition requirement is satisfied if the claims examiner issues in writing a proposed resolution of any matter central to the question of how much compensation an employer owes an employee. **[—11—]**

This court has not squarely addressed the issue in a published case,[5] but we find decisions of our sister circuits instructive. The Fourth Circuit has held that the recommendation requirement was satisfied when "the claims examiner recommended in writing that [the employee's] 'present left knee problems be accepted as a result **{-468-}** of the [incident in question].'" *Newport News Shipbuilding & Dry Dock Co. v. Dir., Off. of Workers' Comp. Programs*, 474 F.3d 109, 113–14 (4th Cir. 2006). Because the employer "did not accept [that] recommendation within fourteen days of its receipt," the employer opened itself up to potential attorney's fees liability. *Id.*

In an identically named case, the Fourth Circuit also held that the recommendation requirement was satisfied when "the District Director . . . stat[ed] that the position of the Office of Workers' Compensation Programs was that [the employer] should begin payments of the [percent disability] rating with which it had no disagreement." *Newport News Shipbuilding & Dry Dock Co. v. Dir., Off. of Workers' Comp. Programs*, 477 F.3d 123, 127 (4th Cir. 2007). Under this instructive precedent, then, a recommendation is issued for the purposes of

[4] The employer has referred to the medical examiner as an IME, but because the doctor was selected by the employer and not the Secretary, that label is incorrect.

[5] In an unpublished decision, this court explained that a recommendation was not issued by a claims examiner when the claims examiner explicitly stated that "she could not issue a recommendation because she lacked the necessary wage and medical information." *Craven v. Dir., Off. of Workers' Comp. Programs,* 407 F. App'x 854, 855–56 (5th Cir. 2011). The memorandum from the claims examiner to the parties specifically explained that "[c]urrent medical information" and "[w]age information should be provided . . . prior to issuing a recommendation with regard to [average weekly wage]." *Id.* at 856 n.2.

§ 928(b) when a claims examiner offers a conclusion on an issue central to the determination of compensation owed. Notably, the opinions do not appear to rest their conclusions on whether, for example, the recommendation states a specific dollar amount owed.

Other cases suggest the same principle by explaining what is *not* a recommendation. The Sixth Circuit held that no recommendation was issued when the claims examiner explicitly stated in the "Recommendation" **[—12—]** section of the post-conference memorandum that no recommendation was being made. *Pittsburgh & Conneaut Dock Co. v. Dir., Off. of Workers' Comp. Programs*, 473 F.3d 253, 263, 265 (6th Cir. 2007). And the Fourth Circuit explained that a recommendation was not issued when the claims examiner simply demanded a claimant provide evidence to support its assertion about three days of lost time. *Virginia Int'l Terminals, Inc. v. Edwards*, 398 F.3d 313, 315, 318 n.* (4th Cir. 2005). So, in these cases in which a recommendation was *not* issued, the claims examiner clearly made no determination on any issue central to the question of whether or how much compensation was due.

In this case, however, the claims examiner *did* make a determination on a central issue in its August 24, 2016 recommendation. Indeed, he did so for multiple issues pivotal to the question of owed compensation. In a document the claims examiner called a "recommendation," he specifically directed that: (1) "[Rivera's] wages used to calculate [average weekly wage] should include those listed as per diem by the employer and added to his other wages to compute a compensation rate in this case"; (2) Rivera had no food or lodging expenses; (3) Rivera's average weekly wage should be calculated by dividing by fifty-two his total earnings in the last year of his work; and (4) Ameri-Force is Rivera's last responsible employer "and [is] responsible for [Rivera's] 35.31% binaural hearing loss plus hearing aids." Each of these conclusions has a determinative effect on the total compensation Rivera was due.

It is true that the recommendation also asked Ameri-Force to submit documentation of Rivera's yearly earnings. Perhaps for that reason, the recommendation did not specify a particular dollar amount Ameri-Force should pay. But the recommendation was nevertheless a recommended disposition under § 928(b). Rivera's yearly earnings were not in dispute between the parties. The disputed issues up until that point were whether *per diem* pay should be included in the average weekly wage, whether Ameri- **[—13—]** Force was the last responsible employer,[6] and the degree of hearing **{-469-}** loss Rivera suffered. The August 24 recommendation offered a conclusion for each of these issues.

What is more, the August 24 recommendation gave Ameri-Force everything necessary to determine the total compensation owed. The parties had already identified the average weekly wage values both including and excluding *per diem* payments. The August 24 recommendation concluded that *per diem* payments should be included. The recommendation then explained that the employer would be liable for Rivera's 35.21% hearing loss and for his hearing aids. As the District Director found, "[t]he Employer had the necessary wage records in its possession to comply with [the claims examiner's] recommendation to add per diem payments and wage payments for the 52 weeks preceding the accident date and to divide that amount by 52 to calculate the proper [average weekly wage]." The BRB did not disturb that finding. Thus, the August 24 recommendation provided all the remaining items necessary to determine the total compensation value, and it described the equation by which to calculate that value. The employer needed only to apply the instructions from the August 24 recommendation to the numbers the employer already possessed, and that would have produced the specific compensation amount due.

Relatedly, as a matter of statutory interpretation, "disposition" could refer to what the August 24 recommendation accom-

[6] By the time the August 24 recommendation was issued, Ameri-Force had agreed that it was the last responsible employer.

plished. When § 928(b) was enacted in its current form, Black's Law Dictionary noted that the term "dispose of" may refer to the determination of suits. *Dispose Of*, BLACK'S LAW DICTIONARY (4th ed. 1968). And it explained that "controversy" can refer to either "a civil action or suit," *or* simply "a litigated question." **[—14—]** *Controversy*, BLACK'S LAW DICTIONARY (4th ed. 1968). So, we may interpret "disposition of the controversy" to apply to situations in which the claims examiner recommends a manner in which a dispute between parties could be resolved. With that understanding in mind, the August 24 recommendation was a disposition in two related but independent senses. First, it expressed a conclusion for all the central issues on which the parties disagreed. Second, it provided everything necessary for the employer to pay the compensation it owed. So, the August 24 recommendation was a recommendation for the "disposition of the controversy."[7]

Because all the criteria for an award of attorney's fees under 33 U.S.C. § 928(b) are satisfied as to the claims examiner's August 24, 2016 recommendation, we REVERSE the decision of the Benefits Review Board and REMAND for further proceedings consistent with this opinion.

(Reporter's Note: Opinion, concurring in part and dissenting in part, follows on p. 294).

---

[7] Rivera also argues that he is entitled to a fee award under § 928(b) based on the claims examiner's July 28, 2016 recommendation, on the ground that after that recommendation Ameri-Force continued litigating the issue of whether it was the last responsible maritime employer. Because Rivera did not present this argument to the BRB, we will not consider it. *See Gallagher*, 219 F.3d at 437.

[—15—] {-469-} ENGELHARDT, Circuit Judge, concurring in part and dissenting in part:

I agree that Rivera's petition was timely filed and that the August 24, 2016 recommendation was a "recommendation" for purposes of § 928(b). On the instant record, however, I part ways with the majority regarding Rivera's entitlement to an award of attorney's fees. Had the claims examiner not issued the September 7, 2016 "Supplemental Informal Conference Recommendation" until *after* the expiration of the fourteen-day period following Ameri-Force's August 29 receipt of the August 24 {-470-} recommendation, I would agree with the majority's determination. But, importantly, that did not occur here. Instead, within those fourteen days, the claims examiner issued the September 7 "Supplemental Informal Conference Recommendation," which recommended a different binaural hearing loss percentage (28.16%) from that set forth in the August 24 recommendation (35.31%). Thus, relative to binaural hearing loss, the September 7 recommendation superseded the August 24 recommendation and triggered a new fourteen-day period for purposes of § 928(b).[1] Ameri-Force timely paid the resulting amount of indemnity benefits—$24,755.46— within those fourteen days. It also timely paid the additional amount of benefits set forth in the September 30, 2016 supplemental recommendation.

As a matter of policy, the informal conference and recommendation process is designed to expedite the resolution of claims through the timely exchange of pertinent information. I think that purpose was served here. That is, the parties conducted themselves in good faith as expected by the statutory [—16—] scheme in narrowing and then resolving the monetary amount due without the necessity of a formal administrative hearing. Accordingly, I dissent with the attorney's fees aspect of the majority's opinion.

[1] Notably, the claims examiner's issuance of the September 7 supplemental recommendation was not unexpected by the parties or contrary to a prior agreement between them. Indeed, the record reveals no objection by Rivera's counsel to the procedures and schedules proposed in Ameri-Force's counsel's August 5, August 29, and September 1 correspondence.

United States Court of Appeals for the Sixth Circuit

United States Court of Appeals
for the Sixth Circuit

No. 20-5514

INGRAM BARGE CO.
VS.
ZEN-NOH GRAIN CORP.

Appeal from the United States District Court for the Middle District of Tennessee at Nashville

Decided: June 28, 2021

Citation: 3 F.4th 275, 9 Adm. R. 296 (6th Cir. 2021).

Before **SILER, WHITE,** and **STRANCH,** Circuit Judges.

[—1—] {-277-} SILER, Circuit Judge:

Typically, only parties to a contract are bound to its terms. This case is no exception. Zen-Noh Grain Corporation was neither a party to nor consented to Ingram **[—2—]** Barge Company's contract for the transportation of goods (a bill of lading) and thus is not bound to the contract's forum selection clause. Therefore, the district court did not have jurisdiction over Zen-Noh, and we AFFIRM the district court's dismissal for lack of personal jurisdiction.

I

Zen-Noh purchased shipments of grains from several companies. The sellers were required to prepay the barge freight and deliver the product to Zen-Noh's grain trading terminal in Convent, Louisiana. But the sellers were not required to use any specific company to deliver the goods. Plaintiff Ingram was chosen.

Ingram then issued a contract to the sellers for the transportation of goods—a negotiable bill of lading in industry parlance. A bill of lading defines the relationships of the parties: the consignor (company arranging shipment); the consignee (company which is owed delivery); and the carrier (company that carries the goods).[1] After the goods have arrived, a consignee presents the bill of lading to receive the goods. *See Evergreen Marine Corp. v. Six Consignments of Frozen Scallops*, 4 F.3d 90, 92 n.1 (1st Cir. 1993). A negotiable bill of lading is a document of title, which is "vested in the holder of the bill." *Id.* at 96.

All the bills issued by Ingram are essentially identical, except two. In most of these bills: "the grain seller (or affiliate) is the consignor; the consignment is to the order of the consignee; Zen-Noh is included as a 'notify' party 'A/C'[2] the consignor/consignee; the freight is described as prepaid; and the signature blocks are for Ingram and the consignor/consignee." In the two exceptions, Zen-Noh is not mentioned at all or is mentioned in the field for consignee. **{-278-}**

Printed on each bill was an agreement to the "Carrier's Grain Transportation Terms" and a link to the Terms on Ingram's website. Importantly, the Terms: (1) purport to bind any entity that has an ownership interest in the goods; and (2) include a forum selection provision selecting the U.S. District Court for the Middle District of Tennessee. **[—3—]**

Ingram updated its Terms in April 2019. Ingram alleges that it notified Zen-Noh of the Terms through an email to CGB Enterprises, Inc. In a declaration, a representative of Ingram says, "to the best of his knowledge, information and belief," that "CGB is a company closely connected with Zen-Noh and Zen-Noh is a part-owner of CGB." The representative also says, again on information and belief, "CGB receives many of Zen-Noh's consigned grain cargos on the Lower Mississippi River and often acts on Zen-Noh's behalf in commercial dealings related to grain transportation." Ingram's email to CGB was sent prior to the use of the invoices at issue in this case.

About three weeks later, Zen-Noh "sent an email to Ingram complaining that Zen-Noh had received invoices for which it did not believe it was liable." Ingram responded that the invoices were "per [the] grain contract." When Zen-Noh requested the grain contract for its review, Ingram replied with a link to the Grain Transportation terms. Zen-Noh

[1] Parties can have multiple roles.

[2] "A/C" means "on account of."

finally answered that it was "not party to the barge affreightment contract as received in your previous email, and as such, is not liable for nor will be paying these invoices."

No one complains that the grains were not shipped and received by Zen-Noh. Instead, Ingram alleges it incurred costs that it claims Zen-Noh must pay. Zen-Noh has already paid Ingram demurrage charges— "penalties related to delayed loading or unloading of goods"—but has not paid for "unrelated expenses that Ingram incurred en route involving 'fleeting,' 'wharfage,' and 'shifting.'" Those costs it says it does not owe. As a result, Ingram filed this lawsuit against Zen-Noh in the Middle District of Tennessee, but the district court dismissed the case for lack of personal jurisdiction.

II

We have jurisdiction over this appeal under 28 U.S.C. § 1291. We review de novo the district court's dismissal for lack of personal jurisdiction under Fed. R. Civ. P. 12(b)(2). *Air Products and Controls, Inc. v. Safetech Intern., Inc.*, 503 F.3d 544, 549 (6th Cir. 2007). The plaintiff carries the burden of establishing the existence of personal jurisdiction, but that burden is relatively slight where, as here, the district court "relies solely on written submissions and affidavits" to resolve the issue. *Id.* Nonetheless, the plaintiff must meet its prima facia showing. **[—4—]** *Id.* The court must view the pleadings and affidavits in a light most favorable to the plaintiff and not weigh "the controverting assertions of the party seeking dismissal." *Id.* (quoting *Theunissen v. Matthews*, 935 F.2d 1454, 1458 (6th Cir. 1991)).

III

Ingram does not allege that Zen-Noh is subject to the court's jurisdiction through general or specific jurisdiction. Rather, it relies on a forum selection clause linked to its bills of lading. And a forum selection clause allows a party to agree "to the jurisdiction of a particular court." *Preferred Capital, Inc. v. Assocs. in Urology*, 453 F.3d 718, 721 (6th Cir. 2006) (citing *M/S Bremen v. Zapata Off-Shore Co.*, 407 U.S. 1 (1972)). **{–279–}**

But a bill of lading is a contract.[3] *See Wemhoener Pressen v. Ceres Marine Terminals Inc.*, 5 F.3d 734, 738 (4th Cir. 1993). "When a contract is a maritime one, and the dispute is not inherently local, federal law controls the contract interpretation." *Dynamic Worldwide Logistics, Inc. v. Exclusive Expressions, LLC*, 77 F. Supp. 3d 364, 373 (S.D.N.Y 2015) (quoting *Norfolk S. Ry. Co. v. Kirby*, 543 U.S. 14, 22–23 (2004)). Under federal common law, these contracts should be construed "by their terms and consistent with the intent of the parties." *Id.* (quoting *Kirby*, 543 U.S. at 31). As such, these contracts bind the parties that negotiated them. *Wemhoener Pressen*, 5 F.3d at 738. Here, Ingram and the grain sellers.

Ingram instead attempts to bind Zen-Noh as a consignee, despite Zen-Noh's classification on most bills as a notify party. *See North Pennsylvania R. Co. v. Commercial Nat. Bank of Chicago*, 123 U.S. 727, 736–37 (1887) (recognizing that notify parties are distinct from consignees). Consignees are considered third-party beneficiaries to bills of lading. *Dynamic Worldwide Logistics*, 77 F. Supp 3d at 374. A bill can bind them, but only with their consent. *See Kawasaki Kisen Kaisha, Ltd. v. Plano Molding Co.*, 696 F.3d 647, 655 (7th Cir. 2012); *In re M/V Rickners Genoa Litig.*, 622 F. Supp. 2d 56, 71 (S.D.N.Y. 2009) *opinion adhered to on reconsideration*, 643 F. Supp. 2d 553 (S.D.N.Y. 2009) *and aff'd sub nom. Chem One, Ltd. V. M/V Rickmers Genoa*, 502 F. App'x 66 (2d Cir. 2012). And a third-party beneficiary can show **[—5—]** consent by: (1) filing suit; (2) its course of conduct; or (3) accepting through its agent.[4]

[3] Ingram cannot simply depend on its own broad contract terms to bind Zen-Noh. To do so simply begs the question. A party cannot "unilaterally employ definitions to bind another by provision to which the other has not consented to be bound." *United States v. Waterman S.S. Corp.*, 471 F.2d 186, 189 n.4 (5th Cir. 1973).

[4] Ingram makes much of Zen-Noh's status as the "ultimate consignee" or owner of the grain, but neither is synonymous with consent. *See Dynamic Worldwide Logistics*, 77 F. Supp. 3d at 374 ("The mere fact that a party is a consignee or third-party beneficiary is insufficient to warrant a finding that

Zen-Noh did not consent in any of these ways. So, even if we treat Zen-Noh as a consignee, the terms of the bills do not reach it.

Lawsuit. Ingram sued Zen-Noh. So, Zen-Noh neither "file[d] a lawsuit under the bill" nor "attempt[ed] to benefit from its terms." *Kawasaki*, 696 F.3d at 655.

Course of conduct. Zen-Noh did not acquiesce to Ingram's grain terms over a long period. Just the opposite. Shortly after Zen-Noh learned of the revised Terms, it informed Ingram that it did not consider itself bound by those terms negotiated by the sellers and Ingram. *Compare APL Co. Pte. Ltd. v. Kemira Water Solutions, Inc.*, 890 F. Supp. 2d 360, 367 (S.D.N.Y. 2012) (holding that "little past dealings" precludes a finding of acceptance through a course of conduct) *with Sea-Land Service, Inc. v. Landis*, No. Civ. A. 94-6153, 1996 WL 4120, at *3 (E.D. Pa. Jan. 3, 1996) (finding acceptance when there was no evidence a defendant rejected the bill's unchanged terms over a decade-long relationship).

Ingram highlights its longstanding relationship with CGB, claiming CGB is affiliated with and partially owned **{–280–}** by Zen-Noh. Yet, even if that is true, that relationship is too attenuated to presume Zen-Noh's acceptance. Ingram also points to Zen-Noh's payment of demurrage charges on some of the shipments. As the district court found, however, those payments may be explained by a separate obligation between Zen-Noh and the sellers. Indeed, Zen-Noh may have "an implied obligation to pay freight charges separate and apart from the operative bill of lading." *APL Co. Pte. Ltd.*, 890 F.Supp. 2d at 367; *see also FT & T Consulting, Inc. v. B.O. Astra Management Corp.*, No. 12-cv-134, 2016 WL 8711085, at *5 (E.D.N.Y. Sept. 30, 2016).

Acceptance by an agent. Zen-Noh and the grain sellers did not have an agency relationship. "A basic principle of agency law is that an agency relationship exists only if the agent is acting on behalf of and subject to the control of the principal." *APL Co. Pte. Ltd*, 890 F. **[—6—]** Supp. 2d at 369 (quoting *Maersk, Inc. v Neewra, Inc.*, 687 F. Supp. 2d 300, 329 (S.D.N.Y. 2009)). Ingram presents no evidence that the grain sellers were "acting on behalf" of Zen-Noh or under Zen-Noh's control when the sellers entered the bills of lading. *Id.* at 369 (collecting cases); *Kawasaki*, 696 F.3d at 655 ("the agency test must fail because [the consignee] did not have the power to control . . ."); *see also Baker v. LeBoeuf, Lamb, Leiby & Macrae*, 105 F.3d 1102, 1106 (6th Cir. 1997) (holding that counterparties cannot be bound to a third-party contract unless the entities are so closely related that being bound to the contract becomes foreseeable). To the contrary, binding Zen-Noh in this way would be "[in]consistent with the intent of the parties." *Kirby*, 543 U.S. at 31. Zen-Noh paid for freight with the expectation that the seller would bear the full responsibility for transport. In other words, Zen-Noh sought to avoid a contractual relationship with Ingram.

IV

While Zen-Noh is a beneficiary of these bills of lading, that "mere fact . . . does not create contractual obligations for that beneficiary." *Dynamic Worldwide*, 77 F. Supp. 3d at 374; *see also Affiliated FM Ins. Co. v. Kuehne + Nagel, Inc.*, 328 F. Supp. 3d 329, 338 (S.D.N.Y. 2018) (declining to enforce a forum selection clause against a third-party beneficiary). Instead, Ingram must show Zen-Noh consented to its bills. It has not. Accordingly, we AFFIRM the district court's dismissal.

(Reporter's Note: Dissenting Opinion follows on p. 299).

[the consignee] was bound by the terms contained in the bills of lading"); *APL Co. PTE v. UK Aerosols LTD.*, No. C 05-0646, 2006 WL 3848784, at *3 (N.D. Cal. Sept. 28, 2006) (finding mere ownership of property does not bind the purchaser to the terms of a bill of lading).

[—7—] {–280–} WHITE, Circuit Judge, dissenting:

I respectfully dissent.

The difference between negotiable and nonnegotiable bills of lading is important in this case. "A negotiable bill of lading is a document of title, while a non-negotiable bill functions more like a receipt." 22 *Williston on Contracts* § 59:10 (4th ed. 2020). Buyers of highly fungible commodities like grain often choose to resell their grain while it is still in transit from the seller. *Wallingford Bros. v. Bush*, 255 F. 949, 950 (8th Cir. 1918). To transfer title of the still-in-transit grain to a new buyer, the original buyer need only endorse the negotiable bill of lading and deliver it to the new buyer. *Allied Chem. Int'l Corp. v. Companhia de Navegacao Lloyd Brasileiro*, 775 F.2d 476, 481 (2d Cir. 1985); Susan Beecher, *Can the Electronic Bill of Lading Go Paperless?*, 40 Int'l Law. 627, 631 (2006) ("the negotiable bill of lading [is] the only document which the shipper may not transmit by fax or email"). The new buyer then presents the bill to the carrier, who "is responsible for releasing the cargo only to the party who presents the original bill of lading. . . . If the carrier delivers {–281–} the goods to one other than the authorized holder of the bill of lading, the carrier is liable for misdelivery." *Allied Chem. Int'l Corp.*, 775 F.2d at 481.

A nonnegotiable bill works differently. Goods sent by way of a nonnegotiable bill are "nontransferable; that is, John Doe cannot, by indorsing that bill to anyone else, give that transferee the right to receive the goods from the carrier." Alan S. Gutterman, *Business Transactions Solutions* § 123:86 (2021). Because title to the goods cannot be transferred mid-shipment when using a nonnegotiable bill, there is no requirement that the buyer present the original bill of lading at the time it accepts the goods from the carrier. *Pere Marquette Ry. Co. v. Chicago & E. I. Ry. Co.*, 255 F. 40, 41–42 (7th Cir. 1918); David A. Bury, *Electronic Bills of Lading: A Never-Ending Story?*, 41 Tul. Mar. L.J. 197, 209 (2016) ("negotiable bills of lading require consignees to present the physical bill of lading to enable the carrier to release the cargo; conversely, non-negotiable alternatives . . . are not burdened by this requirement"). [—8—]

For that reason, the name listed as consignee on a nonnegotiable bill of lading matters a great deal; the carrier must deliver to the named consignee or face liability for misdelivery. *Pere Marquette Ry. Co.*, 255 F. at 41–42. Not so with a negotiable bill. Since a negotiable bill of lading may change hands multiple times mid-shipment, "the consignee or 'notify party' designated on the [negotiable] bill of lading [may] not necessarily [be] the holder of the bill at the time and place of delivery," *Evergreen Marine Corp. v. Six Consignments of Frozen Scallops*, 4 F.3d 90, 92 n.1 (1st Cir. 1993), and these labels accordingly carry little significance. The holder of the negotiable bill is entitled to "the rights and [subject to the] liabilities of the original consignee." *United States v. Wells Fargo & Co.*, 271 F. 180, 182 (2d Cir. 1921). Thus, what matters when dealing with a negotiable bill of lading is who physically presents the bill and accepts delivery of the cargo under it. *Allied Chem. Int'l Corp.*, 775 F.2d at 481. And, because the bill of lading is negotiable, if it purports to bind the consignee to its terms upon acceptance of the goods under it, those who opt to become a party to the transaction by accepting the goods and presenting the bill are bound by its terms.

Ingram Barge's complaint alleges that Zen-Noh became the consignee after the bills of lading were issued, and Zen-Noh does not deny that it physically presented the negotiable bills of lading and accepted delivery of the cargo.[1] The district court and the majority cite the bills' identifying Zen-Noh as merely the "notify" party, and not the consignee, as evidence that Zen-Noh was not a party to the bills and did not consent to be bound by the bills' terms. I disagree with this analysis at a few points. First, Zen-Noh *is* the named consignee on Bill No. ING 19-00901. Second, even if Zen-Noh were listed as the

[1] Had Zen-Noh not presented the bills, Ingram Barge would be liable for misdelivery, and Zen-Noh makes no such claim.

notify party on that bill, as it is on all but one[2] of the other bills in this case, the bills of lading were negotiable, which means that any distinction between the "notify" party and the "consignee" evaporated when, as Ingram Barge alleges, Zen-Noh presented the negotiable bills and accepted delivery of the cargo under the bills. *See Pac. Coast Fruit Dist. v. Pennsylvania R.R. Co.*, 217 F.2d 273, 275 (9th Cir. 1954) **[—9—]** (party not named in original bill of lading became consignee through its actions). It could not **{–282–}** have demanded and accepted the cargo otherwise. *See Allied Chem. Int'l Corp.*, 775 F.2d at 481.

True, neither Zen-Noh nor the named consignees bargained for the terms in Ingram Barge's bills of lading, but, as the majority acknowledges, a bill of lading "can nonetheless bind a non-party buyer where there is consent to be bound." *Kawasaki Kisen Kaisha, Ltd. v. Plano Molding Co.*, 696 F.3d 647, 655 (7th Cir. 2012). The bills of lading in this case clearly stated that "any Consignee hereto is (and will be deemed) bound by [Ingram Barge's] Grain Transportation Terms. The surrender of this original Order Bill of Lading . . . properly endorsed is required before the delivery of the shipment." *See, e.g.*, R. 1-38, PID. 201. Although Zen-Noh told Ingram Barge on June 3, 2019—before accepting any of the cargo at issue here—that it did not believe it was liable for the fleeting, wharfage, and shifting charges Ingram Barge seeks to recoup, that shows only that Zen-Noh was on notice of the terms at issue and nevertheless decided to physically present the bills and accept the cargo under the bills anyway. Absent an express agreement with Ingram Barge to the contrary, Zen-Noh's conduct in stepping into the shoes of the named consignee and accepting the grain pursuant to the negotiable bills of lading demonstrated consent to the terms of Ingram Barge's bills of lading. *See, e.g.*, *Pac. Coast Fruit Dist.*, 217 F.2d at 275 (explaining that "receipt and acceptance of the shipment" would be sufficient to bind consignee to terms of a bill of lading that made the consignee liable for shipping charges, and holding that the consignee was bound to the terms of the bill of lading because the consignee's "unqualified and unequivocal dominion and control of the shipments" was "equivalent to acceptance" of the shipments); *Neilsen v. Jesup*, 30 F. 138, 139 (S.D.N.Y. 1887) ("The general rule undoubtedly is that the consignee and indorsee of the bill of lading who is owner of the goods and of the bill of lading, and who accepts the goods under the bill of lading, is bound by its terms."); *Gage v. Morse*, 94 Mass. (12 Allen) 410, 411 (Mass. 1866) ("The receipt by [consignee] of the cargo, which was to be delivered upon payment of the freight, would have been evidence of an agreement to receive it upon the terms named in the bill of lading[.]"). The majority cites no case holding that a party can unilaterally change the terms of a bill of lading under which it demands and accepts delivery of the cargo. **[—10—]**

The majority contends that neither Zen-Noh's status as the "ultimate consignee" nor as owner of the grain constitutes consent to the bills' terms, and that being a mere beneficiary of the bills of lading does not create contractual obligations for Zen-Noh. Each of those propositions standing alone may be correct, but none is squarely applicable here where Zen-Noh was a consignee, owner and beneficiary *who also* presented the bills and accepted the goods. Indeed, in none of the cases cited by the majority did a consignee physically present a negotiable bill of lading and accept the goods.[3] That factual distinction is critical.

---

[2] Bill No. ING19-00590 does not name Zen-Noh as either consignee or the notify party, but Zen-Noh does not dispute that it presented ING 19-00590 and accepted the cargo.

[3] In *Dynamic Worldwide Logistics, Inc.*, the consignee failed to present the negotiable bill of lading at the time it accepted the goods, thus never evincing knowledge of the bill of lading's terms. 77 F. Supp. 3d at 368. *Affiliated FM Ins. Co. v. Kuehne + Nagel, Inc.* is inapposite, since the third-party beneficiaries were not consignees or owners of the cargo, but subcontractors of the carrier who sought the liability protections of the bill's Himalaya Clause. 328 F. Supp. 3d 329, 338 (S.D.N.Y. 2018). And in the remainder of the cases cited by the majority, the goods were never accepted by the consignee. *Kawasaki Kisen Kaisha, Ltd.*, 696 F.3d at 652 (goods damaged in train derailment); *APL Co. PTE. v. UK Aerosols LTD.*, No. C 05-0646-MHP, 2006 WL 3848784, at *1 (N.D. Cal. Sept. 28, 2006) (goods were "leaking, dangerous and hazardous"

Moreover, presentation of the bills and acceptance of the goods is not the only evidence of consent to be bound that can be found in the record. Zen-Noh paid demurrage **{-283-}** charges owed under the terms of Ingram Barge's bills of lading for some of the shipments at issue. Ingram Barge argues that partial payment of demurrage charges pursuant to the bills of lading is evidence of Zen-Noh's consent to be bound. The majority echoes the district court's speculation—based on no fact apparent in the record—that those payments "may be explained by a separate obligation between Zen-Noh and the sellers" or were paid pursuant to an implied obligation to pay freight charges. One of those theories may prove to be correct, but dismissing Ingram Barge's partial-performance argument based on speculation contravenes our admonition that "the pleadings and affidavits submitted must be viewed in a light most favorable to the plaintiff, and the district court should not weigh 'the controverting assertions of the party seeking dismissal'" when it elects to rule on a Rule 12(b)(2) motion without a hearing or the opportunity for discovery. *Air Prod. & Controls, Inc. v. Safetech Int'l, Inc.*, 503 F.3d 544, 549 (6th Cir. 2007) (quoting *Theunissen v. Matthews*, 935 F.2d 1454, 1458 (6th Cir. 1991)). At this stage, the **[—11—]** district court should have considered Zen-Noh's partial payment of demurrage charges as evidence of Zen-Noh's consent to be bound.

Lastly, I do not disagree with my colleagues' observation that Zen-Noh likely sought to avoid any contractual relationship with the carrier by prepaying the shipping fees to the seller. But Zen-Noh was free to resell the grain or reject the shipment if it did not agree to Ingram Barge's terms. Further, the seller opted to choose Ingram Barge to transport the goods and could have bargained for different terms with Ingram Barge that would not have required the consignee to pay the extra shipping fees. If Zen-Noh believes the terms of Ingram Barge's bills of lading were inconsistent with its separate agreement with the seller, Zen-Noh's recourse is against the seller for violating the terms of that separate agreement. Zen-Noh's understanding of its agreement with the seller has no bearing on the issue before us. Our task here is to determine whether Ingram Barge carried its "relatively slight" burden in making out a prima facie case for personal jurisdiction over Zen-Noh. *Id.* (quoting *Am. Greetings Corp. v. Cohn*, 839 F.2d 1164, 1169 (6th Cir. 1988)). I would hold that it has cleared that low hurdle.

---

and were destroyed by carrier); *APL Co. Pte. v. Kemira Water Sols., Inc.*, 890 F. Supp. 2d 360, 364, 368 (S.D.N.Y. 2012) (hazardous goods—shipped by nonnegotiable bill of lading with terms the consignee never received—leaked during shipment and were rejected by consignee); *In re M/V Rickmers Genoa Litig.*, 622 F. Supp. 2d 56, 62 (S.D.N.Y.), *opinion adhered to on reconsideration*, 643 F. Supp. 2d 553 (S.D.N.Y. 2009), *and aff'd sub nom. Chem One, Ltd. v. M/V Rickmers Genoa*, 502 F. App'x 66 (2d Cir. 2012) (goods were destroyed by an explosion en route).

This page intentionally left blank

United States Court of Appeals for the Seventh Circuit

United States Court of Appeals
for the Seventh Circuit

No. 20-3433

ROEN SALVAGE CO.
VS.
SARTER

Appeal from the United States District Court for the Eastern District of Wisconsin

Decided: November 10, 2021

Citation: 17 F.4th 761, 9 Adm. R. 304 (7th Cir. 2021).

Before **EASTERBROOK**, **ROVNER**, and **KIRSCH**, Circuit Judges.

[—1—] {-762-} **EASTERBROOK**, Circuit Judge:

Donald Sarter drowned after the vessel Monark #2 capsized in Lake Superior. His employer Roen Salvage, which owned Monark #2, filed this federal action under 46 U.S.C. §30505(a), asking the court to limit its liability to $25,000, which it says is the amount of its interest in the vessel. It also asked for exoneration from all liability, a possibility missing from §30505(a) (commonly called the Limitation Act) but mentioned in Rule F(2) of the Supplemental **[—2—]** Rules for Admiralty or Maritime Claims and Asset Forfeiture Actions, an appendix to the Federal Rules of Civil Procedure.

A federal court has exclusive jurisdiction of claims under the Limitation Act, *see* 28 U.S.C. §1333(1), "saving to suitors in all cases all other remedies to which they are otherwise entitled." The district court initially entered an injunction forbidding Julie Sarter, the decedent's spouse, from litigating in any other forum, but she asked the judge to vacate that injunction so that she could proceed under the language we have quoted, commonly known as the Saving-to-Suitors Clause. The judge granted that motion, 2020 U.S. Dist. LEXIS 227813 (E.D. Wis. Dec. 4, 2020), and declined to reinstate the injunction pending appeal, 2021 U.S. Dist. LEXIS 6359 (Jan. 13, 2021). Roen immediately appealed. Our jurisdiction comes from 28 U.S.C. §1292(a)(1) and (a)(3). *See* Fed. R. Civ. P. 9(h)(2).

After a vessel's owner seeks protection under the Limitation Act, a would-be plaintiff often files a concession (sometimes, though inaccurately, called a stipulation) that the federal court's decision about the owner's maximum liability will control even if a state court sets a higher figure in a Saving-to-Suitors action. Julie Sarter made such a concession, in the form of a promise to waive any claim of *res judicata* should Roen return to federal court seeking a cap on its outlay under the Limitation Act. But she declined to make a similar concession about the possibility of exoneration from all liability. She contended that a state court is competent to decide whether the vessel's owner bears any liability at all. The district court agreed with her about that point. Roen contends that this decision conflicts with **{-763-}** *Lewis v. Lewis & Clark Marine, Inc.*, 531 U.S. 438 (2001). **[—3—]**

The first question for us is whether any federal statute entitles a vessel owner to have a federal judge determine exoneration. The answer is no. Certainly §30505(a) does not do so. It reads: "Except as provided in section 30506 of this title, the liability of the owner of a vessel for any claim, debt, or liability described in subsection (b) shall not exceed the value of the vessel and pending freight. If the vessel has more than one owner, the proportionate share of the liability of any one owner shall not exceed that owner's proportionate interest in the vessel and pending freight." And §30506, to which the Limitation Act refers, likewise does not mention exoneration. Thus any entitlement to exoneration lies in the common law of admiralty. That's how the Justices understood Rule F in *Lewis*—as a restatement of old admiralty decisions. It would be hard to see Rule F as a free-standing limit of liability or a reservation of exclusive federal jurisdiction, given the language in the Rules Enabling Act that the federal rules are not supposed to abridge substantive rights. 28 U.S.C. §2072(b). And Fed. R. Civ. P. 82 proclaims that the Rules of Civil Procedure do not affect subject-maker jurisdiction either.

Lewis summarizes the common-law developments that led to the current form of

Rule F. 531 U.S. at 446–50. We need not repeat them. The Court summed up by writing that, when there is only one claimant, or when the total demanded by multiple claimants does not exceed the value set by the Limitation Act, a federal court may permit the substantive claim or claims to proceed in state court under the Saving-to-Suitors Clause. When multiple claims pressed in state court exceed the likely value of the vessel it is appropriate for the federal judge to retain all aspects of the litigation and decide whether the vessel's owner is entitled to exoneration. In all other situations, the Justices stated, it is enough for the federal court to **[—4—]** set the maximum amount of recovery that a state court may allow. Thus "the scope of exclusive federal jurisdiction is proportional to the federal interest in protecting the vessel owner's right to seek limitation of liability." 531 U.S. at 453. To put this otherwise, there is not an *independent* federal right to exoneration, which is derivative from a potential need to control multi-party litigation that may threaten the cap set by the Limitation Act. "[W]here ... the District Court satisfies itself that a vessel owner's right to seek limitation will be protected, the decision to dissolve the injunction [and permit suit in state court] is well within the court's discretion." *Id.* at 454.

Julie Sarter is the only person seeking a remedy against Roen Salvage because of Monark #2's capsizing. The district court can set a maximum level of liability based on the criteria in §30505(a), which will fully protect Roen's federal statutory rights. It was therefore "well within the court's discretion" to permit the substantive claim to proceed in state court.

The parties have spent many pages discussing exactly what concessions (by the would-be plaintiff) or stipulations (by the litigants jointly) are necessary to protect the vessel owner's rights. Our answer is: None. True, the tort claimant in *Lewis* made several concessions, which the Supreme Court deemed sufficient to protect the vessel owner. 531 U.S. at 451–52. But it did not hold that they were *necessary*. Protection also comes from statutes and judicial orders. When lifting or modifying an injunction to permit litigation in state court, a federal district **{–764–}** judge should make any provisos that are essential to safeguard the federal right under §30505(a). The judge could provide, for example, that, if the state court awards damages exceeding the owner's estimate of the vessel's worth, then the federal court will determine that value without regard to the **[—5—]** state judge's conclusion. Litigants do not need to concede or stipulate that federal statutes will be observed, and a state court's attempt to decide an issue that is within the scope of exclusive federal jurisdiction under §1333(a) will not be honored when the vessel owner stands on its right to a federal decision.

Because Julie Sarter has promised that she will not plead *res judicata* should Roen Salvage return to federal court under §30505(a), and because Roen does not possess a right to have a federal court determine its claim to exoneration from liability, we need not remand for the district court to make these matters explicit in its order allowing state litigation. In the future, district judges should choose appropriate language that will obviate the sort of dispute the parties to this case have had about exactly what words a would-be state-court plaintiff must use in order to protect the vessel owner's rights.

AFFIRMED

This page intentionally left blank

United States Court of Appeals for the Eighth Circuit

United States Court of Appeals
for the Eighth Circuit

No. 19-3731

GODFREY
VS.
STATE FARM FIRE AND CAS. CO.

Appeal from the United States District Court for the District of Minnesota

Decided: August 24, 2021

Citation: 11 F.4th 601, 9 Adm. R. 308 (8th Cir. 2021).

Before **SHEPHERD**, **STRAS**, and **KOBES**, Circuit Judges.

[—1—] {–602–} KOBES, Circuit Judge:

Courtney Godfrey sued State Farm Fire and Casualty Company and the Government Employers Insurance Company for liability coverage after she was **[—2—]** injured on her husband's boat. The district court[1] granted summary judgment for the insurers, and we affirm.

I.

Godfrey was seriously hurt when she was thrown from her husband, Ryan Novaczyk's, boat. Godfrey and Novaczyk filed claims for her injuries with State Farm, who insured the boat, and GEICO, who sold Novaczyk an umbrella insurance policy. Both policies had household exclusions: in other words, they declined coverage for injuries to the insured or members of the insured's household. Both insurers denied the personal injury claims because Godfrey and Novaczyk were married and lived together.

Godfrey sued Novaczyk, GEICO, and State Farm. GEICO removed the case to federal court, and Novaczyk was realigned as a plaintiff. Godfrey agreed that the household exclusions applied to her claim, but she argued that they violated Minnesota public policy. She also asked the district court to certify the public policy question to the Minnesota Supreme Court. The district court refused and instead granted summary judgment to the insurers because the exclusions were not prohibited by statute or Minnesota public policy. Godfrey appeals.

II.

The parties agree on the facts and that Minnesota law applies. We apply *de novo* review to the district court's interpretation of the contracts, application of state laws, and summary judgment decisions. *Am. Fam. Mut. Ins. Co., S.I. v. Mid-Am. Grain Distribs., LLC*, 958 F.3d 748, 752 (8th Cir. 2020). "Because we are interpreting Minnesota law, we are bound **{–603–}** by the decisions of the Minnesota Supreme Court, and if the Minnesota Supreme Court has not spoken on a particular **[—3—]** issue, we must attempt to predict how the Minnesota Supreme Court would decide it and may consider relevant state precedent, analogous decisions, considered dicta[,] and any other reliable data." *Engineered Sales, Co. v. Endress + Hauser, Inc.*, 980 F.3d 597, 599 (8th Cir. 2020) (citations omitted) (cleaned up).

Godfrey suggests that the question of umbrella and boatowner's liability insurance coverage arising from spousal negligence creates a novel question of law that we should certify to the Minnesota Supreme Court. We review the district court's decision not to certify a question of law under an abuse of discretion standard. *Anderson v. Hess Corp.*, 649 F.3d 891, 895 (8th Cir. 2011). We also have "an independent discretion of our own to decide whether certification is appropriate." *Knowles v. United States*, 29 F.3d 1261, 1265 n.8 (8th Cir. 1994).

Minnesota's "'well-settled general rule in the construction of insurance contracts' permits parties to 'contract as they desire, and so long as coverage required by law is not omitted and policy provisions do not contravene applicable statutes, the extent of the insurer's liability is governed by the contract entered into.'" *Pepper v. State Farm Mut. Auto. Ins. Co.*, 813 N.W.2d 921, 927 (Minn. 2012) (quoting *Am. Fam. Mut. Ins. Co. v. Ryan*, 330 N.W.2d 113, 115 (Minn. 1983)).

[1] The Honorable Joan N. Ericksen, United States District Judge for the District of Minnesota.

The State Farm and GEICO household exclusions bar recovery here. But Godfrey says Minnesota law and public policy demand we set them aside. She argues that Minnesota would follow a two-step process to abrogate household exclusions: first, abolish family member immunity; and second, invalidate household exclusions in insurance contracts as against public policy. Godfrey Br. 7.

Godfrey points to *Anderson v. Stream*, 295 N.W.2d 595 (Minn. 1980) and *Beaudette v. Frana*, 173 N.W.2d 416 (1969) for the first step. Respectively, those cases invalidated parental and spousal immunity defenses in tort. *Anderson* did note "the prevalence of liability insurance" to "help effectuate th[e] goal [of **[—4—]** compensating injuries]." 295 N.W.2d at 600. But it did not hold that insurance policies must cover household members.

For that, Godfrey points us to *Hime v. State Farm Fire & Cas. Co.*, 284 N.W.2d 829 (Minn. 1979). In *Hime*, the Minnesota Supreme Court considered a conflict-of-laws question for a car accident that occurred in Minnesota but involved a Florida insurance policy. *Id.* at 831–32. In considering the choice-of-law rules, the Minnesota Supreme Court noted that "the courts and legislature of [Minnesota] have condemned household immunity clauses." *Id.* at 833. Godfrey relies too much on that case. The court did a conflict-of-laws analysis, which takes a broad view of state interests. Godfrey also ignores the legislature, whose role the Minnesota Supreme Court recognized in *Hime* when it pointed to Minnesota's no-fault automobile insurance act and noted that the "choice between the Minnesota and Florida laws is determinative of the outcome of this case." *Id.* at 832 n.1. ("Minnesota law has prohibited household or family exclusions in automobile liability insurance policies since 1969 . . . . Under the current Minnesota no-fault automobile insurance act, family and household members are included in the statutory definition of 'insureds.'" (citing Minn. St. 65B.43, subd. 5)). Minnesota has not passed a similar law for boat or umbrella insurance.

In fact, Minnesota consistently enforces household exclusions when "[t]he controlling **{-604-}** statutes do not prohibit such exclusions, nor do they require homeowner's policies to provide liability coverage for claims made by one resident of a household against another." *Ryan*, 330 N.W.2d at 115–116. The authority to change this rule lies with the Minnesota legislature. *See In re Racing Servs., Inc.*, 779 F.3d 498, 505 (8th Cir. 2015) ("If the rule is wrong, the Legislature has ample power to change it. It is the duty of the courts to enforce the law as it exists." (citation omitted)).

Godfrey argues, contrary to *Ryan*, that a statute is unnecessary to show that Minnesota bars household exclusions for non-automotive accidents. And if it was necessary, Minnesota's comparative fault statute, Minn. Stat. § 604.01, subdivs. 1 **[—5—]** and 1a, applies. But we find no language in those provisions, or any other Minnesota law, addressing mandatory coverage or household exclusions beyond Minnesota's statutory mandates for automobile liability insurance that were at issue in *Hime*.

We are bound by Minnesota Supreme Court decisions, not only in *Ryan*, but also in *State Farm Fire & Casualty Co. v. McPhee*, 336 N.W.2d 258, 261 (Minn. 1983) (upholding a household exclusion clause) and *Reinsurance Association of Minnesota v. Hanks*, 539 N.W.2d 793, 797 (Minn. 1995) (upholding a minor-in-the-care-of-insured exclusion clause). The Minnesota Supreme Court looked to *Ryan* and *McPhee* in support of its ruling that the exclusionary clause in *Hanks* was "not void as violative of public policy." *Hanks*, 539 N.W.2d at 797.

It is not our role to expand Minnesota law to invalidate household exclusions. *See Luskin v. State Farm Fire & Cas. Co.*, 141 F.3d 1169 (8th Cir. 1998) (per curiam) (unpublished) ("As a federal court sitting in diversity, we are in no position to extend Minnesota law."). And we do not see an issue of unsettled law. The Minnesota Supreme Court addressed this and declined to revisit the question in *Ryan*,

McPhee, and *Hanks*.[2] *See Vierkant by Johnson v. AMCO Ins. Co.*, 543 N.W.2d 117, 121 (Minn. Ct. App. 1996), *rev. denied* (Minn. Mar. 28, 1996); *Bundul v. Travelers Indem. Co.*, 753 N.W.2d 761, 766 (Minn. Ct. App. 2008), *rev. denied* (Minn. Oct. 1, 2008). Godfrey does not present a close question of state law, so we do not certify the question to the Minnesota court. **[—6—]**

III.

The district court's grant of summary judgment is affirmed.

---

[2] In a Rule 28(j) letter dated March 17, 2021, Godfrey asked us to stay our decision until the Minnesota Supreme Court rules in *Poitra v. Short*, Case No. A20-0491, 2020 WL 7689593 (Minn. Ct. App. Dec. 28, 2020), *rev. granted* (Mar. 16, 2021). The 28(j) letter is not a motion for stay under Federal Rule of Appellate Procedure 8, and it is not clear that the Minnesota Supreme Court's decision in *Poitra* will address anything beyond a homeowner's insurance policy. Godfrey's request is denied.

United States Court of Appeals for the Ninth Circuit

United States Court of Appeals
for the Ninth Circuit

No. 20-35159

PACIFIC GULF SHIPPING CO.
VS.
VIGOROUS SHIPPING & TRADING S.A.

Appeal from the United States District Court for the District of Oregon

Decided: March 29, 2021

Citation: 992 F.3d 893, 9 Adm. R. 312 (9th Cir. 2021).

Before **BOGGS,*** **PAEZ,** and **WATFORD,** Circuit Judges.

* The Honorable Danny J. Boggs, Circuit Judge of the United States Court of Appeals for the Sixth Circuit, sitting by designation.

[—5—] {-894-} BOGGS, Circuit Judge: **{-895-}**

In this admiralty case, appellant Pacific Gulf, in possession of an arbitral award against Adamastos Shipping, tried to collect from appellees Blue Wall and Vigorous Shipping on the grounds that they are either successors to or alter-egos of Adamastos. The district court dismissed the successor-liability claim and granted summary judgment to Blue Wall and Vigorous on the alter-ego claim. We have jurisdiction under 28 U.S.C. § 1291, and we affirm.

I

Brothers George and Efstathios Gourdomichalis operate cargo vessels through their company Phoenix Shipping. Pacific Gulf chartered the M/V *Adamastos*, operated by **[—6—]** Phoenix, from Adamastos,[1] in which the brothers were also officers. Another company, Intergis, subchartered the *Adamastos* from Pacific Gulf. Yet another company, Marubeni, further subchartered her from Intergis to transport soybeans to China.

But the *Adamastos* had a number of problems. Port inspectors at São Francisco, Brazil, found more than 40 defects on the vessel, and, while in port, she broke free of her moorings and ran aground. Phoenix canceled the insurance on the *Adamastos* and abandoned her and her cargo in Brazil. Liability traveled up the charterparty chain, and Pacific Gulf—or, rather, its insurer and subrogee, Michael Else & Co. ("MECO")—was left holding the bag. Pacific Gulf brought arbitration proceedings in England and won an award after Adamastos failed to respond.

The Gourdomichalis brothers were also shareholders, directors, and officers at Blue Wall, whose fleet of eight cargo vessels Phoenix also operated. One of those vessels was the M/V *Vigorous*, which Blue Wall held indirectly through its wholly owned subsidiary Vigorous. Pacific Gulf, unable to collect from the severely undercapitalized Adamastos, instead sought to enforce its award against Blue Wall and Vigorous on the grounds that the brothers dominate and control Blue Wall and Vigorous as part of a single enterprise that includes Adamastos.[2] **[—7—] {-896-}**

In 2018, Pacific Gulf attached the *Vigorous* while she was in port on the Oregon side of the Columbia River. Posting $9.5 million security for the release of the *Vigorous*, the appellees moved to dismiss the verified complaint—as well as its first, second, and third amendments. The district court let the case proceed to discovery, in which well over 100,000 pages of documents were disclosed and at least a dozen depositions taken.

In January 2020, the district court disposed of the case in favor of the appellees. After oral argument, it first dismissed Pacific Gulf's claim based on successor liability. After additional argument two weeks later, the court granted summary judgment to Blue

[1] The vessels in this case are each owned by a corporation sharing its name with the vessel. To distinguish them, we italicize references to the vessels and refer to the corporations in roman type.

[2] We note that this particular suit isn't Pacific Gulf's first broadside against the appellees. In 2015, it had the *Vigorous* arrested in South Africa, whose courts dismissed Pacific Gulf's allegations as groundless. **[—7—]** Pacific Gulf also attached another of Blue Wall's fleet, the M/V *Fearless*, in the Southern District of Texas. The resulting litigation is still ongoing there.

Wall and Vigorous, observing that Pacific Gulf had "come back largely empty handed" from its extensive discovery expedition.

This timely appeal follows.

II

Besides arguing for affirmance, Blue Wall and Vigorous raise a jurisdictional challenge: that Pacific Gulf lacks Article III standing because it did not suffer an injury. A federal court must satisfy itself of its jurisdiction to hear a case, *McGee v. S-L Snacks Nat'l*, 982 F.3d 700, 705 n.2 (9th Cir. 2020), so we briefly address the appellees' challenge.

According to the appellees, MECO satisfied Pacific Gulf's liability by exchanging internal credit and debit notes on its books (Intergis, the company that had subchartered the *Adamastos* from Pacific Gulf, was also insured by MECO). **[—8—]** So Pacific Gulf never paid any cash to Intergis for its liabilities from the *Adamastos* incident. And Pacific Gulf has since withdrawn from the insurance pool, so it will not pay higher premiums. Thus, the appellees say, there is no concrete injury to Pacific Gulf. And because MECO is Pacific Gulf's subrogee, it could only recover what Pacific Gulf could—which is nothing. Furthermore, MECO cannot recover the payments it made to settle Marubeni's claims against Intergis because Intergis was never in privity with Adamastos.

But Pacific Gulf's arbitral award refutes the appellees' basic premise. Even if Adamastos ultimately owes Pacific Gulf no damages, Pacific Gulf is still out at least £5,530 in arbitration costs—plus interest. Peanuts, maybe, compared to the $18.5 million relief at stake, but a concrete, particularized injury nonetheless. *See Uzuegbunam v. Preczewski*, No. 19-968, slip op. at 9 (U.S. Mar. 8, 2021) ("Despite being small, nominal damages are certainly concrete.").

Because Pacific Gulf has standing, we need not determine whether MECO separately has standing. *Council of Ins. Agents & Brokers v. Molasky-Arman*, 522 F.3d 925, 932–33 (9th Cir. 2008).

III

We now consider Pacific Gulf's claim based on successor liability.[3] We review de novo a dismissal for failure to state a claim. *Knievel v. ESPN*, 393 F.3d 1068, **[—9—]** 1072 (9th Cir. 2005). We "accept all factual allegations in the complaint as true and construe the pleadings in the light most favorable to the nonmoving party." *Ibid.* But conclusory legal allegations are "not entitled to the assumption of truth." *Ashcroft v. Iqbal*, 556 U.S. 662, 679 (2009). Rather, **{-897-}** legal conclusions "must be supported by factual allegations." *Ibid.*

Sitting in admiralty, we apply the federal common law in examining corporate identity. *Chan v. Soc'y Expeditions, Inc.*, 123 F.3d 1287, 1294 (9th Cir. 1997).

Transfer of all or substantially all a corporation's assets is a prerequisite to a finding of successor liability. The First Circuit observed in *Carreiro v. Rhodes Gill & Co.*, 68 F.3d 1443, 1448 (1st Cir. 1995), that "successor liability in general, and the 'mere continuation' and 'de facto merger' exceptions in particular, are always discussed and analyzed in the context of inter-corporate asset transfers." Pacific Gulf asserts that "the theory of successor liability recovery is not so narrow" as to require asset transfer as an element, but it cites no legal support for that proposition. Indeed, the First Circuit found only three decisions in which "a litigant sought to impose successor liability in the absence of an asset transfer," all three of which held that "asset transfer was an essential prerequisite to successor liability." *Ibid.* And in our own research of post-*Carreiro* decisions, we have found several cases in accord and none in disagreement. *See, e.g., Nat'l Soffit & Escutcheons, Inc. v. Superior Sys., Inc.*, 98 F.3d 262, 266 (7th Cir. 1996)

[3] Going forward, we refer to the appellants collectively as "Pacific Gulf" because MECO maintains the same position as Pacific Gulf and there is no practical reason to consider them separately.

(applying state law); *Per-Co, Ltd. v. Great Lakes Factors*, 299 F. App'x 559, 562 (6th Cir. 2008) (applying Ohio law); *Premier Cap., LLC v. KMZ, Inc.*, 984 N.E.2d 286, 292–93 (Mass. 2013). We join these courts in holding that maritime law too requires a transfer of all or substantially all of the predecessor's assets to the **[—10—]** alleged successor before successor liability will be imposed on that alleged successor.

Pacific Gulf has failed to plead that essential fact. Pacific Gulf made only a conclusory allegation that Blue Wall and its subsidiaries "comprise successor corporate business entities of" Adamastos. It alleged no transfer of any assets (let alone all or substantially all) from Adamastos to Blue Wall or its subsidiaries. Because Pacific Gulf failed to plead a factual prerequisite to corporate successorship, the district court correctly dismissed the claim based on that theory.

IV

We also agree with the district court that Pacific Gulf's discovery revealed nothing to allow a reasonable juror to rule in its favor on the alter-ego theory.

A

We review de novo a grant of summary judgment. *Szajer v. City of Los Angeles*, 632 F.3d 607, 610 (9th Cir. 2011). If the nonmovant bears the burden of persuasion on the ultimate issue, the movant may make its required initial showing that there is no genuine dispute of material fact, Fed. R. Civ. P. 56(c)(1)(A), by demonstrating that "there is an absence of evidence to support the non-moving party's case." *In re Oracle Corp. Sec. Litig.*, 627 F.3d 376, 387 (9th Cir. 2010). The burden of production then shifts to the nonmovant, who must "go beyond the pleadings and by her own affidavits, or by the 'depositions, answers to interrogatories, and admissions on file,' designate 'specific facts showing that there is a genuine issue for trial.'" *Celotex Corp. v. Catrett*, 477 U.S. 317, 324 (1986) (quoting former Fed. R. Civ. P. 56(e) (1963)). The nonmovant's burden of production at this point "is not a light one"—it "must show **[—11—]** more than the mere existence of a scintilla of evidence" or "some 'metaphysical doubt' as to the material facts at issue." *Oracle Sec. Litig.*, 627 F.3d at 387 (quoting **{-898-}** *Matsushita Elec. Indus. Co. v. Zenith Radio Corp.*, 475 U.S. 574, 586 (1986)). It "must come forth with evidence from which a jury could reasonably render a verdict in the non-moving party's favor," assuming that "all justifiable inferences are . . . drawn in its favor." *Ibid.*

B

To pierce the corporate veil, a party must show that (1) "the controlling corporate entity exercise[s] total domination of the subservient corporation, to the extent that the subservient corporation manifests no separate corporate interests of its own," *Chan*, 123 F.3d at 1294 (quoting *Kilkenny v. Arco Marine Inc.*, 800 F.2d 853, 859 (9th Cir. 1986)), (2) "injustice will result from recognizing [the subservient entity] as a separate entity," *M/V Am. Queen v. San Diego Marine Constr. Corp.*, 708 F.2d 1483, 1489 (9th Cir. 1983), and (3) the controlling entity "had a fraudulent intent or an intent to circumvent statutory or contractual obligations," *ibid.* Whether these elements are established is a fact-intensive inquiry, requiring the court to consider the totality of the record and circumstances. *See Seymour v. Hull & Moreland Eng'g*, 605 F.2d 1105, 1112–13 (9th Cir. 1979) (thoroughly examining the record to review the district court's decision not to pierce the corporate veil).

A review of the case law and scholarly literature reveals a number of indicia that courts have used to determine whether to pierce the corporate veil. *See generally Wm. Passalacqua Builders, Inc. v. Resnick Devs. S., Inc.*, 933 F.2d 131, 139 (2d Cir. 1991); *Associated Vendors, Inc. v. Oakland Meat Co.*, 26 Cal. Rptr. 806, 813–15 (Ct. App. 1962); David H. Barber, *Piercing the Corporate Veil*, **[—12—]** 17 Willamette L. Rev. 371, 372–75 (1981). These indicia include (1) disregarding corporate formalities such as, for example, in issuing stock, electing directors, or keeping corporate records; (2) capitalization that is inadequate to ensure that the business can meet its obligations; (3) putting funds into or taking them out of the corporation for personal, not corporate, purposes; (4) overlap in ownership, directors, officers, and personnel; (5) shared office space, address, or contact information; (6) lack of discretion by the allegedly subservient entity; (7) dealings not at arms-length between the related entities; (8) the holding out by one entity that it is responsible for the debts of another entity; and (9) the use of one entity's property by another entity as its own. *See Seymour*, 605 F.2d at 1110 n.4; *Wm. Passalacqua*, 933 F.2d at 139. This list is, of course, nonexhaustive.

But the mere presence of some of these indicia is not dispositive, nor is it necessarily enough to survive summary judgment. For example, we held in *Chan* that, without more, a single person's common ownership of three corporations was insufficient to prove at trial that the corporations were alter-egos. 123 F.3d at 1294. The Fifth Circuit has held that indirect ownership of all of a corporation's stock, a "number of common officers and directors," and "substantial control" over an alleged subservient corporation's "general policy decisions" were insufficient to "establish a prima facie showing of alter ego" because the entities also observed corporate formalities and there was "no more [control] than appropriate for a wholly-owned subsidiary." *Adm'rs of Tulane Educ. Fund v. Ipsen, S.A.*, 450 F. App'x 326, 330–31 (5th Cir. 2011). Courts have also found that "superficial indicia of interrelatedness" such as shared office space and phone numbers are "not dispositive of the [alter-ego] question," instead looking to a corporation's "practical operation" as "more instructive." *E.g.*, **{-899-}** *Coastal States* **[—13—]** *Trading, Inc. v. Zenith Navigation, S.A.*, 446 F. Supp. 330, 334 (S.D.N.Y. 1977).

C

Pacific Gulf argues that the district court erred by focusing on whether it had presented enough evidence to dispute Blue Wall's "corporate legitimacy." Pacific Gulf cites our invocation in *Chan* of *Kirno Hill Corp. v. Holt*, 618 F.2d 982, 985 (2d Cir. 1980), to claim that corporate legitimacy is not a factor considered in the veil-piercing analysis. Rather, Pacific Gulf claims that the applicable standard is whether it has identified a genuine issue of material fact about "whether the corporate form of the Defendants Blue Wall and Vigorous Shipping was being dominated and controlled by Defendants George and Efstathios Gourdomichalis (and Phoenix Shipping)." Appellants' Br. 19.

Pacific Gulf is wrong in two respects. First, by focusing on isolated language in *Chan*, it misses the other two parts of the inquiry: injustice from failing to pierce the veil and ill intent on the part of the dominating entity. It is true that the Second Circuit employs a disjunctive rule allowing a plaintiff to pierce the corporate veil with only a showing of *either* domination and control *or* fraud. *Kirno Hill*, 618 F.2d at 985; *see also N. Tankers (Cyprus) Ltd. v. Backstrom*, 967 F. Supp. 1391, 1398–401 (D. Conn. 1997) (reconciling the Second Circuit's case law on the point). But, as we stated in *American Queen*, the Ninth Circuit has a conjunctive test: there must be domination and control *and* injustice from not piercing the veil *and* some form of ill intent. 708 F.2d at 1489–90; *see also Seymour*, 605 F.2d at 1109–13 (first articulating the three requirements to pierce the corporate veil in the context of a labor dispute and applying them conjunctively). So *Chan* did not remove the bad-intent **[—14—]** requirement—nor could it have, for a published panel decision may only be displaced by the en banc court or the Supreme Court. *E. Bay Sanctuary Covenant v. Trump*, 950 F.3d 1242, 1284 (9th Cir. 2020). We merely held in *Chan* that the plaintiff there had shown neither domination and control nor fraud and therefore could not pierce the veil. 123 F.3d at 1294. Our reference to the Second Circuit's case law had no precedential effect.

Second, even though Blue Wall's corporate legitimacy is not itself an element of the alter-ego inquiry, the district court was correct to consider it. Evidence of illegitimacy may create a genuine dispute of material fact about the intent of an allegedly dominating entity. On the other hand, if the only evidence produced is consistent with the behavior of the vast number of legitimately operated businesses, an inference of ill intent is not reasonable. *Cf. Matsushita*, 475 U.S. at 588 (holding that, on summary judgment, antitrust plaintiffs "must show that the inference of conspiracy is reasonable in light of the competing inferences of independent action or collusive action that could not have harmed" them).

D

Pacific Gulf's claim is that the Gourdomichalises dominated and controlled Blue Wall, Vigorous, and Adamastos as parts of a single enterprise, so that all of them should be treated as one. Therefore, for its award against Adamastos to be enforceable against the appellees, Pacific Gulf must show *at least* that the brothers dominated and controlled either Blue Wall or Vigorous and used it for a fraudulent purpose. *Am. Queen*, 708 F.2d at 1490. The appellees met their initial burden of production by pointing out the absence of evidence in the record demonstrating either that the Gourdomichalis brothers dominate and **[—15—]** control the appellees or that **{-900-}** the appellees were operated with fraudulent intent. Thus, Pacific Gulf had the burden of producing enough evidence to satisfy a reasonable juror that those two propositions are true. *Celotex*, 477 U.S. at 324.

But much of the evidence Pacific Gulf cites has no connection to Blue Wall or Vigorous at all. That evidence is instead more relevant to the brothers' connection to Adamastos or Phoenix, which even the district court assumed for the purpose of summary judgment.

Stripped to its relevant essentials, Pacific Gulf's resulting argument is that, because Blue Wall's other directors and shareholders exercised little oversight over the brothers' management of the company's fleet and bank accounts, the brothers dominated and controlled Blue Wall and its subsidiaries, including Vigorous.

There are two problems with that argument. First, Pacific Gulf's evidence does not reasonably support the strong inferences it draws. It frequently extrapolates from the ignorance of a sole director on some point to the ignorance of Blue Wall's entire board.

Second, even assuming that Blue Wall's board and owners were completely ignorant of the shipping business and left all the management and operation decisions to the Gourdomichalises, there is not enough to show the required element of fraud. As Pacific Gulf's counsel conceded at oral argument in the district court, it is not "suspicious and uncommon" that the "board of directors [is not] involved in the banking activity and the day-to-day operations of the business." Investors often do not care about the details of business—they just invest their money with purported experts and expect a good return. Mere evidence of common, **[—16—]** legitimate business conduct is not enough for a reasonable inference of fraud.

Pacific Gulf tries to bolster its argument by pointing to overlaps among the businesses. Of course, it is undisputed that the operations of Blue Wall, Vigorous, and Adamastos all involve the Gourdomichalis brothers. Nor is it disputed that Adamastos, Phoenix, and Vigorous all shared the same office or that Blue Wall and Phoenix had the same contact information. But these facts, absent any evidence suggesting wrongdoing, do not reasonably justify a finding of alter-ego. *See Chan*, 123 F.3d at 1294; *Tulane Educ. Fund*, 450 F. App'x at 330–31; *Coastal States*, 446 F. Supp. at 334.

Moreover, Pacific Gulf fails to dispute the evidence presented by Blue Wall and Vigorous, which included a report by an auditor finding no financial mismanagement among Blue Wall, its subsidiaries, Phoenix, and Adamastos. The auditor found no intermingling of funds and no raiding of bank accounts. Even the few potential irregularities that Pacific Gulf points to in Vigorous's bank statements (three payments to Giorgio Armani) were identified as payments on behalf of the master of the *Vigorous*, whose salary was reduced by those same amounts. Pacific Gulf points to no specific evidence disputing the probity of Blue Wall and

Vigorous's books, so we deem that fact undisputed. Fed. R. Civ. P. 56(e)(2)–(3).[4]

Viewing the record as a whole, we agree with the district court that Pacific Gulf came away "empty handed" from **[—17—]** discovery. There is insufficient evidence to support **{–901–}** a finding that the Gourdomichalis brothers operated either Blue Wall or Vigorous as an alter-ego of Adamastos, even after drawing all reasonable inferences in favor of Pacific Gulf.

AFFIRMED.

[4] Pacific Gulf also points to apparent payments for personal goods and services in Phoenix's bank statements. But those payments too were accounted for by the auditor's report, making it unreasonable to infer that the Gourdomichalis brothers were moving funds illicitly to Phoenix's accounts for their own personal use.

United States Court of Appeals
for the Ninth Circuit

No. 20-70541

THOMAS
VS.
CALPORTLAND CO.

On Petition for Review of an Order of the Federal Mine Safety and Health Review Commission

Decided: April 14, 2021

Citation: 993 F.3d 1204, 9 Adm. R. 318 (9th Cir. 2021).

Before **MCKEOWN, HUNSAKER,** and **BUMATAY,** Circuit Judges.

[—3—] {-1205-} **HUNSAKER,** Circuit Judge: **{-1206-}**

Robert Thomas—a dredge operator—claims his former employer CalPortland Company discriminated against him for engaging in protected activities related to safety issues. In this appeal, Thomas challenges the Federal Mine Safety and Health Review Commission's (Commission) conclusion that he failed to prove a prima facie case of discrimination under Section 105(c) of the Mine Safety and Health Act (Mine Act). Interpreting Section 105(c) in light of recent Supreme Court precedent, we conclude the Commission applied the wrong causation standard, and we grant the petition and remand. **[—4—]**

I. BACKGROUND

A. The Sanderling's dredging operation

CalPortland operates the Sanderling, a 220-foot dredge, on the Columbia River. Like its much smaller avian namesake, the Sanderling sucks. Specifically, it sucks sand from the riverbed, deposits it in compartments on the deck, and—with a push from its towboat, the Johnny Peterson—transports the sand to CalPortland's Vancouver, Washington facility. Once there, the crew unloads the sand with water cannons, creating a slurry that flows from the Sanderling to a settling pond via underground pipes.

The Sanderling dredge is not just a boat—it is classified as a surface mine and, accordingly, is regulated by the Mine Act, 30 U.S.C. § 803. The Mine Act subjects mine operators, like CalPortland, to a variety of requirements, including safety standards and employment practices. CalPortland and the Mine Safety and Health Administration (MSHA) often work together collaboratively; for example, MSHA reviewed and approved CalPortland's Sanderling fall-protection safety training. To verify CalPortland's compliance, MSHA inspectors examine CalPortland's mining facilities, including the Sanderling.

The Sanderling's crew includes Thomas, dredge operator, and Joel McMillan, deckhand. Helming the towboat and rounding out the crew is the captain of the Johnny Peterson, a third-party contractor. The shore operations include CalPortland's marine manager, Dean Demers, who oversees and has management authority over the Sanderling and her crew. Demers reports to CalPortland's general manager of aggregates for Oregon material, David McAuley. McAuley works with **[—5—]** CalPortland's safety manager, Jeff Woods, and human resources manager, Candy Strickland.

B. Work-schedule dispute

Thomas started working for CalPortland in 2002 as a deckhand. In 2015, he was promoted to dredge operator—the Sanderling's person in charge (PIC). *See* 30 C.F.R. § 56.18009. Two years later, in July 2017, Demers became CalPortland's marine manager. As marine manager, Demers led safety investigations involving the Sanderling and her crew. He also played a leading role in disciplining Sanderling crew members, in consultation with McAuley and Strickland, but delivering any disciplinary message, including termination, himself.

Sometime in fall 2017, Thomas and McMillan complained to Demers that the lack of other crew members forced them to work long hours, without relief. While Demers responded that "he was working on it," Thomas and McMillan did not believe he was sincere. Although Thomas testified that working such long hours was unsafe, he did not say that he told Demers about his safety concerns and Demers testified that Thomas did not. In response to Thomas's and McMillan's complaints about long hours, Demers moved several CalPortland **{–1207–}** miners from rock barges to the Sanderling to relieve Thomas and McMillan. Thomas and McMillan testified that these miners were inadequately trained, however, and they refused to sign off on the training forms for these miners.

C. Thomas's safety violation

On January 24, 2018, an MSHA inspector spotted Thomas working on the Sanderling without his personal flotation device (PFD) as the dredge arrived in Vancouver. **[—6—]** According to Thomas, he removed his PFD while welding to prevent it from catching fire. According to the MSHA inspector, he saw Thomas on a ladder without his PFD—an egregious safety violation. The inspector and Thomas discussed the incident on deck, and Thomas admitted that he was not wearing his PFD for some period of time but disputed he was on a ladder without it on. Thomas informed Demers of his conversation with the inspector and went home.

D. CalPortland's disciplinary actions

The next morning, Thomas returned to work and discussed the incident again with Demers and the inspector. Thomas and the inspector continued to disagree about whether Thomas was on the ladder without his PFD. After the conversation, Demers and McAuley decided to suspend Thomas pending investigation. As Thomas had already returned to the Sanderling, Demers called ahead and told McMillan he was on his way to "get rid of [Thomas]," instructing McMillan to ensure Thomas did not leave.

On January 29, Demers and Woods interviewed Thomas. They provided Thomas with the MSHA inspector's statement and Thomas responded that "this whole thing is nothing but a sham." Woods left thereafter, and Thomas filled out a more detailed report. Later that afternoon, Strickland, McAuley, and Demers met to discuss the situation and decided that Demers would begin drafting a discipline recommendation. Demers sent his first draft to Strickland—recommending termination—that day.

The following afternoon, Demers mistakenly emailed the second draft of his discipline recommendation—still recommending termination—to the entire barge-scheduling email list, which included Thomas. When Thomas read the **[—7—]** email the morning of January 31, he immediately canceled his scheduled meeting with Demers and hired an attorney, believing he had been terminated.

On February 1, McAuley called Thomas at home. Thomas instructed McAuley to direct all further communications to his attorney. That same day, Strickland decided to begin the voluntary resignation process based on Thomas's refusal to communicate. She sent two letters to Thomas indicating he had until February 8, 2018, to respond or CalPortland would consider him to have voluntarily resigned; Thomas rejected delivery of both letters. On February 9, Strickland sent Thomas another letter confirming Thomas's voluntary resignation; again, Thomas rejected it.

E. Thomas's discrimination claim

Thomas filed a written discrimination complaint with MSHA, alleging he was disciplined and ultimately terminated for engaging in protected activity regarding his safety concerns and his safety violation. MSHA declined to pursue the discrimination claim on Thomas's behalf, and Thomas filed a Section 105(c)(3) action with the Commission, which CalPortland contested. After a hearing, the Administrative Law Judge (ALJ) found for Thomas, concluding that CalPortland took adverse action against him because of his protected activity, including speaking with the MSHA inspector after the inspector observed Thomas's safety violation and reporting his **{–1208–}** concerns about safety and insufficient crew training to CalPortland. CalPortland petitioned for administrative review, which was granted, and the

Commission reversed the ALJ's finding of discrimination and dismissed the case. Thomas now petitions our court for review. **[—8—]**

II. STANDARD OF REVIEW

We review the Commission's interpretation of a statute de novo and its factual findings for substantial evidence. *See Stillwater Mining Co. v. Fed. Mine Safety & Health Rev. Comm'n*, 142 F.3d 1179, 1183 (9th Cir. 1998); *Knox Creek Coal Corp. v. Sec'y of Labor*, 811 F.3d 148, 157 (4th Cir. 2016). If the statute's meaning is plain, "that is the end of the matter," and we need not defer to the Commission's interpretation. *Royal Foods Co. v. RJR Holdings, Inc.*, 252 F.3d 1102, 1106 (9th Cir. 2001); *Chevron v. Natural Resources Defense Council*, 467 U.S. 837, 842–44 (1984); *see also Local Union 1261, Dist. 22, United Mine Workers of Am. v. Fed. Mine Safety & Health Review Comm'n*, 917 F.2d 42, 44 (D.C. Cir. 1990). Substantial evidence means "more than a mere scintilla[] but less than a preponderance;" it is an extremely deferential standard. *NLRB v. Int'l Bd. of Elec. Workers, Local 48*, 345 F.3d 1049, 1054 (9th Cir. 2003) (citation omitted); *Velasquez-Gaspar v. Barr*, 976 F.3d 1062, 1064 (9th Cir. 2020).

III. DISCUSSION

"The purpose of the Mine Act is to ensure the safety of miners." *Cumberland River Coal Co. v. Fed. Mine Safety & Health Review Comm'n*, 712 F.3d 311, 317 (6th Cir. 2013) (citing 30 U.S.C. § 802). "The Mine Act also serves to protect against discrimination or interference with protected activity." *Id.* (citing 30 U.S.C. § 815(c)). In discrimination cases under Section 105(c) of the Mine Act, the Commission has applied the *Pasula-Robinette* framework. *Secretary ex rel. Pasula v. Consolidation Coal Co.*, 2 FMSHRC 2786, 2799 (1980), *rev'd on other grounds sub nom., Consolidation Coal Co. v. Marshall*, 663 F.2d 1211 (3d Cir. 1981); *see also Cumberland River*, 712 F.3d at 317–18. Under this framework, a miner proves a prima facie case of **[—9—]** discrimination by showing that: (1) he engaged in protected activity and (2) was subject to an adverse action motivated "at least partially . . . by his protected activity." *Cumberland River*, 712 F.3d at 318; *see also Donovan ex rel. Chacon v. Phelps Dodge Corp.*, 709 F.2d 86, 88 (D.C. Cir. 1983). The mine operator may then rebut the prima facie case by showing: "(1) the miner was not engaged in any protected activity, or (2) the adverse employment action was not even partially motivated by the miner's protected activity." *Cumberland River*, 712 F.3d at 318. Or, if the mine operator cannot rebut the prima facie case, it may assert an affirmative defense by demonstrating—by a preponderance of evidence—that: (1) the adverse action was also motivated by the miner's unprotected activity; and (2) the adverse action would have been taken in response to the unprotected activity alone. *Id.* at 319.

We have never adopted the *Pasula-Robinette* framework in a published opinion. Indeed, it appears we have resolved only two discrimination appeals under Section 105(c) of the Mine Act, which both resulted in unpublished dispositions. *Bennett v. Fed. Mine Safety & Health Rev. Comm'n*, 12 F. App'x 492 (9th Cir. 2001); *Jaxun v. Fed. Mine Safety & Health Rev. Comm'n*, 408 F. App'x 70 (9th Cir. 2011). And of these two cases, only *Bennett* explicitly cites and applies the *Pasula-Robinette* framework. 12 F. App'x at 494.

On appeal, CalPortland argues that the *Pasula-Robinette* standard should no longer apply to Section 105(c) cases. In his **{–1209–}** reply brief, Thomas agreed that *Pasula-Robinette* conflicts with Supreme Court precedent. Specifically, in their briefing, both parties urged us to construe the word "because" in Section 105(c) to mean "but-for" causation, rather than the *Pasula-Robinette* partially motivated **[—10—]** standard. Citing *Burrage*,[1] *Nassar*,[2] *Gross*,[3] and *Bostock*, the parties claimed that the *Pasula-Robinette* standard conflicts with the Court's instruction that the ordinary meaning of "because" incorporates the "simple and traditional

---

[1] *Burrage v. United States*, 571 U.S. 204, 212–17 (2014).

[2] *Univ. of Sw. Tex. Med. Ctr. v. Nassar*, 570 U.S. 338, 346–60 (2013).

[3] *Gross v. FBL Fin. Servs.*, 557 U.S. 167, 174–80 (2009).

standard of but-for causation." *Bostock v. Clayton Cnty.*, 140 S. Ct. 1731, 1739 (2020) (internal quotation marks omitted) (citing *Nassar*, 570 U.S. at 346, 360). At oral argument, however, Thomas changed his position and now argues that we should apply the *Pasula-Robinette* standard.

The recent Supreme Court precedent cited above strongly supports reading "because" to require a "but-for" causation analysis. In *Burrage*, *Nassar*, *Gross*, and *Bostock*, the Court considered the meaning of "because of" and similar phrases in various statutory schemes and concluded that the ordinary meaning mandates but-for causation. The Court noted, however, that the ordinary meaning may not control when there is "textual or contextual indication to the contrary." *Burrage*, 571 U.S. at 212. For example, in *Bostock*, the Court explained that Congress can avoid imposing liability under a but-for causation theory by drafting legislation that uses terms like "solely" and "primarily" to modify "because of." *Bostock*, 140 S. Ct. at 1739. Such terms would modify the traditional but-for standard, indicating respectively that "actions taken 'because of' the confluence of multiple factors do not violate the law" or "the prohibited factor had to be the main cause of the defendant's challenged employment decision." *Id.* **[—11—]** (noting that Congress can also draft a statute that uses a "motivating factor" causation standard). But absent such modifiers, the Court instructs us that "because of" means "but for." *Id.* And—at least in the Title VII context—a "but-for causation standard means a defendant cannot avoid liability just by citing some *other* factor that contributed to its challenged employment decision." *Id.*

Because we have not previously addressed the applicability of the *Pasula-Robinette* standard in the context now before us, the horizon is clear of binding precedent. *Pedroza v. BRB*, 624 F.3d 926, 931 (9th Cir. 2010) (explaining "an unpublished decision is not precedent"). We begin our interpretive exercise with the plain text of Section 105(c). *See Bottinelli v. Salazar*, 929 F.3d 1196, 1199 (9th Cir. 2019) (beginning and ending its statutory interpretation with the plain text). Section 105(c) prohibits a mine operator from discriminating against a miner "because" the miner engaged in protected activity. 30 U.S.C. § 815(c)(1). It protects against discrimination via the following language:

> No person shall discharge or in any manner discriminate against or cause to be discharged or cause discrimination against or otherwise interfere with the exercise of the statutory rights of any miner, representative of miners or applicant for employment in any coal or other mine subject to this chapter ***because*** such miner, representative of miners or applicant for employment has filed or **{-1210-}** made a complaint under or related to this chapter, including a complaint notifying the operator or the operator's agent, or the representative of the miners at the coal or other mine of an alleged danger or safety or **[—12—]** health violation in a coal or other mine, **or *because*** such miner, representative of miners or applicant for employment is the subject of medical evaluations and potential transfer under a standard published pursuant to section 811 of this title **or *because*** such miner, representative of miners or applicant for employment has instituted or caused to be instituted any proceeding under or related to this chapter or has testified or is about to testify in any such proceeding, **or *because*** of the exercise by such miner, representative of miners or applicant for employment on behalf of himself or others of any statutory right afforded by this chapter.

Id. (emphasis added). We note that Section 105(c) uses the term "because" four times, and each time without any modifiers. We also note that no other provision in Section 105(c) expands upon, or modifies, the substantive protections in the above quoted language—they merely describe the enforcement and adjudication process. *See id.* § 815(c)(2), (3).

The lack of modifiers before or after "because," and the ordinary meaning of "because," plainly indicate that Section 105(c) incorporates the "simple and traditional standard of but-for causation." *Bostock*, 140 S. Ct. at 1739 (internal quotation marks omitted) (citation omitted). Had Congress wished to deviate from this "traditional background principle[] against which [it] legislate[s]," it would have provided a "textual or contextual indication." *Burrage*, 571 U.S. at 212–14 (internal quotation marks omitted) (citing *Nassar*, 570 U.S. at 347). Yet nothing in the text of Section 105(c) or the surrounding provisions indicates that **[—13—]** Congress attempted to deviate from the customary meaning. *See generally* 30 U.S.C. § 815. Section 105(c)'s plain meaning then requires a but-for causation standard for employment discrimination under the Mine Act.

In interpreting a different statute, we recently relied on *Gross* and *Nassar* to discard circuit precedent requiring a "motivating factor" test for causation. *Murray v. Mayo Clinic*, 934 F.3d 1101, 1106 (9th Cir. 2019). In *Mayo Clinic*, the underlying statute, the ADA, used a phrase that "indicate[d] but-for causation" and did "not contain any explicit motivating factor language." *Id.* (internal quotation marks omitted). In holding that the relevant ADA provision required but-for causation, we looked only to the text of the provision at issue. *Id.* (noting also that "[the Court] must be careful not to apply the rules applicable under one statute to a different statute without careful and critical examination" (quoting *Gross*, 557 U.S. at 174)). As *Mayo Clinic* extended the holdings of *Gross* and *Nassar* to a statute not at issue in those cases, we do not venture into uncharted waters by applying the "because means but-for" rule to the Mine Act. Indeed, as *Mayo Clinic* predated *Bostock*—which reinforced and amplified the holdings of *Gross* and *Nassar*—*Bostock* placed an additional marker by which to navigate.

Still, we consider the decisions of our sister circuits and the Commission. It appears that no circuit has considered whether to reject *Pasula-Robinette* based on the cases cited above, *see, e.g.*, *Hopkins Cnty. Coal, LLC v. Acosta*, 875 F.3d 279, 288–89 (6th Cir. 2017); *Harrison Cnty. Coal Co. v. Fed. Mine Safety & Health Rev. Comm'n*, 790 F. App'x 210, 213 (D.C. Cir. 2019). However, in 2016, the Commission reconsidered *Pasula-Robinette* in light of *Gross* and *Nassar* and declined to change direction. **{-1211-}** *Riordan v. Knox Creek Coal Corp.*, 38 FMSHRC 1914, 1920, 2016 **[—14—]** WL 5594252, at *6 (August 23, 2016). Under *Chevron*, we need not consider the Commission's interpretation because the statutory text is unambiguous, but we nonetheless explain why we find unpersuasive the Commission's decision not to adopt but-for causation despite *Nassar* and *Gross*.

In *Riordan*, the Commission stated that "[i]n both *Nassar* and *Gross*, the Supreme Court emphasized that the legislative history and context of the discrimination provisions were essential to interpreting what standard of causation applies" and concluded "the legislative history of the Mine Act affirmatively demonstrates that Congress envisioned such a burden-shifting framework when drafting the discrimination protections of section 105(c)(1)." *Id.* Even assuming the legislative history of the Mine Act weighs as strongly in favor of *Pasula-Robinette* as the Commission asserts, its premise for looking to the legislative history was flawed. In neither *Nassar* nor *Gross* did the Court look to the legislative history to determine the causation standard—much less "emphasize[]" it as the Commission claimed. *See Nassar*, 570 U.S. at 346; *Gross*, 557 U.S. at 175–76. Neither decision even used the phrase "legislative history." Instead, both decisions considered the text of the provision at issue and its context, e.g., how it fits into the statute as a whole and how the statute at issue compares to other similar statutes. *See Nassar*, 570 U.S. at 360 ("Based on these textual and structural indications, the Court now concludes [but-for causation applies]. . ."); *Gross*, 557 U.S. at 175–76 ("[The Court's] inquiry. . . must focus on the text."). Thus, the Commission overstated those decisions by arguing that their holdings flow from an analysis of legislative history. **[—15—]**

IV. CONCLUSION

In the end, the only question we must answer is simple. Section 105(c)'s unambiguous text requires a miner asserting a discrimination claim under Section 105(c) to prove but-for causation. Therefore, as the parties both requested originally, we reject the *Pasula-Robinette* framework. The Supreme Court has instructed multiple times that the word "because" in a statutory cause of action requires a but-for causation analysis unless the text or context indicates otherwise. Section 105(c) contains no such indication. And we drop anchor there because it is for the Commission to apply the but-for standard to this case in the first instance on remand.[4]

The petition for review is **GRANTED** and **REMANDED** to the Commission for further proceedings consistent with this opinion.

[4] We further note the Commission is statutorily bound to review the ALJ's factual findings for substantial evidence, and it errs if it "substitute[s] a competing view of the facts for the view the ALJ reasonably reached." *Donovan ex rel. Chacon*, 709 F.2d at 92. Although we do not reach the issue, the Commission on remand should pay particular attention to Thomas's argument regarding whether the Commission appropriately deferred to the ALJ's factual findings and credibility determinations.

United States Court of Appeals
for the Ninth Circuit

No. 18-71807

SEACHRIS
VS.
BRADY-HAMILTON STEVEDORE CO.

On Petition for Review of an Order of the Benefits Review Board

Decided: April 19, 2021

Citation: 994 F.3d 1066, 9 Adm. R. 324 (9th Cir. 2021).

Before **TASHIMA, BYBEE,** and **COLLINS,** Circuit Judges.

[—6—] {–1071–} **TASHIMA,** Circuit Judge:

This is Ladonna Seachris' ("Seachris") petition to review a decision of the Benefits Review Board ("BRB") upholding a decision of an administrative law judge ("ALJ") awarding Seachris attorney's fees and costs under the Longshore and Harbor Workers' Compensation Act ("LHWCA"), 33 U.S.C. §§ 901–50. We hold that aspects of the decisions under review constitute legal error and are not supported by substantial evidence. Specifically, we hold that the ALJ improperly rejected the fee applicant's evidence of prevailing market rates, erroneously established a paralegal's hourly rate by reference to other ALJ decisions rather than evidence of prevailing market rates in the relevant community, and improperly denied fees for hours reasonably expended. We further hold that the ALJ and the BRB erred in concluding that the LHWCA does not authorize an award of interest on costs. Accordingly, we grant the petition for review and remand to the BRB for further proceedings. We also order the BRB to reassign this matter to a different ALJ on remand.

I. BACKGROUND

A. Robinowitz's Fee Application

In 2006, Seachris, widow of Cloyd E. Seachris,[1] filed a claim for death benefits under the LHWCA. Seachris was represented in the proceedings by attorney Charles Robinowitz. The proceedings were heard by an ALJ in the U.S. Department of Labor's Office of Administrative Law **[—7—]** Judges ("OALJ"). After the ALJ denied the claim and the BRB affirmed, we granted a petition for review and remanded. *Seachris v. Dir., OWCP*, 538 F. App'x 813 (9th Cir. 2013). On remand, in April 2016, the ALJ granted Seachris' claim for benefits.

Seachris' successful prosecution of her claim entitled Robinowitz to an award of "a reasonable attorney's fee." 33 U.S.C. § 928(a).[2] Accordingly, in May 2016, ten **{–1072–}** years after the claim was first filed, Robinowitz filed a Declaration of Attorney Fees and Costs seeking an award of $50,616.75 in attorney's fees and $5,413.95 in costs for work performed between 2007 and 2016.

---

[1] Cloyd Seachris died on October 10, 2005.

[2] Section 928(a) states:

> If the employer or carrier declines to pay any compensation on or before the thirtieth day after receiving written notice of a claim for compensation having been filed from the deputy commissioner, on the ground that there is no liability for compensation within the provisions of this chapter and the person seeking benefits shall thereafter have utilized the services of an attorney at law in the successful prosecution of his claim, there shall be awarded, in addition to the award of compensation, in a compensation order, a reasonable attorney's fee against the employer or carrier in an amount approved by the deputy commissioner, Board, or court, as the case may be, which shall be paid directly by the employer or carrier to the attorney for the claimant in a lump sum after the compensation order becomes final.

33 U.S.C. § 928(a).

Robinowitz requested an hourly rate of $450 for his own legal services. In support of this rate, Robinowitz's **[—8—]** declaration stated that he had over 45 years' experience as an attorney; that his "legal practice emphasizes serious tort and wrongful death claims and workers' compensation claims under the [LHWCA]"; that he has "tried over 200 jury trials, [tried] over 350 court trials, and . . . argued over 150 appeals"; that he has "instructed at [Continuing Legal Education] programs on trial practice and the [LHWCA]"; and that "other lawyers regularly consult [him] for advice on issues under the [LHWCA] as well as on trial practice in civil cases." Robinowitz stated that he has handled "commercial litigation cases," including an Employee Retirement Income Security Act ("ERISA") case and "a large consumer fraud case with over 140 plaintiffs." He further stated that "Longshore cases involve very similar services to these cases. They involve careful review of documents, meeting[] frequently with both expert and lay witnesses, detailed calculation of losses and specific legal research, which is typical trial preparation."

Robinowitz also submitted a 2009 declaration from Portland practitioner Phil Goldsmith. Goldsmith stated that he specializes in class action and financial institution litigation, that most of his compensation comes from court-awarded attorney's fees, that he carefully monitors evidence of local market rates, that he periodically testifies as an expert witness on attorney's fees, and that he has known Robinowitz for many years. Goldsmith stated that "the $400 hourly rate requested" by Robinowitz at that time was "slightly below market rates in Portland for lawyers of comparable skill, experience and reputation." Goldsmith relied in part on a survey of commercial litigation rates compiled by Serena Morones ("Morones Survey") in 2008. According to the Morones Survey, "the average rate [as of January 1, 2008] for lawyers with experience comparable to Mr. Robinowitz was **[—9—]** $446 an hour." Goldsmith also noted that "attorneys that specialize in a specific niche . . . charge a higher rate," and that Robinowitz had "substantial expertise" and experience in LHWCA cases.

Robinowitz also submitted a 2009 affidavit from David Markowitz, another Portland practitioner. Markowitz, the state chairperson of the American College of Trial Lawyers, recounted his experience on the subject of attorney's fees, including his extensive work as an expert witness, arbitrator, and lecturer. Markowitz stated that Robinowitz had a reputation as "a very experienced and accomplished litigator who is able to provide highly qualified representation in [LHWCA] cases as well as a wide variety of business and tort litigation." Markowitz opined that Robinowitz's "attorney fee rate should be set at or above the average rate for attorneys with 30 or more years experience as shown in the Morones Survey of Commercial Litigation Rates," equating to a rate of $404 per hour in 2009. He opined that

> these amounts reflect the prevailing market rates in Oregon for an attorney of Mr. Robinowitz's experience and reputation **{-1073-}** and are rates commensurate with those which he could obtain by taking other types of cases which he is qualified to handle. I have observed from my work in over 100 attorney fee matters as an expert, arbitrator, mediator and attorney in Oregon that these rates are in line with those prevailing in Oregon for similar services by lawyers of reasonably comparable experience and reputation. **[—10—]**

Robinowitz also submitted the 2010 iteration of the Morones Survey. This survey, which includes information from Portland law firms having more than five attorneys specializing in commercial litigation, stated that attorneys with 30 or more years of experience charged an average of $431 per hour as of January 2010.

Robinowitz also submitted portions of the Oregon State Bar 2012 Economic Survey ("2012 OSB Survey"). For Portland attorneys with over 30 years of experience, the 2012 OSB Survey reported a median rate of $350 per hour. For attorneys in the 75th percentile, the rate was $400 per hour; for those in the 95th percentile, it was $500 per hour.

Robinowitz also submitted a 2014 decision by the Ninth Circuit Appellate Commissioner awarding him fees at a rate of $425 per hour for his services in this court. *See Petitt v. Sause Brothers*, No. 12-70740 (9th Cir. Sept. 24, 2014).[3] The Appellate Commissioner looked to the 2012 OSB Survey, which, as noted, reported an hourly rate of $400 for the top 25 percent of Portland attorneys with more than 30 years' experience. The Appellate Commissioner rejected the respondents' contention that the court should instead rely on the OSB Survey's rates for specific practice areas encompassing "Portland plaintiff-side civil litigators. **[—11—]**

Robinowitz also submitted a 2014 decision by the BRB awarding him a rate of $413 per hour for work performed in 2013 and $420 per hour for work performed in 2014. *Petitt v. Sause Brothers*, No. 11-0351 (Ben. Rev. Bd. Apr. 29, 2014).[4] The BRB relied on the 2012 OSB Survey. Rather than looking at the survey's rates for Portland attorneys with at least 30 years' experience, however, the BRB looked at the survey's rates for Portland attorneys practicing in two of the survey's 14 practice areas: plaintiff civil litigation personal injury and plaintiff civil litigation non-personal injury. The BRB placed Robinowitz in the top five percent of lawyers practicing in these areas (the 95th percentile), averaged the rates applicable to these two practice areas, and adjusted the resulting rates for inflation, producing an hourly rate of $413 for work performed in 2013. The BRB adopted the 95th percentile rate because, as the BRB had noted in its prior decision in *Christensen v. Stevedore Services of America*, No. 03-0302, 2010 WL 2256182 (Ben. Rev. Bd. May 13, 2010), Robinowitz had "40 years of experience and demonstrated skill in the successful representation of many claimants before the Board and the Ninth Circuit."

Robinowitz's fee declaration requested an hourly rate of $165 for a paralegal in his office with over 20 years' experience. In support of this rate, Robinowitz relied on the 2009 Goldsmith declaration, which opined that the $150 hourly rate Robinowitz **{–1074–}** requested at that time was "consistent with the rates prevailing in the community." Goldsmith relied on the 2008 Morones Survey of Portland commercial litigation firms, which stated that the average rate for **[—12—]** paralegals at that time was $154 per hour. Robinowitz also relied on the Ninth Circuit Appellate Commissioner's 2014 decision in *Petitt*, which awarded Robinowitz's paralegal a rate of $165 an hour for work performed in 2013. The Appellate Commissioner concluded that this rate was "in line with currently prevailing market rates for Portland paralegal work."

Finally, Robinowitz requested an award of interest on costs to account for delay in payment, noting that Seachris had incurred the litigation expenses in 2011, five years before Robinowitz filed his request for fees and costs.

B. Respondents' Objections

In their objections to Robinowitz's fee declaration, Respondents argued that Robinowitz should be awarded fees at a rate of $358 per hour rather than the $450 he requested. Respondents derived this figure from the practice-area chart in the 2012 OSB Survey rather than the years-of-experience chart. Specifically, Respondents selected the rates applicable to Portland attorneys practicing in two of the survey's 14 practice areas—plaintiff civil litigation personal injury and plaintiff civil litigation non-personal injury. For Portland attorneys in the 75th percentile, the 2012 OSB Survey's rates for these practice areas were $350 and $300

[3] The Appellate Commissioner issued the *Petitt* decision pursuant to Ninth Circuit Rule 39-1.9. Such decisions do not constitute circuit precedent but may be treated as persuasive authority. *See Orn v. Astrue*, 511 F.3d 1217, 1220 (9th Cir. 2008) (noting the Appellate Commissioner's "substantial experience and expertise in ruling on appellate fee requests").

[4] *See also Petitt v. Sause Brothers*, No. 13-0330, 2014 WL 993104, at *4 (Ben. Rev. Bd. Feb. 26, 2014) (awarding Robinowitz a rate of $413 per hour for work performed in 2013).

respectively. Respondents averaged these two rates, adjusted the 2011 rates for inflation, and arrived at a proposed rate of $358 per hour.

Respondents acknowledged the Ninth Circuit Appellate Commissioner and BRB decisions awarding Robinowitz rates of $425 and $420 per hour. They argued, however, that these rates should not control, because "appellate practice involves **[—13—]** a different set of skills than is required to practice before the OALJ."

Relying on *Christensen v. Stevedoring Services of America*, No. 03-0302, 2010 WL 2256182 (Ben. Rev. Bd. May 13, 2010), Respondents also contended that Robinowitz's other evidence of prevailing market rates—the Goldsmith declaration, the Markowitz affidavit, and the Morones Survey—were "not relevant," because "services provided by attorneys with a business litigation practice" are not "comparable" to services performed under the LHWCA.

Finally, Respondents argued that Robinowitz's paralegal should be awarded a rate of $150 per hour rather than the $165 requested. They argued that the Morones Survey was inadequate to support Robinowitz's requested rate because it was "applicable to business litigation." They further argued that, "[i]n other fee decisions involving Mr. Robinowitz, with similar documents and statements offered in support of the requested rate, the paralegal was often awarded $150.00.

C. The ALJ's Fee Decision

The ALJ addressed Robinowitz's request for attorney's fees and costs in a January 2017 order. The ALJ awarded Robinowitz $36,560.50 in attorney's fees and awarded Seachris $5,413.95 in costs.

The ALJ devoted the majority of her decision to the question of Robinowitz's hourly rate. As a threshold matter, the ALJ concluded that Robinowitz had failed to satisfy his initial burden of producing evidence of a prevailing market rate for his services. First, the ALJ declined to give any weight to the Goldsmith declaration, the Markowitz affidavit, **[—14—]** and the Morones Survey because (1) the information contained in this evidence was "too old to be very useful" and "simply too dated to be convincing," and (2) the information **{-1075-}** pertained to rates charged by lawyers handling commercial litigation, which "involve[s] different skills and expertise" than LHWCA work.

Second, the ALJ declined to give any weight to the portion of the 2012 OSB Survey that Robinowitz submitted, faulting him for submitting only part of the report and for relying on the rates for all Portland practitioners, based on years of experience, rather than relying on the rates charged by Portland attorneys in individual practice areas involving "the sort of trial-level skills needed in Longshore practice."

Third, the ALJ declined to give weight to the BRB and Ninth Circuit Appellate Commissioner's decisions awarding Robinowitz rates of $420 and $425 respectively for appellate work. Echoing Respondents, the ALJ reasoned that this evidence was "not convincing," because "[a]ppellate-level Longshore Act work . . . requires skills and expertise that are different than those required to effectively litigate at OALJ."

In sum, the ALJ rejected every piece of evidence offered by Robinowitz in support of his requested hourly rate. Having done so, the ALJ concluded that Robinowitz "has failed to carry his burden of establishing entitlement to the rates claimed in this case." The ALJ then proceeded to determine a reasonable hourly rate independently of the evidence offered by Robinowitz.

In doing so, the ALJ relied almost exclusively on the 2012 OSB Survey. But rather than relying on the OSB Survey rates based on years of experience, as Robinowitz had **[—15—]** proposed, the ALJ relied on the survey's rates applicable to particular practice areas that the ALJ deemed appropriate comparators to LHWCA work. Specifically, the ALJ included three of the survey's 14 practice areas in her analysis: plaintiff civil litigation personal injury, plaintiff civil litigation non-personal injury, and general practice—the practice area that applies to attorneys who devote less than 50 percent of their time to any one practice area. The ALJ calculated a weighted average of these three practice areas, concluded that Robinowitz fell within the 75th percentile (not the 95th percentile, as Robinowitz advocated), and adjusted the resulting rate to account for inflation, producing a rate of $341.92 per hour—far less than the $450 rate proposed by Robinowitz and less even than the $358 rate proposed by Respondents.

The ALJ awarded Robinowitz's paralegal a rate of $150. The ALJ based this rate on other ALJ decisions and federal district court decisions in the District of Oregon.

The ALJ also rejected Robinowitz's request for an award of interest on costs. Citing *Hobbs v. Director, Office of Workers Compensation Programs*, 820 F.2d 1528 (9th Cir. 1987), *abrogated on other grounds as stated in Anderson v. Dir., OWCP*, 91 F.3d 1322, 1324 (9th Cir. 1996), the ALJ ruled that "interest may not be awarded on an award of . . . costs under the Longshore Act."

D. The BRB's Decision

On appeal, the BRB concluded that the ALJ had "addressed, and rationally rejected, the evidence submitted by counsel in support of his requested hourly rate of $450." In particular, the BRB concluded that the ALJ properly "rejected **[—16—]** the Goldsmith declaration, the Markowitz declaration, and the Morones Survey because they are outdated and refer to commercial/business litigation, which the administrative law judge found is not work similar to that practiced by counsel." The BRB also concluded that the "hourly rate awarded represents a reasonable weighted average of the rates established by the 2012 [OSB Survey] in the three practice areas the administrative law judge rationally found **{-1076-}** to be relevant." After correcting an error by the ALJ in adjusting the 2012 OSB Survey rates for inflation, the BRB awarded Robinowitz a rate of $349.85 per hour. The BRB also agreed with the ALJ that the LHWCA "does not permit the paying of interest on costs" and sustained the other challenged aspects of the ALJ's fee order.

Seachris timely petitioned for review.

II. STANDARD OF REVIEW

"In LHWCA proceedings, the [Benefits Review] Board must accept the ALJ's findings unless they are contrary to law, irrational, or unsupported by substantial evidence." *Port of Portland v. Dir., OWCP*, 932 F.2d 836, 838 (9th Cir. 1991). "We review the Board's decisions for errors of law and adherence to the substantial evidence standard." *Id.* Accordingly, "[w]e independently evaluate the evidence in the administrative record to ensure the BRB adhered to the correct standard of review." *Shirrod v. Dir., OWCP*, 809 F.3d 1082, 1086, 3 Adm. R. 620, 621 (9th Cir. 2015). "Because the Board is not a policymaking body, we accord no special deference to its interpretation of the LHWCA." *Port of Portland*, 932 F.2d at 838. **[—17—]**

III. DISCUSSION

A. Robinowitz's Hourly Rate

We begin by reviewing the ALJ's and BRB's decisions regarding Robinowitz's hourly rate.

"The 'lodestar method' is the fundamental starting point in determining a 'reasonable attorney's fee,' and this is true as to computation of attorney's fees under § 928(a) of the LHWCA." *Christensen v. Stevedoring Servs. of Am.*, 557 F.3d 1049, 1053 (9th Cir. 2009) (citation omitted) (citing *City of Burlington v. Dague*, 505 U.S. 557, 562 (1992)). "This method 'requires the court to multiply the number of hours reasonably expended on the litigation by a reasonable hourly rate.'" *Id.* at 1053 n.4 (quoting *Tahara v. Matson Terminals, Inc.*, 511 F.3d 950, 955 (9th Cir. 2007)).

"'[A] reasonable attorney's fee' is one that is 'adequate to attract competent counsel.'" *Blum v. Stenson*, 465 U.S. 886, 897 (1984) (quoting S. Rep. No. 94-1011, at 6 (1976)). "[I]t is necessary," therefore, "that counsel be awarded fees commensurate with those which they could obtain by taking other types of cases," *Christensen*, 557 F.3d at 1053 (quoting *Camacho v. Bridgeport Fin., Inc.*, 523 F.3d 973, 981 (9th Cir. 2008)), and that fees be "sufficient to induce a capable attorney to undertake the representation of a meritorious . . . case," *Perdue v. Kenny A. ex rel. Winn*, 559 U.S. 542, 552 (2010).

To ensure adequate compensation, hourly rates "are to be calculated according to the prevailing market rates in the relevant community," *Blum*, 465 U.S. at 895, meaning the "rates charged to clients of private law firms," *Miele v. N.Y.* **[—18—]** *State Teamsters Conf. Pension & Ret. Fund*, 831 F.2d 407, 409 (2d Cir. 1987). Of course, "there is no private market for attorney's fees under the LHWCA." *Christensen*, 557 F.3d at 1053. LHWCA attorneys do not, and are not permitted to, enter into private fee agreements with their clients. *Id.* (citing 33 U.S.C. § 928(e)).

Hourly rates under the LHWCA, therefore, must be based on the rates charged to clients of private law firms for *similar* work. As *Blum* explains, the rates awarded must be "in line with those prevailing in the community for similar services by lawyers of reasonably comparable skill, experience, and reputation." 465 U.S. at 896 n.11. This ensures that LHWCA attorneys receive **{-1077-}** the same compensation as their private-practice counterparts. *See Missouri v. Jenkins by Agyei*, 491 U.S. 274, 286 (1989) ("A reasonable attorney's fee under § 1988 is . . . comparable to what 'is traditional with attorneys compensated by a fee-paying client.'" (quoting S. Rep. No. 94-1011, at 6 (1976))).

"The evidentiary burdens governing fee motions are well established." *United States v. $28,000.00 in U.S. Currency*, 802 F.3d 1100, 1105 (9th Cir. 2015).

> The applicant has an initial burden of production, under which it must "produce satisfactory evidence" establishing the reasonableness of the requested fee. This evidence must include proof of market rates in the relevant community (often in the form of affidavits from practitioners), and detailed documentation of the hours worked. If the applicant discharges its legal obligation as to the burden of production, the court then **[—19—]** proceeds to a factual determination as to whether the requested fee is reasonable. In the usual case, that factual determination will involve considering both the proponent's evidence and evidence submitted by the fee opponent "challenging the accuracy and reasonableness of the facts asserted by the prevailing party."

Id. (citations omitted) (first quoting *Blum*, 465 U.S. at 896 n.11, and then quoting *Camacho*, 523 F.3d at 980).

We conclude that the ALJ erred in applying these principles.

1. The ALJ erred by concluding that Robinowitz failed to satisfy his initial burden of production

The ALJ concluded that Robinowitz failed to satisfy his initial burden of production. This conclusion is not supported by substantial evidence.

Robinowitz presented substantial evidence that his requested rate of $450 an hour, in 2016, was "in line with those prevailing in the community for similar services by lawyers of reasonably comparable skill, experience, and reputation." *Blum*, 465 U.S. at 896 n.11. This evidence included, among other things: affidavits from two experienced practitioners supporting rates of $400 and $404 respectively in 2009; the 2012 OSB Survey reporting that Portland attorneys with over 30 years' experience billed between $350 (median) and $400 (75th percentile) in 2011; a 2014 Ninth Circuit Appellate Commissioner order awarding Robinowitz $425 for work performed in 2012 and 2013; and **[—20—]** a 2014 BRB decision awarding Robinowitz $413 for work performed in 2013 and $420 for work performed in 2014.

This evidence was more than sufficient to carry Robinowitz's initial burden of production. The ALJ's contrary conclusion is not supported by substantial evidence. The ALJ's concerns at most go to the weight of the evidence, not its sufficiency.

2. The ALJ erred by rejecting Robinowitz's evidence of prevailing market rates as outdated

The ALJ rejected the Goldsmith declaration, the Markowitz affidavit, and the Morones Survey as "too old to be very useful" and "simply too dated to be convincing." We hold that this conclusion is not supported by substantial evidence.

It is true, of course, that fee awards must be "based on current rather than merely historical market conditions." *Christensen*, 557 F.3d at 1055. In *Bell v. Clackamas County*, 341 F.3d 858, 869 (9th Cir. 2003), for example, we held that "it was an abuse of discretion . . . to apply market rates in effect more than two years *before* the work was performed." And it is also true that the parties should provide, and the adjudicator should rely on, the **{–1078–}** most current information available.[5] Evidence of historical market conditions, however, is nevertheless relevant evidence of current market conditions, and reliance on evidence of historical market conditions is particularly appropriate when it is the most **[—21—]** current information available. The ALJ therefore erred by rejecting Robinowitz's evidence on this basis.

ALJs, moreover, must treat the parties' evidence evenhandedly. Here, both parties, and the ALJ herself, relied on dated evidence. Robinowitz relied on 2009 declarations from Goldsmith and Markowitz, the 2010 Morones Survey, and the 2012 Oregon State Bar Survey, which the ALJ criticized as incomplete. Respondents, in turn, relied on excerpts of the 2012 Oregon State Bar Survey. The ALJ rejected Robinowitz's evidence as "too dated to be convincing") but ultimately relied on the very same 2012 Oregon State Bar Survey as the linchpin of her hourly rate determination. By the time the ALJ issued her fee decision in January 2017, the 2011 rates in the 2012 OSB Survey were six years old. The ALJ nevertheless relied on the survey by adjusting the 2011 data for inflation—appropriately so. But the ALJ declined to make similar adjustments to Robinowitz's evidence. We see no reason why she should not have taken the same approach to Robinowitz's evidence, and it was error not to do so.

3. The ALJ erred by rejecting Robinowitz's evidence of commercial litigation rates

The ALJ also rejected the Goldsmith, Markowitz, and Morones evidence because they concern rates charged by attorneys handling commercial litigation. The explanations the ALJ and the BRB offered for rejecting this evidence are unsupported.

The ALJ, for instance, plainly erred by rejecting this evidence on the ground that "commercial litigation . . . is not the market that Petitioner operates in." The question is not **[—22—]** whether Robinowitz qualifies as a commercial litigator; it is whether the rates charged by commercial litigators are relevant comparators—*i.e.*, whether the rates involve "similar services by lawyers of reasonably comparable skill, experience, and reputation." *Blum*, 465 U.S. at 896 n.11.

Turning to that question, the ALJ concluded that commercial litigation is *not* similar to the kind of LHWCA work performed in this case:

> Longshore trial work is relatively straightforward litigation. Effective practice requires familiarity with the peculiar contours of the Act and an ability to understand and work with medical evidence. The process is informal. There are no jury trials. The rules of evidence are considerably relaxed. The rules of procedure are simple, and enforcement is forgiving. Presumptions simplify the case and assist claimants greatly. Hearings, when

[5] Robinowitz would be well advised, in future cases, to exercise more care to offer current practitioner fee data.

necessary, are usually short. Never are there multiple claimants joined in the same claim for adjudication. There may be multiple employers and carriers, but the interests of the respondents are usually adverse. Except in unusual cases, no showing of intent, negligence, or culpability is required.

The sorts of skills and experience possessed by attorneys in Longshore work are not the same as the sorts of skills and experience necessary to engage in mergers and acquisitions, intellectual property law, or **[—23—]** complex and class action litigation. Accordingly, the market rates for such legal work are not very **{-1079-}** informative as to a proxy market for Longshore work.

The ALJ's analysis is valid up to a point. There *are* differences between commercial litigation and LHWCA work. And it *is* reasonable, in identifying appropriate comparators, to distinguish between complex and non-complex litigation. *E.g.*, *DL v. District of Columbia*, 924 F.3d 585, 594 (D.C. Cir. 2019). As we explained in *Davis v. City & County of San Francisco*, 976 F.2d 1536 (9th Cir. 1992), *opinion vacated in part on other grounds*, 984 F.2d 345 (9th Cir. 1993), "[b]oth the Supreme Court and this court have made clear that [reasonable hourly] rates should be established by reference to the fees that private attorneys of an ability and reputation comparable to that of prevailing counsel charge their paying clients for legal work of *similar complexity*." *Id.* at 1545 (emphasis added).

Ultimately, however, the ALJ's reasoning fails for two distinct reasons. First, the ALJ appears to have conflated commercial litigation and complex litigation. These two concepts are not equivalent. Although some commercial litigation qualifies as complex litigation, other commercial litigation does not, *e.g.*, a straightforward commercial debt collection case. *Cf. DL*, 924 F.3d at 594 (rejecting the suggestion that all Individual with Disabilities Education Act ("IDEA") cases qualify as non-complex litigation merely because some IDEA cases do).

Second, the ALJ's analysis proves too much. If commercial litigation differs from "straightforward" and "informal" LHWCA work, then so too do plaintiff civil **[—24—]** litigation work and litigation handled by general practitioners. Yet the ALJ relied on the market rates paid in these practice areas to establish Robinowitz's hourly rate. We can discern no rational basis for the ALJ's selective concerns about the differences between formal and informal litigation. Plainly, an ALJ may not reject commercial litigation as a comparator, arbitrarily, simply because commercial litigation attorneys may charge more than other attorneys. As we explained in *Moreno v. City of Sacramento*, 534 F.3d 1106, 1115 (9th Cir. 2008), the adjudicator's function "is not to 'hold the line' at a particular rate."

In sustaining the ALJ's rejection of Robinowitz's evidence of commercial litigation rates, the BRB cited its earlier decision in *Christensen v. Stevedoring Services of America*, No. 03-0302, 2009 WL 4505490 (Ben. Rev. Bd. 2009). In *Christensen*, the BRB held that "rates paid to commercial/business litigators in Portland do not provide an appropriate basis for setting a market rate," because "a workers' compensation practice and a business litigation practice cannot be viewed as 'similar.'" *Id.* at *2. The BRB offered only a single rationale for treating these two practice areas as dissimilar: "business litigation routinely requires the work of a team of attorneys," such that "certain work is delegated to paralegals or less experienced attorneys at a lower cost to the client; as claimant's counsel is a solo practitioner he cannot delegate work in this manner, nor could he expect a client to pay him $400 per hour to perform all the work himself." *Id.*[6] **[—25—]**

---

[6] The BRB also noted the employer's contention that LHWCA work "is not comparable" to commercial litigation because "there are no lengthy trials, and never any jury trials, in longshore cases," and "the rules of evidence and procedure are relaxed in administrative hearings." *Id.* It is

Even assuming these distinctions were persuasive in *Christensen,* they do not apply here. The record plainly shows that Robinowitz *does* delegate work to less experienced **{-1080-}** attorneys and paralegals: in fact, his fee declaration sought fees not only for his own work (at $450 an hour) but also for an associate attorney (at $225 an hour) and a paralegal (at $165 an hour). Furthermore, although the BRB noted that LHWCA work differs from commercial litigation because it does not involve jury trials or strict evidentiary rules, these same differences exist between LHWCA work and the practice areas that the ALJ and the BRB relied upon to determine Robinowitz's hourly rate—plaintiff civil litigation and litigation by general practitioners. These distinctions, therefore, do not support the ALJ's methodology.

4. The ALJ erred by rejecting Robinowitz's evidence from the 2012 Oregon State Bar Survey

The Oregon State Bar Survey reports hourly rates in two ways. One chart reports the rates charged by Portland attorneys based on their years of experience, irrespective of practice area. The second reports the rates charged by Portland attorneys based on their practice areas, irrespective of their years of experience. Robinowitz relied on the chart reporting data based on years of experience, and the ALJ rejected that evidence on the ground that relying on it would "force me to make a one dimensional fee award by omitting evidence of other [relevant] factors." The ALJ then proceeded to rely on the chart reporting rates by practice area in determining Robinowitz's hourly rate. **[—26—]**

The ALJ's rejection of this evidence is not supported by substantial evidence. First, both charts rely on only a single factor: in one, that factor is years of experience, and in the other, that single factor is practice area. Although the ALJ rejected Robinowitz's survey evidence as "one dimensional," she proceeded to base her rate determination on the equally one dimensional chart reporting rates by practice area. Second, even assuming arguendo that rates based on practice area are *more* probative than rates based on years of experience, the latter rates are at least relevant. Indeed, our case law expressly approves of using the OSB Survey's years-of-experience chart to determine reasonably hourly rates. *See Shirrod,* 809 F.3d at 1089, 3 Adm. R. at 624 (citing *Ramsey v. Cascade Gen., Inc.*, No. 11-0875, 2012 WL 3903607, at *2–4 (Ben. Rev. Bd. Aug. 29, 2012)). The Ninth Circuit Appellate Commissioner, moreover, relied on the years-of-experience chart in awarding Robinowitz fees in *Petitt.*

5. The ALJ's decision to place Robinowitz in the 75th percentile must be vacated

Robinowitz also challenges the ALJ's decision to place him within the 75th percentile of attorneys in the plaintiff civil litigation and general practice areas under the 2012 OSB Survey. He argues that he should have been placed in the 95th percentile. It is undisputed that Robinowitz is a highly experienced attorney, with vast experience and expertise in LHWCA cases. The ALJ, therefore, reasonably could have placed Robinowitz in the 95th percentile, as both this court and the BRB have done on other occasions, albeit with respect to his appellate work. On the other hand, the BRB has placed Robinowitz within the 75th percentile on several other occasions with respect to his trial-level work. This was a judgment call that the ALJ could reasonably have resolved **[—27—]** either way. We nonetheless vacate the ALJ's decision to place Robinowitz in the 75th percentile because that decision appears to have been influenced by an improper factor, namely, the ALJ's unwarranted irritation with a brief that Robinowitz filed on remand from this court.

In our prior decision setting aside the ALJ's denial of benefits, we held that (1) the ALJ "unreasonably characterized Dr. **{-1081-}** Kafrouni's testimony as 'ignor[ing]' and 'dismiss[ing]' [Cloyd] Seachris's other health conditions when Dr. Kafrouni did acknowledge that other conditions in addition

---

[—25—] not clear, however, whether the BRB adopted this rationale advanced by the employer.

to cervical myelopathy contributed to Seachris's immobility and diabetes"; and (2) the ALJ "also erred in finding that Dr. Kafrouni's opinion was unsubstantiated by medical records when the preponderance of the evidence supports Dr. Kafrouni's opinion." *Seachris*, 538 F. App'x at 815. Based on these errors, we held that the "ALJ's credibility determination as to Dr. Kafrouni's testimony was 'patently unreasonable' and 'conflict[s] with the clear preponderance of the evidence.'" *Id.* at 814. We therefore concluded that the "ALJ's determination that the claimant did not establish that the cervical myelopathy caused by Cloyd Seachris's . . . 1979 work injury could have accelerated the immobility and diabetes that contributed to his death *is unsupported by substantial evidence of the record* considered as a whole." *Id.* (emphasis added). Despite the clarity of our instructions that the ALJ's credibility determination was patently unreasonable and that the ALJ's finding of no causation lacked substantial evidence support, the ALJ on remand issued an order requiring Seachris (1) "to identify those parts of Dr. Kafrouni's testimony which acknowledged other medical conditions suffered by the decedent"; and (2) "to identify the medical records in evidence that support Dr. Kafrouni's opinion." Given that these two points mirror **[—28—]** exactly the two defects we had identified in our prior ruling rejecting the ALJ's credibility determination, the ALJ's order effectively required Seachris to file a brief setting out the evidence that justified our reversal. Robinowitz, as counsel for Seachris, reasonably declined this invitation to second-guess our reasons for ruling in his client's favor and instead filed a short brief that reasonably took the position that "[i]n the present case, the Ninth Circuit necessarily held that Dr. Kafrouni's interpretation of the medical evidence was the only permissible one, and that his opinion determines the issue of causation as a matter of law."

Although the ALJ ultimately awarded benefits, the ALJ's subsequent fee order devotes several single-spaced pages to expressing the ALJ's palpable anger with Robinowitz's remand brief, stating that, by filing it, Robinowitz "decided that he needs to discern whether my briefing orders are wise in order to determine whether he needs to comply"; that he had thereby "appoint[ed] himself as a sort of interlocutory appellate judge and nullifies orders deemed unwise"; that "this is not acceptable behavior for an attorney"; that the ALJ "could have initiated a contempt proceeding against [Robinowitz]" but "decided that would simply prolong the litigation"; and that this behavior "would be relevant to the fee decision." There is more than a little irony to these comments, given that the premise of the ALJ's order was apparently that the ALJ was going to re-examine the correctness of *our* holdings. We perceive nothing improper—much less contumacious—in Robinowitz's pointing out that the ALJ's order was inconsistent with our mandate. Moreover, the ALJ's order confirms that Robinowitz's remand brief played a role in her rating of him at the 75th percentile, because the ALJ stated that this "troubling conduct," by itself, would "suggest[] a rating at the **[—29—]** median or lower" and was "not a trial strategy that is adopted by litigators in the top 5% of the bar." In light of these comments, we cannot credit the ALJ's later assertion, in denying reconsideration, that this episode "played no role" in the fee determinations; it obviously did. The BRB clearly erred in accepting that assertion at face value, and a remand is necessary so that the proper percentile rating can be reexamined afresh. **{-1082-}**

6. The ALJ's decision to include the "general" practice area in her analysis is not supported by substantial evidence

Robinowitz argues that the ALJ erred by including the 2012 OSB Survey's general practice area—applicable to attorneys who do not devote at least 50 percent of their time to any one practice area—in her analysis. Robinowitz points out that he is a specialist, rather than a generalist, and that the ALJ may have included the general practice area in the analysis for the improper purpose of holding down his hourly rate.

Robinowitz's argument is well-taken. The ALJ offered no persuasive reason for including the general practice rate in her analysis, and the wide disparity between this rate ($268) and the other rates relied on by the ALJ ($350 and $300) strongly suggests that the ALJ may indeed have been motivated by an improper purpose.[7] We are struck in particular by the ALJ's decision to exclude commercial **[—30—]** litigation as a comparator while including general practice as a comparator. There is no evidence in this record to suggest that LHWCA attorneys in general, or Robinowitz in particular, are comparable to general practitioners in skills, experience, or reputation, but dissimilar to commercial litigators. In fact, general practice, by definition, *excludes* attorneys, like Robinowitz, who specialize (devote more than 50% of their time) in litigation. And, of course, there is abundant evidence in the record to show that Robinowitz was a specialist, with significant experience and success in handling LHWCA cases. We therefore agree with Robinowitz that the record does not support the ALJ's inclusion of this practice area in her analysis.

* * *

In sum, we hold that the ALJ and the BRB committed legal error in determining Robinowitz's hourly rate and that the ALJ's determination of Robinowitz's hourly rate is not supported by substantial evidence. We grant the petition for review on this issue and remand for further proceedings consistent with this opinion. We note that the Oregon State Bar has published an updated survey. The 2017 OSB Survey reports that Portland attorneys with more than 30 years' experience charged a median rate of $425 per hour in 2016. For attorneys in the 75th percentile, the average rate was $495 per hour. These updated rates, which the BRB should take into account on remand, provide further support for Robinowitz's requested rate.

B. Paralegal's Hourly Rate

We next address Seachris' contention that the ALJ erred by awarding Robinowitz's paralegal a rate of $150 per hour **[—31—]** rather than $165 per hour as requested. The ALJ based the $150 rate on two factors: rates awarded by ALJs in other LHWCA cases; and rates awarded by the federal district court in the District of Oregon. We hold that the ALJ erred.

First, the ALJ erred by relying almost exclusively on the rates awarded by other ALJs. As we emphasized in *Christensen*, "the BRB should not be allowed to define 'prevailing market rate' in such a way as to define the 'market' only in terms of what has been awarded by ALJs and the BRB under the LHWCA." 557 F.3d at 1054; *accord Van Skike v. Dir., OWCP*, 557 F.3d 1041, 1046 (9th Cir. 2009).

Second, the ALJ's reliance on the district court's awards is flawed because the decisions upon which the ALJ relied set **{–1083–}** paralegal rates based on survey data pertaining to the western United States as a whole, rather than the relevant Portland community. *Holdner v. Coba*, No. 3:15-CV-2039-AC, 2016 WL 6662687, at *6 (D. Or. Nov. 9, 2016); *Pac. Coast Fruit Co. v. Ron Squires dba Four Seasons Farmers Mkt.*, No. 3:16-CV-00463-BR, 2016 WL 4443166, at *3 (D. Or. Aug. 19, 2016). These decisions therefore do not provide a proper foundation for determining the prevailing market rate in the Portland area. *See Shirrod*, 809 F.3d at 1089, 3 Adm. R. at 624 ("Because the lodestar method requires a 'reasonable attorney's fee' to be based on market rates in the 'relevant community,' we hold that the BRB erred in affirming an attorney's-fee award based on a proxy market rate not tailored to the 'relevant community,' which, in this case, [was] Portland.").

Robinowitz provided the only evidence of market rates for Portland paralegals. Based "on information from Phil Goldsmith and Serena Morones and [his] own knowledge," **[—32—]** Robinowitz stated that "[a] reasonable current hourly rate for [his

[7] These are the 75th percentile rates for the three practice areas selected by the ALJ from the 2012 OSB Survey: $300 for plaintiff civil litigation non-personal injury, $350 for plaintiff civil litigation personal injury, and $268 for general practice.

paralegal's] services is $165." Goldsmith, in turn, testified in 2009 that "the average rate for paralegals was $154 an hour" in the 2008 Morones Survey of commercial litigation rates. Respondents presented no contrary evidence. On this record, therefore, the evidence supported a rate of $165 per hour. We note that this is the rate that the Ninth Circuit Appellate Commissioner awarded to Robinowitz's paralegal in the 2014 *Petitt* decision.[8]

Accordingly, we grant the petition for review on this issue. On remand, the BRB shall award Robinowitz's paralegal a rate of $165 per hour.

C. Reasonable Hours

As noted earlier, *see supra* at 27–28, after we previously held that the ALJ's credibility determination as to Dr. Kafrouni's testimony was "patently unreasonable," *Seachris*, 538 F. App'x at 814, the ALJ on remand ordered Seachris to file a supplemental brief addressing matters that this court had already decided. Accordingly, rather than addressing the issues called for in the ALJ's supplemental briefing order, Robinowitz used his supplemental brief to take issue with the ALJ's interpretation of this court's decision, arguing that "[t]he Ninth Circuit did not remand this case for further consideration of Dr. Kafrouni's testimony . . . . It necessarily remanded for an order allowing widow's benefits to Ms. Seachris . . . ." **[—33—]**

In his subsequent fee application, Robinowitz sought to recover 2.25 hours for preparation of this supplemental brief. The ALJ disallowed one half of that time—1.125 hours—on the ground that Robinowitz's brief was "non-responsive" to the supplemental briefing order. The ALJ nevertheless acknowledged that "[i]t was proper to argue that Claimant's view was that I needed to only enter judgment in her favor."

We hold that the ALJ erred by reducing Robinowitz's hours on this ground. "A district court should exclude from the lodestar amount hours that are not reasonably expended because they are 'excessive, redundant, or otherwise unnecessary.'" *Van Gerwen v. Guarantee Mut. Life Co.*, 214 F.3d 1041, 1045 (9th Cir. 2000) (quoting *Hensley v. Eckerhart*, 461 U.S. 424, 434 (1983)). Here, Robinowitz's hours were neither excessive, redundant, nor unnecessary. As the ALJ conceded, Seachris appropriately **{–1084–}** used her supplemental brief to present her interpretation of the scope of the remand. The ALJ's denial of fees for this time, therefore, is not supported by substantial evidence.

The ALJ's anger over Robinowitz's position on the remand permeates the entire fee order, and it appears that the ALJ improperly reduced Robinowitz's fees for preparing the supplemental brief as a sanction. Although the ALJ later asserted that Robinowitz's performance in this regard played "no role" in the fee award, the record strongly suggests otherwise.

We grant the petition for review on this issue. **[—34—]**

D. Interest on Costs

The ALJ and the BRB erred by holding that the LHWCA does not permit an award of interest on costs to account for delay in payment. The Supreme Court has made clear that interest is available in limited circumstances under federal fee-shifting statutes. *See Perdue*, 559 U.S. at 555 ("[A]n enhancement may be appropriate if the attorney's performance includes an extraordinary outlay of expenses and the litigation is exceptionally protracted. . . . [T]he amount of the enhancement must be calculated using a method that is reasonable, objective, and capable of being reviewed on appeal, such as by applying a standard rate of interest to the qualifying outlays of expenses."). Our decision in *Hobbs*, 820 F.2d at 1530–31, upon which the ALJ relied, addressed *post-judgment* interest and thus has no bearing on the question presented here. We therefore grant the petition for

[8] Nothing in the record suggests that the tasks delegated to a paralegal are so dissimilar in trial versus appellate work as to justify different rates for paralegals in the trial and appellate phases of litigation.

review on this issue. On remand, the BRB should determine whether an award of interest on costs is appropriate because of the "exceptionally protracted" period that this case has been pending—having been filed in 2005—in which costs were incurred between 2007 and 2016, a period five to fourteen years ago.[9]

E. Reassignment

The tone of the ALJ's decision and the manner in which the ALJ evaluated the evidence suggest that the ALJ may not be able to provide Robinowitz with a fair and impartial hearing on remand. Accordingly, we *sua sponte* direct that **[—35—]** the BRB reassign this matter to a different ALJ on remand to avoid the appearance of partiality. *See Smolniakova v. Gonzales*, 422 F.3d 1037, 1054 (9th Cir. 2005) ("We further direct the BIA not to return the case to [Immigration Judge] Anna Ho."); *Nuru v. Gonzales*, 404 F.3d 1207, 1229 (9th Cir. 2005) ("Given his comments during the hearing and our strikingly different appraisal of the record, we order that the case be assigned to a different immigration judge who will afford Nuru the impartiality to which all applicants are entitled."); *Reed v. Massanari*, 270 F.3d 838, 845 (9th Cir. 2001) ("We remand with instructions that the matter be assigned to a different ALJ."); *Milburn Colliery Co. v. Hicks*, 138 F.3d 524, 537 (4th Cir. 1998) ("Finding the ALJ made several errors of law including failing to consider all of the relevant evidence and to adequately explain his rationale for crediting certain evidence, we conclude that review of this claim requires a fresh look at the evidence, unprejudiced by the various outcomes of the ALJ and the [Benefits Review] Board's orders below. Accordingly, we reverse and direct the Board promptly to remand to a new ALJ . . . .").

IV. CONCLUSION

We grant the petition for review and remand for proceedings consistent with this opinion. **{–1085–}**

PETITION GRANTED and REMANDED.

[9] Seachris, of course, has the right to update her application for fees and costs incurred since her initial application was filed in 2016, five years ago.

United States Court of Appeals for the Ninth Circuit

No. 19-17596

LIL' MAN IN THE BOAT, INC.
VS.
CITY AND COUNTY OF S.F.

Appeal from the United States District Court for the Northern District of California

Decided: July 15, 2021

Citation: 5 F.4th 952, 9 Adm. R. 337 (9th Cir. 2021).

Before **MURGUIA** and **CHRISTEN,** Circuit Judges, and **SESSIONS,** District Judge.

* The Honorable William K. Sessions III, United States District Judge for the District of Vermont, sitting by designation.

[—4—] {-954-} **CHRISTEN,** Circuit Judge:

Plaintiff Lil' Man in the Boat (Lil' Man) seeks reversal of a district court order **{-955-}** granting summary judgment on its claim that several municipal entities and officials (collectively, defendants) violated the Rivers and Harbors Act, 33 U.S.C. § 5(b)(2) (RHA), by imposing landing fees on commercial charters operating out of South Beach Harbor Marina in San Francisco Bay. The district court concluded that Congress **[—5—]** did not intend the RHA to restrict the type of fees defendants imposed. We affirm the district court's order dismissing Lil' Man's RHA claim on alternate grounds: we see no indication that Congress intended to create a private right of action in § 5(b)(2).

I

Lil' Man is a commercial charter business that provides transportation and hospitality services in San Francisco Bay. Lil' Man uses South Beach Harbor as a base for its commercial enterprises. Defendants are the City and County of San Francisco; the San Francisco Port Commission; Port officials Elaine Forbes, Peter Daley, and Jeff Bauer; and Harbormaster Joe Monroe. Together, the defendants own, operate, and regulate the Port of San Francisco and the South Beach Harbor.

Until 2016, Lil' Man paid a landing fee of $80 per docking to load and unload passengers at the South Beach Harbor. In 2016, defendants increased the landing fee to $110 and asked Lil' Man and all other commercial vessels to sign a Landing Agreement that altered the terms of the contract for using the marina. In addition to increasing the landing fee, the Landing Agreement required a "gross revenue fee" that applied only in months the vessel docked at the port. The gross revenue fee was to be 7% of the user's monthly gross revenues, in any month that 7% of the user's gross revenues exceeded the user's monthly landing fees.[1] Lil' Man refused to sign the Landing Agreement but twice **[—6—]** paid the gross revenue fee for charters booked prior to implementation of the Agreement.

Lil' Man brought suit in the Northern District of California pursuant to 42 U.S.C. § 1983, alleging the Landing Agreement violated the Tonnage Clause, the dormant Commerce Clause, the First Amendment, and § 5(b) of the RHA, 33 U.S.C. § 5(b). Though Lil' Man's complaint did not specify a particular sub-section of § 5(b), it expressly incorporated the language of § 5(b)(2). Specifically, the complaint alleged the new fees violated the RHA because they were "not reasonable and [were] not charged on a fair and equitable basis;" were "used for purposes other than to pay for the cost of services" to vessels; did not "enhance the safety and efficiency of interstate commerce;" and "impose[d] burdens on interstate commerce." 33 U.S.C. § 5(b)(2)(A)–(C). These allegations make plain that Lil' Man's RHA claim is premised on § 5(b)(2), which allows for the imposition of "reasonable fees charged on a fair and equitable basis."

The First Amendment claim asserted that the Landing Agreement violated Lil' Man's right to petition the government because the Agreement included a provision waiving the right to challenge the fees. The district court granted defendants' motion for judgment on the pleadings with respect to this claim

[1] The gross revenue fee excluded "[s]ums collected for any sales or excise tax imposed directly upon Licensee by any duly constituted governmental authority."

because Lil' Man had not signed the Landing Agreement. After the parties engaged in discovery, they filed cross-motions for summary judgment on Lil' Man's remaining claims.

The district court granted defendants' motion for summary judgment. The court relied on **{-956-}** *Asante v. California Department of Health Care Services*, 886 F.3d 795 (9th Cir. **[—7—]** 2018), and *American Trucking Ass'ns v. City of Los Angeles*, 569 U.S. 641 (2013), to conclude the Landing Agreement did not violate the dormant Commerce Clause because defendants, through the Port, operated as market participants subject to market pressures, and were therefore "exempt from the dormant Commerce Clause." The court ruled that the landing fees did not violate the Tonnage Clause because the fees were charged in exchange for services provided to vessels and not for general revenue-raising purposes. *See Clyde Mallory Lines v. Alabama ex rel. State Docks Comm'n*, 296 U.S. 261, 265–66 (1935); *see also Polar Tankers, Inc. v. City of Valdez*, 557 U.S. 1, 10 (2009).

Turning to the RHA claim, the district court concluded that Congress intended § 5(b) "to clarify existing law with respect to Constitutionally permitted fees and taxes on a vessel, and to prohibit fees and taxes on a vessel simply because that vessel sails through a given jurisdiction." The court granted summary judgment to defendants on the § 5(b)(2) claim because it concluded Congress did not intend § 5(b)(2) to apply to the fees imposed by the Landing Agreement. Lil' Man appeals only the dismissal of this claim and an evidentiary ruling excluding former harbor attendant Paul Dima's declaration from consideration at the summary judgment stage.[2] We have jurisdiction pursuant to 28 U.S.C. § 1291. **[—8—]**

II

We review de novo a district court's order granting summary judgment. *L.F. ex rel. v. Lake Washington Sch. Dist. #414*, 947 F.3d 621, 625 (9th Cir. 2020). We must "determine, viewing the evidence in the light most favorable to the nonmoving party, whether there are any genuine issues of material fact and whether the district court correctly applied the relevant substantive law." *Id.* (quoting *Wallis v. Princess Cruises, Inc.*, 306 F.3d 827, 832 (9th Cir. 2002)). "There is no genuine issue of fact if, on the record taken as a whole, a rational trier of fact could not find in favor of the party opposing the motion." *West v. State Farm Fire & Cas. Co.*, 868 F.2d 348, 350 (9th Cir. 1989). Questions of statutory interpretation are addressed de novo. *United States v. Northrop Corp.*, 59 F.3d 953, 959 (9th Cir. 1995). We may affirm the district court's order on any basis supported by the record. *McSherry v. City of Long Beach*, 584 F.3d 1129, 1135 (9th Cir. 2009).

III

A

33 U.S.C. § 5, commonly known as the Rivers and Harbors Act of 1884, prohibits tolls and operating charges for vessels passing through any lock, canal, canalized river, "or other work for the use and benefit of navigation" belonging to the United States. *See* 33 U.S.C. § 5, 23 Stat. 147 (July 5, 1884). Section 5 has been modestly amended on several occasions, but it was significantly revised in 2002 in conjunction with amendments to the Maritime Transportation Security Act (MTSA) as part of a comprehensive overhaul of the Merchant Marine Act of 1936. *See* MTSA, Pub. L. No. **[—9—]** 107-295, § 101(13), 116 Stat. 2064 (2002); H.R. Rep. No. 108-334, at 180 (2003) (Conf. Rep.). Congress took this step following the September 11, 2001 terrorist attacks on the World Trade Center out of concern that United States ports **{-957-}** were vulnerable to security breaches. *See* MTSA, Pub. L. No. 107-295, § 101(6)–(13), 116 Stat. 2064 (2002). Through the MTSA, Congress established a program that balanced the nation's concern

[2] Because we conclude Lil' Man has no private right of action, we do not reach whether the district court properly excluded Dima's declaration from consideration.

for increased port security with the need to ensure the free flow of interstate and foreign commerce. *See id.*

The 2002 amendment modified § 5's prohibition of tolls and operating charges and allowed the imposition of some charges, consistent with Tonnage Clause and Commerce Clause case law. *See* 33 U.S.C. § 5(b). The current version of § 5(b) provides:

> (b) No taxes, tolls, operating charges, fees, or any other impositions whatever shall be levied upon or collected from any vessel or other water craft, or from its passengers or crew, by any non-Federal interest, if the vessel or water craft is operating on any navigable waters subject to the authority of the United States, or under the right to freedom of navigation on those waters, except for
>
> (1) fees charged under section 2236 of this title;
>
> (2) reasonable fees charged on a fair and equitable basis that-- **[—10—]**
>
> (A) are used solely to pay the cost of a service to the vessel or water craft;
>
> (B) enhance the safety and efficiency of interstate and foreign commerce; and
>
> (C) do not impose more than a small burden on interstate or foreign commerce; or
>
> (3) property taxes on vessels or watercraft, other than vessels or watercraft that are primarily engaged in foreign commerce if those taxes are permissible under the United States Constitution.

33 U.S.C. § 5(b).

As several courts have observed, the 2002 amendment codified Commerce Clause and Tonnage Clause common law.[3] A few courts have considered § 5(b) challenges to fees imposed upon vessels,[4] but we are aware of just one that has squarely considered whether § 5(b)(2) includes a private right **[—11—]** of action. *See Cruise Lines Int'l Ass'n Alaska v. City & Borough of Juneau*, 356 F. Supp. 3d 831, 845–47 (D. Alaska 2018).

In the district court, Lil' Man argued that the fee imposed by the Landing Agreement violates § 5(b)(2) because it was calculated as a percentage of vessels' gross revenues, and not solely to pay for services provided to vessels. Lil' Man further argued that the fees imposed by the Landing Agreement were not imposed on a fair and equitable basis. Defendants urged the district court to dismiss Lil' Man's complaint because § 5(b)(2) does not provide a private right of action, and also argued the new fees were correctly assessed. The district court did not rule on defendants' first argument. Because Lil' Man cannot bring its RHA claim if § 5(b)(2) does not provide a private right of action, we first consider that threshold question. *See Logan v. U.S. Bank Nat'l Ass'n*, 722 F.3d 1163, 1169 (9th Cir. 2013). It is an issue of first impression. **{-958-}**

B

i

"Like substantive federal law itself, private rights of action to enforce federal law must be created by Congress." *Alexander v. Sandoval*, 532 U.S. 275, 286 (2001). "Congress may so empower litigants expressly or implicitly." *UFCW Local 1500 Pension Fund v. Mayer*, 895 F.3d 695, 699 (9th Cir. 2018). If Congress does

---

[3] *See, e.g., Bridgeport & Port Jefferson Steamboat Co. v. Bridgeport Port Auth.*, 566 F. Supp. 2d 81, 102 (D. Conn. 2008), *aff'd*, 567 F.3d 79 (2d Cir. 2009); *State, Dep't of Nat. Res. v. Alaska Riverways, Inc.*, 232 P.3d 1203, 1222 (Alaska 2010).

[4] *See, e.g., Bridgeport*, 566 F. Supp. 2d at 102; *Alaska Riverways, Inc.*, 232 P.3d at 1222; *City of Chicago Through Dep't of Fin. v. Wendella Sightseeing, Inc.*, 143 N.E.3d 771, 777–78 (Ill. App. Ct. 2019), *appeal denied sub nom. City of Chicago v. Wendella Sightseeing, Inc.*, 135 N.E.3d 544 (Ill. 2019).

not provide a private right of action explicitly within a statute's text, we must determine whether Congress implied one. *See Nisqually Indian Tribe v. Gregoire*, 623 F.3d 923, 929–30 (9th Cir. 2010). **[—12—]**

The parties agree that § 5(b)(2) does not expressly provide a private right of action, so we consider the statute's language, structure, context, and legislative history to determine whether a private right of action is implied. *Logan*, 722 F.3d at 1170. "[C]lear and unambiguous terms" are "required for Congress to create new rights enforceable under an implied private right of action." *Gonzaga Univ. v. Doe*, 536 U.S. 273, 290 (2002).

The Supreme Court initially identified four factors relevant to determining whether a statute contains an implied private right of action: "(1) whether the plaintiff is 'one of the class for whose especial benefit the statute was enacted'; (2) whether there is 'any indication of legislative intent, explicit or implicit, either to create [a private right of action] or to deny one'; (3) whether an implied private cause of action for the plaintiff is 'consistent with the underlying purposes of the legislative scheme'; and (4) whether the cause of action is 'one traditionally relegated to state law.'" *Logan*, 722 F.3d at 1170 (quoting *Cort v. Ash*, 422 U.S. 66, 78 (1975)). Since announcing this test, "the Supreme Court has elevated intent into a supreme factor," and *Cort*'s other three factors are used to decipher congressional intent. *Id.* at 1171.

ii

To determine whether Lil' Man is one of a class "for whose especial benefit the statute was enacted," we examine § 5(b)(2)'s text and look for "rights-creating language." *See Sandoval*, 532 U.S. at 288–89. "Statutes that focus on the person regulated rather than the individuals protected create 'no implication of an intent to confer rights on a particular class of persons.'" *Id.* at 289 (quoting *California v. Sierra Club*, 451 U.S. 287, 294 (1981)). The Supreme Court has **[—13—]** explained that "[t]he question is not simply who would benefit from [an] Act, but whether Congress intended to confer federal rights upon those beneficiaries." *Sierra Club*, 451 U.S. at 294.

In *Sandoval*, the Supreme Court considered whether § 602 of the Civil Rights Act, 42 U.S.C. § 2000d-1, created a private cause of action. 532 U.S. at 288–89. The Court compared § 602 to § 601 and cited its decision in *Cannon v. University of Chicago*, 441 U.S. 677 (1979), where the Court had previously recognized that § 601 does create a private right of action. *See Sandoval*, 532 U.S. at 288–89 (quoting *Cannon*, 441 U.S. at 690–91). *Sandoval* explained that the clear focus of § 601 is protecting a class of beneficiaries from discrimination because its text expressly mandates that "[n]o person . . . shall . . . be subjected to discrimination." *Id.* at 288–89 (quoting 42 U.S.C. § 2000d). In contrast, § 602 authorizes federal agencies "to effectuate" § 601 "by issuing rules, regulations, or orders . . . ." *See id.* at 278 (quoting 42 U.S.C. § 2000d-1). The Court observed that the "rights-creating **{–959–}** language so critical to the Court's analysis in *Cannon*" is completely absent from § 602, and held that § 602 does not include an implied right of action. *Id.* at 289–90, 293 (internal quotation marks omitted).

We addressed another statute that lacks rights-creating language, the Investment Company Act of 1940, in *UFCW Local 1500 Pension Fund v. Mayer*, 895 F.3d at 698–99. One section of that statute dictated "[n]o investment company" shall "engage in any business in interstate commerce" unless it registers with the Securities and Exchange Commission. 15 U.S.C. § 80a-7(a)(4). Because the statute's aim was to regulate the conduct of investment companies, we held it did not create a private right of action. *UFCW*, 895 F.3d at 699 **[—14—]** (citing *Northstar Fin. Advisors, Inc. v. Schwab Invs.*, 615 F.3d 1106, 1115–16 (9th Cir. 2010)). We explained that a separate section of the statute, which directed the SEC to take certain actions, was "yet a step further removed from having rights-creating language" because it "focuse[d] neither on the individuals protected nor even on the [parties] being regulated, but on the agenc[ies] that will do the regulating." *Id.* (citing *Sandoval*, 532 U.S. at 289, and 15

U.S.C. § 80a-3(b)(2)) (internal quotation marks omitted). Thus, the statutory language in *UFCW* "doom[ed] any suggestion that Congress intended to create a private right." *Id.*

A statute must also display an intent to create a private remedy in order to create an implied right of action. We have previously recognized the Supreme Court's direction that "[w]ithout evidence of a congressional intent to create both a private right and a private remedy, a private right of action 'does not exist and courts may not create one, no matter how desirable that might be as a policy matter, or how compatible with the statute.'" *UFCW*, 895 F.3d at 699 (quoting *Sandoval*, 532 U.S. at 286–87)). General language or reference to a statute's remedial purpose is not enough to suggest congressional intent to create a remedy; something more is required. *See Transamerica Mortg. Advisors, Inc. v. Lewis*, 444 U.S. 11, 24 (1979) (observing that even a statute intended to protect a class of beneficiaries does not require the conclusion that Congress intended to imply a private cause of action for damages). The absence of remedial language is a key clue that Congress did not intend to imply a private right of action. *Id.*

We examined these concepts thoroughly in *Logan v. U.S. Bank National Ass'n*, 722 F.3d at 1169–73. In that case, we concluded that the Protecting Tenants at Foreclosure Act **[—15—]** (PTFA) does not include a private right of action. *Logan* first observed that, by its terms, the PTFA is aimed at "the regulated party" and is "framed in terms of the obligations imposed on the regulated party . . . while the [tenant] is referenced only as an object of that obligation." *Id.* at 1171. This language indicates that Congress's aim was regulating foreclosure procedures, rather than providing a benefit to tenants. *Id.* We explained that "[s]tatutes containing general proscriptions of activities or focusing on the regulated party rather than the class of beneficiaries whose welfare Congress intended to further do not indicate an intent to provide for private rights of action." *Id.* (citation and internal quotation marks and alteration omitted).

As in *Logan*, nothing in the text or structure of § 5(b)(2) reflects a clear and unambiguous intent to create a private right of action. *Id.* at 1171. To begin, § 5(b)(2) lacks rights-creating language. The statute prohibits non-federal entities from imposing fees or other charges (the obligation) and refers to vessels "only as an object of that obligation." *Id.*; *see also* **{-960-}** 33 U.S.C. § 5(b) ("No . . . fees . . . shall be levied upon or collected from any vessel or other water craft, or from its passengers or crew, by any non-Federal interest . . . ."). This distinguishes § 5(b)(2) from statutes that target a class of beneficiaries as their subject. *See Cannon*, 441 U.S. at 689–90. Section 5(b)(2)'s imposition of an express prohibition on the conduct of non-federal entities—a command we have already held lacks rights-creating language—strongly suggests that § 5(b)(2) is "the kind of general ban" that carries no implied intent "to confer rights on a particular class of persons." *Sierra Club*, 451 U.S. at 294; *UFCW*, 895 F.3d at 699 (citing *Northstar*, 615 F.3d at 1109–10); *see Logan*, 722 F.3d at 1171. **[—16—]**

The absence of an expressly identified remedy in § 5(b)(2) also presents a significant textual clue that Congress did not intend to confer private rights. *See Sierra Club*, 451 U.S. at 294–98. "[E]ven where a statute is phrased in [] explicit rights-creating terms, a plaintiff suing under an implied right of action still must show that the statute manifests an intent 'to create not just a private right but also a private remedy.'" *Gonzaga*, 536 U.S. at 284 (quoting *Sandoval*, 532 U.S. at 286) (emphasis omitted). Section 5(b)(2) does not include any remedial language; rather, it limits the ability of non-federal interests to impose fees on vessels, their passengers, and crews in federally controlled navigable waters. We see no indication that Congress intended § 5(b)(2) to confer an individual benefit upon vessels. Rather, the benefit they receive appears to be ancillary to the statute's goals. *See Sierra Club*, 451 U.S. at 297–98.

iii

Cort also instructs that we may consider legislative history if a statute's text or structure is unclear regarding the intent to create a right of action, or the legislative history squarely contradicts the statute's text. *See Logan*, 722 F.3d at 1171. We find no ambiguity, but note that § 5(b)'s legislative history reinforces the conclusion that the statute does not afford a private right of action.

Legislative history from both the original enactment and intervening amendments helps to divine congressional intent. *See id.* at 1172–73. As originally enacted, the RHA generally prohibited non-federal actors from imposing tolls on vessels and their passengers and crews, thereby facilitating free travel from one port to another. *See* 15 Cong. Rec. 5831–32 (July **[—17—]** 1, 1884) (observing the need for appropriations "to keep commerce moving upon these waters" by avoiding obstructions in navigable channels); H.R. Rep. No. 1544, at 6 (1884). The 1884 Act provided:

> That no tolls or operating charges whatsoever shall be levied or collected upon any vessel or vessels, dredges, or other passing watercraft through any canal or other work for the improvement of navigation belonging to the United States; and for the purpose of preserving and continuing the use and navigation of said canals, rivers, and other public works . . . the Secretary of War . . . is hereby authorized to draw his warrant or requisition from time to time upon the Secretary of the Treasury to pay the actual expenses of operating and keeping said works in repair . . .

23 Stat. 133, 147 (July 5, 1884).

In 1909, Congress amended the statute to add more federally controlled waterways, to expand the meaning of "belonging to the United States," and to allow spending for the purpose of "preserving and continuing the use and navigation of . . . canals and other public works." *See* 35 **{-961-}** Stat. 815 (Mar. 3, 1909). The RHA was not materially amended again until 2002.[5] **[—18—]**

The 2002 amendment added exceptions to the RHA's general ban on tolls and taxes, harmonizing the RHA with Tonnage Clause and Commerce Clause common law that allows local entities to charge fees in exchange for services provided to the vessels. *See* 33 U.S.C. § 5. The amendment was intended to "clarify existing law with respect to Constitutionally permitted fees and taxes on a vessel," and "prohibit fees and taxes imposed on a vessel simply because that vessel sails through a given jurisdiction." H.R. Rep. No. 108–334, at 180 (2003) (Conf. Rep.). On the House floor, the Chair of the Transportation and Infrastructure Committee explained that the bill would prevent "local jurisdictions [from] impos[ing] taxes and fees on vessels merely transiting or making innocent passage through navigable waters . . . ." 148 Cong. Rec. E2143–04 (2002).

The district court appears to have relied heavily on the Committee Chair's floor statement when it concluded that Congress did not intend § 5(b) to apply to the type of fees imposed by the Landing Agreement. But the Conference Committee's report, the Chair's floor statement, and the text of the 2002 amendment make clear that in addition to retaining the prohibition against taxing vessels for merely transiting federally controlled waters, Congress also intended to permit several exceptions to § 5(b)'s general prohibition, including the imposition of fees for services rendered to vessels that enhance the safety and efficiency of interstate and foreign commerce. *See* § 5(b)(2).

Facilitating commerce was clearly a focus of the 2002 amendment, as reflected by the condition in § 5(b)(2)(C) that any fees may not impose "more than a small burden on interstate or foreign commerce." *See also* MTSA, Pub. L. No. 107-295, § 101(12), 116 Stat. 2064 (2002). And as we **[—19—]** have explained, the 2002 amendment brought the RHA in line with Commerce Clause and Tonnage Clause jurisprudence. *See supra*. In all, nothing in the legislative history suggests that Congress contemplated the creation of a

[5] A 1947 supplement to the U.S. Code altered "Secretary of War" to "Secretary of the Army," 33 U.S.C. § 5 (Supp. I 1947), and a 1954 supplement repealed a proviso requiring an itemized statement of expenses, 33 U.S.C. § 5 (Supp. II 1954).

separate private right or private remedy in § 5(b)(2).

iv

Cort's third factor looks to whether an implied private right of action is consistent with the underlying purposes of the RHA. *See Cort*, 422 U.S. at 78. Consideration of this factor also suggests that Congress did not intend to imply a private right of action in § 5(b)(2). Congress adopted a number of provisions governing the use, administration, and navigation of the waters of the United States in Title 33, and § 5(b) is part of this complex regulatory scheme. *See Sierra Club*, 451 U.S. at 289, 297–98 (addressing the Rivers and Harbors Appropriation Act of 1899, 33 U.S.C. § 403); *see also Merrill Lynch, Pierce, Fenner & Smith, Inc. v. Curran*, 456 U.S. 353, 408 (1982) (Powell, J., dissenting) (observing "modern federal regulatory statutes tend to be exceedingly complex" and suggesting the Court should be wary of inferring private rights of action). Because the free movement of commerce and national security are interests historically safeguarded by the federal government, the absence of an implied right of action in § 5(b)(2) is consistent with the overall statutory scheme.[6] **[—20—] {-962-}**

The last *Cort* factor asks us to consider whether the cause of action is traditionally relegated to state law. *Cort*, 422 U.S. at 78. The types of fees at issue here are sometimes challenged pursuant to state law and sometimes challenged pursuant to federal law. *See, e.g., Bridgeport*, 566 F. Supp. 2d at 96–105 (analyzing plaintiffs' claims that passenger fees violated both federal and state law). This factor does not materially affect our analysis given the weight of the other factors. *See Sierra Club*, 451 U.S. at 297 ("Here consideration of the first two *Cort* factors is dispositive.").

v

Lil' Man contends that a private right of action to enforce § 5(b)(2) must be implied because private charters benefit from the RHA's prohibition on local authorities imposing unreasonable fees on vessels that call at their ports. Lil' Man argues that if it cannot bring suit to enforce § 5(b)(2)'s provisions, no one can, and it urges that § 5(b)(2) must not be **[—21—]** left without any enforcement mechanism. We are not persuaded.

First, to the extent Lil' Man argues it cannot vindicate its rights if § 5(b)(2) does not include a private right of action, Lil' Man overlooks that the reasonableness of the Landing Agreement is subject to challenge pursuant to the Tonnage Clause. *See Cruise Lines Int'l*, 356 F. Supp. 3d at 852–53 (considering challenge brought pursuant to the Tonnage Clause to passenger fees imposed upon vessels by non-federal authority); *see also San Carlos Apache Tribe v. United States*, 417 F.3d 1091, 1095–96 (9th Cir. 2005) (explaining that alternate avenue for litigation, via Administrative Procedure Act, weighed against finding private right of action).

---

[6] The existence of another provision in the statutory scheme that *expressly* creates a private right of action supports this conclusion. Section 5(b)(1) permits non-federal interests to impose fees on vessels pursuant to 33 U.S.C. § 2236, part of the Water Resources Development Act of 1986. *See* Pub. L. No. 99-662, § 208, 100 Stat. 4082. That statute allows the imposition of port or harbor dues to finance harbor navigation projects such as removing obstructions to navigation or widening channels **[—20—]** for vessel transit. *See* 33 U.S.C. § 2236(a)(1)–(3). Section 2236 includes an express private right of action for any party aggrieved by the imposition of such fees. *Id.* § 2236(b)(2). Lil' Man does not allege that defendants violated § 5(b)(1) or § 2236. Nor do the parties allege that defendants followed § 2236's procedural steps, including notice and a hearing, before imposing the fees, and Lil' Man does not allege that it filed its complaint within the 180-day window that § 2236 provides. *Id.* § 2236(a)(5), (b)(2). Instead, Lil' Man's complaint explicitly uses the language of § 5(b)(2), which makes no comparable allowance for private claims. We conclude it is "highly improbable that Congress absentmindedly forgot to mention an intended private action" in § 5(b)(2) when it simultaneously incorporated § 2236's private right of action into § 5(b)(1). *Logan*, 722 F.3d at 1170–71 (quoting *Transamerica Mortg. Advisors*, 444 U.S. at 20); *see, e.g., Sandoval*, 532 U.S. at 288–89 (finding no private right of action to enforce § 602 of Title VI of Civil Rights Act).

Second, even if there were no alternative mechanism for private enforcement, this alone would not require us to infer a private right of action. In *California v. Sierra Club*, the Supreme Court construed § 10 of the Rivers and Harbors Appropriation Act of 1899 and determined that it does not include an implied private right of action. 451 U.S. at 292–98. Plaintiffs in *Sierra Club* sought to prevent the State of California from constructing water storage and diversion facilities. *Id.* at 290–91. The statute at issue in *Sierra Club* prohibited "[t]he creation of any obstruction not affirmatively authorized by Congress, to the navigable capacity of any of the waters of the United States . . . ." *Id.* (quoting 33 U.S.C. § 403). The Supreme Court reasoned "Congress was concerned not with private rights but **{-963-}** with the Federal Government's ability to respond to obstructions on navigable waterways," and observed that the statute benefits the public at large because it empowers "the Federal Government to exercise its authority over interstate commerce with respect **[—22—]** to obstructions on navigable rivers caused by bridges and similar structures." *Id.* at 295–96.

The lack of any private enforcement mechanism did not require an alternate conclusion in *Sierra Club*, nor does it here. *See id.* at 297–98; *Three Rivers Ctr. for Indep. Living, Inc. v. Hous. Auth. of City of Pittsburgh*, 382 F.3d 412, 420 (3d Cir. 2004) (explaining "[s]ome statutes create rights in individuals that are only enforceable by agencies . . . or not enforceable at all").[7]

C

We are aware of just one case, *Cruise Lines International*, 356 F. Supp. 3d at 845–47, in which a federal court has directly addressed whether Congress implied a private right of action in § 5(b)(2).[8] In *Cruise Lines*, a trade organization challenged passenger fees imposed by the City of Juneau to fund municipal departments performing services for passengers, projects and services for Juneau's tourist-laden downtown area, and waterfront capital projects. *Id.* at **[—23—]** 837–39. The district court ruled that Congress could not have intended to preclude a private right of action in § 5(b)(2) because Congress crafted the 2002 amendment to mirror federal case law that developed pursuant to the Commerce Clause and Tonnage Clause. *Id.* at 845–47. Reasoning that private plaintiffs had been allowed to enforce the limitations imposed by the Tonnage Clause, the court decided that Congress must have intended to allow private plaintiffs to enforce the same restrictions pursuant to § 5(b)(2). *Id.* at 847 ("Because private plaintiffs have been able to enforce the prohibitions of the Tonnage Clause in courts, Congress must have intended that private plaintiffs would be able to enforce these same prohibitions under Section 5(b) of the RHAA."). We agree with the court's conclusion that Congress intended the 2002 amendment to codify common law that had developed pursuant to the Tonnage Clause and Commerce Clause since the RHA was enacted, but we are obliged to apply *Cort* to determine whether Congress intended to create a private right of action in § 5(b)(2). Having done so, we conclude the amendment was not enacted for the purpose of conferring a benefit on vessels. Rather than including rights-creating language, § 5(b) limits the conduct of non-federal entities for the benefit of the public at large. *See Sierra Club*, 451 U.S. at 298.

We find no indication that Congress intended to create an implied private right of action in § 5(b)(2). Accordingly, we conclude the district court did not err by **{-964-}**

[7] Lil' Man argues that the subject landing fee is per se invalid because it is calculated as 7% of a vessel's gross revenue and the plain text of § 5(b)(2) only permits docking fees that are *solely* related to services rendered to vessels. We do not reach the reasonableness of the fees under § 5(b)(2) because we conclude § 5(b)(2) does not include an implied right of action. Whether the landing fees violate the Tonnage Clause is a question beyond the scope of this appeal because Lil' Man did not appeal the dismissal of its Tonnage Clause claim.

[8] *Bridgeport* questioned whether a private right of action is implied in § 5(b) but it did not resolve the question because the court concluded the challenged passenger fee violated the Tonnage Clause. 566 F. Supp. 2d at 102–03 ("It is not clear to the Court . . . whether there is a private right of action under the statute.").

granting summary judgment on Lil' Man's § 5(b)(2) claim.

AFFIRMED.

United States Court of Appeals
for the Ninth Circuit

No. 20-15810

MAUIA
VS.
PETROCHEM INSULATION, INC.

Appeal from the United States District Court for the Northern District of California

Decided: July 20, 2021

Citation: 5 F.4th 1068, 9 Adm. R. 346 (9th Cir. 2021).

Before **MURGUIA** and **CHRISTEN**, Circuit Judges, and **LYNN**,* Chief District Judge.

* The Honorable Barbara M. G. Lynn, Chief United States District Judge for the Northern District of Texas, sitting by designation.

[—3—] {-1069-} **CHRISTEN**, Circuit Judge: **{-1070-}**

Petrochem Insulation, Inc. (Petrochem) appeals the district court's order denying its motion to dismiss Iafeta Mauia's claims alleging violations of California's wage and hour laws. Mauia alleged that Petrochem failed to provide adequate meal and rest periods to workers on oil platforms off the coast of California. Pursuant to the Outer Continental Shelf Lands Act (OCSLA), 43 U.S.C. § 1331 *et seq.*, all law on the Outer Continental Shelf (OCS) is federal; state law is adopted on the OCS only to the extent it is applicable and not inconsistent with federal law. 43 U.S.C. § 1333(a)(2)(A). The Supreme Court explained in *Parker Drilling Management Services v. Newton* that there must be a gap in federal law before state law will apply on the OCS. 139 S. Ct. 1881, 1892, 7 Adm. R. 36, 41 (2019). Because federal law addresses meal and rest periods, we conclude there is no gap in the applicable federal law. Accordingly, we reverse the district court's order denying Petrochem's motion to dismiss Mauia's state-law claims. **[—4—]**

I

Petrochem provides services to drilling operations located off the coast of California on the OCS. Until 2016, Petrochem employed Mauia as an Onsite Project Manager/Superintendent for scaffolding projects on offshore oil platforms. Mauia was an hourly employee and worked shifts of twelve hours or more. He alleged that Petrochem provided only one meal period after the start of the sixth hour of his shifts, and only two rest periods per twelve-hour shift.

Mauia's operative complaint alleged that Petrochem's meal- and rest-period practices violated California law. Specifically, Mauia alleged that by providing only one meal period that began after the sixth hour of work, Petrochem violated § 512 of the California Labor Code, which mandates that "[a]n employer shall not employ an employee for a work period of more than five hours per day without providing the employee with a meal period of not less than 30 minutes." Cal. Lab. Code § 512(a); *see* 8 Cal. Code Regs. § 11160(10)(A). California also requires that "[a]n employer shall not employ an employee for a work period of more than 10 hours per day without providing the employee with a second meal period of not less than 30 minutes." Cal. Lab. Code § 512(a); *see* 8 Cal. Code Regs. § 11160(10)(B). Mauia sought "meal period premium wages" pursuant to state law in an amount to be determined. *See* Cal. Lab. Code § 226.7.

Mauia also alleged that Petrochem violated California law by providing only two rest breaks during his twelve-hour shifts. *See* 8 Cal. Code Regs. § 11160(11)(A) (requiring employers to "authorize and permit all employees to take rest periods . . . daily at the rate of ten (10) minutes net rest time for every four (4) hours worked"). As with his meal-period **[—5—]** claim, Mauia sought back-pay pursuant to Cal. Lab. Code § 226.7 for the failure to provide rest periods. Finally, Mauia alleged that Petrochem's failure to provide meal and rest periods as required by California law amounted to unfair business practices, and he sought disgorgement and restitution.[1] *See* Cal. Bus. & Prof. Code § 17200 *et seq.*

[1] The district court dismissed some of Mauia's other claims as untimely or because they were

Petrochem moved to dismiss Mauia's state-law claims pursuant to Federal Rule of Civil Procedure 12(b)(6). Its motion argued that California wage and hour laws are inapplicable on the OCS because the Fair Labor Standards Act (FLSA), **{-1071-}** 29 U.S.C. § 201 *et seq.*, addresses meal and rest periods, leaving no gap for California law to fill. *See Parker Drilling*, 139 S. Ct. at 1891, 7 Adm. R. at 40. Petrochem also urged the district court to dismiss Mauia's unfair competition claim because it was derivative of, and dependent upon, the viability of Mauia's meal-and rest-period claims.

The district court denied Petrochem's motion to dismiss. It reasoned that neither the FLSA nor its implementing regulations address meal or rest periods because the federal regulations only concern how and when meal and rest breaks must be compensated as work time; they do not require that employers provide meal and rest breaks. Accordingly, the district court ruled that federal law does not address Mauia's claims, and concluded that California's meal- and rest-break laws were adopted as surrogate federal law for workers on OCS drilling platforms. For the same reasons, the court ruled that Mauia's derivative unfair competition claim survived Petrochem's motion to dismiss. **[—6—]**

The district court recognized that trial courts in our circuit have split on this issue, and certified its order for interlocutory review. A motions panel of our court granted Petrochem's petition for permission to appeal. We have jurisdiction pursuant to 28 U.S.C. § 1292(b), and we reverse the district court's judgment.

II

We review de novo a district court's order denying a Rule 12(b)(6) motion to dismiss. *Fortyune v. City of Lomita*, 766 F.3d 1098, 1101 (9th Cir. 2014). Our review is limited to the complaint, materials incorporated by reference into the complaint, and matters of which we may take judicial notice. *Karasek v. Regents of Univ. of Cal.*, 956 F.3d 1093, 1104 (9th Cir. 2020). We accept as true all well-pleaded factual allegations and construe them in the light most favorable to the non-moving party. *Id.* "A complaint will not survive a motion to dismiss unless it 'contain[s] sufficient factual matter, accepted as true, to state a claim to relief that is plausible on its face.'" *Id.* (alteration in original) (quoting *Ashcroft v. Iqbal*, 556 U.S. 662, 678 (2009)).

III

The OCSLA, 43 U.S.C. § 1331 *et seq.*, extends "[t]he Constitution and laws and civil and political jurisdiction of the United States" to the OCS "to the same extent as if the [OCS] were an area of exclusive Federal jurisdiction located within a State." 43 U.S.C. § 1333(a)(1)(A). The OCSLA provides:

> (2)(A) To the extent that they are applicable and not inconsistent with this subchapter or **[—7—]** with other Federal laws and regulations of the Secretary now in effect or hereafter adopted, the civil and criminal laws of each adjacent State, now in effect or hereafter adopted, amended, or repealed are declared to be the law of the United States for that portion of the subsoil and seabed of the outer Continental Shelf, and artificial islands and fixed structures erected thereon, which would be within the area of the State if its boundaries were extended seaward to the outer margin of the outer Continental Shelf . . . . All such applicable laws shall be administered and enforced by the appropriate officers and courts of the United States.

Id. § 1331(a)(2)(A). The Supreme Court has explained that "all law on the OCS is federal law, administered by federal officials." *Parker Drilling*, 139 S. Ct. at 1886, 7 Adm. R. at 36. "The OCSLA denies States any interest in or jurisdiction over the OCS, and it deems the adjacent State's laws to be federal law '[t]o the extent that they are applicable and not inconsistent with' other federal **{-1072-}** law."

---

resolved by *Parker Drilling*. Those claims are not on appeal.

Id., 7 Adm. R. at 36 (quoting 43 U.S.C. § 1333(a)(2)(A)).

In *Parker Drilling*, the Supreme Court resolved a circuit split concerning how to determine whether a state law is "applicable and not inconsistent with . . . Federal law[]" within the meaning of the OCSLA. 43 U.S.C. § 1333(a)(2)(A); *Parker Drilling*, 139 S. Ct. at 1886–87, 7 Adm. R. at 36–37. The Fifth Circuit had interpreted the OCSLA to require that "'applicable' be read in terms of necessity—necessity to fill a significant void or gap" in federal law. *Cont'l Oil Co. v. London Steam-Ship Owners' Mut. Ins. Ass'n*, 417 F.2d 1030, 1036 (5th Cir. 1969). Our court had interpreted the OSCLA **[—8—]** by giving "applicable" its plain and ordinary meaning. *See Newton v. Parker Drilling Mgmt. Servs., Ltd.*, 881 F.3d 1078, 1090, 6 Adm. R. 314, 321 (9th Cir. 2018), *vacated and remanded by Parker Drilling*, 139 S. Ct. 1881, 7 Adm. R. 36. In *Newton*, we held that an adjacent state's law was "applicable" for purposes of the OSCLA when it "pertained to the subject matter at hand." *Id.* (citing *Applicable*, Funk & Wagnalls Standard Dictionary of the English Language (1958); *Applicable*, Webster's New World Dictionary of the American Language (1972)). We also gave "inconsistent" its ordinary meaning, and held that "applicable" state laws are "inconsistent" with federal law when they are "mutually 'incompatible, incongruous, or inharmonious.'" *Id.* at 1093, 6 Adm. R. at 323–24 (alteration omitted) (quoting *Ecological Rights Found. v. Pac. Gas & Elec. Co.*, 874 F.3d 1083, 1095 (9th Cir. 2017) (quoting Webster's Third New Int'l Dictionary (1971))).

Much like Mauia, Newton worked on oil platforms off the coast of California. *Id.* at 1082, 6 Adm. R. at 314. He worked fourteen-day shifts, with each day consisting of twelve hours on duty and twelve hours on standby. *Id.*, 6 Adm. R. at 314. Though Newton was paid "well above California and federal minimum wage," he was not paid for his standby time. *Id.*, 6 Adm. R. at 314. We reasoned in *Newton* that California's minimum-wage and standby-time laws were applicable to the parties' dispute, and that "the determinative question in Newton's case [was] . . . whether California wage and hour laws are 'inconsistent with' existing federal law." *Id.* at 1093, 6 Adm. R. at 324 (quoting 43 U.S.C. § 1333(a)(2)(A)). Because "the FLSA's savings clause expressly provides that states are free to adopt more protective standards for minimum wages or maximum hours," we held that California's wage-and-hour laws were not inconsistent with federal law, and therefore applied on the OCS. *Id.* at 1097–99, 6 Adm. R. at 327–29. **[—9—]**

The Supreme Court granted certiorari to resolve these competing interpretations of the OCSLA. *Parker Drilling*, 139 S. Ct. at 1886–87, 7 Adm. R. at 36–37. Parker Drilling urged the Supreme Court to adopt the Fifth Circuit's interpretation, but Newton argued "[i]n essence, . . . that state law is 'inconsistent' [with federal law] only if it would be pre-empted under [] ordinary pre-emption principles." *Id.* at 1888, 7 Adm. R. at 37. The Court agreed with Parker Drilling because a "pre-emption analysis is applicable only where the overlapping, dual jurisdiction of the Federal and State Governments makes it necessary to decide which law takes precedence." *Id.* at 1889, 7 Adm. R. at 39. The Supreme Court explained that because the OCS was never part of a state, the "ordinary question in pre-emption cases"—whether a conflict exists between federal and state law—is not present on the OCS. *Id.*, 7 Adm. R. at 39. Instead, the Court reasoned that "like the generally applicable enclave rule, the OCSLA sought to make all OCS law federal yet also 'provide a sufficiently detailed legal framework to govern life' on the OCS." *Id.* at 1890, 7 Adm. R. at 40 (quoting *Shell Oil Co. v. Iowa Dep't of Revenue*, 488 U.S. 19, 27 (1988)). "The text and context of the OCSLA therefore suggest that state law is not adopted to govern the OCS where federal law is on point," and "the OCSLA . . . does not adopt state law 'where there is no gap to fill.'" *Id.* at 1891, 7 Adm. R. at 40 (quoting **{-1073-}** *Lewis v. United States*, 523 U.S. 155, 163 (1998)).

Parker Drilling concluded that "the question is whether federal law has already addressed the relevant issue; if so, state law addressing the same issue would necessarily be inconsistent with existing federal law and cannot be adopted as surrogate federal law. Put another way, to the extent federal law applies to a particular issue, state law is inapplicable." *Id.* at 1889, 7 Adm. R. at 39. Applying this rule to Newton's claims, the Court observed that the FLSA provides a minimum wage and addresses standby time insofar as it **[—10—]** provides that standby time is not work time that must be compensated. *Id.* at 1893, 7 Adm. R. at 42. The Court concluded: (1) there was no gap in federal law to fill; (2) California law governing minimum wage and standby time did not apply; and (3) Newton's state-law claims necessarily failed. *Id.*, 7 Adm. R. at 42.

IV

As *Parker Drilling* instructs, to resolve Mauia's claims we begin by asking "whether federal law has already addressed" the relevant issue. *Id.*, 7 Adm. R. at 39. Mauia's meal- and rest-period claims rely on his allegations that Petrochem provided only one meal break after the beginning of the sixth hour of work, and only two rest breaks during his twelve-hour shifts. Mauia contends that California law applies, and that Petrochem's practices violate California law. We disagree. Because the FLSA addresses meal and rest periods, we conclude that California's meal- and rest-period laws are not adopted as surrogate federal law on the OCS.

The FLSA was enacted to protect employees from working excessive hours for substandard pay. *See Brooklyn Sav. Bank v. O'Neil*, 324 U.S. 697, 706–07 (1945). To achieve this goal, the FLSA sets a minimum hourly wage, and mandates overtime pay for employees working more than forty hours per week. *Id.* at 707; *see* 29 U.S.C. §§ 206(a)(1)(C), 207(a)(1). The FLSA does not require that employers provide meal or rest periods,[2] but its implementing regulations address both meal and rest periods by specifying **[—11—]** that all rest periods and non-bona fide meal periods must be compensated.

Regarding meal breaks, the FLSA's implementing regulations state:

> (a) Bona fide meal periods. Bona fide meal periods are not worktime. Bona fide meal periods do not include coffee breaks or time for snacks. These are rest periods. The employee must be completely relieved from duty for the purposes of eating regular meals. Ordinarily 30 minutes or more is long enough for a bona fide meal period. A shorter period may be long enough under special conditions. The employee is not relieved if he is required to perform any duties, whether active or inactive, while eating. For example, an office employee who is required to eat at his desk or a factory worker who is required to be at his machine is working while eating.
>
> (b) Where no permission to leave premises. It is not necessary that an employee be permitted to leave the premises if he is otherwise completely freed from duties during the meal period.

29 C.F.R. § 785.19. Put simply, if an employee is not "completely relieved from duty" during a meal period, the FLSA requires employers to compensate employees for that time. *Id.* **[—12—]**

Regarding rest breaks, the implementing regulations provide: **{-1074-}**

> Rest periods of short duration, running from 5 minutes to about 20 minutes, are common in industry. They promote the efficiency of the employee and are customarily paid for as working time. They must be counted as hours worked. Compensable time of rest periods may not be offset against other working time such as compensable waiting time or on-call time.

29 C.F.R. § 785.18. In other words, federal law encourages, but does not require, that employers provide rest breaks. And it requires employers to compensate employees for any

---

[2] U.S. DEP'T OF LABOR, *What does the Fair Labor Standards Act NOT require?*, https://webapps.dol.gov/elaws/whd/flsa/screen6.asp (last visited May 21, 2021).

rest breaks that are provided. An employer who fails to abide by these meal- and rest-period regulations is liable to the employees "in the amount of [the employees'] unpaid minimum wages, or their unpaid overtime compensation, . . . and in an additional equal amount as liquidated damages." 29 U.S.C. § 216(b).

The FLSA is not as protective of workers as California law; only the latter mandates that employers provide meal and rest periods of certain duration and at specific intervals. *See* Cal. Lab. Code § 512(a); 8 Cal. Code Regs. § 11160(11). But the fact that federal law does not offer comparable protections does not mean there is a gap in federal law that state law may fill. The FLSA's implementing regulations expressly contemplate meal and rest periods, address how and when these periods must be compensated as work time, and provide a remedy to employees whose employers fail to comply. Because the federal regulations address meal and **[—13—]** rest periods, there is no gap in federal law for state law to fill. *See Parker Drilling*, 139 S. Ct. at 1891, 7 Adm. R. at 40.

The district court approached this analysis differently. It looked first to state law and compared California's wage-and-hour provisions against the protections provided by federal law to determine whether there is a gap between the two schemes. The court found a gap because "California law [] provides a minimum number of meal periods that must be given, when they must be given, and a remedy for the employee if they are not." California law also requires a rest period of ten minutes for each four-hour work period. In contrast, "the [federal] regulation[s] concern[] the computation of hours worked for purposes of determining overtime pay, rather than *regulating* meal or rest periods."

We cannot reconcile the district court's approach with the Supreme Court's decision in *Parker Drilling*. "[T]he only law on the OCS is federal law," *Parker Drilling*, 139 S. Ct. at 1889, 7 Adm. R. at 38, so we must begin with the presumption that federal law applies, and state law is adopted only to fill gaps in federal law. *Id.* at 1891, 7 Adm. R. at 40–41. The fact that federal law does not provide meal- and rest-period protections as robust as California's does not mean that there is a gap in federal law or that federal law does not address meal and rest periods. The result we reach here is consistent with *Parker Drilling*, which made clear that state law plays only a limited role on the OCS. *Id.*, 7 Adm. R. at 40–41.

Mauia further argues that the FLSA's regulations are not applicable to his meal- and rest-period claims because they "fall[] under a part of a subchapter . . . relating to 'hours worked.'" Stated differently, because the federal rules concerning meal and rest periods are folded into the FLSA's **[—14—]** definition of "hours worked" that must be compensated, Mauia sees no "direct federal law counterpart to [the] state law[s]" requiring employers to provide meal and rest periods, and he concludes there is a gap between the two wage-and-hour schemes.

Mauia is correct that the claims at issue in *Parker Drilling* had direct federal counterparts: both the FLSA and California law provide for a minimum wage—although California's is more generous—and **{-1075-}** both federal and California law address whether employees must be paid for standby time. *Id.* at 1893, 7 Adm. R. at 42; *compare* 29 U.S.C. § 206(a)(1), *with* Cal. Lab. Code § 1182.12(b); *compare* 29 C.F.R. § 785.23, *with Mendiola v. CPS Security Sols., Inc.*, 340 P.3d 355, 361 (Cal. 2015). But by urging us to find a gap if there is "no direct federal counterpart" to a state provision, Mauia essentially asks that we revive the type of pre-emption analysis the Supreme Court rejected in *Parker Drilling*. *See* 139 S. Ct. at 1889, 7 Adm. R. at 38–39. Mauia's argument fails because *Parker Drilling* does not require a direct federal counterpart; it requires that we ask whether federal law addresses the relevant issue, not whether federal law addresses it in the same way. *See id.* at 1892–93, 7 Adm. R. at 41–42 (rejecting Newton's claim for standby-time wages under California law because federal law provides that standby time is not compensable).

The FLSA requires that all rest periods must be counted as work time. It also requires that any meal period during which an employee is not "completely relieved from duty" must be counted as work time. 29 C.F.R. §§ 785.18, 785.19. Federal law therefore addresses meal and rest periods, and California law does not provide the rule of decision for meal- and rest-time claims arising on the OCS. We reverse the district court's denial of Petrochem's motion to dismiss **[—15—]** Mauia's California meal- and rest-period claims. Mauia concedes that his unfair competition claim is predicated on Petrochem's alleged violations of California meal- and rest-break laws. Therefore, we also reverse the order denying Petrochem's motion to dismiss his unfair competition claim.

REVERSED.

United States Court of Appeals
for the Ninth Circuit

No. 20-15576

SAN FRANCISCO BAY CONSERVATION & DEV. COMM'N
vs.
UNITED STATES ARMY CORPS OF ENG'RS

Appeal from the United States District Court for the Northern District of California

Decided: August 6, 2021

Citation: 8 F.4th 839, 9 Adm. R. 352 (9th Cir. 2021).

Before **SCHROEDER, SMITH,** and **VAN DYKE,** Circuit Judges.

[—4—] {-841-} SCHROEDER, Circuit Judge:

INTRODUCTION

This case illustrates how the San Francisco Bay Area's economic and environmental destinies are entrusted to multiple governmental agencies, state and federal, and how those agencies must resolve difficult issues when one agency proposes to take action impacting the interests of others. The issues raised here relate to plans proposed by the United States Army Corps of Engineers ("the Corps") for the dredging of the Bay's eleven navigational channels during and after 2017. Federal laws require review of such plans by two California state agencies: the San Francisco Bay Conservation and Development Commission ("the Commission"), as the proposed dredging would affect the coastal environment, and the San Francisco Regional Water Control Board ("the Water Board" or "the Board"), as the proposed plan would affect water quality. The claims before **[—5—]** us are the result of disagreements about where to deposit dredged material, how often to dredge certain channels, and what equipment to use to dredge those channels.

When, in 2015, the Corps submitted its dredging plans for 2017 and subsequent **{-842-}** years to the Commission and Board for approval, those state agencies attempted to receive assurances from the Corps with respect to two aspects of the proposed dredging. First, the Commission sought a commitment from the Corps regarding what to do with the dredged material. It was particularly concerned with how much of the dredged material would be deposited back into the Bay and how much would be committed to beneficial reuse projects such as wetland restoration. Second, in order to protect imperiled native fish, both the Commission and the Board sought to limit the Corps' use of a certain dredging method—hydraulic dredging—in two specific Bay channels. The Corps ended up giving different answers to these two conditions when it made its final decision in early 2017. It refused to comply with the first condition about where to dispose of dredged material. It purported to comply with the second condition by proposing to hydraulically dredge only one of the two channels in question each year and to leave the other undredged until the next year.

By the time the Corps made its final decision, the Commission had filed this action in federal district court pursuant to the Administrative Procedure Act (APA). The Commission contended that the Corps' refusal to comply with the two conditions violated the Coastal Zone Management Act (CZMA) because it violated policies adopted pursuant to that statute and was arbitrary and capricious. San Francisco Baykeeper, an environmental nonprofit organization, intervened, contending the Corps' decision also violated the **[—6—]** Clean Water Act (CWA). The district court granted summary judgment to the Corps, holding it had not violated any applicable provision of law. The Commission and Baykeeper ("Plaintiffs") appeal. The legal issues before us relate only to the Corps' 2017 final decision, not to the subsequent operations conducted pursuant to it.

We affirm the district court. The condition about where to dispose of dredged material was not itself an enforceable policy under the CZMA and its implementing regulations, nor was it tied to any enforceable policy as contemplated by those regulations. *See* 15 C.F.R. §§ 930.4(a)(1), 930.11(h). The Corps was therefore not obligated to comply with that condition. As for the state agencies' condition limiting the Corps' hydraulic dredging in two particular channels, the Corps' final 2017 plan complied with the express terms of that condition. The Corps' plan therefore did not violate the CZMA or the CWA. Nor was the Corps's decision arbitrary or capricious or in violation of any material reporting requirements.

BACKGROUND

A. DREDGING OVERVIEW

Because sediment accumulates in channels over time, dredging—removing sediment from channel beds, often for transport and disposal elsewhere—is required to keep channels navigable. One aspect of this case involves where dredgers may deposit dredged sedimentary material. There are three alternatives: (1) in-Bay disposal sites, which are the cheapest to use but environmentally disfavored; (2) beneficial reuse sites, which are environmentally favored but the most expensive; or (3) ocean disposal sites. The Commission **[—7—]** wanted the Corps to commit to depositing at least 40% of its dredged material at beneficial reuse sites, and no more than 20% at in-Bay sites ("the 20/40 Disposal Condition").

The second aspect of this case deals with the differences between two methods of dredging: hydraulic (or "hopper") dredging and mechanical (or "clamshell") dredging. Hydraulic dredging works by using a suction **{-843-}** to remove material from the channel floor, while mechanical dredging scoops such material in order to remove it. The state agencies sought to limit use of hydraulic dredging in the Richmond Outer Harbor ("Richmond channel") and the Pinole Shoal Channel ("Pinole channel") out of concern for the delta and longfin smelt, two imperiled native fish species. Hydraulic dredging is less expensive than the alternative method of mechanical dredging, but more likely to kill imperiled fish. Both state agencies thus sought to limit the Corps' use of hydraulic dredging in these two channels to one channel per year. The Corps decided to comply with this condition, but in an unexpected manner: by hydraulically dredging only one of the two channels each year in alternating fashion—and, rather than mechanically dredging the other channel, simply leaving it entirely undredged that year. Plaintiffs claim that the Corps' decision violated federal law.

We therefore turn to the two major federal statutes involved, the Coastal Zone Management Act and the Clean Water Act. Our review must include the policies and procedures for federal-state cooperation that these statutes and related regulations prescribe. **[—8—]**

B. APPLICABLE STATUTES AND PROCEDURES

1. The Coastal Zone Management Act (CZMA) and the San Francisco Bay Plan

The Coastal Zone Management Act was enacted in 1972 "to preserve, protect, develop, and where possible, to restore or enhance, the resources of the Nation's coastal zone." 16 U.S.C. § 1452(1). The coastal zone includes both the coastal waters and the adjacent shorelands. 16 U.S.C. § 1453(1). The CZMA, invoking cooperative federalism, encourages states to develop management programs for their coastal zones. 16 U.S.C. § 1451(i). Once approved by the National Ocean and Atmospheric Administration (NOAA), each such state-submitted coastal zone management program becomes the governing federal standard for federal agency activity involving that coastal zone. 16 U.S.C. §§ 1455, 1456(c)(1)(A); 15 C.F.R. § 930.11(h).

California has a federally approved management program for the San Francisco Bay Area. One of the central components of this management program is a comprehensive coastal conservation and development plan known as the San Francisco Bay Plan ("Bay Plan"), San Francisco Bay Conservation & Dev. Comm'n (May 2020), https://bcdc.ca.gov/pdf/bayplan/bayplan.pdf. The creation of the Bay Plan preceded the CZMA because the California Legislature acted before Congress did. *See Acme Fill Corp. v. S.F. Bay Conservation & Dev. Comm'n*, 232 Cal. Rptr. 348, 353 (Ct. App. 1986). The 1965

McAteer–Petris Act, Cal. Gov. Code § 66600 *et seq.*, created the Commission in 1965, and the Commission completed and adopted the Bay Plan over the following three years. *Acme Fill*, 232 Cal. Rptr. at 353. Thus, by the time Congress enacted the CZMA in **[—9—]** 1972, California already had a statutory scheme and comprehensive coastal management program in place. *Id.* In 1977, NOAA formally approved the management program for the San Francisco Bay Area, and the Commission and its Bay Plan were accordingly wholly incorporated into the CZMA's federal scheme. *Id.* at 350; *see* Bay Plan, at 9.

The Bay Plan contains dozens of findings and policies on dredging and other topics, so it is no surprise that the Commission has periodically amended the Bay Plan since its adoption a half-century ago. *See id.*, Letter (before Table of Contents). **{–844–}** The CZMA allows states to amend their coastal zone management programs, but, importantly, it mandates that any amendment must be approved by NOAA in order to render it legally enforceable against the federal government. 16 U.S.C. § 1455(e); 15 C.F.R. § 930.11(h); *see* Coastal Zone Management Act Program Changes, National Oceanic and Atmospheric Organization (May 21, 2021), https://coast.noaa.gov/czmprogramchange/#/public/home (click "Learn About Program Changes") ("State programs are not static—laws and issues change. Changes to programs, including new or revised enforceable policies, must be submitted to NOAA for approval through the program change process."). Such federal approval of plan amendments has been required since the CZMA's inception in 1972. Pub. L. No. 92-583 § 306(g), 86 Stat. 1280, 1285 (1972); 16 U.S.C. § 1455(e).

Disposal of dredged material in the San Francisco Bay Area, in particular, has been shaped by extensive federal-state cooperative efforts. Between 1990 and 1999, numerous federal and state agencies—the Corps, the Environmental Protection Agency (EPA), the Commission, the regional Water Board, and the State Water Resources Control **[—10—]** Board—developed a Long-Term Management Strategy (LTMS) meant to guide the agencies' decisions about placement of dredged material in the Bay Area over the next 50 years. *See* LTMS Volume 1, Executive Summary, at 1-1 to 1-2 (Aug. 1998), https://www.spn.usace.army.mil/Portals/68/docs/Dredging/LMTS/1998/1-%20execsummary .pdf. The LTMS endorsed a "long-term approach" of "low in-Bay disposal (approximately 20 percent), medium ocean disposal (approximately 40 percent), and medium upland/wetland reuse (approximately 40 percent)" while acknowledging that these goals "cannot be achieved immediately." *See id.* at 1-1, 1-11, 1-16. These long-term numerical targets from the LTMS line up with the figures from the disposal condition that the Commission communicated to the Corps in 2015.

The LTMS itself has never undergone NOAA approval, however, and is therefore unenforceable under the CZMA. *See* 16 U.S.C. § 1455. The LTMS did inform several NOAA-approved amendments to the Bay Plan in 2001, as outlined in the Final LTMS Management Plan, at ES-1, 10-1 (July 2001), https://www.spn.usace.army.mil/Portals/68/docs/Dredging/ LMTS/entire%20LMTF.pdf. Plaintiffs' argument relies on three of the Bay Plan's dredging policies, all adopted as part of the 2001 amendments. *See id.* at 10-1 to 1-10. These three policies envision reducing the disposal of dredged material back into the Bay and increasing reuse of such material for environmentally friendly purposes:

> *Bay Plan Dredging Policy 1:*
> Dredging and dredged material disposal should be conducted in an environmentally and economically sound manner. Dredgers should reduce disposal in the Bay and certain **[—11—]** waterways over time to achieve the LTMS goal of limiting in-Bay disposal volumes to a maximum of one million cubic yards per year [1.0 mcy/yr]. The LTMS agencies should implement a system of disposal allotments to individual dredgers to achieve this goal only if voluntary efforts are not effective in reaching the LTMS goal . . . . **{–845–}**

Bay Plan Dredging Policy 3:
Dredged materials should, if feasible, be reused or disposed outside the Bay and certain waterways. Except when reused in an approved fill project, dredged material should not be disposed in the Bay and certain waterways unless disposal outside these areas is infeasible . . . .

Bay Plan Dredging Policy 5:
[D]redging projects should maximize use of dredged material as a resource consistent with protecting and enhancing Bay natural resources, such as creating, enhancing, or restoring tidal and managed wetlands . . . .

Id. at 10-5 to 10-6; Bay Plan, at 54.

Plaintiffs rely on these Bay Plan Policies because, while the LTMS itself is not itself enforceable, the Bay Plan is. Plaintiffs argue that these Policies empowered the Commission to, at its discretion, instruct the Corps to abide by the LTMS' 20% and 40% figures. According to the Plaintiffs, such a condition was necessary in order to ensure **[—12—]** that the Corps' actions would be consistent with the Bay Plan Policies. *See* 15 C.F.R. §§ 930.4(a)(1), 930.11(h).

Consistency between federal actions and a state's enforceable policies is a major theme of the CZMA. In order to achieve this consistency, the CZMA and its regulations spell out step-by-step procedures for coordination and cooperation between state and federal agencies. *See* 16 U.S.C. § 1456; 15 C.F.R. Part 930.

Any federal agency that seeks to carry out activity "affect[ing] any land or water use or natural resource of the coastal zone" must first submit a planning document known as a consistency determination ("CD") to the state agency. 16 U.S.C. § 1456(c)(1). The CD must explain the federal plans and how they are, "consistent to the maximum extent practicable with the enforceable policies of approved State management programs." *Id.* § 1456(c)(1)(A), (c)(2). NOAA regulations further clarify that this standard requires federal actions to be "fully consistent with the enforceable policies of management programs[,] unless full consistency is prohibited by existing law applicable to the Federal agency." 15 C.F.R. § 930.32(a)(1).

The state agency then responds to the CD. The state may concur, conditionally concur, or object to the CD. *Id.* §§ 930.4, 930.6, 930.43. A conditional concurrence is a communication from the state telling the federal agency that it must meet certain conditions in order to be deemed consistent with the state's policies. *Id.* § 930.4. If the state conditionally concurs in the CD, the state must "identif[y] . . . specific enforceable policies of the management program" and explain why its conditions are "necessary to ensure consistency with [those] specific enforceable policies." *Id.* **[—13—]** § 930.4(a)(1). If the federal agency rejects the conditions in the state's conditional concurrence, the concurrence effectively becomes an objection. *Id.* § 930.4(b).

The federal agency may not proceed with a proposed action over the state's objection unless the agency concludes that the action is "fully consistent with the enforceable policies of the management programs" or that "full consistency is prohibited by existing law applicable to the Federal agency." *Id.* §§ 930.32, 930.43(d)(1)–(2). A federal agency may generally not evade an "enforceable policy of a management program" solely on the basis of cost. *Id.* § 930.32(a)(3).

The CZMA issues in this litigation concern chiefly whether the 20/40 Disposal Condition is anchored in an "enforceable policy" that the Corps may not evade on the basis of cost.

2. The Clean Water Act (CWA)

Like the CZMA, the Clean Water Act requires state approval before proceeding with certain environmentally consequential actions. More specifically, any activity that "may result in any discharge into the navigable waters" requires a federal permit issued by the Corps. 33 U.S.C. §§ 1311(a), 1341(a)(1). The Corps, in turn, may not issue such a permit without obtaining a **{-846-}** water quality certification (WQC) from the appropriate state agency—in this case, the Water Board—unless the state agency waives the certification requirement. *Id.* § 1341(a)(1). Where, as here, it is the Corps' activity that will result in discharge, the Corps does not process and issue permits to itself. 33 C.F.R. § 336.1(a)(1). The Corps must nonetheless obtain a WQC **[—14—]** from the Water Board in order to perform dredging—or, more precisely, in order to discharge dredged material into the navigable waters. *See* 33 U.S.C. §§ 1323(a), 1344(t), 1362(6).

The WQC represents the state agency's conclusion that the proposed activity will comply with the applicable state water quality standards. *See id.* § 1341. State agencies enjoy substantial latitude in this certification process: in addition to limitations on chemical discharges and other restrictions contemplated by the CWA, an issuing state agency may set forth in a WQC "any other appropriate requirement of State law." *Id.* § 1341(d); *see PUD No. 1 of Jefferson Cnty. v. Washington Dep't of Ecology*, 511 U.S. 700, 713 (1994) (interpreting "appropriate" to encompass, "at a minimum," certain limitations related to state water quality standards). Once a requirement is included in the WQC, it becomes a binding condition that is incorporated into any relevant federal permit. 33 U.S.C. § 1341(d). Generally, federal agencies may not reject or alter the conditions imposed by state agencies' WQCs. *See, e.g.*, *Snoqualmie Indian Tribe v. FERC*, 545 F.3d 1207, 1218 (9th Cir. 2008).

C. THE CORPS' 2017 DREDGING PROPOSAL AND RESPONSES

The events giving rise to this case began when the Corps submitted its dredging proposals for 2017 and later years to the Commission and Water Board pursuant to 16 U.S.C. § 1456(c)(2) and 33 U.S.C. § 1323. Both state agencies approved the proposals subject to certain conditions. The issues before us concern the Corps' obligations to comply with those conditions. **[—15—]**

1. The Commission's Letter of Agreement ("LOA")

In March 2015, the Corps submitted its dredging proposal to the Commission for approval in the form of a consistency determination ("CD"), as required by the CZMA. 16 U.S.C. § 1456(c). The CD proposed dumping up to 48 percent of the Corps' dredged material back into the Bay, and it did not propose reducing hydraulic dredging in the Bay.

In June 2015, the Commission responded to the Corps with a proposed LOA conditionally concurring in the Corps' CD. The Commission's LOA stated the conditions under which it would approve the Corps' dredging proposal. The two conditions relevant here concerned reducing the volume of material deposited in the Bay and limiting the use of hydraulic dredging equipment:

> *Special Condition II.B ("the 20/40 Disposal Condition"):*
> The Corps would, in 2017, "reduce [its] in-Bay disposal volume to meet the LTMS goals of a maximum of twenty percent in-Bay disposal and a minimum of forty percent beneficial reuse."
>
> *Special Condition II.J.2.a ("the Hydraulic Dredge Condition"):*
> The Corps would, in fiscal year 2017, "use a maximum of one hydraulic hopper dredge in either [the] Richmond . . . or Pinole . . . channels."

The proposed LOA also directed the Corps to obtain funding to accomplish these changes, citing to the Corps' **[—16—]** own regulations. *See* 15 C.F.R. § 930.32. A representative **{-847-}** of the Corps signed the LOA on June 23, 2015.

2. The Water Board's Water Quality Certification ("WQC") and Provision 10

During the same period that the Corps was negotiating with the Commission, the Corps was pursuing a parallel approval process with the Water Board for the Corps' proposed dredging plans through 2024. In February 2015, the Corps wrote a letter to the Water Board requesting a WQC for its dredging proposal. The Board issued a conditional WQC to the Corps in May 2015. The WQC contained several conditions, only one of which is relevant here.

Provision 10 of the WQC called for hydraulic dredging to be used in, at most, one of the Richmond and Pinole channels in any given year. Provision 10 was therefore in substance the same as the Commission's Hydraulic Dredge Condition (Special Condition II.J.2.a). The relevant language in Provision 10 provided that, beginning in fiscal year 2017, the Corps was to either (1) "[l]imit hopper [hydraulic] dredge use to a maximum of one in-Bay federal channel, either the Richmond [channel] or the Pinole [channel]" or (2) avoid hopper dredge use in any in-Bay channels.

As a matter of historical practice, whether hydraulically or mechanically, the Corps had typically dredged both channels every year. All parties were aware of this. The language of Provision 10, however, did not refer to this historical practice, nor did it expressly call for annual dredging of each channel. It called only for limiting hydraulic dredging to one of the two channels per year. **[—17—]**

3. The Corps' Rejection of the Agencies' Conditions

In November 2015, the Corps wrote a letter to the Commission rescinding its earlier acceptance of the LOA and the conditions set forth in it. Citing funding limitations and the need to maintain flexibility in planning, the Corps' letter took issue with both the LOA conditions—i.e., the 20/40 Disposal Condition and the Hydraulic Dredge Condition. The Corps' principal reason was cost. The letter cited the relevant federal standard making cost an important criterion. *See* 33 C.F.R. §§ 335.7, 336.1. The letter stated that the LOA conditions "exceed[ed] the constraints established by the federal standard, defined as the 'least costly, environmentally acceptable factor, consistent with engineering requirements . . .'" and concluded that the Corps "lack[ed] the necessary authority to comply with" those conditions. *See* 33 C.F.R. § 336.1(c)(1).

The Corps sent a similar letter to the Water Board the same day formally disavowing Provision 10 of the WQC. The letter went further and stated that the Corps would not perform any dredging of the Richmond or Pinole channels unless the Board removed Provision 10 from the WQC.

4. The Corps' Final Decision ("Course of Action #2")

The record developed in this case reflects that, after further discussion with the Commission and the Board, the Corps was considering four potential courses of action ("COAs"):

- COA #1: status quo dredging and placement (annually dredging both the Richmond and Pinole channels, either hydraulically or mechanically, and **[—18—]** disposing of dredged material at sites previously deemed acceptable);
- COA #2: dredge in accordance with the WQC, but not the LOA (reducing hydraulic dredging by dredging only **{-848-}** one of the Richmond and Pinole channels each year in alternating fashion, and making no commitments with respect to in-Bay disposal or beneficial reuse);
- COA #3: dredge in accordance with the LOA and the WQC (reducing hydraulic dredging and describing a number of alternatives for doing so, and committing to decreasing in-Bay disposal and increasing beneficial reuse); or
- COA #4: defer all maintenance dredging of San Francisco Bay Channels.

Internal Corps memos recommended COA #2, which, according to the Corps' analysis, would have only a minimal impact on navigation safety. By comparison, the Corps' analysis indicated that full compliance with the LOA and WQC dredging and disposal requirements—i.e., COA #3—would, given funding constraints, result in "less than half of the typical annual maintenance [being] accomplished in any year" and a corresponding increase in navigational risk.

The Corps decided to adopt COA #2 in January 2017. The Corps publicly announced a month later that it would not dredge the Richmond channel in 2017.

As relevant here, this decision was a final action with two consequences. It made clear that the Corps would leave one **[—19—]** of the Richmond and Pinole channels undredged each year, and it made no commitment with respect to disposal of dredged material. It thereby rejected the Commission's 20/40 Disposal Condition.

D. DISTRICT COURT PROCEEDINGS

The Commission originally filed this suit in district court in September 2016, seeking a declaration that the Corps was required to conduct dredging as outlined in the Commission's LOA, and related relief. After the Corps adopted COA #2 several months into the litigation, San Francisco Baykeeper, a regional non-profit environmental organization, intervened as an additional plaintiff in the litigation. Plaintiffs jointly filed an amended complaint in June 2017 challenging both the Corps' rejection of the Commission's conditions and its adoption of COA #2. The amended complaint took particular issue with the Corps' cost-based rationales for these actions.

The parties filed cross-motions for summary judgment. Plaintiffs' joint motion argued that the Corps' actions violated the CZMA because lack of funding could not excuse the Corps from its obligation to act fully consistently with the conditions of the LOA. According to Plaintiffs, the LOA's conditions were enforceable because they were necessary to ensure the Corps' operations' consistency with enforceable policies of the Bay Area management plan—primarily Bay Plan Dredging Policies 1 and 5. Plaintiffs also contended that the Corps had violated the CWA, violated certain regulatory reporting requirements, and acted arbitrarily and capriciously in violation of the APA. The Corps' opposition and cross-motion argued (1) that the conditions in the Commission's LOA were not themselves, and were not based on, enforceable policies; (2) that the Corps had not violated the **[—20—]** CWA because COA #2 complied with Provision 10 of the WQC; (3) that the Corps had also complied with its reporting regulations; and (4) that all the Corps' actions were reasonable.

The district court granted summary judgment to the Corps. It considered first the contention that the Corps was required to abide by the 20/40 Disposal Condition from the LOA in order to ensure compliance with the Bay Plan Dredging Policies. The district court concluded that the Bay Plan Policies were generalized policy statements **{-849-}** and that the Corps was therefore not legally obligated to accept the 20/40 Disposal Condition in the absence of direct support from any enforceable policy. Next, with respect to Provision 10 of the WQC (and the Commission's equivalent Hydraulic Dredge Condition), the district court found that "COA #2 meets the letter of that requirement, because the Corps is in fact using a hydraulic dredge in only one channel each year." Reasoning that "the Corps' plan does not violate the maximum limits on dredging imposed by the state agencies" and that Plaintiffs had not shown "a basis to force the Corps to do more dredging than it has agreed to carry out," the district court concluded that Plaintiffs "cannot prevail." The district court entered judgment in favor of the Corps.

Plaintiffs timely appeal. Plaintiffs argue that the Corps' adoption of COA #2 violated the CZMA because the Commission's conditions are linked to federally enforceable policies; that the Corps violated the CWA by failing to comply with Provision 10; and that the Corps' action was arbitrary and capricious in violation of the APA, as well as in violation of the Corps' own procedural regulations. **[—21—]**

DISCUSSION

A. Plaintiffs' claim that the Corps must comply with the Commission's 20/40 Disposal Condition fails because the condition is not supported by any enforceable policy.

Plaintiffs contend that the Corps was required to comply with the conditions in the Commission's LOA, including the 20/40 Disposal Condition. That condition required the Corps to meet specific targets: to "reduce [its] in-Bay disposal volume to meet the LTMS goals of a maximum of twenty percent in-Bay disposal and a minimum of forty percent beneficial reuse." Plaintiffs' central argument is that the Corps' refusal to comply was based solely on cost and therefore unlawful. They correctly identify federal regulations that prohibit federal agencies from citing a general lack of funds in order to avoid compliance with an enforceable policy of an approved coastal zone management program. 15 C.F.R. § 930.32(a)(3) ("Federal agencies shall not use a general claim of a lack of funding or insufficient appropriated funds . . . as a basis for being consistent to the maximum extent practicable with an enforceable policy of a management program.").

The problem for Plaintiffs is that the statute and implementing regulations require compliance only with the "enforceable policies" of approved management programs. *See, e.g.*, 16 U.S.C. §§ 1455, 1456(c)(1)(A); 15 C.F.R. §§ 930.32(a)(3), 930.39. Governing regulations specify that this federal approval must come from NOAA. 15 C.F.R. § 930.11(h), (l). The specific numerical targets in the 20/40 Disposal Condition—no more than 20% of the Corps' dredged material disposed of in the Bay, and no less than **[—22—]** 40% of it committed to beneficial reuse—are not drawn from any provision of a NOAA-approved program. Nor does any provision resembling or contemplating the terms of the 20/40 Disposal Condition appear in any NOAA-approved program. The Corps was therefore not required to comply with the condition.

The 20% and 40% figures instead derive from the LTMS, which, as Plaintiffs acknowledge, has never received NOAA approval. Plaintiffs' argument is that the 20/40 Disposal Condition can be traced back to and made enforceable by three dredging policies found in the NOAA-approved Bay Plan. The Bay Plan does have the requisite federal approval as part of the NOAA-approved management program for the San Francisco Bay Area. NOAA first approved the Bay Plan in **{-850-}** 1977, and it has approved subsequent amendments to the Bay Plan. *See Acme Fill*, 232 Cal. Rptr. at 350; Bay Plan, at 9. The Bay Plan's provisions are therefore enforceable.

Plaintiffs specifically maintain that the 20/40 Disposal Condition is based on Policies 1, 3, and 5 of the Bay Plan. These express the overall goals of the LTMS as they relate to dredged material. Policy 1 describes achieving, "over time," "the LTMS goal" of 1.0 mcy/yr or less of dredged material deposited back into the Bay. Policy 3 provides that dredged material "should, if feasible, be reused or disposed outside the Bay." Policy 5 calls for maximizing reuse of dredged material. Bay Plan, at 54.

These policies speak in fairly general terms and do not contain any ratio- or percentage-based targets. Plaintiffs point out that policies need not be so specific in order to be enforceable. It is true that CZMA regulations provide that, to be enforceable, a policy "need not establish detailed criteria **[—23—]** such that a proponent of an activity could determine the consistency of an activity without interaction with the State agency." 15 C.F.R. § 930.11(h). Policies must, however, provide some meaningful guidance as to what is and is not permissible; accordingly, the previous sentence in the regulation requires policies to "contain standards of sufficient specificity to guide public and private uses" in order to be enforceable. *Id.* Bay Plan Dredging Policies 1, 3, and 5 do provide general policy guidance for dredgers to deposit dredged material outside of the Bay and maximize reuse where possible. But they do not appear to contemplate requiring any specific ratios or allocations among different sites for the disposal of dredged materials, much less imposing such requirements on an individual basis; yet that is what the Commission attempted to impose here.

The language of Policy 1 in fact disfavors any mandatory limitations on deposits in the Bay. The policy explicitly endorses only "voluntary efforts" to reduce in-Bay disposal until and unless such efforts fail. Bay Plan, at 54. Plaintiffs acknowledge that voluntary compliance efforts have not yet failed. Policy 1 therefore does not support the imposition of a mandatory in-Bay deposit limitation on the Corps. Similarly, Policy 1's source, the Final LTMS Management Plan, describes a two-phase plan for managing in-Bay disposal, with numerous steps the Commission and the Board must satisfy before transitioning from voluntary compliance efforts (Phase I) to binding allotments imposed on individual dredgers (Phase II). *See* Final LTMS Management Plan, at 6-1 to 6-7.

Plaintiffs have not shown any textual or practical connection between the 20/40 Disposal Condition and the Bay Plan Policies that they rely upon. The only numerical **[—24—]** reference in any of those Policies is Policy 1's target of 1.0 mcy/yr for in-Bay disposal. Bay Plan, at 54. But the policy describes that figure as a goal to be achieved "over time" and as an aggregate limit, not one subject to enforcement against individual dredging entities like the Corps. *Id.*

We therefore must conclude that the 20/40 Disposal Condition is unenforceable. It is not "necessary to ensure consistency with" enforceable policies pursuant to 15 C.F.R. § 930.4(a)(1). Nor is the 20/40 Disposal Condition "based on enforceable policies" as permitted under 15 C.F.R. § 930.11(h). The Corps was not required to comply with the condition.

B. Plaintiffs' Clean Water Act (CWA) claim fails because the Corps' plan complied with Provision 10 of the Water Quality Certification (WQC).

The key condition that the Water Board's WQC imposed on the Corps was **{-851-}** labeled Provision 10. Like the Commission's Hydraulic Dredge Condition, Provision 10 of the WQC placed a limit on the amount of hydraulic dredging the Corps could do in the Richmond and Pinole channels. Specifically, Provision 10 provided that the Corps would either (1) "[l]imit hopper [hydraulic] dredge use to a maximum of one in-Bay federal channel, either the Richmond [channel] or the Pinole [channel]" or (2) avoid hopper dredge use in any in-Bay channels. This limitation on hydraulic dredging, as opposed to mechanical or other types of dredging, was intended to protect imperiled native fish species. **[—25—]**

The Corps does not dispute that the CWA required it to comply with the conditions specified in the Board's WQC, including Provision 10. *See* 33 U.S.C. § 1341. The Corps instead argues that the course of action it eventually adopted, COA #2, complied with the plain language of Provision 10 and therefore with the CWA. Under COA #2, the Corps proposed to dredge only one of the Richmond and Pinole channels each year in alternating fashion, thereby leaving the other channel undredged until next year. Based on past practice and their representations before the court, this is not at all what the Commission and Board intended. They wanted the Corps to switch from hydraulic dredging to mechanical dredging in order to protect imperiled fish, not reduce the frequency of the Corps' dredging.

Plaintiffs therefore argue Provision 10 required the Corps to transition from hydraulic dredging to mechanical dredging in at least one of the Richmond and Pinole channels, while still dredging both channels annually in accordance with past practice. They contend COA #2 represented an unlawful refusal to fully implement Provision 10. Provision 10, however, only directs the Corps to limit its use of hydraulic dredging. COA #2 does exactly that. In the district court's words, "COA #2 meets the letter of that requirement, because the Corps is in fact using a hydraulic dredge in only one channel each year."

Plaintiffs point to past practice. They emphasize that, in past years, the Corps had typically dredged both channels every year, whether hydraulically or mechanically.

Plaintiffs also point out that all parties were initially operating with the understanding that both channels were to be dredged annually, and that hydraulic dredging traps and kills more fish than mechanical dredging does, since it requires removing **[—26—]** much more water from the channel. The Corps does not dispute this history.

Given the cooperative federal-state process dictated by the CWA, however, the issue before this court is whether the Corps' plan complied with the condition that the Water Board imposed: Provision 10. The requirements set forth in a WQC are what is legally enforceable under the CWA. *See* 33 U.S.C. § 1341(d) ("[An] [a]ppropriate requirement of State law set forth in [a water quality] certification . . . shall become a condition on any Federal license or permit subject to the provisions of this section."). Under the CWA, the "appropriate requirement[s] of State law" that federal agencies must follow result from a cooperative approval process involving federal agencies like the Corps and state agencies like the Board. *Id.* The requirement that resulted from this process, Provision 10, did not mandate any dredging beyond the limited hydraulic dredging proposed in COA #2.

Plaintiffs argue that the Corps' adoption of COA #2 is nonetheless unlawful because it reflected an improper plea of insufficient funding to evade the Commission's conditions. *See* 15 C.F.R. § 930.32(a)(3). Plaintiffs cite to **{-852-}** *Ohio v. U.S. Army Corps of Engineers*, 259 F. Supp.3d 732 (N.D. Ohio 2017), where the Corps refused to accommodate the state's WQC condition and would not dredge the channel in question unless it received non-federal funds for that purpose. *Id.* at 742–43. Its refusal on the basis of cost was held to be unlawful. *Id.* at 754. The difference is that, here, the Corps did not refuse to comply with the WQC condition. It complied with Provision 10's specific terms. The decision in *Ohio* is therefore inapposite. **[—27—]**

C. The Corps' adoption of COA #2 was not arbitrary or capricious or in violation of any material reporting requirements.

Plaintiffs contend that the Corps' decision was arbitrary and capricious in violation of the APA both because COA #2 is a generally unreasonable means of complying with Provision 10 and because the Corps did not adequately explain and justify its decision to depart from past dredging practices. *See* 5 U.S.C. § 706(2)(A); *FCC v. Fox Television Stations, Inc.*, 556 U.S. 502, 514–15 (2009).

These arguments ignore that the Corps engaged in a lengthy cooperative process of negotiations, one embedded in the CZMA and the CWA. COA #2 did not appear out of the blue. Rather, it was one of several alternatives the Corps considered in response to discussions with the state agencies about conditions that had, in turn, been crafted in response to the Corps' initial dredging plans. It is hard to see how the adoption of COA #2 could be arbitrary and capricious when, as we have seen, it complied with the relevant enforceable policies and with Provision 10. The Corps' course of action was thus not irrational. The Corps' deliberations reflect the agency's understanding that COA #2 represented a change relative to its historical practice. *See FCC v. Fox*, 556 U.S. at 515–16.

Plaintiffs also suggest that the Corps' 2017 adoption of COA #2 has turned out to be problematic because the Corps had to dredge the Pinole channel on an emergency basis in 2020. Such subsequent developments are not relevant to the issues before us, which relate to the validity of the Corps' decision to adopt COA #2 in 2017. *See Lands Council v. Powell*, 395 F.3d 1019, 1029–30 (9th Cir. 2005) (quoting *Sw.* **[—28—]** *Ctr. for Biological Diversity v. U.S. Forest Serv.*, 100 F.3d 1443, 1450 (9th Cir.1996)) ("[R]eview of an agency decision typically focuses on the administrative record in existence at the time of the decision . . . ."). We have earlier denied Plaintiffs' request that we take judicial notice of subsequent events. We express no opinion as to whether the 2020 dredging may be relevant in other, later proceedings related to how the Corps conducted its dredging operations or on the effects of those operations.

Finally, Plaintiffs contend that the Corps failed to comply with various procedural regulations contained in 33 C.F.R. Part 337 and dealing for the most part with internal reporting requirements. For example, Plaintiffs argue that the Corps was required by 33 C.F.R. § 337.8(a)(3)–(4) to report to higher echelons on certain funding considerations but did not do so. Even assuming without deciding that the Corps failed to follow these regulations, Plaintiffs have not explained what relief would be warranted by such violations or how such violations might affect the validity of COA #2. Nor have they cited any authority—statutory, regulatory, or judicial— for setting aside an agency decision on such a basis.

We understand Plaintiffs' concerns that the Corps' chosen course of action represents a departure from understandings the parties had in the past and may lead to problems in the future. Nevertheless, we **{-853-}** must agree with the district court that the adoption of COA #2 did not violate any applicable law.

CONCLUSION

The judgment of the district court is **AFFIRMED**.

United States Court of Appeals
for the Ninth Circuit

No. 20-70147

MARTIN
VS.
SUNDIAL MARINE TUG & BARGE WORKS, INC.

On Petition for Review of an Order of the Benefits Review Board

Decided: September 2, 2021

Citation: 12 F.4th 915, 9 Adm. R. 363 (9th Cir. 2021).

Before **WARDLAW** and **HURWITZ,** Circuit Judges, and **BOLTON,*** District Judge.

* The Honorable Susan R. Bolton, United States District Judge for the District of Arizona, sitting by designation.

[—4—] {-917-} **HURWITZ,** Circuit Judge:

Rick Martin applied for disability and medical benefits under the Longshore and Harbor Workers' Compensation Act (the "Act"), 33 U.S.C. §§ 901–950, after injuring both knees while working for Sundial Marine Tug & Barge Works, Inc. After extended agency proceedings, the Benefits Review Board ("BRB") affirmed a decision of an administrative law judge ("ALJ") awarding Martin benefits and relying on § 910(a) to calculate Martin's average weekly wage. This petition for review from Martin followed. We have jurisdiction under **{-918-}** 33 U.S.C. § 921(c) and we hold that the ALJ did not err in applying § 910(a) to calculate Martin's average weekly wage at the time of injury.[1]

I

"We review BRB decisions for errors of law and for adherence to the statutory standard governing the Board's review of the administrative law judge's factual determinations." *Todd Shipyards Corp. v. Black*, 717 F.2d 1280, 1284 (9th Cir. 1983) (cleaned up). "The BRB must accept the ALJ's findings unless they are contrary to the law, irrational, or unsupported by substantial evidence." *Id.* **[—5—]**

II

A

Under the Act, a benefits award is based on the claimant's "average weekly wage." 33 U.S.C. § 910. The statute sets forth three different formulas for determining the average weekly wage:

> Except as otherwise provided in this chapter, the average weekly wage of the injured employee at the time of the injury shall be taken as the basis upon which to compute compensation and shall be determined as follows:
>
> **(a)** If the injured employee shall have worked in the employment in which he was working at the time of the injury, whether for the same or another employer, during substantially the whole of the year immediately preceding his injury, his average annual earnings shall consist of three hundred times the average daily wage or salary for a six-day worker and two hundred and sixty times the average daily wage or salary for a five-day worker, which he shall have earned in such employment during the days when so employed.
>
> **(b)** If the injured employee shall not have worked in such employment during substantially the whole of such year, his average annual earnings, if a six-day worker, shall consist of three hundred **[—6—]** times the average daily wage or salary, and, if a five-day worker, two hundred and sixty times the average daily wage or salary, which an employee of the same class working substantially the whole of such immediately preceding year in the same or in similar employment in the same or

[1] In a separate memorandum disposition filed contemporaneously with this opinion, we address Martin's challenge to the BRB decision insofar as it denies reimbursement of certain medical expenses.

> a neighboring place shall have earned in such employment during the days when so employed.
>
> **(c)** If either of the foregoing methods of arriving at the average annual earnings of the injured employee cannot reasonably and fairly be applied, such average annual earnings shall be such sum as, having regard to the previous earnings of the injured employee in the employment in which he was working at the time of the injury, and of other employees of the same or most similar class working in the same or most similar employment in the same or neighboring locality, or other employment of such employee, including the reasonable value of the services of the employee if engaged in self-employment, shall reasonably represent the annual **{–919–}** earning capacity of the injured employee.

Id.

At issue is whether Martin's average weekly wage should have been calculated under § 910(a) or § 910(c); the parties agree that § 910(b) does not apply. The ALJ and the BRB applied § 910(a), under which the **[—7—]**

> average weekly wage is calculated by: 1) dividing the total earnings of the claimant during the fifty-two weeks preceding the injury by the number of days actually worked; 2) multiplying that figure by either 260 or 300, depending on whether the claimant worked a five- or six-day week (in this case, five); and 3) dividing that figure by fifty-two.

Matulic v. Dir., Off. of Workers' Comp. Programs, 154 F.3d 1052, 1056 (9th Cir. 1998). In contrast, § 910(c) "does not prescribe a fixed formula." *Id.* Under that subsection, which Martin claims should apply, the ALJ must "consider the employee's ability, willingness and opportunity to work," *Palacios v. Campbell Indus.*, 633 F.2d 840, 843 (9th Cir. 1980) (cleaned up), with regard to "(1) the previous earnings of the injured employee in the job at which the employee was injured, and (2) previous earnings of similar employees, or (3) other employment of the injured employee," *id.* at 842.

B

Sundial made weekend work available on a voluntary basis. Martin testified that he generally worked five days per week but worked overtime on weekends when possible. The parties initially stipulated to the use of § 910(a) before the ALJ. But, in a reply brief filed after the record closed, Martin's counsel sought a wage determination under § 910(c) to account for days worked in excess of 260 after "rechecking the calculations."

The ALJ found that in the 52 weeks before his injury, Martin had earned $47,498.41 and had worked 264 days (including four days of overtime). Notwithstanding Martin's invocation of § 910(c), the ALJ used § 910(a) to **[—8—]** calculate Martin's average weekly wage, citing the stipulation and noting that "[t]here is no requirement that a 5-day worker work exactly 260 days in the preceding year."

On appeal, citing *Stevedoring Services of America v. Price*, 382 F.3d 878 (9th Cir. 2004), the BRB affirmed the ALJ's use of § 910(a) because Martin had worked more than 75 percent of the available working days for a five-day worker, but increased the average weekly wage to correct a calculation error. The BRB also held that the ALJ "properly held claimant to his stipulation that his average weekly wage for his 2004 injuries should be calculated pursuant to Section 10(a), as that stipulation is not contrary to law." The BRB vacated a portion of the ALJ's opinion treating a separate issue and remanded for further consideration of that issue. In a subsequent appeal, Martin renewed his objections to the ALJ's use of § 910(a) to calculate his average weekly wage, and the BRB affirmed the ALJ's calculation as law of the case. This timely petition for review followed.

III

A

Sundial first argues that Martin is bound by his initial stipulation that § 910(a) applies. Because whether § 910(a) or (c) applies is a legal question, *see Matulic,* 154 F.3d at 1057, we decline to find Martin bound by the stipulation. *See Sanford's Est. v. Comm'r of Internal Rev.*, 308 U.S. 39, 51 (1939). The "policies underlying the exhaustion doctrine" are satisfied here; the BRB determined **{-920-}** that the stipulation was "not contrary to law" only after concluding on the merits that § 910(c) did not apply. *See W. Radio Servs., Co. v. Qwest Corp.*, 530 F.3d 1186, 1203 (9th Cir. 2008). **[—9—]**

B

Martin does not dispute that he was a five-day worker. But he contends that using § 910(a) to determine the average weekly wage of a five-day worker who worked 264 days during the relevant year violates the statutory scheme.

As an initial matter, we reject both parties' contentions that our decisions in *Matulic* and *Price* resolve this question. *Matulic,* upon which *Price* relies, held that § 910(a) presumptively applies when a claimant works more than 75 percent of the 260-day measuring year for five-day workers. *Matulic*, 154 F.3d at 1058. But, no prior Ninth Circuit case addresses whether a five-day worker who worked *more* than 260 days should have his average weekly wage calculated under § 910(a). *See, e.g., Matulic*, 154 F.3d at 1056 (claimant worked 82 percent of 260 working days); *Gen. Constr. Co. v. Castro*, 401 F.3d 963, 976 (9th Cir. 2005) (77 percent); *Price*, 382 F.3d at 884 (76 percent).

Nor does *Matulic* resolve the issue now before us in Martin's favor. The holding in *Matulic* that § 910(a) could be reasonably and fairly applied when a claimant "works more than 75% of the workdays of the measuring year," 154 F.3d at 1058, recognized that the Act is to be construed "in favor of the worker" and that "some 'overcompensation' is built into the [the Act's] system institutionally," *id.* at 1057. It thus found that using the statutory presumption in § 910(a) for a five-day worker who had worked more than 75 percent of 260 days in the previous year "well within the realm of theoretical or actual 'overcompensation' that Congress contemplated." *Id.* at 1058. But that does not mean that § 910(a), whose formula employs a multiplier of 260 for five-day workers, does not apply whenever a five-day worker works more than 260 days. Nor does the general statement in *Matulic* that "the statutory formula may benefit **[—10—]** the employer," *id.* at 1057, compel a particular outcome here. The portion of the statute *Matulic* referred to in making that observation was § 906(b)(1), which contains a formula that sets a ceiling for compensation for disability for a high-earnings claimant at twice the applicable fiscal year's national average weekly wage. *See id.* at 1057 n.3. That subsection is not implicated here. The question whether § 910(a) can "reasonably and fairly be applied," *id.* § 910(c), when a five-day worker works more than 260 days is thus one of first impression.

We have stated that the § 910(a) formula "presumptively applies" in calculating a five-day worker's average weekly wage. *Trachsel v. Rogers Terminal & Shipping Corp.*, 597 F.3d 947, 950 (9th Cir. 2010). Being a five-day worker is not the end of the inquiry; we still must analyze whether use of § 910(a) would be unreasonable or unfair under the circumstances of the case before us. *Matulic*, 154 F.3d at 1057; *see also Tri-State Terminals, Inc. v. Jesse*, 596 F.2d 752, 756 (7th Cir. 1979) ("Even if a claimant is engaged in full-time employment, however, [910(a)] will not apply if [it] can not reasonably and fairly be applied.") (cleaned up). There is a "high threshold," however, that must be met to overcome the statutory presumption. *Matulic*, 154 F.3d at 1057.

We find the statutory presumption is not rebutted as a matter of law simply because § 910(a) would slightly underestimate earning capacity because the claimant worked in excess of 260 days. The statute plainly contemplates some inaccuracy in calculating the average weekly wage. *See* **{-921-}** *id.*

(describing congressional intent to create "an efficient," but not "entirely accurate" method of calculating earning capacity). And it does not provide that § 910(a) is inapplicable if more than 260 days were worked. Nor does **[—11—]** the fact that Martin worked 264 days by itself make use of the § 910(a) formula unreasonable or unfair. Martin is incorrect that the § 910(a) formula entirely fails to account for his increased earnings, as the starting point for the § 910(a) calculation is the total amount of compensation earned in the previous year.

The legislative history of the Act suggests that Congress did not envision application of § 910(c) under these circumstances. Prior to 1948, the Act included only a formula employing a 300-day multiplier for six-day workers. *See* S. REP. NO. 80-1315, at 6 (1948), *as reprinted in* 1948 U.S.C.C.A.N. 1979, 1982. In 1948, responding to the rise of five-day work weeks, Congress amended the Act to provide a 260-day multiplier "so that the particular provision can be made useful in the 5-day week employments." *Id.* Tellingly, in enacting this amendment, Congress did not choose simply to discard a presumptive multiplier for full-time employees in favor of the *actual* days worked.

Congress also appears not to have envisioned application of § 910(c) to a claimant who worked full-time for a single employer during the previous year. The Senate Report concerning the 1948 amendments indicates that § 910(c) is intended for use where the "employment itself . . . does not afford a full year of work"; where the work week is shorter than 5 or 6 days; or where there is "seasonal, intermittent, discontinuous, and like employment which affords less than a full workyear or workweek." 1948 U.S.C.C.A.N. at 1982. The report also provides:

> The measurement of an employee's capacity to earn should not be limited to his earnings in the particular employment in which he was engaged when injured, but should be gaged **[—12—]** [sic] by what the employee is capable of earning in all employments in which he was employed during the year prior to injury, otherwise harsh results necessarily follow.

Id. at 1983. None of the situations Congress spoke to are present here. The use of § 910(a) in this case is thus not the kind of "harsh result" Congress sought to avoid in enacting § 910(c). *See* 1 ROBERT FORCE & MARTIN J. NORRIS, THE LAW OF MARITIME PERSONAL INJURIES § 5:7 (5th ed. 2020) ("Although 33 U.S.C.A. § 910(c) provides for unusual situations, it should not be resorted to when the employee has an established earnings record.").

Martin emphasizes that we should "construe broadly [the Act's] provisions so as to favor claimants in the resolution of benefits cases." *Price v. Stevedoring Servs. of Am.*, 697 F.3d 820, 843 (9th Cir. 2012) (en banc). But that does not mean that the claimant always wins. As the Supreme Court has noted, the Act is "not a simple remedial statute intended for the benefit of the workers," but was instead "designed to strike a balance between the concerns of the longshoremen and harborworkers on the one hand, and their employers on the other." *Morrison-Knudsen Constr. Co. v. Dir., Off. of Workers' Comp. Programs*, 461 U.S. 624, 636 (1983). The Court has also stressed that the maxim that "the statute at hand should be liberally construed to achieve its purposes" does not provide courts the freedom to "add features that will achieve the statutory 'purposes' more effectively." **{-922-}** *Dir., Off. of Workers' Comp. Programs v. Newport News Shipbuilding & Dry Dock Co.*, 514 U.S. 122, 135–36 (1995) (cleaned up). Martin asks us to do just that, effectively amend § 910 to add language providing that § 910(a) does not apply "if the claimant worked more than 260 days." **[—13—]**

We are also mindful that the Act was designed to provide for "efficient resolution of a class of private disputes." *Id.* at 131. The presumption that § 910(a)—whose fixed multiplier serves "administrative conven-ience," *Matulic*, 154 F.3d at 1057 (quoting *Duncanson-Harrelson Co. v. Dir., Off. of Workers' Comp. Programs*, 686 F.2d 1336,

1342 (9th Cir. 1982))—applies is a critical statutory element of that program. We therefore hold that the ALJ and BRB did not err in using the § 910(a) formula to calculate Martin's weekly wage.[2]

PETITION FOR REVIEW DENIED.

[2] We do not address whether the use of § 910(a) would be unreasonable if a nominal five-day worker worked substantially more days than 260 or whether such a worker effectively becomes a six-day worker.

This page intentionally left blank

United States Court of Appeals for the Eleventh Circuit

United States Court of Appeals
for the Eleventh Circuit

No. 19-13012

BULAND
VS.
NCL (BAHAMAS) LTD.

Appeals from the United States District Court for the Southern District of Florida

Decided: March 29, 2021

Citation: 992 F.3d 1143, 9 Adm. R. 370 (11th Cir. 2021).

Before **W. PRYOR,** Chief Judge, **J. PRYOR** and **CARNES,** Circuit Judges.

[—1—] {–1146–} W. PRYOR, Chief Judge:

These cross-appeals involve a jury trial about negligent medical treatment of a passenger aboard a cruise ship. The jury awarded the injured passenger more **[—2—]** than $2,000,000 in damages, which the district court remitted to an award of just over $1,700,000. But the passenger argues that the district court erred by excluding testimony about damages for loss of earning capacity from his expert economist and by granting a directed verdict for the cruise line on that issue. And the cruise line argues that the district court erred by refusing to give its requested jury instruction about medical negligence at sea and by denying its motion for a new trial. We reject the arguments for both the passenger and the cruise line and affirm. **{–1147–}**

I. BACKGROUND

Andre Ow Buland is a citizen of Trinidad and Tobago. For over 12 years, he worked as the chief financial officer of several large corporations in Trinidad. He made around $135,000 a year in his last five years in that role. But the job was stressful, so Ow Buland resigned to pursue development projects for a few real properties he owned instead.

Before turning to real-estate development, Ow Buland decided that he first needed a vacation. He and his wife departed for a five-day cruise from Miami to Jamaica and back. They boarded the *Norwegian Pearl*, a cruise ship owned and operated by NCL (Bahamas) Ltd., a Bermuda company doing business as Norwegian Cruise Line. **[—3—]**

Ow Buland woke up early in the morning of the third day of the cruise with stomach pain. He felt weak and had acid reflux pain all day. After he vomited at dinner, he went to the ship infirmary.

The ship's doctors administered a blood test, a chest x-ray, and an electrocardiogram. The medical tests confirmed Ow Buland was having a heart attack, so the doctors admitted him to the ship's intensive care unit. Based upon a remote consultation with the Cleveland Clinic and not knowing if there were facilities to treat an arterial blockage in the closest port city, the ship's doctors concluded it was safest for Ow Buland to stay on the ship for treatment.

The ship carried thrombolytic medications, which are clot-busting medicines used to treat heart-attack patients. But the ship's doctors decided it was too risky to treat Ow Buland with a thrombolytic. He had been experiencing symptoms for too long already, and he had recently undergone medical procedures that created a risk thrombolytics could cause life-threatening internal bleeding.

The ship's medical staff monitored Ow Buland in the intensive care unit until the ship arrived in Miami a day and a half later. An ambulance waiting at the port took him to the hospital. Ow Buland was admitted to Mount Sinai Hospital in Miami Beach, where he underwent a cardiac catheterization and had four stents implanted. He returned home to Trinidad and eventually got a pacemaker. He continues to suffer from medical problems caused by the damage to his heart. **[—4—]**

Ow Buland sued NCL for negligence. He alleged that its medical staff failed to diagnose and properly manage his status and failed to evacuate him from the ship. And he claimed damages including the "loss of [the] capacity to earn money." He invoked both diversity-of-citizenship, 28 U.S.C. § 1332, and admiralty jurisdiction, *id.* § 1333.

Because the parties initially proceeded under the assumption that the district court had diversity jurisdiction, both requested a jury trial. But our intervening decision in *Caron v. NCL (Bahamas), Ltd.* clarified that diversity jurisdiction was unavailable. 910 F.3d 1359, 1365, 6 Adm. R. 471, 473 (11th Cir. 2018) ("[Section] 1332(a)(2) does not grant jurisdiction over a suit between a corporation incorporated solely in a foreign state and another alien . . . ."). Ow Buland's complaint fell only within admiralty jurisdiction, which meant the parties did not have a right to a jury trial. Fed. R. Civ. P. 9(h)(1), 38(e). But the district court granted Ow Buland's unopposed motion to try the case to a jury by the parties' consent. *Id.* R. 39(c)(2).

Ow Buland retained Gary A. Anderson, Ph.D., as a damages expert. Dr. Anderson is an economist, and Ow Buland offered him to testify about the value of Ow Buland's lost earning capacity. Dr. Anderson **{-1148-}** prepared three models to estimate Ow Buland's lost-earning-capacity damages. Each model assumed Ow Buland's pre-injury earning capacity was equal to his salary when he resigned as a chief financial officer. The models varied in their assumptions about Ow Buland's **[—5—]** post-injury earning capacity. One model assumed Ow Buland could obtain a part-time teaching job that would pay $14,570 a year. Another assumed he could sit on corporate boards and earn $14,990 a year. A third model, based on Ow Buland's pursuit of real estate development opportunities, was later withdrawn as unrealistic. Dr. Anderson selected the potential career options for the models based on a discussion with Ow Buland.

NCL moved for partial summary judgment on the availability of damages for loss of earning capacity. It argued that Ow Buland had no competent evidence to establish the magnitude of any diminished capacity because Dr. Anderson was not a vocational expert and his analysis was based only on Ow Buland's subjective opinions about the work he could perform after his heart attack, not his actual post-injury earning capacity. NCL withdrew that motion, but later moved *in limine* to exclude Dr. Anderson's testimony on loss of earning capacity. It argued that the assumptions underlying Dr. Anderson's models were unsupported and that his testimony was unreliable. The district court granted the motion to exclude.

The parties proceeded to a five-day jury trial. At the close of evidence, NCL moved for a directed verdict on the issue of lost earning capacity. The district court agreed that Ow Buland failed to prove the extent of any impairment of his earning capacity with enough certainty for a jury to determine a reasonable award of damages. It granted NCL's motion for a directed verdict. **[—6—]**

The district court instructed the jury using a pattern instruction for medical negligence. It refused NCL's request to modify the pattern instruction to add emphasis that doctors at sea are not held to the same standard of care as doctors on land. The jury found NCL negligent and awarded $1.2 million in non-economic damages, $800,000 in future medical expenses, and $84,000 in lost services. Ow Buland later accepted remittitur, and the award was reduced to $1,712,862.

NCL moved for a new trial. It based its motion on the failure of the district court to give the jury a maritime-specific instruction about medical negligence and on Ow Buland's experts' failure to acknowledge the differences between cruise-line medicine and land-based medicine. The district court denied the motion.

II. STANDARDS OF REVIEW

"We review a district judge's exclusion of expert testimony only for abuse of discretion" and defer to that decision "unless it is manifestly erroneous." *Chapman v. Procter & Gamble Distrib., LLC*, 766 F.3d 1296, 1305 (11th Cir. 2014) (internal quotation marks omitted). We review a directed verdict *de novo. Cook ex rel. Estate of Tessier v. Sheriff of Monroe Cnty.*, 402 F.3d 1092, 1114 (11th Cir. 2005). We "examine the evidence in a light most favorable to the non-moving party" and affirm if "there is no legally sufficient evidentiary basis for a reasonable jury to find for the non-moving party on that issue." *Id.* (internal quotation marks omitted). And we review the denial of a motion for a new trial for [—7—] abuse of discretion. *Brochu v. City of Riviera Beach*, 304 F.3d 1144, 1155 (11th Cir. 2002). When a party moves for a new trial based on the sufficiency of the evidence but does not move for a directed verdict on that basis, our review is limited to "inquir[ing] into whether *any* evidence **{-1149-}** supported submission of the issue" to the jury. *Coker v. Amoco Oil Co.*, 709 F.2d 1433, 1437 (11th Cir. 1983).

III. DISCUSSION

We divide our discussion in three parts. First, we explain the basis for admiralty jurisdiction over complaints of medical negligence brought by passengers of cruise ships. Second, we address the exclusion of testimony from Ow Buland's damages expert and the directed verdict for NCL on lost-earning-capacity damages. And third, we address NCL's motion for a new trial.

A. Cruise-Line Medical Negligence Claims Are Cognizable in Admiralty Jurisdiction.

The parties agree that the district court had admiralty jurisdiction. But we are obligated to review our subject-matter jurisdiction *sua sponte*. *Nance v. Comm'r, Ga. Dep't of Corr.*, 981 F.3d 1201, 1204 (11th Cir. 2020). Because we have never explained the basis for admiralty jurisdiction over a complaint of medical negligence brought by a cruise-ship passenger, we do so here before turning to the merits of the appeal.

The judicial power of the United States extends "to all Cases of admiralty and maritime Jurisdiction." U.S. Const. art. III § 2, cl. 1. By statute, Congress gave **[—8—]** the district courts original jurisdiction of "[a]ny civil case of admiralty or maritime jurisdiction." 28 U.S.C. § 1333. Traditionally, the determination of whether a tort fell within the admiralty jurisdiction of the federal courts turned on whether the wrong occurred on navigable waters. *See Exec. Jet Aviation, Inc. v. City of Cleveland*, 409 U.S. 249, 253 (1972) (explaining the traditional rule of locality). But the Supreme Court later clarified that a tort must also have "a significant connection with traditional maritime activity" to fall within maritime jurisdiction. *Foremost Ins. Co. v. Richardson*, 457 U.S. 668, 674 (1982).

A tort falls within admiralty jurisdiction when two conditions are satisfied. First, "the incident occurred on navigable water, or the injury was caused by a vessel on navigable water." *Caron*, 910 F.3d at 1365, 6 Adm. R. at 473. And second, "the incident is connected with maritime activity." *Id.*, 6 Adm. R. at 473. The second condition requires courts to "assess the general features of the type of incident involved to determine whether the incident has a potentially disruptive impact on maritime commerce," and to "determine whether the general character of the activity giving rise to the incident shows a substantial relationship to traditional maritime activity." *Jerome B. Grubart, Inc. v. Great Lakes Dredge & Dock Co.*, 513 U.S. 527, 534 (1995) (internal quotation marks and citations omitted).

Both conditions are satisfied in this appeal. First, the medical negligence occurred on the navigable waters between Jamaica and Miami. Second, the **[—9—]** medical negligence is connected to the traditional maritime activity of providing care and comfort to ship passengers. Medical negligence aboard a cruise ship has "a potentially disruptive impact on maritime commerce," *id.* (internal quotation marks omitted), because, among other reasons, failure to provide reasonable medical care under the circumstances may force a cruise ship to make an unplanned stop and disrupt the cruise for other passengers. And "the general character of the activity giving rise to the incident"—here, caring for sick passengers—"shows a substantial relationship to traditional maritime activity." *Id.* (internal quotation marks omitted). **{-1150-}**

It has long been the case that "[a] contract for passage by water implies something more than ship room and transportation. It includes reasonable comforts, necessaries, and kindness, and suitable food and the common means of relief in cases of sickness." *Defrier v. The Nicaragua*, 81 F. 745, 745 (S.D. Ala. 1897) (citing *Chamberlain v. Chandler*, 5 F. Cas. 413, 414 (C.C.D. Mass. 1823) (No. 2,575)

(Story, J.)). The Passenger Act of 1882 also imposed a duty to provide medical care for passengers:

> [E]very steamship or other vessel carrying or bringing emigrant passengers, or passengers other than cabin passengers, exceeding fifty in number, shall carry a duly qualified and competent surgeon or medical practitioner . . . who shall be provided with surgical instruments, medical comforts, and medicines proper and necessary for diseases and accidents incident to sea-voyages, and for the proper medical treatment of such passengers during the voyage . . . . **[—10—]**

Pub. L. No. 47-374, § 5, 22 Stat. 186, 188. To be sure, today's "state-of-the-art cruise ships . . . , complete with well-stocked modern infirmaries and urgent care centers," have come a long way from "nineteenth-century steamships." *Franza v. Royal Caribbean Cruises, Ltd.*, 772 F.3d 1225, 1239, 2 Adm. R. 582, 591 (11th Cir. 2014). But caring for sick passengers is a "traditional maritime activity," *Jerome B. Grubart, Inc.*, 513 U.S. at 534 (internal quotation marks omitted), even if performed in a more sophisticated way today. The district court had admiralty jurisdiction over Ow Buland's complaint about a maritime tort.

B. The District Court Did Not Err by Excluding Testimony from Ow Buland's Expert Economist and Granting a Directed Verdict on Loss of Earning Capacity.

"An award for impaired earning capacity is intended to compensate the worker for the diminution in [his] stream of income." *Jones & Laughlin Steel Corp. v. Pfeifer*, 462 U.S. 523, 533 (1983). The *en banc* former Fifth Circuit explained that calculating such an award "involves four steps: estimating the loss of work life resulting from the injury or death, calculating the lost income stream, computing the total damage, and discounting that amount to its present value." *Culver v. Slater Boat Co.*, 722 F.2d 114, 117 (5th Cir. 1983) (en banc). "The base figure" arrived at before discounting to present value "is the difference between what a person could have earned 'but for' the accident and what he is able to earn upon returning to work in his partially disabled state." *Masinter v. Tenneco Oil* **[—11—]** *Co.*, 867 F.2d 892, 899 (5th Cir. 1989), *mandate recalled and modified*, 934 F.2d 67 (5th Cir. 1991).

Ow Buland challenges two orders related to his request for damages for loss of earning capacity. We first discuss the exclusion of testimony about loss of earning capacity from Ow Buland's economic expert. We then discuss the directed verdict on lost-earning-capacity damages.

1. Dr. Anderson's Testimony Was Unreliable Because It Was Based on Unsupported Assumptions About Ow Buland's Post-Injury Earning Capacity.

The district court did not abuse its discretion by excluding Dr. Anderson's testimony on the value of Ow Buland's lost earning capacity. Federal Rule of Evidence 702 establishes the prerequisites for expert testimony to be admissible into evidence:

> (1) [T]he expert [must be] qualified to testify competently regarding the matters he intends to address; (2) the methodology by which the expert reaches his **{-1151-}** conclusions [must be] sufficiently reliable as determined by the sort of inquiry mandated in *Daubert* [*v. Merrell Dow Pharmaceuticals, Inc.*, 509 U.S. 579 (1993)]; and (3) the testimony [must] assist[] the trier of fact, through the application of scientific, technical, or specialized expertise, to understand the evidence or to determine a fact in issue.

City of Tuscaloosa v. Harcros Chems., Inc., 158 F.3d 548, 562 (11th Cir. 1998) (footnote omitted). "The *Daubert* requirement that the expert testify to scientific knowledge—conclusions supported by good grounds for each step in the analysis—means that any step that renders the analysis unreliable under the **[—12—]** [*Daubert*] factors renders the expert's testimony inadmissible."

Kilpatrick v. Breg, Inc., 613 F.3d 1329, 1341 (11th Cir. 2010) (alteration rejected) (internal quotation marks omitted).

Dr. Anderson used the following steps to estimate the present value of Ow Buland's lost earning capacity. First, he used Ow Buland's actual history of earnings as his pre-injury earning capacity. From there, he assumed modest yearly salary increases over the course of Ow Buland's working life, added the value of fringe benefits, and adjusted for mortality and taxes. Then, he subtracted the amount Ow Buland would be expected to earn in each of several post-injury careers. Finally, he discounted the difference to present value and reported the resulting number as Ow Buland's loss of earning capacity. Based on that methodology, Dr. Anderson's testimony was reliable only to the extent the hypothetical careers it was based on approximated Ow Buland's actual post-injury earning capacity.

Dr. Anderson's assumption that Ow Buland did not have career opportunities more lucrative than working as a part-time university teacher or member of a corporate board was entirely speculative. Dr. Anderson testified in his deposition that he "identified [the] alternative scenarios for prospective post injury employment pursuant to [a] discussion with Mr. Ow Buland." He "rel[ied] on the testimony of [an expert cardiologist] that . . . [Ow Buland] is not capable of **[—13—]** performing the work of a [chief financial officer]." And he also relied on a letter from a recruiting director explaining that "senior finance professionals [in Trinidad and Tobago] typically . . . work extended hours on a consistent basis" and suggesting that Ow Buland "may be more suited to a flexible working arrangement that would allow him to control his working hours in line with his physical limitation."

To be admissible under *Daubert*, an expert's opinion must be "supported by good grounds for each step in the analysis." *Id.* (internal quotation marks omitted). Dr. Anderson did not have good grounds to support his assumption that there was no middle ground between Ow Buland's suggestions about the kinds of part-time work he could perform and the work as a senior finance professional he could no longer perform. The unsupported assumption made his testimony unreliable. The district court did not abuse its discretion by excluding Dr. Anderson's testimony on loss of earning capacity.

2. NCL Was Entitled to a Directed Verdict Because Ow Buland Did Not Prove the Amount of His Lost-Earning-Capacity Damages.

Ow Buland argues that at trial he "presented more than sufficient lay and medical testimony to establish a permanent injury, and a significant diminution in his ability or capacity to earn income." He contends that his pre-injury earning capacity is evident from his previous salary as a **{-1152-}** chief financial officer, and that his medical experts established that the injury prevented him from returning to a **[—14—]** stressful full-time job. And he contends that he testified to his ability to work as a part-time university teacher or member of a corporate board with specificity about what he could earn in those positions.

But there is a significant gap between the 10-hour workweek Ow Buland testified he could handle and the 60-hour workweek his medical experts testified he could no longer handle. "[T]ort law requires an aggrieved plaintiff to prove [his] damages with a reasonable degree of certainty." *Guyana Tel. & Tel. Co. v. Melbourne Int'l Commc'ns, Ltd.*, 329 F.3d 1241, 1248 (11th Cir. 2003); *see also* Restatement (Second) of Torts § 912 (Am. L. Inst. 1979). A jury award for lost earning capacity must be supported by record evidence of the upper limit of the plaintiff's post-injury earning capacity. *See Myers v. Griffin-Alexander Drilling Co.*, 910 F.2d 1252, 1253, 1255 (5th Cir. 1990).

Ow Buland failed to present evidence that "the part-time jobs *he believes* he is qualified and capable of performing, such as sitting on corporate boards, and part-time university level teaching," represent the full extent of his post-injury earning capacity. Without evidence establishing that fact, any jury award for lost earning capacity would have been unduly speculative. Because there was no legally sufficient evidentiary basis for the jury to award Ow Buland damages for loss of earning capacity, the district court correctly granted NCL's motion for a directed verdict. *See* Fed. R. Civ. P. 50(a). **[—15—]**

C. NCL Is Not Entitled to a New Trial.

NCL cross-appeals from the order denying its motion for a new trial. It argues that it is entitled to a new trial because the district court erred by refusing to give the jury a standard-of-care instruction that was tailored to the maritime medical malpractice context, and because Ow Buland's expert witnesses testified to the standard of care in a land-based emergency room, not one at sea. We address NCL's arguments in turn.

1. The District Court Correctly Instructed the Jury.

We have explained that "[i]t is indisputable that cruise lines must treat their passengers with 'ordinary reasonable care under the circumstances.'" *Franza*, 772 F.3d at 1253, 2 Adm. R. at 604 (quoting *Keefe v. Bahama Cruise Line, Inc.*, 867 F.2d 1318, 1322 (11th Cir. 1989)). And we have explained how that duty, which is the standard for all maritime torts, applies in the context of medical negligence. "Implicit in this variable standard is the notion that cruise lines will not always be held to the same standard of care that would guide treatment onshore. This is as it should be, since standards of care typically vary among differently situated healthcare providers." *Id.*, 2 Adm. R. at 604.

The district court instructed the jury in accordance with *Franza*. It explained that reasonable care is defined in the light of "*all relevant surrounding circumstances*" and that medical negligence is "doing something that a reasonably **[—16—]** careful physician would not do *under like circumstances* or failing to do something that a reasonably careful physician would do *under like circumstances*." A district court "enjoys broad discretion to formulate jury instructions provided those instructions are correct statements of the law." *United States v. Lebowitz*, 676 F.3d 1000, 1014 (11th Cir. 2012). The instruction given correctly stated the law, and the exact wording of it fell within the discretion of the district court.

The district court did not abuse its discretion by choosing a more general formulation **{-1153-}** of the instruction than the one NCL requested. NCL argues the district court should have instructed the jury that "[r]easonable care on the part of a physician *in an admiralty case involving medical malpractice*" is defined in reference to "similar and reasonably careful physicians *in the same maritime environment*," and that medical negligence is "doing something that a reasonably careful physician *in the same maritime environment* would not do under like circumstances or failing to do something that a reasonably careful physician *in the same maritime environment* would do under like circumstances." That proposed instruction is as accurate as the instruction the district court gave. But it is up to the litigants—not the district court—to present the evidence and to make the case to the jury about which circumstances are relevant to the standard of care in a case of medical negligence. **[—17—]**

2. Sufficient Evidence Supported the Verdict Against NCL.

NCL also argues that a new trial is necessary because Ow Buland "did not establish the requisite standard of care applicable to a physician facing a cardiac emergency at sea or then prove that NCL's doctors did not meet the applicable standard of care." We understand this to be an argument that the evidence was insufficient to support the jury's verdict. But NCL did not move for a directed verdict based on Ow Buland's failure to prove a violation of the correct standard of care. After the close of evidence, it moved for a directed verdict on four grounds: failure to prove past medical expenses, failure to prove any alleged breach exacerbated the damage caused by the heart attack, failure to prove future medical expenses, and failure to prove lost earning capacity. But it did not argue that Ow Buland failed to prove a breach of the correct standard of care until it moved for a new trial.

"[A]n appellate court cannot examine the sufficiency of the evidence supporting the jury's verdict unless the objecting party filed a timely motion for directed verdict with the trial court." *Coker*, 709 F.2d at 1437. When a party allows an issue to go to the jury without first objecting to the sufficiency of the evidence, our review on appeal is limited to "inquir[ing] into whether *any* evidence supported submission of the issue." *Id.* The issue before us is "whether there was **[—18—]** an absolute absence of evidence to support the jury's verdict." *Wilson v. Attaway*, 757 F.2d 1227, 1237 n.3 (11th Cir. 1985) (internal quotation marks omitted).

Some evidence supported the jury's finding that NCL did not exercise reasonable care under the circumstances. The district court observed that "[NCL] had the ability to administer a thrombolytic . . . [and the] decision was made not to . . . . [It] had the ability to go to the nearest port and disembark . . . and [NCL] didn't do that, and that's a circumstance . . . the jury certainly could and probably did consider." And the district court pointed out that NCL offered testimony "that the facilities onboard the ship were at least the equivalent of a land-based emergency room," which the jury could have relied on to find that NCL failed to treat Ow Buland as well as it could have even under the circumstances. Some evidence existed to support the jury's finding that NCL failed to provide reasonable care under the circumstances. So we cannot disturb the verdict based on Ow Buland's alleged failure to prove a breach of the proper standard of care. NCL is not entitled to a new trial.

IV. CONCLUSION

We **AFFIRM**.

United States Court of Appeals
for the Eleventh Circuit

No. 19-13690

TRAVELERS PROPERTY CAS. CO. OF AM.
vs.
OCEAN REEF CHARTERS LLC

Appeal from the United States District Court for the Southern District of Florida

Decided: May 6, 2021

Citation: 996 F.3d 1161, 9 Adm. R. 377 (11th Cir. 2021).

Before **JORDAN, PRYOR,** and **BRANCH,** Circuit Judges.

[—1—] {–1162–} JORDAN, Chief Judge:

The Supreme Court held in *Wilburn Boat Co. v. Firearm's Fund Ins. Co.*, 348 U.S. 310, 316 (1955), that in the field of marine insurance state law should be applied **[—2—]** where there is no established federal maritime rule governing the issue at hand. For over 60 years, *Wilburn Boat* has sown confusion with respect to the treatment of warranties in marine insurance policies. *See, e.g.*, 2 Thomas Schoenbaum, Admiralty and Maritime Law § 19:15 (6th ed. 2020) (asserting that *Wilburn Boat* has "caused endless mischief"); Gerard J. Mangone, United States Admiralty Law 247 (1997) (noting that *Wilburn Boat* "has since troubled many maritime lawyers"); I Alex L. Parks, The Law and Practice of Marine Insurance and Average 13 (1987) ("*Wilburn [Boat]* cast the law of marine insurance into a state of turmoil.").

In this case the district court held on summary judgment that, under Eleventh Circuit precedent, federal maritime law requires strict compliance with captain and crew warranties in a marine insurance policy. And because Ocean Reef Charters breached those warranties, there was no coverage for the loss of its yacht under a policy issued by Travelers Property Casualty Company.

Doing our best to make sense of *Wilburn Boat* and its progeny, we reverse. We **{–1163–}** conclude that there is no entrenched maritime rule governing captain or crew warranties, and that as a result Florida law applies to determine the effect of Ocean Reef's breaches.

I [—3—]

As this is an appeal from the grant of summary judgment, our review is plenary, and we view the facts in the light most favorable to Ocean Reef Charters. *See Tolan v. Cotton*, 572 U.S. 650, 651 (2014).

A

This case concerns the demise of the *M/Y My Lady*, a 92-foot Hatteras yacht. Ocean Reef, the owner of the *M/Y My Lady*, insured it with Travelers for a one-year term from October of 2016 to October of 2017. The 2016-17 policy, a renewal of annual policies issued in the two prior years, contained two express warranties that are at issue in this case. First, the captain warranty required Ocean Reef to employ a full-time professional captain approved by Travelers: "It is warranted you employ a professional captain for the yacht . . . Such captain shall be full time and approved by us." Second, the crew warranty required Ocean Reef to have one full- or part-time professional crew member onboard: "You [shall] employ 1 full time or part time professional crew for your yacht[.]"

Ocean Reef purchased the 2016-17 policy through its insurance agent, Keen Battle Mead & Company, located in Homestead, Florida. Travelers negotiated and issued the policy through its producing agent, Hull & Company, based in Fort Lauderdale, Florida. Travelers delivered the policy to Hull at its Florida address and Hull in turn delivered the policy to Keen Battle in Hialeah, Florida. The policy **[—4—]** named Ocean Reef as the insured with a New York address, but listed Key Largo, Florida, as the primary mooring location for the *M/Y My Lady*.

Ocean Reef did not employ a professional captain for the *M/Y My Lady* in early September of 2017, when Hurricane Irma was heading towards Florida. Nor did it have any crew onboard.

Eyeing the impending storm, Richard Gollel—the named operator of the *M/Y My Lady*—contacted Michael McCall, his former captain (who had previously been approved by Travelers and who was then in Massachusetts). Mr. Gollel asked Captain McCall whether he could move the yacht to a more protected location from its mooring near Mr. Gollel's residence in Pompano Beach, Florida. Captain McCall initially agreed to the request, but, according to Ocean Reef, he changed his mind and advised Mr. Gollel that there was no way to move the yacht safely.

Mr. Gollel then sought permission to move the *M/Y My Lady* himself, but Hull (Travelers' agent) told Keen Battle (Ocean Reef's agent) that the yacht should not be moved. So Mr. Gollel did his best to secure the yacht by, among other things, adding extra fenders and mooring lines. The extra mooring lines proved ineffective when a year-old dock piling—to which the port bow line was attached—gave way as Hurricane Irma struck land on September 10-11, 2017. The yacht drifted onto other pilings and hit the sea wall, before eventually becoming holed and sinking at the dock. The damage resulted in a total constructive loss under the Travelers policy. **[—5—]**

B

Shortly after the *M/Y My Lady* sank, and while she was still submerged, Travelers filed this lawsuit against Ocean Reef. Travelers denied coverage six weeks later, asserting that Ocean Reef had breached the captain and crew warranties in the policy. **{–1164–}**

Following discovery, the parties filed cross-motions for summary judgment. Travelers argued that federal maritime law requires strict compliance with express warranties in marine insurance contracts, and that a breach bars coverage even if it is unrelated to the loss. Ocean Reef countered that Florida's so-called "anti-technical statute" should instead apply, and that under that statute the breaches did not preclude coverage because they were unrelated to the loss. *See* Fla. Stat. § 627.409(2) ("A breach . . . does not void the policy or contract, or constitute a defense to a loss thereon, unless such breach or violation increased the hazard by any means within the control of the insured."). Ocean Reef presented lay and expert testimony that the failure to have a captain and crew did not increase the hazard to the *M/Y My Lady*, and that the yacht sunk due to the unforeseeable failure of the dock piling.

The district court granted Travelers' motion for summary judgment, concluding that "the Eleventh Circuit has fashioned an entrenched rule of admiralty: express warranties in maritime insurance contracts *must* be strictly construed in the **[—6—]** absence of some limiting provision in the contract." *Travelers Property Casualty Co. v. Ocean Reef Charter LLC*, 396 F. Supp. 3d 1170, 1176 (S.D. Fla. 2019). Ocean Reef appealed, and we set the case for oral argument.

II

This case concerns the interpretation of a marine insurance policy, which gives rise to federal admiralty jurisdiction. *See Wilburn Boat*, 348 U.S. at 313; *St. Paul Fire and Marine Ins. Co. v. Lago Canyon, Inc.*, 561 F.3d 1181, 1184 (11th Cir. 2009). "As this case lies in admiralty, federal maritime conflict of laws control." *Cooper v. Meridian Yachts, Ltd.*, 575 F.3d 1151, 1161 (11th Cir. 2009).

So what law do we apply to determine the effect of Ocean Reef's breaches of the captain and crew warranties? To figure out the answer, we look to the Supreme Court's frequently criticized decision in *Wilburn Boat*.

A

Perhaps unsurprisingly, the facts in *Wilburn Boat* bore no resemblance to the clashes and controversies on the high seas that formed the basis of American admiralty jurisprudence. The case involved a houseboat located on an artificial inland lake between Texas and Oklahoma. *See* 348 U.S. at 311. The insurance policy included two warranties of relevance—one providing that the boat could not be sold or otherwise transferred, and another providing that the boat could be used only for private pleasure purposes. *See id.* Both warranties were breached, and the **[—7—]** boat was subsequently destroyed by a fire unrelated to the breaches. *See id.* The owner made a claim under the policy, which the insurer denied due to the breaches. *See id.* The owner argued that Texas law should determine the effect, if any, of the breaches, but the Fifth Circuit sided with the insurer. It held that federal maritime law applied, and that there was an established maritime rule requiring literal compliance with all express warranties in marine insurance policies. The owner's breaches, therefore, voided coverage. *See id.* at 312-13.

When the case came before it, the Supreme Court posed two questions: "(1) Is there a judicially established federal admiralty rule governing these warranties? (2) If not, should we fashion one?" *Id.* at 314. Answering those questions, the Court reversed and remanded for application of Texas law.

The Court first concluded that there was no established federal maritime rule "requiring strict fulfillment of marine insurance warranties," explaining that "[w]hatever **{-1165-}** the origin of the 'literal performance' rule may be, we think it plain that it has not been judicially established as part of the body of federal admiralty law in this country." *Id.* at 314, 316. The Court acknowledged that one of its early cases referenced a rule requiring strict compliance with marine warranties, but did not think that the case applied a federal maritime rule. *See id.* at 315 (discussing *Hazard's Administrator v. New England Marine Ins. Co.*, 33 U.S. (8 Pet.) 557, 580 (1834)). **[—8—]**

Moving on to the second question, the Court declined to fashion a uniform federal rule governing breaches of warranties in marine insurance policies, and opted instead for the application of state law. It considered adopting the old common-law rule requiring literal and strict compliance with warranties, but thought that rule was "harsh." *Id.* at 320. Noting that the choice as to what rule to adopt involved policy considerations best left to Congress, the Court concluded that it was going to "leave the regulation of marine insurance where it has been—with the [s]tates." *Id.* at 322.

Justice Reed, joined by Justice Burton, registered a strong dissent in *Wilburn Boat*. First, he asserted that English law and American law required strict compliance with marine insurance warranties. *See id.* at 325-26 (citing English and American authorities). Second, he lamented the detrimental effect the Court's decision would have, including a lack of uniformity in federal maritime law. *See id.* at 327-28. As he put it, "[s]tate authority, . . . although it may provide remedies, does not extend to changing the general substantive admiralty law." *Id.* at 331. Third, he believed that the applicability of state law with respect to warranties would adversely affect the certainty needed by vessel owners and insurers: "What law is to govern—that of the [s]tate where the insurance contract was issued, the [s]tate of the accident, or the [s]tate of the forum? It seems an unreasonable interference with maritime activity to allow the many states to declare the substantive law of marine insurance." *Id.* at 334. Fourth, he thought that the Court's decision could not be **[—9—]** limited to the unique facts in *Wilburn Boat*: "The considerations which lead me to favor a uniform rule are not changed simply because a relatively small boat was here involved, or the number of [s]tates through which it passed were few, or because its ultimate destination was a small lake." *Id.* at 334-35.

B

One problem with *Wilburn Boat*, as commentators have pointed out, is that it rests on a flawed premise. At the time the case was decided, "all the major admiralty [appellate courts in the United States] had long accepted the literal performance rule." 2 Schoenbaum, Admiralty and Maritime Law, at § 19:15. This rule derived from English common law and applied to all express warranties in marine contracts. *See id.* ("English law applied the rule of automatic discharge as a consequence of breach of warranty."). Indeed, the Supreme Court itself had referenced a rule of strict compliance with marine warranties in the early 1800s. *See*

Hazard's Administrator, 33 U.S. at 583 (a misrepresentation that a ship was "coppered" would void the policy, and it was "immaterial in what way the loss may arise"). Another problem is that *Wilburn Boat* undermines uniformity in admiralty law. *See* Joel K. Goldstein, *The Life and Times of* Wilburn Boat*: A Critical Guide (Part II)*, 28 J. Mar. L. & Com. 555, 558 (1997) ("By holding that state law governed the issues presented, *Wilburn* frustrated the effort to create uniform law regarding marine insurance. In so doing, it represented a departure **{-1166-}** from the approach which animated **[—10—]** . . . earlier cases involving marine insurance."); Grant Gilmore & Charles L. Black, Jr., The Law of Admiralty 69 (2d ed. 1975) ("[I]t is hard to say what is to be governed by a federal maritime law, if the question of the effect of a breach of warranty in a marine policy is not so governed.").

Wilburn Boat poses difficult choice-of-law questions in cases involving breaches of express warranties. The Supreme Court denied the existence of a then-entrenched federal maritime rule on the subject, and declined to fashion a uniform maritime rule, while at the same time seemingly instructing courts in future cases to look to whether there exists such a rule. *See Wilburn Boat*, 348 U.S. at 316-18. So the challenge for us is to find a way to give meaning to the Court's opinion in express-warranty cases.

The Supreme Court has given us little help on the matter. In the 65 years since *Wilburn Boat* was decided, the Court has cited the case just 13 times. Only two of those cases are relevant here, and neither one dealt with an express warranty in a marine insurance policy.

In *Kossick v. United Fruit Co.*, 365 U.S. 731 (1961), the Supreme Court considered an alleged oral agreement by a shipowner to assume responsibility for any improper or inadequate treatment of a seaman at a public health hospital. The Court held that "several considerations point to an accommodation favoring the application of maritime law." *Id.* at 741. It distinguished but did not overrule **[—11—]** *Wilburn Boat*, noting that "[a] concurring opinion and some commentators have preferred to refer [that] decision to the absurdity of applying maritime law to a contract of insurance on a houseboat established in the waters of a small artificial lake between Texas and Oklahoma." *Id.* at 742 (citations omitted). It then declared: "Needless to say the situation presented here has a more genuinely salty flavor than that." *Id.*

As a matter of linguistics, or even intuition, we are unsure what to make of this sentence in *Kossick*. How "genuinely salty" is salty enough? Where, for example, does a dispute stemming from an incident in brackish water fall on the scale? *See American Dredging Co. v. Miller*, 510 U.S. 443, 452-53 (1994) (comparing *Wilburn Boat* and *Kossick*: "It would be idle to pretend that the line separating permissible from impermissible state regulation is readily discernible in our admiralty jurisprudence, or indeed is even entirely consistent within our admiralty jurisprudence."). Whatever the precise meaning of *Kossick*, we concluded relatively quickly that it did not overrule *Wilburn Boat*. *See Irwin v. Eagle Star Ins. Co.*, 455 F.2d 827, 829-30 (5th Cir. 1972) ("Despite the language in *Kossick* tending to limit the *Wilburn Boat* opinion to its facts, we believe that *Kossick* did an incomplete job of burying the *Wilburn Boat* obeisance to state contract law in certain cases involving marine contracts."). **[—12—]**

In 2004, the Supreme Court cited *Wilburn Boat* for the principle that "not every term in every maritime contract can only be controlled by some federally defined admiralty rule." *Norfolk Southern Railway Co. v. Kirby*, 543 U.S. 14, 27 (2004) (quoting *Wilburn Boat*, 348 U.S. at 313). The Court went on to say that "[a] maritime contract's interpretation may so implicate local interests as to beckon interpretation by state law," but added that "when state interests cannot be accommodated without defeating a federal interest . . . then federal substantive law should govern." *Id.* The *Norfolk Southern* choice-of-law formulation is obviously different than the one set out in *Wilburn Boat*. But **{-1167-}** *Norfolk Southern* involved a so-called Himalaya clause (which extends liability limitations to downstream parties) in a bill of lading, a very different issue than the breach of an express warranty in a marine insurance policy. We therefore do not think that *Norfolk Southern* constituted a stealth overruling of *Wilburn Boat. See Shalala v. Illinois Council on Long Term Care, Inc.*, 529 U.S. 1, 18 (2000) ("This Court does not normally overturn, or so dramatically limit, earlier authority *sub silentio*.").

By not squarely addressing *Wilburn Boat* in the 65 years since its issuance, the Supreme Court has left the lower federal courts at sea without a rudder or compass. If we were writing on a blank slate, we would consider holding that there should be a uniform maritime rule regarding the effect of a breach of an express warranty in a marine insurance policy—and from there determine what that uniform **[—13—]** rule should be. *See generally DeLovio v. Boit*, 7 F.Cas. 418, 443 (C.C.D. Mass. 1815) (Story, J.) (noting the "advantages resulting to the commerce and navigation of the United States, from a uniformity of rules and decisions in all maritime questions"); 1 Benedict on Admiralty § 111 (7th rev. ed. 2020) (explaining that the "fundamental purpose" of the grant of admiralty jurisdiction was to "preserve adequate harmony and appropriate uniform rules relating to maritime matters" and to "bring them within the control" of the federal government); Goldstein, *The Life and Times of* Wilburn Boat, 28 J. Mar. L. & Com. at 557 ("[T]he uniformity idea has long antecedents regarding marine insurance.").

The slate, however, is not blank. It is covered in graffiti, and we must somehow make sense of the layers of paint.

C

Wilburn Boat remains on the books, and we are bound by its treatment of warranties in marine insurance policies despite the ample criticism the decision has received. As we read *Wilburn Boat*, it instructs us "to look to see if the *specific* warranty at issue is (or should be) the subject of a uniform or entrenched federal admiralty rule." *Great Lakes Reinsurance (UK) PLC v. Rosin*, 757 F.Supp.2d 1244, 1257 (S.D. Fla. 2010). That is the way we interpreted *Wilburn Boat* early on. *See, e.g., Koninklyke Nederlandsche Stoomboot Maalschappy, N.V. v. Strachan Shipping Co.*, 301 F.2d 741, 743 (5th Cir. 1962) (observing that although *Wilburn Boat* "held **[—14—]** that marine insurance contracts should be governed by state law, there can be no doubt that a clearly established federal judicially-fashioned maritime rule governs a stevedore's breach of warranty to perform services in a workmanlike fashion"); *Fireman's Fund Ins. Co. v. Wilburn Boat Co.*, 300 F.2d 631, 647 n.2 (5th Cir. 1962) (explaining that *Wilburn Boat* "held that state law is to be applied in the field of marine insurance only where 'entrenched federal precedent is lacking' with respect to a specific issue").[1]

We recognize that there is language in some of our cases pronouncing the existence **{-1168-}** of an entrenched maritime rule as to the breach of all marine warranties. For example, in *Lexington Ins. Co. v. Cooke's Seafood*, 835 F.2d 1364, 1366 (11th Cir. 1988), we said—without citing to or even acknowledging *Wilburn Boat*—that "admiralty law requires the strict construction of express warranties in marine insurance contracts," and that "breach of the express warranty by the insured releases the insurance company from liability even if compliance with the warranty would not have avoided the loss." And in *Hilton Oil Transport v. Jonas*, 75 F.3d 627, 630 **[—15—]** (11th Cir. 1996), we similarly explained that the breach of an express maritime warranty deprives the

[1] Over the years, our cases discussing or applying *Wilburn Boat* have admittedly not been uniform. *See Rosin*, 757 F.Supp.2d at 1253-56 (surveying Fifth and Eleventh Circuit precedent through 2010); Graydon S. Staring, Wilburn Boat *is a Dead Letter: R.I.P.*, 42 J. Mar. L. & Com. 465, 478-82 (2011) (same). Our sister circuits have also taken divergent approaches to *Wilburn Boat. See* 8 Benedict on Admiralty, at § 12:03 (noting that "the lower courts have not been consistent" in applying *Wilburn Boat*). For a sampling of post-*Wilburn Boat* cases in other circuits, see *Albany Ins. Co. v. Anh Thi Kieu*, 927 F.2d 882, 886 (5th Cir. 1991); *Calhoun v. Yamaha Motor Corp., U.S.A.*, 40 F.3d 622, 627 (3d Cir. 1994); *Advani Enterprises, Inc. v. Underwriters at Lloyd's*, 140 F.3d 157, 162 (2d Cir. 1998); and *Lloyd's of London v. Pagan-Sanchez*, 539 F.3d 19, 24 (1st Cir. 2008).

insured of coverage under a "judicially established and entrenched federal admiralty rule," even if the breach is unrelated to the loss.

The district court relied on these cases to conclude that "the Eleventh Circuit has fashioned an entrenched federal rule of admiralty: express warranties in maritime insurance contracts *must* be strictly construed in the absence of some limiting provision in the contract." *Ocean Reef Charters*, 396 F. Supp. 3d at 1176. The district court's view is understandable given the mess we have created, but we cannot take the broad pronouncements in *Cooke's Seafood* and *Hilton Oil* at face value. Doing so would eviscerate *Wilburn Boat* and its holding that there is no established federal maritime rule requiring strict fulfillment of all warranties in marine insurance policies. *See* 2 Schoenbaum, Admiralty and Maritime Law, at § 19:15 (explaining that cases which hold that "the literal performance rule still applies to warranties as a matter of *federal* law. . . . choose to ignore the Supreme Court's mandate [in *Wilburn Boat*] that state law applies to insurance warranties").

As a subsequent panel, we accept and treat as binding the specific holdings in *Cooke's Seafood* and *Hilton Oil*, which are that the breach of a navigation limit warranty bars coverage as a matter of maritime law even when the breach is unrelated to the loss. *See Cooke's Seafood*, 835 F.2d at 1367; *Hilton Oil*, 75 F.3d at 630. There is, after all, authority for the proposition that there exists an entrenched **[—16—]** federal maritime rule governing navigation limit warranties. *See generally Fla. Marine Towing, Inc. v. United Nat'l Ins. Co.*, 686 So.2d 711, 713 (Fla. App. 1997) ("Federal courts have recognized that . . . strict construction of navigational limit warranties has been an established admiralty rule of the federal judiciary.") (quotation omitted).

We decline, however, to read those cases as purporting to overrule *Wilburn Boat* with respect to the treatment of all warranties in maritime insurance policies. The Supreme Court, and only the Supreme Court, has the prerogative of overruling its own decisions. *See Bosse v. Oklahoma*, 137 S.Ct. 1, 2 (2016). Unlike some commentators, *see, e.g.*, Staring, *Dead Letter*, 42 J. Mar. L. & Com. at 484-85, we cannot scuttle *Wilburn Boat* just because we might disagree with it. We instead harmonize *Wilburn Boat* with *Cooke's Seafood* and *Hilton Oil* by limiting the latter cases to the specific warranty they addressed. *See Rosin*, 757 F. Supp. 2d at 1257. This approach may be messy and do little to solve the overall doctrinal confusion, but we think it is the only path open to us if we are going to be faithful to *Wilburn Boat*.[2] **[—17—] {-1169-}**

For the same reason, we narrowly construe *Aguirre v. Citizens Casualty Co. of New York*, 441 F.2d 141, 146 (5th Cir. 1971), which held that the breach of an express warranty of seaworthiness voids coverage even if unrelated to the loss because "[t]he seaworthiness standard is solidly entrenched in federal maritime jurisprudence." We read *Aguirre* as applying an entrenched maritime rule with respect to seaworthiness warranties, *see* Thomas R. Beer, *Established Federal Admiralty Rules in Maritime Insurance Contracts and the* Wilburn Boat *Case*, 1 U.S.F. Mar. L. J. 149, 158-59 (1989) (stating that "[t]he standard of seaworthiness is solidly entrenched in American maritime law"), but do not understand it to hold that there is an entrenched federal maritime rule requiring strict compliance with all marine warranties. Such a broad interpretation would, again, be contrary to *Wilburn Boat*.

D

As this case does not involve a navigation limit warranty or a seaworthiness warranty,

---

[2] We note, as well, that before *Cooke's Seafood* and *Hilton Oil* we had confirmed in a number of cases that state law governs the interpretation of marine insurance policies unless there is an entrenched maritime rule on the particular issue at hand. *See, e.g., Strachan Shipping*, 301 F.2d at 743; *De Bardeleben Marine Corp. v. United States*, 451 F.2d 140, 147 n.18 (5th Cir. 1971); *Walter v. Marine Office of America*, 537 F.2d 89, 94 (5th Cir. 1976). These earlier decisions also counsel against an expansive reading of *Cooke's Seafood* and *Hilton Oil*.

Cooke's Seafood, *Hilton Oil*, and *Aguirre* do not control or dictate the outcome. The precise questions for us under *Wilburn Boat* are whether there exist entrenched federal maritime rules governing captain or crew warranties. The answer to those questions is no.

The two cases we have located addressing the breach of a captain warranty have each applied state law. *See Yu v. Albany Ins. Co.*, 281 F.3d 803, 808-09 (9th **[—18—]** Cir. 2002) (Hawaii law); *Northern Assurance Co. of America v. Rathbum*, 567 F.Supp.2d 316, 319 (D. Conn. 2008) (Connecticut law). Although both of these cases alluded to a purported maritime rule of strict compliance with marine warranties, neither one adopted such a federal rule, and as we have noted such a broad rule would conflict with *Wilburn Boat*. A third case, *Capital Coastal Corp. v. Hartford Fire Ins. Co.*, 378 F. Supp. 163, 172 (E.D. Va. 1974), addressed the breach of a warranty requiring that the vessel be manned by a specific captain. The district court in *Capital Coastal* held that all warranties had to be literally fulfilled, and in support cited to two pre-*Wilburn Boat* cases from the Sixth Circuit—one applying federal maritime law and another applying state insurance law. *See id.* To the extent that *Capital Coastal* relied on a supposed entrenched maritime rule requiring strict compliance with all warranties in marine insurance policies, we do not give it much weight, as it did not cite or discuss *Wilburn Boat*. *Cf. Rosin*, 757 F. Supp. 2d at 1257 (holding that "there is no established and entrenched federal precedent concerning the effect of a breach of a 'named operator' warranty").

As for the crew warranty, we have found no American cases or authorities recognizing or announcing an entrenched maritime rule. There is, however, an old and often-cited English case which held that the breach of a crew warranty voided a marine insurance policy even though the breach was cured before the loss and was unrelated to the loss. *See DeHahn v. Hartley*, 1 T.R. 343, 345-46, 99 E.R. 1130 **[—19—]** (K.B. 1786) (warranty required crew of at least 50 but ship initially sailed with 46). In the words of Chief Justice Mansfield, "[a] warranty in a policy of insurance is a condition or contingency, and unless that be performed, there is no contract." *Id.* For several reasons, *DeHahn* does not change our conclusion that there is no entrenched federal maritime rule governing breaches of crew warranties. First, Travelers does not claim that such an established federal rule exists. Second, in his *Wilburn Boat* dissent **{–1170–}** Justice Reed cited *DeHahn* to support his view that English law required strict compliance with warranties in marine insurance policies, *see* 348 U.S. at 325 n.1, but the majority was not persuaded by his contention. If *Wilburn Boat* held, in the face of cases like *DeHahn*, that there was no entrenched maritime rule in the United States requiring strict compliance with warranties in marine insurance policies, we do not think we can rely on *DeHahn* today as authority for such a rule with respect to crew warranties.

All of this means that Florida law, specifically Fla. Stat. § 627.409(2), governs the effect of Ocean Reef's breaches of the captain and crew warranties. On remand, the district court will need to apply § 627.409(2), and consider any other related arguments raised by the parties. *See generally Pickett v. Woods*, 404 So.2d 1152, 1153 (Fla. App. 1981) (explaining that § 627.409(2) was "designed to prevent the insurer from avoiding coverage on a technical omission playing no part in the loss"); *Eastern Ins. Co. v. Austin*, 396 So. 2d 823, 824-25 (Fla. App. 1981) (concluding that **[—20—]** the term "hazard" in § 627.409(2) "refer[s] to danger to the insured vessel itself"). It appears that, under Florida law, the burden of proving a breach and "a resulting increase of the hazard" is on the insurer. *See Fla. Power and Light Co. v. Foremost Ins. Co.*, 433 So. 2d 536, 536-37 (Fla. App. 1983).

E

As noted, the Supreme Court in *Wilburn Boat* considered the then-existing English rule requiring literal performance of marine warranties to be "harsh," 348 U.S. at 320, and some commentators have theorized that the Court's disdain for that rule led to its bewildering decision. *See* 2 Schoenbaum,

Admiralty and Maritime Law, at § 19:15 ("There is evidence of another reason for [the *Wilburn Boat*] decision: dissatisfaction with the English law of warranties."). English law, however, has recently turned full circle and we take a moment to note the change on the other side of the pond.

The United Kingdom Insurance Act of 2015 abandoned the literal compliance rule, so that now "rescission is no longer the [automatic] remedy for breach of warranty." Hugh D. Baker, *Sailing to Calmer Seas: The United Kingdom Insurance Act 2015 and Its Potential Effect on United States Marine Insurance Markets and Law*, 41 Tul. Mar. L. J. 159, 180 (2016). Instead, a breach only suspends coverage until it is cured. *See* Insurance Act 2015, c.4 (U.K.), at §10. In addition, an insured who breaches a warranty and fails to cure can recover if it "shows that the non- **[—21—]** compliance with the term could not have increased the risk of the loss which actually occurred in the circumstances in which it occurred." *See id.* at § 11(3). If there are still "special reasons for keeping in harmony with the marine insurance laws of England, the great field of this business," *Queen Ins. Co. of America v. Globe & Rutgers Fire Ins. Co.*, 263 U.S. 487, 493 (1924), it will be interesting to see what effect the Act has on American maritime law (and on how *Wilburn Boat* is viewed). *See* 2 Schoenbaum, Admiralty and Maritime Law, at § 19:15 ("It is likely that the new U.K. law will encourage U.S. courts to formalize these doctrines."); Attilio M. Costabel, *The UK Insurance Act 2015: A Restatement of Marine Insurance Law*, 27 St. Thomas U. L. Rev. 133, 166 (2015) ("[T]he . . . Act will surely have influence on the law of marine insurance, both in the United States and at the home of the Act in the United Kingdom.").

III

In the 1975 edition of their treatise on admiralty law, Grant Gilmore and Charles **{-1171-}** L. Black, Jr., wrote that "[i]t is utterly impossible to be at all sure . . . how the Supreme Court will at last resolve the[ ] perplexities and contradictions" created by *Wilburn Boat. See* Gilmore & Black, The Law of Admiralty, at 70. Since then, more than 45 years have passed, yet we are no closer to an answer. Maybe, just maybe, this case will prove tempting enough for the Supreme Court to wade in and **[—22—]** let us know what it thinks of *Wilburn Boat* today. As they say, "[h]ope springs eternal . . . ." Alexander Pope, *An Essay on Man*, Epistle I, l. 95 (1733).

"It may be that *Wilburn Boat* was a bad (or at least badly written) decision." *Rosin*, 757 F. Supp. 2d at 1256. But we are stuck with it, and finding no established maritime rule governing captain and crew warranties, we hold that Florida law governs. We reverse the district court's order granting summary judgment to Travelers, and remand for further proceedings.

REVERSED AND REMANDED.

United States Court of Appeals
for the Eleventh Circuit

No. 19-14181

UNITED STATES
vs.
NUNEZ

Appeal from the United States District Court for the Southern District of Alabama

Decided: June 17, 2021

Citation: 1 F.4th 976, 9 Adm. R. 385 (11th Cir. 2021).

Before **W. PRYOR,** Chief Judge, **GRANT** and **TJOFLAT,** Circuit Judges.

[—1—] {–979–} W. PRYOR, Chief Judge: **{–980–}**

These appeals present several issues about the convictions of four drug smugglers under the Maritime Drug Law Enforcement Act. Three threshold issues involve jurisdiction: whether a vessel lacks nationality when, upon request by the **[—2—]** Coast Guard, no member of the crew identifies himself as the master or individual in charge and the vessel otherwise lacks any indicia of nationality or registry; whether a district court must hold an evidentiary hearing to determine jurisdiction under the Act; and whether the district court erred by delaying a jurisdictional ruling. The remaining two issues are whether sufficient evidence supports the smugglers' convictions and whether the district court deprived them of a fair trial by limiting their cross-examinations of witnesses. We conclude that the United States had jurisdiction over the smugglers' stateless vessel, no evidentiary hearing was required for that ruling, and any error in delaying it was harmless. We also conclude that sufficient evidence supported the smugglers' convictions because their indictments did not obligate the government to prove that they knew the identity of the controlled substance they carried. And because the district court afforded them a meaningful opportunity to present a complete defense, we affirm their convictions.

I. BACKGROUND

On Christmas Eve 2018, the United States Coast Guard intercepted a small, homemade boat on the verge of sinking in choppy waters of the high seas between the Dominican Republic and Puerto Rico. The crew of a Coast Guard airplane first spotted the boat while patrolling the narcotics-trafficking route northeast of the Dominican Republic and northwest of Puerto Rico. The guardsmen considered the **[—3—]** boat suspicious because it carried a large number of fuel containers, lacked a visible name or registration number, and used no navigation lights. They reported it to a nearby Coast Guard cutter, the *Richard Dixon*, which detached a small "over-the-horizon" boat to intercept the suspicious boat.

The Coast Guard's boat caught up to the suspicious boat about 50 nautical miles from the coast of the Dominican Republic. It approached with its lights off and shined a spotlight when it was 20 or 30 feet away from the suspicious boat. Coast guardsmen saw "frantic" activity aboard the suspicious boat as two men threw things overboard. When the guardsmen stopped the boat, **{–981–}** they found six bales in the water tied to each other and to a seventh bale still inside the boat. The suspicious boat was small—just 20 or 25 feet long—and between the four men, seven bales, and a dozen 30-gallon fuel containers, little space remained aboard. The guardsmen took a photo of the boat, which is reproduced below.

[—4—]

A Coast Guard officer asked the men "who was the master, who was in charge." No one answered, so he asked who piloted the boat. One of the men answered that they all took turns. The others appeared to agree, based on their body language. The boat had a hand tiller that each person could operate for only about three hours at a time. The men said they were traveling from Santo Domingo in the Dominican Republic to Dorado, Puerto Rico. They estimated they had been traveling for five or six days, although they later said they had been on the water for between five and seven hours. As winds gusted, the waters grew choppy, so the Coast Guard moved the men into the over-the-horizon boat.

Then the guardsmen searched the smugglers' boat. They found that the serial number had been filed off its outboard motor. And the boat contained no fishing or recreational equipment and only a few personal items.

With the search complete, the bales gathered, and the four smugglers safe, the Coast Guard destroyed the boat by throwing a flare next to the fuel containers. The over-the-horizon boat returned the smugglers to the *Richard Dixon*. On board, the four men identified themselves as Pedro Dino Cedado Nunez, Manely Enriquez, Angel Castro Garcia, and Mike Castro Martinez.

The *Richard Dixon* brought the smugglers to Saint Thomas in the Virgin Islands about 10 days later. There, a Homeland Security agent met the smugglers **[—5—]** and flew with them to Mobile, Alabama. He interviewed all four men individually that day.

Garcia confessed that two people he did not know offered him $5,000 to travel to Puerto Rico, and he agreed to go. When the agent referred to the boat as carrying "one hundred kilos of cocaine," Garcia denied knowledge of the quantity but did not deny knowing the boat was carrying cocaine. **{-982-}** The agent responded, "But, that is what it was. . . . You were taking cocaine and you were going from the Dominican Republic to Puerto Rico." "That's where we were going," Garcia confirmed. Garcia also reported that he told the other three men not to throw the bales overboard because they were "already caught."

Martinez and Enriquez provided similar confessions. Martinez said a friend offered him $5,000 to "take some things" to Puerto Rico. He knew when he got onto the boat that the bales contained drugs. He said he was not in charge of the boat, and he laughed when the agent asked if there was a captain. And he said all four men decided together to turn around and return to the Dominican Republic when the engine started sputtering. For his part, Enriquez said a man he knew offered him $5,000 to take the boat to Puerto Rico. He knew that he was transporting drugs.

The bales weighed about 180 kilograms, and the four men stipulated that they contained cocaine. The cocaine had a street value of $25 or $30 million. **[—6—]**

The United States charged the men under the Maritime Drug Law Enforcement Act with possessing cocaine with intent to distribute and conspiring to distribute and to possess cocaine with intent to distribute. 46 U.S.C. §§ 70503(a)(1), 70506(b). The indictment alleged that they "did willfully, knowingly and unlawfully conspire with each other . . . to distribute and possess with the intent to distribute approximately 182 kilograms of cocaine." The defendants pleaded not guilty.

Before trial, the government moved for a ruling that the United States had jurisdiction over the smugglers' boat as a stateless vessel under the Maritime Drug Law Enforcement Act. It attached the statements of three guardsmen about their encounter with the boat and its crew. The guardsmen reported that they searched the boat for "indications of nationality" or "markings, paperwork[,] or identification numbers" but found none. The smugglers moved to dismiss the indictment for lack of jurisdiction and requested an evidentiary hearing.

At a pretrial hearing, the district court made a provisional finding of jurisdiction because the Coast Guard intercepted the vessel in international waters, it contained "no flag[,] no vessel registration documents[, and] no other indicia of nationality," and "[n]o crew member claimed nationality or registry of the vessel." It rejected the argument that an evidentiary hearing was required under the Act, especially when the smugglers did not contest the jurisdictional facts and had not **[—7—]** identified any evidence they hoped to introduce. The district court told the smugglers they could question the government's witnesses about the jurisdictional evidence outside the jury's presence during the trial.

Before trial, the government also moved *in limine* to bar the smugglers from introducing evidence about the conditions of their confinement on the *Richard Dixon*. All four smugglers objected. After discussing the matter during a pretrial hearing, the judge granted the motion. But he said that he might revisit the ruling during the trial if the evidence appeared to be relevant.

The trial lasted two days. As soon as the jury was sworn, all four smugglers moved for a mistrial on jurisdictional grounds. The judge offered them an opportunity to contest the jurisdictional facts by immediately questioning the government's witnesses. Nunez declined because he "was not afforded an opportunity to subpoena the witnesses [he] wanted," but he did not identify any additional witnesses he would have called if he had the chance. The judge **{-983-}** reiterated that the smugglers would be allowed to cross-examine the government's witnesses about jurisdictional issues as they testified.

Garcia's counsel cross-examined a Coast Guard petty officer about where the men were detained on the *Richard Dixon*. The petty officer answered that they were placed on "the top deck of the cutter towards the back where we place all our detainees and migrants." He stated that he did not know if they were shackled. The **[—8—]** government objected after a few questions, and the district court sustained the objection. After further argument, the district court clarified that the defense could present evidence about the smugglers' transportation from Saint Thomas to Mobile immediately before they gave their incriminating statements, but they could not present more evidence about their detention on the *Richard Dixon*.

Later, Garcia's counsel sought to ask the Homeland Security agent who interviewed the men whether he knew that they had been kept shackled and on the deck of a ship for the preceding "14 . . . or 15 days." The district court refused to allow the line of questioning, but it allowed the attorney to ask the agent if he was "aware of any circumstance that might have caused [the smugglers] duress or stress before [he] met them[.]"All four defendants objected to the ruling.

None of the defendants sought to introduce or elicit on cross-examination any evidence about jurisdiction. At the end of the trial, all four smugglers moved for acquittal on the ground that the government had failed to prove jurisdiction. The district court responded that "to the extent I need to make a separate ruling, . . . I find that we have subject matter jurisdiction in this court over this case."

All four smugglers also moved for a judgment of acquittal based on insufficient evidence at the close of the government's case and again after they rested. The district judge denied the motions. The jury convicted each smuggler on both charges. Martinez, Garcia, and Enriquez received concurrent sentences of 188 **[—9—]** months in prison on each count. Nunez received concurrent sentences of 152 months of imprisonment on each count.

II. STANDARDS OF REVIEW

A few different standards govern our review. We review the interpretation of the Maritime Drug Law Enforcement Act *de novo* and underlying jurisdictional findings of fact for clear error. *United States v. Tinoco*, 304 F.3d 1088, 1114 (11th Cir. 2002). We review a decision about whether to grant an evidentiary hearing for abuse of discretion. *United States v. Barsoum*, 763 F.3d 1321, 1328 (11th Cir. 2014). We review the sufficiency of the evidence *de novo* and view the evidence in the light most favorable to the government. *United States v. Estrada*, 969 F.3d 1245, 1265 (11th Cir. 2020). We also review *de novo* whether the exclusion of evidence violated a constitutional guarantee. *United States v. Ruan*, 966 F.3d 1101, 1154 (11th Cir. 2020). If it did, we will reverse unless the error was "harmless beyond a reasonable doubt." *United States v. Hurn*, 368 F.3d 1359, 1362–63 (11th Cir. 2004) (quoting *Chapman v. California*, 386 U.S. 18, 24 (1967)).

III. DISCUSSION

We divide our discussion in four parts. We first explain why the United States had jurisdiction over the smugglers' vessel. Next, we reject the smugglers' argument that the district court was obliged to grant them an evidentiary hearing on jurisdiction and conclude that any error in delaying a jurisdictional ruling was **[—10—]** harmless. **{-984-}** We then explain that sufficient evidence supports the challenged convictions. We finally decide that the ruling limiting evidence about the smugglers' confinement at sea did not infringe their right to present a complete defense, and alternatively any error was harmless.

A. Jurisdiction Existed Under the Maritime Drug Law Enforcement Act.

The Maritime Drug Law Enforcement Act prohibits knowing possession of controlled substances with intent to distribute aboard "covered vessel[s]." 46 U.S.C. § 70503(a)(1). A "covered vessel" is the first link in a chain of facts that determines subject-matter jurisdiction. *United States v. De La Garza*, 516 F.3d 1266, 1271–72 (11th Cir. 2008). The required proof of those facts reflects concern for "smooth relations between sovereigns in the domain of international waters." *Tinoco*, 304 F.3d at 1109. In keeping with those concerns, covered vessels are vessels of the United States; any vessel, if the individual in question is a United States citizen or resident alien; and "vessel[s] subject to the jurisdiction of the United States." 46 U.S.C. § 70503(e). This appeal involves only the third category.

A vessel is "subject to the jurisdiction of the United States" if it is in the customs waters of the United States or the territorial waters of a foreign nation that consents to the enforcement of United States law, if it is "a vessel without nationality," or in a few other circumstances. *Id.* § 70502(c)(1). And the Act **[—11—]** describes three ways to establish that a vessel lacks nationality when the government encounters the master or individual in charge of the vessel:

> [T]he term "vessel without nationality" includes—
>
> (A) a vessel aboard which the master or individual in charge makes a claim of registry that is denied by the nation whose registry is claimed;
>
> (B) a vessel aboard which the master or individual in charge fails, on request of an officer of the United States authorized to enforce applicable provisions of United States law, to make a claim of nationality or registry for that vessel; and

> (C) a vessel aboard which the master or individual in charge makes a claim of registry and for which the claimed nation of registry does not affirmatively and unequivocally assert that the vessel is of its nationality.

Id. § 70502(d)(1).

Section 70502(d)(1) does not list every circumstance in which a vessel lacks nationality. It uses the word "includes," which ordinarily introduces only examples. Antonin Scalia & Bryan A. Garner, *Reading Law: The Interpretation of Legal Texts* § 15, at 132–33 (2012). And its use of the term "includes" differs materially from the use of the phrase "includes only" in the next subsection. 46 U.S.C. § 70502(e). That material variation confirms that the three circumstances enumerated in section 70502(d)(1) provide only examples of when a vessel lacks nationality, not an exhaustive list. Scalia & Garner, *Reading Law* § 25, at 170–73. To determine what other vessels are "vessel[s] without nationality," we interpret that term against the backdrop of its "reasonably well developed meaning" in customary international law. *United States v. Rosero*, 42 F.3d 166, 170–71 (3d Cir. **[—12—]** 1994) (Alito, J.); *see also United States v. Matos-Luchi*, 627 F.3d 1, 4 (1st Cir. 2010).

Under customary international law, any nation may grant ships the right to sail under its flag. Convention on the High Seas art. 4, *opened for signature* **{-985-}** Apr. 29, 1958, 13 U.S.T. 2312, 450 U.N.T.S. 82. A vessel registered to a nation is ordinarily subject to that nation's exclusive jurisdiction. Craig H. Allen, *The Peacetime Right of Approach and Visit and Effective Security Council Sanctions Enforcement at Sea*, 95 Int'l L. Stud. 400, 413 (2019). Association with a single nation protects the vessel from most interference by other nations. *Id.* at 413 & n.67.

A ship seeking the protection of nationality will usually make its association with its flag state obvious—classically, by flying a flag and carrying official documents as evidence of its association with its flag state. *See* Convention on the High Seas art. 5(2) ("Each State shall issue to ships to which it has granted the right to fly its flag documents to that effect."); *United States v. Obando*, 891 F.3d 929, 934–38, 6 Adm. R. 442, 444–48 (11th Cir. 2018). If a country decides to attribute its nationality to a vessel, that decision must be "disclos[ed]" so that the attribution of nationality is "cognoscible" or "ascertainab[le]." H. Meyers, *The Nationality of Ships* 156 (1967); *see also* Myres S. McDougal et al., *The Maintenance of Public Order at Sea and the Nationality of Ships*, 54 Am. J. Int'l L. 25, 27 & n.7 (1960). **[—13—]** Ordinarily, this disclosure occurs through some combination of carrying official documents on the vessel, flying the nation's flag, and entry in a national registry of vessels. *See* Meyers, *The Nationality of Ships* 177–78.

The smugglers' vessel offered none of these customary signs of nationality. It carried no documents, it flew no flag, and it had no name or identifying numbers that would permit entry into a national registry. No one on the vessel verbally claimed that it had any nationality, nor was the vessel "in a position to provide evidence" of any nationality, so it falls within the meaning of "vessel without nationality" in international law and under the Act. *Matos-Luchi*, 627 F.3d at 6 (internal quotation marks omitted).

Another provision of the Act points in the same direction. The Act describes three exclusive ways that a master or individual in charge may make a "claim of nationality or registry":

> A claim of nationality or registry under this section includes only—
>
> (1) possession on board the vessel and production of documents evidencing the vessel's nationality as provided in article 5 of the 1958 Convention on the High Seas;
>
> (2) flying its nation's ensign or flag; or
>
> (3) a verbal claim of nationality or registry by the master or individual in charge of the vessel.

Id. § 70502(e); *see Obando*, 891 F.3d at 933, 6 Adm. R. at 444. The smugglers and their boat could make no "claim of nationality or registry," and it is hard to see how a boat with no claims of nationality could be anything other than a vessel without nationality. **[—14—]**

The smugglers' boat had no master or individual in charge who could make a verbal claim of registry under section 70502(e). During the interception of the boat, a Coast Guard officer asked the smugglers who was the master or individual in charge, and no one claimed to be. The evidence showed that the smugglers were equals; each man took turns driving the boat, and Martinez said everyone decided together to turn around when the boat started having engine problems. Martinez even laughed when a federal agent asked him if the boat had a captain. The record contains no evidence of a hierarchy among the smugglers.

The smugglers argue that their equality means either that they were *all* in charge or that they took turns being in charge. And at oral argument, counsel argued that when no one has been designated as the **{-986-}** individual in charge, the person currently navigating the boat is in charge. We disagree.

These arguments misunderstand maritime law. In this context, "individual in charge" refers to someone with authority over the vessel's personnel, not someone with temporary control of navigation. The Act pairs the words "master" and "individual in charge" because they bear associated meanings in a variety of maritime statutes. *See Home Depot U. S. A., Inc. v. Jackson*, 139 S. Ct. 1743, 1751 (2019); *Mississippi ex rel. Hood v. AU Optronics Corp.*, 571 U.S. 161, 169–70 (2014); Scalia & Garner, *Reading Law* §§ 31, 39, at 195–98, 252–55. **[—15—]**

In maritime law, an individual in charge of a vessel is someone with command authority. For example, one statute limits the circumstances in which "[a]n owner, charterer, managing operator, master, individual in charge, *or other person having authority*" may order an officer to take charge of a vessel's deck watch. 46 U.S.C. § 8104(a) (emphasis added). Another statute requires the "owner, charterer, managing operator, master, or individual in charge" to enter a written employment agreement with each seaman. *Id.* § 10302(a). And the seaman must sign the agreement "in the presence of the master or individual in charge." *Id.* § 10305(2). Another statute requires the "master or other individual in charge" of certain vessels to report complaints of sexual offenses to the government. *Id.* § 10104(a). And yet another requires "the master or individual in charge" to provide a seaman with documents "[o]n discharging [him] and paying [his] wages." *Id.* § 10311(a).

The record also fails to support the smugglers' argument. When asked, no smuggler claimed to be in charge during the interception. That fact is inconsistent with the theory that everyone was in charge and with the theory that everyone took turns being in charge. Martinez denied ever being in charge when questioned later. And the record contains no other evidence to support either theory. The vessel lacked a master or individual in charge. **[—16—]**

The smugglers argue that the vessel was not stateless because the Act specifies that a vessel lacks nationality when the master or individual in charge fails to make a claim of nationality "on request of an officer of the United States authorized to enforce applicable provisions of United States law," *id.* § 70502(d)(1)(B), and no request was made during the interception. But this requirement applies only when the master or individual in charge is aboard the vessel; here, no one was in charge. And section 70502(e) makes clear that only a master or individual in charge can make a verbal claim of registry; the Coast Guard was not required to ask the crew for such a claim.

We conclude that the district court had jurisdiction under the Act. The smugglers' vessel had no indicia of nationality: no registry papers, identification markings, flag, or verbal claim of nationality by anyone, let alone a master or individual in charge. In the absence of any claim of registry, the vessel lacked nationality.

Our conclusion is consistent with our precedents. We have held that a vessel lacked nationality under the Act when it lacked indicia of nationality or registry, the captain concealed himself among the crew, and neither captain nor crew made a claim of nationality or registry when they were questioned. *United States v. De La Cruz*, 443 F.3d 830, 832 (11th Cir. 2006). We also have held that a district court had jurisdiction under the Act when a vessel "was not flying any flag and had no **[—17—]** indicia of nationality." **{-987-}** *De La Garza*, 516 F.3d at 1271–72 (internal quotation marks omitted). And we have held that jurisdiction existed when guardsmen could not identify a master and did not ask for the individual in charge; they instead asked each person on board for a claim of nationality, so "any individual who possessed the authority to make a claim of registry . . . was given the opportunity to do so at the request" of a Coast Guard officer. *United States v. Cabezas-Montano*, 949 F.3d 567, 589 n.14, 8 Adm. R. 364, 375 n.14 (11th Cir. 2020).

To the extent customary international law prescribes procedures for determining whether a vessel is stateless, it does not undermine our conclusion. It is well established that a ship can have only one nationality; if it attempts to claim association with more than one nation for its own convenience, it loses association with any nation and becomes stateless. Convention on the High Seas art. 6. Customary international law does not otherwise define the conditions under which a nation may conclude that a vessel is stateless or any examination necessary to reach that conclusion. The most important source, the Convention on the High Seas of 1958, provides that a nation's warship may visit a suspicious ship that falls within one of several categories (a ship suspected of piracy, for example), in large part to verify that ship's right to fly its flag. *Id.* art. 22(1)–(2). If suspicion persists, the warship may conduct "a further examination" aboard the ship. *Id.* But even in that context, the Convention does not specify how that examination must proceed, **[—18—]** who may make a claim of nationality, or what conclusions to draw if the vessel lacks a master or individual in charge.

Scholarly articles and treatises also offer little guidance. For example, one scholar recently explained that an examination aboard a vessel suspected of statelessness "typically continues until either there are no longer any reasonable grounds for suspecting the vessel's claim of nationality or the examination is completed." Allen, *The Peacetime Right of Approach and Visit*, at 424. The article fails to mention any mandatory questions during an onboard examination or define the consequences for the nationality of a vessel if it lacks a master or individual in charge. Another article describes the controversy over what to do with a vessel that claims no registration as "far from settled" but argues that "the underlying philosophy" of customary international law requires a vessel to affirmatively claim nationality and provide evidence supporting its claim. Andrew W. Anderson, *Jurisdiction over Stateless Vessels on the High Seas: An Appraisal Under Domestic and International Law*, 13 J. Mar. L. & Com. 323, 341 (1982). Likewise, a prominent treatise states that "a ship which obscures the cognoscibility of its [nationality] repeatedly, deliberately, and successfully may be treated as stateless." Meyers, *The Nationality of Ships* 351 (internal quotation marks omitted). But the treatise does not address whether a vessel deliberately obscures its nationality **[—19—]** when it lacks a master or individual in charge and bears no flag or markings of nationality.

We acknowledge that the only other circuit to consider a similar set of facts reached the opposite conclusion, *United States v. Prado*, 933 F.3d 121, 130–32 & n.5, 7 Adm. R. 92, 95–98 & n.5 (2d Cir. 2019), but its reasoning fails to persuade us. The Second Circuit concluded that jurisdiction was lacking when three men in a go-fast boat, none of whom identified himself as the master, were not asked for a claim of nationality or registry. *Id.*, 7 Adm. R. 92, 95–98 & n.5. It reasoned that "failure to volunteer a claim of nationality does not suffice" to create jurisdiction because the statute is clear that a vessel is stateless only if the master fails to claim registry upon request. *Id.* at 131, 7 Adm. R. at 96. And it concluded that even if no **{-988-}** one identified himself as the master, the Coast Guard should have asked each crew member if he wished to make a claim of nationality or registry. *Id.* at 131 & n.5, 7 Adm. R. at 96 & n.5. But *Prado*'s reasoning fails to grapple with the non-exhaustive nature of the examples in section 70502(d)(1) or to consider the possibility that a vessel may not have a master or individual in charge.

B. The District Court Was Not Obligated to Hold an Evidentiary Hearing on Jurisdiction, and Its Delayed Final Ruling Was Harmless Error.

The smugglers also argue that the district court erred when it declined to hold an evidentiary hearing. They argue that the Confrontation Clause required an evidentiary hearing so that they could cross-examine the government's witnesses **[—20—]** and call their own witnesses. And they argue that the Act itself requires an evidentiary hearing on jurisdiction. We reject both arguments.

The Confrontation Clause does not require an evidentiary hearing because the Act makes clear that jurisdiction is a "preliminary question[] of law to be determined solely by the trial judge"; it is not an element of the crime. 46 U.S.C. § 70504(a). For that reason, we have previously held that the admission of documentary evidence to prove jurisdiction under the Act, without affording the defendant an opportunity to cross-examine the declarant, does not violate the Confrontation Clause. *United States v. Campbell*, 743 F.3d 802, 806, 2 Adm. R. 543, 545 (11th Cir. 2014).

The Act too does not oblige a district court to hold an evidentiary hearing in every prosecution under the Act. The smugglers identify no language in the Act that creates such a requirement, and we do not see any.

The smugglers point to three decisions as suggesting the need for an evidentiary hearing, but none supports their argument. In *United States v. Iguaran*, we remanded for additional factual development because the record contained no facts supporting jurisdiction, but we did not require the district court to hold an evidentiary hearing. 821 F.3d 1335, 1337–38, 4 Adm. R. 457, 457–59 (11th Cir. 2016). We instead instructed the district court to provide the parties with "an opportunity to submit evidence" about jurisdiction. *Id.* at 1338, 4 Adm. R. at 459 (internal quotation marks omitted). In **[—21—]** *United States v. Aikins*, the Ninth Circuit held that a district court must allow "a full presentation of the evidence" if a jurisdictional fact is disputed. 923 F.2d 650, 657 (9th Cir. 1990). But the smugglers never identified a jurisdictional fact they disputed, and in any event, the Ninth Circuit later superseded that opinion on rehearing with a new opinion that lacks the language the smugglers rely upon. *See United States v. Aikins*, 946 F.2d 608 (9th Cir. 1990). The last decision the smugglers cite does not address evidentiary hearings at all; it addresses whether a jurisdictional question under a different statute should have been submitted to the jury. *Gough v. Rossmoor Corp.*, 487 F.2d 373, 376–77 (9th Cir. 1973).

A district court does not abuse its discretion when it declines to hold an evidentiary hearing in the absence of a factual dispute or proffer of evidence to be presented by the requester of the hearing. *See United States v. Cooper*, 203 F.3d 1279, 1285 (11th Cir. 2000). The smugglers have never identified any facts proved by the government that they contest. Nor have they identified additional evidence they wanted to introduce at an evidentiary hearing. The district court did not abuse its discretion by declining to hold a hearing about uncontested facts. **{-989-}**

The smugglers also argue that the district court erred by waiting until the end of the trial to make a final determination of jurisdiction, but any error was harmless. To be sure, the district court was obliged to determine whether it had jurisdiction before the trial started; after all, the Act refers to jurisdiction as a **[—22—]** "preliminary question[]." 46 U.S.C. § 70504(a). The district court made only a provisional finding of jurisdiction before trial as a concession to the smugglers to allow them to cross-examine the witnesses for the prosecution about jurisdiction during trial. After the smugglers failed to do so and otherwise failed to introduce any new evidence about jurisdiction, the district court made a final determination of jurisdiction immediately before the jury began deliberating. The smugglers suffered no prejudice from the delay of that ruling.

C. Sufficient Evidence Supported the Convictions of Martinez, Garcia, and Enriquez.

Martinez, Garcia, and Enriquez argue that the government failed to present sufficient evidence at trial that they knew they were transporting drugs. We disagree. Martinez and Enriquez admitted during their interrogations in Mobile that they knew they were agreeing to transport drugs before they left the Dominican Republic. And Garcia made incriminating statements that stopped just short of admitting to knowledge.

Admissions of knowledge aside, the men were in a small boat that contained nothing but fuel, 400 pounds of cocaine, and a few personal items. There was little room for anything else. And they were promised a lot of money for the trip.

Sufficient circumstantial evidence of knowledge exists when the government proves the obvious presence of a large quantity of contraband, a lengthy voyage, and suspicious behavior surrounding apprehension. *Tinoco*, 304 F.3d at 1123. By **[—23—]** any measure, 400 pounds of cocaine, worth about $25 or $30 million, is a large quantity of contraband. And the smugglers' journey had already stretched for five or six days. The contraband was obvious because it was in the open on the deck. The boat had no other supplies or equipment to explain why it was 50 nautical miles from shore. And the crew engaged in suspicious behavior by traveling at night with no navigational lights and attempting to destroy the contraband when the Coast Guard arrived. *See United States v. Cruickshank*, 837 F.3d 1182, 1189–90, 4 Adm. R. 472, 473–75 (11th Cir. 2016).

Martinez and Garcia argue that the government needed to prove that they knew they were transporting cocaine. The indictment alleged that they "did willfully, knowingly and unlawfully conspire with each other . . . to distribute and possess with the intent to distribute approximately 182 kilograms of cocaine." We take the opportunity to clarify our precedents on this issue.

Ordinarily, controlled-substance offenses require the government to prove the defendants' mens rea only with respect to controlled substances generally. *United States v. Lewis*, 676 F.2d 508, 512 (11th Cir. 1982). In the context of the Act, for example, the government ordinarily must prove only that the defendants knew they were transporting a controlled substance, not that they knew the controlled substance was cocaine. *See* 46 U.S.C. § 70503(a)(1). **[—24—]**

We departed from this longstanding rule in *United States v. Narog*, 372 F.3d 1243 (11th Cir. 2004). An indictment charged several defendants with conspiring to possess and distribute pseudoephedrine "knowing and having reasonable cause to **{–990–}** believe that the listed chemical would be used to manufacture a controlled substance, that is, methamphetamine." *Id.* at 1246; *see* 21 U.S.C. § 846. The district court instructed the jury that "the government need not prove that a Defendant knew or had reasonable cause to believe the exact nature of the controlled substance to be manufactured," and that it needed to prove only that "a Defendant knew or had reasonable cause to believe that the pseudoephedrine would be used to manufacture *some* controlled substance." *Narog*, 372 F.3d at 1247 (emphasis added) (internal quotation marks omitted). We reversed, holding that the language the government used in the indictment required it to prove that the defendants knew the pseudoephedrine would be used to manufacture methamphetamine and that the judge constructively amended the indictment by instructing the jury otherwise. *Id.* at 1247–50. We reasoned that by including the identity of the controlled substance in the indictment, "the government essentially charged a subset of the statutory crime," so the district court "'altered an essential element of the crime charged'" when it instructed the jury otherwise. *Id.* at 1249.

Narog is contrary to our earlier precedents. *Narog* reasoned that the government was required to prove mens rea with respect to the specific controlled **[—25—]** substance at issue because the indictment charged a subset of the offense. 372 F.3d at 1249. A subset offense is one in which "the elements of the [subset] offense are a subset of the elements of the charged offense." *Schmuck v. United States,* 489 U.S. 705, 716 (1989). And an element is any fact that must be proven to the jury. *Apprendi v. New Jersey,* 530 U.S. 466, 477–78 (2000). But our prior panel precedents make clear that a defendant's mens rea with respect to the identity of the controlled substance is not an element of a controlled-substance offense; the indictment therefore did not charge a subset offense. *Narog* depends on the opposite conclusion, so it is inconsistent with our earlier decisions.

Two decisions that predate *Narog* make this point especially clearly. Our predecessor court held in *United States v. Restrepo-Granda* that "knowledge that the substance [at issue] is a particular narcotic need not be proven," and that "knowledge that such substance is a controlled substance" would suffice. 575 F.2d 524, 527 (5th Cir. 1978). The indictment in question charged that the defendant "'knowingly and intentionally did unlawfully possess [with] intent to distribute approximately 1943.6 grams of Cocaine-Hydrochloride.'" *Id.* at 526. So, long before *Narog*, we held that the mens rea with respect to the specific controlled substance was not an element of the crime. Likewise, we held in *United States v. Gomez* that "a defendant need not be found to know the particular drug involved in order to receive" the enhanced penalties for some drugs that apply under one **[—26—]** statute, 21 U.S.C. § 841(b)(1). 905 F.2d 1513, 1514 (11th Cir. 1990). The indictment in *Gomez* charged the defendant with possession of cocaine and possession with intent to distribute cocaine. *Id.* So *Gomez* makes clear that, even keeping in mind the principle that "the core crime and [any] fact[s] triggering [a] mandatory minimum sentence together constitute a new, aggravated crime, each element of which must be submitted to the jury," *Alleyne v. United States,* 570 U.S. 99, 113 (2013), mens rea with respect to the specific controlled substance is not an element of the crime.

These holdings are inconsistent with the holding in *Narog* that an indictment **{-991-}** can charge a subset offense that requires it to prove knowledge of the specific controlled substance at issue. *Narog,* 372 F.3d at 1249. The indictment could not have charged such a subset crime because knowledge of the specific controlled substance is not an element of a controlled-substance offense. *Gomez,* 905 F.2d at 1514; *Restrepo-Granda,* 575 F.2d at 527. When two decisions conflict, the earlier decision controls. *U.S. Sec. & Exch. Comm'n v. Ginsburg,* 362 F.3d 1292, 1298 (11th Cir. 2004); Bryan A. Garner et al., *The Law of Judicial Precedent* § 36, at 303 (2016). To be sure, no one appears to have raised a subset or constructive amendment argument in *Restrepo-Granda* or *Gomez.* But the "argument that [*Narog*] should not be [controlled] by [those decisions] because this point was not really argued in th[ose] case[s] runs afoul of our decisions that a prior panel **[—27—]** precedent cannot be circumvented or ignored on the basis of argument not made to or considered by the prior panel." *Tippitt v. Reliance Std. Life Ins. Co.,* 457 F.3d 1227, 1234 (11th Cir. 2006). *Narog* is not binding, and we reject the smugglers' argument that the government failed to supply required proof that they knew they were transporting cocaine.

We distinguished *Narog* in two later decisions, but neither affects our conclusion today. In each decision, we concluded, notwithstanding *Narog,* that the indictment did not require proof of the mens rea with respect to the specific substance mentioned in the indictment. *United States v. Achey,* 943 F.3d 909, 912, 915–16 (11th Cir. 2019); *United States v. Sanders,* 668 F.3d 1298, 1311–12 (11th Cir. 2012). Their outcomes, and the reasoning necessary to those outcomes that the indictments did not require proof of knowledge of the type of controlled substance, are thus consistent with our older decisions. *See* Garner et al., *The Law of Judicial Precedent* § 4, at 44–45. And neither decision attempted to reconcile *Narog* with our earlier precedents.

D. The District Court Did Not Deprive Martinez, Garcia, or Enriquez of a Meaningful Opportunity to Present a Complete Defense.

The Constitution guarantees criminal defendants a meaningful opportunity to present a complete defense. *Holmes v. South Carolina*, 547 U.S. 319, 324 (2006); *Crane v. Kentucky*, 476 U.S. 683, 690 (1986). Martinez, Garcia, and Enriquez argue that the district court deprived them of this right when it prohibited **[—28—]** them from cross-examining the government's witnesses about more than the basic details of their 10-day outdoor confinement on the *Richard Dixon*. But the district court did not infringe on their right, and alternatively any error was harmless.

The right to a meaningful opportunity to present a complete defense is "subject to reasonable restrictions." *United States v. Scheffer*, 523 U.S. 303, 308 (1998). An evidentiary ruling may violate the right if it "infringe[s] upon a weighty interest of the accused." *Holmes*, 547 U.S. at 324 (alteration adopted) (internal quotation marks omitted). But an evidentiary ruling does not infringe a weighty interest because the excluded testimony only "would have been helpful." *United States v. Gillis*, 938 F.3d 1181, 1195 (11th Cir. 2019). Nor does an evidentiary ruling infringe on a defendant's rights when it prevents him merely from "increas[ing] the quantity of witnesses who would tell the jury what other witnesses already said." *United States v. Mitrovic*, 890 F.3d 1217, 1222 (11th Cir. 2018).

The district court prevented the smugglers only from introducing cumulative **{-992-}** evidence, so it did not infringe their weighty interests. It allowed Garcia's counsel to elicit testimony that the smugglers were confined on the deck of the Coast Guard cutter and that they might have been shackled. And the record contained evidence that the smugglers were aboard the cutter for 10 days. After the government objected to additional cross-examination on the point, the district court **[—29—]** ruled that the time aboard the *Richard Dixon* was too remote from the interrogation to bear strongly on the credibility of the smugglers' confessions, so the matter did not warrant further cross-examination. To be sure, absent an instruction to move on, the smugglers could have asked additional questions of the same Coast Guard officer or asked the same questions of other Coast Guard witnesses. But the district court allowed the smugglers to place the key facts before the jury, so it did not violate the smugglers' right to defend themselves. *Id.*

Even if it had, any error was harmless. A constitutional error may be harmless if there was ample evidence to convict absent the error. *United States v. Pon*, 963 F.3d 1207, 1239–40 (11th Cir. 2020). The government presented a video recording from the patrol plane, credible testimony that the smugglers attempted to throw the cocaine overboard when the Coast Guard approached, the confiscated cocaine, photos of the boat showing that the smugglers sat just inches away from the cocaine, and expert testimony that the smugglers' behavior was typical of cocaine importation from Colombia through the Dominican Republic into Puerto Rico. And the smugglers were able to introduce "the essence of" the desired testimony. *United States v. Harris*, 916 F.3d 948, 959 (11th Cir. 2019). They introduced evidence that they were held on the deck of the *Richard Dixon*, that they might have been shackled, and that they were intercepted at sea on December **[—30—]** 24 and were not put ashore until January 3. Those facts were enough to permit them to challenge the credibility of their interrogations.

IV. CONCLUSION

We **AFFIRM** the smugglers' convictions.

United States Court of Appeals
for the Eleventh Circuit

No. 19-14324

GOODLOE
VS.
ROYAL CARIBBEAN CRUISES, LTD.

Appeal from the United States District Court for the Southern District of Florida

Decided: June 21, 2021

Citation: 1 F.4th 1289, 9 Adm. R. 396 (11th Cir. 2021).

Before **JORDAN**, **PRYOR**, and **BRANCH**, Circuit Judges.

[—2—] {-1291-} PRYOR, Circuit Judge:

Laura Goodloe brought this wrongful death suit on behalf of the estate of her deceased father, Richard Puchalski, against Royal Caribbean Cruises ("RCL"). Mr. Puchalski died of a heart attack after seeing a doctor on board an RCL cruise ship. In the district court, a jury found RCL liable and awarded pecuniary and substantial non-pecuniary damages. RCL now appeals the award of non-pecuniary damages.

The question before us—whether Ms. Goodloe can recover non-pecuniary damages—depends on the law that applies here. General maritime law does not allow non-pecuniary damages for wrongful death, but the Supreme Court has held that state law may supplement general maritime law for damages in wrongful death suits for deaths that occur within state territorial waters. *Yamaha Motor Corp., USA v. Calhoun*, 516 U.S. 199, 216 (1996). The district court found that Florida law governs the award of damages in this case. On appeal, RCL argues that this was error and that Wisconsin law should apply instead. After careful consideration of the facts and circumstances of this case, and with the benefit of oral argument, we affirm. **[—3—]**

I. BACKGROUND

Mr. Puchalski, a Wisconsin citizen, and his wife took a cruise aboard an RCL cruise ship. While the ship was docked in Juneau, Alaska, he began experiencing shortness of breath and went to the ship's infirmary. He was examined by the ship's physician, Dr. Amanda Saunders, and given prescription medication—an ACE inhibitor, a beta blocker, and a diuretic. Mr. Puchalski returned to his quarters, where he collapsed. He was taken to a hospital in Juneau and from there was airlifted to an intensive care unit in Anchorage, Alaska, where he died several days later.

Ms. Goodloe, on behalf of Mr. Puchalski's estate, sued RCL, a Liberian corporation headquartered in Florida. She brought the suit in the Southern District of Florida as required by the forum selection clause on Mr. Puchalski's cruise ticket. She **{-1292-}** alleged two claims for relief, negligent medical care and treatment by RCL employees or actual agents and negligence against RCL itself based on its apparent authority over those employees or actual agents.

Before trial, the parties raised the issue of whether Ms. Goodloe could recover non-pecuniary damages on her claims. The dispute turned on a choice-of-law question: whether Wisconsin or Florida law should supplement general maritime law as allowed by *Calhoun*, 516 U.S. at 215–16. Florida law would have authorized non-pecuniary damages. *See* Fla. Stat. § 768.21 (allowing damages for **[—4—]** loss of companionship and mental pain and suffering). Wisconsin law would not have. *See* Wis. Stat. §§ 895.03, 895.04(4) (capping non-pecuniary damages in wrongful death actions to $350,000 for deaths that are caused within Wisconsin and providing no remedy for deaths that happen outside the state). Rather than litigate this choice-of-law question before trial, the parties agreed to address it only if a damages award made it necessary.

Following a four-day trial, the jury found RCL liable and awarded damages. After a stipulated reduction and application of the jury's comparative fault percentages to the damages award, the total award to Ms. Goodloe was $3,384,073.22 in damages, $3,360,000 of which represented non-pecuniary losses. The non-pecuniary award implicated the unresolved choice-of-law question, so RCL filed a Motion for Remittitur arguing that Wisconsin law should apply under the maritime choice-of-law test established in *Lauritzen v. Larsen*, 345 U.S. 571 (1953). To support its argument, RCL emphasized that Wisconsin was Mr. Puchalski's domicile before his death and he received his cruise ticket in Wisconsin. RCL argued that because Wisconsin law does not provide for the recovery of damages for deaths caused outside the state, the award in this case should be reduced to include only pecuniary damages, which are allowed under maritime law. **[—5—]**

The district court denied RCL's Motion for Remittitur and determined that Florida law governs damages in this case. In reaching this decision, the district court stated that "the *Lauritzen* factors, at their core, aim to identify the state with the most significant relationship to the action." Doc. 182 at 21.[1] It also noted that RCL was headquartered in Florida and the ticket had a Florida forum selection clause. The district court then contrasted Wisconsin law's territorial limitation with Florida law's lack of one. Because Wisconsin's wrongful death law does not apply to deaths occurring outside the state, the court concluded that Wisconsin law should not be applied in a case pending in Florida to a death that occurred in Alaska. Therefore, the court applied Florida law and denied the motion.

This appeal followed.

II. STANDARD OF REVIEW

Generally, we review the denial of a motion for remittitur under an abuse of discretion standard. *Moore v. Appliance Direct, Inc.*, 708 F.3d 1233, 1237 (11th Cir. 2013). "A ruling based on an error of law is an abuse of discretion." *Smith v. Casey*, 741 F.3d 1236, 1244 (11th Cir. 2014) (alteration adopted) (internal quotation marks omitted). A conflict-of-laws issue "present[s] a legal question which appellate courts review *de novo*." *Grupo Televisa, S.A. v. Telemundo* **[—6—]** *Commc'ns Grp., Inc.*, 485 F.3d 1233, 1239 (11th Cir. 2007). In this case, we consider the conflict-of-laws issue of which state's law should supplement federal maritime law. Our standard **{-1293-}** of review thus is *de novo*, even though the question comes to us on review of the district court's denial of a motion for remittitur.

III. DISCUSSION

Because Mr. Puchalski's death occurred in navigable waters, general maritime law governs the case and provides the wrongful death cause of action. General maritime law does not, however, provide a comprehensive remedy for all deaths that occur in state territorial waters. Instead, state statutes may supplement maritime law and allow for remedies beyond those afforded by maritime law alone. *Calhoun*, 516 U.S. at 215–16.

Relying on *Calhoun*, the parties here agree that state law can supplement general maritime law and, depending on the remedies offered by state law, provide additional remedies. They disagree over which state's law should apply. RCL argues for Wisconsin law, which caps non-pecuniary damages at $350,000 for wrongful deaths caused in Wisconsin. Wis. Stat. § 895.04(4). Wisconsin does not apply its own law to deaths that happen outside of the state.[2] *Id.* § 895.03; *see also* **[—7—]** *Waranka v. Wadena Ins. Co.*, 847 N.W.2d 324, 329 (Wis. 2014) ("If no Wisconsin wrongful death cause of action arises under

[1] "Doc." numbers refer to the district court's docket entries.

[2] Wisconsin's wrongful death statute provides:

> Whenever the death of a person shall be caused by a wrongful act, neglect or default and the act, neglect or default is such as would, if death had not ensued, have entitled the party injured to maintain an action and recover damages in respect [—7—] thereof, then and in every such case the person who would have been liable, if death had not ensued, shall be liable to an action for damages notwithstanding the death of the person injured; *provided, that such action shall be brought for a death caused in this state.*

Wis. Stat. § 895.03 (emphasis added).

Wis. Stat. § 895.03, . . . Wis. Stat. § 895.04 terms and limitations do not apply."). Ms. Goodloe urges us to apply Florida law, which, by contrast, allows for non-pecuniary damages with no cap and applies regardless of where the death is caused.[3] *See* Fla. Stat. §§ 768.19 (cause of action), 768.21 (damages). If Florida law supplements, the damages award stands. If Wisconsin law supplements, the fact that the death occurred outside Wisconsin forecloses the availability of non-pecuniary damages.

The Supreme Court's decision in *Calhoun* did not address how we should resolve the choice-of-law issue, 516 U.S. at 216 n.14, however, and we have not previously addressed how to resolve a domestic choice-of-law question under **[—8—]** maritime law. The parties point to *Lauritzen,* in which the Supreme Court addressed how to resolve *international* choice-of-law questions in maritime tort cases. 345 U.S. at 571. We agree with the parties that the test established in *Lauritzen* applies here, but it must be adjusted for application in the domestic choice-of-law context. Applying a modified *Lauritzen* test to the facts of this case, we conclude that Florida law supplements the remedies available under maritime tort law. **{-1294-}**

A. Modified *Lauritzen* Test for Domestic Choice-of-Law Questions Arising Under Maritime Law

In deciding how to apply *Lauritzen* in the domestic context, we begin with a brief discussion of the case itself and then explain how its factors apply in a domestic choice-of-law analysis. In *Lauritzen,* a Danish seaman was injured while working on a Danish ship that was docked in Cuba. *Id.* at 573. He brought a claim under the Jones Act against the ship's owner in the Southern District of New York, where he had joined the crew and signed his employment contract. *Id.* The shipowner argued that Danish law, rather than the federal Jones Act, applied, and that the seaman had received all the damages he was entitled to under Danish law.[4] *Id.* at 574–75. **[—9—]**

To decide which law applied, the Court analyzed seven factors or points of contact that "alone or in combination, are generally conceded to influence choice of law to govern a tort claim, particularly a maritime tort claim." *Id.* at 583. In discussing the factors, the Court did not establish a rigid test for determining which jurisdiction's law to apply. Instead, it provided a framework to help determine which sovereign has the most significant connection to the case and the greatest interest in having its law applied. *Id.* at 582 ("Maritime law, like our municipal law, has attempted to avoid or resolve conflicts between competing laws by ascertaining *and valuing* points of contact between the transaction and the states or governments whose competing laws are involved." (emphasis added)); *see Calhoun v. Yamaha Motor Corp., U.S.A.*, 216 F.3d 338, 346 (3d Cir. 2000) ("[T]he *Lauritzen* factors, viewed as a whole, represented a departure from the application—in admiralty cases—of the lex loci delecti rule and a move toward analyzing which state had the most significant relationship to the incident and the dominant interest in having its law applied."). The factors the Court considered were: (1) place of the wrongful act, (2) law of the flag, (3)

---

[3] Florida's wrongful death statute provides:

> Damages may be awarded as follows:
>
> (1) Each survivor may recover the value of lost support and services from the date of the decedent's injury to her or his death, with interest, and future loss of support and services from the date of death and reduced to present value . . .
>
> (2) The surviving spouse may also recover for loss of the decedent's companionship and protection and for mental pain and suffering from the date of injury. . . .
>
> (5) Medical or funeral expenses due to the decedent's injury or death may be recovered by a survivor who has paid them.

Fla. Stat. § 768.21.

[4] Neither party argued for the application of Cuban law.

allegiance or domicile of the injured, (4) allegiance or domicile of the defendant shipowner, (5) place of contract, (6) inaccessibility of the foreign forum, and (7) law of the forum. *Id.* at 584–92. In a later Jones Act suit by a noncitizen seaman against a noncitizen shipowner, the Court added an eighth factor: the shipowner's base of operations. **[—10—]** *Hellenic Lines Ltd. v. Rhoditis*, 398 U.S. 306, 309 (1970). Other factors, such as the structure of the remedial schemes under each nation's laws, may also be considered. *See Lauritzen*, 345 U.S. at 575–76 (evaluating the Dutch scheme for torts by sailors against shipowners as an indication of the Netherlands' interest in the suit).

Both parties agree that *Lauritzen* applies in this case. Indeed, one of our sister circuits has used *Lauritzen* to resolve a domestic choice-of-law dispute in a maritime tort case, *Calhoun v. Yamaha Motor Corp*, on remand from the Supreme Court. However, two of the *Lauritzen* factors address concerns not present in a domestic choice-of-law analysis. First, the law of the flag, central to the Court's decision in *Lauritzen*, 345 U.S. at 584–85, applies purely in the international context. A ship's flag indicates its nationality; thus, the law of the flag signifies a country's interest in a case against its shipowner national. *Id.* at 584. There is no comparable indicator in a domestic choice-of-law dispute.

Second, the inaccessibility of the foreign forum is potentially relevant only in an international context. Domestically, federal courts routinely apply the law of states **{-1295-}** other than the forum. By contrast, in international choice-of-law cases the question of accessibility may be more pressing, as other countries may require a tort to be litigated in their own courts. *See id.* at 590 (noting that Panama allows **[—11—]** seamen's suits under Panamanian law to be brought only in Panamanian courts). That consideration does not exist here.

We are left with six *Lauritzen* factors to consider when conducting a domestic choice-of-law analysis under maritime law: (1) place of the wrongful act, (2) domicile of the injured, (3) domicile of the defendant, (4) place of contract, (5) law of the forum, and (6) location of the defendant's base of operations.[5] As the Third Circuit explained in *Calhoun*, the *Lauritzen* factors help us to "analyz[e] which state had the most significant relationship to the incident and the dominant interest in having its law applied." 216 F.3d at 346; *see Scott v. E. Air Lines*, 399 F.2d 14, 28–29 (3rd Cir. 1967) (en banc) (applying *Lauritzen* and observing that choice-of-law rules under federal maritime jurisdiction were designed to "take into account the interest of the State having significant contact with the parties to the litigation" (internal quotation marks omitted)); *see also Piamba Cortes v. Am. Airlines, Inc.*, 177 F.3d 1272, 1299–1303 (11th Cir. 1999) (completing a choice-of-law analysis, although not under admiralty jurisdiction, by identifying the points of contact and then weighing the relative interests of Florida and Colombia in having their laws applied in a tort action); Restatement (Second) Conflict of Laws §§ 6(2), 145 (Am. L. Inst. 1988) (establishing factors to assist courts facing choice-of-law **[—12—]** questions in tort cases to weigh competing jurisdictions' contacts with the dispute and the parties and their interests in having their laws applied). Next, we apply these factors to this case.

B. Under a Domestic *Lauritzen* Analysis, Florida Law Applies Here.

Having laid out the appropriate factors to consider, we now turn to which state has the most significant relationship to the case and the dominant interest in having its law applied. Of the six factors we use to guide our analysis, two—the domicile/base of operations of the shipowner and the law of the forum—point to Florida. One—the decedent's domicile—points to Wisconsin. The remaining factors, as we will explain, do not point significantly toward either state. Based on the *Lauritzen* factors, Florida has a slightly stronger connection to the case than Wisconsin, although not so strong as to be

[5] In a case like this one, where a single state is both the defendant's domicile and the location of its base of operations, these two factors merge into a single factor.

dispositive. But when we value and compare the two states' interests, *see Lauritzen*, 345 U.S. at 582, as expressed through their wrongful death laws, we conclude that Florida law should apply here. RCL argues, despite Florida's connection and interests, that applying Florida law would conflict with our precedent or lead to untenable outcomes in future cases. Ultimately, though, we find its arguments unconvincing.

We begin by examining each state's connections to this case using the *Lauritzen* factors. Wisconsin's sole connection is as the domicile of the deceased. Florida has two connections to the case. First, Florida is RCL's domicile and base **[—13—]** of operations. Although RCL is incorporated in Liberia, its operations are headquartered in Florida. It has no claim to domicile in any other state.

Florida is also the forum state. RCL argues that we should give no weight to the forum-state factor because the forum in a tort case is often fortuitous and therefore **{-1296-}** no indication of any real connection to the case. RCL is correct that the Supreme Court has said the forum state often has little interest in a given case because its connection to the tort or the parties was fortuitous. *See Lauritzen*, 345 U.S. at 590–91 (determining that the forum state's interest was of little importance to a choice-of-law analysis solely because the plaintiff happened to file there); *cf. Scott v. E. Air Lines*, 399 F.2d 18, 28 (3d Cir. 1967) (en banc) (applying *Lauritzen* and refusing to apply the law of Massachusetts, where the crash took place, in part because the location of the crash was "adventitious"). But the fortuitous nature of the connection to the forum state limits the weight we give to the forum-state factor, not whether we can consider it as a factor at all. Moreover, here, the forum was not fortuitous. RCL chose—and mandated—the Southern District of Florida as the forum through the forum selection clause it included in the passenger ticket contract. Of course, forum selection clauses are distinct from choice-of-law provisions and do not dictate that the law of the forum be applied. We have located no caselaw addressing whether we should give the forum state any weight in our choice-of-law analysis where the forum is mandated by a forum **[—14—]** selection clause. But we cannot say that a Florida company's choice to require that all suits against it be filed in a federal district court in Florida is irrelevant in determining Florida's connection to a case. *Cf. Carnival Cruise Lines, Inc. v. Shute*, 499 U.S. 585, 593–94 (1991) (identifying the benefits to cruise lines and litigants of forum selection clauses).

The two remaining *Lauritzen* factors, the place of the wrongful act and the place of contract do not favor either Florida or Wisconsin. Alaska is the place of the wrongful act, but neither party argues that Alaskan law should control. We therefore do not include this factor in our analysis. *Id.* at 584 (discarding Cuban law in choice-of-law analysis because neither party argued for it, even though the wrongful act occurred in the Havana harbor).

As to the place of contract, the parties disagree about where the contract was formed. RCL maintains that it was formed in Wisconsin, where the Puchalskis received their cruise tickets and where their travels began. Ms. Goodloe argues that the place of contract was Connecticut because a Connecticut travel agent purchased and received the tickets from RCL on the Puchalskis' behalf and then sent them from Connecticut to the Puchalskis. Fortunately, we need not resolve this question to complete our analysis. In *Lauritzen*, the Supreme Court said the place of contract should have little bearing on the choice-of-law analysis in a maritime tort case. *Id.* at 588–89. There, the Court declared the location fortuitous **[—15—]** and gave it little weight. *Id.* On the facts before us, where the contract was formed seems similarly fortuitous, so we do not factor it into our choice-of-law analysis.

Based on the relevant *Lauritzen* factors, Florida has a slightly stronger connection to this case. It is both the forum state and the domicile/base of operations of the defendant corporation, whereas Wisconsin's sole connection is as the domicile of the deceased. But *Lauritzen* does not counsel us to merely count each state's points of contact and choose the state with the most connections. We turn now to comparing the two states' relative interests in having their laws applied here. This juxtaposition makes clear that Florida law should govern.

In an international choice-of-law case outside the maritime tort context, we have held that "Florida . . . retains an interest in ensuring that a compensatory damages **{-1297-}** award against its own domiciliary defendants is not excessive." *Piamba Cortes*, 177 F.3d at 1301.[6] Because RCL is a domiciliary of Florida, Florida's **[—16—]** "interest would be furthered by applying Florida's compensatory damages scheme to this case," even though the damages award against RCL would be lower if Wisconsin's law were applied. *Id.* Florida courts apply Florida law in wrongful death suits brought against Floridians, even when the death happened outside of Florida. *See Harris v. Berkowitz*, 433 So. 2d 613, 613–15 (Fla. Dist. Ct. App. 1983) (applying Florida law in a wrongful death suit over a death that occurred in Maine). By contrast, Wisconsin law does not govern, and thereby express an interest in, all wrongful death suits concerning its domiciliaries. Wisconsin's wrongful death statute has a strict territorial limitation; the statute and the accompanying damages cap do not apply to deaths caused outside of Wisconsin. *Waranka*, 847 N.W.2d at 329 ("[T]he plain language of the wrongful death statute, Wis. Stat. § 895.03, prevents its application to deaths caused outside of the state."). If a Wisconsin plaintiff brings a wrongful death action against a Wisconsin defendant in a Wisconsin forum, the court will nonetheless apply the law of the state where the death was caused. *Id.* at 332. This indicates Wisconsin's interests would not be served by applying Wisconsin law to this case. Applying Florida law, however, would further Florida's interests in wrongful death suits involving its domiciliaries.

In sum, Florida has a slightly stronger connection to this case than Wisconsin, though not so strong as to be dispositive. Instead, Florida's interest **[—17—]** dominates because its wrongful death law applies to deaths that happen outside of the state. We note, too, that this is not a case in which the plaintiff argues for the application of her home state's law, as was the case in the Third Circuit's decision in *Calhoun*. Here, the defendant is attempting to use Wisconsin law as a sword against a Wisconsin resident plaintiff. We therefore agree with the district court that Florida's law should supplement general maritime law in this case.

Before concluding, we address two counter arguments RCL makes against the application of Florida law. First, RCL argues that applying Florida law here would conflict with our decision in *Piamba Cortes*. In that case, American Airlines, a Delaware corporation headquartered in Texas, and two of its pilots, both Florida citizens, were sued for a Colombian citizen's death after an airplane crash in Colombia. *Piamba Cortes*, 177 F.3d at 1276–79. The parties disagreed over whether, under choice-of-law principles, Florida or Colombian law governed damages. The defendants urged the application of Colombian law because Florida law allowed for generous non-pecuniary damages in wrongful death suits, whereas Colombian law capped non-pecuniary damages. *Id.* at 1299–1300. After looking at each jurisdiction's **{-1298-}** connections and evaluating the respective interests of the two **[—18—]** jurisdictions, among other factors, we held

[6] *Piamba Cortes* was governed not by maritime law but by the Warsaw Convention. *Id.* at 1276. Noting that the case could be seen as arising under diversity or federal question jurisdiction, we applied the conflict-of-laws rules of both the forum state and federal common law because they were identical: both used the factors set forth in §§ 6(2) and 145 of the Restatement (Second) of Conflicts of Law to determine whether Florida or Colombian law should apply. *Id.* at 1296–1303 & n.19. Although the factors the Restatement directs courts to consider are not identical to the factors set out in *Lauritzen*, like *Lauritzen*, the Restatement's test looks at each jurisdiction's connections to the dispute and weighs them to determine which state has the "most significant relationship to the occurrence and the parties." Restatement (Second) Conflict of Laws § 145. The Restatement also resembles *Lauritzen* in that it invites the examination of, among other things, the "relative interests of [the] states in the determination of the particular issue." *Id.* at § 6(2).

that Florida law should apply.[7] *Id.* at 1300–03.

RCL points to our statement in *Piamba Cortes* that "Florida . . . possesses no interest in compensating domiciliaries of other jurisdictions more richly than they would receive in their own courts." *Id.* at 1301. Relying on this statement, RCL contends that we should not apply Florida law here because Ms. Goodloe would be compensated more richly under Florida law than she would in a Wisconsin court under Wisconsin law. RCL's argument ignores *Piamba Cortes*'s holding and reasoning, however. Following the quote on which RCL relies, we explained that Florida also possessed an interest in ensuring that judgments against its own residents were not excessive. *Id.* In this case, Florida has the same interest in protecting its residents from excessive damages awards. And here, as in *Piamba Cortes*, we reject the argument that we must apply Florida law simply because it **[—19—]** would result in a lower damages award against a Florida domiciliary. Although we did not explicitly say so in *Piamba Cortes*, Florida's legislature apparently does not view awards of non-pecuniary damages as excessive because, if it did, Florida law would not authorize their recovery. Applying *Lauritzen* to this case, we reach a similar conclusion. Although Florida has no apparent interest in allowing Ms. Goodloe to recover a larger award than she would receive in a Wisconsin court under Wisconsin law, it has another compelling interest that weighs in favor of applying Florida law.

Second, RCL argues that if we conclude Florida law applies here, it necessarily will apply in every wrongful death action against a cruise ship company based in Florida or with a forum selection clause requiring venue in Florida. This is not so. If, for example, Wisconsin's wrongful death law covered deaths caused outside of Wisconsin, we might well have reached a different conclusion. Applying *Lauritzen* to the facts and circumstances of this case, we conclude that Florida has the stronger interest in having its law applied. But our holding does not mean that Florida law will always apply to wrongful death cases against cruise ship companies based in Florida.

IV. CONCLUSION

For the foregoing reasons, we affirm the district court's ruling that Florida law governs the award of damages in this case. **[—20—]**

AFFIRMED.

---

[7] In conducting our analysis in *Piamba Cortes*, we noted, on the one hand, that although Florida law expressed an interest in shifting the losses in wrongful deaths from the survivors to the wrongdoers, the state had no interest in compensating other jurisdictions' domiciliaries more richly than courts in their own jurisdictions would. 177 F.3d at 1301. On the other hand, we observed, the state's interest in protecting its domiciliaries against excessive compensatory damages awards weighed in favor of applying Florida law. *Id.* After examining these and other interests, we found that Colombia's "compelling" interest in compensating its own domiciliaries injured on its soil was "slightly" weightier than Florida's interest in ensuring that its own domiciliaries did not face excessive damages awards. *Id.* We then explained that "[t]his conclusion, however, does not end our analysis under section 6(2) [of the Restatement], and we must proceed to examine the remaining factors." *Id.* After analyzing the remaining factors—including the ease of applying Florida law compared to Colombian law—we concluded that Florida law should apply, even though Colombia's compensatory damages scheme would have resulted in a much lower damages award against Florida's domiciliaries. *See id.* at 1299, 1301–03.

United States Court of Appeals
for the Eleventh Circuit

No. 20-10452

YUSKO
vs.
NCL (BAHAMAS), LTD.

Appeal from the United States District Court for the Southern District of Florida

Decided: July 12, 2021

Citation: 4 F.4th 1164, 9 Adm. R. 403 (11th Cir. 2021).

Before **MARTIN, GRANT,** and **BRASHER,** Circuit Judges.

[—1—] {-1165-} **BRASHER,** Circuit Judge: **{-1166-}**

This appeal requires us to decide whether a shipowner is liable under maritime law when its employee negligently injures a passenger. After falling during a dance **[—2—]** competition on a cruise ship, passenger Joann Yusko sued the ship's owner NCL (Bahamas), Ltd., for negligence. She alleged that her partner in the competition—a professional dancer and cruise ship employee—released her hands as she leaned away from him during a dance move, causing her to fall backward and hit her head on the deck. The district court granted summary judgment in favor of NCL because NCL did not have actual or constructive notice of a risk-creating condition on the ship. But the district court applied the wrong standard. Our precedent assumes—and today we expressly hold—that when a passenger makes a maritime negligence claim against a shipowner based on an employee's negligence under a theory of vicarious liability, the passenger need not establish that the shipowner had actual or constructive notice of a risk-creating condition. Accordingly, we reverse and remand.

I. BACKGROUND

NCL owns a cruise ship called the *Norwegian Gem.* Near the end of 2017, Yusko—who was 64 years old at the time—boarded the *Norwegian Gem* for a ten-day cruise. One evening during the cruise, Yusko volunteered to participate in a dance competition called "Dancing with the Stars." The "stars" in question were crewmembers employed by the ship, and the competition was an informal event where passengers were judged based on how entertaining they were.

The organizers of the competition paired Yusko with crewmember and **[—3—]** professional dancer Michael Kaskie. While dancing, Kaskie performed multiple dance movements in which he spun Yusko while holding her arms. Yusko danced for less than a minute before falling backward and hitting her head during one of those movements. After the fall, Yusko received treatment onboard the ship and completed the cruise. Upon her return home, multiple physicians diagnosed her with a traumatic brain injury as a result of her fall.

Yusko sued NCL in the United States District Court for the Southern District of Florida. In her amended complaint, Yusko alleged that NCL through its agents and employees was negligent in (1) its own failure to exercise reasonable care under the circumstances and (2) Kaskie's failure to act reasonably and in a manner that would keep Yusko safe.

After discovery, NCL moved for summary judgment. In its order granting NCL's motion, the district court cited our decision in *Keefe v. Bahama Cruise Line, Inc.*, 867 F.2d 1318 (11th Cir. 1989). Relying on that decision, it held that a shipowner is not liable to a passenger under maritime negligence law unless it has actual or constructive notice of the risk-creating condition that caused the passenger's injury. Because Yusko had not shown that NCL had notice of the risk-creating condition that led to her injury—*i.e.*, Kaskie's allegedly negligent dancing—the district court granted NCL's motion for summary judgment. Yusko timely appealed. **[—4—] {-1167-}**

II. STANDARD OF REVIEW

We review a district court's grant of summary judgment *de novo*, viewing all the evidence—and drawing all reasonable factual inferences—in favor of the nonmoving party. *See Amy v. Carnival Corp.*, 961 F.3d 1303, 1308, 8 Adm. R. 424, 426 (11th Cir. 2020). "A grant of summary judgment is proper if the movant shows that there is no genuine dispute as to any material fact and the movant is entitled to judgment as a matter of law." *Id.*, 8 Adm. R. at 426 (internal quotation marks omitted) (quoting FED. R. CIV. P. 56(a)). "But it is improper if a reasonable jury could find for the non-moving party." *Id.*, 8 Adm. R. at 426.

III. DISCUSSION

We have previously held that a passenger cannot succeed on a maritime negligence claim against a shipowner unless that shipowner had actual or constructive notice of a risk-creating condition. *See Keefe v. Bahama Cruise Line, Inc.*, 867 F.2d 1318, 1322 (11th Cir. 1989). On appeal, Yusko contends that the district court should not have assessed her negligence claim under that standard. She argues that the notice requirement from *Keefe* applies only to maritime negligence claims based on a theory of direct liability. And she argues that her negligence claim is based on a theory of vicarious liability. Under principles of vicarious liability, Yusko argues, NCL is liable for its employee Kaskie's negligence, even if it is not **[—5—]** directly liable for anything that it did or failed to do.[1] She therefore concludes that—contrary to the district court's analysis—she was not required to establish that NCL had notice.

We agree with Yusko. We have applied the notice requirement when a shipowner is alleged to be *directly* liable for a passenger's injuries through, for example, the negligent maintenance of its premises. But the notice requirement does not—and was never meant to—apply to maritime negligence claims proceeding under a theory of vicarious liability.

We begin with some basic principles. General maritime law governs tort claims, like this one, that arise on ships sailing in navigable waters. *See Keefe*, 867 F.2d at 1320. The Supreme Court has authorized the lower federal courts to develop this law and formulate "flexible and fair remedies in the law maritime." *Franza v. Royal Caribbean Cruises, Ltd.*, 772 F.3d 1225, 1231–32, 2 Adm. R. 582, 585 (11th Cir. 2014) (quoting *United States v. Reliable Transfer Co.*, 421 U.S. 397, 409 (1975)). Congress has neither imposed nor barred tort liability where—as here—a passenger sues a shipowner for its employee's negligence during recreational activities like dancing. **[—6—]** We are therefore "obliged to exercise our broad discretion in admiralty and maritime to develop [the] law" regarding this issue. *Id.* at 1232, 2 Adm. R. at 586.

When Congress has not spoken on a maritime matter, we rely on common law principles. *See Chaparro v. Carnival Corp.*, 693 F.3d 1333, 1336 (11th Cir. 2012). To prove negligence under common law, a plaintiff must show that (1) the tortfeasor had a duty to protect the plaintiff from a particular injury, (2) the tortfeasor breached that duty, (3) the breach actually and **{-1168-}** proximately caused the plaintiff's injury, and (4) the plaintiff suffered actual harm. *See id.* Common law also recognizes vicarious liability and allows an employer to be held liable for its employee's torts if committed during the scope of the employment. *See* Restatement (Third) Of Agency § 7.07 (2006).

For its part, the notice requirement at the center of the parties' dispute originated in *Keefe*, in which we addressed the scope of a shipowner's duty to keep its passengers safe. There, a passenger on a cruise ship slipped and fell on a wet surface while dancing and sued the shipowner for negligently maintaining its floor. *See Keefe*, 867 F.2d at

[1] NCL argues that Yusko waived this vicarious-liability argument by failing to raise it in the district court. We disagree. Count II of Yusko's amended complaint raises a claim based on the "failure of ship's employee/agent who was the assigned dancing partner of Plaintiff to act reasonably and in a manner that would keep Plaintiff safe." That kind of negligence is the hallmark of vicarious liability. Moreover, in her response to NCL's motion for summary judgment, Yusko argued that the "negligent act that [she] has alleged in this case is NCL's *employee's* dangerous *manner* of dancing" and the "no-notice defense does not apply."

1320. We had to determine "the correct standard of care against which a shipowner's conduct must be measured." *Id.* at 1321. And we held "that the benchmark against which a shipowner's behavior must be measured is ordinary reasonable care under the circumstances." *Id.* at 1322. In evaluating the shipowner's duty to exercise ordinary reasonable care in that case, we held, "as a **[—7—]** prerequisite to imposing liability, that the carrier [must] have had actual or constructive notice of the risk-creating condition, at least where, as here, the menace is one commonly encountered on land and not clearly linked to nautical adventure." *Id.*

The following year, we reiterated that notice requirement in *Everett v. Carnival Cruise Lines*, 912 F.2d 1355, 1358 (11th Cir. 1990). There, a passenger on a cruise ship tripped and fell over a metal threshold for a fire door and sued the shipowner for negligence. *Id.* at 1357. Relying on *Keefe*, we held again that, for the passenger's negligence claim to succeed, the shipowner must "have had actual or constructive notice of the risk-creating condition." *Id.* at 1358 (quoting *Keefe*, 867 F.2d at 1322). We then remanded the case for a new trial because the district court had failed to apply *Keefe*'s notice requirement. *Id.* at 1359.

Over the intervening decades, we have continued to require plaintiffs in maritime negligence cases to establish notice on the part of a shipowner. For example, in *Chaparro*, a passenger left a cruise ship to explore an island and was killed by gang-related gunfire. *See* 693 F.3d at 1335. Her parents and brother sued the shipowner for negligently failing to warn her about the island's crime problems, gang violence, and potential for shootings. *See id.* In our analysis, we repeated the notice requirement and held that "a cruise line owes its passengers a duty to warn of *known* dangers beyond the point of debarkation in places where passengers are **[—8—]** invited or reasonably expected to visit." *Id.* at 1336 (emphasis added) (citing *Carlisle v. Ulysses Line Ltd., S.A.*, 475 So.2d 248, 251 (Fla. Dist. Ct. App. 1985)).

More recently, we applied the notice requirement in *K.T. v. Royal Caribbean Cruises, Ltd.*, 931 F.3d 1041, 1046, 7 Adm. R. 507, 509 (11th Cir. 2019). There, a cruise-ship passenger sued a shipowner for negligently failing to monitor the ship's public areas and to prevent her from becoming intoxicated and sexually assaulted by other passengers. *Id.* at 1043, 1045, 7 Adm. R. at 507, 508–09. In reversing the district court's decision to dismiss, we noted that the passenger had alleged that the shipowner had actual knowledge of sex crimes and violence between passengers and foresaw that alcohol would be served to minors like the plaintiff to intoxicate and assault them. *Id.* at 1044, 7 Adm. R. at 508. Accepting the truth of those allegations as we were required to do, we concluded that the notice requirement had been satisfied. *Id.* at 1045, 7 Adm. R. at 508–09.

Against this backdrop, NCL argues that the district court below correctly required Yusko to establish notice as a part of her negligence claim. This is so, NCL argues, because the notice requirement applies regardless **{-1169-}** of whether a negligence claim is based on a shipowner's direct negligence or its vicarious liability for an employee's negligence. We disagree.

As an initial matter, NCL's argument erroneously conflates the very different concepts of direct and vicarious liability. Our caselaw's notice requirement defines the scope of a shipowner's duty to exercise ordinary reasonable care to passengers. **[—9—]** If a shipowner breaches that duty in a way that injures a passenger, then it may be directly liable to that passenger under maritime law. In both *Keefe* and *Everett*, the passengers sued the shipowners for negligent acts committed by the shipowners themselves—the negligent creation or maintenance of their premises. Similarly, in *Chaparro*, the passenger sued the shipowner for its negligent failure to warn of known dangers on the island where the ship had stopped. And in *K.T.*, the passenger sued the shipowner for negligently failing to monitor its premises and prevent the events that led to her sexual assault by other passengers. In all these cases, the notice requirement governed because the passengers alleged wrongdoing by the shipowner itself.

But the scope of a shipowner's duty has nothing to do with vicarious liability, which is not based on the shipowner's conduct. When the tortfeasor is an employee, the principle of vicarious liability allows "an otherwise non-faulty employer" to be held liable "for the negligent acts of [that] employee acting within the scope of employment." *Langfitt v. Fed. Marine Terminals, Inc.*, 647 F.3d 1116, 1121 (11th Cir. 2011). Unlike a party that is directly liable for a tort, a party that is vicariously liable "has not committed any breach of duty to the plaintiff but is held liable simply as a matter of legal imputation of responsibility for another's tortious acts." Restatement (Third) of Torts: Apportionment Liab. § 13 cmt. b (2000); *see also* 1 American Law of Torts § 4:1 (2021) ("'Vicarious liability' is a term generally **[—10—]** applied to legal liability that arises solely because of a relationship and not because of any act of negligence by the person held vicariously liable for the act of another."). In other words, an employer can be held liable under a vicarious liability theory even if it has not violated any duty at all. *See Meyer v. Holley*, 537 U.S. 280, 285–86 (2003) ("The principal is liable for the acts and negligence of the agent in the course of his employment, although he did not authorize or did not know of the acts complained of[.]" (quoting *New Orleans, M., & C.R. Co. v. Hanning*, 15 Wall. 649, 657 (1873)). Accordingly, it makes very little sense to rely on caselaw about the scope of a shipowner's duty where, as here, the shipowner's duty is irrelevant.

NCL's argument is also inconsistent with our precedent about vicarious liability. At first glance, it might seem that the scope of *Keefe* is as sweeping as NCL argues. After all, we did not expressly limit the notice requirement to any particular theory of liability. But our maritime precedent on employee-caused torts plainly contemplates such a limitation.

For starters, we held in *Franza* that a passenger can rely on a theory of vicarious liability "to impute to a cruise line liability for the medical negligence of its onboard nurse and doctor." 772 F.3d at 1228, 2 Adm. R. at 582. We acknowledged that, usually, a "shipowner is only liable to its passengers for medical negligence if its conduct breaches the carrier's more general duty to exercise reasonable care under the circumstances." *Id.* at 1233, 2 Adm. R. at 586 (internal quotation marks omitted) (quoting *Kermarec v.* **[—11—]** *Compagnie Generale Transatlantique*, 358 U.S. 625, 632 (1959)). But we observed that the plaintiff "d[id] not argue that [the shipowner] violated this duty directly" **{-1170-}** and that she instead sought to hold it "vicariously liable under the doctrine of respondeat superior, precisely because [its] medical employees allegedly failed to treat her father with appropriate care." *Id.*, 2 Adm. R. at 586. In approving this theory, we explained that "the Supreme Court and all of the federal circuits have for many years generally applied [vicarious liability] rules across a rich array of maritime cases." *Id.* at 1235, 2 Adm. R. at 588. And we noted that "we have regularly permitted passengers to invoke respondeat superior"—a species of vicarious liability—to sue an employer for its employee's negligence. *Id.* at 1234, 2 Adm. R. at 587 (emphasis omitted). Accordingly, we held that the shipowner could be held vicariously liable for the negligence of its medical personnel without notice of a risk-creating condition.

Likewise, in *Doe v. Celebrity Cruises, Inc.*, we were asked to determine what standard of care governed when a ship's crewmember sexually assaulted a passenger. *See* 394 F.3d 891, 893 (11th Cir. 2004). We held that shipowners are strictly liable for such intentional torts, regardless of their lack of notice. *See id.* at 913 (relying on *New Jersey Steam–Boat Co. v. Brockett*, 121 U.S. 637 (1887), and *New Orleans & N.E.R. Co. v. Jopes*, 142 U.S. 18 (1891)). We distinguished *Keefe* and *Everett* as "physical-condition cases" that had no bearing on a shipowner's liability for "a crew member assault on a passenger." *Id.* at 910. In doing so, we **[—12—]** expressly cabined the scope of those cases—along with their notice requirement—to allow vicarious liability for intentional sexual assaults.

Notwithstanding *Franza* and *Doe*, NCL argues that, unless we import a notice requirement into our vicarious liability caselaw, the notice requirement in our direct liability caselaw will be superfluous. After all, NCL argues, both Yusko and the passenger in *Keefe* were injured while dancing on a cruise ship, so why should the latter's claim potentially fail and the former's claim potentially succeed? Although there is some intuitive pull to this argument, we are ultimately unconvinced. A plaintiff is the master of his or her complaint and may choose to proceed under a theory of direct liability, vicarious liability, or both. It may be true that, in some cases, it will easier for a passenger to proceed under a theory of vicarious liability than under one of direct liability. But common sense suggests that there will be just as many occasions where passengers are limited to a theory of direct liability. Sometimes, as in *Keefe*, a passenger will not be able to identify any specific employee whose negligence caused her injury. In other cases, a passenger will seek to hold a shipowner liable for maintaining dangerous premises (as in *Everett*), for failing to warn of dangerous conditions off-ship (as in *Chaparro*), or for negligence related to the actions of other passengers (as in *K.T.*). Accordingly, we are confident that the notice requirement will have a robust field of operation despite our decision not to extend it to vicarious liability. **[—13—]**

In short, we hold that a passenger need not establish that a shipowner had actual or constructive notice of a risk-creating condition to hold a shipowner liable for the negligent acts of its employees. Consequently, the district court erred in granting summary judgment based on Yusko's inability to establish that NCL had actual or constructive notice of a risk-creating condition.

IV. CONCLUSION

For the reasons above, we **REVERSE** the district court's grant of summary judgment in favor of NCL and **REMAND** the **{-1171-}** case for further proceedings consistent with this opinion.

United States Court of Appeals
for the Eleventh Circuit

No. 19-10562

MCINTOSH
VS.
ROYAL CARIBBEAN CRUISES, LTD.

Appeal from the United States District Court for the Southern District of Florida

Decided: July 27, 2021

Citation: 5 F.4th 1309, 9 Adm. R. 408 (11th Cir. 2021).

Before **JORDAN, PRYOR,** and **BRANCH,** Circuit Judges.

[—1—] {-1310-} **JORDAN,** Circuit Judge: **{-1311-}**

A "cruise to nowhere" usually involves a ship sailing into international waters for several days without any intermediate port calls. On such a cruise, it's **[—2—]** supposedly the journey, and not the destination, that matters. This maritime negligence case involves a different type of "cruise to nowhere"—one that never departed. The *Liberty of the Seas*, owned by Royal Caribbean Cruises, was scheduled to sail from Galveston, Texas, on August 27, 2017. But Hurricane Harvey—a Category 4 storm that eventually made landfall in Texas and Louisiana—had other ideas, and Royal Caribbean cancelled the cruise on the date of its scheduled departure and offered refunds to the would-be passengers.

One of those passengers, Nikki McIntosh filed, on behalf of other similarly situated passengers, a class-action complaint against Royal Caribbean on several tort theories, including negligence, intentional infliction of emotional distress, and negligent infliction of emotional distress. She alleged that Royal Caribbean canceled the cruise and offered refunds only on the day the *Liberty of the Seas* was set to sail. Because the ticket contracts provided that no refunds would be given for passenger cancelations within 14 days of the voyage, and because Royal Caribbean repeatedly told passengers that they would lose their entire payments for the cruise if they canceled, the plaintiffs claimed that they were forced to travel to Galveston and nearby areas (like Houston) as Hurricane Harvey approached. She alleged that, while in Texas, they were forced to endure hurricane-force conditions, and suffered physical and emotional injuries. **[—3—]**

In a series of orders, the district court ruled that the case could not proceed as a class action due to a class-action waiver in the passengers' ticket contracts; that the complaint failed to plead damages sufficient to satisfy the amount-in-controversy requirement for diversity jurisdiction under 28 U.S.C. § 1332; that the plaintiffs had not established maritime jurisdiction under 28 U.S.C. § 1333(1); and that the claims for intentional and negligent infliction of emotional distress failed as a matter of law. After the district court ruled that the case could not proceed as a class action, over 100 plaintiffs filed a joint amended complaint asserting individual claims. Based upon these rulings, the court dismissed the plaintiffs' second amended complaint with prejudice.

The plaintiffs now appeal, challenging the district court's jurisdictional and merits rulings.

I

We exercise plenary review to determine whether the district court had subject-matter jurisdiction. *See, e.g., Romero v. Drummond Co., Inc.*, 552 F.3d 1303, 1313 (11th Cir. 2008).

II

The district court, acting *sua sponte*, ruled that the plaintiffs could not aggregate their emotional distress claims to satisfy the $75,000 amount-in-controversy requirement for diversity jurisdiction under 28 U.S.C. § 1332. The court **[—4—]** reasoned that the plaintiffs were not seeking to enforce rights in which they had a common and undivided interest. The court also summarily stated that the plaintiffs' claims did not arise under federal maritime law so as to provide for jurisdiction under **{-1312-}** 28 U.S.C.

§ 1333(1). We consider each of these rulings below.

A

In ruling that diversity jurisdiction was lacking, the district court committed two errors, one procedural and one substantive. Each one provides an independent basis for reversal.

First, the district court failed to give the plaintiffs notice of its intent to *sua sponte* address the matter of diversity jurisdiction. A federal court has an independent duty to ensure that it has subject-matter jurisdiction. *See, e.g., Arbaugh v. Y&H Corp.*, 546 U.S. 500, 514 (2006). And that means that it can take up the issue of such jurisdiction on its own. *See Morrison v. Allstate Indem. Co.*, 228 F.3d 1255, 1261 (11th Cir. 2000). But when it does so, it must give the parties notice and an opportunity to be heard. Its failure to do so here, therefore, was error. *See Day v. McDonough*, 547 U.S. 198, 210 (2006) ("Of course, before acting on its own initiative, a court must accord the parties fair notice and an opportunity to present their positions.") (citation omitted); *Lipofsky v. New York State Workers Comp. Bd.*, 861 F.2d 1257, 1258 (11th Cir. 1988) (holding that if a court raises on its own the issue of venue or personal jurisdiction, it "may not dismiss without first giving the **[—5—]** parties an opportunity to present their views on the issue") (citation omitted); *Republic Nat'l Bank of Dallas, et al. v. Crippen*, 224 F.2d 565, 566 (5th Cir. 1955) (explaining that the denial of the right to be heard is a violation "of due process which is never harmless error").

Second, putting aside the aggregation of damages issue, the district court failed to consider whether any individual plaintiff had satisfied the $75,000 amount-in-controversy requirement. *See Exxon Mobil Corp. v. Allapattah Serv., Inc.*, 545 U.S. 546, 549.

When a court conducts a facial review of a complaint to determine whether it has diversity jurisdiction, it must accept the plaintiff's factual allegations. *See Morrison v. Amway Corp.*, 323 F.3d 920, 924 n.5 (11th Cir. 2003). And, taking those factual allegations as true, the court can dismiss only if it is convinced "to a legal certainty" that the claims of the plaintiff in question will not exceed $75,000 (the current jurisdictional threshold). *See Hunt v. Washington State Apple Advert. Comm'n*, 432 U.S. 333, 346 (1977); *Horton v. Liberty Mutual Ins. Co.*, 367 U.S. 348, 354 (1961); *Fastcase, Inc. v. Lawriter, LLC*, 907 F.3d 1335, 1342 (11th Cir. 2018); *Deen v. Egleston*, 597 F.3d 1223, 1228 (11th Cir. 2010).

But where, as here, a plaintiff "pleads an unspecified amount of damages, [she] bears the burden of proving by a preponderance of the evidence that the claim on which jurisdiction is based exceeds the jurisdictional minimum. This additional **[—6—]** requirement is 'warranted because there is simply no estimate of damages to which a court can defer.'" *Fastcase*, 907 F.3d at 1342 (citation omitted). Because the district court acted *sua sponte*, it did not give the plaintiffs an opportunity to satisfy their burden. Nevertheless, based on our review of the record, we are convinced that at least some of the plaintiffs sufficiently pled damages over $75,000.

The plaintiffs alleged that, as a result of Royal Caribbean's delay in canceling the **{-1313-}** cruise and offering refunds, they had to travel to Galveston and nearby areas in Texas that were in a state of emergency due to Hurricane Harvey. They had to spend days in those locations trapped by a "devastating storm," often without power, and with limited food and water. And, as a result, they were "injured about their body and extremities," sustaining physical pain and suffering; mental and emotional anguish; temporary, permanent, and/or physical disability; impairment; and disfigurement. They also incurred medical expenses for the care and treatment of their injuries.

These alleged injuries and expenses—accepted as true—are sufficient to plead damages that exceed the $75,000 amount-in-controversy requirement. *See, e.g., Parker v. Four Seasons Hotels, Ltd.*, 845 F.3d 807, 809 (7th Cir. 2017) (claimed injuries and damages caused by the explosion of a shower glass door in a hotel room exceeded the $75,000 amount-in-controversy requirement, even though the plaintiff recovered only $12,000, because at the time of filing, she brought claims in good **[—7—]** faith for compensatory and punitive damages exceeding $150,000). And if there were any doubt, it is erased by the plaintiffs' individual requests for punitive damages. *See, e.g.*, *Holley Equip. Co. v. Credit Alliance Corp.*, 821 F.2d 1531, 1535 (11th Cir. 1987) ("When determining the jurisdictional amount in diversity cases, punitive damages must be considered.").[1]

That does not mean, however, that diversity jurisdiction exists. Alienage diversity under 28 U.S.C. § 1332(a)(2) "must be complete," such that "an alien on both sides of a dispute will defeat jurisdiction." *Caron v. NCL (Bahamas) Ltd.*, 910 F.3d 1359, 1364, 6 Adm. R. 471, 472 (11th Cir. 2018). Based on this principle, we held in *Caron* that § 1332(a)(2) "does not grant jurisdiction over a suit between a corporation incorporated solely in a foreign state and another alien, regardless of the corporation's principal place of business." *Id.* at 1365, 6 Adm. R. at 473. Here it appears from our review of the record that Royal Caribbean is a citizen of Liberia, where it is incorporated, and that at least some of the plaintiffs are residents of other countries (e.g., Canada, Mexico, and the Philippines). On remand, therefore, the district court will need to address whether there is complete alienage diversity. **[—8—]**

We add one more observation. The district court dismissed the plaintiffs' complaint with prejudice for lack of subject-matter jurisdiction. That was incorrect. If subject-matter jurisdiction does not exist, dismissal must be without prejudice. *See Stalley ex rel. U.S. v. Orlando Reg'l Healthcare Sys., Inc.*, 524 F.3d 1229, 1232 (11th Cir. 2008) ("A dismissal for lack of subject matter jurisdiction is not a judgment on the merits and is entered without prejudice."). And if there was no subject-matter jurisdiction, the court should have vacated its rulings on the merits of the plaintiffs' claims (unless it was going to issue alternative holdings on the merits for purposes of appeal in case diversity jurisdiction existed).

B

On remand, the district court should also consider whether there is maritime **{–1314–}** jurisdiction. In one of its orders, the district court said that maritime law applied to the plaintiffs' claims. *See* D.E. 24 at 3. But in a later order, the district court summarily stated that the plaintiffs had not alleged any facts demonstrating federal-question (i.e., maritime) jurisdiction. *See* D.E. 48 at 4.

Congress has given the federal courts original jurisdiction in "[a]ny civil case of admiralty or maritime jurisdiction, saving to suitors in all cases all other remedies to which they are otherwise entitled." 28 U.S.C. § 1333(1). The plaintiffs alleged that, in the event diversity jurisdiction did not exist as to some or all of them, the case was "brought under the admiralty and maritime jurisdiction" of the district **[—9—]** court, and that the claims asserted "ar[ose] under" the general maritime law of the United States. *See* Second Am. Compl., D.E. 30, at ¶¶ 81, 82, 84.

We express no view on whether the torts alleged by the plaintiffs arise under or are governed by federal maritime law. On remand, even though diversity jurisdiction may exist as to some or all of the plaintiffs, the district court will need to address whether any of their claims arise under federal maritime law because the elements of a tort can differ under maritime law and state law.

In determining whether federal maritime law governs any of the plaintiffs' claims, the district court will have to apply the location/connection test articulated by the

---

[1] Because Royal Caribbean does not raise the issue, we do not consider whether all of the plaintiffs could collectively allege that they suffered the same injuries. *See United States v. Sineneng-Smith*, 140 S. Ct. 1575, 1579 (2020) (explaining the principle of party presentation). If Royal Caribbean suspects that some or all of the plaintiffs are exaggerating or misstating their alleged injuries, it can take discovery and file appropriate Rule 12(b)(1) motions mounting a factual attack on the allegations.

Supreme Court in cases like *Jerome B. Grubart, Inc. v. Great Lakes Dredge & Dock Co.*, 513 U.S. 527, 534 (1995) ("[A] party seeking to invoke federal admiralty jurisdiction pursuant to 28 U.S.C. § 1333(1) over a tort claim must satisfy conditions both of location and of connection with maritime activity."). Generally speaking, the "locality prong of the test for admiralty jurisdiction is satisfied if the incident occurred on 'navigable waters' or 'the injury suffered on land was caused by a vessel on navigable waters,'" while the connection prong "requires two determinations: (a) whether the incident has a potentially disruptive impact on maritime commerce; and (b) whether the activity shows a substantial relationship to a traditional maritime activity." 1 Thomas Schoenbaum, Admiralty and Maritime **[—10—]** Law § 3:5 (6th ed. & Nov. 2020 update). *See also* 1 Steven F. Friedell, Benedict on Admiralty § 171 (7th rev. ed. & Dec. 2020 supp.).

We recognized a claim for negligent infliction of emotional distress under federal maritime law in *Chaparro v. Carnival Corp.*, 693 F.3d 1333, 1337–38 (11th Cir. 2012), but that case was factually different. *Chaparro* involved cruise ship passengers on a shore excursion who were trapped on a bus and witnessed a fatal shooting near a beach. The plaintiffs here never embarked on their cruise. The district court will therefore have to determine whether *Chaparro* extends to the circumstances alleged here under the *Great Lakes* location/connection test. *Cf. Archawski v. Hanioti*, 350 U.S. 532, 533 (1956) (allegation that a ship owner accepted money to take passengers on a trip, and then abandoned the voyage, "stated a claim for breach of a maritime contract"); *Wallis v. Princess Cruises, Inc.*, 306 F.3d 827, 840–41 (9th Cir. 2002) (stating, in a case involving on-board activity, that "[a] cruise line's treatment of paying passengers clearly has potential to disrupt commercial activity, and certainly has substantial relationship to traditional **{-1315-}** maritime activity").[2] **[—11—]**

Should the district court conclude that there is maritime jurisdiction, it will need to apply the "zone of interest" test we adopted in *Chaparro* to the negligent infliction of emotional distress claim. That test—which includes an "impact rule"—also "allows recovery if a plaintiff is 'placed in immediate risk of physical harm by [the defendant's negligent] conduct.'" *Chaparro*, 693 F.3d at 1337–38 (alteration in bracketed material) (quoting *Stacy v. Rederiet Otto Danielsen, A.S.*, 609 F.3d 1033, 1035 (9th Cir. 2010)).[3]

III

We reverse the dismissal of the plaintiffs' complaint for lack of subject-matter jurisdiction, and remand for further proceedings consistent with this opinion. Because of the uncertainty over jurisdiction, we do not address the class action waiver or the plaintiffs' claims for intentional infliction of emotional distress and negligent infliction of emotional distress.

REVERSED AND REMANDED.

---

[2] In a factually similar case, we concluded in an unpublished decision that there was maritime jurisdiction, but we did not explain our conclusion. *See Heinen v. Royal Caribbean Cruises LTD.*, 806 F. App'x 847, 849 n.1 (11th Cir. 2020). We therefore do not view *Heinen* as helpful or persuasive.

[3] Some federal courts have also recognized a claim for intentional infliction of emotional distress under maritime law. *See, e.g.*, *Wallis*, 306 F.3d at 841–42; *Sangha v. Navig8 Ship Mgmt. PTE Ltd.*, 440 F. Supp. 3d 1286, 1300–01 (S.D. Ala. 2020); *Broberg v. Carnival Corp.*, 303 F. Supp. 3d 1313, 1317 (S.D. Fla. 2017). These courts have generally adopted, as the federal maritime rule, the standard set forth in § 46 (and its comment d) of the Restatement (Second) of Torts (1965). *See, e.g.*, *Wallis*, 306 F.3d at 841–42. That standard is the same one used by Florida courts to evaluate claims of intentional infliction of emotional distress. *See Metropolitan Life Ins. Co. v. McCarson*, 467 So.2d 277, 278–79 (Fla. 1985).

United States Court of Appeals
for the Eleventh Circuit

No. 20-13666

TURNER
VS.
COSTA CROCIERE S.P.A.

Appeal from the United States District Court for the Southern District of Florida

Decided: August 19, 2021

Citation: 9 F.4th 1341, 9 Adm. R. 412 (11th Cir. 2021).

Before **NEWSOM, BRASHER,** and **MARCUS,** Circuit Judges.

[—1—] {-1343-} MARCUS, Circuit Judge: **[—2—]**

Plaintiff Paul Turner appeals the district court's order dismissing his putative class **{-1344-}** action complaint against Costa Crociere S.p.A., an Italian cruise operator, and its American subsidiary Costa Cruise Lines, Inc. (together, the "Defendants"). The Defendants operate and market the cruise ship *Costa Luminosa.* Turner alleges that the Defendants' negligence contributed to an outbreak of COVID-19 aboard the *Costa Luminosa* during his transatlantic voyage beginning on March 5, 2020. The district court dismissed Turner's complaint on *forum non conveniens* grounds because his passage ticket contract includes a forum selection clause requiring that all claims associated with his cruise be litigated in a court in Genoa, Italy. After careful review, we affirm.

These are the relevant facts as alleged in the complaint. Turner, a Wisconsin resident, purchased a ticket for a transatlantic cruise aboard the *Costa Luminosa* departing from Fort Lauderdale, Florida. By purchasing the ticket, he agreed to the attached "General Conditions of Passage Ticket Contract" (the "Contract"). Section 2(a) of the Contract provides:

> Any claim, controversy, dispute, suit, or matter of any kind whatsoever arising out of, concerned with, or incident to any Cruise or in connection with this Contract shall be instituted only in the courts of Genoa, Italy, to the exclusion of the courts of any other country, state, or nation. Italian law shall apply to any such proceedings, without effect to Italian choice-of-law principles.

What might have been a dream vacation for Turner turned into something of a nightmare. Right before Turner's cruise, the *Costa Luminosa* had conducted **[—3—]** another cruise out of Fort Lauderdale. During this voyage, on February 29, 2020, the ship had to dock in the Cayman Islands and evacuate a 68-year-old Italian passenger who presented with symptoms consistent with COVID-19. The passenger tested positive for COVID-19 and eventually died, though the Defendants did not learn of the positive test until after March 8.

On March 4, the night before Turner's cruise, Costa Cruise Lines emailed all passengers to let them know that while the World Health Organization had raised the alert level for COVID-19, Costa Cruise Lines remained in contact with health authorities and would make the "most appropriate decisions" and take the "most adequate measures" to ensure "the highest level of safety for its guests and crewmembers." Costa also told passengers concerned about the virus that the ship was safe. It did not hire any experts to verify that the ship had been sufficiently cleaned after the COVID-19-positive passenger disembarked. It also allegedly failed to refuse boarding privileges to passengers and crewmembers who showed COVID-19 symptoms or had travelled to high-risk areas such as China.

Shortly after departing, on March 8, the *Costa Luminosa* docked in Puerto Rico in order to transport a northern Italian couple with COVID-19 symptoms to the hospital. The couple later tested positive. Ship staff did not inform passengers of the couple's circumstances in Puerto Rico; passengers found out a day later after the ship had already departed for a seven-day journey across the Atlantic to the Canary **[—4—]** Islands. Costa Cruise Lines did not instruct passengers to isolate, despite the issuance of

CDC guidance instructing cruise ships to quarantine individuals who had had high-risk exposures to the virus. The ship assured passengers that it maintained 24-hour medical facilities, but Turner visited the medical facility and found that it was closed for much of the day. Meanwhile, **{-1345-}** several other passengers on the *Costa Luminosa* became ill with symptoms of COVID-19. Eventually, but not immediately, the captain ordered all passengers to quarantine. When all passengers finally disembarked in France on March 19, thirty-six of the seventy-five passengers tested positive for COVID-19. Turner himself contracted the virus.

Turner sued the Defendants in the United States District Court for the Southern District of Florida, seeking damages for himself and a putative class of his fellow *Costa Luminosa* passengers. He alleged claims arising under general maritime law for negligence, negligent misrepresentation, negligent infliction of emotional distress, and intentional infliction of emotional distress, as well as a claim for misleading advertising under Fla. Stat. § 817.41.

The Defendants filed a motion to dismiss on *forum non conveniens* grounds, arguing that the forum selection clause required Turner to litigate his claims in Italy. The district court agreed, finding that Turner's claims fell within the scope of the forum selection clause; that the forum selection clause was enforceable, did not contravene public policy, and was not fundamentally unfair; and that the *forum non* **[—5—]** *conveniens* factors as modified by the forum selection clause favored dismissal. Italy provided an adequate alternative forum and the balance of public interest factors, like Italy's relationship with the dispute—Costa Crociere is the largest tour operator in Italy—weighed in favor of dismissal. Turner appealed.

On appeal, Turner "assume[s]" that his claims fall within the scope of the forum selection clause's terms, but argues that the clause is unenforceable. He further argues that since the forum selection clause does not control, the district court erred by engaging in the modified *forum non conveniens* analysis that applies in the presence of a valid forum selection clause pursuant to *Atlantic Marine Const. Co. v. U.S. Dist. Ct. for W. Dist. of Texas*, 571 U.S. 49, 60–66 (2013). We disagree.

We review the enforceability of a forum selection clause de novo. *Rucker v. Oasis Legal Fin., L.L.C.*, 632 F.3d 1231, 1235 (11th Cir. 2011); *Lipcon v. Underwriters at Lloyd's, London*, 148 F.3d 1285, 1290–91 (11th Cir. 1998). In this case arising under federal general maritime law, federal law determines the enforceability of the forum selection clause. *See Carnival Cruise Lines, Inc. v. Shute*, 499 U.S. 585, 590 (1991). Forum selection clauses "are presumptively valid and enforceable unless the plaintiff makes a strong showing that enforcement would be unfair or unreasonable under the circumstances." *Rucker*, 632 F.3d at 1236 (internal quotation marks and citation omitted). A plaintiff can defeat this presumption by showing that (1) the clause "'was induced by fraud or overreaching; **[—6—]** (2) the plaintiff would be deprived of its day in court because of inconvenience or unfairness; (3) the chosen law would deprive the plaintiff of a remedy; or (4) enforcement of the clause would contravene public policy.'" *Id.* (citing *M/S Bremen v. Zapata Off-Shore Co.*, 407 U.S. 1 (1972)).

Turner attempts to invoke the second (unfairness) and fourth (public policy) exceptions, but to no avail. Even when "the forum selection clause establishes a remote forum," a plaintiff seeking to establish that a forum selection clause is unenforceable due to inconvenience or unfairness **{-1346-}** "'bear[s] a heavy burden of proof.'" *Shute*, 499 U.S. at 592 (citation omitted). A plaintiff who relies on inconveniences that were "foreseeable at the time of contracting" in order to meet this burden can prevail only by showing "that trial in the contractual forum will be so gravely difficult and inconvenient that he will for all practical purposes be deprived of his day in court." *Bremen*, 407 U.S. at 17–18.

Turner claims that enforcing the forum selection clause would be fundamentally unfair because requiring him and fellow class members to travel to Italy to prosecute their claims "would significantly expose (and/or increase) the risk of complicating their [COVID-19] symptoms and/or contracting COVID-19 again," an inconvenience that was unforeseeable due to the unique nature of the COVID-19 **[—7—]** pandemic.[1] Even assuming that travel difficulties and risks associated with COVID- 19 are any less foreseeable than medical difficulties that would attend more standard personal injuries that were plainly foreseeable when Turner agreed to the forum selection clause, Turner still has not met his burden of proving that pursuit of his claims in Italy would subject him to fundamental unfairness. The reason is basic: he has not established that he would have to travel to Italy in order to pursue his case. *See Effron v. Sun Line Cruises, Inc.*, 67 F.3d 7, 11 (2d Cir. 1995) ("A plaintiff may have his 'day in court' without ever setting foot in a courtroom."). The Defendants produced an affidavit from an Italian attorney explaining that Turner would not be required to attend routine proceedings in person and that even for those events that required attendance, he could possibly either arrange for appointment of a special attorney to attend on his behalf or request that the event take place in the United States via international rogatory.

Turner vaguely characterizes these representations as "unsupported," but, notably, he did not file any declarations or any other evidence to counter them. In **[—8—]** the district court, Turner did not even dispute the Italian attorney's statements. He therefore has not met *his burden* to "'clearly show that enforcement [of the forum selection clause] would be unreasonable and unjust.'" *Est. of Myhra v. Royal Caribbean Cruises, Ltd.*, 695 F.3d 1233, 1240 (11th Cir. 2012) (citation omitted), *superseded by statute on other grounds as stated in Caron v. NCL (Bahamas), Ltd.*, 910 F.3d 1359, 1364 n.2, 6 Adm. R. 471, 472 n.2 (11th Cir. 2018). We emphasize that our holding on this point is narrow: on this particular record, Turner has not presented evidence sufficient to meet his "'heavy burden of proof'" on his claim of unfairness. *Shute*, 499 U.S. at 592 (citation omitted).

Turner's next claim, that the forum selection clause in his ticket contract contravenes **{-1347-}** public policy, likewise goes nowhere. He says that the clause contravenes 46 U.S.C. § 30509(a), which provides:

> (1) In general.--The owner, master, manager, or agent of a vessel transporting passengers between ports in the United States, or between a port in the United States and a port in a foreign country, may not include in a regulation or contract a provision limiting—
>
> > (A) the liability of the owner, master, or agent for personal injury or death caused by the negligence or fault of the owner or the owner's employees or agents; or
> >
> > (B) the right of a claimant for personal injury or death to a trial by court of competent jurisdiction.
>
> (2) Voidness.--A provision described in paragraph (1) is void.

Turner contends that the forum selection clause effectively limits the Defendants' liability for negligently causing personal injury. It limits the forum for his claims to **[—9—]** Italy, and, according to Turner, Italy

[1] Turner also suggests that the selection of an Italian forum, even though Costa Cruise Lines is based in Pembroke Pines, Florida and the cruise departed from Fort Lauderdale, indicates that the inconvenience was not foreseeable and that the forum selection clause is unreasonable. *See Bremen*, 407 U.S. at 17 (noting that an agreement to litigate "essentially local disputes in a remote alien forum" might weigh in favor of finding the clause unreasonable or "might suggest . . . that the parties did not have the particular controversy in mind when they made their agreement"). But the selection of an Italian forum is not remote to this dispute; defendant Costa Crociere, the owner of both co-defendant Costa Cruise Lines and the *Costa Luminosa* itself, is headquartered in Italy. Moreover, Turner's cruise was scheduled to stop at three Italian ports before it canceled these plans due to the pandemic.

has prohibited foreign travel due to COVID-19 and medical complications from COVID-19 would make it unfeasible for him to travel there anyway. But as we have just explained, Turner has not shown that travel and medical issues will prevent him from being able to litigate in Italy, much less done so "strong[ly]" enough to overcome the presumption in favor of forum selection clause enforceability. *Rucker*, 632 F.3d at 1236.

More to the point, both we and the Supreme Court have directly rejected the proposition that a routine cruise ship forum selection clause is a limitation on liability that contravenes § 30509(a), even when it points to a forum that is inconvenient for the plaintiff. *Shute*, 499 U.S. at 596–97 ("[R]espondents cite no authority for their contention that Congress' intent in enacting § [30509(a)] was to avoid having a plaintiff travel to a distant forum in order to litigate. The legislative history of § [30509(a)] suggests instead that this provision was enacted in response to passenger-ticket conditions purporting to limit the shipowner's liability for negligence or to remove the issue of liability from the scrutiny of *any* court by means of a clause providing that 'the question of liability and the measure of damages shall be determined by arbitration.' There was no prohibition of a forum-selection clause.") (citations omitted) (emphasis added); *Est. of Myhra*, 695 F.3d at 1246 ("We hold that 46 U.S.C. § 30509(a) does not bar a ship owner from including a forum- **[—10—]** selection clause in a passage contract, even if the chosen forum might apply substantive law that would impose a limitation on liability.").

Turner's final move is to claim that the district court abused its discretion by failing to apply proper *forum non conveniens* analysis. "It is . . . well settled in our decisional law that we may only reverse a district court's dismissal based on *forum non conveniens* if it constitutes a clear abuse of discretion." *Aldana v. Del Monte Fresh Produce N.A., Inc.*, 578 F.3d 1283, 1288 (11th Cir. 2009) (cleaned up). Normally, to obtain a *forum non conveniens* dismissal, "'the moving party must demonstrate that (1) an adequate alternative forum is available, (2) the public and private factors weigh in favor of dismissal, and (3) the plaintiff can reinstate his suit in the alternative forum without undue inconvenience or prejudice.'" *GDG Acquisitions, LLC v. Gov't of Belize*, 749 F.3d 1024, 1028 (11th Cir. 2014) (alteration adopted and citation omitted). The presence **{-1348-}** of a forum selection clause, however, modifies this analysis in important ways. "First, the plaintiff's choice of forum merits no weight. Rather, as the party defying the forum-selection clause, the plaintiff bears the burden of establishing that transfer to the forum for which the parties bargained is unwarranted." *Atl. Marine*, 571 U.S. at 63. Second, "[a] binding forum-selection clause requires the court to find that the forum *non conveniens* private factors entirely favor the selected forum." *GDG Acquisitions, LLC*, 749 F.3d at 1029. The Supreme Court has instructed that "a valid forum-selection clause **[—11—]** [should be] given controlling weight in all but the most exceptional cases." *Atl. Marine*, 571 U.S. at 63 (internal quotation marks and citation omitted).

Thus, our conclusion that the forum selection clause is enforceable and applies here compels us to reject most of Turner's remaining arguments, each of which proceeds from the mistaken premise that the district court should not have applied the *forum non conveniens* analysis in its modified, forum-selection-clause form. Turner says that the district court abused its discretion by refusing to defer to his chosen forum and by deeming the private interest factors to weigh in favor of the Italian forum. But because of the valid forum selection clause, each of these steps was consistent with—indeed, required by—the modified approach set forth in *Atlantic Marine*.

This leaves Turner with one last complaint about the district court's analysis, namely that when it analyzed the public *forum non conveniens* factors, it failed to consider one particular factor, "the unfairness of burdening citizens in an unrelated forum with jury duty." *See Piper Aircraft Co. v. Reyno*, 454 U.S. 235, 241 n.6 (1981) (the public factors include "the administrative difficulties flowing from court congestion; the 'local interest in having localized controversies decided at home'; the interest in having the trial of a diversity case in a forum that is at home with the law that must govern the action; the avoidance of unnecessary problems in conflict of laws, or in the application of foreign law; and the unfairness of burdening citizens **[—12—]** in an unrelated forum with jury duty."); *see also Fresh Results, LLC v. ASF Holland, B.V.*, 921 F.3d 1043, 1049 (11th Cir. 2019).

This argument, too, misses the mark. For one thing, district courts are not required to consider *all* of the public factors, they may choose to discuss only those that are *relevant*. *Fresh Results*, 921 F.3d at 1051. The district court carefully considered several public factors including the administrative difficulties associated with the Southern District of Florida's busy docket (though it gave this factor little weight), the interest of the United States in making sure United States citizens generally have access to an American forum, Italy's interest in adjudicating claims related to its tourism industry, the likely need to apply Italian law based on the Contract's choice-of-law clause, and the fact that key events took place not in Florida but on board the *Costa Luminosa* as it sailed across the Atlantic. The district court's analysis of these factors was thorough and persuasive. Therefore, even if Turner's proposed additional factor, the unfairness of burdening the allegedly unrelated Italian forum, weighed in favor of keeping the case in Florida, we would be hard pressed to conclude that it was a "clear error of judgment" for the district to grant the motion to dismiss. *Cf.* **{-1349-}** *Aldana*, 578 F.3d at 1288, 1296 ("Nor are we convinced that the overall balance of private interests would be significantly affected by the second private interest cited by the dissent.") (citation omitted). Moreover, as we've explained—and as the district court itself recognized when analyzing whether the **[—13—]** forum selection clause was enforceable—Italy bears a significant relationship to this dispute; it therefore would not be unfair to burden Italian jurors with resolving it. Turner has not shown any shortcoming that counsels a departure from the "substantial deference" we normally afford to the district court's reasonable balancing of the *forum non conveniens* factors. *Id.* at 1288 (quoting *Piper*, 454 U.S. at 257).

In short, the forum selection clause is enforceable and applies to Turner's claims, and the district court acted well within its discretion when it granted the Defendant's motion to dismiss on *forum non conveniens* grounds.

AFFIRMED.

United States Court of Appeals for the District of Columbia Circuit

United States Court of Appeals
for the District of Columbia Circuit

No. 19-3051

UNITED STATES
vs.
MORENO-MEMBACHE

Appeal from the United States District Court for the District of Columbia

Decided: April 27, 2021

Citation: 995 F.3d 249, 9 Adm. R. 418 (D.C. Cir. 2021).

Before **TATEL, MILLETT,** and **KATSAS,** Circuit Judges.

[—2—] {-250-} MILLETT, Circuit Judge: **{-251-}**

Plea agreements are at once ordinary and extraordinary. Ordinary because they resolve nearly 98% of criminal cases in the federal system every year.[1] And extraordinary because of what they entail for individual defendants. A guilty plea is not only the defendant's admission in open court that he committed a crime, but also a "grave and solemn act" through which the defendant waives a panoply of constitutional rights, including his rights to a jury trial and to put the government to its heavy burden of proof. *See Brady v. United States*, 397 U.S. 742, 748 (1970). Because of the vital interests at stake, "when a plea rests in any significant degree on a promise or agreement of the prosecutor, so that it can be said to be part of the inducement or consideration, such promise must be fulfilled." *Santobello v. New York*, 404 U.S. 257, 262 (1971).

In this case, Antonio Moreno-Membache entered a guilty plea on the understanding that the government would not argue that he was ineligible for a sentence reduction because of his alleged supervisory or managerial role in a drug-smuggling conspiracy. That promise would eliminate a statutory barrier to Moreno-Membache seeking relief under the Safety Valve provision of the Sentencing Reform Act of 1984, 18 U.S.C. § 3553(f)(4), from his mandatory minimum sentence.

The government understood its promise differently, arguing that it retained the ability to oppose any Safety Valve relief and characterizing the relevant language in the plea **[—3—]** agreement as "inelegant[]" and "unnecessary." Oral Arg. Tr. 17:1–3, 21:8–9.

The question before this court is whether the language of the plea agreement is ambiguous because the law demands clarity when constitutional rights are waived. We hold that the plea agreement is ambiguous as to the government's ability to oppose Safety Valve relief on the ground that Moreno-Membache was a supervisor or manager in a drug conspiracy. Controlling precedent requires that the ambiguity be resolved in favor of the defendant. For that reason, we vacate Moreno-Membache's sentence and remand for a new sentencing proceeding, untainted and uninfluenced by the government's breach of the plea agreement and the evidence it introduced in the process.

I

A

In June 2012, the United States Coast Guard surveilled the *Mistby*, a so-called "go-fast" boat, off the coast of Panama.[2] When the Coast Guard approached, the *Mistby* fled. As the Coast Guard pursued the boat, the *Mistby*'s crew began dumping **{-252-}** cargo overboard. To no avail. The Coast Guard soon interdicted the *Mistby* and retrieved the discarded cargo, which amounted to more than 220 kilograms of cocaine and more than 235 kilograms of marijuana.

Moreno-Membache was not a member of the *Mistby*'s crew, nor was he present when the ship was stopped. *See* **[—4—]** *United*

[1] *See Federal Judicial Caseload Statistics, Table D-4,* U.S. COURTS (2020), https://www.uscourts.gov/statistics/table/d4/federal-judicial-caseload-statistics/2020/03/31 (last accessed April 26, 2021).

[2] A "go-fast" boat is "a type of boat that can travel at high rates of speed and thus is considered a favored vehicle for drug smuggling operations." *United States v. Tinoco*, 304 F.3d 1088, 1117 (11th Cir. 2002).

States v. Mosquera-Murillo, 902 F.3d 285, 287–288, 6 Adm. R. 505, 505–06 (D.C. Cir. 2018). Instead, he was arrested and extradited to the United States after a joint investigation of the Colombian and United States governments concluded that he was involved in the conspiracy that ultimately resulted in the *Mistby*'s failed journey. *Id.*, 6 Adm. R. at 505–06.

In January 2016, Moreno-Membache pled guilty to conspiracy to "knowingly and intentionally distribute, and possess with intent to distribute * * * on board a vessel subject to the jurisdiction of the United States" both (i) five kilograms or more of cocaine, and (ii) 100 kilograms or more of marijuana. J.A. 130 ¶ 1. The charge was a violation of the Maritime Drug Law Enforcement Act ("Maritime Drug Act"), 46 U.S.C. §§ 70503, 70506(b), and the Controlled Substances Import and Export Act, 21 U.S.C. § 960(b)(1)(B), (b)(2)(G).

Under the Maritime Drug Act, the conspiracy charge to which Moreno-Membache pled carries a mandatory minimum sentence of ten years in prison. 46 U.S.C. § 70506(a) (stating that violators of the Maritime Drug Act shall be punished as provided in 21 U.S.C. § 960(b)); *see* 21 U.S.C. § 960(b)(1)(B), (b)(2)(G) (providing for ten-year mandatory minimum).

A separate statutory provision, known as the Safety Valve, allows district courts to approve sentences below a mandatory minimum in certain circumstances. Sentencing Reform Act of 1984, Pub. L. No. 98-473, § 212(a), 98 Stat. 1987, 1989–1990 (codified at 18 U.S.C. § 3553(f)). Specifically, the Safety Valve provision sets out five eligibility criteria for obtaining relief. 18 U.S.C. § 3553(f). The offense (i) must not have resulted in death or serious bodily injury to any person, and the defendant (ii) must not have a significant criminal history, (iii) must not have used or threatened violence or possessed a firearm or other dangerous weapon in connection with the **[—5—]** offense, (iv) must not be "an organizer, leader, manager, or supervisor of others in the offense, as determined under the sentencing guidelines," and (v) must truthfully provide all relevant information and evidence concerning the offense to the government. 18 U.S.C. § 3553(f)(1)–(5).

Also relevant to this appeal, Moreno-Membache's plea agreement was a "C-Plea." Referencing Federal Rule of Criminal Procedure 11(c)(1)(C), a "C-Plea" is one that makes the government's recommended sentence "binding on the court 'once the court accepts the plea agreement[.]'" *Freeman v. United States*, 564 U.S. 522, 529 (2011) (quoting FED. R. CRIM. P. 11(c)(1)(C)); *accord United States v. Goodall*, 236 F.3d 700, 703 (D.C. Cir. 2001). A C-Plea presents the district court with a take-it-or-leave-it proposition: The court must either accept or reject the plea; it may not modify the plea's terms, including the proposed sentence. *See Goodall*, 236 F.3d at 703 (citing *United States v. Cunavelis*, 969 F.2d 1419, 1422 (2d Cir. 1992)).

Under the C-Plea, the government and Moreno-Membache agreed to a sentence of 120 months (the mandatory minimum sentence), unless the district court determined that Moreno-Membache was eligible for relief under the Safety Valve provision. J.A. 131 ¶ 7. So the district court could either accept the 120-month sentence or find that Moreno-Membache deserved a **{–253–}** lesser sentence under the Safety Valve provision. But the district court could not impose a longer sentence.

Under the plea agreement, Moreno-Membache expressly preserved his ability to seek relief from his mandatory minimum sentence under the Safety Valve provision. J.A. 132 ¶ 9; *see also* J.A. 132 ¶¶ 6, 7. And the government preserved its right to argue both that (i) the Safety Valve provision is categorically inapplicable to Moreno-Membache's conviction **[—6—]** under the Maritime Drug Act, and (ii) Moreno-Membache does not meet the Safety Valve eligibility criteria. J.A. 132 ¶ 9.

In the same paragraph of the plea agreement in which the government preserved its Safety Valve arguments, the government also surrendered its ability "to seek any of the adjustments set out in U.S.S.G. Chapter 3, Part B." J.A. 132 ¶ 9. That part of the Sentencing Guidelines includes, as relevant here, sentencing enhancements for a defendant's aggravating role in the offense. U.S. SENTENCING GUIDELINES MANUAL § 3B1.2 (U.S. SENTENCING COMM'N 2004) ("U.S.S.G."). A defendant plays an "aggravating role" when he acts as an organizer, leader, manager, or supervisor in the criminal operation. *Id.*

B

The district court initially ruled that the Safety Valve provision had no application to the Maritime Drug Act crimes to which Moreno-Membache had pleaded guilty. *See United States v. Mosquera-Murillo,* 172 F. Supp. 3d 24, 38 (D.D.C. 2016). This court reversed, holding that the Safety Valve was available for such offenses. *Mosquera-Murillo,* 902 F.3d at 296, 6 Adm. R. at 513.

On remand, the district court turned to Moreno-Membache's request for relief under the Safety Valve provision. *United States v. Mosquera-Murillo,* No. 13-cr-00134-BAH, 2018 WL 6267765, at *1 (D.D.C. Nov. 30, 2018). Turning to the five statutory criteria for relief, the district court concluded as to the first and third criteria that Moreno-Membache had no serious criminal history and that the crime did not result in serious injury or death to any person. *Id.* at *5. The district court also declined to address the fifth criterion, which is whether Moreno-Membache fully shared all relevant information about his criminal activities with the government. [—7—] *Id.* So the district court's analysis of Moreno-Membache's eligibility for relief under the Safety Valve provision turned on the two remaining criteria: whether Moreno-Membache performed some leadership or supervisory role in the offense "as determined under the sentencing guidelines," and whether he possessed a weapon in conjunction with the crime, 18 U.S.C. § 3553(f)(2) & (4).

With respect to acting as a leader or supervisor, Moreno-Membache contended that the government expressly surrendered its right to argue that he had served such a role when it "agree[d] not to seek any of the adjustments set out in U.S.S.G. Chapter 3, Part B[,]" J.A. 132 ¶ 9, which necessarily included arguing that he served as an organizer, leader, manager, or supervisor in the conspiracy, *see* U.S.S.G. § 3B1.1 cmt. n.2; Joint Status Report at 4–5, 7–8, *Mosquera-Murillo,* No. 13-cr-00134-BAH (D.D.C. Nov. 19, 2018), ECF No. 271. The government disagreed and would present evidence that Moreno-Membache was ineligible for relief under the Safety Valve provision because of his alleged supervisory or managerial role in the offense. Joint Status Report at 6, *Mosquera-Murillo,* No. 13-cr-00134-BAH (D.D.C. Nov. 19, 2018), ECF No. 271.

The district court ruled that the plea agreement preserved the government's ability to argue that Moreno-Membache **{-254-}** was ineligible for Safety Valve relief because of his supervisory or managerial role. The district court reasoned that, in the plea agreement, the government waived only its right to seek an increase in Moreno-Membache's guideline sentence because of his alleged leadership status. The district court also pointed to other provisions of the plea agreement that allowed the government to "inform the Court and the Probation Office" of facts relevant to sentencing, J.A. 132 ¶ 8, and to "dispute [—8—] sentencing factors or facts material to sentencing," J.A. 133 ¶ 12.

After conducting an evidentiary hearing, the district court found that Moreno-Membache was a supervisor or manager of crew members involved in the offense. *United States v. Mosquera-Murillo,* No. 13-cr-00134-BAH, 2019 WL 3037533, at *12–15 (D.D.C. July 11, 2019).

With respect to the other Safety Valve criterion pertaining to the use of a firearm in conjunction with the offense, the district court credited a law enforcement agent's description of two cooperating co-conspirators' claims that Moreno-Membache possessed a firearm. The captain of the *Mistby* reportedly said that he saw Moreno-Membache with a firearm at a planning meeting. *Mosquera-Murillo,* 2019 WL 3037533, at *15. And a "streetwise" crewmember reportedly said that he saw what appeared to him to be the outline of a firearm in Moreno-Membache's waistband, but he did not see the firearm itself. *Id.*

Based on its findings as to Moreno-Membache's supervisory or managerial status and possession of a firearm in conjunction with the crimes, the district court ruled that Moreno-Membache was ineligible for relief from the Maritime Drug Act's mandatory minimum sentence under the Safety Valve provision. The court then sentenced Moreno-Membache to the mandatory minimum of 120 months in prison. Moreno-Membache filed a timely notice of appeal.

II

The district court had jurisdiction to hear this case under 18 U.S.C. § 3231, which gives the district courts of the United States original jurisdiction over "all offenses against the laws of the United States." This court has jurisdiction to hear the **[—9—]** appeal of the final judgment in this case under 28 U.S.C. § 1291.

To determine whether a party has breached the terms of a plea agreement, we generally apply principles of contract law. *United States v. Henry*, 758 F.3d 427, 431 (D.C. Cir. 2014); *United States v. Jones*, 58 F.3d 688, 692 (D.C. Cir. 1995). We interpret the terms of the plea agreement *de novo*. *Henry*, 758 F.3d at 431. Consistent with constitutional principles and the settled rule that contracts are construed against their drafters, we construe any ambiguities in the plea agreement against the government. *In re Sealed Case*, 702 F.3d 59, 65 (D.C. Cir. 2012).

III

A

1

At the heart of this case is the ninth paragraph of Moreno-Membache's plea agreement. That paragraph reads, in relevant part:

> The government *agrees not to seek any of the adjustments set out in U.S.S.G. Chapter 3, Part B.* The Defendant is permitted to request relief under Safety Valve provisions, and the Government is permitted to argue that the Safety Valve provisions do not apply to the maritime offense to which the Defendant has agreed to plead guilty and that, in any **{-255-}** event, the Defendant does not meet the criteria to qualify for Safety Valve relief.

J.A. 132 ¶ 9 (emphasis added). **[—10—]**

The question is whether the government's express agreement not to seek any adjustment under Chapter 3, Part B of the Sentencing Guidelines—including arguing that Moreno-Membache qualified for a supervisory or managerial role enhancement—foreclosed it from nevertheless arguing that Moreno-Membache was ineligible for Safety Valve relief because he was a supervisor or manager "as determined under the sentencing guidelines," 18 U.S.C. § 3553(f)(4).

Under settled precedent, ambiguity in the meaning of a plea agreement must be resolved against the government. *Henry*, 758 F.3d at 431; *Jones*, 58 F.3d at 691. Here, the scope of the government's waiver of its right to argue that Moreno-Membache had a supervisory or managerial role in the offense is, at a minimum, ambiguous, and Moreno-Membache reasonably read the plea agreement as foreclosing the government's opposition to his eligibility for Safety Valve relief on that basis.

To start with, the statutory Safety Valve criterion regarding supervisory and managerial roles expressly references the sentencing guidelines. *See* 18 U.S.C. § 3553(f)(4). And Section 5C1.2 of the Sentencing Guidelines, which specifically implements the Safety Valve criterion in Section 3553(f)(4), provides that a criminal defendant is disqualified from Safety Valve relief only if he "*receives* an adjustment for an aggravating role under § 3B1.1." U.S.S.G. § 5C1.2 cmt. n.5 (emphasis added). In other words, the Safety Valve criterion only seems to proscribe relief for those who are actually given an "organizer, leader, manager, or supervisor" adjustment under the Sentencing Guidelines. That is what the government under Paragraph Nine expressly surrendered by forgoing its ability to argue that Moreno-Membache should "receive[]" a supervisory adjustment under Section 3B1.1. **[—11—]** And Moreno-Membache in fact never "receive[d]" any such adjustment under the Sentencing Guidelines.

Because the government's ability to oppose Moreno-Membache's eligibility for Safety Valve relief on the grounds of his supervisory or managerial status textually hinged on that status actually being "determined" under the Sentencing Guidelines and Moreno-Membache actually "receiv[ing]" such an adjustment, the plea agreement, at the very least, can reasonably be read to foreclose the government from pursuing such an argument at sentencing.[3]

Reinforcing our conclusion, the government candidly acknowledged at oral argument that Paragraph Nine was "inelegantly drafted." Oral Arg. Tr. 21:8–9. Which seems to be a deft way of admitting that the agreement was unclear. Because Moreno-Membache reasonably read that inelegant phrasing as foreclosing the government from arguing his ineligibility for Safety Valve relief based on his asserted supervisory or managerial status, that is the reading we must give the agreement's text.

The government's only counter is to read Paragraph Nine as simply promising that it would not seek any additional adjustments **{–256–}** to Moreno-Membache's sentence. That cannot be. Remember, Moreno-Membache's plea agreement was a "C-Plea" that, by its very terms, already precluded the government from seeking any additional adjustments or enhancements to Moreno-Membache's sentence. *See, e.g., Freeman*, 564 U.S. **[—12—]** at 529 (quoting FED. R. CRIM. P. 11(c)(1)(C)). So there was no reason for the plea agreement to include language prohibiting the government from seeking an adjustment under Chapter 3, Part B of the Sentencing Guidelines other than to preclude the government's opposition to Safety Valve relief on the basis of an asserted supervisory or managerial role.

In other words, the language of the plea agreement either meant something under Moreno-Membache's reading or meant nothing under the government's. We are loath to assume that a defendant surrendered a panoply of constitutional rights in exchange for a meaningless and valueless promise. *See* 11 WILLISTON ON CONTRACTS § 32:5 (4th ed. Supp. Nov. 2020) ("An interpretation which gives effect to all provisions in the contract is preferred to one which renders part of the writing superfluous, useless, or inexplicable."); *cf. United States v. Franco-Lopez*, 312 F.3d 984, 991 (9th Cir. 2002) ("[W]e prefer a contractual interpretation that gives some effect to the government's apparent promises contained in the agreement[.]"). At a minimum, whether the government's promise was meaningful or meaningless is textually ambiguous.

2

Of course, Paragraph Nine's language cannot be read in isolation. Because a plea agreement is a contract, it must be read as a whole. *United States v. Schwartz*, 511 F.3d 403, 405 (3d Cir. 2008) (Plea agreements "must be interpreted as a whole and no part should be ignored.") (quoting CALAMARI & PERILLO, CONTRACTS §3.13 (5th ed. 2003)); *see also* 11 WILLISTON ON CONTRACTS §32:5 (4th ed. Supp. Nov. 2020). In that regard, the district court pointed to two other provisions in the agreement that, in its view, preserved the government's ability to oppose Safety Valve relief on the basis of Moreno- **[—13—]** Membache's asserted supervisory or managerial status. Neither provision resolves, nor even addresses, the relevant ambiguity.

The district court pointed to Paragraphs Eight and Twelve of the agreement, both of

[3] To be clear, whether a criminal defendant must actually receive an aggravating role adjustment under the Sentencing Guidelines to be ineligible for Safety Valve relief is not the question in this case. The only question is whether Moreno-Membache reasonably read the plea agreement that way, in light of Paragraph Nine and the incorporated Sentencing Guidelines provision. He did.

which preserved the government's ability to advise the court of "facts pertinent to the sentencing process," J.A. 132 ¶ 8, and "facts material to sentencing," J.A. 133 ¶ 12. But those provisions are more naturally read as allowing the government to introduce evidence bearing on those other sentencing and Safety Valve factors not expressly waived in Paragraph Nine. That, in fact, is exactly what the government has done in arguing that Moreno-Membache is ineligible for the Safety Valve because of his possession of a firearm to facilitate the offense.

The district court offered a second rationale for finding that the plea agreement was unambiguous. It reasoned that the Sentencing Guidelines commentary defining an "organizer, leader, manager, or supervisor" as a person "who receive[d] an adjustment for an aggravating role" does not limit the court's ability to determine Safety Valve eligibility because the court, "not the government, makes the final determination of the applicability of such a role enhancement." *See Mosquera-Murillo*, 2018 WL 6267765, at *6. So in the district court's view, the government's promise not to present evidence did not prevent the court itself from finding that a role enhancement applied. *See id.* Maybe. But the issue here is not about the power of the **{-257-}** court, but whether the *government*'s conduct breached the plea agreement when it asked the court to find that Moreno-Membache was a supervisor or manager as part of the sentencing proceeding and submitted evidence to that end on which the court relied. Or, more specifically, whether the plea agreement's ambiguous language could reasonably be **[—14—]** understood by Moreno-Membache as foreclosing that argument and introduction of evidence by the government.

In sum, based on the plain text of the plea agreement, the correlative wording of the Sentencing Guidelines, and the longstanding rule that ambiguity in a plea agreement is interpreted against the government, we hold that the government breached its agreement with Moreno-Membache when it argued that he was ineligible for Safety Valve relief because of any supervisory or managerial role he might have played in the offense. With so much at stake for the defendant, it is not too much to hold the government that drafted the plea agreement responsible for the misunderstanding that arose from a confusing, unclear ("inelegant[]"), and "unnecessary" hollow promise in the agreement, Oral Arg. Tr 21:8–9, 17:1–3.

B

The government argues that, regardless of his supervisory or managerial status, Moreno-Membache is still ineligible for Safety Valve relief because he "possess[ed] a firearm or other dangerous weapon" in connection with the conspiracy, *see* 18 U.S.C. § 3553(f)(2).

Specifically, the government argued to the district court that Moreno-Membache was ineligible for Safety Valve relief because he attended one *Mistby* planning meeting with a 9-millimeter pistol. The government supported this account with the testimony of a special agent who reviewed transcripts of interviews with the *Mistby*'s captain (a cooperating co-conspirator), who stated he saw the firearm, and a crewmember (another cooperating co-conspirator), who asserted he saw what appeared to be the outline of a gun in Moreno-Membache's waistband. J.A. 226–227. **[—15—]**

But to render a defendant ineligible for relief, his possession of the firearm must have had "the potential of facilitating the drug trafficking offense." *United States v. Erazo*, 628 F.3d 608, 611 (D.C. Cir. 2011) (alteration omitted) (quoting *United States v. DeJesus*, 219 F.3d 117, 122 (2d Cir. 2000)); *see* 18 U.S.C. § 3553(f)(2) (firearm must be possessed "in connection with the offense").

In this case, the district court grounded its finding of facilitation on Moreno-Membache's "supervisory role" guarding the narcotics. *Mosquera-Murillo*, 2019 WL 3037533, at *16. Specifically, the district court found that Moreno-Membache "had responsibility for supervising others in the storage and movement of the cocaine that ultimately was loaded onto the *Mistby*." *Id.* at *14. The district court therefore found that, because

Moreno-Membache played a supervisory role in safeguarding the cocaine and possessed a firearm, his firearm had the potential of facilitating the drug trafficking offense. *See id.* at *16; *see also Erazo*, 628 F.3d at 611.

Because the district court specifically tied its facilitation determination to its prior finding that Moreno-Membache acted as a manager or supervisor, we are unable to disentangle the district court's firearm determination from the government's arguments in breach of the plea agreement asserting Moreno-Membache's supervisory or managerial position. As a result, "the interests of justice and appropriate recognition of the duties of the prosecution in **{-258-}** relation to promises made in the negotiation of pleas of guilty will be best served by remanding the case[.]" *Santobello*, 404 U.S. at 262; *see Pepper v. United States*, 562 U.S. 476, 507 (2011) ("Because a district court's 'original sentencing intent may be undermined by altering one portion of the calculus,' an appellate court when reversing one part of a defendant's sentence 'may vacate the entire sentence so that, on remand, the trial court can reconfigure the **[—16—]** sentencing plan[.]'") (formatting modified; first quoting *United States v. White*, 406 F.3d 827, 832 (7th Cir. 2005), then quoting *Greenlaw v. United States*, 554 U.S. 237, 253 (2008)); *United States v. Wolff*, 127 F.3d 84, 86 (D.C. Cir. 1997).

The dissenting opinion asserts that the district court's analysis of Moreno-Membache's firearm and his supervisory role were sufficiently distinct because, if Moreno-Membache guarded the cocaine while possessing a firearm, it would not matter if he was a lowly laborer in the conspiracy or a kingpin. Dissenting Op. 3–4. While we agree on the law, we disagree on the facts. When it found that Moreno-Membache guarded drugs, the district court expressly predicated its determination upon its specific *finding* that Moreno-Membache "had a supervisory role," *Mosquera-Murillo*, 2019 WL 3037533, at *16, an issue it likely would not have reached had the government complied with the plea agreement.

The dissenting opinion separately contends that the firearm could be connected to the offense because one cooperating co-conspirator claimed to have seen Moreno-Membache with a pistol at a planning meeting and another cooperating co-conspirator said that he saw what he perceived to be the outline of a pistol in Moreno-Membache's waistband at the *Mistby*'s launch site. But that was not the basis for the district court's facilitation finding. And this court is ill-equipped to make such a factual finding.[4] **[—17—]**

Remand will allow the district court to make an independent determination regarding the firearm criterion, uninfluenced in any way by any of the government's improper argument or evidence presented to support Moreno-Membache's asserted supervisory or managerial status. More to the point, on remand Moreno-Membache will finally receive what he bargained for—a sentencing hearing freed of the government's argument or evidence that he was a manager or supervisor in the conspiracy.

IV

For all of those reasons, we reverse the ruling of the district court, vacate Moreno-Membache's sentence, and remand to the district court for further proceedings consistent with this opinion.

So ordered.

---

[4] *Cf. United States v. Vaval*, 404 F.3d 144, 155 (2d Cir. 2005) (remanding for resentencing even though the district court was not influenced by the government's breach of the plea agreement because, "in order to preserve the integrity of plea bargaining procedures and public confidence in the criminal justice system, a defendant is generally entitled to the enforcement of a plea **[—17—]** agreement without showing tangible harm resulting from a breach"); *see also United States v. Yah*, 500 F.3d 698, 704 (8th Cir. 2007) (remanding for resentencing, even where "[t]he district court specifically stated that the government's [breach] was irrelevant" to the imposed sentence because "'[t]he fact that the district court stated the government's remark did not influence its decision does not ameliorate the government's breach.'") (quoting *United States v. McCray*, 849 F.2d 304, 305 (8th Cir. 1988)).

*(Reporter's Note: Dissenting Opinion follows on p. **426**).*

[—1—] {-258-} **KATSAS**, Circuit Judge, dissenting:

Antonio Moreno-Membache, who belonged to a smuggling operation in Colombia, {-259-} pleaded guilty to an offense carrying a minimum prison sentence of ten years. The plea bargain preserved his ability to seek a lower sentence under 18 U.S.C. § 3553(f), popularly known as the Safety Valve, which permits a sentence below statutory minima if the district court makes five findings favorable to the defendant. One of them is that the defendant was not an "organizer, leader, manager, or supervisor of others in the offense." *Id.* § 3553(f)(4). Another is that the defendant did not "possess a firearm ... in connection with the offense." *Id.* § 3553(f)(2). The district court here found that Membache satisfied neither requirement, so it imposed a ten-year sentence. *United States v. Mosquera-Murillo*, No. 13-cr-00134-BAH, 2019 WL 3037533, at *12–16 (D.D.C. July 11, 2019).

In vacating the sentence, my colleagues reason in two steps. First, the government breached the plea bargain by arguing that Membache was ineligible for Safety Valve relief because he supervised others in the offense. *Ante* at 9–14. Second, evidence of such supervision may have improperly influenced the district court's finding that Membache possessed a firearm in connection with the offense. *Id.* at 14–17. I will assume the first point for the sake of argument. But as explained below, I disagree with the second.

A

Section 3553(f)(4) disqualifies a defendant from Safety Valve relief if he "possess[ed] a firearm ... in connection with the offense." Possession happens "in connection with the offense" if the firearm has the "potential of facilitating" the offense, *United States v. Erazo*, 628 F.3d 608, 611 (D.C. Cir. 2011)—as when, for example, a firearm is "present in order to protect contraband," *United States v. Evans*, 888 F.2d 891, 896 (D.C. Cir. 1989). The defendant must prove eligibility for Safety Valve relief by a preponderance of the evidence. *United* [—2—] *States v. Mathis*, 216 F.3d 18, 29 (D.C. Cir. 2000). We review findings about such eligibility only for clear error. *United States v. Gales*, 603 F.3d 49, 53 (D.C. Cir. 2010).

The district court did not clearly err in finding that Membache possessed a firearm in connection with his offense. In his guilty plea, Membache acknowledged membership in an organization that grew and stored large amounts of cocaine and marijuana in Colombia, then used speedboats to smuggle the drugs into Panama. Two members of the organization told the government that Membache possessed a firearm in connection with the smuggling. The captain of the ill-fated *Mistby* saw Membache carry a 9-millimeter pistol—and at one point openly display it—during a planning meeting before the boat's launch. A *Mistby* crew member likewise saw Membache with a pistol tucked into his waistband at the launch site. The district court credited these statements and thus concluded that Membache possessed a firearm. *Mosquera-Murillo*, 2019 WL 3037533, at *15–16. The court then found that Membache possessed the firearm "in connection with" his offense because his job included "safeguarding" the contraband. *Id.* at *16. That conclusion rested in part on statements from five co-conspirators—including two of Membache's brothers—that Membache was responsible for guarding and moving the drugs in Colombia. *Id.* at *6–7.

Membache asks us to disregard this evidence because it was introduced through the hearsay testimony of a government investigator. But sentencing courts may consider all evidence of a defendant's "background, character, and conduct," 18 U.S.C. § 3661, including reliable hearsay, *United States v. Leyva*, 916 F.3d 14, 26 (D.C. Cir. 2019). And we review the decision {-260-} to consider hearsay only for abuse of discretion. *Id.* at 25. Here, the district court noted that the co-conspirators' statements corroborated one another, the captain's statements [—3—] about Membache were consistent, and an intercepted phone call verified some of the captain's other statements. *Mosquera-Murillo*, 2019 WL 3037533, at *14–16. Under these circumstances, the district court did not abuse its discretion in considering the co-

conspirators' statements. *See, e.g.*, *Leyva*, 916 F.3d at 25–26; *United States v. Jones*, 744 F.3d 1362, 1367–68 (D.C. Cir. 2014).

B

My colleagues take a different approach. They do not contest the factual support for the finding that Membache possessed a firearm in connection with his offense. Instead, they worry that this finding may have rested on "improper argument or evidence" that Membache supervised others. *Ante* at 17. And they order the district court to reconsider the firearm issue without any "argument or evidence" that Membache was a supervisor. *Id.* This approach is wrong for two reasons.

First, the question whether Membache possessed a firearm in connection with his offense is distinct from the question whether Membache supervised others. The district court recognized this by devoting separate sections of its opinion to the evidence bearing on each question. *See Mosquera-Murillo*, 2019 WL 3037533, at *12–16. To be sure, in addressing the firearm issue, the court did make one reference to Membache's supervisory role: "Moreover, as already established, Membache had a supervisory role in the *Mistby* offense, and played a role in safeguarding cocaine while it was transported throughout Colombia onto go-fast vessels for shipment elsewhere. Given this role in guarding the narcotics, his firearm had the potential of facilitating the drug trafficking offense." *Id.* at *16 (cleaned up). The court's analysis focused on Membache's conduct in "safeguarding" or "guarding" illegal drugs, not on his exact position in the criminal **[—4—]** enterprise. And that focus makes sense, for the court's conclusion—that the firearm helped Membache guard the contraband—follows regardless of whether Membache acted as one pawn among many, as a mid-level supervisor, or as a high-level organizer. Similarly, once the court credited testimony that Membache (i) displayed a pistol "at a planning meeting prior to the launch of the *Mistby*" and (ii) possessed a pistol "at the launch site of the *Mistby*," *Mosquera-Murillo*, 2019 WL 3037533, at *15, the conclusion that he possessed the weapon "in connection with the offense" follows inexorably. The court's stray reference to "supervisory role" made no difference in its resolution of the firearm issue.

In any event, the plea bargain permitted the government to present all evidence relevant to the firearm issue. The agreement expressly allowed the government both to argue that Membache "does not meet the criteria to qualify for Safety Valve relief" and to "inform the Court" of "all relevant information concerning the offenses committed." J.A. 132. To be sure, the agreement also barred the government from seeking "any of the adjustments set out in" chapter 3.B of the Sentencing Guidelines, *id.*, which contains adjustments for the defendant's "role in the offense," U.S.S.G. § 3B1. And because the Safety Valve requires a finding that "the defendant was not an organizer, leader, manager, or supervisor of others in the offense, *as determined under the sentencing guidelines*," 18 U.S.C. § 3553(f)(4) (emphasis added), there is at least arguably no distinction between statutory arguments under section 3553(f)(4) and guideline-adjustment arguments under chapter 3.B. But **{-261-}** whatever the force of this point to bar the government from opposing Safety Valve relief under section 3553(f)(4), it cannot possibly bar the government from opposing Safety Valve relief under section 3553(f)(2)—or from introducing any evidence relevant to that provision. So if Membache's supervisory role were relevant to the firearm **[—5—]** question, the government could introduce evidence of it for that purpose, and the district court could so consider it. *See* 18 U.S.C. § 3661 ("No limitation shall be placed on the information concerning the background, character, and conduct of a person convicted of an offense which a court of the United States may receive and consider for the purpose of imposing an appropriate sentence."). At most, that is how the district court assessed the firearm issue.

In sum, the district court was permitted to consider all evidence bearing on whether Membache possessed a firearm in connection with his drug trafficking, and the court permissibly resolved that question against him. Because that was enough to foreclose Safety Valve relief, I would affirm Membache's ten-year sentence.

United States Court of Appeals
for the District of Columbia Circuit

No. 19-7009

DISTRICT NO. 1, PAC. COAST DIST., MARINE ENG'RS BENEFICIAL ASS'N
vs.
LIBERTY MARITIME CORP.

Appeal from the United States District Court for the District of Columbia

Decided: May 25, 2021

Citation: 998 F.3d 449, 9 Adm. R. 429 (D.C. Cir. 2021).

Before **SRINIVASAN,** Chief Judge, and **ROGERS** and **PILLARD,** Circuit Judges.

[—2—] {-452-} SRINIVASAN, Chief Judge:

This case stems from a number of labor disputes between Liberty Maritime Corporation and a maritime labor union that represents certain Liberty employees. The parties' collective bargaining agreement provides for resolution of disputes under oversight of an arbitrator appointed by mutual agreement. The union contends that Liberty violated the agreement by unilaterally selecting an arbitrator. Liberty maintains that the arbitrator was validly appointed.

The central issue we confront is who decides whether the arbitrator was validly (i.e., mutually rather than unilaterally) appointed: the challenged arbitrator himself, or instead a court? The district court concluded that the collective bargaining agreement assigns to the arbitrator himself the authority to determine the validity of his own appointment. We disagree and understand the agreement to leave that issue for resolution by a court. We thus vacate the district court's judgment and remand for the court to determine whether the challenged arbitrator was validly appointed.

I.

A.

District No. 1, Pacific Coast District, Marine Engineers' Beneficial Association, AFL-CIO, whom we will refer to as MEBA, is a union that has long represented deck and marine engineering officers **{-453-}** employed by Liberty Maritime Corporation. MEBA and Liberty are parties to a decades-old collective bargaining agreement.

Section 2 of the agreement, entitled "Grievance Procedure and Arbitration," states that "[a]ll disputes relating to the interpretation or performance of this Agreement shall be **[—3—]** determined in accordance with the provisions in this Section." Agreement of District No. 1, Pacific Coast District, MEBA (AFL-CIO) and Liberty Maritime Corporation ("Agreement") § 2(a), J.A. 45–46. Those provisions call for establishment of a Licensed Personnel Board charged with "resolv[ing] any grievance" either party may have. Agreement § 2(b), J.A. 46. The Board is comprised of four representatives: two chosen by MEBA and two chosen by Liberty.

An arbitrator serves as the chair of the Board and presides over its meetings. If the Board resolves a matter by majority vote, that decision becomes final. But in the event the Board cannot reach a majority resolution, the arbitrator serves as the tiebreaker. A decision by the arbitrator is final and binding on both parties. Agreement §§ 2(b)–(c), J.A. 46–47.

The agreement specifies that the "Arbitrator will be appointed by mutual agreement." Agreement § 2(d), J.A. 47. The agreed-upon arbitrator serves "for a one (1) year period, renewable for one (1) year periods by mutual consent." *Id.* In the event of the arbitrator's termination during the one-year term, "the parties will agree within fifteen (15) days upon a successor." *Id.* If the parties cannot agree on a successor, "the parties shall request an agreed upon agency to designate five (5) names from among which each party shall have the right to strike two (2), and the Agency shall designate a successor who shall serve for the balance of the contract year." *Id.* The term "agreed upon agency," according to a supplemental memorandum of understanding between the parties, is "intended to mean either the United States Secretary of Labor or the American Arbitration Association." J.A. 150. **[—4—]**

B.

Despite the existence of the procedures for resolution of grievances set forth in Section 2 of the collective bargaining agreement, the parties long refrained from invoking those procedures when a grievance arose. Instead, when either party raised a grievance, the parties would request a list of qualified arbitrators from the American Arbitration Association (AAA). The parties would then take turns striking names from the list and choose the last remaining person as the arbitrator.

In April 2018, however, Liberty informed MEBA of its interest in invoking the Section 2 procedures to resolve a number of outstanding grievances. MEBA responded that it did "not believe there is any reason to resurrect the licensed personnel board procedures," noting that the parties had "never followed these procedures." J.A. 314. MEBA instead proposed to select an arbitrator "from a panel of arbitrators issued by AAA." *Id.*

On June 12, 2018, Liberty advised MEBA that it was invoking the Section 2 procedures and identified the two Liberty representatives it was appointing to the Licensed Personnel Board. Liberty also called a meeting of the Board to take place on June 18, at which, Liberty stated, the first order of business would be to choose the arbitrator. MEBA again objected to Liberty's invocation of the Section 2 procedures. The parties exchanged a flurry of emails over the course of a week, culminating in MEBA's providing the names of its two Board representatives. **{-454-}**

Although MEBA ultimately agreed to participate in the Section 2 process, it objected to a revised meeting date (June 26) chosen by Liberty because MEBA's attorney would be **[—5—]** unable to attend. Liberty declined to select another date because, in its view, the parties' attorneys need not join the meeting. MEBA's Board representatives, though, refused to attend the meeting without the participation of counsel. Undeterred, Liberty's two Board representatives met on June 26 and proceeded to appoint an arbitrator.

MEBA then brought this action in the district court. MEBA challenged the arbitrator's appointment on the ground that he had been unilaterally rather than mutually appointed. MEBA's complaint seeks both declaratory and injunctive relief: a declaration stating that Liberty could not unilaterally appoint an arbitrator consistent with Section 2 of the collective bargaining agreement, and an injunction barring Liberty from participating in arbitration proceedings overseen by the challenged arbitrator. Liberty filed a motion to dismiss MEBA's complaint, arguing that the arbitrator had been validly appointed.

The district court treated Liberty's motion to dismiss as a motion to compel arbitration, reasoning that both parties plainly intended to arbitrate their underlying disputes. *Dist. No. 1, Pac. Coast Dist., Marine Eng'rs' Beneficial Ass'n v. Liberty Mar. Corp.*, No. 18-1618, 2019 WL 224291, at *3 (D.D.C. Jan. 15, 2019). The court then addressed whether the parties' dispute over the validity of the arbitrator's appointment should be resolved by the challenged arbitrator himself or instead by the court. The court read the collective bargaining agreement to assign that issue for resolution by the arbitrator. The court thus granted Liberty's motion to dismiss and referred the parties to arbitration. *Id.* at *5–6. MEBA now appeals. **[—6—]**

II.

While Liberty does not contest our jurisdiction over MEBA's appeal, we must assure ourselves of our appellate jurisdiction. We generally possess jurisdiction over appeals from final decisions of the district court. 28 U.S.C. § 1291. Here, the district court purported to dismiss MEBA's complaint "without prejudice." *Liberty Mar. Corp.*, 2019 WL 224291, at *6. The district court's "without prejudice" dismissal raises the question of whether the court's order was final and appealable. We conclude that it was.

In *Ciralsky v. CIA*, 355 F.3d 661, 666 (D.C. Cir. 2004), we explained that there is a distinction between a district court's dismissal of a *complaint* without prejudice and a district court's dismissal of an *action* without prejudice. When a court dismisses a complaint without prejudice, the plaintiff generally can "amend his pleading and continue the litigation." *Id.* (internal quotation marks omitted). But the "dismissal of an action—whether with or without prejudice—is final and appealable." *Id.* That is because, when a district court dismisses an action, it terminates the case. *Id.* at 667. Even if the dismissal of the action is denominated "without prejudice," such that claim preclusion principles would not bar the filing of a new action, "that does not change the fact that, in the absence of such an affirmative act" of initiating a new action, the initial "case is at an end." *Id.*

As we recognized in *Ciralsky*, though, "it is not always clear whether a district court intended its order to dismiss the action or merely the complaint." *Id.* To answer that question, the court in *Ciralsky* examined three sources: (i) the language used by the district court in effecting its dismissal, (ii) the language of the dismissal **{-455-}** motion granted by the court, and (iii) the course of the litigation. *See id.* at 667–68. **[—7—]**

Here, while the district concluded its opinion by stating that it was dismissing the "complaint," the context makes evident that the court in fact sought to dismiss the action in the sense of bringing the case to an end. The same was true in *Ciralsky*: there, too, the district court "spoke several times of dismissing the complaint," but the circumstances indicated that the court believed it was dismissing the action, i.e., ending the case. *Id.* at 667. The three sources we examined in *Ciralsky* in reaching that conclusion all likewise point to a dismissal of the action here.

First, the district court concluded its memorandum opinion granting Liberty's dismissal motion by stating that, "because there are no issues left for this court to resolve, I easily conclude that it is appropriate to dismiss this case in its entirety." *Liberty Mar. Corp.*, 2019 WL 224291, at *6 (internal quotation marks omitted). That language bespeaks a final dismissal of an action—i.e., an end of the case—not merely a dismissal of the complaint. There is little doubt "that the district court thought the order had terminated the action." *Ciralsky*, 355 F.3d at 667. After all, the court said that "there are no issues left . . . to resolve" and that it was "appropriate to dismiss this case in its entirety." *Liberty Mar. Corp.*, 2019 WL 224291, at *6 (internal quotation marks omitted).

Second, although Liberty's motion referenced dismissal of the complaint, the motion in substance sought dismissal of the action. Liberty's chief argument was that the collective bargaining agreement gives the arbitrator, not a court, the authority to determine the validity of his own appointment. As a result, Liberty contended, "'all of the claims are subject to resolution by the arbitrator,' and the Court should dismiss them." Defendant's Mot. to Dismiss at 2, J.A. 439 (citing *W & T Travel Servs., LLC v. Priority One Servs., Inc.*, 69 F. Supp. **[—8—]** 3d 158, 174 (D.D.C. 2014)). Liberty noted parenthetically that, in the cited decision, *W & T Travel Servs.*, the court had "dismiss[ed] a suit," i.e., an action. *Id.* And Liberty's submission that MEBA's claims should be resolved in arbitration proceedings, not in the court, necessarily contemplated bringing the action before the court to an end. Liberty correspondingly sought a dismissal "with prejudice." *Id.* at 14, J.A. 451.

Third, the course of the litigation confirms that, in granting Liberty's dismissal motion, the district court effected a dismissal of the action, not just the complaint. When the court granted Liberty's motion, the court in both its opinion and its order expressly stated that "the parties are referred to arbitration." *Liberty Mar. Corp.*, 2019 WL 224291, at *6. That resolution terminated the litigation before the court, shifting the proceedings to an arbitral forum. *Cf. Green Tree Fin. Corp. v. Randolph*, 531 U.S. 79, 82 (2000) (order compelling arbitration is a final, appealable decision for purposes of the Federal Arbitration Act).

For those reasons, we hold that the district court's grant of dismissal amounted to a final decision as to the action, not just the complaint. We thus possess appellate jurisdiction to consider MEBA's appeal.

III.

The underlying question in MEBA's action is whether the arbitrator selected by Liberty's designated Board members was "appointed by mutual agreement" in accordance with the terms of the parties' collective bargaining agreement. The issue we face on appeal is who decides that underlying question: does the challenged arbitrator **{-456-}** himself decide whether he was validly **[—9—]** appointed by mutual agreement, or is that instead a decision for a court?

The parties agree that the issue of who decides is governed by the parties' intent as manifested in their collective bargaining agreement. Liberty contends, and the district court agreed, that the agreement calls for the arbitrator himself to resolve whether he had been appointed by mutual agreement. MEBA argues that the parties left that decision to a court. We agree with MEBA.

As an initial matter, MEBA contends that the district court erred by treating Liberty's motion to dismiss as a motion to compel arbitration. That treatment, in MEBA's view, resulted in the district court's applying an unduly lenient standard when granting Liberty's motion. We have no need to resolve that issue: even assuming the district court permissibly converted the motion to dismiss into a motion to compel arbitration, we conclude that the court should not have compelled arbitration. Rather, the question whether the arbitrator was validly appointed by mutual agreement should be answered by a court, not by the contested arbitrator himself.

A motion to compel arbitration is decided on a summary judgment standard. *See Aliron Int'l, Inc. v. Cherokee Nation Indus., Inc.*, 531 F.3d 863, 865 (D.C. Cir. 2008); Fed. R. Civ. P. 56(c). The issue is "whether or not there had been a meeting of the minds on the agreement to arbitrate" the dispute at hand. *Aliron Int'l*, 531 F.3d at 865 (internal quotation marks omitted). There was no such meeting of the minds here to empower the challenged arbitrator himself to decide whether he was validly appointed by mutual agreement.

Our analysis proceeds in two steps. First, we assess whether the dispute over the arbitrator's appointment involves **[—10—]** the kind of question that is presumptively for judicial rather than arbitral resolution. We answer that question yes. Second, we assess whether the parties' collective bargaining agreement overcomes that presumption through a clear and unmistakable assignment of power to the challenged arbitrator himself to decide the validity of his own appointment. We find no clear and unmistakable provision to that effect in the agreement, meaning that the matter has been left for resolution by a court.

A.

The Supreme Court has explained that "arbitration is a matter of contract, and courts must enforce arbitration contracts according to their terms." *Henry Schein, Inc. v. Archer & White Sales, Inc.*, 139 S. Ct. 524, 529 (2019). The parties to an arbitration agreement "may agree to have an arbitrator decide not only the merits of a particular dispute but also gateway questions of arbitrability, such as whether the parties have agreed to arbitrate or whether their agreement covers a particular controversy." *Id.* (internal quotation marks omitted). The gateway issue in this case is whether the arbitrator was validly appointed by mutual agreement.

We note at the outset that, in assessing whether that gateway issue is for a court or instead for the contested arbitrator himself to resolve, we assume that the issue is one that parties *could* "agree to have an arbitrator decide" if they so intend. *Id.* That may not always be the case. The Supreme Court has observed, for instance, that "before referring a dispute to an arbitrator, the court determines whether a valid arbitration agreement exists."

Id. at 530; *see* **{-457-}** *New Prime Inc. v. Oliveira*, 139 S. Ct. 532, 538 (2019); *Rent-A-Center, West, Inc. v. Jackson*, 561 U.S. 63, 71 (2010). Insofar as the threshold question "whether a valid arbitration agreement exists" then is necessarily for "the court [to] determine[]," *Henry Schein*, 139 **[—11—]** S. Ct. at 530—such that it cannot be delegated to an arbitrator—MEBA makes no argument that the gateway issue in this case is of that type. We thus assume that parties could enable a contested arbitrator herself to decide whether she was validly appointed by mutual agreement, and we proceed to assess whether the parties did so here.

1.

The Supreme "Court has consistently held that parties may delegate threshold arbitrability questions to the arbitrator, so long as the parties' agreement does so by 'clear and unmistakable' evidence." *Id.* (quoting *First Options of Chicago, Inc. v. Kaplan*, 514 U.S. 938, 944 (1995)). That is, the "question whether the parties have submitted a particular dispute to arbitration, i.e., the question of arbitrability, is an issue for judicial determination unless the parties clearly and unmistakably provide otherwise." *Howsam v. Dean Witter Reynolds, Inc.*, 537 U.S. 79, 83 (2002) (formatting modified) (internal quotation marks omitted). A "question of arbitrability" then is presumptively for a court to decide, unless the parties clearly and unmistakably assign it to the arbitrator.

The Supreme Court has explained, though, that the "clearly and unmistakably" standard does not govern every gateway issue that could be characterized as a "question of arbitrability." "Linguistically speaking, one might call any potentially dispositive gateway question a 'question of arbitrability,' for its answer will determine whether the underlying controversy will proceed to arbitration on the merits." *Id.* But some gateway issues, the Court has held, "are presumptively for the arbitrator, not for the judge." *Id.* at 85.

So how do we determine whether a given gateway issue is a "question of arbitrability" such that it is presumptively for a **[—12—]** court to decide (absent a clear and unmistakable provision to the contrary), or instead falls outside that category such that it is presumptively for the arbitrator to decide? The answer, the Supreme Court has instructed, turns on whether the parties would likely have expected a court or instead an arbitrator to decide the issue. *See id.* at 83–85.

In particular, a gateway issue will qualify as a "question of arbitrability"—and thus presumptively decided by a court—"where contracting parties would likely have expected a court to have decided the gateway matter, where they are not likely to have thought that they had agreed that an arbitrator would do so, and, consequently, where reference of the gateway dispute to the court avoids the risk of forcing parties to arbitrate a matter that they may well not have agreed to arbitrate." *Id.* at 83–84. Examples of such questions of arbitrability include a "dispute about whether the parties are bound by a given arbitration clause" and "a disagreement about whether an arbitration clause in a concededly binding contract applies to a particular type of controversy." *Id.* at 84; *see Henry Schein*, 139 S. Ct. at 529; *First Options*, 514 U.S. at 943.

On the other hand, the Supreme "Court has found the phrase 'question of arbitrability' *not* applicable in other kinds of general circumstances where parties would likely expect that an arbitrator **{-458-}** would decide the gateway matter." *Howsam*, 537 U.S. at 84. For instance, "procedural questions which grow out of the dispute and bear on its final disposition are presumptively *not* for the judge, but for an arbitrator, to decide." *Id.* (internal quotation marks omitted). That includes questions about whether "prerequisites such as time limits, notice, laches, estoppel, and other conditions precedent to an obligation to arbitrate have been met." *Id.* at 85 (internal quotation marks and emphasis omitted). Those sorts of threshold procedural issues fall "within the class of gateway **[—13—]** procedural disputes that do not present what [the Supreme Court's] cases have called 'questions of arbitrability,'" such that "the strong pro-court presumption as to the parties' likely intent does not apply." *Id.* at 85–86.

2.

Where, then, does that leave us with respect to the gateway issue in this case—viz., whether the arbitrator was validly appointed by mutual agreement or instead invalidly selected by unilateral action? Does that gateway issue qualify as a question of arbitrability, presumptively decided by a court? Or is it instead the kind of gateway issue that is presumptively decided by an arbitrator—here, the disputed arbitrator himself? The answer, as explained, turns on whether the issue is one that parties likely would have expected is for a court to decide or instead likely would have expected is for the arbitrator to decide. We believe the former.

Courts enforce arbitral awards "[b]ecause the parties have contracted to have disputes settled by an arbitrator *chosen by them* rather than by a judge." *United Paperworkers Int'l Union, AFL-CIO v. Misco, Inc.*, 484 U.S. 29, 37 (1987) (emphasis added). Arbitration thus essentially presupposes a consensually chosen arbitrator. In the event of a disagreement between the parties over whether an arbitrator was consensually chosen in accordance with the terms of their contract, it is unlikely that the parties would have expected resolution of the dispute by the disputed arbitrator herself.

Consider the respective positions of parties when there is a dispute about whether an arbitrator has been mutually agreed upon. One party believes the arbitrator has been validly appointed by joint affirmation. The other party believes the arbitrator has been impermissibly foisted upon it by the **[—14—]** opposing side acting alone. In that context, why would the parties expect that the disputed arbitrator herself would resolve the legitimacy of her own appointment, as opposed to a neutral third party (a court) deciding the matter? Neither party presumably would want to risk being put in a position in which an arbitrator whom it believes has been unilaterally imposed upon it by the opposing party is nonetheless given power to decide for herself whether she can act as the final arbiter of disputes between them.

Rather, this is the sort of "circumstance where contracting parties would likely have expected a court" to "decide[] the gateway matter, where they are not likely to have thought that they had agreed that [the challenged] arbitrator [herself] would do so." *Howsam*, 537 U.S. at 83. At the least, it is appropriate to *presume* that parties would not intend for the challenged arbitrator herself to decide the validity of her own appointment absent a clear and unmistakable indication that the parties intended to give her that authority.

Imagine what would happen in a situation involving not just one disputed arbitrator but two, with each side asserting that its preferred arbitrator was validly **{-459-}** appointed by mutual agreement but that the opposing side's preferred arbitrator was invalidly appointed unilaterally. If the validity of an arbitrator's appointment were deemed an issue for the arbitrator herself to resolve, which of the two disputed arbitrators would decide the matter? If they each deemed themselves validly appointed, how would the stalemate get resolved? The more sensible course, and the one more in keeping with parties' likely expectations, is to presume—absent a clear and unmistakable indication to the contrary—that the gateway question of whether an arbitrator has been validly appointed by mutual agreement is for a court to decide, not for the challenged arbitrator herself. **[—15—]**

That conclusion is reinforced by the understanding that courts have presumptive responsibility to decide whether a "particular type of controversy" lies within an arbitrator's authority. *Id.* at 84; *see Green Tree Financial Corp. v. Bazzle*, 539 U.S. 444, 452 (2003) (plurality opinion); *AT & T Technologies, Inc. v. Communications Workers of Am.*, 475 U.S. 643, 651–52 (1986). If courts are given presumed power to decide whether a particular matter falls within an arbitrator's authority because "contracting parties would likely have expected a court to have decided" the question, *Howsam*, 537 U.S. at 83, courts should also be presumed to decide whether the arbitrator who would exercise that authority (potentially over many matters) was validly appointed in the first place.

While the Supreme Court has not specifically addressed that issue, a group of three Justices considered it in *Green Tree Financial Corp. v. Bazzle*, and their resolution accords with ours. The issue in *Bazzle* was whether the parties' arbitration agreement allowed for class arbitration. The lead plaintiffs and the defendant company had agreed on an arbitrator to resolve their dispute, *see* 539 U.S. at 449 (plurality opinion), and the question was whether that agreed-upon arbitrator could also arbitrate the claims of the entire plaintiff class. The Justices making up the majority viewed that issue to concern "*what kind of arbitration proceeding* the parties agreed to." *Id.* at 452; *see id.* at 454–55 (Stevens, J., concurring in the judgment and dissenting in part). That sort of question, the majority held, was for the arbitrator to decide. *See id.* at 452–53 (plurality opinion).

Chief Justice Rehnquist, joined by Justices O'Connor and Kennedy, conceived of the matter differently. In their view, the question whether the arbitrator could arbitrate the entire class's claims concerned not *what* kind of arbitration **[—16—]** proceeding the parties had agreed to, but rather *who* is the arbitrator chosen to resolve each class member's claims. *See id.* at 458–59 (Rehnquist, C.J., dissenting). As those Justices saw it, allowing the single arbitrator chosen by the named plaintiffs and defendant company to resolve the claims of the entire class of plaintiffs would violate the agreement's provision calling for selection of arbitrators by mutual consent. That provision, to those Justices, meant that there needed to be mutual agreement on a specific arbitrator for *each* class member's claims, which they believed had not been accomplished by the initial agreement on a single arbitrator. *See id.* at 459.

Of particular relevance here, in reaching that conclusion, those Justices explained that "the choice of arbitrator is as important a component of the agreement to arbitrate as is the choice of what is to be submitted to him." **{-460-}** *Id.* at 456–57. And because a dispute over what has been submitted to the arbitrator was "a question for the courts under" the Supreme Court's precedents, rather than a question for an arbitrator, a dispute over "how the arbitrator should be selected" was also an issue "for the courts." *Id.* at 457. Although those three Justices expressed that view in a dissenting opinion, the majority suggested no disagreement with the proposition that a dispute over "how the arbitrator should be selected" is for a court to resolve. Rather, because the Justices in the majority believed that the case instead concerned what kind of arbitration proceeding the parties had agreed to, they had no occasion to disagree with the notion that questions about the selection of an arbitrator are presumptively for a court.

Liberty, though, expresses a contrary view in this case. According to Liberty, a disagreement about "how the arbitrator should be selected" is ultimately a procedural issue. It should thus presumptively be assigned to the arbitrator for resolution, **[—17—]** Liberty submits, akin to "procedural questions which grow out of the dispute and bear on its final disposition." *Howsam*, 537 U.S. at 84 (internal quotation marks omitted). We are unpersuaded by Liberty's argument.

True, the Supreme Court in *Howsam* explained that gateway procedural issues such as "waiver, delay, or a like defense to arbitrability" are generally for the arbitrator, not a court, to resolve. *Id.* (internal quotation marks omitted). But that is not because of any categorical rule that a gateway issue amenable to characterization as "procedural" necessarily lies with the arbitrator. Rather, it is because threshold procedural issues like waiver, timeliness, notice, and estoppel, are ones as to which "parties would likely expect that an arbitrator would decide the gateway matter." *Id.*

The pivotal question is: what would parties likely expect? And for all the reasons we have explained, when the issue is whether an arbitrator was validly appointed by mutual agreement, parties would likely expect resolution by a court, not by the challenged arbitrator herself. *See Bazzle*, 539 U.S. at 457 (Rehnquist, C.J., dissenting) ("[T]he parties' agreement as to how the arbitrator should be selected is much more akin to the agreement as to what shall be arbitrated, a question for the courts . . . than it is to allegations of waiver, delay, or like defenses to arbitrability, which are questions for the arbitrator under *Howsam*.") (internal quotation marks omitted).

B.

While we thus decide that the gateway issue of whether the arbitrator was appointed by mutual agreement is a "question of arbitrability" within the meaning of the Supreme Court's decisions, that means that the issue is only *presumptively* for a court to resolve. *See Howsam*, 537 U.S. at 83. The **[—18—]** presumption is overcome if parties clearly and unmistakably assign a question of arbitrability to the arbitrator. *See id.* Here, however, there was no clear and unmistakable agreement by the parties to give the challenged arbitrator himself the power to determine the validity of his own appointment.

1.

In arguing that the parties agreed to empower the arbitrator to decide whether his appointment came about by mutual agreement, Liberty principally relies on a reference to the American Arbitration Association in the collective bargaining agreement. That reference appears in the **{-461-}** provisions setting out how the parties will select a replacement arbitrator in the event of an arbitrator's termination in the midst of her one-year term: if the parties cannot agree within fifteen days on a successor arbitrator who will serve the remainder of the term, they must "request an agreed upon agency" to "designate a successor" through a prescribed process, Agreement § 2(d), J.A. 47, and the "agreed upon agency" is in turn defined to "mean either the United States Secretary of Labor or the American Arbitration Association," Supp. Mem. (1969), J.A. 150.

Liberty's reliance on that reference to the AAA proceeds in multiple steps. First, Liberty observes, the AAA rules governing labor arbitrations provide that an arbitrator "shall have the power to rule on his or her own jurisdiction, including any objections with respect to the existence, scope, or validity of the arbitration agreement." AAA Labor Arbitration Rule 3(a), https://www.adr.org/sites/default/files/Labor_Arbitration _Rules_3.pdf. Second, Liberty submits, that rule encompasses a disagreement about whether the arbitrator was validly appointed in the first place. Third, Liberty asserts, if parties to an arbitration agreement incorporate AAA arbitration rules, they thereby delegate to an arbitrator the authority to decide **[—19—]** gateway questions of arbitrability such as the scope of the arbitrator's jurisdiction. And fourth, Liberty contends, the parties in this case intended to incorporate the AAA rules when they mentioned the AAA in the agreement. The upshot, according to Liberty, is an agreement by the parties to give the challenged arbitrator himself the power to decide whether he was validly appointed.

We see no such agreement from the mere reference to the AAA, much less a clear and unmistakable agreement of the kind that would be necessary to overcome the presumptive assignment of the gateway arbitrability question in this case to a court. First, while we have no need to resolve the matter here, it is far from clear that an arbitrator's ostensible power under AAA Labor Arbitration Rule 3(a) to decide "her own jurisdiction" on matters such as "the existence, scope, or validity of the arbitration agreement," extends to deciding whether she was validly appointed in the first place. Assigning an arbitrator authority to decide the scope of the arbitration agreement, for instance, would seem to presuppose agreement on the arbitrator who would make that decision. And even if the parties attempt to give an agreed-upon arbitrator the power to decide the scope of their arbitration contract, that conferral of authority would not necessarily carry with it the power to decide whether she is their agreed-upon arbitrator to begin with. Nonetheless, we will assume arguendo that the second step of Liberty's argument is correct.

With regard to the third step of Liberty's reasoning, virtually every court of appeals to address the issue agrees that when parties expressly incorporate the AAA rules, they thereby clearly and unmistakably delegate to an arbitrator the power to decide gateway questions of arbitrability (including questions about the arbitrator's own "jurisdiction"). *See Oracle Am., Inc. v. Myriad Grp. A.G.*, 724 F.3d 1069, 1074 (9th Cir. 2013) **[—20—]** (cataloging cases). While our court has not specifically addressed the issue in the context of the AAA rules, we have reached the same conclusion when parties incorporate the rules of the United Nations Commission on International Trade Law, which contain a parallel provision assigning to an arbitrator the authority to rule on her own jurisdiction. *See Chevron Corp. v. Ecuador*, 795 F.3d 200, 207–08 (D.C. Cir. 2015). **{-462-}**

We note, though, that the Supreme Court has "express[ed] no view" on whether parties' explicit incorporation of AAA rules establishes a clear and unmistakable delegation of threshold arbitrability questions to the arbitrator. *Henry Schein*, 139 S. Ct. at 531; *see id.* at 528. There were several references to that issue when the Court recently heard oral argument after granting review a second time in the *Henry Schein* case, but the Court has dismissed the writ of certiorari as improvidently granted, without issuing an opinion. *See* Transcript of Oral Argument at 9–10, 18–19, 31–33, 40–41, 63–66, *Henry Schein, Inc v. Archer & White Sales, Inc.*, 141 S. Ct. 656 (2021) (No. 19-963). For our purposes, then, we will assume the soundness of the third step of Liberty's reasoning, as we did with the second step.

Liberty's argument nonetheless falls short at its fourth and final step. The parties' mention of the AAA in their agreement does not embody an incorporation of the AAA rules, let alone a clear and unmistakable incorporation. For starters, the parties initially added the reference to the AAA in 1969, long before the relevant AAA rule giving the arbitrator power to decide her own jurisdiction even came into being: MEBA notes that the rule first appeared in the AAA rules for labor disputes in 2013, and Liberty does not dispute the point. *See* MEBA Br. 26; *see also* American Arbitration Association, Handbook on Commercial Arbitration 83 & n.84 (2d ed. 2010) (explaining **[—21—]** that the AAA first introduced the relevant language to any of its rules in the late 1990s).

At any rate, even assuming the AAA rule concerning an arbitrator's power to decide her own jurisdiction was in effect at the relevant time, the reference to the AAA in the parties' agreement simply does not mention (much less incorporate) the AAA rules. Compare, for instance, the agreement in *Henry Schein*. There, the parties agreed that disputes arising under the agreement would be resolved "by binding arbitration in accordance with the arbitration rules of the American Arbitration Association." 139 S. Ct. at 528 (internal quotation marks omitted). Here, by contrast, the agreement contains its own rules for the conduct of proceedings to resolve grievances. Agreement § 2, J.A. 45–52. The agreement's reference to the AAA instead concerns the selection of an arbitrator, and only as a third-tier fallback matter: the AAA becomes salient only if (i) the agreed-upon arbitrator were to be terminated in the midst of her one-year term, (ii) the parties cannot agree on a successor, and (iii) the parties opt to consult the AAA rather than the Secretary of Labor for help in choosing a successor arbitrator to serve for the balance of the year. And even if all of those contingencies were to come to pass, the agreement does not expressly (or necessarily) call for applying the AAA rules for any disputes that may arise during that brief period.

In this case, it bears recalling, the AAA had no evident involvement in the selection of the challenged arbitrator. He was chosen by Liberty's designated members of the Licensed Personnel Board (without the input of MEBA's designated Board members), raising the question whether he was validly appointed by mutual agreement. It is true that the AAA could in theory play a role under the agreement in appointing an arbitrator in circumstances far removed from this case. But the possibility of the AAA's involvement in selecting an arbitrator **[—22—]** in one highly contingent situation addressed by the agreement was not a clear and unmistakable incorporation in all situations of the AAA rule giving an arbitrator power to decide questions about her jurisdiction. **{-463-}**

2.

While Liberty principally relies on the agreement's reference to the AAA in arguing that the parties agreed to delegate gateway arbitrability questions to the arbitrator, Liberty also notes the breadth of matters falling within the grievance procedures' coverage. The coverage provision states: "All disputes relating to the interpretation or performance of this Agreement shall be determined in accordance with the provisions in this Section," i.e., the grievance and arbitration procedures. Agreement § 2(a), J.A. 46. We have previously described that provision as "quite broad" in scope. *Dist. No. 1, Pac. Coast Dist., Marine Eng'rs' Beneficial Ass'n, AFL-CIO v. Liberty Mar. Corp.*, 815 F.3d 834, 846, 4 Adm. R. 490, 498 (D.C. Cir. 2016).

While the agreement may describe the coverage of the grievance procedures in "quite broad" terms, that description did not clearly and unmistakably give the challenged arbitrator himself the power to decide the validity of his own appointment. The coverage language pertains centrally to disputes about the myriad substantive provisions in the agreement: matters such as wages, hours of labor, working conditions, safety equipment, discharges of workers, vacations, holidays, severance, and the like. Agreement i–ii, J.A. 31–32. Insofar as the coverage language could be seen to speak to disputes about the grievance procedures themselves, that language does not rise to the level of a clear and unmistakable delegation of gateway questions of arbitrability to an arbitrator. **[—23—]**

For example, in *AT&T Technologies, Inc., v. Communications Workers of America*, 475 U.S. 643, 649 (1986), the Supreme Court invoked the general rule that "the question of arbitrability" is ordinarily "for judicial determination," "[u]nless the parties clearly and unmistakably provide otherwise." The parties' collective bargaining agreement in that case provided for arbitration of "any differences arising with respect to the interpretation of this contract or the performance of any obligation hereunder," "provided that such dispute is not excluded from arbitration by other provisions of this contract." *Id.* at 645 n.1 (internal quotation marks omitted). The Court described that arbitration provision as "broad" in reach. *Id.* at 650. But the Court nonetheless held that a gateway question about whether a particular dispute was subject to arbitration (or instead excluded from arbitration) "was for the court, not the arbitrator, to decide," and thus "should not have been referred to the arbitrator." *Id.* at 651–52. The same is true in this case of the dispute over whether the challenged arbitrator was validly appointed by mutual agreement.

C.

Because the dispute over whether the arbitrator was appointed by mutual agreement poses a question of arbitrability for resolution by a court, we will remand this case for the district court to conduct that inquiry in the first instance. Before doing so, however, we address a threshold disagreement between the parties about the meaning of the mutual-agreement requirement. In Liberty's view, that requirement calls for the four party-appointed members of the Licensed Personnel Board to agree on the arbitrator. In MEBA's view, the parties themselves—not the Board members—must mutually agree on the arbitrator. We believe MEBA's understanding is correct. **[—24—]**

The relevant language of the collective bargaining agreement states that the "Arbitrator will be appointed by mutual agreement for a one (1) year period, renewable for one (1) year periods by mutual consent." **{-464-}** Agreement § 2(d), J.A. 47. Read in isolation, the reference to "mutual agreement" does not necessarily point to the Board members or the parties. But consider the immediately ensuing sentence, discussed previously, which states: "In the event of the termination of the Arbitrator, *the parties will agree* within fifteen (15) days upon a successor, failing which, *the parties shall request* an agreed upon agency to designate five (5) names from among which each party shall have the right to strike two (2), and the Agency shall designate a successor who shall serve for the balance of the contract year." *Id.* (emphases added). That sentence expressly calls for "the parties," not the Board members, to agree on a successor to replace a terminated arbitrator. In that light, the previous sentence is best read likewise to call for mutual agreement of the parties, not the Board members.

A contrary reading would lead to an anomalous result: the Board members would bear responsibility for appointing the arbitrator, but in the event of that arbitrator's termination, the parties themselves—for the first time—would need to agree on a successor to complete the balance of the term. The more sensible reading would give the parties themselves responsibility for appointing the arbitrator throughout—whether the initial choice or any ensuing choice of a successor.

Other provisions of the agreement fortify that reading. Section 2(e), for example, states, "The Arbitrator must render a decision within fifteen (15) days after the hearing has been closed unless the parties have otherwise extended such time by mutual consent." J.A. 48. That provision plainly speaks in terms of mutual consent of the parties. And Section 2(d) uses **[—25—]** the identical language of "mutual consent" to describe who can renew the arbitrator's appointment for successive terms.

To be sure, one provision of the agreement refers to a decision to be made by mutual agreement of the Board members: Section 2(b) states, "If said Board resolves any grievance either by majority vote or by mutual agreement, said grievance shall be deemed settled." J.A. 46. But the language of that sentence expressly points to a mutual agreement of the Board members. Section 2(d)'s requirement that "[t]he Arbitrator will be appointed by mutual agreement," by contrast, does not expressly speak in terms of either the Board members or the parties themselves. But the immediately ensuing sentence, as explained, resolves any ambiguity, making clear that the provisions governing the selection of the arbitrator contemplate a mutual agreement by the parties.

With respect to whether the parties here mutually agreed to the appointment of the challenged arbitrator, we remand to the district court to decide the issue. MEBA contends that the arbitrator was not selected by mutual agreement of the parties. And while Liberty has argued thus far that the Board members should be deemed to have mutually agreed on the arbitrator, Liberty is free to contend on remand that Section 2(d)'s requirement of an agreement by the parties themselves was satisfied.

D.

Before concluding, we note that a recent decision of a New York state court in a case involving the same parties is no obstacle to our deciding this appeal. *See Dist. No. 1, Pac. Coast Dist., Marine Eng'rs' Beneficial Ass'n v. Liberty Mar. Corp.*, No. 655407/2018 (N.Y. Sup. Ct. 2021). MEBA initiated that separate litigation after it filed this lawsuit. In the state court **[—26—]** proceedings, MEBA sought to vacate arbitration awards issued by the challenged arbitrator. Here, by contrast, **{-465-}** MEBA seeks to enjoin those arbitration proceedings, but it does not request vacatur of particular arbitration awards.

The collective bargaining agreement contemplates precisely that type of bifurcated litigation. Section 2(o) of the agreement begins, "Any action to enjoin a grievance or arbitration proceeding under this Agreement shall be instituted in the federal courts of the District of Columbia." J.A. 51. But the provision then goes on to say, "Any action to modify or vacate an arbitration award shall be instituted in the courts of the State of New York." *Id.* Consistent with the agreement, MEBA sought to enjoin an arbitration proceeding in the federal courts of the District of Columbia before instituting an action to vacate arbitration awards in the state courts of New York. And while Liberty alerted us to the state court decision, Liberty has not argued that we should not decide this appeal.

* * * * *

For the foregoing reasons, we vacate the district court's order compelling arbitration and remand for the district court to determine whether the arbitrator was appointed by mutual agreement of the parties.

So ordered.

United States Court of Appeals for the Federal Circuit

United States Court of Appeals
for the Federal Circuit

No. 20-1909

TAYLOR ENERGY CO.
VS.
DEPARTMENT OF THE INTERIOR

Appeal from the United States District Court for the Eastern District of Louisiana

Decided: March 9, 2021

Citation: 990 F.3d 1303, 9 Adm. R. 442 (Fed. Cir. 2021).

Before **PROST,** Chief Judge, **PLAGER** and **O'MALLEY,** Circuit Judges.

[—2—] {–1305–} O'MALLEY, Circuit Judge:

Appellants, United States Department of the Interior, et al. (collectively, "Interior"), appeal the decision of the United States District Court for the Eastern District of Louisiana, transferring this case to the United States Court of Federal Claims ("Claims Court"). Order, *Taylor Energy Co. LLC v. United States Dep't of Interior*, No. 18-14065 (E.D. La. Mar. 31, 2020), ECF No. 71; J.A. 1–2 (*Transfer Order*). Because we hold that the Claims Court does not have subject matter jurisdiction over this case, we reverse and remand to the district court for further proceedings.

I. BACKGROUND

A. Factual Background

In 1994, Taylor Energy Company, LLC ("Taylor") became the lessee and operator of oil and gas properties in the Gulf of Mexico, located on the Outer Continental Shelf, offshore Louisiana. *Taylor Energy Co. LLC v. United States*, 975 F.3d 1303, 1307, 8 Adm. R. 581, 583 (Fed. Cir. 2020). In 2004, Hurricane Ivan destroyed Taylor's offshore operations at the site, causing oil to leak from the wells into the waters of the Outer Continental Shelf. *Id.* at 1308, 8 Adm. R. at 583. Three federal statutes—the Outer Continental Shelf Lands Act ("OCSLA"), the Clean Water Act, and the Oil Pollution Act—and their implementing regulations, require Taylor to decommission the site and stop the oil leaks. To comply with its statutory and **{–1306–}** regulatory obligations, Taylor and Interior developed a plan to decommission the wells and associated facilities. **[—3—]**

Taylor's leases at the site terminated in June 2007, and it ultimately decided to leave the offshore oil production business in 2008. Pursuant to OCSLA regulations, Interior approved Taylor's assignments of its active leases to third parties on the condition that Taylor set aside part of the proceeds from those lease sales in order to provide sufficient funding for its decommissioning obligations. Although Interior's regulations generally provide for a bond to ensure sufficient funding of decommissioning obligations, 30 C.F.R. §§ 556.900(a)–(d), 556.901(d), the regulations also authorize Interior to accept equivalent financial assurances, *id.* § 556.904. Here, Interior required additional financial assurance and Taylor decided to establish and contribute to a "lease-specific abandonment account" in an amount equal to Interior's initial estimate of the decommissioning costs. *Taylor*, 975 F.3d at 1307–09, 8 Adm. R. at 582–84.

Taylor and Interior entered into three agreements in 2008—the Trust Agreement, the Disbursement Agreement, and the Bond Agreement. These agreements addressed how Taylor would fund the trust account and how Interior would disburse payments from it. The Trust Agreement requires Taylor to comply with the regulatory decommissioning requirements. The Disbursement Agreement establishes procedures for approving and disbursing funds from the trust account. The Bond Agreement required Taylor to deposit $666,280,000 into the trust account, consistent with the cost estimate in the Trust Agreement. *Id.* at 1308–09, 8 Adm. R. at 584. Taylor deposited that amount on the agreed upon schedule.

The agreements require Taylor to seek reimbursement from its insurance policies for work performed at the site and prevent Taylor from receiving payment from the trust account for costs covered by such reimbursement. The Trust Agreement specifically provides that "[n]o disbursements will be given for amounts reimbursed to [Taylor] by insurance proceeds." J.A. 28. The Bond Agreement further provides that "Taylor will not be entitled to payment under **[—4—]** the Trust Agreement for costs reimbursed by insurance companies," but that Taylor will be able to reduce or offset required deposits if the work is completed with insurance or other funds. J.A. 27–28. In compliance with the agreements, Taylor secured contracts, began decommissioning work, submitted insurance claims, and requested disbursement from the trust account.

In August 2009, Taylor sent a letter to Interior proposing that Taylor "make the full final deposit into the trust account," without any offsets, and "retain all insurance proceeds it has received and will receive in the future as reimbursement for work performed." J.A. 16. Interior rejected Taylor's proposal on August 28, 2009 ("the 2009 Decision"). The agency explained that Taylor: (1) must make the full deposit due because Taylor had "not yet completed any phase of the 'Work,' as defined by the Trust Agreement"; and (2) must reimburse the trust account for any disbursements Taylor received that duplicated reimbursement from Taylor's insurance company. J.A. 17. Taylor appealed the 2009 Decision to the Interior Board of Land Appeals ("IBLA"), seeking to compel Interior to accept Taylor's proposal to keep the proceeds of any future payouts under its insurance policies.

While its administrative appeal was pending, Taylor continued its decommissioning work, including plugging and abandoning **{-1307-}** wells and removing damaged equipment and debris. As the decommissioning progressed, Taylor temporarily suspended work pending assessment of certain risks. During the periods of suspension, Taylor incurred downtime costs associated with its decommissioned rig, because Taylor was required to pay its contractor when the rig was idle. J.A. 30.

In August 2011, Taylor sent a letter to Interior, requesting reimbursement from the trust account for rig downtime costs. Interior denied the request on November 7, 2011 ("the 2011 Decision"), finding that Taylor had been **[—5—]** overcompensated by the trust. Taylor timely appealed the 2011 Decision to the IBLA.

In a single consolidated opinion issued in October 2018, the IBLA affirmed Interior's 2009 and 2011 Decisions ("the IBLA Decision"). According to the IBLA, the agency's "2009 and 2011 Decisions reflect a proper construction of the Agreements." J.A. 41. The IBLA concluded that Interior properly denied: (1) Taylor's requests to retain insurance proceeds in lieu of offsetting them against the final supplemental deposits to the trust account; and (2) the disbursement of trust account funds for rig downtime costs. *Id.*

B. Related Case

In a related case involving the same Trust Agreement at issue here, Taylor filed suit against the government in the Claims Court in January 2016, asserting a variety of contract claims and alleging violation of Louisiana law. The government moved to dismiss that complaint under Rules 12(b)(1) and 12(b)(6). In particular, the government argued that the court lacked jurisdiction because the statute of limitations barred Taylor's claims.

The Claims Court dismissed Taylor's complaint for failure to state a claim in April 2019. *Taylor Energy Co. LLC v. United States*, 142 Fed. Cl. 601, 612 (2019). The court addressed and rejected the government's limitations argument, and thus denied the government's motion to dismiss under Rule 12(b)(1). *Id.* at 608–09. But the court dismissed Taylor's contract claims for failure to state a claim. In doing so, the court noted that the "IBLA, on behalf of Interior, has determined that Taylor remains obligated to decommission its wells under federal law." *Id.* at 611. The court noted that "Taylor has decided not to challenge the IBLA's decision" and explained that the court "cannot second guess the IBLA." *Id.* And the court rejected Taylor's argument that it "must separate Taylor's regulatory **[—6—]** obligations under the Trust Agreement from its regulatory obligations under the OCSLA." *Id.* at 612.

Taylor appealed the Claims Court's decision to this court, and we affirmed in September 2020. At the outset, we rejected "Taylor's attempt to disguise its regulatory obligations as contractual ones." *Taylor*, 975 F.3d at 1306, 8 Adm. R. at 581. Although Taylor argued that Louisiana state law should control, we explained that, "[i]n the context of OCS-based claims, state law does not apply if federal law addresses the relevant issue." *Id.* at 1312, 8 Adm. R. at 587. Because the issues underlying Taylor's claims were governed by federal law, we held that the Claims Court correctly dismissed for failure to state a claim.

In a footnote, we explained that "[a]n IBLA decision must be appealed to a United States district court" and that "[n]either the Claims Court nor this court is empowered to review IBLA decisions." *Id.* at 1311 n.6, 8 Adm. R. at 586 n.6 (citing 5 U.S.C. §§ 701–706 and **{–1308–}** *Underwood Livestock, Inc. v. United States*, 89 Fed. Cl. 287, 290 (2009), *aff'd*, 417 F. App'x. 934, 939 (Fed. Cir. 2011)). We further noted that IBLA decisions have a binding effect on related lawsuits before the Claims Court. *Id.*, 8 Adm. R. at 586 n.6.

C. Procedural History

In December 2018, Taylor filed this action against Interior in the Eastern District of Louisiana, seeking judicial review of the IBLA's October 2018 final agency decision, which affirmed Interior's 2009 and 2011 Decisions. Specifically, Taylor filed suit under the Administrative Procedure Act ("APA"), 5 U.S.C. §§ 701–706, asking the district court to "[r]everse, set aside, and vacate the IBLA Decision affirming [Interior's] 2009 and 2011 Decisions" and to "[d]eclare that the 2009 Decision and 2011 Decision are arbitrary, capricious, contrary to law and an abuse of discretion." Complaint at 1 & 10, *Taylor Energy Co. LLC v. U.S. Dep't of the Interior*, No. 2:18-cv-14065 (E.D. La. Dec. 20, **[—7—]** 2018), ECF No. 1; J.A. 4, 13. Taylor also asked the district court to instruct Interior to disburse the funds.

The same day that Taylor filed its complaint in district court, it filed a second complaint in the Claims Court, alleging breach of contract. That case involved the same operative facts as the district court case. In a footnote, Taylor informed the Claims Court that it had filed a substantially similar lawsuit against the same defendants in district court under the APA. Taylor stated that the district court case "was filed in an abundance of caution in the event jurisdiction in this Court under the Tucker Act is deemed to be improper" and that "Taylor Energy intends to seek a stay of the APA proceeding pending this Court's determination of subject matter jurisdiction." J.A. 207 n. 2.

In February 2019, the government moved to dismiss the Claims Court suit for lack of subject matter jurisdiction pursuant to 28 U.S.C. § 1500. The government explained that: (1) Taylor filed a "substantially similar" complaint in district court before it filed the complaint with the Claims Court; and (2) there is no dispute that the two suits have the same operative facts. In response, Taylor stipulated to dismissal of the Claims Court action without prejudice.

After the Claims Court dismissed Taylor's complaint pursuant to § 1500, Taylor moved to transfer the Louisiana district court action to the Claims Court. In doing so, Taylor argued that: (1) the district court does not have jurisdiction over Taylor's claims "because in essence the case is a breach of contract case involving the government's incorrect interpretation of agreements with Taylor"; and (2) because the Claims Court's April 2019 decision dismissed Taylor's claims in that case under Rule 12(b)(6)—not Rule 12(b)(1)—the court necessarily "found that it has subject matter jurisdiction to address claims under the Trust Agreement." Mtn. to Transfer at 6, *Taylor Energy Co. LLC v. U.S. Dep't of the Interior*, No. 2:18-cv-14065 (E.D. La. Apr. 26, 2019), ECF No. 30–1; J.A. 196. **[—8—]**

Taylor attached to the transfer motion an amended complaint that it proposed to file in the Claims Court if the case were transferred. The proposed amended complaint asserted a breach of contract claim, not a claim filed pursuant to the APA, but the complaint continued to ask the court to "reverse, set aside, and vacate" the IBLA Decision. Specifically, the proposed complaint asked the court to "reverse, set aside, and vacate the IBLA Decision affirming [Interior's] 2009 and 2011 Decisions, which constituted separate breaches **{–1309–}** of the applicable contract between Taylor and the United States and award Taylor Energy monetary damages in the amount of $10,433,905.12 plus applicable interest." First Am. and Restated Complaint at 11, *Taylor Energy Co. LLC v. U.S. Dep't of the Interior*, No. 2:18-cv-14065 (E.D. La. Apr. 26, 2019), ECF No. 30–6; J.A. 329.

Interior opposed the transfer, arguing that the Claims Court had already determined that it must defer to the IBLA. The government maintained that, "if Taylor wishes to challenge the Interior Board of Land Appeals' decision, it must do so in district court under the [APA]." Resp. Mem. in Opp'n. at 2, *Taylor Energy Co. LLC v. U.S. Dep't of the Interior*, No. 2:18-cv-14065 (E.D. La. May 14, 2019), ECF No. 34; J.A. 351.

In a two-page order issued in March 2020—without the benefit of our September 2020 decision in the related case—the district court granted Taylor's motion to transfer. In doing so, the court stated that the issue presented was "whether it has subject matter jurisdiction over Taylor Energy's breach of contract claims asserted against the Federal Defendants." *Transfer Order* at 1. The court explained that "the Tucker Act . . . provides the exclusive basis for the assertion of contract claims against the United States." *Id.* And the court found "the reasoning set forth by the Court of Federal Claims" in the April 2019 decision—"to be controlling." *Id.* The district court therefore transferred the case to the Claims Court. **[—9—]**

Interior timely appealed the district court's transfer order to this court. We have jurisdiction under 28 U.S.C. § 1292(d)(4)(A).

II. DISCUSSION

"Our review of the district court's decision granting or denying transfer of an action to the Court of Federal Claims is de novo because the district court's underlying determination is one of jurisdiction." *Acceptance Ins. Cos. Inc. v. United States*, 503 F.3d 1328, 1332 (Fed. Cir. 2007).

The federal transfer statute provides that a case may be transferred to a "court in which the action or appeal could have been brought." 28 U.S.C. § 1631. The propriety of the transfer order at issue here turns on whether this case properly belongs before the district court under the APA, or before the Claims Court under the Tucker Act, 28 U.S.C. § 1491.

The APA provides for judicial review of certain agency actions in the federal district courts. 5 U.S.C. §§ 701–706. Specifically, the APA provides for judicial review of final agency actions if "there is no other adequate remedy in a court," *id.* § 704, and if the plaintiff is "seeking relief other than money damages," *id.* § 702. The Tucker Act, on the other hand, provides the Claims Court jurisdiction over "any claim against the United States founded . . . upon any express or implied contract with the United States, or for liquidated or unliquidated damages in cases not sounding in tort." 28 U.S.C. § 1491(a)(1). The Tucker Act itself does not create any substantive right to monetary damages. *United States v. Mitchell*, 445 U.S. 535, 538 (1980). Rather, a plaintiff must plead an independent contractual relationship, constitutional provision, federal statute, or executive agency regulation that provides a substantive right to money damages. *Cyprus Amax Coal Co. v. United States*, 205 F.3d 1369, 1373 (Fed. Cir. 2000). **[—10—]**

On appeal, Interior maintains that the district court erred in transferring this case to the Claims Court because "judicial **{–1310–}** review of the IBLA decision may proceed *only* in district court." Appellants' Br. 15. Specifically, Interior argues that, because the IBLA Decision is binding on the Claims Court, the court cannot provide Taylor with an "adequate remedy," and Taylor's only option for judicial review is in district court under the APA.[1] As explained below, Interior is correct.

In determining whether a suit belongs in a district court under the APA, or in the Claims Court under the Tucker Act, the question is "can the Court of Federal Claims provide an adequate remedy under the Tucker Act for the alleged wrong?" *Suburban Mortg. Assocs., Inc. v. U.S. Dep't of Hous. & Urban Dev.*, 480 F.3d 1116, 1125 (Fed. Cir. 2007). We have held that, "if a Tucker Act suit in the Court of Federal Claims provides an adequate remedy, APA review in the district court is not available." *Nat'l Ctr. for Mfg. Scis. v. United States*, 114 F.3d 196, 199 (Fed. Cir. 1997). **[—11—]**

Here, the record is clear that the Claims Court cannot provide an adequate remedy. In its proposed First Amended and Restated Complaint for Breach of Contract, Taylor purports to assert a breach of contract claim, but asks the Claims Court to "reverse, set aside, and vacate the IBLA Decision affirming BOEM's 2009 and 2011 Decisions" on grounds that they were "arbitrary and capricious, an abuse of discretion, and otherwise not in accordance with the law." First Am. and Restated Complaint at 11, *Taylor Energy Co. LLC v. U.S. Dep't of Interior*, No. 2:18-cv-14065 (E.D. La. Apr. 26, 2019), ECF. No. 30-6; J.A. 329.

As we recently noted, judicial review of IBLA decisions may proceed only in district court under the APA. *Taylor*, 975 F.3d at 1311 n.6, 8 Adm. R. at 586 n.6. Specifically, we explained that "[n]either the Claims Court nor this court is empowered to review IBLA decisions." *Id.*, 8 Adm. R. at 586 n.6 (citing *Underwood Livestock, Inc. v. United States*, 89 Fed. Cl. 287, 290 (2009), *aff'd*, 417 F. App'x 934, 939 (Fed. Cir. 2011)). We further noted that "both this court and the Supreme Court have recognized the binding effect of IBLA decisions on related lawsuits before the Claims Court." *Id.*, 8 Adm. R. at 586 n.6 (citing *United States v. Utah Constr. & Mining Co.*, 384 U.S. 394, 422–23 (1966), and *Aulston v. United States*, 823 F.2d 510, 514–15 (Fed. Cir. 1987)). Because the Claims Court must accept the IBLA Decisions affirming Interior's actions—and thus cannot "set aside" those agency decisions as Taylor requests—the Claims Court cannot provide Taylor with an "adequate remedy."

In *Aulston*, for example, we determined that the Claims Court "properly held that it lacked the power to decide appellants' Fifth Amendment taking case in its present procedural posture in view of the [IBLA's] prior adjudication that appellants **{-1311-}** had no ownership rights." 823 F.2d at 511. That is, "where the administrative agencies of the Interior Department have decided [the factual question at issue], the Court of Claims could not review or overturn that administrative determination even though that court **[—12—]** indisputably had jurisdiction over 'taking' claims." *Id.* at 514. We further explained that "[t]he authority to review Interior's administrative decision lay initially in the district courts and then in the regional courts of appeals." *Id.*

Taylor seeks to distinguish *Aulston* on grounds that it involved a taking claim, rather than a contract claim. But nothing in *Aulston* suggests that its application is so limited. Claims founded either upon the Fifth Amendment or on an alleged contract with the government may generally be filed in the Claims Court under the Tucker Act. Importantly, however, the Claims Court may not award any "adequate relief" for either type of claim when there is a controlling and contrary IBLA decision, as is the case here.

[1] Interior also argues that the district court erred in finding the Claims Court's April 2019 opinion dismissing Taylor's complaint "controlling" on jurisdiction. We agree. The court's jurisdictional analysis in that earlier case was limited to finding that the six-year statute of limitations—a jurisdictional bar—had not run. *Taylor*, 142 Fed. Cl. at 612. Notably, Taylor did not challenge the IBLA's decision in that case, and thus the court did not expressly address the jurisdictional issue presented here. *See id.* at 611 ("Taylor has decided not to challenge the IBLA's decision."). It is well established that, "[w]hen an issue is not argued or is ignored in a decision, such decision is not precedent to be followed in a subsequent case in which the issue arises." *Nat'l Cable Television Ass'n, Inc. v. Am. Cinema Eds., Inc.*, 937 F.2d 1572, 1581 (Fed. Cir. 1991).

Taylor cites the Claims Court's decision in *Griffin & Griffin Exploration, LLC v. United States*, 116 Fed. Cl. 163 (2014), for the proposition that courts "regularly find that the [Claims Court] has exclusive jurisdiction over cases involving a claim for money damages arising out of a contract, even when reviewing an administrative decision, like the IBLA decision at issue here." Appellee's Br. 26. In *Griffin*, the plaintiffs sought damages arising out of the government's alleged breach of contract involving two oil and gas leases. 116 Fed. Cl. at 167. The Bureau of Land Management ("BLM") determined that the Griffin leases were improperly issued because of a prior lease for the same property. BLM canceled the leases and the IBLA affirmed the BLM's decision. *Id.* The plaintiffs filed suit in the Claims Court alleging breach of contract and seeking over $30 million in damages. *Id.* The court found that it had subject matter jurisdiction over the breach of contract claim. Although the court agreed with the government that "Congress has invested the federal district courts with exclusive jurisdiction to review IBLA decisions pursuant to the [APA]," and agreed that "the IBLA's findings in this case are fatal to one aspect of plaintiffs' contract claims," the court found that "the government's arguments regarding the binding nature of the IBLA's determinations do not **[—13—]** go to this Court's subject matter jurisdiction over plaintiffs' contract claims; they go to the merits of those claims." *Id.* at 172.

As the government points out, *Griffin* is not binding on this court, and does not address the issue of "adequate remedy." To the extent *Griffin* suggests that the Claims Court has jurisdiction where there is an IBLA decision addressing and resolving the exact issue on which the plaintiff bases a contract claim, it is incorrect. We have recently clarified that the Claims Court cannot provide adequate relief in these circumstances. *Taylor*, 975 F.3d at 1311 n.6, 8 Adm. R. at 586 n.6. Because the IBLA decision is binding on the Claims Court, and may not be reviewed by the Claims Court, the court cannot provide an "adequate remedy." Only the district court has jurisdiction over a challenge to an IBLA decision.

Taylor also cites the Fifth Circuit's decision in *Amoco Production Co. v. Hodel*, 815 F.2d 352 (5th Cir. 1987), for the proposition that, "even though this suit involves review of an administrative decision . . . it is fundamentally a breach of contract suit in which Taylor Energy seeks recovery of $10,433,905.12 in monetary damages." Appellee's **{–1312–}** Br. 29–30. *Amoco* involved "a dispute over the valuation of royalties due [to] the federal government from a gas lease on the Outer Continental Shelf." 815 F.2d at 353. Amoco filed suit in district court, seeking declaratory and injunctive relief from a decision of the IBLA affirming Interior's "assessment of extra royalties and penalties due for gas produced and sold by Amoco from a lease off the Louisiana shore." *Id.* The government moved to dismiss for lack of subject matter jurisdiction, arguing that Amoco's claim was actually a disguised claim for a money judgment in excess of $10,000, and that therefore jurisdiction was proper in the Claims Court pursuant to the Tucker Act. *Id.* The district court denied the motion to transfer and found in favor of the government on the merits. **[—14—]**

On appeal, the Fifth Circuit in *Amoco* found that the district court lacked jurisdiction, vacated the judgment of the district court, and remanded with instructions to transfer the case to the Claims Court. *Id.* at 354. In doing so, the court explained that the provision of the OCSLA at issue there—43 U.S.C. § 1339—"creates a right to monetary relief against the government, that is, that can fairly be interpreted as mandating compensation by the federal government." *Id.* at 360. Because the OCSLA itself created a right to receive compensation from the federal government, the Tucker Act provided for jurisdiction in the Claims Court. *Id.*

Unlike *Amoco*, here, the OCSLA provisions at issue impose a regulatory duty on Taylor—the obligation to decommission the site. The Trust Agreement is a "regulatory instrument in its entirety," not a contract that provides Taylor with a remedy for breach by the government. *Taylor*, 142 Fed. Cl. at 612 ("[T]he Trust Agreement implements Taylor's federal regulatory obligations under the

OCSLA . . . including Taylor's obligation to retain adequate funding."); *see also Anderson v. United States*, 344 F.3d 1343, 1356–57 (Fed. Cir. 2003) (holding that regulatory boilerplate provisions, added by the government as a regulator, are not contracts). And, as the IBLA determined, the trust account is a "lease-specific abandonment" account that serves to provide security for the performance of that obligation. *Taylor*, 975 F.3d at 1311, 8 Adm. R. at 586 (noting that "the IBLA characterized the trust account as a 'lease-specific abandonment account'"). Neither the provisions of OCSLA at issue nor Interior's regulations contain any language "mandating compensation" or otherwise providing a right to monetary damages.

Although Taylor captions its proposed amended complaint as a breach of contract claim, the allegations contained therein, as well as the relief requested, reveal that Taylor is, in fact, seeking APA review of the agency's actions. Taylor expressly asks the court to reverse, set aside, **[—15—]** and vacate the IBLA Decision. As Interior points out, "[i]f Taylor were to establish in district court that it is entitled as a matter of law to the requested relief, including an order instructing Interior to disburse the funds, then the district court would have jurisdiction to award that relief or to set aside Interior's decisions or to remand to Interior, as appropriate." Appellants' Br. 23. In contrast, the Claims Court is bound by the IBLA Decision and thus cannot award Taylor the relief it seeks. Because Taylor is challenging the IBLA Decision, it must do so in district court under the APA.

III. CONCLUSION

For the reasons explained above, the Claims Court does not have jurisdiction **{-1313-}** over this case. We therefore reverse the transfer order and remand to the district court for further proceedings.

REVERSED AND REMANDED

COSTS

No costs.

Tables of Authority

This page intentionally left blank

Table of Cases

This page intentionally left blank

Table of Cases[1]

Page

[1] Cases named solely after ships, *see, e.g.*, *The Pennsylvania*, 86 U.S. (19 Wall.) 125 (1873), are alphabetized under the letter "T." Cases where the United States is the plaintiff are alphabetized by defendant under the letter "U."

B

C

D

E

F

G

H

I

J

K

L

M

N

O

P

Q

R

S

T

U

V

W

Y

Z

This page intentionally left blank

Table of Statutes and Rules

This page intentionally left blank

TABLE OF STATUTES AND RULES[1]

PAGE

TREATIES/INTERNATIONAL

[1] As cited in the opinions reported.

FEDERAL

CONSTITUTION

MISCELLANEOUS

Statutes

Rules

Regulations

STATE

This page intentionally left blank

Index

This page intentionally left blank

INDEX

PAGE

A

B

C

D

E

F

G

H

I

J

L

M

N

O

P

R

S

T

U

V

W

Y

This page intentionally left blank

www.ingramcontent.com/pod-product-compliance
Lightning Source LLC
LaVergne TN
LVHW060016210926
848481LV00013B/3718
* 9 7 8 1 7 3 3 7 7 9 0 6 7 *